Fourth Edition

The Dilemmas of Corrections

Contemporary Readings

Kenneth C. Haas
University of Delaware

Geoffrey P. Alpert
University of South Carolina

WAVELAND
PRESS, INC.
Prospect Heights, Illinois

For information about this book, write or call:
  Waveland Press, Inc.
  P.O. Box 400
  Prospect Heights, Illinois 60070
  (847) 634-0081

Contents

PART III
THE COURTS AND CORRECTIONS   225

PART IV

THE REHABILITATION DEBATE: WHAT WORKS?   333

PART V

CORRECTIONS IN THE COMMUNITY   437

—— PART VI —————————————————————
CRITICAL PROBLEMS AND ISSUES
IN CORRECTIONS   527

Preface

Prisons, as they were established in the United States, were to be positive contributions to the new world. They were to be institutions in which the idle, the unmotivated, the hooligans, and the cruel were sent to be transformed into active energetic, useful, and kind members of society. Somehow, somewhere, something went wrong. Critics have offered too few constructive solutions for change and too many quick-fixes. One of the more insightful comments was made by George Bernard Shaw in his 1925 book *Imprisonment:*

> Although public vindictiveness and public dread are largely responsible for [the cruelty], some of the most cruel features of the prison system are not understood by the public, and have not been deliberately invented or contrived for the purpose of increasing the prisoner's torment. The worst of these are (a) unsuccessful attempts at reform [and] (b) successful attempts to make the working of the prison cheaper for the state and easier for the officials. . . . (pp. 80-81).

Shaw was commenting on the problems of English prisons that he observed in the early 1900s. Today these problems are especially prevalent in the United States, and they exist for more prisoners than Shaw ever imagined. On June 30, 1997, an estimated 1,725,842 men and women were incarcerated in U.S. prisons and jails. 1,218,256 of these people were confined in state or federal prisons, and 567,079 were locked up in local, city, or county jails. Approximately 4 million others were under probation, parole, or some other type of correctional supervision.

Our purpose in bringing together the readings in the fourth edition of *The Dilemmas of Corrections* is to present a timely, issue-oriented perspective on corrections. From the vast number of articles and reports on corrections, we have chosen forty-two that demonstrate what George Bernard Shaw noted so many years ago: there have been recurring attempts to reform shabby prison operations; there have been recurring attempts to find simple answers for complex penal problems; and more and bigger prisons have been constructed. What Shaw also told us is that these attempts are nearly always well intentioned and nearly always leave a legacy of failure.

A close analysis of the literature on corrections reveals a tendency to criticize each and every aspect. What is written about prisons and jails tends to leave the reader with the impression that practitioners do nothing at all, or actively and maliciously oppress a selected segment of society. While it may be a trend to damn every aspect of corrections, it is in many ways unfair. As we read these articles, we can reflect upon Shaw's comments and keep in mind that most administrators and line staff want to do what is right and what is decent. Unfortunately, the political and budgetary restraints placed upon correctional officials make it extraordinarily difficult to manage prisons and other correctional programs effectively.

Our compilation of materials includes some of the outstanding essays and studies that have been published in books, research reports, and professional journals. In addition, we have brought together new material from several of the best criminologists in the country. These original contributions offer readers the most recent theories and research findings in the field of corrections. Part I provides an overview of the scope and structure of the U.S. correctional system and addresses the all-important question: Who goes to prison and why? Our second section describes the pains of imprisonment felt by those who are incarcerated. What really happens when the bars slam shut? Part III examines the impact the judiciary has had on the correctional system and the prisoners. No book on corrections would be complete without a section on rehabilitation, and our fourth section offers an up-to-date overview of the continuing debate over the effectiveness of correctional treatment programs. The fifth section explores the theory and practice of what has come to be called community-based corrections. Corrections outside the traditional walls and fences may be a sensible alternative to warehousing criminals, but the movement toward community corrections has not succeeded in reducing the nation's reliance upon prisons.

Part VI was added in the second edition of *The Dilemmas of Corrections*. This section now contains readings on nine problems and issues that undeniably are among the most pressing and troublesome in the field of corrections today. The first four articles in this section examine the problems involved in meeting the special needs of four distinct types of offenders: mentally ill inmates, elderly prisoners, incarcerated adolescent females, and juvenile offenders with learning disabilities. The next two selections offer insights into two controversial issues in correctional administration—the difficult policy choices concerning how best to prevent the spread of AIDS in U.S. prisons and the hotly debated question of whether private corporations can do a better job of running prisons than do government agencies. The final three chapters analyze the costs and benefits of "get tough" policies in corrections. The first of these chapters tackles the tricky issues surrounding the question of the cost-effectiveness of "locking them up." Next, the recent trend toward imposing so-called "shaming punishments" on certain offenders is examined from both a legal and a policy-effectiveness perspective. The final chapter offers a correctional official's thoughts on whether the high economic costs of capital punishment result in any social benefits for crime victims or anyone else.

Part I

Who Goes to Prison?

Introduction

Many Americans undoubtedly believe that the United States is one of the most lenient nations in the world in punishing offenders. However, the U.S. imprisonment rate is the second highest in the world and it is rising rapidly. As of 1995, the rate of incarceration in the United States (600 inmates per 100,000 population) was surpassed only by that of Russia (690 per 100,000). Moreover, the best available data indicate that U.S. prisoners serve longer terms than their counterparts anywhere else in the world. With nearly 600,000 inmates incarcerated in local, city and county jails and over 1.2 million adults behind bars in state and federal prisons as of June 30, 1997, it is important to find out who is "selected" to be placed in these facilities and who is not. Our first group of readings addresses these and related issues.

We begin with "Prisons as Punishment: An Historical Overview," a chapter in Leonard Orland's provocative 1975 book, *Prisons: Houses of Darkness*. This article provides an excellent history of our present penal system. It traces the history of criminal punishments from Anglo-Saxon England to the twentieth-century American corrections system. It is not surprising that the approach to criminal punishment pursued in the American colonies in the seventeenth and eighteenth

1

centuries was very similar to the approach that had long prevailed in England: this included use of the stocks, the pillory, and the public cage, as well as hangings, whippings, and banishment.

In 1879, however, Philadelphia's Quakers had a new idea; they opened the Walnut Street Jail—the world's first penitentiary for the housing of convicted felons. Although the Walnut Street Jail—and the many other penitentiaries that soon opened—emphasized solitude, forced labor, and an ordered, disciplined life, these new institutions were viewed by many as a progressive, humane alternative to the harsh and primitive punishments of the past. As Orland chronicles the past 200 years of correctional history—a seemingly endless cycle of scandal and reform—readers may come to agree that despite all of the reform movements, "the prison has steadfastly remained a nineteenth-century institution."

Certainly one thing that never seems to change is that prisons are primarily filled by people who are poor, powerless, undereducated, unemployed, and members of minority groups. In the second article in Part I, Jessica Mitford offers some explanations for minority overrepresentation in U.S. prisons. She invites readers to consider the history of society's efforts to pinpoint a "criminal type." This selection has been reprinted from Mitford's controversial, hard-eyed examination of the inadequacies and hypocrisies of the U.S. prison system, *Kind and Usual Punishment: The Prison Business.* Her thesis in "The Criminal Type" is that although crimes are committed at all levels of U.S. society, the criminal justice process sees to it that the prisons are overwhelmingly filled with the young, the poor, the black, and the brown.

Of course, it has long been documented that race, ethnicity, and social class are of major importance in determining who goes to prison. African Americans, for example, account for approximately 12 percent of the total U.S. population; yet they are grossly overrepresented in U.S. prisons, comprising nearly 50 percent of the national prison population. For the most part, this reflects the disproportionately high arrest and incarceration rates for African-American men. Our third article focuses on the reasons for the high rate of African-American-male involvement in the criminal justice system. In "'Lock 'Em Up and Throw Away the Key': African-American Males and the Criminal Justice System," Marc Mauer updates the thought-provoking chapter he contributed to the third edition of *The Dilemmas of Corrections.* Mauer argues that while the criminal justice system does not bear all of the blame for the overrepresentation of black males in U.S. correctional populations, its impact on black men nonetheless has been devastating. Mauer examines the many and complex factors that have created this situation, and he suggests a number of reforms that may lessen the negative impact that the justice system has had on African-American males.

Virtually all of the available data on the scope and structure of the U.S. correctional system and on the demography of the U.S. correctional population stems from the work of the Bureau of Justice Statistics (BJS), a branch of the U.S. Justice Department. Thus, we are fortunate to have as our fourth selection an article by a BJS statistician who has analyzed some of the most recent and important trends in the U.S. correctional population. Allen Beck shows that the number of adults under some form of correctional supervision (including probation and parole) reached an all-time high of nearly 5.5 million as of the end of 1996. Beck explains some of the reasons for the dramatic growth in the correctional population, stressing changes in the composition of the jail and prison populations. He also offers some thoughts on the question of whether the recent increases in the jail, prison, probation, and parole populations will continue into the twenty-first century.

As mentioned earlier, the United States is one of the world leaders in the use of incarceration, ranking second only to Russia among the nations for whom trustworthy data are available. We are pleased to add to the fourth edition of *The Dilemmas of Corrections* a large portion of a recently published study on the international use of incarceration. In June 1997, The Sentencing Project—an independent Washington D.C.-based organization known for its timely and innovative studies on criminal justice issues—released its latest report examining the extent to which different nations make use of imprisonment as a way to deal with convicted and suspected criminal offenders. The author of the report is Marc Mauer, also the author of our earlier piece on the problems African-American men face in the U.S. criminal justice system.

In "Americans Behind Bars: U.S. and International Use of Incarceration," Mauer brings together data for 1995 on the incarceration rates of 59 nations. It is particularly telling to note that no other Western democracy even comes close to the U.S. incarceration rate of 600 inmates per 100,000 people. For example, the U.S. rate is 6 to 10 times higher than the rates found in Denmark, England, France, Germany, Ireland, The Netherlands, Spain, Sweden, Switzerland and other Western European nations.

Mauer's analysis of some of the "get tough" sentencing practices in the United States—mandatory sentences, "three strikes and you're out" laws, an increasing willingness to impose lengthy sentences on nonviolent drug offenders—explains why the United States shares the world lead in building and populating prisons. These trends continue and yet, as Mauer demonstrates, there is no clear and consistent relationship between incarceration rates and crime rates. American readers of this report may want to consider two obvious questions: (1) Is there something unusual in our culture, our political system, our view of human behavior, or perhaps in our beliefs about the value of punishment that can explain why we have so eagerly embraced a "get tough" ideology of crime control? (2) Could it be that we are right and virtually all other democratic nations are wrong in their approach to combatting crime?

Another question that demands our attention is the extent to which public attitudes toward punishing criminals are responsible for high imprisonment rates and so many overcrowded prisons. This is one of the issues analyzed in the sixth and final selection in Part I. In "The American Prison Crisis: Clashing Philosophies of Punishment and Crowded Cellblocks," Ben Crouch, Geoffrey Alpert, James Marquart and Ken Haas argue that the current prison crisis stems from a failure to develop a consistent policy of imprisonment premised on a clear understanding of what prisons can and cannot be expected to accomplish. The authors discuss several of the traditional justifications for criminal punishment: retribution, general deterrence, specific deterrence, incapacitation, and rehabilitation. They conclude that unless and until Americans and correctional policymakers decide which of these goals can be accomplished within current budgetary restraints and develop a consistent and widely accepted prison policy, the present prison crisis will only get worse.

1

Prisons as Punishment
An Historical Overview
Leonard Orland

The English Heritage

Places of criminal detention are ancient institutions. Indeed, the ancient cuneiform symbol for "prison" is a combination of the symbols for "house" and "darkness."[1] Although the description "house of darkness" remains accurate, and suggested the title of this volume, the earliest prisons were quite different from those of today. The early institutions functioned only to detain prisoners prior to trial; they were not used to punish people after conviction. The idea of sending men to prison as postconviction punishment did not arise until the early decades of the nineteenth century. Ironically, the prison was born not amid the tyranny of Europe's divine-right monarchs or Asia's Draconian potentates, but rather among the free citizens of the United States of America.

Source: Reprinted with the permission of The Free Press, a Division of Simon & Schuster from *Prisons: Houses of Darkness* by Leonard Orland. Copyright © 1975 by The Free Press.

In Anglo-Saxon England, the practice of imposing a term of imprisonment for a specified period of time was unknown; guilty felons were either killed, mutilated, or sold into slavery. There were penal slaves in England through the twelfth century, "a voteless minority amidst Saxon freemen."[2] In Anglo-Saxon England, imprisonment was considered useless. It did not satisfy revenge; it kept the criminal idle, and it was costly.[3] It was not the notion of punishment itself that was strange to the Anglo-Saxon legal tradition, but the idea of using imprisonment to punish. Prior to the Norman Conquest, the law declared criminals to be outlaws and banished them. It was the right and duty of every man to pursue an outlaw, to ravage his land, to hunt him down, and to slay him like a wild beast. Outlaws were the ancestors of convicts, and the wilderness was the first penal colony.

English penal law prior to the twelfth century had also established an elaborate system of pecuniary payment to the injured party. Every injury was atoneable by a "bot" (a money compensation paid to the injured man or his relations). The fine levied depended on the nature and extent of the damage and the rank and importance of the injured person. Every man had his class and his value, and every form of aggression against a free man, from a theft or a blow which deprived him of a tooth to a mortal wound, had its appointed fine. Maine commented that "it is curious to observe how little the men of primitive times were troubled with . . . scruples . . . as to the degree of moral guilt to be ascribed to the wrongdoer," how "completely they were persuaded that the impulses of the wronged person were the proper measure of the vengeance he was entitled to exact," and "how literally they imitated the rise and fall of his passions in fixing their scale of punishment."[4]

Early English law also relied extensively on physical punishment, as opposed to a fine or imprisonment. When physical punishment was imposed, it was severe. Death was imposed by hanging, by beheading, by burning, by drowning, and by stoning, as well as castration, flogging, and body mutilation. In medieval England, a man forfeited, for coining, his hand, which, once amputated, was nailed over the mint. One of the earliest surviving English criminal statutes, enacted by King Cnut in the eleventh century, was quite explicit: "Let his hands be cut off, or his feet, or both, according as the deed may be, and if then he hath wrought greater wrong, then let his eyes be put out, or his nose and his ears and the upper lip be cut off, or let him be scalped, so that punishment be inflicted and also the soul preserved."[5]

Although mutilation ultimately disappeared from English law, the brutality of Anglo-Saxon criminal punishment continued unabated into the eighteenth century. In the thirteenth century, offenders were commonly broken on the wheel for treason.[6] A 1530 act authorized poisoners to be boiled alive.[7] Burning was the penalty for high treason and heresy, as well as for murder of a husband by a wife, or of a master by a servant. Unlike the punishment of boiling, that of burning remained lawful in England until 1790. In practice, and as a kindness, women were strangled before they were burned. The right hand was taken off for aggravated murder. Ordinary hangings were frequent, and drawing and quartering, where the hanged offender was publicly disemboweled and his still-beating heart held up to a cheering multitude, was not uncommon.

In addition, until the mid-nineteenth century, English law permitted a variety of "summary" punishments. Both men and women (the latter until 1817) were flagellated in public for minor offenses. For more serious misdemeanors there was the pillory, which was not abolished in England until 1837. With his face protruding through its beams and his hands through the holes, the offender was helpless. Sometimes he was nailed through the ears to the framework of the pillory with the hair of his head and beard shaved; occasionally he was branded. Thereafter, some offenders were carried back to prison to endure additional tortures.

The prison as we know it today—a barred and walled institution to house felons after conviction—emerged from several closely related English institutions which housed pretrial detainees. These institutions date back to the twelfth century. As early as 1166, Henry II declared that "gaols" (jails) were to be erected in walled towns or within royal castles, but their sole function was to confine prior to punishment. A related development occurred in 1553, when Bishop Ridley's place at St. Bridget's Well was selected for locking up and whipping beggars, prostitutes, and nightwalkers. Subsequently, similar places of detention became known as "Bridewells." In 1597, Parliament[8] authorized the erection of houses of correction; in 1609, each county was ordered to build a house of correction.[9] The gaol, the house of correction, and the Bridewell were the progenitors of the contemporary prison.

These institutions quickly deteriorated into places of filth and pain. Then, as now, there was a vast discrepancy between theory and practice. Thus, thirteenth-century law declared that it was forbidden "that anyone be tormented before judgment [because] the law wills that no one be placed among vermin and putrefaction, or in any horrible or dangerous place, or in the water, or in the dark, or any other torment."[10] But this ideal was never realized. Captives were confined under inhuman conditions until the next king's "assize" (term of court)—which could be a matter of months, or years.

John Howard's *The State of the Prisons*, the most influential of eighteenth-century denunciations of detention conditions, reported that in 1777, despite the heavy toll taken by the gallows for no fewer than 240 separate capital offenses, "many more persons were destroyed by gaol fever than were put to death by all the public executions in the kingdom.'' There are prisons, Howard declared, "into which whoever looks will, at first sight of the people confined there, be convinced, that there is some great error in the management of them." Some inmates "are seen pining under diseases . . . expiring on the floors, in loathsome cells, of pestilential fevers, and the confluent smallpox." All types of prisoners were confined together: "debtors and felons, men and women; the young beginner and the old offender. . . . Few prisons separate men and women in the day-time. .·. . The insane, where they are not kept separate, disturb and terrify other prisoners.''[11]

The conditions described by Howard were attributable in large part to the fact that the wardens, keepers, and gaolers (who either purchased their positions or were rewarded their posts for services rendered) were unpaid by the Crown and, consequently, exacted fees and charges from the inmates. Until the eighteenth century, the gaolers used instruments of torture, including the thumbscrew and skullcap, to exact those fees and charges. Prisoners were loaded with heavy irons unless they paid for lighter ones. They were flogged with ropes or whips and confined in damp dungeons and in darkness. The living were sometimes confined with the dead. Prisoners were deliberately exposed to starvation and smallpox or, in some cases, murdered by their keepers.

To recapitulate: the early criminal dispositions were outlawry and banishment, pecuniary compensation, gaol, mutilation, and death. In succeeding centuries, partially in response to the growing mercantile expansion of the Empire, English penal law adopted two other closely related ways of dealing with convicted felons—consignment to galleys and transportation. Both of these policies were based on premises not unlike those underlying the contemporary prison: to dispose of a convicted felon other than by execution, to benefit the state, and to rationalize the result as an act of mercy.

In 1602, Elizabeth I appointed a commission to establish a system of involuntary galley servitude for the condemned as an alternative to death. The Elizabethan scheme permitted prisoners, "except when convicted of wilful Murther, Rape and Burglarye," to be reprieved and sent to the galleys, "wherein as in all things, our desire is that justice may be tempered with clemency and mercy . . . and the offenders to be in such sort corrected and punished that even in their punishment they may yield some profitable service to the Common Welth.''[12]

By the end of the sixteenth century, sailing ships began to replace boats pulled by oars, thus eliminating the need for convicts as galley conscripts. The successor to galley service was transportation. Again, English penal law was responding to external economic conditions. Faced with a rising gaol population at home and an acute need for cheap labor in the American colonies, the Crown conceived the policy of conditionally pardoning felons and transporting them to the American colonies. An estimated fifty thousand convicts were thus transported from England to the American colonies, a fact invariably ignored by the Daughters of the American Revolution.

Transportation as a penal policy can, of course, be traced to Roman roots. The English policy originated in a 1597 measure for the "punyshment of Rogues, Vagabonds and Sturdy Beggars," who, after being flogged, were committed "to the House of Correction or . . . to the Gaole"; thereafter, "such of the Rogues . . . as thought fit . . . shall be . . . banyshed out of this Realme . . . and shall be conveied unto such parts beyond the seas as shall be . . . assigned by the Privie Counsell."[13] Shipments of convicts to the American colonies began in 1618, encouraged by legislation which granted land to colonists who imported convicts. By custom, the convict, upon his arrival, assumed the status of indentured servant rather than convict. The terms of penal indenture, ranging from one to five years, were fixed by the colonial legislatures, and the colonial population, particularly in Virginia, readily absorbed the convicts. At the conclusion of the bondage term, the servant was customarily freed and supplied with tools and, occasionally, with land.

With the abrupt termination of transportation to America at the onset of the Revolution in 1776, the convict population in English gaols began to expand greatly. Much of the excess convict population was warehoused in obsolete prison hulks, permanently anchored in British waters. In 1786, a royal commission found the hulks overflowing with the captives who had been accumulating since the loss of America. The Crown responded by returning to the policy of transportation. But now the destination was Australia, which, fortuitously, had been discovered by Captain Cook in 1770. In late 1787, an expedition of eleven vessels, with 564 male and 192 female criminals aboard, commenced the first of many eight-month voyages to Australia. But there was an important distinction between transportation to America and transportation to Australia. In America, the convict, upon arrival, usually was already half-free—an indentured servant who would become a freeman upon completion of his term. The convict transported to Australia, however, was sent to a penal colony, separate from free settlers, and maintained his status as a convict until released.

The conditions under which felons were transported to Australia were grotesque. One contemporary account indicates that prisoners had been "shipped off in chains" and that the inmates, upon arrival at Sydney Harbor, presented "a sight truly shocking to the feelings of humanity . . . some half and others entirely naked, unable to turn or help themselves. . . . The smell was so offensive that I could scarcely bear it."[14] In 1795, English transportation was abandoned, for all time, as the result of opposition by the Australian free settlers. In the eight-year interim, however, an estimated 135,000 criminals had been shipped to Australia under uniformly inhuman conditions.

Thus, as the early English law had sent its lawbreakers into the forest to live as outlaws, later, seafaring English merchants banished their felons to new and larger wildernesses. Ironically, it was from this innovation, the practical economic notion of populating colonies with society's outcasts, that the modern penitentiary grew. For, in fact, it was the American descendants of those transported pariahs who created still another place to which society could send its rejects, what we now call the prison and what they termed "the penitentiary."

The Penitentiary

Not surprisingly, the approach to criminal punishment pursued in the American colonies in the seventeenth and eighteenth centuries was not unlike that prevailing in England at the same time. Thus, eighteenth-century colonial criminal codes authorized and criminal courts inflicted the traditional English punishments: fines, whippings, use of the stocks, the pillory, and the public cage, as well as banishment and hanging. Although the fine and the whip were most widely used, branding was also inflicted with some frequency. The colonial codes broadly defined capital offenses, and colonial courts did not hesitate to exact the death penalty; an estimated 20 percent of the punishments meted out by New York's colonial courts were capital.

A sentence of imprisonment as punishment was as uncommon in early America as it was in England. David Rothman, the preeminent historian of American penology, gives us reasons: the colonists did not believe that a jail could rehabilitate and placed little faith in reform. Prevailing Calvinist doctrine that stressed the depravity of man "hardly allowed for such optimism." The openness of the frontier was another note-worthy factor. "Institutionalization seemed unnecessary," Rothman observes, "when numerous offenders could be marched beyond the town line and not be seen again."[15]

Thus, until the end of the eighteenth century, prisons as places of punishment were as unknown in America as they had been in England. But within the succeeding four decades, Americans conceived and created the prison as a penal institution, in the form that is still with us today. Hence, familiarity with the American historical experience in the decades between 1790 and 1830 is crucial to an understanding of the contemporary American prison.

Two forces help to explain why and how Americans invented the penitentiary and shaped the future of prisons in the United States as well as in Europe for the next 150 years. One was the shift of the burgeoning agrarian population to the developing industrial complexes of the new Republic. The other was the emergence of the Enlightenment notion of "right reason," which began seriously to challenge the prevailing Calvinist doctrine of the depravity of man. Increasingly, Americans questioned ideas inherited from England. They perceived traditional mechanisms of social control as obsolete and devised new procedures. With the turn of the century, the colonists turned from romantic revolutionary zeal to the practical ideal of government by reason. In that period of flux, two enlightenment documents, one a law book, the other a penal tract, received unparalleled distribution. The influence they had on the development of American criminal law and penal policy is difficult to overestimate.

The first was Sir William Blackstone's *Commentaries on the Laws of England*. To the eighteenth-century lawyer, judge, and legislator, Blackstone was law, and law was Blackstone. It is not surprising, therefore, that American penal reformers took serious heed of Blackstone's pronouncement that "crimes are more effectively prevented by the *certainty* than the *severity* of the punishment," because "excessive severity of law," hinders law enforcement.[16] Blackstone's stance on this issue was not original. Rather, it reflected a view initially put forward in an enlightenment penal tract that was widely read in the American colonies, Beccaria's *On Crimes and Punishments*. To Beccaria, "the severity of punishment of itself emboldens men to commit the very wrongs it is supposed to prevent." Criminals "are driven to commit additional crimes to avoid the punishment for a single one." Those places "most notorious for severity of penalties have always been those in which the bloodiest and most inhumane of deeds were committed."[17] The central thesis of this work became enshrined as dogma in the eighteenth century, and remained as a fundamental tenet of penology. Even today, common wisdom is, to echo Beccaria's notion, that "certainty of punishment, even if it be moderate, will always make a stronger impression than the fear of another which is more terrible but combined with the hope of impunity."

An influential group of Quaker Pennsylvania reformers took this message to heart. William Bradford of Philadelphia declared in 1773: "Moderate punishments strictly enforced, will be a curb as effectual as the greatest severity." The Pennsylvania reformers, like John Howard, believed strongly in the desirability of separate confinement of each prisoner. Isolation from "the society of his fellow prisoners, in which society the worse are sure to corrupt the better," wrote the reformer William Paley in 1785, "is calculated to raise up in him reflections on the folly of his choice and to expose his mind to such better and continued sentence as may produce a lasting alteration in the principles of his conduct."

In May 1787, a group led by Benjamin Franklin and William Rush organized the Philadelphia Society for Alleviating the Miseries of Public Prisoners. The Society's first object of concern was the Walnut Street jail, constructed in 1772. By 1786, conditions in the jail had deteriorated substantially, approximating those in their British counterparts. The Society's first action was to petition the Pennsylvania Executive Council to declare that the only desirable method of penal reform was "solitary confinement to hard labor, and total abstinence." The Pennsylvania legislature responded, in 1789, by designating the Walnut Street jail as a place for the reception of serious offenders from all parts of the Commonwealth. The Act of 1789 directed the commissioners of Philadelphia County to erect in the yard of the jail "a suitable number of cells six feet in width, eight feet in length and nine feet in height," which, "without the necessary exclusion of air and light, will prevent all external communication, for the purpose of confining the more hardened and atrocious offenders, who have been sentenced to hard labor for a term of years."[18]

Although antiquarians still debate the point, in all probability the Walnut Street jail, as modified by the Act of 1789, was the first penitentiary in the world for the housing of convicted felons. Solitude and forced labor were its chief characteristics, and the name of the institution reflected its function: "penitentiary" was derived from the Latin "to repent." The objective was clear: "to turn the thought of the convict inwards upon himself, and to teach him to think." Thus the Pennsylvania reformers saw themselves as simultaneously implementing the reform program of John Howard, the penal philosophy of Beccaria, the legal reforms of Blackstone, and their own Quaker predisposition toward the efficacy of prayer and solitude in reforming the soul.

The culmination of the Pennsylvania reformers' efforts came in 1829, with the opening of the Eastern Penitentiary of Philadelphia. Known as Cherry Hill, America's first architecturally designed penitentiary was built at a cost of three quarters of a million dollars, a staggering amount at that time. It was conceived by the famous architect John Haviland to implement the principle of separate confinement. The Walnut Street jail, constructed four decades earlier, had been an ordinary large frame house, indistinguishable from other large-size buildings. The design of Cherry Hill was in marked contrast. "Breaking out from a central rotunda, like the spokes of a huge wheel," a penal historian noted of Cherry Hill, "the seven massive stone corridors of the prison provided easy access to the rows of cells that flanked them. Each of the four hundred large solitary cells, 8 by 15 and 12 feet high in the center of their vaulted roofs, could be entered only from these corridors, but each was provided with an individual exercise yard, likewise securely walled about to prevent any communication between the convicts."[19]

Intense efforts were made to ensure that the prisoner was in complete solitude from the moment he entered the institution. "Over the head and face of every prisoner who came into this melancholy house," Charles Dickens observed in his *American Notes*, "a black hood is drawn; and in this dark shroud, an emblem of the curtain dropped between him and the living world, he is led to his cell from which he never again comes forth, until his whole term of imprisonment has expired."[20] The success of the Pennsylvania architects and reformers in achieving their goals was graphically described by Tocqueville and Beaumont in an 1833 treatise, far less known than Tocqueville's *Democracy in America* but hardly less readable or perceptive, *On the Penitentiary System in the United States.* "When the convict arrives in the prison," Beaumont and Tocqueville wrote, "he is conducted to his solitary cell, which he never leaves." The result is that the "silence within these vast walls, which contains so many prisoners, is that of death."[21]

The penitentiary movement spread rapidly in the 1820s. New York opened the Auburn State Prison in 1819 and the Sing Sing Prison in 1825. In 1827, Connecticut opened a penitentiary at Wethersfield; in 1829 Massachusetts opened its maximum security penitentiary at Charlestown and Maryland erected its penitentiary in Baltimore. The following year, the New Jersey penitentiary at Trenton received its first inmates. These other American prisons followed New York's approach of modified solitude—"the congregate" system—rather than Pennsylvania's system of complete solitude.

In the first half of the nineteenth century, there was vigorous debate as to the relative merits of the New York and Pennsylvania penitentiary system. However, with the perspective of time, the similarities between New York's "congregate" system and Pennsylvania's "solitary" system seem more apparent than do their differences. While Pennsylvania stood quite alone in enforcing complete solitude, both the Pennsylvania and New York (Auburn State) systems had a common basis—the isolation of the prisoners. The differences between the Pennsylvania and Auburn State systems related to control of the inmates during the day. At Cherry Hill, prisoners were isolated twenty-four hours a day. In the Auburn system, as well as in systems founded upon the same model (as in Vermont, New Hampshire, and Ohio), prisoners were locked up in their solitary cells at night only. During the day they worked together in common workshops, and, as they were subject to the law of rigorous silence, though physically together, they were in fact isolated. "Labor in common and in silence," Beaumont and Tocqueville wrote, "forms then the characteristic trait which distinguished the Auburn [i.e., New York] system from that of Philadelphia."

These differences in theory were reflected by differences in architecture. Cherry Hill employed outside-cell construction, while the designers of the Auburn prison used inside-cell construction. The unique design of Auburn—back-to-back interior cells within a hollow building—was the result not so much of rational calculation as of simple economy. The size of a cell at Cherry Hill was quite generous, so that the inmate could use it as a workshop. In contrast, the Auburn cell was tiny, measuring only 7 feet long and 3 feet 6 inches wide. "Any light or air that might penetrate the cell" at Auburn, as a penal historian noted, "could only enter by small and heavily barred niches built into the outer building shell that surrounded the cell blocks. The cells were obviously too small for any degree of comfort, usually too damp in summer and too cold in winter."[22]

One of the ironies of American penal history is that the hastily conceived and economy-minded construction features of Auburn State and its methods of discipline served for years as the pattern for most state penitentiaries in the United States. The Vermont, New Hampshire, and Ohio institutions, built in the 1830s, were explicitly patterned on the Auburn State design, as were the Georgia and Kentucky prisons, built in the 1840s, and most of the twenty-three other prisons built in the United States between 1830 and 1870. In 1973, six prisons built prior to 1830 and seventeen built between 1830 and 1870 were still in operation.[23] The result is the perpetuation not only of antiquated physical facilities, but of prison construction without a basis in architectural theory. There is, in fact, no theory of prison architecture in the United States; prison architecture, to date, blindly follows the historical pattern of preoccupation with security.

The principle of isolation—total in Pennsylvania, partial in New York—constituted the *raison d'etre* of penitentiary life in the decades following the 1820s. Isolation led directly to a system of harsh penal discipline and rigid control of the inmate population. Such rigid control and discipline, including restrictions on correspondence and visits, are understandable in light of the theories of crime and punishment prevalent in nineteenth-century America. What is far less understandable is that this approach to incarceration has endured. It still constitutes the central mode of institutional control of prison inmates in the mid-twentieth century.

The system of rigid control began with attempts to cut off completely, on pain of punishment, all communication with the outside world. The principle of "absolute separation" as the sole means to prevent "mutual pollution" was adopted in Pennsylvania, Beaumont and Tocqueville explained, "in all its rigor," on the theory that "perfect isolation secures the prisoner from all fatal communication." Each individual, an early Pennsylvania tract noted,[24] "will necessarily be made the instrument of his own punishment; his conscience will be the avenger of society"; separated from "evil society" the prisoner's "corruption" will be arrested. The prisoner "will be compelled to reflect on the error of his ways, to listen to the reproaches of conscience, to the expostulations of religion." Denied all newspapers, correspondence, and visits, even from relatives, he was, by design, totally secluded from the world.

New York's efforts at enforcing complete silence were equally rigorous. The rules at Auburn State in the 1830s provided that convicts were to "receive no letters or intelligence from or concerning their friends, or any information on any subject out of prison."[25] A decade later, the commissioner of prisons in Maine, reflecting a view widely held by prison administrators, declared that "information on events of current interest, and glimpses of the outer world, have a tendency to unsettle the convict's mind and render him restless and uneasy."[26] Sadly enough, these views, too, are still held today.

The Connecticut prison regulations of the 1830s sum up the prevailing approach to incarceration in the first quarter of nineteenth-century America. Inmates were exhorted to be "industrious, submissive, and obedient"; to "labor diligently in silence"; they were forbidden to "write or receive a letter" or to communicate in any manner "with or to persons" without the warden's permission; they were prohibited from engaging in conversation "with another prisoner" without permission or to "speak to, or look at, visitors."[27]

These rules were enforced, sometimes with great difficulty in congregate systems, by a variety of punitive measures. Discipline was relatively easy to enforce at Cherry Hill. Indeed, this was the self-proclaimed virtue of the system. As Beaumont and Tocqueville described it, "The discipline is as simple as the system itself. . . . The only chastisement is imprisonment in a dark cell with reduction of food. It is rare that more than two days of such discipline are required to curb the most refractory prisoner." Punishment in congregate systems, they note, "could not have the same character of simplicity." In a survey of prevailing modes of penal punishment in the 1830s, they remark: "At Sing Sing, the only punishment for those who infringe the established order is that of the whip. The application of this disciplinary means is there very frequent; and the least fault is punished with its application." At Auburn, whipping was the primary mode of punishment, while in Virginia, Maryland, Pennsylvania, and Massachusetts, solitary confinement, with a small allowance of bread and water, prevailed. Connecticut employed a combination of whipping, use of chains, solitary confinement, and subjection to severe hunger to enforce discipline.

What was beginning to happen in the middle decades of the nineteenth century was that the congregate American penitentiaries, in their efforts to enforce the rules of isolation and silence, began to revert to the physical tortures characteristic of the seventeenth-century English gaols. The whip became common in Auburn, Charleston, and Wethersfield; Pennsylvania used the iron gag; Maine preferred the ball and chain; and Connecticut favored the cold shower. The use of the iron gag was justified in Pennsylvania on the ground that inmates were "men of idle habits, vicious propensities and depraved passions."[28] Ohio's warden justified the use of the whip by declaring that "whenever the Penitentiary becomes a pleasant place of residence, whenever [there is] a relaxation of discipline, . . . then it loses all its influence for good upon the mind of men disposed to do evil."[29] This view, too, is still widely held today, although few would publicly argue for a return of the lash.

The Auburn system of penal discipline established a pattern of rigidity, strictness, and monotony that is still with us today. At Auburn-type institutions, Beaumont and Tocqueville noted, "with daybreak, a bell gives the sign of rising; the jailers open the doors." The prisoner's "labor is not interrupted until the hour of taking food." There is no recreation. In the evening, "the convicts leave the workshops to retire to their cells." Everything "passes in the most profound silence, and nothing is heard in the whole prison but the steps of those who march." The "order of the day is that of the whole year"; one hour "follows with overwhelming uniformity the others, from the moment of his entry into the prison to the expiration of his punishment."

Almost a century later, in 1939, the attorney general of the United States, reviewing the history of the penal disciplinary system of silence and isolation, observed:

> With non-communication went a whole new "prison discipline" and so effectively did its advocates do their work during the second quarter of the nineteenth century that even today prison officers protest in horror against anything which might upset the discipline. This discipline meant that prisoners did not communicate with each other, that they walked to and from work or meals in lockstep so as to show both hands to the guards at all times, that they ate in silence face to back, to prevent communications through signals, that they stood with folded arms and downcast eyes when an officer appeared, that they did not gaze at or communicate with visitors, that they were allowed only a limited number of visitors under strict supervision, that their communications through letters with the outside world were strictly limited, that they were allowed few or no newspapers, that they lived in a prison within a prison, i.e., in interior cells, which made contact with the outer world difficult. To enforce such rules meant the organization of new punishment to add to the old. As punishment for every violation of these non-communication rules was considered essential in maintaining discipline, soon all orders of the prison were enforced through the fear of punishment.[30]

One of the most tragic aspects of the history of the American prison is that the concept of isolation, originally conceived as a means of rehabilitating convicts, became an end in itself. Brutal punishment for violating the isolation rules also became an end in itself, and the notion of rehabilitation, as the *raison d'être* of silence, somehow became lost.

It is quite remarkable how widely accepted the idea of the penitentiary became in the first half of the nineteenth century in America. The intellectual debate centered on whether the Pennsylvania or New York system was better, not on whether the penitentiary as such was good. Few were prepared to side with Dickens, who condemned the very *idea* of the penitentiary as punishment:

> The system . . . I believe . . . In its effects, to be cruel and wrong. In its intention, I am well convinced that it is kind, humane and meant for reformation; but I am persuaded that those who devised this system . . . and those benevolent gentlemen who carry it into execution, do not know what it is that they are doing. I believe that very few men are capable of estimating the immense amount of torture and agony which this dreadful punishment, prolonged for years, inflicts upon its sufferers; and, in guessing at it myself, and in reasoning from what I have seen written upon their faces, and what to my certain knowledge they feel within, I am only the more convinced that there is a depth of terrible endurance in it which none but the sufferers themselves can fathom, and which no man has a right to inflict upon his fellow creature. I hold this slow and daily tampering with the mysteries of the brain to be immeasurably worse than any torture of the body; and because its ghastly signs and tokens are not so palpable to the eye and sense of touch as scars upon the flesh, because its wounds are not upon the surface, and it exhorts few cries that human ears can hear, therefore I the more denounce it, as a secret punishment which slumbering humanity is not roused up to stay.[31]

Although Dickens's penchant for institutional reform made him more sensitive to prevailing prison conditions than other contemporary observers, by the middle of the nineteenth century, he was no longer alone in this view. Disillusion with prisons began to emerge, for reasons that are not entirely clear.

The Reformatory

The prison as an institution was greatly affected by Reconstruction and its concomitant reform movements. In the wake of the cataclysmic social and political upheaval that was the Civil War, criticism of the prison became widespread. Politically, abolitionists had envisioned and

accomplished the extinction of slavery; philosophically, transcendental-
ists envisioned a new moral and social order. It is not unlikely that the
sudden elimination of institutionalized racial bondage and the search
for a more noble society of men contributed to an increasing skepticism
toward the theory that prison was a suitable place to achieve penitence
and rehabilitation.

The most thorough account of prisoners available at this time was the
1867 report[32] to the New York legislature. The report traced the transformation of the prison from the theoretical ideal, never achieved, of
an institution for rehabilitation to the reality of the prison as a place
where punishment was inflicted in the name of reformation. "There is
not a state prison in America," the report concluded, "in which the
reformation of the convicts is the one supreme object" or "which . . .
seeks the reformation of its subjects as a primary object." The problem,
to most nineteenth-century reformers, was not the institution but its
"program." Prison programs "are all . . . lacking in the breadth and
comprehensiveness of their scope; all lacking in the aptitude and
efficiency of their instruments; and lacking in the employment of a wise
and effective machinery to keep the whole in healthy and vigorous
action."

The response of the reformers was to develop a new "program": the
much-heralded, but ultimately abortive, "reformatory." New York's
Elmira Reformatory opened in 1876; within the next twenty-five years,
a dozen reformatories were constructed. The theoretical basis for the
reformatory lay in a melange of the nineteenth-century prison reform
ideas of Maconochie in Australia and Crofton in Ireland.

In 1840, Maconochie became superintendent of the penal colony at
Norfolk, an island off the coast of Australia. He promptly instituted a
"mark system" under which the inmate could, by good behavior, "earn"
redeemable marks that could be used as credit either for food and
supplies or toward early release. The objective "was to graduate conduct,
as well as its reward." Maconochie assumed that marks "would soon
be greedily coveted as wages" and that their loss "for misconduct would
supply the place of lashes for minor offenses." The inmate, at his option,
could convert marks into "indulgences" at the cost of prolonging
detention, or, by "steadfastness and self-denial," could earn release.[33]
The objective was to make the prisoner's condition resemble, as closely
as possible, that of a debtor required to be imprisoned, or otherwise
retained, till his debt was paid.

A variant of Maconochie's mark system was adopted by Sir Walter
Crofton when he became chairman of Irish prisons in 1854. Crofton
employed a four-stage system of incarceration. First, the inmate would
be placed in solitary confinement for three months, initially on a reduced
diet, so that "the idler will generally have learned to associate industry

with pleasure."[34] The second stage of imprisonment involved the inmate in a process of passing through four grades, which were dependent on his good conduct and educational and vocational progress. In the third or "intermediate" stage, "industry" was the ruling principle, the testing ground for conditional release on "ticket of leave," which was Crofton's fourth and final stage.

These primitive positive-reinforcement ideas of Maconochie and Crofton had great impact on the American penal reform movement in the final third of the nineteenth century. This movement had reached its height in 1870, when the National Congress on Penitentiary and Reformatory Discipline convened in Cincinnati. The reformers declared there that "the supreme aim of prison discipline is the reform of criminals, not the infliction of vindictive suffering." In furtherance of this goal, the Cincinnati reformers turned to Maconochie and Crofton. They argued that Crofton's ideas were adaptable to the United States and that fixed sentences of imprisonment ought to be replaced by sentences of indeterminate length.[35]

The Elmira Reformatory was seen as the perfect testing ground for the ideas of Maconochie and Crofton. The underlying assumptions of their approach was that criminals could be reformed; that reformation was the "right of the convict" and the "duty of the State"; that every prisoner must be given "special treatment"; that the way to achieve this was to permit prisoner authorities "to lengthen or shorten the duration of this term of incarceration."

The Elmira Reformatory opened in 1879 to house young adults from sixteen to thirty years old who were being imprisoned for the first time. Architecturally, it was a typical Auburn-like prison. Its central features were a greater emphasis on education (at a time in American life when public education was rapidly developing and was seen as an answer to many social problems); an insistence that all sentences be "indeterminate" (i.e., with a maximum but no minimum, so that all prisoners could be released on parole); and the implementation of a parole release program in which all inmates were to be graded on achievement and conduct. Inmates were to pass through three grades: All inmates were initially placed in the second grade, and thereafter were either demoted to the third grade for bad conduct or promoted to the first grade on the basis of good marks. Only first-grade inmates were eligible for parole.

The popularity of the reformatory system peaked at the turn of the century. Its eulogy was written in 1931 by a national commission chaired by George Wickersham. "The reformatory movement," the Wickersham Commission reported, "began with a great flourish." It was conceived as a new and far-reaching attack upon the older penal system. It sought to introduce an institution that would take the younger prisoner and

"save him from contact with the older and more hardened inmate."
"Unfortunately," the Wickersham Commission concluded, "these early
hopes" were unfulfilled. The reformatory "does not reform"; indeed,
it is "not a reformatory at all."[36]

Whatever the shortcomings of the reformatory as an innovative
correctional institution, the legacy of the reformatory movement is still
very much with us. In particular, two aspects of the Elmira experiment
have become enshrined as essential components of the twentieth-century
American scheme of correctional justice. The first, a direct descendant
of Maconochie's "mark" system, is the notion of "good time." Under
good time legislation, prevalent in most states, an inmate can earn
reductions in his sentence by good conduct and industriousness. In
Connecticut, for example, an inmate can "earn" five days a month by
not misbehaving; he can "earn" an additional two days a month for
"meritorious work" and still another five days a month by "working"
a seven-day rather than a five-day week. The consequence is that the
inmate can convert thirty-day months into twenty-day months and
twelve-month years into ten-month years. The other side of the coin,
from the inmate's point of view, is that if he does not adhere to the
prison's regulations—in terms of both work and discipline—he risks
"losing" the "good time" he has "earned." The second enduring
contribution of the reformatory movement is the notion of the
indeterminate sentence and parole, now the dominant feature of the post-
conviction criminal justice system in the United States.

American penal history is replete with reform movements. The
hallmark of that history may well be that despite these movements, the
prison has steadfastly remained a nineteenth-century institution. The
contemporary American prison has witnessed the birth and death of
Emile Durkheim and Sigmund Freud. Nevertheless, the prison has
managed to remain cloistered from the widespread influence of these
and most other twentieth-century theoreticians.

Notes

[1] Taylor, *History of the Alphabet* 21 (1899).
[2] Ives, *A History of Penal Methods* 5 (1914).
[3] Pollock and Maitland, II *History of English Law* 514 (1895).
[4] Maine, *Ancient Law* 389 (1906).
[5] Thorp, *Laws of Cnut*, fol. ed. 169 (1840).
[6] Bracton, *DeLegibus*, lib. iii f. 118.
[7] 22 Hen. VIII c. 9.
[8] 39 Eliz. 4.
[9] 7 Jac. I. c. 4.
[10] *Mirror of Justice* 52 (Whittaker's ed.)
[11] Howard, *The State of the Prisons* 10 (1780).

[12] Rymer, *De Commissione Speciali pro Condempnatis ad Galleas Transferendis*, tom. XVI. 446.

[13] 39 Eliz. c. 4; Statutes of the Realm, Vol. IV. p. 2 at 899 (1819).

[14] Ives, *supra*, n.2 at 132.

[15] Rothman, *The Discovery of the Asylum* 51 (1971).

[16] IV Blackstone, *Commentaries**753 (1892).

[17] Beccaria, *On Crimes and Punishments* 43 (1764, reprinted 1963). See Maestro, *Cesare Beccaria and the Origins of Penal Reform* (1973).

[18] Teeters and Shearer, *The Prison at Philadelphia, Cherry Hill* 9 (1957).

[19] McKelvey, *American Prisons* 11 (1936).

[20] Dickens, *American Notes* 155, 156 (1842).

[21] Beaumont and Tocqueville, *On the Penitentiary System in the United States* (1833, reprinted 1964).

[22] Barnes and Teeters, *New Horizons in Criminology* 340 (1959).

[23] National Advisory Commission on Criminal Justice Standards and Goals, *Report on Corrections* 343 (1973).

[24] Rothman, *supra*, n.15 at 85.

[25] *Id.* at 95.

[26] *Id.* at 96.

[27] Beaumont and Tocqueville, *supra*, n.21 Appendix B.

[28] Rothman, *supra*, n.15 at 102.

[29] *Ibid.*

[30] *The Attorney General's Survey of Release Procedures* (1940).

[31] Dickens, *supra*, n.20.

[32] Wines and Dwight, *Report on the Prisons and Reformatories of the United States and Canada* (1867).

[33] Maconochie, "The Mark System of Prison Discipline" (1855) in Glueck and Glueck, "History and Aims of the Reformatory Movement," *500 Criminal Careers* 16 (1960).

[34] *Id.* at 18.

[35] See *Transactions of the National Congress on Penitentiary on Reformatory Discipline* (1871, reprinted 1970).

[36] National Commission on Law Observance and Enforcement, *Report on Penal Institutions* 51 (1931).

2

The Criminal Type
Jessica Mitford

Time was when most crimes were laid at the door of the Devil. The English indictment used in the last century took note of Old Nick's complicity by accusing the defendant not only of breaking the law but of "being prompted and instigated by the Devil," and the Supreme Court of North Carolina declared in 1862: "To know the right and still the wrong pursue proceeds from a perverse will brought about by the seductions of the Evil One."

With the advent of the new science of criminology toward the end of the nineteenth century, the Devil (possibly to his chagrin) was deposed as primary cause of crime by the hand of an Italian criminologist, one of the first of that calling, Cesare Lombroso. Criminals, Lombroso found, are born that way and bear physical stigmata to show it (which presumably saddles God with the responsibility, since He created them). They are "not a variation from a norm but practically a special species, a subspeicies, having distinct physical and mental characteristics. In general all criminals have long, large, projecting ears, abundant hair, thin beard, prominent frontal sinuses, protruding chin, large cheekbones." Furthermore, his studies, consisting of exhaustive

Source: From *Kind and Usual Punishment* by Jessica Mitford. Copyright © 1973 by Jessica Mitford. Reprinted by permission of Alfred A. Knopf, Inc.

examination of live prisoners and the skulls of dead ones, enabled him to classify born criminals according to their offense: "Thieves have mobile hands and face; small, mobile, restless, frequently oblique eyes; thick and closely set eyebrows; flat or twisted nose; thin beard; hair frequently thin." Rapists may be distinguished by "brilliant eyes, delicate faces" and murderers by "cold, glassy eyes; nose always large and frequently aquiline; jaws strong; cheekbones large; hair curly, dark and abundant." Which caused a contemporary French savant to remark that Lombroso's portraits were very similar to the photographs of his friends.

A skeptical Englishman named Charles Goring, physician of His Majesty's Prisons, decided to check up on Lombroso's findings. Around the turn of the century he made a detailed study of the physical characteristics of 3,000 prisoners—but took the precaution of comparing these with a group of English university students, impartially applying his handy measuring tape to noses, ears, eyebrows, chins of convicts and scholars alike over a twelve-year period. His conclusion: "In the present investigation we have exhaustively compared with regard to many physical characteristics different kinds of criminals with each other and criminals as a class with the general population. From these comparisons no evidence has emerged of the existence of a physical criminal type."

As the twentieth century progressed, efforts to pinpoint the criminal type followed the gyrations of scientific fashions of the day with bewildering results. Studies published in the thirties by Gustav Aschaffenburg, a distinguished German criminologist, show that the pyknic type (which means stout, squate, with large abdomen) is more prevalent among occasional offenders, while the asthenic type (of slender build and slight muscular development) is more often found among habitual criminals. In the forties came the gland men, Professor William H. Sheldon of Harvard and his colleagues, who divided the human race into three: endomorphs, soft, round, comfort-loving people; ectomorphs, fragile fellows who complain a lot and shrink from crowds, mesomorphs, muscular types with large trunks who walk assertively, talk noisily, and behave aggressively. Watch out for those.

Yet no sooner were these elaborate findings by top people published than equally illustrious voices were heard in rebuttal. Thus Professor M.F. Ashley Montagu, a noted anthropologist: "I should venture the opinion that not one of the reports on the alleged relationship between glandular dysfunctions and criminality has been carried out in a scientific manner, and that all such reports are glaring examples of the fallacy of *false cause*...to resort to that system for an explanation of criminality is merely to attempt to explain the known by the unknown."

Practitioners of the emerging disciplines of psychology and

psychiatry turned their attention early on to a study of the causes of criminality. Dr. Henry Goddard, Princeton psychologist, opined in 1920 that "criminals, misdemeanants, delinquents, and other antisocial groups" are in nearly all cases persons of low mentality: "It is no longer to be denied that the greatest single cause of delinquency and crime is low-grade mentality, much of it within the limits of feeble-mindedness." But hard on his heels came the eminent professor Edwin H. Sutherland of Chicago, who in 1934 declared that the test results "are much more likely to reflect the methods of the testers than the intelligence of the criminals" and that "distribution of intelligence scores of delinquents is very similar to the distribution of intelligence scores of the general population...Therefore, this analysis shows that the relationship between crime and feeblemindedness is, in general, comparatively slight." In *New Horizons in Criminology*, Harry E. Barnes and Negley K. Teeters go further: "Studies made by clinical psychologists of prison populations demonstrate that those behind bars compare favorably with the general population in intelligence. Since we seldom arrest and convict criminals except the poor, inept, and friendless, we can know very little of the intelligence of the bulk of the criminal world. It is quite possible that it is, by and large, superior."

Coexistent with these theories of the criminal type was one that declares the lawbreaker to be a deviant personality, mentally ill, of which more later.

It may be conjectured that prison people were not entirely pleased by the early explanations of criminality; perhaps they welcomed the rebuttals, for if the malfeasant is that way because of the shape of his ears, or because of malfunctioning glands, or because he is dim-witted, none of which he can help—why punish? In this context, George Bernard Shaw points out, "As the obvious conclusion was that criminals were not morally responsible for their actions, and therefore should not be punished for them, the prison authorities saw their occupation threatened, and denied that there was any criminal type. The criminal type was off." The perverse old soul added that he knows what the criminal type is—it is manufactured in prison by the prison system: "If you keep one [man] in penal servitude and another in the House of Lords for ten years, the one will shew the stigmata of a typical convict, and the other of a typical peer." Eugene V. Debs expressed the same thought: "I have heard people refer to the 'criminal countenance.' I never saw one. Any man or woman looks like a criminal behind bars."

Skull shape, glands, IQ, and deviant personality aside, to get a more pragmatic view of the criminal type one merely has to look at the composition of the prison population. Today the prisons are filled with the young, the poor white, the black, the Chicano, the Puerto Rican.

Yesterday they were filled with the young, the poor native American, the Irish or Italian immigrant.

Discussing the importance of identifying the dangerous classes of 1870, a speaker at the American Prison Congress said: "The quality of being that constitutes a criminal cannot be clearly known, until observed as belonging to the class from which criminals come...A true prison system should take cognizance of criminal classes as such." His examination of 15 prison populations showed that 53,101 were born in foreign countries, 47,957 were native-born, and of these, "full 50 percent were born of foreign parents, making over 76 percent of the whole number whose tastes and habits were those of such foreigners as emigrate to this country."

At the same meeting, J.B. Bittinger of Pennsylvania described the tastes and habits of these dissolute aliens: "First comes *rum*, to keep up spirits and energy for night work; then three fourths of their salaries are spent in *theaters and barrooms*...many go to *low concert saloons* only to kill time...they play *billiards* for *drinks*, go to the *opera*, to the *theater*, *oyster suppers* and *worse*...they have their peculiar literature: dime novels, sporting papers, illustrated papers, obscene prints and photographs." Commenting on the large numbers of foreign-born in prison, he added: "The figures here are so startling in their disproportions as to foster, and apparently justify, a strong prejudice against our foreign population."

The criminal type of yesteryear was further elaborated on in 1907 by J.E. Brown, in an article entitled "The Increase of Crime in the United States": "In the poorer quarters of our great cities may be found huddled together the Italian bandit and the bloodthirsty Spaniard, the bad man from Sicily, the Hungarian, Croation and the Pole, the Chinaman and the Negro, the Cockney Englishman, the Russian and the Jew, with all the centuries of hereditary hate back of them."

In 1970 Edward G. Banfield, chairman of President Nixon's task force on the Model Cities Program, updated these descriptions of the lower-class slum-dweller in his book *The Unheavenly City: The Nature and Future of the Urban Crisis*, an influential book that is required reading in innumerable college courses. Since it is reportedly also recommended reading in the White House, presumably it reflects the Administration's conception of the criminal classes as they exist today. "A slum is not simply a district of low-quality housing," says Mr. Banfield, "Rather it is one in which the style of life is squalid and vicious." The lower-class individual is "incapable of conceptualizing the future or of controlling his impulses and is therefore obliged to live from moment to moment...impulse governs his behavior...he is therefore radically improvident; whatever he cannot consume immediately he considers valueless. His bodily needs (especially for sex) and his taste for 'action' take precedence over everything else—and certainly over any work routine." Furthermore he "has a feeble, attenuated sense of self...

"The lower-class individual lives in the slum and sees little or no reason to complain. He does not care how dirty and dilapidated his housing is either inside or out, nor does he mind the inadequacy of such public facilities as schools, parks and libraries; indeed, where such things exist, he destroys them by acts of vandalism if he can. Features that make the slum repellent to others actually please him."

Most studies of the causes of crime in this decade, whether contained in sociological texts, high-level governmental commission reports, or best-selling books like Ramsey Clark's *Crime in America*, lament the disproportionately high arrest rate for blacks and poor people and assert with wearying monotony that criminality is a product of slums and poverty. Mr. Clark invites the reader to mark on his city map the areas where health and education are poorest, where unemployment and poverty are highest, where blacks are concentrated—and he will find these areas also have the highest crime rate.

Hence the myth that the poor, the young, the black, the Chicano are indeed the criminal type of today is perpetuated, whereas in fact crimes are committed, although not necessarily punished, at all levels of society.

There is evidence that a high proportion of people in all walks of life have at some time or other committed what are conventionally called "serious crimes." A study of 1,700 New Yorkers weighted toward the upper income brackets, who had never been arrested for anything, and who were guaranteed anonymity, revealed that 91 percent had committed at least one felony or serious misdemeanor. The mean number of offenses per person was 18. Sixty-four percent of the men and 27 percent of the women had committed at least one felony, for which they could have been sent to the state penitentiary. Thirteen percent of the men admitted to grand larceny, 26 percent to stealing cars, and 17 percent to burglary.

If crimes are committed by people of all classes, why the near-universal equation of criminal type and slum-dweller, why the vastly unequal representation of poor, black, brown in the nation's jails and prisons? When the "Italian bandit, bloodthirsty Spaniard, bad man from Sicily," and the rest of them climbed their way out of the slums and moved to the suburbs, they ceased to figure as an important factor in crime statistics. Yet as succeeding waves of immigrants, and later blacks, moved into the same slum area the rates of reported crime and delinquency remained high there.

No doubt despair and terrible conditions in the slums give rise to one sort of crime, the only kind available to the very poor: theft, robbery, purse-snatching; whereas crimes committed by the former slum-dweller have moved up the scale with his standard of living to those less likely to be detected and punished: embezzlement, sale of fraudulent stock, price-fixing. After all, the bank president is not likely to become a bank robber; nor does the bank robber have the opportunity to embezzle depositors' funds.

Professor Theodore Sarbin suggests the further explanation that police are conditioned to perceive some classes of persons (formerly immigrants, now blacks and browns) as being actually or potentially "dangerous," and go about their work accordingly: "The belief that some classes of persons were 'dangerous' guided the search for suspects...Laws are broken by many citizens for many reasons: those suspects who fit the concurrent social type of the criminal are most likely to become objects of police suspicion and of judicial decision-making." The President's Crime Commission comments on the same phenomenon: "A policeman in attempting to solve crimes must employ, in the absence of concrete evidence, circumstantial indicators to link specific crimes with specific people. Thus policemen may stop Negro and Mexican youths in white neighborhoods, may suspect juveniles who act in what the policemen consider an impudent or overly casual manner, and may be influenced by such factors as unusual hair styles or clothes uncommon to the wearer's group or area...those who act frightened, penitent, and respectful are more likely to be released, while those who assert their autonomy and act indifferent or resistant run a substantially greater risk of being frisked, interrogated, or even taken into custody."

An experiment conducted in the fall of 1970 by a sociology class at the University of California at Los Angeles bears out these observations. The class undertook to study the differential application of police definitions of criminality by varying one aspect of the "identity" of the prospective criminal subject. They selected a dozen students, black, Chicano, and white, who had blameless driving records free of any moving violations, and asked them to drive to and from school as they normally did, with the addition of a "circumstantial indicator" in the shape of a phosphorescent bumper sticker reading "Black Panther Party." In the first 17 days of the study these students amassed 30 driving citations—failure to signal, improper lane changes, and the like. Two students had to withdraw from the experiment after two days because their licenses were suspended; and the project soon had to be abandoned because the $1,000 appropriation for the experiment had been used up in paying bails and fines of the participants.

The President's Crime Commission Report notes that "the criminal justice process may be viewed as a large-scale screening system. At each stage it tries to sort out the better risks to return to the general population," but the report does not elaborate on *how* these better risks are sorted. Professor Sarbin suggests an answer: "To put the conclusion bluntly, membership in the class 'lawbreakers' is *not* distributed according to economic or social status, but membership in, the class 'criminals' *is* distributed according to social or economic status...To account for the disproportionate number of lower class and black prisoners, I propose that the agents of law enforcement and justice engage in decision-making against a backcloth of belief that people can be readily classified into two types, criminal and non-criminal."

This point is underlined by Professor Donald Taft: "Negroes are more likely to be suspected of crime than are whites. They are also more likely to be arrested. If the perpetrator of a crime is known to be a Negro the police may arrest all negroes who were near the scene— a procedure they would rarely dare to follow with whites. After arrest, negroes are less likely to secure bail, and so are more liable to be counted in jail statistics. They are more liable than whites to be indicted and less likely to have their cases *nol prossed* or otherwise dismissed. If tried, negroes are more likely to be convicted. If convicted, they are less likely to be given probation. For this reason they are more likely to be included in the count of prisoners. Negroes are also more liable than whites to be kept in prison for the full terms of their commitments and correspondingly less likely to be paroled."

As anyone versed in the ways of the criminal justice system will tell you, the screening process begins with the policeman on the beat: the young car thief from a "nice home" will be returned to his family with a warning. If he repeats the offense or gets into more serious trouble, the parents may be called in for a conference with the prosecuting authorities. The well-to-do family has a dozen options: they can send their young delinquent to a boarding school, or to stay with relatives in another part of the country, they can hire the professional services of a psychiatrist or counselor—and the authorities will support them in these efforts. The Juvenile Court judge can see at a glance that this boy does not belong in the toils of the criminal justice system, that given a little tolerance and helpful guidance there is every chance he will straighten out by the time he reaches college age.

For the identical crime the ghetto boy will be arrested, imprisoned in the juvenile detention home, and set on the downward path that ends in the penitentiary. The screening process does not end with arrest, it obtains at every stage of the criminal justice system.

To cite one example that any observer of the crime scene—and particularly the black observer—will doubtless be able to match from his own experience: a few years ago a local newspaper reported horrendous goings-on of high school seniors in Piedmont, a wealthy enclave in Alameda County, California, populated by executives, businessmen, rich politicians. The students had gone on a general rampage that included arson, vandalism, breaking and entering, assault, car theft, rape. Following a conference among parents, their lawyers, and prosecuting authorities, it was decided that no formal action should be taken against the miscreants; they were all released to the custody of their families, who promised to subject them to appropriate discipline. In the very same week, a lawyer of my acquaintance told me with tight-lipped fury of the case of a nine-year-old black ghetto dweller in the same county, arrested for stealing a nickel from a white classmate, charged with "extortion and robbery," hauled off to juvenile hall, and, despite the urgent pleas of his distraught mother, there imprisoned for six weeks to wait for his court hearing.

Thus it seems safe to assert that there is indeed a criminal type—but he is not a biological, anatomical, phrenological, or anthropological type; rather, he is a social creation, etched by the dominant class and ethnic prejudices of a given society.

The day may not be far off when the horny-handed policeman on the beat may expect an assist in criminal-type-spotting from practitioners of a new witchcraft: behavior prediction. In 1970, Dr. Arnold Hutschnecker, President Nixon's physician, proposed mass psychological testing of six- to eight-year-old children to determine which were criminally inclined, and the establishment of special camps to house those found to have "violent tendencies." Just where the candidates for the mass testing and the special camps would be sought out was made clear when Dr. Hutschnecker let slip the fact he was proposing this program as an alternative to slum reconstruction. It would be, he said, "a direct, immediate, effective way of attacking the problem at its very origin, by focusing on the criminal mind of the child."

The behavior-predictors would catch the violence-prone *before* he springs, would confine him, possibly treat him, but in any event would certainly not let him out to consummate the hideous deeds of which he is so demonstrably capable. Their recurring refrain: "If only the clearly discernible defects in Oswald's psychological makeup had been detected in his childhood—had he been turned over to us, who have the resources to diagnose such deviant personalities—we would have tried to help him. If we decided he was beyond help, we would have locked him up forever and a major tragedy of this generation could have been averted." They refer, of course, to Lee Harvey Oswald, who allegedly gunned down President Kennedy, not to Russell G. Oswald, the New York Commissioner of Corrections who ordered the troops into Attica, as a result of which 43 perished by gunfire.

3

"Lock 'Em Up and Throw Away the Key"
African-American Males and the Criminal Justice System
Marc Mauer

The Crisis and Consequences
of Criminal Justice Control

Discussion regarding the crisis of the African-American male has continued for a number of years. Whether or not the African-American male is an "endangered species," clearly the dimensions of this crisis are broad. Perhaps nowhere are they so startling as within the criminal justice system. Consider:

- As of 1995, almost one in three (32 percent) African-American males twenty to twenty-nine years old was under the control of the criminal justice system—prison, jail, probation, or parole. This compared with one in sixteen white males and one in eight Hispanic males.[1]

- By 1992, the number of African-American males in prison and jail, 583,000, exceeded the number of African-American males enrolled in higher education, 537,000.[2]

Source: Revised especially for *The Dilemmas of Corrections*.

- Forty-nine percent of all prisoners in the United States are African-American males. Black males comprise 41 percent of those condemned on death row.
- At current levels of imprisonment, a black boy born today has a 28 percent chance of serving time in a state or federal prison at some point in his lifetime.[3]

These statistics only begin to describe the complexity of the criminal justice crisis, a crisis defined by the pervasiveness of the criminal justice system in the lives of black men, and its devastating consequences for the health and survival of the black community.

The problems African-American males face in the criminal justice system are not new, of course. Lynching as a form of "justice" defined a significant period in our history. The fact that 90 percent of the 455 men executed for rape were black tells us much about the system's contributions to the perpetuation of racism.

Certainly, in recent years, change has taken place within the criminal justice system. Blacks and other minorities are now much more prominent in a variety of leadership positions in the criminal justice system—police chiefs, judges, and wardens. But, as the videotaped beating of Rodney G. King in Los Angeles in 1991 told us only too well, long-established patterns of abuse still exist.

Despite some positive changes, the most dramatic and ominous trend within the justice system is its vast expansion, dating back more than two decades. Since 1973, an unprecedented growth in the system has taken place. Even though the justice system has long been a primary feature of the life cycle for many African-American men, never before have we had a period in which so many black males have come under the control of the system. In this sense, we can only surmise what the consequences of this situation will be for current and future generations.

For the young African-American men caught up in the system, their prospects for engaging in a productive career and family life will be severely postponed and diminished. Employers, educational institutions and potential marriage partners display little enthusiasm for the young man who has little work history or potential earnings, and whose long-term stability in the community is uncertain.

There are those who would say that, unfortunate as this situation may be for the black community, these, after all, are black "criminals," who are being placed under criminal justice supervision. Had they not chosen a life of crime, they would not be suffering the ill effects of the justice system. Furthermore, the black community is being afforded protection from those who rape, rob, and assault its citizens with such frequency.

When the African-American community is experiencing high crime rates, this argument is persuasive for many. Further, if it could be demonstrated that the high incarceration rate of African-American men was having a sustained impact on crime, some would argue that this would justify the financial and human cost of such policies.

What we see instead is a twenty-year progression of criminal justice policies that have had little effect on crime but have taken a great toll on human lives. Consider the decade of 1985-95, for example, a period in which the nation's prison and jail populations doubled. If one assumes that a high incarceration level should have a significant impact on crime, then we should have seen dramatic results during this period. Yet, overall, the crime rate changed little during this period.

Even more disturbing to the "law and order" perspective is that trends in crime rates were not consistent during this period. From 1985 to 1991, crime increased by a total of 13 percent. Then, from 1991 to 1995, crime rates declined, by a total of 11 percent. Thus, in a decade, prison populations increased and crime went up; then prison populations continued to increase and crime went down. The cause-and-effect relationship is far from clear.

Advocates of a continued "get tough" approach to crime control face the challenge of defining an optimal level of control, a point at which such a policy will begin to have a demonstrable impact. If one out of three young African-American men under the control of the system is not sufficient to reduce crime substantially, does the control level need to be increased to one out of two, or three of four? Would society tolerate such levels if it were young white men involved in the system?

Aside from the human costs to the African-American community, the overall financial costs to the nation are substantial and are increasingly problematic for the health of our communities. A conservative estimate of the costs of incarceration for the 583,000 African-American males in prison and jail is $11 billion a year. Corrections costs nationally are more than $30 billion annually, and represent the fastest-growing expenditure in state budgets.[4] Rising criminal justice costs are resulting in painful choices for state and local officials faced with cutbacks in education, transportation, and other services.

Why Are So Many African-American Men Involved in the Criminal Justice System?

If we are to begin to develop strategies by which to reduce the disproportionate effect of the criminal justice system on African-American men, we need to understand the complex factors that have created this situation. These include criminal justice policies and socioeconomic issues affecting the African-American community.

Crime Rates

A starting point for an analysis is to look at why so many African-American men enter the justice system in the first place. Except for the relative handful who have been unjustly convicted, clearly all the African-American men in the system have committed a crime—or have been charged with a crime, as is the case for the pretrial detainees in jail.

Do African-American men commit more crimes than men of other ethnic and racial groups, or do their high numbers in the criminal justice system reflect a discriminatory system?

We can see that African-American males do have higher offense levels for a range of crimes. Homicide rates are perhaps the best indicator of this, since virtually all homicides are reported to the police, and the rates of arrest, prosecution, and conviction are also high. Overall, African Americans make up 54 percent of all arrests for murder, clearly very disproportionate to their representation in the total population.[5] While arrest data may reflect some racial bias in police priorities, it is unlikely that the overall arrest rates for homicides are dramatically different than actual offense rates.

Victimization studies conducted by the Justice Department confirm the higher offense rate of black males for a number of crimes. These studies, in contrast to Federal Bureau of Investigation crime reports that only account for crimes reported to the police, survey households to determine levels of victimization regardless of whether crimes are reported to the police. Thus, the victimization studies yield a higher, but presumably more accurate, rate of actual crime. For violent crimes, blacks are the perceived perpetrators for 25.5 percent of single offender crimes, about twice their proportion of the total population.[6] Although these figures are for all blacks, not just males, the vast majority of crimes for blacks and whites alike are committed by males.

Other studies show that for crimes against persons—rape, robbery, assault, and larceny—black males eighteen to twenty are convicted of these crimes at a rate five times that of white males in this age group.[7] It would be surprising, indeed, if African-American male offending rates for certain crimes were not higher than for white males. For, if we believe that even some causal relationship exists between social and economic conditions and crime rates, then certainly the black community, with its disproportionate levels of poverty and other social ills, should exhibit higher rates of crime as well.

If we accept the fact that African-American males commit serious crimes at higher rates than white males, and both groups at much higher rates than for women of any race, then an explanation of why this is so is needed. The historical legacy of racism is certainly critical to any analysis. But the dramatic increases in criminal justice populations over the past twenty years suggest other factors as well.

Structural Changes in the U.S. Economy

Not all poor people commit crimes, nor do all wealthy people refrain from committing crimes. We need only look at the large numbers of law-abiding poor people or the savings and loan speculators of the late 1980s to see this. Yet, it is also true that the stresses, strains and lack of income produced by poverty create needs and temptations that lead some poor people to criminal activity.

While poverty has always existed, and the black community has experienced it in great numbers, the economic changes that the United States has undergone in the last twenty years have had a profound effect on the life prospects of the black community. As the manufacturing economy has been replaced in large part by the service economy, urban areas have experienced severe dislocations, leaving them with fewer jobs, eroding tax bases, and financially strapped families. Relatively high-wage manufacturing has been replaced by lower-wage service work. An automobile worker in Detroit with a high school education who could support a family on a single income now may have a son selling computer software at half the salary of his father. These structural changes have created the framework for a political climate based on social divisions, racism, as well as a less charitable view of one's neighbors and community.

The Criminal Justice Response

The beginnings of the "get tough" movement can be traced to the late 1960s, but the framework for its success is clearly ingrained within the priorities of the criminal justice system. Living in a time of high crime rates and daily crises in the criminal justice system, we tend to forget that the system is one in which conscious and unconscious policy options are being made every day that affect our crime-control responses.

In the most basic way, our history of criminal justice control is one of controlling the crimes of the poor. One need only visit almost any prison in the country to note the vast inmate population of low-income and primarily non-white prisoners. Nowhere in the Constitution is it written that theft of an automobile shall be taken more seriously than insider trading, yet in practice, that has been an unwritten assumption of our system.

Some would contend that, while it is unfortunate to focus on crimes of the poor, their "street crimes" are more violent than those of the wealthy, and so close attention is warranted. Looking at street crimes, or the FBI's crime rate index, though, we find that only about 13 percent are violent.

Further, what constitutes a "violent" offense? Many offenses of environmental pollution or workplace safety are much more violent in their long-term consequences than individual street crimes. Do we pay more attention to street crimes because they are immediate and direct, or because they are more likely to involve non-white offenders than are white-collar crimes?

How do these priorities manifest themselves in daily routines of law enforcement? Many of them are built into the discretionary nature of the system, starting with the cop on the beat, and working through the prosecutor, judge, and parole board. If the local police officer sees two drunken men staggering down the street, one a white in a three-piece suit and the other a disheveled looking African American, who is more likely to be arrested and who will probably get a call home for a ride?

Resource allocation within the criminal justice system also tells us much about the priorities placed on various crimes. The total national loss for all street crimes is estimated at $11 billion a year, compared with $175 billion to $231 billion a year for white-collar crime.[8] Until relatively recently, little attention was paid to white-collar offenses. Although this has changed somewhat with higher rates of apprehension and conviction beginning in the 1980s, the system remains one that is overwhelmingly focused on crimes of the poor.

The Rise of the "Get Tough" Movement

The "formal" inauguration of the "get tough" on crime movement can in many ways be seen in the 1968 presidential campaign. Before that, criminal justice reform, while perhaps not in vogue, was considered a worthy topic of discussion. Public support for the death penalty was at an all-time low, only a handful of executions took place during the 1960s, and incarceration rates had been declining for almost a decade.

But underlying this seemingly liberal public atmosphere were the growing seeds of a more repressive social climate. Crime rates, particularly in urban areas, increased markedly in the 1960s, leading to the "white flight" and heightened security measures that now are common-place. The impact of the civil rights movement, the urban rebellions of 1967, and the social divisions caused by the Vietnam War polarized America, often along racial lines. In a world seemingly changing by the day, those who could not, or would not, understand the changes sought a return to "normalcy"—or, as captured by Richard M. Nixon—"law and order."

Mr. Nixon's successful campaign captured these themes well for this targeted audience. Upon taking office, he moved to quickly implement "tough" crime-control policies. Under the guise of criminal code reform, the Nixon administration took a draft bill prepared under President Lyndon B. Johnson and developed the notorious S.1, a compilation of some of the most repressive legislation concerning civil rights and civil liberties seen in many years.

The "get tough" movement has since broadened from the brainchild of the Republican administration to a political statement and policies that have worked equally well for Democrats and Republicans. Liberal and conservative governors boast of their achievements in building prisons and in incarcerating greater numbers of offenders. Politicians try to outdo one another on their support for the death penalty and more repressive crime-control measures.

The movement reached its zenith, in terms of public attention, in the 1988 presidential campaign, as George Bush's media advisors succeeded in making Willie Horton a household name. Little attention was paid to the overwhelming success rates of most prison furlough programs, or even Governor Michael S. Dukakis' boasting of his own prison construction accomplishments while in office.

Unfortunately, the "get tough" movement has meant more than just empty campaign slogans. Once elected, legislators have often pursued repressive criminal justice policies with a vengeance. This has been through mandatory minimum sentences, "three strikes" laws, cutbacks in parole and "good time," and other policies that have cumulatively served to swell our institutional populations.

The overall dimensions of this buildup are staggering. Since 1973, the prison population has quintupled from just over 200,000 to 1.1 million by 1996.[9] Probation and parole populations have experienced similar increases, rising 165 percent and 213 percent, respectively, from 1980 to 1994.[10] Since the 1976 Supreme Court ruling reinstating the death penalty, the death rows of this nation have swelled quickly, with well over 3,000 inmates now awaiting execution.

For African-American males, already starting with substantial numbers in the criminal justice system, this movement has brought the current crisis. Even more distressing is that African-American and Hispanic rates of criminal justice control are increasing at an even greater rate than for whites. Much of this increasing disparity is a result of the renewed "war on drugs."

An irony of the "get tough" movement is that after twenty years of implementing "tough" policies, an image of the criminal justice system as being "soft on crime" still exists—"revolving-door justice," "soft" judges, and "coddling" prisoners.

Seemingly, the public has an insatiable appetite for "tough" rhetoric on crime. However, this craving for "toughness" may have been misrepresented in the media and by pollsters. A distinction needs to be made between getting tough and controlling crime. If we can control crime and do it in a cost-effective manner through less repressive policies, we should expect public support to be forthcoming.

The "War on Drugs": A War on the Poor?

While overall crime rates have not changed substantially during the 1980s, certainly nowhere near explaining the rise in prison populations, the renewed war on drugs has fueled much of the dramatic increase:

- Adult arrests for selling and manufacturing drugs increased nearly fourfold from 1980 to 1989, to 404,275 from 102,714. Arrests for drug possession more than doubled, to 843,488 from 368,451.[11]
- Drug offenders make up an increasingly larger share of the federal prison population, rising to 59 percent of all prisoners in 1994 from 25 percent in 1980.[12]

Although drug use cuts across class and racial lines, drug law enforcement has been disproportionately directed toward the inner cities and, thereby, African-American and Hispanic drug use. The National Institute of Drug Abuse has reported that African Americans comprise 12 percent of the people who use drugs regularly, and 16 percent of regular cocaine users. Yet, more than 48 percent of those arrested for heroin and cocaine drug charges in 1988 were black.[13] Delaware Prosecutor Charles Butler once observed: "Sure, it's true we prosecute a high percentage of minorities for drugs. The simple fact is, if you have a population, minority or not, that is conducting most of their illegal business on the street, those cases are easy pickings for the police."[14]

Thus, although drug prosecutions and convictions are up nationally, blacks are making up an increasingly greater percentage of those figures. From 1984 to 1995, the black share of drug arrests nationally rose from 30 percent to 37 percent.[15] Unless dramatic change takes place in how the war on drugs is waged—currently two-thirds of federal funding is devoted to law enforcement—we can expect ever larger numbers of African-American males to swell our prisons over the next decade.

Racism and the Criminal Justice System

The evidence upon which to determine whether the criminal justice system has a racist effect is not as clear as one might expect. On the one hand, as we have seen, African-American males are convicted of serious offenses at greater rates than are white males. In this regard, if the criminal justice system responds to those offenses equally, then the determination of racial bias would have to be sought in social and economic conditions preceding the criminal justice system.

But in the most extreme case, capital punishment, the evidence is quite strong for a racially determined outcome. Several authoritative studies in recent years have concluded that the race of offender and victim in a potentially capital case play a strong role in determining in which cases a prosecutor will seek the death penalty and when it will be imposed by a judge or jury.[16] The studies find that the black offender-white victim combination is far more likely to result in a death sentence than any other pairing. (When presented with this evidence, a Supreme Court majority responded by saying that an overall pattern of racism was not sufficient to overturn death statutes, and that death-row inmates would need to prove specific racial bias in their own cases.)

Looking at other offenses, though, the research literature is more mixed. Alfred Blumstein, for example, found that 76 percent of the disparity in incarceration could be explained by factors unrelated to race, primarily seriousness of offense and prior criminal history. The remaining 24 percent, he concluded, might be explained by race or by other factors.[17] A RAND study of sentencing in California determined that race was not a factor in sentencing when other variables were controlled for, although with the key exception of drug offenders.[18]

How does this evidence fit with the experience of black defendants and prisoners, as well as their attorneys, who report on racially determined criminal justice outcomes every day? The seeming contradiction may depend on which part of the system is being examined. As described previously, much of the disparity in the justice system may lie in the early stages, at the level of arrest and prosecution. Thus, a black drug offender and a white one may be treated equally at sentencing, but the black offender may be more likely to be arrested and prosecuted in the first place. Therefore, we cannot necessarily conclude that the system is fair even if the sentencing outcome appears to be so.

Several studies demonstrate these dynamics and the racially dispro-portionate outcomes they produce. The United States Sentencing Commission, in examining the impact of federal mandatory sentencing statutes, found that prosecutors used their discretion to plea-bargain below the mandatory minimum sentence in a manner that "appears to be related to the race of the defendant."[19]

A comprehensive study of plea-bargaining practices in California documents similar patterns. An analysis of 700,000 cases by the *San Jose Mercury News* concludes that, "At virtually every stage of pre-trial negotiation, whites are more successful than non-whites."[20]

Life Prospects for Black Males

Perhaps the most troubling explanation for the high rate of criminal justice control for African-American men relates to the real and per-ceived lack of opportunity and sense of hopelessness about the future. For young African-American men growing up today, the perception of the criminal justice system is a radically different one than for young white men. With one in three young African-American men coming under the control of the system, black men find it hard not to view the justice system as almost an inevitable part of one's life cycle. This is not to say that it is a "rite of passage," but that it is a part of growing up that is taken for granted almost as much as going to college is assumed for many young whites.

This sense of limited opportunity, of course, is not just a perception, but one based on disturbing reality. As the National Center for Children in Poverty at Columbia University has documented, one of every two African-American children under the age of six is now living in poverty— as are 40 percent of Hispanic children.[21] Unless current policies are altered seriously, this group represents the next generation of "prison-bound" offenders.

How Can We Respond to the High Criminal Justice Control Rate?

Much of the solution to the high rate of African-American male involvement in the criminal justice system lies, of course, in addressing racism and social and economic inequities, and in strengthening com-munity support of young people. In the course of developing these broad strategies, though, we should not neglect reforms within the criminal justice system that can contribute to a lessening of the system's negative impact on black males.

Following is an outline of policy reforms to address the problem:

Increase Diversion from the Criminal Justice System

Many young and first-time offenders are only stigmatized by their experiences with the criminal justice system, without necessarily receiving appropriate supervision or support. Opportunities exist to divert many of these offenders to organizations and individuals who can better focus on the problems of black, Hispanic, and poor youth. Such organizations as 100 Black Men exist in many communities, and they can be used by the courts to divert defendants, and to develop preventive measures to work with "at-risk" youth before they become enmeshed in the justice system.

Focus the "War on Drugs" on Prevention and Treatment

The law enforcement approach to drug abuse is hardly a new strategy. It has been tried for decades, with few results. The consequences of current and proposed policies of large-scale arrests of casual users as well as dealers threatens to overload completely the judicial and corrections systems, while avoiding discussions on the more profound underlying issues.

A comprehensive study by the Special Committee on Criminal Justice in a Free Society of the American Bar Association's Criminal Justice Section illustrates the problem well. The committee reported that, of approximately 34 million serious crimes committed against persons or property in 1986, 31 million never resulted in arrest and only several hundred thousand resulted in felony convictions and imprisonment. Even if we assume that a good number of those offenders had committed multiple crimes that were not detected, we are still left with a situation in which law enforcement can only result in the prosecution of a small portion of overall criminal activity.

With such widespread drug use in our society, continued excessive reliance on the criminal justice system can only have a limited effect on drug crimes—at great cost. In some jurisdictions, criminal justice officials have recognized and responded to the limitations of incarceration. Pretrial diversion programs in several jurisdictions now screen drug defendants and refer some to treatment programs in lieu of prosecution. The former police chief in New Haven, Connecticut, discontinued mass drug arrests, and used his officers to go door-to-door in certain communities encouraging residents to make use of treatment programs sponsored by the city.

The larger policy question, of course, is whether drug treatment or law enforcement is a financial priority. Decisions made by Congress and both Democratic and Republican administrations have resulted in two-thirds of the monies allocated for anti-drug efforts being spent on law enforcement. Only one-third has gone to treatment and prevention.

With waiting lists to enter drug treatment of six months or more in many communities, can we really say that the criminal justice system is our only alternative, and that nothing else has worked?

Reduce Lengthy and Inefficient Prison Terms

Mandatory sentencing laws and lengthier prison terms have resulted in high costs, with only relatively modest gains in crime control. Prisoners are prevented from committing crimes in the community while they are locked up, but this represents only a small fraction of all crimes. A 1978 report by the National Academy of Sciences concluded that to achieve a 10 percent reduction in crime, New York would have had to increase its prison population more than twofold and Massachusetts more than threefold.

The massive increase in incarceration and in the lengthening of prison terms provides almost no long-term benefits in reducing recidivism. The most recent Justice Department study of this issue shows that recidivism rates, while very high, are virtually identical for prisoners who serve from one to five years.[22] Therefore, "getting tough" results in high corrections costs, but leaves us with offenders who are no less likely to commit future crimes.

Reducing lengthy prison terms by itself is not the answer to crime control problems. What it would accomplish, though, is to relieve the burden on an overcrowded system, reduce the impact of the system on minorities, and free up tax dollars for more preventive measures.

Sentence to Ameliorate Racial Disparities

Judges, prosecutors, defense attorneys, and probation officers all have a unique and important opportunity to lessen the drastic effect that the justice system has had on African-American males. The opportunity comes at sentencing. The courtroom sentencing process should include a full examination of the circumstances of victim and offender, and an analysis of community support and supervision mechanisms that may contribute to appropriate sentencing options. The goals of this process should be:

- To assess public safety concerns.

- To restore victims to the extent possible.
- To order appropriate and constructive sanctions in the community.
- To reduce the chances that offenders will return to the system.

While such a process may sound unrealistic to some, it is actually very similar to that used in sentencing many white-collar offenders.

Use More Alternatives to Incarceration

For far too long, we have equated punishment with prison. Aside from incarceration being by far the most costly component of the criminal justice system, it has also not proved to be very productive in reducing crime. If we want our justice system to punish, treat or supervise offenders, a variety of community-based sanctions exist that can accomplish this without resorting to imprisonment in all cases. These programs vary, but they include restitution to victims, community service and intensive probation supervision. They also include provisions for treatment programs, education, and employment.

Programs that provide alternative sentencing options for judges have long been established, and they have proven to be more appropriate than incarceration in many cases. Far too often, though, they are not well financed or they fail to have clear goals for diverting offenders from prison. In some jurisdictions, too, white offenders are more likely to receive the benefits of alternative sentencing, while African Americans continue to receive prison terms in large numbers. Programs providing alternatives to incarceration need to be monitored to ensure that black and Hispanic offenders are appropriately represented in these sanctions.

Conclusion

The criminal justice system is not the primary cause of the distressing plight of African-American males, nor is it unique in its operations regarding racial disparities. Its impact on African-American males and the African-American community, though, is potentially devastating for the life prospects of current and future generations. Of particular significance is that long-established trends in the criminal justice system have worsened considerably over the past two decades, with little relief in sight.

The potential for political and community change does exist, even if reform forces appear to be weak at times. Two factors appear to be critical in developing broad public support for change. First is the escalating cost of building and operating prisons. Those who are increasingly conscious of limited resources and the competition for tax dollars may be receptive to arguments based on the fiscal crisis that a growing corrections bureaucracy will create.

Tied in with this is the limited effectiveness of the justice system in controlling crime. Aside from the enormous cost of courts and prisons, most Americans still do not feel safe in their homes and communities. A strategy designed to link these issues, along with alternative crime-control proposals, can build a broad coalition to support more effective, and less destructive, policies.

Notes

[1] Marc Mauer and Tracy Huling. *Young Black Americans and the Criminal Justice System: Five Years Later*. The Sentencing Project, October 1995.

[2] Marc Mauer. *Americans Behind Bars: The International Use of Incarceration, 1992-1993*. The Sentencing Project, September 1994.

[3] *Lifetime Likelihood of Going to State or Federal Prison*, Bureau of Justice Statistics, March 1997.

[4] National Conference of State Legislatures, *State Budget Actions, 1994*, November 1994.

[5] FBI. *Uniform Crime Reports, 1995*, 1996.

[6] *Criminal Victimization in the United States, 1993*. Bureau of Justice Statistics, 1995.

[7] Elliott Currie. *Confronting Crime: An American Challenge*. Pantheon, New York, 1985, p. 154.

[8] John Irwin and James Austin. *It's about Time*. National Council on Crime and Delinquency, 1987.

[9] *Prison and Jail Inmates at Midyear 1996*, Bureau of Justice Statistics, January 1997.

[10] *Correctional Populations in the United States, 1994*, Bureau of Justice Statistics, June 1996.

[11] *Drug and Crime Facts: 1990*. Bureau of Justice Statistics, August 1991.

[12] *Correctional Populations in the United States, 1994*

[13] Sam Meddis. "Whites, Not Blacks, At the Core of Drug Crisis." *USA Today*, December 20, 1989.

[14] Barry Bearak. "Big Catch: Drug War's Little Fish." *Los Angeles Times*, May 6, 1990.

[15] FBI. *Uniform Crime Reports*, various years.

[16] See "USA: The Death Penalty." Amnesty International, London, 1987.

[17] Alfred Blumstein. "Racial Disproportionality of U.S. Prison Populations Revisited." *University of Colorado Law Review*, Vol. 64, No. 3, 1993.

[18] Stephen Klein, Joan Petersilia, Susan Turner. "Race and Imprisonment Decisions in California." *Science*, February 16, 1990.

[19] "Mandatory Minimum Penalties in the Federal Criminal Justice System." United States Sentencing Commission, August 1991.

[20] Christopher Schmitt. "Plea Bargaining Favors Whites as Blacks, Hispanics Pay Price." *San Jose Mercury News*, December 8, 1991.

[21] Spencer Rich. "Report Says Children Under 6 Have Highest Poverty Rate." *Washington Post*, April 15, 1990.

[22] Allen J. Beck and Bernard E. Shipley, "Recidivism of Prisoners Released in 1983," Bureau of Justice Statistics, April 1989.

4

Trends in U.S. Correctional Populations
Why has the Number of Offenders Under Supervision Tripled Since 1980?
Allen J. Beck

Since 1980, the estimated number of adults in the United States under some form of correctional supervision, including those on probation, in local jails, in state or federal prisons, or on parole, has tripled—increasing by more than 3.6 million in sixteen years. The year 1996 marked a record high of over 5.5 million adults under correctional supervision. At year-end 1996, nearly 3.2 million adults were on probation, 1.1 million were in the physical custody of state and federal prisons, and more than 700,000 were on parole. At midyear 1996, more than 510,000 adults were also held in local jails (table 1).

The percentage of adults under correctional supervision rose from 1.1 percent in 1980 to 2.8 percent in 1996.[1] At year-end 1996 an estimated 1 out of every 35 adults were under correctional supervision—1 in every 20 adult men and 1 in every 125 women.

Source: Prepared especially for *The Dilemmas of Corrections.*

Table 1. Changes in the size of U.S. adult correctional populations, 1980-96

Year	Total correctional population[1]	Probation	Jail[2]	Prison	Parole
1980	1,840,400	1,118,097	182,288	319,598	220,438
1985	3,011,500	1,968,712	254,986	487,593	300,203
1990	4,348,000	2,670,234	403,019	743,382	531,407
1991	4,535,600	2,728,472	424,129	792,535	590,442
1992	4,762,600	2,811,611	441,781	850,566	658,601
1993	4,944,000	2,903,061	455,500	909,381	676,100
1994	5,141,300	2,981,022	479,800	990,147	690,371
1995[3]	5,335,100	3,077,861	499,300	1,078,542	679,351
1996	5,523,100	3,180,363	510,400	1,127,669	704,709
Percent change					
1995-96	4%	3%	2%	5%	4%
1980-96	200%	184%	180%	253%	220%
Average annual percent change					
1980-96	7.1%	6.8%	6.6%	8.2%	7.5%
1990-96	4.1%	3.0%	4.0%	7.2%	4.8%
1980-90	11.6%	11.0%	10.8%	13.4%	12.3%

Note: Counts for probation, prison, and parole population are for December 31 of each year. Jail population counts are for June 30 each year. Prisoner counts are for those in custody only.
[1]A small number of individuals may have multiple correctional statuses; consequently, the total number of persons under correctional supervision is an overestimate.
[2]The jail population counts for 1993-96 are estimated and exclude persons supervised outside of jail facilities.
[3]Parole counts for 1995 dropped from the previously reported total of 700,174 due to changes in reporting methods in New Jersey and the federal system.
Source: Correctional Populations In the United States, 1996.

Supervision rates were the highest among black males. In 1996, an estimated 16 percent of all adult black males were under correctional supervision, compared to 3.5 percent of all adult white males (table 2). In 1980, 7.2 percent of adult black males and 1.5 percent of adult white males were under supervision. In both years black males age 20 to 29 had the highest supervision rates (13.2 percent in 1980 and 29.2 percent in 1996). Among white males in their twenties, 3.1 percent were under supervision in 1980; 7.5 percent in 1996.

These statistics are both alarming and profoundly disturbing. Behind them lies a high rate of crime and widespread offending, with enormous societal and individual costs. Combined criminal justice expenditures by all levels of government reached 100 billion dollars in 1994; $32

**Table 2. Estimated number of males under correctional supervision,
by race, age, and year**

	Estimated number[1]			Percent of all persons in age category[2]		
	1980	1991	1996	1980	1991	1996
White males	1,023,400	2,402,000	2,808,900	1.5 %	3.1 %	3.5 %
18-19[3]	99,700	161,300	136,300	2.7	5.5	4.4
20-24	311,800	580,000	599,000	3.4	7.2	8.0
25-29	230,300	552,200	569,700	2.7	6.4	7.1
30-34	143,300	437,900	510,700	1.9	4.7	5.8
35-59	95,500	275,500	416,600	1.6	3.2	4.4
40 or older	142,800	395,100	576,600	0.5	1.0	1.3
Black males	565,600	1,422,000	1,748,100	7.2 %	14.8 %	16.0 %
18-19[3]	43,000	98,400	97,400	7.3	17.7	16.2
20-24	170,800	340,200	390,900	13.0	26.0	29.4
25-29	149,500	345,500	376,600	13.5	26.4	28.9
30-34	101,700	285,100	343,300	11.4	22.1	24.4
35-59	43,600	183,200	241,900	6.5	16.0	17.2
40 or older	57,000	169,600	298,000	2.0	5.0	6.1

Note: All numbers have been estimated based on BJS surveys and censuses.
[1]Data were rounded to the nearest 100.
[2]Percents were based on the total resident population, obtained from the Bureau of the Census,
U.S. Population Estimates, by Age, Sex, Race, and Hispanic Origin:1990 to 1995, PPL-41.
Population estimates for 1996, by sex, race, and age, were adjusted for the census undercount.
[3]Excludes youthful offenders.
Source: Correctional Populations In the United States, 1996.

billion of this amount was for corrections.[2] Balanced against this was incalculable amounts of squandered human capital—the damaged and lost lives of both victims and offenders.

These statistics reflect the complexity of the interaction between crime and criminal justice policies. The statistics that follow suggest that the dramatic growth and change in the nation's correctional populations is only partially explained by trends in crime and changing patterns of offending. Correctional populations have also been affected by changes in criminal justice policies, including the unprecedented and far-reaching war on drugs; enactment of new laws that increase the severity and certainty of punishment; adoption of mandatory minimum sentences and sentencing enhancements for certain offenses and offenders; and introduction of sentencing guidelines that limit the discretion of judges and parole boards.

The tremendous growth of the U.S. correctional populations and changes in their composition illustrate the interaction between crime and social policy. Though the number of adults arrested increased by nearly 50 percent between 1980 and 1996, the number under correctional supervision tripled. To better understand this growth in corrections, we draw on findings from data collected and analyzed by the Bureau of Justice Statistics (BJS).[3] By consolidating these findings, we can develop a detailed profile of the nation's correctional populations. These findings not only document the nature and extent of the growth for each population but identify factors that account for this growth.

I. Recent Changes in U.S.Correctional Populations

Changing Demographic Characteristics

Correctional populations in the United States have changed dramatically since 1980. The number of female inmates in jails and prisons has increased at a faster rate than the number of males (table 3). Although more than 9 of every 10 inmates are male, the percentage of female inmates has been steadily rising. Between 1983 and 1996, the percentage of females among jail inmates rose from 7 percent to 11 percent; since 1980, the percentage female among state inmates rose from 4 percent to 6 percent. Women also represent a growing percentage of the probation and parole populations. In 1996, 21 percent of probationers and 11 percent of parolees were female, up from 16 percent and 7 percent, respectively, in 1985.

Statistics on race and Hispanic origin were first compiled on persons under community supervision in 1985. These statistics show that an increasing percentage of inmates are from minority groups. While Hispanics are considered a minority, table 3 shows Hispanics listed separately because the characterization of "Hispanic" is not considered a racial classification, but rather an ethnic one.

In both prisons and jails, Hispanics are the fastest growing minority group—increasing between 1980 and 1996 from 10 percent to 17 percent of state inmates and from 15 percent to 28 percent of federal inmates. Hispanics (of any race) represented 18 percent of all jail inmates in 1996, up from 13 percent in 1983. Overall, the percentage of non-Hispanic whites dropped from 46 percent to 37 percent among jail inmates and from 40 percent to 35 percent among state prison inmates.

Table 3.   Adults under correctional supervision, by sex, race, Hispanic origin, and year

	Probation		Local jails		State prisons	
	1985	1996	1983	1996	1980	1996
Sex						
Male	84 %	79 %	93 %	89 %	96 %	94 %
Female	16	21	7	11	4	6
Race						
White	70 %	64 %	59 %	53 %	52 %	47 %
Black	29	35	40	43	47	51
Other	1	1	1	4	1	2
Hispanic origin	14 %	15 %	13 %	18 %	10 %	17 %

	Federal prisons		Parole	
	1980	1996	1985	1996
Sex				
Male	94 %	93 %	93 %	89 %
Female	6	7	7	11
Race				
White	62 %	57 %	54 %	53 %
Black	36	40	44	46
Other	1	3	2	1
Hispanic origin	15 %	28 %	17 %	20 %

Sources: *Probation Data Survey, 1985 and 1996; Census of Jails, 1983; Annual Survey of Jails, 1996; National Prisoner Statistics, 1980 and 1996; Parole Data Survey, 1985 and 1996.*

Between 1983 and 1996, the percent of jail inmates who were black, Asian, Native American, or Pacific Islanders rose from 41 percent to 47 percent. The percent among state prison inmates rose from 48 percent in 1980 to 53 percent in 1996, and the percent among federal inmates rose from 37 percent to 43 percent.

By the end of 1996 just over a third of probationers and nearly half of parolees were black, while two-thirds of probationers and half of parolees were white. Persons of other races accounted for 1 percent of each population. Hispanics, who may be of any race, constitute 15 percent of probationers and 20 percent of parolees.

Table 4. Adults under correctional supervision, by age and year

	Probation	Local jails		State prisons		Federal prisons*
	1995	1983	1996	1979	1991	1996
Age						
17 or younger	1 %	1 %	2 %	1 %	1 %	0 %
18-24	26	40	29	36	21	9
25-34	37	39	37	42	46	37
35-44	25	12	24	14	23	31
45-54	8	5	6	5	7	16
55 or older	3	2	2	2	3	7

Note: All numbers have been estimated based on BJS surveys and censuses.
Detail may not add to total because of rounding.
*Excludes unsentenced prisoners.

Jail and prison populations are also becoming more middle-aged (table 4). In 1996, 24 percent of jail inmates were between the age of 35 and 44 compared to 12 percent in 1983. The percent under the age of 25, however, dropped from 41 percent in 1983 to 31 percent in 1996. A similar change occurred among inmates in state prisons. In 1991, the most recent year for which age data were collected, 23 percent of state inmates were in the 35 to 44 age group, up from 14 percent in 1979. Despite growing concerns about the number of older inmates and their special needs, the percentage of inmates age 55 or older has remained nearly constant—about 2 percent of inmates in jail and state prison and 7 percent of federal inmates.

With respect to age, the probation population closely resembles the jail population. The first national survey of adults on probation, conducted in 1995, found an estimated 27 percent were under age 25; 37 percent were between 25 and 34; 25 percent were between 35 and 44; and 11 percent were 45 or older.[4]

Changing Offense Composition

The offense distributions of the nation's correctional populations have also significantly changed since 1980, reflecting underlying changes in criminal activity and responses of the criminal justice system.

As with other characteristics of the state inmate population, the distribution of offenses changed between 1980 and 1995 (table 5). The percentage of state prisoners serving time for violent crimes fell from 59 percent in 1980 to 47 percent in 1995. An estimated 12 percent of inmates in 1995 and 16 percent in 1980 were serving a sentence for

Table 5. Adults under correctional supervision, by offense and year

Most serious offense	Probation		Local jails		State prisons		Federal prisons		Parole
	1991	1995	1983	1996	1980	1995	1980	1995	1991
All offenses	100 %	100 %	100 %	100 %	100 %	100 %	100 %	100 %	100 %
Violent offenses	16 %	17 %	31 %	26 %	59 %	47 %	34 %	13 %	26 %
Homicide	1	1	5	3	16	12	4	1	4
Sexual assault	2	4	4	3	7	10	*	<1	4
Robbery	2	2	11	7	25	14	24	7	11
Assault	8	9	9	12	8	9	2	3	5
Other violent	2	2	2	1	3	2	4	2	1
Property offenses	34 %	29 %	39 %	27 %	30 %	23 %	24 %	9 %	36 %
Burglary	7	6	14	8	17	11	1	<1	15
Larceny/theft	16	10	12	8	5	5	13	2	12
Motor vehicle theft	1	1	2	3	2	3	**	<1	2
Fraud	7	7	5	5	4	3	10	7	5
Other property	3	4	5	3	3	3	**	1	1
Drug offenses	24 %	21 %	9 %	22 %	6 %	23 %	25 %	60 %	30 %
Possession	14	10	5	12	2	--	--	<1	10
Trafficking	8	10	4	9	4	--	--	59	18
Other/unspecified	2	2	1	1	0	--	--	0	2
Public-order offenses	25 %	31 %	21 %	24 %	4 %	7 %	11 %	18 %	7 %
Weapons	1	2	2	2	1	--	4	9	2
DWI/DUI	16	17	70	7	0	--	--	0	3
Other public-order	8	12	12	15	3	--	7	9	2
Other offenses	1 %	1 %	1 %	<1 %	--	<1 %	7 %	0 %	1 %

Note: All numbers for probation, jails, state prisons, and parole have been estimated based on BJS surveys and censuses. Federal prison numbers are from the Federal Bureau of Prisons for 1980 and from BJS' federal justice database for 1995.

--Not available.
*Included in other violent.
**Included in larceny/theft.

homicide (murder or manslaughter). Among individual offense categories, robbery showed the largest decrease, from 25 percent of all inmates in 1980 to 14 percent in 1995. The only violent offense that showed an increase was sexual assault, from 7 percent to 10 percent.

Property offenders accounted for 23 percent of all state inmates in 1995, down from 30 percent in 1980. Most of this decline resulted from a decreasing percentage of inmates sentenced for burglary.

The percentage of inmates in state prison for a drug crime rose significantly, from 6 percent in 1980 to 23 percent in 1995. Nearly 12 times as many inmates were serving a state prison sentence for a drug law violation in 1991 (225,000) as in 1980 (19,000). Inmates sentenced for a drug offense accounted for 30 percent of the total increase in the state prison population from 1980 to 1995.

Offenders in federal prisons are quite different from those in state prisons. Nearly 60 percent of all sentenced federal inmates in 1995 were in prison for a drug offense, up from 25 percent in 1980. One in 7 inmates were in prison for a violent offense, down from 1 in every 3 inmates in 1980. Nine percent were in prison for a weapons offense, up from 4 percent. Approximately two-thirds of the growth in the federal prison population since 1980 is the result of increasing numbers of drug offenders.

As with the prison inmate populations, the distribution of offenses in local jails has changed since the 1980s. Between 1983 and 1996 the number of inmates in jail for drug law violations increased dramatically. In 1983 about 1 in every 10 inmates were in jail for a drug offense; in 1996 more than 1 of every 5 were in jail for drugs. From 1983 to 1996 the increase in the number of persons in jail for drug offenses accounted for nearly a third of the total increase in the jail population.

The percentage in jail for violent offenses decreased from 31 percent in 1983 to 26 percent in 1996. Among violent offenses the largest decrease was for robbery, from 11 percent to 7 percent. The percentage in local jails for property offenses also declined, from 39 percent to 27 percent. Burglary and larceny/theft, the two most prevalent types of offenses in 1983, decreased from 26 percent to 16 percent in 1995.

Comparable data on the offense distributions of the nation's probation populations were collected in 1991 and 1995. Though trends in composition cannot be ascertained, the data in both years reveal that offenses for which persons serve time on probation most closely resemble those for which inmates serve time in local jails. An estimated 17 percent of persons on probation in 1995 were violent offenders, proportionately fewer than any other correctional population. More than 1 in 5 probationers were drug offenders (including 10 percent for drug trafficking and 10 percent for drug possession). The most common offenders on probation were those sentenced for driving while intoxicated (17 percent).

Persons under local, state, or federal parole supervision following a sentence to jail or prison differ greatly from those on probation in the types of offenses for which they had been sentenced. Two-thirds of parolees in 1991 (the only year for which data were collected) had been convicted and served time for either a property or drug offense. Whereas 16 percent of probationers in 1991 were violent offenders, 26 percent of parolees had been convicted of a violent crime. Drug traffickers were the largest single group of offenders on parole (18 percent), followed by burglars (15 percent), and those sentenced for larceny/theft (12 percent).

Criminal Histories of Offenders under Supervision Vary

Despite the enormous growth in the total number of inmates and shifts in the types of offenses for which inmates were incarcerated, the criminal backgrounds of prison inmates remained largely unchanged during the 1980s. In each of the state prison surveys conducted, approximately 8 of 10 state inmates were recidivists, that is, either sentenced to probation or incarcerated for a prior offense (table 6). In 1991 an estimated 19 percent of state inmates were first-time offenders, up from 17 percent in 1979.

Table 6. Criminal histories of inmates in jails and prisons, by year

Criminal history	Percent of jail inmates			Percent of state prison inmates			Percent of federal inmates
	1983	1989	1996	1979	1986	1991	1991
Total	100 %	100 %	100 %	100 %	100 %	100 %	100 %
No previous sentence	20 %	22 %	29 %	17 %	18 %	19 %	43 %
Current violent	8	7	10	12	13	13	5
Current nonviolent	12	16	19	5	5	6	39
Violent recidivists	37 %	30 %	34 %	54 %	53 %	49 %	23 %
Current and prior violent	11	8	12	19	19	17	7
Current violent only	12	10	9	26	22	19	6
Prior violent only	13	12	13	8	11	13	9
Nonviolent recidivists	43 %	48 %	37 %	29 %	29 %	32 %	34 %

Note: Data based on reports by inmates of their past sentences to probation or incarceration.
Detail may not add to total due to rounding.

Sources: Survey of Inmates in Local Jails, 1983, 1989, and 1996; Survey of Inmates in State Correctional Facilities, 1979, 1986, and 1991; Survey of Inmates in Federal Correctional Facilities, 1991.

In jails, however, the number of first-time offenders has grown significantly. An estimated 29 percent of all jail inmates in 1996 had no prior sentences to probation or incarceration, compared to 22 percent in 1989 and 20 percent in 1983.

Though data on the criminal histories of federal inmates in the 1980s are not available, the 1991 survey revealed that federal inmates have generally shorter and less serious criminal backgrounds than state or local inmates. About 62 percent of federal inmates, 94 percent of state inmates, and 81 percent of local jail inmates in the most recent surveys were either recidivists or serving a sentence for a violent crime. Federal inmates (43 percent) were more likely than state prison inmates (19 percent) and local jail inmates (29 percent) to have never been on probation or in a correctional facility before.

Data from the 1995 probation survey revealed that more than half of all adults on probation had a prior sentence to probation or incarceration, 45 percent as an adult and 9 percent as a juvenile. About 30 percent of probationers had been previously incarcerated in jail or prison, while 42 percent had previously been on probation. More than 10 percent of all probationers were first-time drug offenders.

Reported Drug Use on the Rise

While the number of inmates serving time for drug law violations increased dramatically, the number of inmates reporting past use of cocaine or crack rose sharply (table 7). The largest increases have been reported by jail inmates. Half of all jail inmates in 1996 said they had used cocaine or crack at some time in their lives, compared with 38 percent in 1983. Among convicted jail inmates, 24 percent said they had used cocaine or crack in the month before their current offense, up from 12 percent in 1983, and 15 percent said they were under the influence of cocaine or crack at the time of the offense, up from 6 percent.

Similar increases in cocaine and crack use were reported by state inmates. In 1991 a quarter of all inmates had used cocaine or crack in the month before their current offense; in 1979, 13 percent. In 1991, 14 percent reported that they were under the influence of cocaine or crack at the time of the offense; in 1979, only 5 percent reported such usage.

On every measure of past use, drug use by jail inmates has increased. An estimated 84 percent of all jail inmates in 1996 said they had used drugs in the past (up from 76 percent in 1983); 55 percent of convicted inmates said they had used drugs in the month before the offense (up from 46 percent); and 36 percent said they were under the influence of drugs at time of the offense (up from 30 percent).

Table 7. Drug use by persons on probation, in jail or in prison, by type of drug and year

Measure and type of drug use	Percent of probationers 1995	Percent of jail inmates 1983	Percent of jail inmates 1996	Percent of State prison inmates 1979	Percent of State prison inmates 1991	Percent of Federal inmates 1991
Total	100 %	100 %	100 %	100 %	100 %	100 %
Ever used drugs	69 %	76 %	84 %	78 %	79 %	60 %
Marijuana	66	73	78	75	74	53
Cocaine/crack	31	38	50	37	50	37
Heroin/opiates	8	22	24	30	25	14
Used drugs in the month before the offense*	32 %	46 %	55 %	56 %	50 %	32 %
Marijuana	25	39	37	48	32	19
Cocaine/crack	9	12	24	13	25	15
Heroin/opiates	2	8	9	12	10	6
Under the influence at time of the offense*	14 %	30 %	36 %	32 %	31 %	17 %
Marijuana	10	17	18	18	11	6
Cocaine/crack	4	6	15	5	14	8
Heroin/opiates	1	6	6	9	6	4

Note: Data are based on self-reported drug use prior to the current offense for which the probationers or inmates were sentenced. Detail may not add to total because the probationer or inmate may have used more than one type of drug. Other drugs not shown separately were included in the totals.
*Reported by convicted inmates only.
Sources: Survey of Inmates in Local Jails, 1983 and 1996; Survey of Inmates in State Correctional Facilities, 1979 and 1991; Survey of Inmates in Federal Correctional Facilities, 1991; Survey of Adults on Probation, 1995.

Among state inmates, however, reported use of all types of drugs other than cocaine or crack declined or remained unchanged between 1979 and 1991. In each survey more than three-quarters of all state inmates reported some drug use in their lifetime. More than half said they had used drugs in the month before their offense, and at least 30 percent were under the influence of drugs at the time of their offense.

Though federal inmates are much more likely than those in state prisons or local jails to be serving time for a drug offense, they report significantly lower levels of past drug use. In 1991, when the first survey of federal inmates was conducted, 60 percent said they had used an illegal drug in the past; 32 percent had used drugs in the month before their current offense; and 17 percent said they were under the influence of drugs at the time of the offense.

Probationers report levels of past drug use similar to those of federal inmates. An estimated 69 percent of all probationers in 1995 said they had used drugs in the past; a third said they had used drugs in the month before their offense; and 14 percent said they were under the influence of drugs when they committed the offense. Compared to jail and prison inmates, probationers report significantly lower levels of past use of cocaine, crack, and heroin.

II. Factors Behind the Growing Number of Offenders under Supervision

Increasing Number of Adult Arrests

Underlying the dramatic growth of the correctional populations during the 1980s was a rise in the number of arrests, from nearly 8.3 million adult arrests in 1980 to almost 12 million in 1990 (table 8). Although the total grew by 45 percent, for some offenses the percent increase was substantially greater, e.g., simple assault (up 115 percent), drug abuse violations (up 114 percent), and aggravated assault (up 74 percent).

Table 8. Number of adult arrests for selected offenses, 1980, 1990, and 1996

	1980		1990		1996		Percent change	
	Number	Rate[1]	Number	Rate[1]	Number	Rate[1]	1980-90	1990-96
Total	8,258,800	5,050	11,980,700	6,467	12,286,200	6,275	45.1	2.5
UCR, Part I, Violent offenses								
Murder[2]	18,200	11	19,800	11	16,200	8	8.8	(18.2)
Forcible rape	26,700	16	33,300	18	27,400	14	24.7	(17.7)
Robbery	102,200	62	127,300	69	106,100	54	24.6	(16.7)
Aggravated assault	236,600	145	410,700	222	444,900	227	73.6	8.3
UCR, Part I, Property offenses								
Burglary	282,800	173	289,800	156	229,800	117	2.5	(20.7)
Larceny/theft	745,300	456	1,088,400	588	983,900	503	46.0	(9.6)
Motor vehicle theft	75,600	46	119,800	65	102,600	52	58.5	(14.4)
Other UCR offenses								
Other sex offenses[3]	55,600	34	90,500	49	78,700	40	62.8	(13.0)
Other assaults	401,200	245	863,000	466	1,095,100	559	115.1	26.9
Forgery, fraud, embezzlement	358,600	219	368,600	199	565,600	289	2.8	53.4
Drug abuse violations	471,200	288	1,008,900	545	1,295,300	662	114.1	28.4
Driving under the influence	1,393,900	852	1,790,900	967	1,448,200	740	28.5	(19.1)
Weapons	141,300	86	180,900	98	163,400	83	28.0	(9.7)

Note: The number of adult arrests was estimated by multiplying the total number of arrests by the proportion of known arrests of persons age 18 or older, as reported annually by the FBI. Estimates were rounded to the nearest 100. Negative numbers are in parentheses.
[1]Number of arrests per 100,000 adults in the U.S. population.
[2]Includes nonnegligent manslaughter.
[3]Excludes forcible rape and prostitution.
Source: Crime in the United States, 1980, 1990, and 1996.

Since 1990 the total number of adult arrests has increased only slightly (up 2.5 percent by 1996). Except for aggravated assault, arrests for the major indexed offenses actually declined. The sharpest declines were recorded for burglary (down 21 percent) and murder (down 18 percent). These declines were offset by increases in the number of arrests for drug abuse violations (up 28 percent) and other assaults (up 27 percent).

Increasing Number of Offenders Sentenced to Probation

The increases in arrests for drug abuse offenses, assaults other than aggravated assault, and larceny/theft contributed significantly to the growth in the adult probation population. Upon conviction for felony offenses, more than half of offenders in state courts received a sentence to straight probation or probation combined with a period of incarceration (table 9). Since these three types of offenses represent nearly half of all felons and misdemeanants sentenced to probation, any rise in the number of arrests for these offenses will have a direct impact on the size of the probation population.

Table 9. Felons sentenced to probation, by offense, 1986, 1990, and 1994

Most serious offense	Number sentenced to probation			Percent of all felons sentenced to probation		
	1986	1990	1994	1986	1990	1994
Total	306,303	445,074	429,694	53 %	54 %	49 %
Violent offenses						
Murder	901	1,542	1,176	9 %	14 %	10 %
Rape	5,386	7,401	7,101	27	41	35
Robbery	10,593	14,064	10,980	25	30	24
Aggravated assault	18,126	29,690	30,375	47	55	47
Property offenses						
Burglary	51,487	52,316	42,810	50 %	48 %	44 %
Larceny	4,951	65,237	57,707	55	58	51
Fraud	--	39,483	37,942	--	68	59
Drug offenses						
Possession	--	64,989	67,697	-- %	61 %	62 %
Trafficking	47,951	86,331	76,784	62	51	46
Weapons offenses	--	11,383	15,532		55 %	50 %

Note: Data based on all felony convictions in state courts. Probation cases include persons with sentences to straight probation and those with split sentences (in combination with a sentence to jail or prison).
--Not available.
Source: National Judicial Reporting Program, 1986, 1990, 1994.

Counts of the number of persons entering probation closely track the increasing number of arrests during the 1980s and the subsequent leveling off since 1990. During this time, the number of entries to probation more than doubled, from 753,500 in 1981 to more than 1.6 million in 1990, and then declined. Only in 1996 was the record high entry rate of 1990 surpassed.

Rise in Jail Population Linked to Arrests, Felony Convictions, Drug Offenses, and Prison Backups

The increase in the number of arrests during the 1980s also resulted in a growing number of admissions to local jails. During 1993, when the last jail census was conducted, the estimated number of new admissions totaled nearly 9.8 million, up from an estimated 6 million in the annual period ending June 30, 1983.[5] Among inmates facing felony charges, the likelihood of being held in a local jail prior to the disposition of the case rose only slightly (from 34 percent in 1988 to 37 percent in 1992).[6]

The impact of more arrests and jail admissions, however, was compounded by a growing number of felons receiving a sentence to jail. Between 1986 and 1992, the number of convicted felons sentenced to confinement in local jails almost doubled, from an estimated 122,400 to 232,300. In 1994, the number dropped to an estimated 222,100.[7]

Growth in the local jail population has not been the result of longer sentences. In both 1988, the first year in which comparable data were collected, and 1992, felons sentenced to a local jail received a mean maximum sentence of 7 months. In 1994, the mean dropped to 6 months.[8] The largest source of growth in jail inmates in the 1980s was drug law violators. Based on data from the inmate surveys in 1983, 1989, and 1996, the number of jail inmates charged with or convicted of drug offenses rose from 20,600 in 1983, to 90,500 in 1989, to 112,300 in 1996. Drug offenders accounted for more than 40 percent of the total increase in the jail population from 1983 to 1989 but less than 20 percent of the increase from 1989 to 1996. The number of violent offenders grew from an estimated 88,500 in 1989 to 134,200 in 1996. This increase represents about 39 percent of the total growth in the jail population since 1989.

The jail population has also grown as a result of crowding in state prisons (table 10). Based on annual reports of state correctional officials, the number of prison inmates held in local facilities grew from 10,143 in 1985 (4 percent of all jail inmates) to more than 50,000 in 1993 (11 percent of jail inmates). Since 1993 the number has dropped to 31,508 (6 percent of all jail inmates).

Table 10. Jail inmates: Trends in selected populations, 1985-96

Year	Number of juveniles[2]	Adult inmates		State prisoners held in jails due to overcrowding[1]	
		Percent convicted	Percent female	Number	Percent of all jail inmates
1985	1,629	49	8.0	10,143	4.0
1990	2,301	49	9.2	17,574	4.3
1991	2,350	49	9.3	18,304	4.3
1992	2,804	49	9.2	38,006	8.5
1993	4,300	49	9.6	50,966	11.1
1994	6,700	50	10.0	45,618	9.4
1995	7,800	44	10.2	27,858	5.5
1996	8,100	49	10.8	31,508	6.1

[1]Data represent the number of state prisoners held in local jails because of prison crowding.
[2]Juveniles are persons defined by state statute as being under a certain age, usually 18, and subject initially to juvenile court authority even if tried as adults in criminal court. In 1994 the definition was changed to include all persons under age 18.
Sources: Annual Jail Survey, 1985, 1990-92, 1994-96; Census of Jails, 1993; National Prisoner Statistics, 1985, 1990-96.

Higher Probabilities of Incarceration

Compounding the impact of more adult arrests for selected serious offenses was the increase in the rate of sending offenders to prison (table 11). Except for murder and non-negligent manslaughter, the number of admissions to state prison per 1,000 arrests for serious crimes rose significantly from 1980 to 1990. During this time period, the likelihood of incarceration upon arrest increased fivefold for drug violations and increased threefold for weapons offenses. The likelihood of going to prison increased by more than 50 percent for larceny/theft, motor vehicle theft, and sexual assault other than rape. Similarly, as the number of offenders convicted in federal courts rose from 29,943 in 1980 to 47,494 in 1990, the percentage sentenced to prison rose from 46 percent to 60 percent.

As a result, the total number of admissions to state prisons from courts rose from 131,215 sentenced prisoners in 1980 to 323,069 in 1990 (an increase of more than 145 percent). The number of offenders sentenced to federal prisons in U.S. district courts rose from 13,766 to 28,659 (an increase of 108 percent).

Table 11. Court commitments to state prisons relative to adult arrests for selected offenders, 1980-95

	Number of new court commitments to state prison per 1,000 arrests							
	1980	1985	1990	1991	1992	1993	1994	1995
Violent offenses								
Murder*	621	488	460	459	521	484	540	576
Rape	182	159	229	218	224	199	230	250
Other sexual assault	61	103	112	115	132	150	145	163
Robbery	245	238	233	262	262	251	260	265
Aggravated assault	45	47	56	58	58	56	55	58
Property offenses								
Burglary	107	141	160	159	159	155	156	157
Larceny/theft	14	20	24	23	29	25	25	26
Motor vehicle theft	40	50	72	64	85	69	70	74
Fraud	19	23	24	32	24	24	24	23
Drug offenses	19	34	103	102	104	93	80	81
Weapons offenses	11	22	34	40	43	39	48	57

Note: The ratio is the number of new court commitments per 1,000 adult arrests for each offense category. The number of admissions is limited to persons with a sentence of more than 1 year.
*Includes nonnegligent manslaughter.
Sources: National Prisoner Statistics (NPS-2/3), 1980; National Corrections Reporting Program, 1985, 1990-95; Crime in the United States, 1980, 1985, 1990-95.

Since 1990 the rates of sending offenders to prison have changed. For drug law violations the chances of going to state prison have dropped—from 103 admissions per 1,000 arrests to 81 admissions per 1,000 in 1995. For property crimes, such as burglary, larceny/theft and motor vehicle theft, and aggravated assault, the chances of going to prison have remained unchanged. For those arrested for rape, other sexual assaults, robbery, and weapons offenses, the chances of going to prison have continued to rise. Consequently, the number of admissions to prison since 1990 has risen only modestly (up 11 percent).

More Probation and Parole Violators Entering Prison

Due to the compounding nature of these factors, the total number of admissions to state prisons rose from 159,300 in 1980 to nearly 512,600 in 1995. During this time the relative size of the two principal sources of admissions to prison—court commitments and returned conditional release violators—changed. Court commitments accounted

Table 12. Trends in state prison admissions and releases, 1980-96

	Admissions to state prison			Releases from state prison			
			Percent			Percent of all releases	
		Admission	new court		Release	Parole	Mandatory
Year	Number	rate[1]	commitments	Number	rate[2]	board	release
1980	159,286	57.1 %	82.4 %	143,543	32.8 %	54.8 %	18.8 %
1985	240,598	57.9 %	76.1 %	206,988	31.5 %	42.5 %	30.4 %
1990	460,739	72.7 %	70.1 %	405,374	37.0 %	39.4 %	28.8 %
1991	466,285	67.6	68.0	421,687	36.5	39.7	29.9
1992	480,676	65.6	69.5	430,198	35.5	39.5	29.5
1993	475,100	60.9	66.9	417,838	33.3	38.8	31.6
1994[3]	498,919	58.0	64.5	418,372	30.8	35.0	35.6
1995	521,970	55.7	64.7	455,139	31.2	32.3	39.0
1996	512,594	51.1	63.7	467,241	30.8	30.4	38.0

Note: All data are limited to prisoners with a sentence of more than 1 year
and exclude escapees, AWOLs, and transfers.
[1]The number of admissions per 100 state prisoners at the beginning of each year.
[2]The number of releases per 100 state prisoners at the beginning of year plus
the number admitted during the year.
[3]Admissions and releases in Alaska were estimated for 1994.
Source: Correctional Populations in the United States, 1996.

for a decreasing share of admissions (64 percent in 1995, down from
82 percent in 1980), while probation and parole violators had an
increasing share (34 percent in 1995, up from 17 percent in 1980)
(table 12). The increase in the number of conditional release violators
accounted for more than 40 percent of the growth in admissions to
state prisons during this period.

Data from BJS inmate surveys reflect the impact of this changing
composition of state prison admissions. In the 1991 survey, about 45
percent of state inmates said they were either on probation or parole for
a prior offense at the time of their current arrest, up from 34 percent in
the 1979 survey.[9] When translated into the number of inmates, probation and parole violators totaled more than 356,000 state prisoners in
1991 compared to fewer than 96,000 in 1979.

Increasing Time Served in Prison and
Declining Release Rates

Data on prison admissions and releases collected annually in the
National Corrections Reporting Program (NCRP) suggest that a major
source of growth in the state prison population is increasing time
served. Data for 1995 show that state prisoners released for the first

Table 13. State prison admissions and releases: Trends in sentencing and time served, 1985, 1990 and 1995

	1985	1990	1995
New court commitments			
Most serious offense (percent)			
Violent	35.1 %	27.2 %	28.8 %
Drug	13.2	32.0	30.8
Maximum sentence			
Mean	78 mo	70 mo	72 mo
Median	48	48	48
10 years or more (percent)	19.7 %	17.9 %	19.6 %
Minimum time to be served[1]			
Mean	31 mo	38 mo	43 mo
Median	18	24	24
First releases[2]			
Most serious offense (percent)			
Violent	31.9 %	25.3 %	24.7 %
Drug	12.4	27.5	32.2
Maximum sentence			
Mean	65 mo	65 mo	61 mo
Median	36	48	48
Time served in prison[3]			
Mean	20 mo	22 mo	25 mo
Median	14	13	15
10 years or more (percent)	0.6 %	1.4 %	1.7 %

Note: Data were obtained from the National Corrections Reporting Program.
[1]The estimated shortest time that each admitted prisoner is expected to serve before becoming eligible for first release.
[2]Excludes persons who had previously been conditionally released from prison and then were returned to prison for the same offense.
[3]Excludes time spent in jail and credited to the current sentence.
Source: National Corrections Reporting Program, 1985, 1990, 1995.

time on their current offense (that is, first releases) served on average 25 months in prison (table 13). The amount of time served was 5 months shorter in 1985 (20 months) and 3 months shorter in 1990 (22 months).

These data, however, reflect the time served by prisoners actually released. Some prisoners will die in prison, and some with very long sentences will not show up among released prisoners for many years.

As a result, these measures of time served tend to understate the actual time served by persons entering prison and are insensitive to recent changes in sentencing and release policies.

Data on the projected average minimum time to be served by persons entering prison reveal more clearly that time served has increased. In 1995, taking into account parole eligibility requirements, good-time credits, and other early release allowances, persons entering state prison were expected to serve an average of 43 months in prison, up from 38 months in 1990 and 31 months in 1985.

Prison release rates have also declined since 1990. The number of persons released each year relative to the number of persons in prison during the year (that is, the number of inmates at the beginning of the year plus those admitted during the year) peaked in 1990 (37 per 100 inmates) and then declined sharply in 1996 (31 per 100).

In combination with increasing amount of time served, the declining rates of release since 1990 have been a major factor in the continued growth of the state prison population. Without these countervailing trends, the prison population would have mirrored more closely the leveling off in arrests and small growth in admissions. Had the 1990 release rate of 37 per 100 inmates remained constant through 1996, the state prison population would have been about 15 percent smaller. Instead of a total increase of about 32 percent in 6 years, the population held in state prison would have increased by only 13 percent.

Federal Offenders Are Serving More Time

In addition to the combined effects of the rise in the number of convictions in U.S. district courts and the increasing percentage sentenced to prison, an increase in time served has also affected the growth of the federal prison population. The effect of sentencing guidelines and other reforms introduced by the Sentencing Reform Act of 1984 has been an increase in the time served in prison overall (table 14). The average time served by persons released from federal prison rose from 15 months in 1986 to 27 months in 1995 (an 80 percent increase). For violent offenses, the time served by first releases increased from 46 months to 52 months, and for drug offenses from 21 months to 38 months.

Rise in Parole Population Linked to Trends in Prison Releases

Between 1980 and 1990, the nation's parole population grew at an average annual rate of more than 12 percent. Only the state and federal prison populations grew at a faster rate (13 percent). As with the other

Table 14. Federal prison admissions and releases: Trends in sentencing and time served, 1980, 1986, 1990, and 1995

	1980	1986	1990	1995
New court commitments[1]	13,766	23,058	28,659	31,805
Most serious offense (percent)				
Violent	12.9 %	7.9 %	7.1 %	7.1 %
Drug	26.7	40.2	49.2	44.2
Maximum sentence (mean)				
All offenses	44 mo	53 mo	57 mo	61 mo
Violent	125	132	89	91
Drug	47	62	81	82
First releases[2]				
Time served in prison (mean)				
All offenses	--	15 mo	18 mo	27 mo
Violent	--	46	53	52
Drug	--	21	27	38

Note: Data are based on prisoners of any sentence length, as reported in BJS' federal justice database.
--Not available.
[1]Persons entering prison directly from a sentence by a court.
[2]Excludes persons who had previously been conditionally released from prison and then were returned to prison for the same offense.
Source: Compendium of Federal Justice Statistics, 1986, 1990, 1995.

correctional populations, the average rate of growth has dropped since 1990 to less than 5 percent.

Despite a national trend toward "truth in sentencing" and the abolition of parole, the overall percentage of prisoners released from prison to supervision in the community declined only slightly from 1980 (73 percent) to 1996 (68 percent). There was a steady decline in the percentage of inmates released by parole boards, down from 55 percent in 1980 to 30 percent in 1996. This drop was offset by dramatic increases in mandatory parole releases (19 percent in 1980 and 38 percent in 1996).

As with the state prison population, growth in the parole population was the result of large increases in parole entries. Between 1981 and 1990, the number of adults entering parole nearly tripled, from 132,700 to 358,800 (table 15). Since 1990, however, parole entries have increased by less than 20 percent.

Table 15. Adults under parole supervision: Trends in entries and exits, selected years

Year	All adults on parole			State parole discharges only			
	Number of entries	Number of exits	Percent under active supervision	Percent successful	Percent unsuccesful	Time served on parole (months)	
						Successful	Unsuccessful
1981	132,700	129,700	--	--	--	--	--
1985	183,400	173,000	82	70	26	19	19
1990	358,800	284,200	82	57	41	22	19
1992	379,200	342900	81	49	49	17	20
1994	412,000	397,500	75	44	54	21	23
1996	427,600	400,196	78	--	--	--	--

¹Missing data for parole entries and exits in 1992, 1994, and 1996 were estimated by multiplying the ratio of all entries (or exits) to the beginning of year population of all states times the population at the beginning of year population in each non-reporting state.
Estimates were rounded to the nearest 100.
-- Not available.
Sources: Parole Data Survey, 1981, 1985-96, National Corrections Reporting Program, 1985, 1990-94.

Finally, NCRP data on annual discharges from state parole supervision reveal a sharp drop in the percent of parolees who successfully complete their term of community supervision. As a percentage of all discharges, offenders successfully completing parole declined from 70 percent in 1985 to 44 percent in 1994. The average time served under parole supervision remained largely unchanged—21 months for those successfully completing parole and 23 months for those returned to prison.

III. Will These Trends Continue?

The growth in the nation's correctional populations over the last 16 years is unparalleled. The magnitude of this growth for both institutional and community corrections was not predicted. Despite the enormous improvements in the amount and quality of statistical information, it is still difficult to forecast future trends. The evidence suggests that factors underlying past growth are complex and interrelated.

Careful study of these numbers suggests that the future should not be projected simply from past experience. The recent decline in crime may continue, but how the criminal justice system responds to this decline will affect the numbers and types of persons under supervision. Less crime does not necessarily imply that fewer persons will be under correctional supervision. We see in the growth since 1980 the influences of policy changes at every step in the criminal justice process—from law enforcement, to prosecution, to sentencing, and to corrections.

More effective law enforcement combined with real changes in levels of criminal activity may cause crime rates to fall even further. These trends, however, may be offset by the gloomy forecast by demographers of an increase in the numbers of youth soon to enter the high-crime-prone ages. The impact of future demographic trends and changing levels of crime on the number of offenders under supervision will continue to be influenced by changes in criminal justice policies.

Prison and jail populations may continue to rise, as states are encouraged to adopt truth-in-sentencing, increase length of stay for violent offenders, and increase prison capacity. Small increases in currently low probabilities of incarceration relative to arrest may offset declining crime rates and fewer arrests. Budgetary considerations may ultimately limit the size and growth of the prison and jail populations.

Probation and parole populations may also continue to rise as governments look to more cost effective methods of supervising the offender populations. Increased use of intermediate sanctions, split sentences, and community-based alternatives to incarceration may continue to fuel growth in the probation population. In the near term, the parole population may grow more slowly, as states abolish parole, limit discretion of parole boards, and limit good-time. However, the overwhelming majority of offenders who are sent to prison will eventually be released, and if current practices continue, more than two-thirds will be subject to some form of post-custody supervision.

Notes

[1] *Correctional Populations in the United States, 1996.* Washington, DC: U.S. Department of Justice, Bureau of Justice Statistics.

[2] *Justice Expenditure and Employment Extracts: 1994.* Washington, DC: U.S. Department of Justice, Bureau of Justice Statistics.

[3] Dillingham, Steven D., and Greenfeld, Lawrence A., (1991). "An Overview of National Corrections Statistics," in *Federal Probation,* June, pp. 27–34.

[4] Bonczar, Thomas P. (1997). *Characteristics of Adults on Probation, 1995.* Washington, DC: U.S. Department of Justice, Bureau of Justice Statistics.

[5] Perkins, Craig A., Stephan, James J., and Beck, Allen J. (1995). *Jails and Jail Inmates 1993–94.* Washington, DC: U.S. Department of Justice, Bureau of Justice Statistics.

[6] Reaves, Brian A. and Perez, Jacob. (1994). *Pretrial Release of Felony Defendants, 1992.* Washington, DC: U.S. Department of Justice, Bureau of Justice Statistics.

[7] *Felony Sentences in State Courts, 1986, 1992, and 1994.* Washington, DC: U.S. Department of Justice, Bureau of Justice Statistics.

[8] Langan, Patrick, A. and Brown, Jodi M. (1997). *Felony Sentences in State Courts, 1994.* Washington, DC: U.S. Department of Justice, Bureau of Justice Statistics.

[9] Cohen, Robyn L. (1995). *Probation and Parole Violators in State Prison, 1991.* Washington, DC: U.S. Department of Justice, Bureau of Justice Statistics.

5

Americans Behind Bars
U.S. and International Use of Incarceration
The Sentencing Project

Overview

Beginning in 1991, The Sentencing Project has issued a series of reports examining the use of incarceration internationally. These analyses have revealed wide variations in the degree to which nations make use of incarceration as punishment for offenses and hold offenders awaiting trial. These disparities have existed both within and across the industrialized world and the developing world.

Since the time of our last report in 1994, criminal justice policies in the United States have continued to become more punitive. Mandatory sentencing laws continue to proliferate and nearly half the states, along with the federal government, have adopted some form of "three strikes and you're out" laws.

During the course of the decade of the 1990s, Russia (previously the Soviet Union) and the United States have shared the world lead in the

Source: Slightly abridged from *Americans Behind Bars,* June 1997. © 1997 by The Sentencing Project (Washington, DC); used with permission.

use of incarceration. With new data from 1995, we now provide an updated view of the use of incarceration in 59 nations for which data are available.

Trends in the International Use of Incarceration

As we have described in previous reports, assessments of the use of incarceration by different nations provide some perspective on a society's approach to crime and social problems, but also raise a series of further questions. The comparative use of incarceration is a type of benchmark for the complex interaction between crime rates, criminal justice policies, social interventions, and societal problem-solving techniques. In the United States and other nations, these issues are compounded by considerations of race, ethnicity, politics, and other variables.

A high rate of incarceration is an indication that a nation has some type of problem. This may be a high rate of crime, or violent crime, for which large-scale imprisonment is viewed as necessary or appropriate. Higher than average rates of incarceration could result from more punitive criminal justice policies than comparable nations; that is, more severe punishments for relatively similar offenses. They may also reflect the consequences of social policy decisions which affect the population's standard of living and propensity to commit crime. Whatever the case, the imprisonment of large numbers of a nation's population is generally considered to be a regrettable status, either reflective of a crime problem that has not been controlled through more pro-active interventions and/or an indication of a society which imposes harsher sanctions than are felt necessary by other nations.

Conversely, a relatively low rate of incarceration raises a series of questions as well. A low rate of crime might provide an explanation for such a situation. A nation's social and economic structure or policies that emphasize a more pro-active approach to crime control might result in fewer resources being devoted to building prisons. Also, in developing nations with limited resources, the fiscal cost of incarceration may be viewed as too high a price to pay compared to other necessities, and so the crime control and punishment apparatuses may be more limited in their approaches.

Data for 1995, as seen in table 1 and figure 1, indicate that Russia and the United States remain as the leading world incarcerators of the 59 nations for which we have current statistical information.[1] The Russian rate of incarceration is 690 per 100,000 and the U.S. rate is 600 per 100,000. These rates are generally 6–10 times the rates for most nations in western Europe.

Table 1. International Rates of Incarceration, 1995

Nation	Number of Inmates	Rate of Incarceration per 100,000	Nation	Number of Inmates	Rate of Incarceration per 100,000
Austria	6,761	85	Lithuania	13,228	360
Bangladesh	44,111	37	Luxembourg	469	115
Belarus	52,033	505	Macau	439	107
Belgium	7,401	75	Malaysia	20,324	104
Brunei Darussalam	312	110	Malta	196	55
Bulgaria	9,684	110	Moldova	10,363	275
Cambodia	2,490	26	Netherlands	10,143	65
Canada	33,882	115	New Zealand	4,553	127
China	1,236,534	103	Northern Ireland	1,740	105
Cook Islands	45	225	Norway	2,398	55
Croatia	2,572	55	Philippines**	17,843	26
Cyprus	202	30	Poland	65,819	170
Czech Republic	19,508	190	Portugal	12,150	125
Denmark	3,421	65	Romania	45,309	200
England/Wales	51,265	100	Russia	1,017,372	690
Estonia	4,034	270	Scotland	5,697	110
Fiji	961	123	Singapore**	8,500	287
Finland	3,018	60	Slovakia	7,979	150
France	53,697	95	Slovenia	630	30
Germany	68,396	85	Solomon Islands	150	46
Greece	5,897	55	South Africa*	110,120	265
Hong Kong	12,741	207	South Korea	61,019	137
Hungary	12,455	120	Spain	40,157	105
Iceland	113	40	Sweden	5,767	65
India	216,402	24	Switzerland	5,655	80
Ireland	2,032	55	Thailand	106,676	181
Italy	47,323	85	Turkey	49,895	80
Japan	46,622	37	Ukraine	203,988	390
Kiribati	91	130	United States	1,585,401	600
Latvia	9,608	375			

* The rate of incarceration for South Africa is based on a different population base than in our previous report and so should not be used for comparative purposes.

** The incarceration rates for the Philippines and Singapore are understated. The rate for the Philippines only includes national facilities, and not any regional or local institutions. The Singapore rate does not include an additional 7,608 persons detained in drug rehabilitation centers managed by the Prison Service.

FIGURE 1

INCARCERATION RATES FOR SELECTED NATIONS, 1995

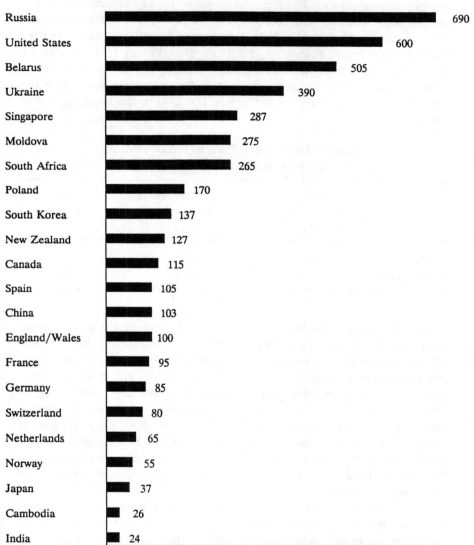

Rate of Incarceration per 100,000 Population

As seen in table 2, the Russian rate of incarceration has been increasing at a faster rate than that of the United States since 1993, the time of our previous analysis.[2] The Russian rate rose by 24 percent during this period, while the U.S. rate increased by 14 percent. In the past several years, serious crime has reportedly been increasing in Russia. Murder rates, for example, rose from 15.5 per 100,000 in 1992 to 21 per 100,000 in 1994.[3] In the United States, though, the prison population increases have come about at a time of declining crime rates, with murder rates declining from 9.3 to 9.0 per 100,000 in the same period of 1992–94.

Table 2. Increase in Rate of Incarceration
Russia and United States, 1993–1995

Nation	Rate of Incarceration 1993	Rate of Incarceration 1995	Percent Change
Russia	558	690	24
United States	528	600	14

Within Europe, the nations of the former Soviet bloc tend to have higher rates of incarceration on average. For example, the rate per 100,000 population in Belarus is 505 and in Ukraine, 390. Other eastern European nations, though, experienced a decline from previous high rates of incarceration, generally coinciding with their change of governments in 1989–1990, and now maintain more modest rates. Poland's rate of incarceration of 170 per 100,000, for example, is roughly double that of most of western Europe, but represents a considerable decline from its rate of 270 in 1985. (Obviously, no comparative data are available for Russia for 1985 since it had been part of the Soviet Union at that time.)

In a report conducted for an affiliate of the United Nations, Roy Walmsley has documented a general trend toward an increased use of incarceration in the industrialized world.[4] Many observers believe that these trends are a result of economic dislocation in many nations, increasing immigration and rising ethnic tensions, and, in some instances, harsher drug policies. Looking at the ten-year period 1985–95, Walmsley finds that much of western Europe experienced a rise in the use of imprisonment, as can be seen in table 3.

Table 3. Trends in National Prison Populations 1985–1995

Nation	1985 Rate of Incarceration	1995 Rate of Incarceration	Percent Change
Austria	120	85	-29
Belgium	65	75	+15
Cyprus	30	30	—
Czech Republic	270	190	-30
Denmark	65	65	—
England/Wales	90	100	+11
Estonia	455	270	-41
Finland	80	60	-25
France	75	95	+27
Germany*	90	85	-6
Greece	35	55	+57
Hungary	220	120	-45
Ireland	55	55	—
Latvia	640	375	-41
Lithuania	405	360	-11
Netherlands	35	65	+86
Norway	45	55	+22
Poland	270	170	-37
Portugal	90	125	+39
Romania	260	200	-23
Scotland	100	110	+10
Slovakia	225	150	-33
Slovenia	70	30	-57
Spain	60	105	+75
Sweden	50	65	+30
Turkey	90	80	-11
United States	313	600	+92

* The rate of incarceration for Germany in 1985 only includes the former West Germany, in order to provide a comparative basis for the 1995 data.

Although the increase in the use of imprisonment during this period is as high as 86 percent in the Netherlands and 75 percent in Spain, for most of western Europe, any increase is well below the rise of 92 percent in the United States during this time frame.

Also notable is the fact that rates of incarceration in several nations were either stable (Cyprus, Denmark, Germany and Ireland) or declined during this period (Austria, Finland, Turkey). This appears to have been a result of conscious policy changes in most instances.

In Germany, for example, decisions by prosecutors and judges have led to a long-term increase in the use of fines and conditional dismissals as alternatives to short prison terms. Between 1982 and 1990, the prison population declined from 39,000 to 33,000. A National Institute of Justice report on the impact of these policy changes found that in those regions where there was little change in imprisonment policies the number of offenders rose by 7 percent, while in those jurisdictions that implemented more alternative sentencing the number of offenders declined by 13 percent.[5] While the researchers recognized that a cause and effect relationship was difficult to establish, in looking at juvenile crime they also concluded that, "when youths are imprisoned for offenses, they are more likely to later embrace criminality than are young people given alternative sanctions."[6]

In Finland, changes initiated by court and prison officials have led to the greater use of non-custodial sanctions for theft, drunk driving, and other offenses. Public opinion surveys of attitudes toward punishments show a significant rise in support for community service sentencing over time, rising from 36.8 percent of the public in 1989 to 55.9 percent in 1992.[7] Researchers studying this trend suggest "that the public may become more supportive of alternatives to imprisonment after their formal adoption as a sentencing option."

Crime and Incarceration in the United States, 1985–1995

In recent years in particular, there has been a great deal of debate in the United States regarding the crime control impact of incarceration. The declines in crime during the past several years, including the 7 percent drop in violent crime in the FBI's preliminary report for 1996, have led many political leaders to claim that rising incarceration has been a major causative factor in this decline.

While incarceration clearly has some impact on crime, an analysis of trend data for the ten-year period we have examined in incarceration, 1985–95, shows a more complex picture than is sometimes presented. As seen in table 4, despite a four-year decline beginning in 1992 (and continuing through 1996 as well), rates of crime in 1995 were still as high as ten years previously, and violent crimes were up by 23 percent.

Also displayed here are trend reports that include the preliminary 1996 crime data. Here too, there is essentially no change in overall crime rates for the 1985–96 period, a smaller increase in violent crimes, but a drop in murder, aided largely by the 11 percent decline for 1996.

Table 4. Crime Rates 1985–1995/96

| | Rate per 100,000 | | | Change | |
Crime	1985	1995	1996*	1986–95	1985–96
Index Crimes**	5207	5278	5120	1 %	-2 %
Property Crimes	4651	4593	4455	-1 %	-4 %
Violent Crimes	57	685	637	23 %	14 %
Murder	7.9	8.2	7.3	4 %	-8 %

* Rate based on percentage change reported by FBI in preliminary UCR report for 1996.

** Index Crimes are the FBI categories of murder and non-negligent manslaughter, rape, robbery, aggravated assault, burglary, larceny, motor vehicle theft, and arson. Index Crimes represent the sum of Violent Crimes and Property Crimes, but may not add exactly due to rounding.

One important factor that is often overlooked in analyses of crime rates is the significance of drug crimes. FBI reports of index crimes, commonly referred to as "the crime rate," do not include drug offenses in their calculations. While there is no accurate means of measuring drug offenses, the number of drug arrests serves as a general indication of trends in this area, although this is at least in part a reflection of law enforcement priorities.

In the decade of 1985–95, drug arrests nationally increased by 82 percent, rising from 811,000 to 1,476,000. Thus, the relative stability of the overall crime rate must be tempered by the fact that there may have been a shift in offenders committing drug crimes rather than offenses that would otherwise have been included in the index crime data.

A more detailed examination of the ten-year trends provides some perspective on the contention that the "get tough" policies of recent years are responsible for the 1990s decline in crime. Within this ten-year period, we see two distinct crime trends—a rise in both overall crime and violence from 1985 to 1991, and then a decline in both indicators from 1991 to 1995.

Thus, as seen in figure 2 and table 5, as the rate of incarceration increased by 54 percent from 1985 to 1991 (an average of 9 percent a year), index crimes rose by 13 percent and violent crimes by 36 percent. Then, from 1991 to 1995, the rate of incarceration rose by 24 percent (an average of 6 percent a year), while index offenses declined by 11 percent and violent crimes by 10 percent.

Overall, no simple correlation between incarceration and crime can be ascertained. As imprisonment increased steadily for ten years, trends in crime rates were inconsistent. This certainly suggests that the

Figure 2   Incarceration and Crime

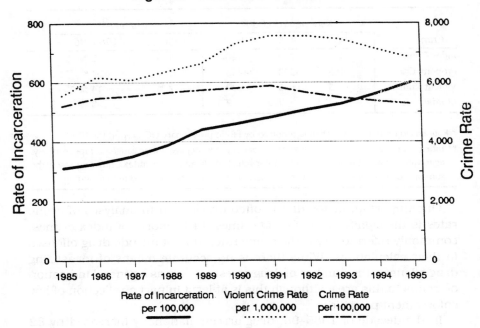

Crime rate is expressed per 100,000 population, but violent crime rate
is expressed per 1,000,000, so as to better indicate trends.

Table 5. Crime Rates and Incarceration

Crime	Rate per 100,000					
	1985	1991	Change	1991	1985	Change
Index	5207	5898	+13	5898	5278	-11
Property	4651	5140	+11	5140	4593	-11
Violent	557	758	+36	758	685	-10
Murder	17.9	9.8	+24	9.8	8.2	-16
Incarceration	313	483	+54	483	600	+24

relationship between these factors is far more complex than political rhetoric would make it appear. It is possible, for example, that the experience among different states would be more instructive than national data, perhaps depending on the types of offenders who are incarcerated or the relative length of imprisonment.

Research in this area is somewhat mixed, although most leading experts in the field believe that the impact of increased imprisonment on crime is modest at best. Leading scholars of the history of the prison, Norval Morris and David Rothman, for example, conclude that "research into the use of imprisonment over time and in different countries has failed to demonstrate any positive correlation between increasing the rate of imprisonment and reducing the rate of crime."[8]

Other Factors Influencing Crime

If the relationship between incarceration and crime during this ten-year period is inconsistent, how else can we understand changes in crime in recent years? Several factors appear to contribute to a more comprehensive analysis of this issue.

Demographics

Changes in the age composition of the population are known to affect crime rates, since males in the age group 15–24 commit a disproportionate amount of crime. Demographic trends of the past fifteen years help to understand some of the changes in crime rates, although as with incarceration rates, these are not always consistent. From 1980 to 1995, the number of young males in the population declined by 13.5 percent nationally, which coincided with a decline in overall crime of 11.3 percent, although not a continuous one. These trends are parallel for two periods, 1980–84 and 1991–95, when crime rates were declining. The rise in crime rates for the period 1984–91, which is inconsistent with the declining young male population during this period, may be explained by other factors.

Crack and the Drug Trade

The introduction of crack in urban areas beginning in the mid-1980s may account for the seeming inconsistency noted in the declining number of young males and rising crime rates in the period 1984–91. As crack use spread quickly, young entrepreneurs lured by the promise of quick money entered this new arena of the drug trade. The violence associated with these activities peaked in the late 1980s, but by most accounts appears to have subsided by the 1990s. Some of this decline is related to drug dealers being killed or incarcerated. Street-level research also indicates that drug-dealing activities may have moved to safer indoor locations and that younger teens are less enticed by the trade after seeing its impact on their older siblings and neighbors.

Guns and Violence

The most disturbing aspect of the increase in juvenile homicides since 1984 has been the substantial increase in the number of firearms-related homicides. Many observers believe that much of this increase was due to the widespread use of guns by those entering the crack trade and subsequently, by other young people believing they needed protection in dangerous neighborhoods. The Justice Department has reported that while the number of victimizations not involving firearms remained steady between 1984 and 1994, the number of homicides with firearms tripled during this period, accounting for the entire increase in juvenile homicide victimizations.[9]

Policing

In recent years, significant changes have taken place in many police departments across the country. The most prominent of these has been in New York City, where former Police Commissioner William Bratton's aggressive management strategy is claimed to have been a significant contributing factor to the sharp decline in crime rates. Other cities have instituted community policing strategies in recent years as well. While most of these changes are too new to have been thoroughly evaluated, it appears that they have had at least some impact on the falling crime rates of the 1990s.

The Dynamics of Incarceration and Crime

The reasons for the limited impact of continuing efforts to raise the level of imprisonment are several. First, the criminal justice system responds to crime after it has been committed. A majority of crimes are never even reported to the police and, of those that are, only a relatively small percentage result in arrest, conviction, and incarceration.

The demographics of crime commission show us that young males commit a disproportionate amount of crime, but that most of them "grow out" of their high crime rate years when they reach their twenties. Thus, incarcerating offenders in their 20s and 30s may have some incapacitating effect, but does not generally address the crime potential of succeeding generations of teenagers.

New research by Canela-Cacho, Blumstein, and Cohen also casts light on a significant factor necessary to evaluate increased imprisonment, that of the diminishing returns of higher rates of incarceration.[10] In any criminal justice system, serious and violent offenders will almost always be incarcerated, generally for long periods of time. Thus, the vast majority of convicted murderers, rapists, and armed robbers are incarcerated in every state.

In recent years, though, the number of inmates has continued to rise, at a rate far greater than any increase in particular offense rates. This therefore suggests that the additional number of inmates in prison on the whole represent less serious offenders than those who were incarcerated previously. For example, a large drug ring may have one "kingpin," a number of high-level dealers, and hundreds of street-level sellers. Since the kingpin and high-level dealers are almost always incarcerated if and when they are convicted, any increase in the number of drug sellers in prison is more likely to come from the ranks of the lower level offenders. Thus, while incarcerating any given drug user or seller may result in some gains in crime control, for each succeeding offender who is locked up there will generally be diminishing impacts on public safety.

As seen in table 6, from 1985 to 1994 (the most recent year for which data are available), drug offenders accounted for more than a third (36 percent) of the increase in the number of offenders in state prisons and more than two-thirds (71 percent) of the increase in federal prisoners.[11] While there is no way of calculating how much of this increase represented "kingpins" or lower-level offenders, it is highly likely that a substantial portion are the lowest level dealers in the trade.

This trend can be seen within the federal system where sentencing data for drug traffickers sentenced in 1992, virtually all of whom received a prison term, has been analyzed by the U.S. Sentencing Commission.[12] The Commission's analysis found that 11 percent of the traffickers were considered high-level dealers, 34 percent mid-level dealers, and 55 percent street-level dealers or couriers. It should also be noted that these figures are for federal drug traffickers, generally considered to be the most serious drug cases in the system. A similar analysis for state drug offenders or for cases of drug possession would likely find an even smaller proportion of high-level offenders.

Table 6. Increase in Prison Population, 1985–1994

Inmate Population	1985	1994	Increase	% of Total Increase
State Prisons				
Total	415,812	906,112	454,300	100
Drug Offenders	38,900	202,100	163,200	36
Federal Prisons				
Total	27,607	87,515	59,908	100
Drug Offenders	9,482	51,823	42,341	71

The new research on offender crime rates has attempted to estimate the degree to which diminishing returns affect crime control estimates of incarceration. The authors conclude that among the three states they studied, offenders who are not arrested and remain free average 1–3 robberies and 2–4 burglaries a year, while incarcerated offenders had committed these crimes at a rate 10–50 times higher.[13]

Research on the net impact of incarceration on crime control has recently been summarized in a comprehensive National Institute of Justice study on crime prevention prepared for Congress:

> It is clear that the most serious offenders such as serial rapists should be incapacitated. However, locking up those who are not high-rate, serious offenders or those who are at the end of their criminal careers is extremely expensive.[14]

Even a leading academic proponent of the value of incarceration, James Q. Wilson, has stated that, due to the phenomenon of diminishing returns and the difficulty of increasing deterrence, "Very large increases in the prison population can produce only modest reductions in crime rates."[15]

The debate on the relationship between incarceration and crime has unfortunately tended to obscure the complexity of understanding crime control. It has long been known that a broad set of circumstances affect the likelihood of crime commission. In addition to criminal justice factors such as police deployment and sentencing policy, these include such factors as spatial location, opportunity, individual values, economics, demographics, and neighborhood organization. By continuing to engage in a public debate which primarily looks only at imprisonment, policymakers obscure a complex issue and divert attention from a range of productive responses.

The New York City Decline in Crime

Much attention in recent years has been directed to the dramatic decline in murder rates and crime generally in New York City. Crime rates have been declining in New York since 1991, and the decline accelerated following the implementation of more strategic policing by former Police Commissioner William Bratton in 1994. Overall violent crime rates declined by 34 percent from 1990 to 1995 and property crime rates by 39 percent during that period. While it is too early to evaluate fully the impact of the changes in policing on the decreases in crime, it is possible to examine changes in incarceration during this period.

As seen in table 7, during the time when New York City's crime rate was declining significantly, its state prison population (a majority of which is composed of offenders from New York City) increased by 25 percent, well below the national average of 43 percent for that period. Within the city's jail system, the number of inmates actually declined by 9 percent, compared to the national average increase of 25 percent.

Therefore, it appears that whatever impact the changes in policing may have had on crime did not come about primarily through a higher prison and jail population caused by more arrests. The impact of policing or arrest policies may work in other ways, though. Police officials have contended that more arrests for "quality of life" crimes may disrupt an escalation toward more serious criminal behavior or that a sustained police presence in a crime-ridden community may have a deterrent impact.

Additional factors appear to have worked in favor of a reduction in crime in New York. These include changes in the drug distribution market and a decline in "turf wars," demographic shifts, and changes in community behaviors resulting in younger people avoiding potential situations of conflict. The New York experience remains a fascinating

Table 7. Increase in Incarceration, 1990–1995
New York City and National

	Change in State Prison Population		Change in Jail Inmate Population	
	New York	*National*	*New York City*	*National*
1990–95	+25%	+43%	9%	+25%

subject for ongoing analysis. What should not be lost in this examination, though, is what appears to be the relatively limited role that increased incarceration has played in these developments.

More Prisoners, Less Education

In the political focus on calls for increased incarceration as a form of punishment, there has been virtually no attention devoted to the impact of imprisonment on offenders or for the community to which most will return. Even aside from any humanitarian concerns, we know that more than 95 percent of those sentenced to prison will someday be released. From a crime control perspective, if prisoners returning to the community are more likely to engage in crime upon the completion of their sentence, incarceration becomes counterproductive, especially if there are meaningful alternative options.

One area of study involves the educational levels of persons in prison and the extent to which efforts are made to address educational deficiencies during the period of imprisonment. Surveys of the Bureau of Justice Statistics demonstrate that 41 percent of state prison inmates in 1991 had either not completed high school or obtained a GED.[16] Research by the Department of Education concludes that prisoners are far more likely to perform at the lowest levels of literacy testing than the general population. About one in three inmates tested at a Level 1 (of 5) on the prose literacy scale, compared to one in five in the household population.[17] Finally, assessments of incarcerated juvenile populations have estimated that 30–50 percent of inmates may be defined as learning disabled, compared to 3–6 percent in the general population.[18]

These issues are significant not because they should serve to condone criminal activity, but because it is known that addressing these educational deficits has been shown to reduce future rates of recidivism. A number of studies have demonstrated that inmate participation in either GED programs or post-secondary education can lead to lower rates of recidivism. One of the more comprehensive analyses in this area was a review of a sample of 1,205 inmates released from federal prison in 1987.[19] For inmates successfully completing one or more courses for each 6 months of their prison term, 35.5 percent recidivated, compared to 44.1 percent of those who completed no courses during their incarceration.

Despite the existence of this research, though, the impact of public policy decisions in recent years has been to cut back significantly on the extent of prison-based education. The most direct policy decision was the congressional decision of 1994 to eliminate Pell grants for prisoners who wished to pursue higher education. Even though prisoners constituted less than 1 percent of all persons receiving Pell grants, members of Congress created a climate where "deserving" students were pitted against inmate recipients. As a result of this decision, post-secondary education has essentially been decimated in prisons nationwide.

A 1994 survey by *Corrections Compendium* further documented the decline of inmate education. The survey of prison officials nationally found that within a five year period, 16 states had cut funding for one or more education programs, including Adult Basic Education, GED, and special education.[20]

While cutting back on supposed "frills" for prisoners may make for good politics, it clearly does not result in good crime control policies. It is unfortunate, to say the least, that public discussion on these issues is as narrow as the sound bites which pervade policy debates.

Conclusion

Whether intended or not, the Cold War between the United States and the former Soviet Union now continues between the United States and Russia in their race to incarcerate ever more of their citizens. Despite the large-scale human and fiscal costs to both societies, crime rates continue at high rates despite all-time record rates of incarceration.

The increases in incarceration in some other industrialized nations indicate that trends in the United States are not necessarily unique, although the scale of imprisonment in the United States dwarfs that of these other nations.

If there is a primary lesson to be learned from the past decade's near doubling of the rate of incarceration in the United States it is that imprisonment is hardly a panacea for reducing crime, and its continuing increase may distract us from more effective and less costly responses. As we have seen in the case of New York City, whatever combination of factors may have contributed to the reduction in crime, these did not include a higher than average increase in the use of incarceration.

While a certain level of incarceration is necessary, continued expansion of the prison system is likely to lead to diminishing returns and a host of unintended consequences. Other strategies for addressing crime appear to be more promising. These include:

- Reducing gun violence—Department of Justice data show that the entire increase in juvenile homicides in recent years is gun-related. Coordinated efforts to disrupt gun markets in Boston and other cities show promise in reducing the scale of violence.
- Targeted policing—While there is still debate about the degree to

which strategic changes in policing in New York City have affected the crime rate, clearly these initiatives have inspired a healthy reexamination of the role of police in reducing crime.

- Addressing substance abuse—Criminal justice interventions that include drug courts, prison-based therapeutic communities, and prosecutorial diversion have demonstrated reductions in recidivism. Given the substantial overlap between substance abusers and offenders, efforts to increase treatment access both within and outside the criminal justice system can be expected to produce additional benefits.

- Mobilizing communities—For quite some time, the role of the community in preventing and responding to crime has been undervalued. In recent years, though, locally-based efforts to involve communities in crime prevention have been growing rapidly through restorative justice programs and coordinated police-community activities. These efforts have the potential to both provide greater safety and enable citizens to reclaim their communities.

The one strategy that has clearly not been effective in fighting crime has been that of political demagoguery. Political sound-bites may help to win elections by narrowing the debate on crime control, but they do little to help citizens engage in an informed debate. Political leaders might do well to instead examine the research and experiences of practitioners and communities that are attempting to develop more constructive approaches to these problems.

Sources

Data on national rates of incarceration were obtained from: Roy Walmsley, "Prison Populations in Europe and North America: Some Background Information," The European Institute for Crime Prevention and Control, HEUNI, 1997; Andre Kuhn, "Incarceration Rates in Europe and the USA," paper presented at the American Society of Criminology, Chicago, November 1996; and, for South Africa, the Department of Correctional Services.

Crime rates and incarceration rates for the United States and New York were obtained from the FBI *Uniform Crime Reports* and annual prison reports of the Bureau of Justice Statistics. Jail incarceration rates were obtained from the New York City Board of Correction.

Notes

[1] Available data are primarily from Europe, Asia, and North America, and therefore, do not generally include countries in Africa and South America.
[2] While we reported a U.S. rate of incarceration of 519 for the U.S. for 1993, here we use the Justice Department figure of 528, based on more updated information.

3 Lee Hockstadter, "Russia's Criminal Condition," *Washington Post*, February 26, 1995.

4 Roy Walmsley, "Prison Populations in Europe and North America: Some Background Information," The European Institute for Crime Prevention and Control, HEUNI, 1997.

5 Christian Pfeiffer, "Alternative Sanctions in Germany: An Overview of Germany's Sentencing Practices," National Institute of Justice, February 1996.

6 Ibid.

7 Jan J. M. van Dijk and Patricia Mayhew, *Criminal Victimization in the Industrialized World*, Ministry of Justice, The Netherlands, November 1992.

8 Norval Morris and David J. Rothman, "Introduction," in *The Oxford History of the Prison*, Oxford University Press, 1995, p. xii.

9 "Juveniles Offenders and Victims: 1996 Update on Violence," Office of Juvenile Justice and Delinquency Prevention, February 1996.

10 Jose A. Canela-Cacho, Alfred Blumstein, and Jacqueline Cohen, "Relationship Between the Offending Frequency of Imprisoned and Free Offenders," *Criminology*, Vol. 35, No. 1, 1997.

11 Data calculated from *Correctional Populations in the United States, 1994*, Bureau of Justice Statistics, June 1996.

12 United States Sentencing Commission, *Cocaine and Federal Sentencing Policy*, February 1995.

13 Canela-Cacho, op. cit.

14 Doris Layton MacKenzie, "Criminal Justice and Crime Prevention," in Lawrence W. Sherman, et al., *Preventing Crime: What Works, What Doesn't, What's Promising*, National Institute of Justice, 1997.

15 James Q. Wilson, "Crime and Public Policy," in James Q. Wilson and Joan Petersilia, editors, *Crime*, Institute for Contemporary Studies, 1995, p. 501.

16 Allen Beck, et al., "Survey of State Prison Inmates, 1991," Bureau of Justice Statistics, 1993.

17 Karl O. Haigler, Caroline Harlow, Patricia O'Connor, and Anne Campbell, "Literacy Behind Prison Walls," National Center for Education Statistics, October 1994.

18 Nancy Cowardin, "Learning Disabilities and Illiteracy in the Juvenile and Criminal Justice System," The Almansor Center, South Pasadena, California, 1997.

19 Miles D. Harer, "Recidivism Among Federal Prison Releasees in 1987: A Preliminary Report," Federal Bureau of Prisons, March 11, 1994.

20 Jamie Lillis, "Prison Education Programs Reduced," *Corrections Compendium*, March 1994.

6

The American Prison Crisis
Clashing Philosophies of Punishment and Crowded Cellblocks

Ben M. Crouch
Geoffrey P. Alpert
James W. Marquart
Kenneth C. Haas

Introduction

Media attention has heightened people's concern about the American correctional institutions (prisons and jails). Headlines such as the following greet citizens:

Ex-convict commits rape within four hours after release from prison

Federal judge condemns violent and unsanitary conditions in prison—orders immediate reform

Inmate performs abdominal surgery on self after prison medical staff deny treatment

Prison officials release convicts early to relieve overcrowding

Source: Prepared especially for *The Dilemmas of Corrections*.

Who Goes to Prison?

Such stories are often taken as evidence of the fai...
reform and care for prisoners adequately. For ma...
to house and control all of the offenders sentence...
crisis not just for prisons but for community safety...
corrections, however, do not simply result from a sud...
evil people, incompetent prison officials, or a natural,...
process. The current prison crisis—a combination of high im...
rates, the resulting overcrowding, and society's uncertainty a...
to control crime—reflects political decisions and conflicts that hav...
place over the 200 years of correctional history in the United St...

The crowding and control problems in American prisons are not ne...
A major reason for these problems is that in spite of our extensive use...
of prisons, we do not have a unified and widely accepted prison policy...
Our failure to develop a consistent prison policy results from the many
conflicting definitions of what prison can or should accomplish. For
example, we expect prisons to keep honest citizens honest (general
deterrence), deter offenders from additional law-breaking behavior
(specific deterrence), isolate criminals from the community
(incapacitation), inflict a just measure of suffering on them (retribution),
and yet somehow ''cure'' them of their anti-social attitudes and behavior
(rehabilitation). These traditional rationales for incarcerating criminals
may seem reasonable, but are they compatible? Are they achievable?
The answer, it would appear, has always been ''no.'' As the New York
Prison Commission argued in 1852, ''most men who have been confined
for long terms are distinguished by a stupor of both the moral and
intellectual facilities. . . . Reformation is then out of the question.''[1]

In the 1990s the most pressing political crisis in the prison system
is crowding. Simply stated, we are sending more offenders to prison
than can be accommodated, but the situation is anything but simple.
The tremendous growth of prison populations in the 1980s and 1990s
has been compounded by uncertainties about which crimes are deserving
of imprisonment, how many people we should lock up, what we expect
prisons to do with those people, and how much we are willing to spend
on incarceration.

This chapter focuses on the issue of crowding. By placing prison
crowding in a social, historical, and ideological context, we hope to show
that this crisis involves more than prisons themselves. As with other
social problems, the prison crisis is fueled by the fact that many
subgroups in society (including middle-class voters, inner-city residents,
legislators, and academics) have conflicting values and ideas about how
we should react to crime and criminals. To this end, we describe prison
crowding and its implications for American corrections. Then we turn
to the social and ideological forces that have shaped this crisis. Finally,

; to overcrowded conditions in

·isons

·isons by the Edna McConnell
in the late 1970s and early

storage rooms, hallways
ng over into tents. . . .
_..ine in cells not much wider
_..ina's century-old Central Prison some
_..ed with four inmates and bunks line the walkways.
_..nd New York State, in what one observer called "a move with
ominous symbolism," lifted a cap on the population of the Attica
State Correctional Facility which was placed there in 1971 after a
riot which left 43 people dead.[2]

With almost every state prison system operating at or beyond capacity, these conditions persist today. At the end of 1993, state prisons were estimated to be operating at between 18 and 29 percent above capacity, while the federal system was estimated to be 36 percent over capacity.[3] Moreover, this extensive use of prison is relatively recent. From 1980 to 1993, the nation's prison population increased by 188 percent—from 329,821 to a record high of 948,881. More to the point, in 1980 the imprisonment rate was 139 prisoners per 100,000 population. By 1993, however, the rate of imprisonment stood at 351 prisoners per 100,000 residents.[4] This rise in prison population made the United States one of the world's leaders in its rate of imprisonment, and outstripped the capacity of prisons to house offenders.[5]

Crowding can be physically and mentally harmful to prisoners. Research indicates that prisoners in open living areas (e.g., large rooms with many beds divided only by waist-high partitions) use medical clinics more frequently and have higher blood pressure levels than do prisoners in individual cells. In addition, high-density cell use is likely to make health problems such as colds and flu more difficult to control. Finally, crowded prisons are likely to have higher rates of prisoner assault and misconduct.[6]

Even when crowding does not lead to illness or violence, it undermines the already limited privacy of prison life. For example, because of inadequate housing, a Texas prison had to place three men in a nine-by-five-foot cell designed for only two; the third man had a mattress on the floor. That man was often stepped on at night and suffered indignities when his cell mates used the toilet. The rapid increase in prisoners stretched the security staff's ability to deliver such minimum services as showers, meals, and laundry. The "clock" was used as never before to accommodate the prisoners' needs. The swelling inmate population forced the guards, for example, to begin serving the inmates' breakfast at 3:30 A.M., lunch at 9:30 A.M., and the evening meal at 3:30 in the afternoon. Crowded cellblocks also produce tremendous levels of noise and limit prisoners' activities. As the same prisoner told a federal judge who was investigating crowding,

> It was impossible to [read or study]. The radios would stay up so high that they'd almost knock your eardrums out and then they had the television in the day room, which was packed, men sitting on the floor. . . . It was just so many people could get in there and that would be it and the rest of them would have to go back to their cells. They wouldn't get no recreation.[7]

By limiting personal space, crowding exposes prisoners daily to constant and unwelcome contact with others. Commenting on this problem, a prisoner stated:

> Like, for three years I haven't sat without an elbow on each side of me. I never have been able to put my elbows up to the table in three years. . . . You may be done eating and have to sit there and push together, bodies real close and smell everybody together for twenty minutes before you can get up to move.[8]

Crowding is also a problem for the prison staff because dense populations are harder to supervise and control. For example, in Texas prisons between 1971 and 1982, the prison population doubled while the number of officers remained virtually the same. The guards began to rely increasingly on elite, powerful prisoners known as "building tenders" to keep order. The building tenders routinely used excessive force on other prisoners. Thus, crowding undermined official control and led to prisoner abuse.[9] Moreover, an overcrowded prison usually entails temporary housing, nonroutine transfers of prisoners during the day, and strained laundry and kitchen services, all of which make it more difficult for the staff to maintain a stable, safe institution.

Finally, crowded correctional institutions affect other elements of the justice system. For example, when state prisons have no room for offenders who have been sentenced to incarceration, those offenders must remain in county jails. While only 5.4 percent of state prisoners nationwide were in county jails in 1993, the percentage is much higher in many states and counties. Texas is the national leader in this regard, with 30 percent of its 71,103 sentenced prisoners incarcerated in local jails rather than in state prisons.[10]

This "backlog" of state prisoners in jails, makeshift facilities such as "tent cities," old military barracks, and motels creates a tremendous financial, management, and security burden for the counties. It can also create friction between the counties and the state. In Texas, for example, nine large counties sued the state to accept convicts who were still in local jails or pay the counties to house prisoners the state prison could not accept. As of this writing, nearly 30,000 state prisoners are housed in Texas county jails. State prison inmates in several local jails have rioted in response to the crowding conditions, causing extensive damage to the jails.

There are many sources of the current prison crisis. We stated earlier that to understand the crisis, we must look not just to the prison but to changing conditions and differences in values in American society. In the following sections we develop this theme. We begin our analysis by exploring how social change has affected people's perceptions of crime. We then review the different ideas or theories as to what it is we expect prisons to achieve. These differing ideas have meant that prisons have at different times emphasized prisoner rehabilitation, prisoners' constitutional rights, and, more recently, an explicitly punitive approach. Each of these ideas, which we will discuss below, was sponsored by different groups. Religious groups and some academic researchers pushed prisoner rehabilitation programs, federal judges moved to protect prisoners' civil liberties, and conservative legislators pressed for a more punitive system. We conclude by arguing that the conflict between pressure to imprison increasing numbers of offenders and resistance to that pressure from various sources is at the heart of the current prison crisis.

Citizen Perceptions of Crime and Social Change

Criminal behavior threatens society. At the individual level, citizens fear injury and personal financial loss; at the community level, crime threatens social order. While researchers have at various times declared offenders to be biologically deficient, mentally defective, poorly trained, or lacking social controls, to most citizens they are simply evil. The public wants criminals to be dealt with in a way that not only controls their behavior but symbolizes society's anger and desire to exclude, hurt, or eliminate law violators.[11] A wide range of punishments have served this purpose over the centuries. Before prisons came into routine use about 200 years ago, criminals were killed, exiled, mutilated with whips and hot irons, and placed in stocks or pillories.[12] Though prison has replaced corporal punishment as today's most common response to serious crime, Americans have remained consistent in wanting to have criminal behavior punished severely.

Citizen Perceptions and Punishment Rationales

This conservative public orientation toward criminals is the foundation for four age-old punishment rationales or philosophies. The first is *retribution* or *just deserts*, which holds that society or the state is morally obligated to punish offenders. Moreover, retributive theory requires that the offender's punishment must be commensurate to the seriousness of the crime and the offender's blameworthiness. Modern retributivists do not insist on a strict "eye for an eye" equivalence between a crime and its punishment, but they do insist that the severity of punishments should be graded according to the gravity of the crime and the offender's culpability.[13] A second rationale for punishment is *incapacitation* or *self-defense*. Here the concern is to make offenders easy to identify or remove them from society. A "T" branded on the cheek of a thief, a scarlet letter sewn to a dress, and the modern practice of requiring offenders to display bumper stickers or license plates that announce their offenses illustrate this rationale. Eliminating offenders from society for a period of time (prison) or forever (death) also serves this purpose. The third rationale, *specific deterrence*, is intended to keep offenders from committing additional crimes. And the fourth, *general deterrence*, assumes that seeing or knowing that criminals are punished for their crimes will cause nonoffenders to think twice about risking the punishment that follows criminal acts.

These traditional rationales reflect relatively little concern for the offender. Citizens and legislators are inclined to allow prisoners to be warehoused in any quarters that are available and give administrators wide discretion over their care and control. After all, the argument goes, although prison is an unpleasant or even painful experience, it is what criminals deserve and may deter crime. Once local judges and juries sent offenders "up the river," prison officials understood that they were expected to keep them quiet, safely locked away, and out of the news, all as inexpensively as possible.

In the 1950s and early 1960s prison officials were able to meet these expectations, but that was a time when crime rates were relatively low and prison populations were decreasing nationally; controlling the size of prison populations was relatively easy. But in the late 1960s and 1970s, violent crime rose dramatically. The result was public fear and pressure on the state for protection through more effective punishment. Let us examine the social changes that were responsible for these trends.

Social Changes and Public Concern about Crime

The first of these social changes involves the *baby boom*, the tremendous rise in the birthrate immediately after World War II. By the time the birthrate peaked in about 1960, it had set a dramatically large number of young persons on course to pass through adolescence and adulthood in the late 1960s. By the late 1960s and the early 1970s these youths were fifteen to twenty-nine years old, the age when crime and violence are most likely. Thus, as the baby boomers entered this dangerous age in great numbers, crime and violence increased sharply.

Fundamental changes in technology and the economy coincided with this sudden rise in the number of young people, putting many of them at a disadvantage in the workplace. Throughout the 1950s, the U.S. economy was dominated by manufacturing. However, by the early 1960s this type of industry, illustrated by assembly-line production, began to give way to automation; service and technical jobs began to grow much faster than manufacturing jobs did. These changes increased the demand for more skilled and better-educated workers and lowered the demand for unskilled workers with minimal education. Moreover, these changes occurred just as the baby boomers began to look for jobs and the "good life." They reduced job opportunities for many American youths, but poor urban minorities were the most severely affected,[14] with a limited ability to participate in the marketplace. Facing an array of social problems in often deprived urban ghettos and barrios, many members of the underclass turned to crime and drugs.[15]

These broad demographic and economic changes altered the extent and nature of crime in the United States. Media portrayals of rising crime, along with personal experiences of crime, heightened peoples' concern about violence, drugs, and social order. National Opinion Research Center data indicate, for example, that the proportion of citizens in national polls agreeing that courts are too lenient on criminals rose from just over 70 percent in 1972 to nearly 90 percent by 1978 and then remained stable through the 1980s.[16] When asked to name the most important thing that could be done to reduce crime, people most frequently selected "cut the drug supply" and "harsher punishments"[17] (table 1). Given the prevailing public notion that incarceration is the only "real" punishment,[18] the sense that crime is a growing threat increases pressure to lock up more offenders for longer periods of time.

While the violent crime rate increased in the 1960s, it decreased in the 1980s. This suggests that public perceptions of crime are not always closely correlated with national crime trends. One reason for this is that the media tend to exaggerate the extent of violent crime. However, even while serious crimes decreased nationally, many urban areas continued to experience high crime rates. Gunfire and violent deaths are daily

**Table 1 Attitudes toward Crime Reduction Measures
in the United States, 1981 and 1989**

Question: *What is the most important thing that can be done to help reduce crime?*

	1981 percent*	1989 percent*
Cut drug supply	3	25
Harsher punishment	38	24
Teach values, respect for law	13	12
Reduce unemployment	22	10
More police	11	5
Try cases faster	6	2
Other	13	21
No opinion	11	14

*Totals add to more than 100 percent due to multiple responses.

Source: U.S. Bureau of Justice Statistics, Washington, D.C., U.S. Government Printing Office, 1989, p. 145.

events in some Washington, D.C. neighborhoods, and in Houston there were as many robbery-homicides in the first six months of 1991 as there were in all of 1990.

While such conditions cause the public to demand more incarceration, they are not the only sources of pressure on lawmakers. Pressure also comes from citizen, academic, legal, and legislative interest groups which want to reform the prison system.

Ideology and Reform

Many groups and organizations have tried to reform prisons and prisoners. These reformers have been concerned about prisoners' souls, their reintegration into society, and their constitutional rights. In this section we review three reform efforts and the theories that lie behind them. The first stresses the rehabilitation of individual prisoners, the second focuses on prisoners' constitutional rights, and the third emphasizes justice and uniformity in the sentencing and punishment process (the "just deserts" philosophy).

Rehabilitation

In the 1790s a group of Pennsylvania Quakers proposed a prison system in which offenders, with the help of solitude and the Bible, could be led to see the error of their ways. The idea caught on, and by the early nineteenth century every American state and territory and most European countries had developed institutions aimed at the rehabilitation of offenders.

Throughout the nineteenth century and into the twentieth century, however, prison practices seldom approached this ideal. Pressed to house increasing numbers of inmates, American prisons were typically not uplifting places of personal reform but warehouses where inmates often lived in idleness and danger. The public and its officials were usually indifferent to what happened to those behind the walls.

In the 1950s prisons began to receive much more attention as a series of riots occurred in which prisoners violently protested their living conditions. Partly because of these riots, sociologists began studying prison organizations and their impact on individual prisoners. The result was a renewal of interest in prisoner welfare and rehabilitation.

In time, most state and prison officials embraced rehabilitation and the treatment programs it involved. Experts contended that despite similarities in offenses, offenders are different from each other, with unique needs and personal problems which require individual treatment programs. Prison sentences thus should be open-ended to allow time to treat offenders' problems. The states therefore adopted *indeterminate sentencing laws* which permitted prison officials rather than judges to decide when a prisoner was "cured" and ready for release.

Sensing the possibility of a better life inside as well as outside the institution, prisoners came to have high expectations about reform, often accepting both the notion that they needed treatment and the idea that the new correctional institutions could help them. Many found, however, that the changes were superficial and that their reintegration into society was elusive. Because California officials were avid proponents of rehabilitation, prisoners there were particularly disgruntled by the system's failure to deliver treatment.[19] This disappointment was one factor behind the increasing numbers of prisoners who began suing state prisons in federal court in an effort to improve prison conditions.

Prisoners' Constitutional Rights

Through the first half of this century, federal courts refused to respond to prisoners' complaints. Because of the Constitution's separation of judicial (courts) and executive (prisons) powers or their own ignorance about prisons, federal judges felt that they should not interfere in prison operations even when prisoners complained that abuse and crowding violated their civil rights. Also, many prison officials were able to answer prisoners' claims by making their institutions appear to be both strict and helpful to prisoners.

In the 1960s, when prison populations were stable, state prisons were often able to deal with the public's general demand that prisons be tough *and* with the ideal of rehabilitation with little concern about outside intervention. The Stateville prison in Illinois and the Texas prison system are well-known examples of how this was done. These prisons met public expectations by keeping prisoners compliant and operations efficient through a highly authoritarian control system which emphasized secrecy, strict loyalty to superiors, and tightly controlled rewards for staff members and prisoners.[20] At the same time, they projected a progressive, rehabilitation-oriented image through well-publicized vocational and educational programs.

In the 1970s federal judges began to look behind the walls and apply constitutional standards to prison operations in many states, including Illinois and Texas.[21] In major cases involving judicial intervention, prison crowding has typically been a central issue; crowding and its associated abuses were routinely found to violate the U.S. Constitution's ban on cruel and unusual punishment. In addition to reducing prison populations, judges ordered prison officials to ease solitary confinement (prisoners cannot be kept in filthy conditions and made to use a crude toilet they cannot flush), limit the discretion of guards in punishing prisoners (guards cannot beat or have their prisoners beat "troublemakers"), and increase prisoners' access to courts (officials had to provide inmates with "adequate law libraries"). Clearly, prisoners found a powerful champion in the courts.

Court intervention to improve prison conditions and limit crowding was on a collision course with trends promoting a more punitive attitude toward offenders and greater degrees of incarceration. One of these trends, as we have seen, was public concern about crime. Another was the claim by some sociologists and psychologists in the mid-1970s that prison rehabilitation programs were seldom successful, a conclusion applauded by conservative officials, politicians, and citizens. A third trend was the emergence of the "just deserts" philosophy.

Just Deserts Philosophy

In the late 1970s a number of influential scholars began to criticize the criminal justice system for providing different prison sentences for similar crimes. These scholars argued that this practice violated the ideals of fairness and justice. They asserted that the length of offenders' sentences should not depend on when officials think offenders are rehabilitated. Instead, prisoners should know exactly how long they will be incarcerated and the sentence should be based not on offenders' needs or involvement in a treatment program but on their crimes and criminal histories. This argument, known as the just deserts philosophy, holds that a fair and explicit brand of retribution should replace rehabilitation, which was viewed as a philosophy that leads to uncertainty and sentencing disparities.

By the early 1980s most states had subscribed to this philosophy and had begun to dismantle their indeterminate sentencing laws. The new laws typically set mandatory minimum sentences for many crimes and either eliminated or drastically reduced opportunities for parole. Since the new laws involved fixed or predetermined sentences, judges' discretion in sentencing was greatly reduced.

These new laws translated into increases in both the amount of time prisoners served and the number of people in prison. Heeding calls to get tough, legislators usually determined the new, fixed sentence for a given crime by taking the average time prisoners had served for that crime under the old laws. This strategy meant that no one convicted of that crime under the new laws would serve less than the old average sentence. As a result, more offenders arrived in prison with sentences longer than those faced by similar offenders in the past. Between 1980 and 1987, the average sentence given to offenders increased from 44 to 55 months.[22] By 1991, average sentence length increased to 150 months.[23]

Emphasis had shifted from "correcting" offenders to putting as many offenders as possible in prison, often with long mandatory sentences. In addition, the "war on drugs," declared by the federal government in the early 1980s, "dumped" tens of thousands of prisoners into an already packed correctional system. The impact of this "get tough" strategy was enormous. For example, in 1986, 38,500 prisoners were serving a sentence for a drug conviction. By 1991, the number of prisoners serving a sentence for a drug charge swelled to 150,300.[24] "Get tough" attitudes, the fall from favor of rehabilitation, and changes in sentencing practices largely explain recent increases in prison use in this country, but they do not explain the prison crisis. The crisis emerges when rising incarceration rates encounter constitutional and fiscal obstacles to prison growth. Incarcerating large numbers of offenders without adding bed space goes against court-determined limitations on the number of prisoners who can be housed in existing facilities. Most courts have held that prisoners should have forty-five square feet in a cell (about the size of a mid-sized car) and sixty square feet in a dormitory; a higher density can be interpreted as unconstitutional crowding.

Thus, at the heart of the present prison crisis is the conflict between demands for retribution, protection, and deterrence through the imprisonment of offenders and court decisions holding that over-crowding cannot be tolerated. At a time when state resources are being stretched to provide social services for citizens, the prison crisis presents states with difficult financial choices.

Responding to the Prison Crisis

Decisions about how to use prison resources are always political. Officials try to integrate the desire for protection from crime and the demand that predators be punished with the goal of dealing justly with individual offenders. That these interests often are in conflict does not diminish the fact that they are both valid societal goals. In the 1990s, as communities demand more incarceration for offenders, state officials must somehow achieve these goals in properly managed prisons.

It is useful to think of responses to the prison crisis in terms of short-range and long-range approaches. Short-range approaches attempt to manage the prison crisis over the next several years. Long-range approaches try to address the societal conditions that produce offenders.

Short-Range Approaches

The most obvious response to pressure for incarceration is simply to build enough safe, legal prisons to house all the people who are sentenced to prison. Most states have added bed space, and some, such as Texas, Ohio, and California, have attempted to build enough prison space to meet demand. However, with new prison space costing $100,000 per cell, construction is very expensive. Even when new prisons are built, space continues to lag behind demand. However, this is only one problem with prison expansion. A very different one is that state officials may find that large and powerful correctional bureaucracies that have a vested interest in full prisons will bring pressure to keep prisons filled even when demand for prison beds is falling.

Lacking the resources for new prisons, some states have turned to private prison companies. These companies develop prison space and then accept and supervise a percentage of the state's prisoners (usually minimum-security prisoners) for a fee. The idea is that private contractors can run prisons more economically than state bureaucracies can. Several concerns have been raised about privatization as a comprehensive solution. First, while private prisons may be more efficient and thus more profitable than state-run institutions, their profits depend on full capacity; pressure to keep the prisons full thus can encourage prison use when it is unnecessary and delay the timely release of prisoners.

A second problem concerns legal liability since prisoners are wards of the state but are under the care and control of private business. For example, if a state prisoner is abused in a private prison, is the state legally responsible for the abuse if that prisoner sues because of mistreatment in an institution the state does not run? Finally, some people doubt that prison entrepreneurs can foster rehabilitation. Though downplayed today, rehabilitation remains an objective, and its advocates fear that it might fall to the profit motive in private facilities.

The states have used two other strategies to limit prison construction, both of which can create political difficulties. The first involves releasing prisoners before the end of their sentences or their normal parole dates to make room for incoming prisoners. The problem here is that citizens and politicians become upset when they learn that the time offenders spend locked away is far less than their original sentences. Community distress is especially great when the media give wide coverage to a serious crime committed by an offender who was released early from prison. The second strategy is to divert offenders into nonincarceration programs in the community. Over the last decade many states have used electronic monitoring to keep convicted offenders in or near their own homes. Usually the program involves attaching a small transmitting device to an offender's ankle. Through that person's telephone or more specialized equipment, the device automatically notifies officials if the person moves a specified distance from home.

Most serious offenders who are diverted from prison, however, go into a probation program such as Intensive Supervision Probation (ISP). Probation is much less expensive than incarceration and thus can limit pressure on prison bed space. However, probation programs, especially ISP, may involve very close supervision and surprise drug testing. Ironically, such conditions can make probation seem as punitive as prison to some offenders. For example, in a Texas study of approximately 1,000 newly imprisoned men, nearly half (49 percent) indicated they would rather go to prison for a full year than spend five years on probation in the community.[25]

Diversion from prison may also be accomplished through "intermediate sanctions,"[26] or punishments which fall between probation and prison and do not necessarily call for close supervision. Examples include a greater use of fines, community service, and restitution programs. Public support for these programs is often limited because they do not seem to be sufficiently punitive.

These short-range strategies all attempt to balance societal pressure for punishment with fiscal and legal constraints on punishment options. Building prisons is a slow process that creates both a backlog of prisoners and a sense that the state is not doing enough to protect citizens. Non-

incarceration programs in the community are cheape
meet community expectations for being tough.

Long-Range Approaches

Prisons remain dumping grounds for unskilled, poor, powe
angry people. Prisoners overwhelmingly come from areas wher
and drug use are high and opportunities for personal or family adv
ment are limited. These patterns almost guarantee a steady strea
new and repeat prisoners. For example, young African-American ma
as a group are particularly disadvantaged economically[27] and are als
overrepresented in prison. The proportion of African-Americans in state
and federal prisons increased from 21 percent in 1926 to over 43 percent
in the late 1980s. In 1993, the comparable figure for inmates of African
descent was 47.4 percent.[28] At current incarceration rates, nearly one
in five African-American males will serve a prison term sometime in
his life, compared with one in thirty white males.[29] While some discrimination certainly occurs within the criminal justice system, it does
not account for all of the overrepresentation of African-American males
in the system according to research evidence.[30] When violent crime
victims were asked in large household surveys to characterize their
assailants in terms of race and age, young African-Americans were
significantly more likely to be named than were other groups. The
evidence suggests that the frequent criminality—and subsequent
imprisonment—of these Americans are linked to their low economic
status and the dearth of educational and employment opportunities. It
is also telling that in 1991, 53 percent of African-American inmates grew
up in single parent homes (compared to 40 percent of Hispanic and 33
percent of Anglo inmates).[31]

These findings argue for long-range approaches to the prison crisis,
such as expanding educational and occupational opportunities and
strengthening families. Among other outcomes, these strategies could
reduce crime and drug use. Of course, such strategies are difficult and
expensive and cannot eliminate prisons. Still, they address the
fundamental societal conditions that are the root causes of crime and
the prison crisis.

Will citizens, who fear crime and want offenders locked away, support
such fundamental changes? The answer is a qualified "yes." In 1989,
a national poll asked citizens whether they preferred trying to lower the
crime rate by attacking the social and economic problems that lead to
crime through better education and job training or by increasing the
number of prisons, police officers, and judges. Sixty-one percent said
that we should attack the social problems that cause crime, while only
32 percent supported an expanded criminal justice system.[32]

clusion

's in the 1990s and beyond? In the
ublic demands that offenders be
rol crowding. To this end, they
nge strategies discussed above
nd fiscal realities.

next several years with these
ing some relief. Evidence suggests,
rtion of young persons in the population
es, crime rates will also decline.[33] As a result,
s may fall as well. Imprisonment rates may also
use of changing crime patterns or the diversion of some
offenders into community programs. For example, California's
sons, which have the largest populations in the nation, recently
reported a drop in admissions, which officials attributed to a sharp
decline in the number of drug offenders being sent to prison. Whether
this is a national trend is unclear.

Adding to the prison crisis will be a fundamental change in the overall
composition of the prisoner population. There is one social fact about
prison from which there is no escape: prisons are a reflection of the wider
society. Prison managers will have to contend with a broad array of
special-needs prisoners. Programs will have to be implemented for the
expected increases in prisoners with HIV/TB/hepatitis, women prisoners,
youthful offenders, inmates sentenced to life without parole, geriatric
prisoners, death-sentenced offenders, illegal aliens, and medically,
physically, and mentally disabled prisoners.

There is little reason to be optimistic about the size of the prison
population. For the immediate future, conditions in American cities will
continue to produce high crime rates for which citizens and legislators
will continue to seek increased incarceration. Therefore, despite public
support for addressing the fundamental causes of crime in our
communities, we can expect some version of the present prison crisis
to be with us well into the next century.

Notes

[1] Quoted in David J. Rothman, The Discovery of the Asylum: Social Order and Disorder in the New Republic. Boston: Little, Brown and Co., 1970, p. 244.

[2] Cited in Bert Useem and Peter Kimball, States of Siege: U.S. Prison Riots 1971–1986. New York: Oxford University Press, 1989, p. 82.

[3] Bureau of Justice Statistics, Survey of State Prison Inmates, 1993:6–7.

[4] Bureau of Justice Statistics, op. cit., pp. 1–2.

[5] Marc Mauer, "Americans Behind Bars: One Year Later." Washington, D.C.:The Sentencing Project, 1992.

[6] Gerald G. Gaes, "The Effects of Overcrowding in Prison." In Michael Tonry and Norval Morris (eds.), *Crime and Justice: A Review of Research*, vol. 6. Chicago: University of Chicago Press, 1985, pp. 95–146.

[7] Steve Martin and Sheldon Ekland-Olson, *Texas Prisons: The Walls Came Tumbling Down*. Austin: Texas Monthly Press, 1987, p. 141.

[8] Hans Toch, *Living in Prison: The Ecology of Survival*. New York: Free Press, 1977, p. 31.

[9] Ben M. Crouch and James W. Marquart, *An Appeal to Justice: Litigated Reform of Texas Prisons*. Austin: University of Texas Press, 1989.

[10] Bureau of Justice Statistics, op. cit., p. 5.

[11] Franklin Zimring and Gordon Hawkins, *The Scale of Imprisonment*. Chicago: University of Chicago Press, 1991, p. 187.

[12] Graeme Newman, *The Punishment Response*. Philadelphia: Lippincott, 1978.

[13] Kenneth C. Haas, "The Triumph of Vengeance Over Retribution: The United States Supreme Court and the Death Penalty." *Crime, Law and Social Change*, 21:127–154, 1994.

[14] William Wilson, *The Truly Disadvantaged: The Inner City, the Underclass and Public Policy*. Chicago: University of Chicago Press, 1987. See also Robert Sampson, "Urban Black Violence: The Effect of Male Joblessness and Family Disruption," *American Journal of Sociology* 93:348–382, 1987.

[15] Carl Taylor, *The Dangerous Society*. East Lansing: Michigan State University Press, 1990. See also David Bazelon, *Questioning Authority: Justice in Criminal Law*. New York: Knopf, 1988.

[16] Zimring and Hawkins, op. cit., pp. 128–129.

[17] Bureau of Justice Statistics, *Sourcebook of Criminal Justice Statistics, 1989*. Washington, D.C.: U.S. Government Printing Office, 1990, p. 145.

[18] Michael Sherman and Gordon Hawkins, *Imprisonment in America: Choosing the Future*. Chicago: University of Chicago Press, 1981, p. 122.

[19] John Irwin, *Prisons in Turmoil*. Boston: Little, Brown, 1980.

[20] See James Jacobs, *Stateville*. Chicago: University of Chicago Press, 1977; Crouch and Marquart, op. cit.

[21] Richard Hawkins and Geoffrey Alpert, *American Prison Systems: Punishment and Justice*. Englewood Cliffs, NJ: Prentice-Hall, 1989, chaps. 11 and 12.

[22] Bureau of Justice Statistics, op. cit., p. 505.

[23] Bureau of Justice Statistics, *Survey of State Prison Inmates, 1991*:7.

[24] Bureau of Justice Statistics, op. cit., p. 4.

[25] Ben M. Crouch, "Is Incarceration Really Worse? Analysis of Offender Preferences for Prison over Probation." *Justice Quarterly*, Spring 1993. See also Joan Petersilia, "When Probation Becomes More Dreaded Than Prison," *Federal Probation*, March 1990, pp. 23–28.

[26] Norval Morris and Michael Tonry, *Between Prison and Probation: Intermediate Punishments in a Rational Sentencing System*. New York: Oxford University Press, 1990.

[27] Jewel Gibbs, *Young Black and Male in America*. Dover, MA: Auburn House, 1988.

[28] Bureau of Justice Statistics, *Survey of State Prison Inmates, 1993*:9.

[29] Lawrence Greenfeld and Patrick Langan, "Trends in Prison Populations," presented before the National Conference on Punishment for Criminal Offenses, Ann Arbor, Michigan, 1991.

[30] Alfred Blumstein, "Prison Population: A System Out of Control." In Tonry and Morris, op. cit., vol. 10, p. 245.

[31] Bureau of Justice Statistics, *Survey of State Prison Inmates, 1991*:4.

[32] Bureau of Justice Statistics, op. cit., p. 158.

[33] Darrell Steffensmier and Miles Harer, "Did Crime Rise or Fall During the Reagan Presidency? The Effects of an 'Aging' U.S. Population on the Nation's Crime Rate." *Journal of Research on Crime and Delinquency* 28:330–359, 1991.

[34] John Hurst, "California Bucks Prison Growth Trend." *Houston Chronicle*, September 2, 1991, p. 3A.

Part II

The Realities of Prison Life

Introduction

In *Rhodes v. Chapman*, a 1981 decision holding that, by itself, the double-celling of inmates for long periods of incarceration does not violate Eighth Amendment standards, the U.S. Supreme Court declared that "to the extent that [prison] conditions are restrictive and even harsh, they are part of the penalty that criminal offenders pay for their offenses against society." Emphasizing that facilities housing persons convicted of serious crimes "cannot be free of discomfort," the Justices concluded that "[t]he Constitution does not mandate comfortable prisons." This undoubtedly is a sentiment that enjoys widespread public approval. It is not uncommon to hear people who have never even visited a jail or prison refer to America's prisons as "country clubs" or "Holiday Inns."

Such stereotyping, of course, obscures the fact that no two prisons are exactly alike. There are some prisons, primarily federal prison camps specializing in white-collar offenders, which come complete with modern recreational facilities, a variety of work and therapy opportunities, and expansive visiting hours. However, anyone who reads the evidence accrued in the hundreds of lawsuits brought to the courts by state prisoners in the past few years can only conclude that too many American prisons are depressing, rat-infested, heavily overcrowded fortresses that have created perverse societies in which violence, homosexual rape, and other assorted cruelties are everyday occurrences.

Scholars have carefully documented the fact that imprisonment inevitably leads to anxiety, pain, and stress. In his classic 1958 work, *The Society of Captives*, a detailed study of a large, maximum security prison in New Jersey, Gresham Sykes described the most severe psychological and social problems that accompany incarceration. These "pains of imprisonment" included the loss of liberty, autonomy, security, goods and services, and heterosexual relations. These deprivations, according to Sykes, arouse intense anxiety and bitter resentment in prisoners, and, ironically, they pressure prisoners to seek refuge in the antisocial values of the prison community, thus destroying any prospects of rehabilitation and provoking the very types of behavior prisons are supposed to suppress.

Just how violent, degrading, and emasculating is life in the prisons of the 1990s? To what extent are prisoners brutalized by their fellow prisoners, guards, and other staff members? What effects does prison life have on prisoners and how do those other prisoners—the guards—adapt to the stresses of daily confrontations with a hostile, abusive, and potentially violent inmate population? These are among the questions discussed in Part II.

Our first selection, "Target Violence," is the third chapter of Daniel Lockwood's excellent book, *Prison Sexual Violence*. This book examines the causes, consequences, and possible cures of sexual aggression in men's prisons. In "Target Violence," Lockwood focuses on the prisoner who reacts violently to men who make aggressive sexual approaches to him. Lockwood provides numerous horrifying examples of victim-precipitated violence as he explores the links between fear, anger, and sexual violence. It is especially interesting that most prisoners and most staff members support violence against sexual aggressors because they believe it to be the best self-defense available. This selection speaks volumes about the prevalence of prison violence by both aggressors and targets, and it depicts the harsh realities of life in a cannibalistic society where the strong prey on the weak.

In some respects, the conditions and practices in women's prisons are similar to those found in men's prisons in that both male and female prisoners suffer the same losses of liberty and autonomy, and must find ways to cope with the "pains of imprisonment." However, women's prisons, though increasingly overcrowded, tend to be smaller in size than men's prisons, and female prisoners are less likely than are male prisoners to engage in acts of extreme physical and/or sexual violence against one another. Nevertheless, women's prisons are places where rehabilitation is rare, where health care usually falls well below accepted medical standards, and where rules and regulations seem designed to harass and humiliate rather than to correct. In particular, women prisoners are often treated as "girls," as children in institutions in which paternalism and infantilization are dominant features of everyday life. Women prisoners, as Jean Harris has deftly chronicled in her 1988 book, *"They Always Call Us Ladies": Stories from Prison*, are reduced to infancy by petty, arbitrarily enforced rules that tell them to walk and talk like "ladies," to avoid cursing, and to "act like grown women" when they go "shopping" at the prison commissary.

Without doubt, the treatment of imprisoned women reflects sexist attitudes that are deeply entrenched in our culture and the myth and folklore that have pervaded the study of female offenders. This is one of the themes taken up by Richard Hawkins in "Inmate Adjustments in Women's Prisons," the second article in Part II. Hawkins explores the leading research studies on the realities of life in women's prisons. These studies reveal the existence of a prison subculture in which many female prisoners establish homosexual relationships and form pseudo-families in which such traditional family roles as "husband," "wife," "father," "brother," and "daughter" can be played. These and other social roles existing in women's prisons form an inmate subculture that new students of corrections may find shocking.

Correctional staff, of course, also become a major part of the prison community. Accordingly, our next article concerns staff-prisoner victimization in U.S. prisons. "The Victimization of Prisoners by Staff Members" is taken from Lee Bowker's *Prison Victimization*, a comprehensive overview of the sexual, social, psychological, and economic victimization of prisoners and prison staff. Readers may be shocked by the many well-documented accounts of psychological mistreatment, physical torture, and sexual assaults against both adults and juveniles by sheriffs, deputies, guards, and other correctional officials. But as Bowker explains, there are at least two intriguing theoretical explanations—total institutions theory and role theory—that can help us understand why the dynamics of prison life bring out the very worst impulses in inmates and staff alike.

Prisoners and prison guards view one another with distrust, suspicion, and hostility. Nevertheless, sociological research on the prison community has revealed that the custodial staff seek to attain discipline and order not by imposing inflexible rules on prisoners, but by maintaining an elastic system of rewards and punishment in which the guards deliberately fail to enforce the full range of institutional regulations in exchange for the cooperation of inmate leaders in preventing widespread rulebreaking. In "Prison Guards and Snitches: Social Control in a Maximum Security Institution," James Marquart and Julian Roebuck explain how the guards in a maximum security penitentiary were able to use the most prestigious, aggressive, and feared inmates as "rats" or "snitches." This contradicts previous research portraying "rats" as weak, pitiful outcasts. Most intriguingly, Marquart and Roebuck show that it was the non-informing, ordinary prisoners and the lower ranking guards who were labeled as deviant and who were relegated to a lower status position in the prison under study.

How can researchers get the facts on the realities of life in a particular prison or in prisons generally? Traditionally prison research has been conducted by social scientists who use survey methodology and other techniques. Over the years, prisoners and guards have been interviewed and/or polled on a wide range of topics. Another valuable research strategy is to enter a prison as an observer—someone known to inmates and staff alike as an outsider (a "prof" or "doc") who is there for the explicit purpose of studying the internal dynamics of the prison. Although these research techniques have led to the collection of valuable quantitative and qualitative data, they may offer only a limited view of the actual behavior of prisoners and prison staff.

In our next selection, James Marquart discusses a research technique that arguably offers unusually penetrating insights into the "real world" of the prison—actually becoming a prison guard in order to study inmate and staff behavior. In "Doing Research in Prison: The Strengths and Weaknesses of Full Participation as a Guard," Marquart makes it clear that a full-participation research strategy is filled with potential problems, including but not limited to ethical dilemmas and threats to the safety and well-being of the researcher. Clearly this is not a type of research that will appeal to everyone. But readers will enjoy Marquart's account of his work as a guard at a large, maximum-security Texas prison, and they will also come away with a good understanding of the benefits and costs of studying prisons from the inside.

Prison guards are sometimes referred to as a society's forgotten prisoners, and with good reason. In most states, correctional officers are underpaid, undertrained, and overworked. They have one of the most frustrating, stress-filled, and dangerous jobs imaginable. Accordingly, the last selection in Part II examines the plight of the prison guard. Ben Crouch's "Guard Work in Transition" offers an insightful and detailed examination of how changes in American prisons over the past three decades have created new and difficult problems for today's guards. Crouch, a nationally recognized expert on the sociology of guarding, has updated this chapter especially for the fourth edition of *The Dilemmas of Corrections*. He explores such issues as guard stress, the dangerousness of guard work, the increasing racial and sexual integration of guard forces, the nature and extent of guard deviance on the job, and guard reactions to the growing professionalization and bureaucratization of American prisons.

7

Target Violence
Daniel Lockwood

Most prison violence involves inmates assaulting each other (Cohen et al., 1976). One reason is that violent men and men from violent subcultures live in prison. As violence behind the walls becomes acceptable behavior, prison itself becomes a "subculture of violence" (Conrad, 1966). When otherwise peaceful men live with prisoners who are dangerous or perceived to be dangerous, they become distrustful and fearful. These feelings of vulnerability cause those who have not been violent before to arm themselves and prepare themselves psychologically for fighting. Thus, in prison, sexual aggression results in two main types of violence: (1) Aggressors use violence to intimidate targets, and (2) targets of aggressors react violently to sexual approaches. This chapter examines the latter class of violent behavior, i.e., target violence precipitated by aggressive sexual approaches.

Hans Toch, as a member of the California Task Force on Institutional Violence, constructed a typology of prisoners in violent encounters (Toch, 1965). He calls the man whom I discuss here the "Homosexual Self-Defender." This prisoner, according to Toch, uses violence against men who make sexual approaches to him in order to be left alone.

Source: Reprinted by permission of the publisher from Chapter Three by Daniel Lockwood, *Prison Sexual Violence*, 38-58. Copyright 1980 by Elsevier Science Publishing Co., Inc.

According to Toch, "The effort here is to get out of a corner by eliminating whoever is blocking the exit" (1965).

> Following a heated altercation between inmates S and L, S obtains a razor blade, enters L's cell, and cuts L about the face and chest. S testifies that L had visited him to involve him in homosexual activities, and had been pressuring him. Other inmate sources point out that S has been under pressure from several homosexuals. (Toch, 1965)

Observers describe similar target reactions in a number of settings (Huffman, 1960; Thomas, 1967). Following the riot of 1971, the New York State Special Commission on Attica (1974) interviewed inmates in Attica, who frequently voiced their belief that violence is the only way to ward off sexual attacks. The Commission noted:

> The irony was not lost on the inmates. They perceived themselves surrounded by walls and gates, and tightly regimented by a myriad of written and unwritten rules; but when they needed protection, they often had to resort to the same skills that had brought many of them to Attica in the first place. (p. 101)

When targets fight aggressors, it reminds us of victim-precipitated homicide (Schultz, 1964). Offenders are incited to assaultive responses by the aggressive actions of their victims. Victims of targets (sexual aggressors), like many homicide victims in the street, often have been previously arrested for crimes of violence. Their patterns of conduct involve them in situations that provoke others to hostile reactions. In prison, a physical environment enforcing contact between antagonists, the probability of an aggressor provoking a violent response may be even greater than in the street. As Albert Cohen points out, prisons create "back-against-the-wall situations" because threatened men often lack the option of withdrawing (Cohen et al., 1976). When interactions contain potential for conflict, confinement itself hastens violence.

A study of violence in six California prisons in 1963 and 1964—one of the few sources classifying inmate assaults—indicates the kinds of contribution that sexual aggression can make to prison violence. The report breaks inmate-to-inmate assaults into the following categories.

Accidental, real, or imagined insult combined with hypersensitivity	35%
Homosexual activities	25%
Pressuring (for possessions)	15%
Racial conflict	12%
Informant activities	9%
Retaliation for past assaults	7%

Incidents attributed to homosexuality divide almost equally between homosexual rivalry (12 percent) and homosexual force (13 percent) (Toch, 1965). However, as we shall see in this chaper, it is possible for sexual aggression to play a role in the other categories listed above.

Prevalence

I define physical violence to include instances where one person was forcefully touched by another, this being marked by vehement feelings or the aim to injure or abuse. According to such a definition, 51 percent of 150 incidents in my study involved physical violence. About half of these were initiated by aggressors using force against unprovoking targets. Targets began the rest. These were clearcut violent responses to sexual approaches targets perceived as aggressive.

The Violent Transaction

We followed a method suggested by Toch, who states:

> In this type of approach, each move is seen as the rational response by one player to the play of another. The focus is on logical possibilities left open by preceding moves and on logical implications of each move for successive moves. These possibilities and implications can be conceptualized and qualified (1969, p. 35).

Diagramming 114 transactions (incomplete cases were left out), we grouped them according to the aggressor's first move. They fall into the following four categories:

1. Incidents begun by sexual overtures accompanied by offensive remarks and gestures (N = 42)
2. Incidents begun by polite propositions (N = 36)
3. Incidents begun by physical attacks (N = 21)
4. Incidents begun by verbal threats (N = 15).

With an examination of the largest group, we see that over half of these transactions, begun by aggressors directing offensive remarks or gestures to targets, quickly escalated to violence. The moves in those sequences culminating in violence commonly follow this pattern:

1. a. Aggressor(s) makes offensive sexual overture.
   b. Target tries to withdraw or target responds with force or threats and a fight starts.
2. a. Aggressor repeats overture, accompanied by threats.
   b. Target uses physical force against aggressor and a fight starts or target answers with counterthreat and a fight starts.

I use an example of this transaction from Coxsackie, a prison housing 700 youths ranging in age from 16 to 21. The target is a white marijuana dealer from Florida. The aggressor is black, a violent offender from New York City. During an incident an officer looks on but is out of earshot:

C2-27: While I was taking a shower he said to me, "You're all right and you're going to be mine later." There was two or three saying it, but they had one spokesman....They were in the shower and they were waiting to have me turn around so that they could see my ass....They were saying that I was going to be theirs and they would take care of me and buy me cigarettes and that I would be their main squeeze.

And I said, "Well you can see me later, but we're going to fight about it, because you're not going to get anything out of me."

So he said, "Okay, Angel, that's okay, I'll play it rough with you and then after you break then you'll be mine."

So I rinsed off and then I got the fuck out....So I'm over there by the door and as he was going out he put his arm around me and as he did that, I pushed his arm away and I said, "I don't play that, man."

And he said, "Well, you're going to play what I want you to play."

And I said, "Definitely not — I don't want to hassle."

And he said, "You're going to be mine." And he leaned over and said that he was going to whisper something in my ear and I told him to back off, gave him a shove and he came back fighting. I hit him a couple of times and then the guards broke it up and then we were both locked up for the same amount of time.

An important feature of this fight is that before the violence, the target tries to withdraw, but cannot. As he tells us:

C2-27: I figured that he would want to hassle, so I got my clothes on and I went away from his group of people and then I went out the door and stayed away from him and I thought that maybe he would keep away from me that way and go on to somebody else. And I noticed that he was talking to some other people and giving them the same thing. I thought, if he's hassling somebody else, I'm not any hero and I'm not going to go defend somebody else.

Cornered, his back against the wall, the target starts the fight (i.e., by shoving the aggressor)—only after his antagonist has repeatedly propositioned him, threatened him, and attempted to whisper endearments in his ear. Because prison restricts movement, the transaction escalates to violence, even though one of the participants wants to retreat.

Why does the target finally shove the aggressor, thereby changing a verbal encounter to a physical one? Mindful that an officer is supervising the shower area, why can't the target limit himself to verbal responses? Whether his reaction springs from panic or the cool decision to make a preemptive strike, the root cause is fear. Following the aggressor's initial move, the target's thoughts are a mixture of fear and self-doubt.

C2-27: I was saying, "What could I do if all three of these guys came and jumped me?" I could probably hit a couple of them but I'm thinking of all these martial arts that I'm going to break into and all I've seen is Kung Fu on T.V. And there was nothing to pick up and I didn't have any shoes that I could kick them with.

If this target had felt safe, the fight might have been avoided. But prisons are places of fear where violence feeds on itself and breeds more violence. If this target had been able to withdraw, the fight might have been avoided. But prison prohibits free movement and men in antagonistic transactions lash out when cornered. If the target had been separated from abusive and threatening comments, the incident would never have occurred. But society deposits its bullies and exploiters in prison. Inevitably, behind the walls, they continue these patterns of behavior, directing their aggression against weaker prisoners instead of free citizens.

Forty-two incidents, like the above example, began with propositions accompanied by offensive remarks or gestures. Twenty-four (or 57 percent) ended in violence. Many incited sharp target reactions from the very first: 12 targets, for example, fought with aggressors immediately following their offensive overtures.

Does target violence work? Or is it senseless, an overreaction to a situation that could be resolved by talking over the problem? To examine this question, let us compare, still within the category of incidents begun by offensive remarks or gestures, targets responding violently to targets trying to ignore or respond politely to these sexual overtures. Only one target who responded without violence succeeded in ending this type of incident. In the other transactions in this category, the nonviolent target response was met in the following ways:

1. Seven aggressors repeated the offensive remark or gesture;
2. Four aggressors leveled sexual threats at targets; and
3. Four aggressors attacked targets.

Polite refusals, thus, tended to encourage aggressors to continue their offensive behavior. We know violent responses to unwanted sexual overtures are normative expectations of the convict community. Unfortunately, in some instances, they may actually be necessary for surviving incarceration with dignity.

We also grouped 36 incidents sequentially that opened with requests for sex—propositions. Twelve of these incidents evolved into physical violence. This escalation usually occurred in one of two ways. In the first, the target replied to the request for sex with a polite refusal, or ignored the request. Following this response, the aggressor reacted violently or accompanied a renewed request with threats. In the second sequence, the target, hearing the request, reacted with the use of force. In one-third of these incidents, targets responded with threats of their own before propositioners made violent or threatening moves. These threats ended half of these incidents, while the others escalated to higher levels of force.

The messages being communicated—that the propositioner wanted sex with the target, and that the target wanted the aggressor to stay away—tended to be confused by threats on both sides. In this scenario, threats often escalated into physical violence. Some targets heard a proposition and snarled back. Others attempted to reason with propositioners and ended up snapping back when their reasoning failed. Aggressors, beginning their approaches with requests for sex, were drawn into conflict for varying reasons. For example, a refusal might suggest the necessity for developing threats or violence. On the other hand, a refusal might be perceived as insulting. In these cases of violence, the sexual motive changes into a reaction to the sting of wounded pride.

We also grouped 21 incidents beginning with sexual attacks and 15 that began with extreme threats. Following these expressions of force, six targets submitted to sexual assault, because of the level of force exerted. Many immediately began to fight with their assailants. Officers then appeared and the incidents ended short of sexual penetration. Completed rapes depended more on the presence or absence of security than on any type of target response. Most incidents that began with immediate threats moved directly into physical violence. In four cases, violence occurred because aggressors used force when their threats were met with target attempts to withdraw peacefully. In nine cases, targets initiated the violence by responding to the threats with physical force. This set of incidents exemplifies both patterns of sequences resulting in physical violence. Aggressors escalate from threats to physical force, and targets escalate from being the objects of threats to being the initiators of physical violence.

In conclusion, the results of diagramming 150 incidents of sexual aggression may be stated simply. Attacks and threats are often answered by physical violence or threats. Targets tend to answer propositions with threats and aggressors tend to threaten or employ force when propositions have been declined. Thus, dialogue escalates to threats and threats escalate to violence. We could expect little less when violent men enter such transactions.

Fear, Anger, and Violence

We coded the psychological impact of sexual aggression, tabulating the incidence of specific emotions in each interview. The results of this laborious process showed *fear* and *anger* to be the feelings most often associated with the experience. These are concomitants of violent behavior in both animal and human interactions.

We will first examine the contribution of anger to target violence. By our definition, targets are recipients of unwanted sexual approaches. Because these approaches are unwanted — obnoxious and offensive — they cause frustration. Targets must often suffer frustration for long periods of time, while aggressors, who play the prison "pimp" role, take pride in their persistence. Because sexual problems are often unshareable problems, men do not talk about them, and they are sometimes afraid to vent their true feelings to aggressors. Frustration, having no release, dams up until it breaks in a flood of aggression. A prisoner tells us:

ARE-4: And when he sat down, he had a cup of coffee in his left hand and he put his right arm around my whole shoulders....And I got so irritated. Nothing would stop him, nothing. Neither threats nor making just sense, or trying to show him my point of view in the situation. Nothing. Nothing would deter it. So he sat down and put his arm around my shoulders and I realized that this was it. I had come to the end of my rope and put up with this crap for long enough. It all happened so fast. I had just come to the end of my rope. And when I jumped up he stood up immediately. I poked at him with that fork, and he backed up because he really thought that I was going to stab him. I was so angry, but I really wasn't going to stab him. I just wanted to make him realize that I could become violent. And like I said, "Back up and if you ever touch me I'll kill you." And I was just ready to enact it. I was at the end. All this pressure just came out at one time.

Aggressors often select targets who seem to have emotional problems that make them more vulnerable. This strategy backfires where targets have difficulty managing aggressivity and hostile feelings. Such men may be locked up because temper control is one of the components of their criminal behavior.

C2-29: The guys were fooling around and grabbing me by the ass. He said I was a pussy and he is going to break me. So I picked him up and I threw him against the wall. When he come off the wall I just beat the pulp out of him. I kind of just lost my head and I know that if I get in that state I am really going to break because, you know, after a while it builds up. You can't take it no longer.

AR-16: He will make a false move and that is when my whole body starts shaking. Like I have got a bad temper and I don't take no shit from nobody. I was close enough to kill one of these dudes around here. I am all nervous and anything could happen.

Of course, confinement can make any prisoner, regardless of his personality, unduly sensitive to irritations. Sexual approaches may impinge on a man already troubled by family worries, resentments over authority, or any of the other possible difficulties of confinement. Sexual pressure in some cases caps a sediment of accumulated aggravations. A target who killed his aggressor tells us:

B-6:   At that certain time, I had a whole lot on my mind. He caught me at the wrong time to talk to me about that stuff. If it was another time, I don't believe that I would have tried to kill him or would have tried to do anything to him. I had a whole lot of little things on my mind. It was the time. When I finished, I felt sorry for him. I really shouldn't have done that, but I did it.

Rationales for Violence

While some target violence relates to unscheduled explosions of rage, in other cases prisoners say they fight aggressors to carry out calculated aims. Violence, men tell us, becomes the medium for a message and a cool strategy for self-defense.

Defining Sexual Identity

Some targets say they become violent to show others they are straight and mean to stay that way. Most targets dread the gay label. When approached for sex, some avail themselves of the opportunity to attack aggressors so they can publicly demonstrate their disdain of homosexuality. While part of targets' fear revolves around anxiety about being stigmatized, men also feel that if others believe they are gay they will be open to further victimization. This fear relates to the tendency for prisoners to think of targets as "sissies" or "squeeze."

C2-30:   It was mostly the same guy and I had to take it out on him because it was getting to a point, you know, everybody in the institution was thinking I was a punk or squeeze or a pussy and stuff like that. I had to to something about it in order to stop it. I had to prove to these other people that I wasn't a pussy or punk or anything else. I had to prove to these other people in my way and their way that I wasn't what he thought I was.

C2-29:   And people was thinking, the people that was looking on at that time, that this guy — well, maybe this guy is a pussy or something. This guy is fooling around with his ass. There must be something wrong with him. He must be a pussy.

    So I turned around and I caught him fooling around. So I told him, "Do it once more and I am going to bust you in the face." The people, that is the worst thing in this place, the people look on and they always have their ratings. And they have to gossip. They are like ladies and they really build it up and it runs around the institution.

CR-28: The guy right next to me, they grab his ass. He just lets it go by and so they call him a squeeze. I told him, "The next time that they touch your ass, you turn around and swing, or otherwise they are going to think that you are a squeeze."

Showing You Believe in the Convict Code

Those identifying with the convict code feel they must answer threat with threat. Such men cannot discuss the problem with the staff, for that shows they are rats. Similarly, the subcultural inmate sometimes cannot reason with an aggressor because he sees talk as a sign of weakness, uncoolness, or as an unacceptable attribute of straight society. Self-respect for prisoners upholding the convict code means favoring private solutions. The correct course of action calls for facing the challenge and responding to it forcefully.

AUI-2: See, when a guy first comes in a lot of guys will say, "Well, I don't want to hit the guy because I am thinking about the parole board." But, really, that is the very best way to deal with it. You could report the incident but that is snitching and I feel myself that if you have to knock the guy's head off to handle the problem, knock the guy's head off. You have to establish yourself as a man and you have to live with yourself. You have to look at yourself every morning in the mirror.

• • •

I: Did you think of any other ways to solve this problem?

AR-41: No, not really. Because what he said was already out in the open. If I talked to him, then everybody else would say I'm trying to cop out. So the only way I seen to solve the problem was to actually get out and fight, prove to him that I ain't going to go to no police and inform on anybody.

Showing You are Tough

Targets sometimes assert that they are violent because they wish to show others they are tough. Fighting is a way of communicating to all other potential aggressors—not just the men in the immediate incident—that one is not to be messed with. Discouraging the immediate approach becomes secondary to raising one's status. The assumption is that a violent demeanor is necessary for survival in prison, and that an aggressive image is a positive and worthwhile attribute of one's public personality, which must be consciously cultivated.

ARE-2: Now, if you were to go out and hit somebody across the head with a pipe and almost kill them, then people would think twice again. They would say, "That dude is crazy and he might try to kill me if I ask him that." And, so, then you know you can go where you want to go.

C2-23: Now, each and every inmate goes through a trial period here where someone is going to say, "I want your ass." But if he straightens it out himself and he gets into a fight with the guy, it will show everyone that he is not going to take that kind of shit. He will be all right.

AR-41: I felt kind of different because, like, when I walked through the yard there was people in it that went to school also and they were telling their friends, "This little guy will cut you if you even attempt to do anything to him. He's a dude to stay away from." And you see people looking at you as you're walking by, like saying, "Should I approach him, will he cut me too?" Stuff like this going through their minds.

C2-27: I wanted to protect myself and the only way that you can protect yourself is with violence. And it was getting to the point where after a while I was starting to do pushups every night. And then as I would get tired, I said that I would kick that guy's ass as I got stronger. I noticed that there was a bunch of them around, I thought when he hit me, "This is it, that will show the other guys when I get into a fight with this one that I'm not going to quit." So I fight and get punched a few times and I punch him a few times and they see that I'm a man.

Violence as a Means of Curbing Violence

Violence can be a simple matter of using preemptive self-defense. At a certain point the target begins to believe that the aggressor is on a course escalating toward a forceful attempt at sexual assault. He then fights to alter this self-conceived prediction. Even men who are approached with nonviolent propositions may project into the future, see themselves as probably victims, and react violently.

C2-43: I was going to grab a bench or a piece of pipe or something and I figured if I hit one of them and they got to bleeding or something they might stop monkeying around.

A-1: A lot of times fear will make you do things like that. The first time that somebody gives you some lip, you stab him. It's a warning: "Look, I don't want to be pushed around." If somebody comes to you, they can say a word wrong and if you don't react to that one word in the right way, you lose something and then they will test you a little further. If you fail then you're in trouble.

Documenting Violence Effectiveness

Violence as a pragmatic solution is a formula upheld by most inmates. But how does this theory work in actual practice? Is violence, in fact, a successful way to meet the violence problem? On one level, the answer is "yes." In concrete incidents, some men have found violence to be a satisfactory ploy. Targets can report violent responses that have curbed aggressive approaches, and some men who try reasoning with aggressors find them unresponsive until these targets project a more aggressive stance. The effectiveness of protective aggression in certain cases strengthens the norms supporting violence as a solution to forceful sexual approaches.

AR-1:   I stood my ground right then and there and I said, "Look, you just stay clear or else I am going to put a pipe right across your head." And I wasn't fooling. And that is the last time he has ever bothered me.

AR-41: The Spanish dude, after I cut him, he comes back and he says, "Listen, I'm sorry for what I did."
        I said, "Do you really mean that? Then I'm sorry for cutting you."
        I had to put it straight right then, "I'll do it again if you try it again."
        And he says, "No, no, everything's all right."

C2-23: He hit me and then I went after this guy, I beat him — I beat him real good. So about a week later he came back downstairs and all of a sudden he shook my hand and said, "Let's be friends." The only way to get respect from them is to put a foot in their ass.

AR-7:   He went to the hospital and I got locked up. I got a two-day keep-lock even though the administration knew basically that he was behind it. And after that, we more or less became friends, I suppose. We were talking to each other.

ARE-2: A dude pushed a guy and cut him with a knife. And ever since then people don't do nothing. They talk about it among themselves but whenever he's around, people want to be friends with him.

Negotiating from Weakness

At the same time forces pull men toward violent solutions, other drives push them away from resolving the conflict by verbal negotiation. Especially for those on the brink of feeling powerless, the willingness to negotiate may be seen as an additional symbol of weakness, a further step toward vulnerability. Targets also feel that verbal sparring with aggressors can sink them into deeper trouble than they are in already. Lacking confidence in their bargaining ability, some targets fear that fast-talking "players" will easily manipulate any conversation to serve their ends.

C2-29: You talk to the guy and he bullshits his way out and says this and that and tries to twist your words and throws them back to you. And it doesn't work. He doesn't listen. And the only way he is going to listen at this point is to punch him in the mouth. You can't do anything else.

A-1:   I think they can talk themselves into it deeper. I think that you can talk yourself out of it if you're very slick and if you're mean and have a mean rap. If you have the right eyes, and the right look in your eyes, and the right way of how anger should appear in your eyes, and how hate should appear, and malice, and how to project fear into somebody else's eyes, if you can do that, you can do it, you can talk your way out of it. But the thing is that if you're too scared, then you lose.

C2-23:   You try to talk to them—you try to talk sense to them and say, "Now, look, I am an inmate and you are an inmate."

And they will say, "Ah—don't tell me that pussy shit." They will tell you that, you know. So, I figured that talking was no good with this guy. There is only one way to handle him and that is to fight with him.

A-1:   I hadn't even tried to talk them out of it, because I wasn't that good at expressing myself and I couldn't project fear into someone. I couldn't project hostility. There was something that I couldn't do.

Peer and Staff Support

The attitudes and behaviors associated with target violence are in part social behavior, learned in prison from other inmates and staff. Targets are generally new to the prison where they are harassed by sexual aggression; they may look to others for guidance. Peers, often men who have been targets themselves, may advise new men to consider violence favorably. Men who have never used weapons are supplied with "shanks" and "pipes" by their more experienced friends. Others are supplied with arguments through which guilt is neutralized. The target's violent response is an explicit normative expectation of the prison community. This is passed on to new men by experienced inmates as part of the process of "prisonization."

AR-23:   And I went out in the yard and I told my brother what was happening. The next thing you know one of my brother's friends came up and gave me a shank and told me that if a guy come up at me to stick him.

C2-52:   He just told me to grab anything that I can and just beat them. Whether it is a chair or whatever and just go after them.

C2-22:   This black dude was going to jump a friend of mine and so I talked to him and I said, "Look, man, the knife drawer is open. Grab one of them butcher knives and bring it upstairs. That is all." He took the knife out of the drawer and put it in the back of his pants and went upstairs and stuck it in the pillow and sewed the pillow back up. And if this dude come over, he would have got stabbed.

C2-28:   I just said, "Look-it, you just pick up something and you hit that dude. Or else you go and you make yourself a blade and you stab the dude—do anything." I says, "If the dude is going to rip you off, you kill the dude— that is all."

AR-36:   He was the water man and he was pretty straight. He came right out and he told me, "You are a little guy and you can expect trouble, you know, but if anything happens, don't even question it, just crack their skull and it will be over with — that is all."

C2-30: I go over and pull him over in the corner and talk to him right then and there and tell him, "These guys are trying to get over on you. The best thing for you to do is to hang out with the white guys and try and get to know people. Lift weights. Try boxing and do what you can. Learn how to fight if you can't fight."

C2-23: I told him that the best thing to do, in front of everyone, while this guy was popping shit to him, is to hit the guy. There is no other way that this thing is going to be resolved unless you hit the guy.

C2-44: I don't know how many times I told him, "If a dude run up on you, popping you some shit, just hit him in his face. If you lose, you lose — so what? You get locked up for seven days and you come downstairs and the dude will think twice before running up on you again. Because they are going to know that you will hurt him."

AR-6: So I tried to talk about it with some of the white guys that was here. They was living on this tier with me. And they tried to give me solutions. The majority of them told me to hit this guy, anybody that come up to you, just hit him.

The advocacy of violence is spread by the old to the young and by the experienced to the inexperienced. Thus, in observing how targets are readied to behave violently, we see a process whereby a subculture upholding violence spreads its message. Moreover, the learning that occurs in these peer groups is not academic. It answers an immediate problem of pressing concern to the learner.

Staff

Staff members also support target violence so that the square or isolate inmate who identifies with officialdom can learn violent norms just as well as the group member who identifies with his peers. Why do staff uphold violent solutions? Some staff members have cultural origins similar to those of many inmates in the prison. They are working-class men themselves and hold norms supporting "masculine" responses to intimidation. In addition, staff, like inmates, belong to the prison community. This community, as a norm of its own, holds that a violent response is one of the simplest and most effective ways of handling an aggressive sexual approach. Finally, staff, especially officers, sometimes can think of no options that they know to work as well as a violent response.

C2-20: And the C.O. came in and asked what had happened and I told him that this guy had tried to take me off and I was just protecting myself. So then the C.O. said, "I'll shut the door and you do what you think is the best." And so I fucked the guy up and sent him to the hospital.

AR-46: In Attica, they told me to take a pipe to them if they bother you sexually. Take a pipe to them — that was the officers. I was told that in '65 and so I started using one.

C2-51: The officer with me in the hall — he said, "You should have hit him in the nuts." And I said, "I am not a dirty fighter." He said, "That don't make no difference, man, you just do that." And I guess after a while I found out that he was right. So after a while, after I took it under deep study, I had the trouble and I hit him in the nuts.

AR-36: He [lieutenant] said, being a little guy, if anything like that should happen, hit the guy with the first thing available and try and knock him down. Try and do it in front of a hack or somebody and then he will come down and break it up. Once they do, you will go to the box. And once you get to the box, tell the hacks that you want to see me. I will come up, see what I can do. That is about the only thing that I can tell you.

• • •

I: So you spoke to the priest about this sex pressure, too? Did he offer you any advice?

C2-52: He just told me to do what I think is best and just fight if I have to.

• • •

I: You went to your company officer?

C2-23: Right, I went and said, "Look, this guy is bothering me, man. He keeps coming out with these sexual remarks and I want somebody to do something about this guy — tell him something." He said, "Well, there is nothing that we can do about it, and there is nothing that the brass can do about it, so hit him." He came right out and told me just like that.

During informal conversations, as when an officer on his rounds pauses to discuss an inmate's problem with him, the staff advise targets to be violent. Staff also offer this advice as part of the formal delivery of counseling services. Administrators, counselors, and even chaplains participate in giving such advice. The message that is communicated through official channels is essentially the same message as the men receive from their peers. Its content mirrors the themes we have reviewed: Violence will win you respect; it will deter future approaches; it will cause the aggressor bothering you to back off. Prison records show staff pleased with such advice, convinced of its effectiveness. When one inmate applied for transfer, his counselor wrote:

> Because of his youthful appearance, other inmates saw him as a prime material for homosexual activities. Through counseling and an individually tailored body building program, John has developed self-confidence and asserted his individuality. Having made his adjustment here, he should be able to hold his own in a camp setting.

When prisoners fight, they face stiff discipline. Formal procedures can remove privileges and sentence men to solitary confinement. In some cases of sexual aggression, however, informal arrangements suspend disciplinary proceedings, enabling staff to back up their advice with supportive leniency. When staff view inmate violence as justified and practical, formal measures to stop violence may be suspended. Staff may make private arrangements to overlook a fight provided it is in the service of survival. Staff thus monitor and even encourage instrumental inmate assaults on other inmates.

C2-37: I said, "Well, there is a nigger wanting to make me a kid." I says, "Before I give my ass up to any nigger, I would fucking kill him." So he [staff] says, "Well, you have got a point there." He says, "Yeah, all right, I am going to let you go." I said, "Any keep-lock or anything?" And he says, "You have got one day keep-lock and the next time any nigger or anything comes up on you, you do the same thing."

C2-31: One sergeant told me, "Put a bat across this dude's head and I will go to court and testify that you told me about this shit."

AR-36: When I went through my orientation, the senior lieutenant told me that if anything like that should happen, "Hit him, and when you go to the box, send the word and I will come up and talk to you. I will do what I can to get you out of trouble."

C2-30: I asked Sergeant Brown. And he told me to go ahead. "Pick up the nearest thing around you and hit him in the head with it. He won't bother you no more." I went over to another sergeant and I asked him and he said, "Pick up the nearest damn thing to you and just hit him with it, that is all." I looked at him and I said, "All right. If I do this I ain't going to get locked up for it, am I?" He looks at me and he says, "No." Because I am using self-defense.

Problems with Violent Solutions

The violent response to sexual approaches may be effective for some, but not for others. As Bartollas et al. (1976) point out, such values, in institutions, are "functional for aggressive inmates...the code clearly works to the disadvantage of the weak" (p. 69). Such men take into prison ideas opposed to violence while others have limited experience with violence. Men may also have types of personality that make violent behavior a difficult—or impossible—solution for them. According to Toch (1977) norms that prescribe violence create a difficult situation for inmates to whom violence is "ego alien."

A-7: The minute I think about what to do to a guy and how they butcher them and this and that, all that runs through my mind is blood. That scares the hell out of me. I don't like this. I wouldn't want to cut up anybody just like I wouldn't want them to cut me up....I am not a fighter, man, that's not my bag and I won't do it. I hardly did any fighting out on the streets. And they just told me to take a guy, take a club, and club him. And I never did that to a guy.

APC-14: If you are an aggressive person, like a bigmouth, you stand a chance of people steering away from you. But if you're reserved, they'll run all over you. But I'm quiet and I don't think that I have got to adjust to them people. In other words, if I have got to be getting up and saying, "Hey, motherfucker," and make up lies that I did this and that, just to keep them away from me, then I could do it. But it's not my thing.

APCC-4: It wasn't easy because I felt that he would see through me. Because I'm not that way naturally. And I thought that he would see through me and laugh at me.

While some violent reactions to sexual approaches are informally tolerated by officials, fear of institutional discipline restrains many men. They want to avoid punishment, losing good time, or being sentenced anew. Such repercussions are particularly likely when the target exceeds the limits of violence tolerated by authorities. For example, the man who murdered the aggressor who propositioned him received a sentence of five years. Another target sliced a man across the face, giving him a wound requiring 22 stitches, and he received a sentence of 22 years. This man also received a wide range of punishments available to the prison administration. He tells us:

AR-35: They took me to special housing unit called the guard house and they put me in a stripped cell. No bed. No nothing. Just a toilet bowl and a sink. They left me there 38 days—just feeding me—took all my clothes and everything. I didn't have anything except for a toilet bowl and a sink and after a while I had an inmate sneak me a blanket and when the officers come by I would have to sneak it back to him. Then they took me to court and prosecuted me—assault in the first degree. They gave me 22 years. Before I went to trial, I was placed in a security cell for 38 days and taken to the superintendent's hearing and was prosecuted. And I had been punished about four or five times for that crime.

The fear of disciplinary infractions or of new charges puts some targets in a dilemma. Should they consider their long-term welfare or fight to alleviate an aggressor's pressure? Peer and staff support may facilitate personal aggression but cannot grant immunity to consequences. This means that the fear of punishment may outweigh the perceived benefits of violence.

Fear of punishment complicates the problem "solved" by the norm of violence. Similarly, the norms are no "solution" for those unable to fight because they are unprepared, socially and psychologically, to

meet tough urban sexual aggressors. These men are in especially difficult positions. Unable to avail themselves of the escape provided by the
convict culture, they are plagued by feelings of inadequacy. Knowing
that violence is the "correct" course of action but not being able to
implement it, they are failures in the convict world. The normative
advice cannot help them, and they must seek other, perhaps less
attractive, solutions to the problem. These are the men who often go to
the solitary confinement of protective custody —"protection
companies" — men who may live in fear throughout their stay in prison
(Lockwood, 1977a).

Conclusion

About half of 152 incidents of sexual aggression I examined involved
physical violence. Half of this violence came from aggressors who
attempted to coerce targets; the rest came from targets who reacted to
threats or perceived threats. Violent reactions are instrumental for
targets in the sense that they end more incidents than any other
reactions. After fights, targets tell us, aggressors leave them alone.
They move around the prison with less fear and feel better about
themselves.

Most men we interviewed had attitudes and values supporting
violent solutions to the problem of being a target. Prisoners see
violence as the medium for the message that one is straight, uninterested in sexual involvement, or that one is tough, not a prospect to "get
over on." Others say that violence is the best self-defense available.
Reacting with force unambiguously lets the aggressor know the
consequences of his behavior if he persists. In prison, target violence
usually leads to an improved self-image and a more favorable status
among other prisoners. Fellow inmates, looked to for guidance, school
new inmates to accept this solution. Staff support target violence and
back up their counsel with a flexible disciplinary process, exempting
some inmates from punishment when they fight to uphold their
manhood.

Other psychological factors complement these ideas supporting
inmate violence. Anger characterizes the target emotional response.
The irritation caused by aggressors can itself lead to targets exploding
in unpredictable and uncalculated ways. As in ethology, fear and
anger are linked to aggression. Threatened men, angered men, become
aggressive and turn aggressors into victims.

References

Bartollas, C., Miller, S.J., and Dinitz, S. 1976. *Juvenile Victimization.* New York: Sage Publications.

Cohen, A.K., Cole, G.F., and Bailey, R.G. 1976. *Prison Violence.* Lexington, MA: Lexington Books.

Conrad, J.P. 1966. "Violence in Prison." *Annals of the American Academy of Political and Social Sciences.* 364: 113-119.

Huffman, A. 1960. "Sex Deviation in a Prison Community." *Journal of Social Therapy.* 6: 170-181.

Lockwood, D. 1977a. "Living in Protection." In *Survival in Prison.* Toch, H., ed. New York: The Free Press.

New York State Special Commission on Attica. 1974. *Attica.* New York: Praeger.

Schultz, L.G. 1964. "The Victim-Offender Relationship." *Crime and Delinquency* 14: 135-141.

Thomas, P. 1967. *Down These Mean Streets.* New York: New American Library.

Toch, H. 1965. "Institutional Violence Code, Tentative Code of the Classification of Inmate Assaults on Other Inmates." Unpublished Manuscript, California Department of Corrections Research Division.

Toch, H. 1977. *Living in Prison.* New York: The Free Press.

8

Inmate Adjustments in Women's Prisons

Richard Hawkins

Prisons for women are the symbolic backwaters of the correctional stream. Separate institutions for women have a shorter history than men's prisons in America. They are few in number and small in inmate population size, in part a reflection of the lack of female involvement in criminal behavior. In light of increasing criminal activities by women *and* the greater probability that women will receive prison time as punishment today, women's institutions are moving into the spotlight.

Up until about a decade ago, women represented only about four percent of the total inmate population. Now that percentage is close to six percent. The numbers of female inmates has increased at twice the rate of men in the 1980s in large part due to more women being arrested for drug use (Fletcher et al., 1993:6). In spite of these trends, a major dilemma remains for women in prison: there has never been enough of them.

Most states have separate institutions for women (see Freedman, 1981:144–145). But the relatively small numbers of female inmates in

Source: Prepared especially for *The Dilemmas of Corrections*.

state and federal institutions, unlike county jails where the number of women is closer to the number of men, means that separate women's institutions have not been cost effective (Gibson, 1976; Resnik, 1983). The result is that women are disadvantaged compared to men in American penal institutions. For example, the small number of women inmates means most states with institutions separate from men's have only one prison. Location is seldom centralized and settings are often rural. Women remain isolated from friends and relatives who cannot afford visitation trips. The distances are even greater in the federal system where only four institutions house female inmates.

The separate institutions which have been established for women lack an inmate population base to sustain multiple programs. For example, a national study of forty adult women's correctional institutions conducted in 1980 found that 40 percent had fewer than 100 inmates, 42 percent had between 100 and 300, and the remaining 18 percent had over 300 women in the facility (Neto, 1981:70). A very visible consequence of this size problem is the lack of inmate rehabilitation work. One study found an average of 2.7 educational and vocational programs per women's institution versus 10 programs per men's prison (Simon, 1975:76). When prison officials try to explain the reasons for such differences, an economy of scale issue has been used to justify fewer services and programs for women prisoners.

Women's failure to achieve equal access to prison programs is being recognized as an equal protection problem under the Fourteenth Amendment. Class-action lawsuits initiated by female inmates continue to document the imbalance in programs. In Michigan, evidence in court revealed that women inmates had access to only five "job-training opportunities" while men had some twenty vocational programs:

> Men printed a newspaper; women made personal calendars. Men learned welding, women did small handicrafts—again for personal use. Men apprenticed as machinists, tool-and-die makers, and electricians and were then permitted to practice those trades in prison industries. There were no apprentice programs for women and no industries in their prison. (Resnik, 1983:111)

A federal court concluded that the Michigan system constituted significant discrimination against women inmates.

Economic reasons for the disadvantaged position of female prisoners is only part of the story. Even more important is the long-standing influence of sexism which has come to shape the structure of women's prisons and their programs. The focus on domesticity by early reformers fostered a stereotypic work and program response: Women should be taught to cook, sew and clean; they should develop those skills which would make them dutiful wives; job training was unnecessary because all they needed was a good man to support them in marriage after release (Gibson, 1976). This "domestic science" training could be put into practice in institutional work assignments, which reduced the need for an outside cooking and maintenance staff.

The thin line between institutional training and inmate exploitation was frequently crossed in women's prisons. Institutional work replaced education and viable job-training for the labor market after release; the exploitation of women at prison jobs complemented the nineteenth-century vision of true womanhood—"purity, piety, domesticity, and submissiveness" (Freedman, 1981:54). This philosophy continues to dominate most women's institutions today in spite of challenges from feminist groups (Fletcher et al., 1993).

Sexism reinforced the emphasis on control of female inmates by creating extreme submissiveness. Again the family model was invoked in that adult women inmates were seen and treated like errant children:

> Just as some superintendents in the past called their charges "the girls," so later prison personnel have continued to view inmates "as being weak, like children," and have treated them accordingly. . . . [A result has been] the paternalistic view that women and children are inherently dependent, while men, even when incarcerated, retain a degree of adult status. (Freedman, 1981:154–55)

This child-like submissiveness can be seen in the emphasis on inmate discipline and staff expectations of appropriate behavior. The fact that women are treated as children is evident in these examples of minor institutional infractions (which in some women's institutions can lead to punishment of up to 30 days in isolation): "walking on the grass, rattling doors and yelling, failure to return towels, or having torn sheets" (Glick and Neto, 1977:42). The same study found "foul language" an infraction in eleven of fourteen prisons for women.

Institutional personnel, like parents, will often manifest an excessive concern with cleanliness. Women who harbor minor vices such as smoking experience clean-up work as punishment. An example is found in a Wisconsin women's institution:

> It is our policy that if you smoke you will be expected to wash your room walls once every other month. If you do not smoke, you should wash them once every three months. . . . If the housekeeper or other staff member in your residential building determines that your room is in need of washing earlier than provided, you will be asked to do so. (Cited in Gibson, 1976:115)

Such excessiveness in governing women inmates has been characterized as "pastel fascism," where inmate control "is glossed over and concealed by a superficial facade of false benevolence and concern for the lives of inmates" (Balkan et al., 1980:220).

The domestic model of inmate residential architecture and rules represents the twofold impact of sexism in women's prisons. A chauvinistic imposition of dependency while in the institution is combined with programs designed to prepare women to return to (or achieve for the first time) the presumed shelter of a traditional relationship with a man upon release. This dual focus is especially ironic as a basis for inmate control because "prison discipline attempts to school women into a domesticity which (a) many of them see as one source of their trouble in the first place, and (b) many of them have already rejected" (Carlen, 1982:122).

The form of discipline just described sets women's institutions off from men's prisons. Due to a combination of viewing women as more passive (another sexist assumption) and a greater focus on treatment in women's prisons (due to a tradition of defining female lawbreaking as an individual pathology) women are more likely to be placed in minimum or medium security facilities. But behind the well-manicured campus settings and the homey cottage facades which make up women's prisons lies the reality of a heavy rule-laden system of control. Psychological coercion rather than architectural barriers serve as omnipresent restrictions. As a result, women have developed unique ways of adjusting to their incarceration. While these ways are not found in men's institutions, the deprivations of incarceration are likely more similar than different (see Carlen, 1994). This fact should not preclude a look at how women have worked out the problems of their incarceration.

Establishing Kinship

The major orientation which structures and shapes the inmate social system for women is sex roles and to a lesser degree consensual homosexual relationships. A kinship or extended family structure is found in women's institutions. It is made up of inmates who take on certain family roles such as mother, father, aunt, grandmother, child and in some cases even in-laws (Giallombardo, 1966). This "playing at family" is given some reality by the fact that some women take on various male roles, e.g. husband, father, etc. Marriages are created and given a legitimacy through formal ceremonies (marriages) complete with marriage license, officiating "judge" and a cluster of witnesses (who are present at the "wedding" and even sign the license). Relatives from the kinship structure attend and even help arrange the wedding ceremony.

Overcoming institutional objections to "courtship" and "marriage" becomes a time-consuming task. A great deal of planning is required (as is true for heterosexual weddings on the outside). Marriage ceremonies must be secret, but still permit family and witnesses to attend. Weddings may occur surreptitiously during organized events in such places as the auditorium or the chapel. In some women's institutions, the Friday night film is referred to by inmates (and staff) as family night at the movies. Whether or not a wedding is scheduled, the seating arrangements at films and other events allow "family" members from different cottages or dorms to be together (Giallombardo, 1974).

These large pseudo families or extended kinship networks are found in separate women's prisons and to some extent in co-correctional settings (Propper, 1981). They provide the informal structure which exercises considerable influence and control over each inmate's behavior. Nuclear families may have from two to ten or more members. Kinship roles of aunt, cousin, brother, sister, etc. create ties to other families or relatives. While control and allegiance are stronger in the nuclear family, they can extend to other "relatives" (Giallombardo, 1966:164). These interlacing kinship ties cut across racial lines and span different living units of the institution. Kinship networks may include over one hundred inmates (Giallombardo, 1966:175).

Sex Roles

Along with kinship roles, gender-based social roles are seen in prison. Those acting out masculine roles are called "studs," "butches," or "pimps." Feminine roles are represented by the label "fems" (or "femmes"), "broads," or "foxes" (Giallombardo, 1974; Heffernan, 1972). Family and kinship roles tend to follow these gender distinctions, e.g., femmes will be mothers, aunts, sisters, and studs will be brothers, husbands, and fathers. But some sex roles are found outside the family roles. A "stud broad" may be single; femmes may be unattached. "Chippies" and "tricks" are prison prostitutes who seek out sexual customers among the studs. "Cherries" tend to be younger inmates who have not been exposed to homosexual activity; they may be children in the family structure (Giallombardo, 1966).

As these are social roles, not biological ones, the dynamics of role selection are of interest. Fewer inmates select a masculine role, which creates a sex-ratio problem. This means studs are in high demand and a certain status is accorded those taking this role. Competition among femmes for marriage or some other form of relationship to a stud is fierce, and arguments, fights, and other conflicts are likely to develop. Such conflicts are often mediated by family members.

Role switching is a frequent occurrence. A stud may fall for another stud, switching to a femme role to establish a relationship—what inmates term "dropping the belt" (Giallombardo, 1966). If an inmate frequently switches roles, negative labels like "popcorn" are used to signal disapproval and loss of status (Giallombardo, 1974:190). Role switching breaks up marriages and leads to confusion in the kinship structure. If an uncle or brother drops the belt and marries another stud, does she become an aunt or a sister?

In addition to role switching, divorce is another source of family role disruption. Femmes who are unattached may seek to break up marriages. Chippies and tricks may tempt away stud broads. At other times, femmes permit extra-marital affairs, as seen in the role of "commissary hustler." Rose Giallombardo, in her study of Alderson, the federal women's prison, describes the role:

> The "commissary hustler" establishes a single homosexual alliance [with a femme] , but also establishes relationships with a number of inmates in other cottages for economic purposes. This is called "mating for commissary reasons. . . ." The commissary hustler presents a commissary list to the tricks scattered throughout the prison, and they, in turn, supply the commissary hustler with needed material items. The function of all the tricks in this "polygynous" system is an economic one. The "wife" in the cottage takes precedence over all others. (1966:125-26)

"Doing the shopping" takes on a unique form in women's prisons. The relationships of sex roles and family structure to the sub rosa economic structure of women's prisons is discussed below; our point here is that such extramarital activity may break up the original relationship, representing another threat to family stability.

Homosexual Activity

There is much confusion in the literature on women's prisons between taking on a sex role identification, being in a family and kinship system, and engaging in intimate sexual activity with other inmates. It is possible to be in a family role, but not be engaged in homosexual activity. Heffernan (1972:102-3) in her study of a Virginia prison for adult women found that 49 percent of the inmates were involved in "familying" (kinship roles) but only 38 percent designated themselves as "players" (engaged in homosexual behavior). Giallombardo's (1966:151) research at Alderson does not distinguish sex roles from involvement in sexual activity; she reports 86 percent of the inmates played at some variation of the stud or femme role.

Juvenile institutions also have pseudo-kinship structures and homosexual activity. In a study of four female institutions and three co-ed facilities, all for juveniles, Propper (1981:52) reports that 48 percent were involved in a "make-believe-family role." Careful to make a distinction between family and sexual behavior, Propper used self-reported acts to measure homosexual involvement. She found 17 percent of her total sample admitted to homosexual activities, with variations of 6 to 29 percent in different institutions. Giallombardo (1974:248) in research in three juvenile institutions for girls reports family involvement rates of 84 percent, 83 percent, and 94 percent. Unfortunately Giallombardo, as in her Alderson research, does not separate family role involvement and sexual activity.

Failure to make this distinction has created an impression that homosexual behavior is rampant in women's institutions. This is probably not the case; what does appear to be true is that family roles are likely to be found, but homosexual activity is less frequent. Some reasons for this difference: (a) inmates in roles of stud and femme who are married may not be sexually intimate; (b) a number of femmes may lack partners for sexual activity due to the sex-ratio problem—too few studs available; (c) family roles which preclude homosexual contact may be widespread, e.g., sister-sister or mother-daughter; and (d) inmates in family roles may be counseled not to participate in homosexual relationships. Giallombardo (1966) found that younger inmates were cast as children and were encouraged not to get emotionally involved if their sentence was short. (These inmates were called "cherries" or "institutional virgins.")

On the other hand, homosexual relationships can occur outside of a family structure. Propper (1981:154) found that homosexual experiences were just as likely to be found among inmates outside of make-believe families as within family roles. Consequently it is possible to find women's prisons without kinship structures, but where homosexual activity does occur (Ward and Kassebaum, 1965; Mawby, 1982). Membership in prison families does not automatically imply sexual activity. And conversely, family and kinship structures will involve some sexual activity going on outside of kinship structures.

As a general rule, kinship and family structures will include a larger proportion of inmates than will those involved in actual sexual activity, for the reasons mentioned by Propper (1981:155):

> Participation in make-believe families seems to be less motivated by a desire for sexual gratification than by a need for security, companionship, affection, attention, status, prestige, and acceptance.

The role of the staff must also be recognized in the differences between family involvement and sexual activity. Action of the staff may support a family model. Institutional design and philosophy create a home-like environment. Also, many staff members may tolerate kinship systems and inmate families because they help to keep the level of inmate conflict down. Homosexual acts, on the other hand, may be harder to ignore, create more punitive reactions, and be seen as a potential source of inmate aggression (fights over partners, etc.). Ironically, attempts by staff to break up assumed homosexual liaisons may create jealousy and conflict, thereby increasing the aggression level in women's institutions (Bowker, 1977:89).

Classification decisions made by prison staff may be based on stereotypes of homosexuality. At times, this may set up a labeling situation where the inmate is pushed in the direction of institutional homosexuality. A new inmate describes her experiences to Kathryn Burkhart:

> When I got to Riker's Island, the guards asked me right off if I was a butch or a fem. I didn't know what they were talking about. I had very long hair . . . down to here. But they took me down to the beauty shop and cut my hair and right away I was called a "butch." People started calling me "he" even though I have four children. It was a very confusing thing. (Burkhart, 1976:374)

In other cases, decisions to separate inmates by a new cottage placement or isolation in solitary confinement may be based on attributions of homosexual activity. This makes friendship formation a problem in prison; as one female inmate said, "You can't have a friend here because if you sit with another woman or buy something for her at the canteen, the staff thinks you're homosexuals" (cited in Propper, 1981:63). In this manner staff reaction may prevent personal friendship, indirectly fostering a larger, protective affiliation by kinship attachment.

Staff members often give ambiguous messages to inmates. Correctional officers tend to know the members of kinship groups and recognize that these groups provide controls over inmate behaviors. Tolerant attitudes of acceptance may result, as seen in this comment by a cottage supervisor:

> After you've been in a cottage a short time, you know who the ones are that are involved in homosexuality, but we don't put [on] any labels unless you see them in bed . . ., and if they respect you so that you don't see anything, what more can you ask? (Giallombardo, 1966:44–45)

The closer the staff is to the living arrangements of the inmates, the more tolerance is likely to develop (Giallombardo, 1974:244; Polsky, 1962). In general, the staff is more likely to tolerate make-believe families than they are actual homosexual involvement, as the latter is likely to be seen as very serious behavior (Propper, 1981:158). But as Giallombardo notes, "the ambivalence of many staff members concerning courtship, marriage and kinship ties leads many of the adolescent offenders to believe that these relationships are acceptable to staff" (1974:245).

One feature of kinship, but especially homosexual liaisons, which does produce a negative response is the interracial nature of many of these activities. As early as 1913, an article appeared entitled "A Perversion Not Commonly Noted" (Otis, 1913) which described the shocking practice of courting between black and white girls at a reform school. Adult institutions were experiencing similar discoveries about the same time. At Bedford Hills in 1915, "it was the revelation of homosexual attachments between black and white inmates that proved a source of embarrassment for the administration" (Freedman, 1981:140). The scandal prompted an investigation of the institution, which resulted in a recommendation for racially segregated living units. Historians have come to question the motives for such a response; "either the taboo against interracial sex surfaced as a stronger one than against homo- sexuality (for surely intraracial sex would continue), or the entire incident served as an excuse to segregate black women" (Freedman, 1981:140).

Today, the true extent of interracial sexual activity is difficult to assess because prison researchers have not systematically investigated race. The fact that race has not emerged as a critical variable in studies of women's prisons implies that it has neither the same meaning nor the conflict potential it has in men's institutions (Kruttschnitt, 1983). Kinship groups are racially integrated (Giallombardo, 1966:159). Interracial marriages do occur, and in some prisons, interracial homosexual activity is frequent. Van Wormer (1978; 1981) found many of the homosexual relationships at an Alabama prison for women were interracial, with black women more likely to take the stud role and white inmates the femme role. Ward and Kassebaum (1965:136) found that butches were more likely to be white, but the difference by race was not statistically significant in their California prison sample. James Fox (1982:100–102) found interracial families at Bedford Hills prison for women (as did Giallombardo at Alderman), but he did not focus on types of homosexual roles taken by these family members.

An explanation of interracial dating, sexual activity and family membership in women's prisons could take two forms. The first would focus on dominance and leadership. If black women, because of ghetto socialization and a greater likelihood of being a single parent in charge of a family prior to incarceration, become dominant figures in prison, they may be cast into the masculine role by other inmates. Or they may seek out masculine, protective roles for themselves (Propper, 1981:143 cites studies to support this contention). As butches or stud broads are infrequent roles in prison, women seeking out sexual relationships, or constructing family units (without corresponding sexual involvement), are likely to find that black inmates are key figures in these configura- tions. Interracial homosexuality and kinship structures are the result.

A second explanation, which might operate alongside the first, deals with identity. If women are seeking temporary relationships and structures, they may want to guard against permanent relationships. They may also wish to distance themselves from their sexual activity, i.e., they may seek to maintain a self-definition of heterosexuality even though they are involved in homosexual activities. If female inmates can convince themselves that "this is only play" or "this is not really me," they maintain a situated definition of their behaviors. Given cultural prohibitions against interracial dating (and even more so against interracial homosexual activity), both partners can be involved but convince themselves that "this cannot last." If this identity hypothesis is valid, we would expect to find frequent interracial "dating" in co-educational prisons (to be discussed below). In co-ed facilities, women could seemingly choose to associate with men of the same race. However research at a co-ed prison, Pleasanton in California, reveals "the frequent association of white women with black men" (Lambiotte, 1980:240). Lambiotte suggests there are shared expectations that prison romances in co-ed institutions will not last or carry on upon release. This implies a distancing explanation.

The Importance of Kinship

We now turn to the question of why extended family systems evolved to structure inmate relationships in women's prisons. The answers to the question tend to stress importation factors; for example, Giallombardo asserts that women are culturally conditioned to depend on family roles. Furthermore, the sex-role socialization of women serves to encourage displays of emotions (while males learn to repress them), to tolerate displays of affection between women (but not between men), and to stress passive responses to deprivations (rather than aggressive counter-actions). Cultural expectations of marriage and family for women, although changing in recent years, are still important for women. When these "preconditions" are imported into a structured environment based to some extent on a family model (both in terms of policy and architectural layout), kinship systems result. The importation explanation asserts that participation in the pseudo-kinship system becomes a substitute for the family roles left behind. If this is the case, we would expect less involvement in kinship groups for these types of female prisoners: first offenders (who may maintain ties to the outside); women on short sentences; those with more frequent contacts with outsiders (letters, visits) and unmarried, younger inmates. This appears to be true (Heffernan, 1972:102–103; Giallombardo, 1966).

As we have seen, membership in kinship groups is more frequent than participation in homosexual activity. Giallombardo (1974:169) says that kinship ties occur earlier than sexual involvements. Kinship membership is usually stable, although marriages and divorces alter the sexual roles played by some in the family unit. Families provide a sense of belonging and identification; they structure courtship and marriage decisions and represent support systems when one-to-one sexual relationships or close friendships break up. Families and extended kin networks keep inmates involved in "family affairs," which permits women to do easy time (Giallombardo 1966:134). Just as in male prisons, those who are isolated and those who cannot psychologically distance themselves from external ties will do hard time.

Idleness, lack of inmate rehabilitation and training programs, and the absence of other forums by which inmates could organize and associate in women's prisons has meant the kinship system has played a central role. But given changes in sex role socialization and more women entering the work force, the pressures to re-create the family unit in prison may be declining. Formal inmate clubs and organizations could become the new focus of inmate identification in the future. Inmate structures in women's prisons may lose their uniqueness, becoming more like the inmate structures in men's institutions. While kinship structures in adult women's institutions may decline in importance, this is not likely to be the case in juvenile institutions for women. To understand why, we need to make a distinction in terms of the type of family that is being replicated behind bars.

In adult women's institutions, the inmates are deprived of their conjugal family membership. Granted that the majority of women in prison were not married at the time of incarceration, a great many have been married or do have children (Glick and Neto, 1977). For them, the conjugal family is important. For juveniles, there are two family ties— their family of origin (consanguineous family) and their anticipated marriage (conjugal family). It is hypothesized that this dual-family concern among adolescent female offenders accounts for their high rates of kinship involvement (Giallombardo, 1974), and for their relatively low rates of participation in homosexual activities (Propper, 1981). In other words, women in juvenile facilities may be acting out roles more in accord with their family of origin, i.e., sister-sister; mother-daughter; such roles do not require involvement in sexual activities. For teenagers, conjugal families are likely approached through fantasy before really becoming sexually active.

In adult institutions, these consanguineous family ties are not critical. When other mechanisms for association are present, the overall rates of sexual involvement may decline as kinship networks are reduced in importance. But it is unlikely that kinship systems will disappear in women's prisons (they should remain strong in juvenile institutions). To see why kinship will not go away, the economic aspects of prison adjustment must be considered.

For Love or Money: Kinship and Economic Exchange

The economic link of family membership and style of living in prison is critical to understanding why women create and participate in kinship systems. The sub rosa economy is not handled by a distinct system of prison rackets as in men's institutions. The family members in women's prisons look out for each other, providing goods and services to those kinfolk in need. The kinship networks become the major conduit of illicit goods and services; other bases of economic exchange on a broad scale are seldom found.

One reason for this failure to develop prison rackets of the type found in men's prisons is a lower commitment to the inmate code. The relatively high level of snitching in women's prisons makes it difficult or impossible for full-scale inmate rackets to develop (Ward and Kassebaum, 1965:54). By having kinship networks provide for the distribution of illicit goods and services, the sex roles of the family are made more realistic. The stud or butch in the husband role is responsible for seeing that economic needs are met. The husband may become a commissary hustler or even turn over the breadwinning duties to the wife. Some husbands divorce their spouse to improve their economic advantage;

> some of the "husbands" would not hesitate leaving one partner to play an initially active role in attracting a new "wife" if she "had the looks and the money." (Heffernan, 1972:25)

While economic considerations may disrupt marriages, kinship systems tend to benefit inmates. This concern with "taking care of their own" means that prison administrators have few effective ways to control rule-breakers. Staff actions, like taking away commissary privileges, "are not felt to be depriving by inmates in prison families, as no inmate who has kinship ties 'goes without' when such privileges are removed" (Giallombardo, 1966:170). The larger family structure provides a safety net for those who might be "jilted" or even exploited economically in the marriage alliance; an inmate in a Virginia prison describes such a situation:

> A girl comes in here and asks the family for 25 dollars, and goes and spends it on her "husband," buys "him" clothes and canteen, and then when "he's" got everything, "he" goes off to another "wife." (Heffernan, 1972:93)

Events like this mean that some inmates develop a very cynical attitude toward "love" relationships. As another inmate in the same institution put it: "Women say 'I love you, can't do without you,' when you give them cigarettes. Then you're nothing next week." (Heffernan, 1972:102). Awareness of economic as well as emotional exploitation within marriage relationships may deter some from romantic involvements. However, these "abstainers" are likely to avail themselves of the advantages of kin membership, i.e., economic security, companionship and protection.

Self Identity and Personal Crisis

The assault on personal identity is more intensive in women's prisons than in men's. Status-stripping occurs in various ways. Identity pegs such as rings and jewelry are often prohibited. Cosmetics use is forbidden, or the few provided fail to meet the bare necessities of appearance. Even items of personal hygiene may be limited and dispensed to inmates in embarrassing ways. Personal clothing is usually not permitted. Prison-issue clothes are drab and often well-worn. Certain types of dress may be uniformly required of all inmates, which prevents the use of clothing to set forth a unique identity.

Restrictions on the type of apparel and how clothing could be worn are coupled with numerous other rules which make female inmates feel like children. "You have to eat everything on your plate. You can't even decide for yourself what you want to eat" (Burkhart, 1976:129). The family model in women's prisons reinforces this child-like imagery for inmates. Prisoners are often referred to as "girls" by the staff, implying an immaturity and an inability to make decisions. Such treatment may even carry over to the thinking patterns of the inmate, as illustrated by a woman at Bedford Hills:

> I find myself sometimes, if I'm writing a letter, I'll say, "the girls here. . . ." The officers make you feel as if you're definitely not equal. They look down to you, so you begin to look at yourself as a child. (Fox, 1988:214)

Denied control over clothes, cosmetics and hygiene, inmates find it difficult to create a strong feminine identity; lapsing into a child-like dependency becomes the easy response to incarceration (Carlen, 1982:119).

The fragile identities which result from these practices are more susceptible to stress. Little things may precipitate a crisis as seen in this inmate's account of an institutional haircut:

. . . the inmates do it, and if they don't like somebody they'll do
an awful job on it. But I watched, and then when they cut it, this
one side was so much shorter than the other. I looked terrible. So
I was all upset. I went back to quarantine, and I took a tin can, and
I cut my arm. (Fox, 1975:188)

The entering inmate, in compensating for the threat to her identity,
seeks out available sources of attachment and commitment. As we have
seen, many find affiliation in the kinship structure; a smaller number
seek commitment in a homosexual relationship. For those who remain
unattached, personal crises (mental breakdown, self-mutilation and
suicide) become real possibilities. From "their unrewarded search for
love and trust, they may conclude that they are unworthy and worthless"
(Fox, 1975:196). Failure to affiliate in a setting where most inmates are
in quasi-family systems means self-hatred may occur.

Research on women in crisis permits three generalizations to be made.
First, women in danger of a breakdown become preoccupied with
support from significant others. Those in kin systems may find it; others,
deterred by prison rules against close personal contact between inmates,
may find no support. If support is not available from loved ones outside
of prison (as it is often not), a break may occur. Second, it appears that
when women do break in prison, "they tend to do so explosively, with
a considerable display of randomly aggressive behavior" (Fox,
1975:199). Destructive violence and assault become signs of failure to
adapt (or they may also be triggered by failure in love relationships when
jealousy prompts fighting). And the third point is that prison is more
injurious to women than to men. "Whereas men can defend themselves
against pain [and breakdown] through variations on their manly stance,
women have no such recourse" (Fox, 1975:202). In short, violence and
aggression serve as mechanisms of a "healthy" adjustment for men; for
women, the same actions are seen as being out of control, i.e., undergoing a personal crisis—not adjusting to prison. In this way, sex role
socialization handicaps the woman in her adjustment to incarceration.

The sources of personal crisis are not all inside the prison; unlike men,
a heavy "burden of family ties" follows many women into prison. Those
with young children are especially vulnerable to depression and personal
breakdown. Even when active members of a prison family, young
mothers have real difficulty doing easy time, i.e., letting the problems
of the outside world be downplayed or forgotten. We now examine these
external problems of inmates with children.

The Costs of Motherhood

Two of three women in prison have one or more children under 18
years of age (Baunach, 1982:168). Depression and worry about the lives

of the children left behind have many sources. Custody issues must be faced by those without relatives who will care for offspring; foster home placement—while not that frequent—is decided by state welfare agencies rather than the mother. In cases of legal separation and divorce, a woman's incarceration increases the chances that legal custody will be given to the husband or his relatives. Even when supportive relatives care for the child, there is the fear that they may be unwilling to return the child after release.

Mothers sent to jail or prison face the dilemma of telling their children why they have been incarcerated. Young children may not be told because they will not understand; this postponement contributes to maternal anxiety. Some mothers of older children try to hide their imprisonment, encouraging relatives to speak of "vacation" or being "away at school." Such deception is not likely to be successful for long. Most mothers prefer to tell children they are in prison and provide some rationale (Baunach, 1982:161). While this approach carries the risk that children may reject their mother, most inmates feel it is better to tell the child directly than let strangers or acquaintances do it.

The initial pains of separation are replaced by a sense of helplessness. Guilt over imagined neglect and the anxiety of not knowing how children are adjusting to school, for example, feed this helpless feeling. The infrequent visits by children to prison may compound the anxiety, as described by one woman:

> The hardest thing is that I know I can't be home and that I have a son there. He was up to see me in May and asked me when I was coming home, and I just cried. I didn't know what to say to him. And he said he wanted to stay with me. And that bothered me a lot. (Fox, 1975:191–2)

Part of this helplessness is due to fears over what the mother's incarceration means in the child's daily life. "Sometimes children of prisoners have been the target of teasing by schoolmates aware of their mother's background [and they] have great fun 'playing the dozens' on other children's mothers" (Burkhart, 1976:413). Deprived of any power to protect their children, the mother in prison can experience self-hatred. Those in on drug charges, or who have drug problems, may be "down" for the first time and "have an opportunity to consider the effects of their behavior upon themselves and their children" (Baunach, 1982:157). Guilt, compounded by powerlessness, becomes the enemy of the mother with children on the outside. Things do not necessarily improve as release from prison approaches.

Mothers returning to their families after serving their sentences face the problems of reestablishing the mother role. A woman's children have likely learned to survive quite well without her. They may openly reject her because of her former inmate status; more likely they have come to rely on others for things usually provided by their mother. In addition to reestablishing control over her family, the returning inmate faces problems of seeking employment, housing and all the other reentry tasks. Failures in these areas may be taken out on children, which further weakens the tenuous ties of mother and child. Trouble in achieving that illusive "good mother" role may create pressure to revert to crime. This is especially true for those women who serve as single parents (a rather high proportion of inmates). Ironically, their return to crime is usually taken as a sign of neglect and disregard for their children—the exact opposite of what the true situation is likely to be. (See Baunach, 1985, for a complete documentation of mothers' problems.)

While the costs of motherhood are high, even more problems await those women who are pregnant at the time they are incarcerated or who become pregnant during their sentence. Risks of pregnancy after incarceration are high because of co-ed prisons, conjugal visits, furloughs and work release, and even the possibility of sexual intercourse or rape by prison staff (Holt, 1982:524-5). As incarceration usually removes women from the various chemical and technological means of birth control, pregnancy is a very real health problem for women in prison (Resnik and Shaw, 1981; McGurrin, 1993).

The termination of a prison pregnancy may not be possible even if desired by the inmate. "Although it is the policy of the federal prison system to arrange and pay for an inmate's abortion, this practice has not gained acceptance on the state level" (Holt, 1982:527). On the other hand, inmates may be forced into an abortion by prison officials; at times abortions may be induced without the consent or knowledge of the inmate (Holt, 1982:527). Such situations produce a significant challenge for prisoners' rights for pregnant inmates (e.g., McHugh, 1980; McGurrin, 1993).

Karen Holt, in an article entitled "Nine months to life—the law and the pregnant inmate" (1982), describes the patchwork policies of different states for those women who go through with their pregnancy. In some states, such as California, the mother is allowed to keep the child with her in prison for up to two years, and in some cases even longer. At the other extreme in states like Florida, the Department of Corrections takes responsibility for the newborn child and arranges a custody hearing for placement of the child (Holt, 1982:537). Most other states fall in between these extremes, but the risk of loss of custody is high for mothers having children in prison. The federal system, while liberal in regard to providing both birth control and abortions to inmates, has a rather severe policy on children born in custody; ". . . current practice is to separate the mother and child, usually within several days of birth, and to exclude the child from visitation except if permitted to enter [the prison] when visitors attend under general visiting rules'' (Resnik and Shaw, 1981:80). Inmates without relatives who will accept the child and bring him or her to prison for visitation lose all chance of contact with the newborn. Awareness of such a policy may force some federal inmates to seek an abortion who might not do so under a more liberal policy.

In light of these numerous problems, the burdens of motherhood for women prisoners are complex and urgent. A national policy is needed for integrating prison mothers and their children. Programs should be established which would serve the woman who gives birth in prison as well as the inmate with dependent children who are left behind by incarceration. A key to such programs is the way inmates are included:

> There is need for alternative programs, perhaps in the community, which house mothers and children together. One of the key aspects of this approach is the voluntary involvement of inmate-mothers in the development, implementation, and operations of the programs. Adherence to the medical model that suggests that offenders are ''sick and must be cured'' prior to release means that things must be done to or for the offender rather than with her. However, this antiquated model is antithetical to the development of a sense of responsibility among inmate-mothers. Involvement in the decision-making process means that inmate-mothers themselves are given the opportunity to determine the focus and direction of the program. (Baunach, 1982:167)

In theory, these programs could be logistically provided in three settings: (1) community-based programs which would allow mothers and children to live away from the prison, (2) special cottages permitting young children to live with the mother within the prison, and (3) some form of extended visitation for family members (e.g. , overnight, weekends) coupled with parental training or counseling sessions (Chapman, 1980:122). The last category is the most frequent program in American prisons for women, while Europe has utilized the live-in philosophy. For example, overnight visits of children are permitted in California and Mississippi prisons. New York uses trailers on prison grounds for family visitation of up to 30 hours in length. Nebraska permits visits of five consecutive days each month where children live and eat with their mothers.

Special programs like parenting training are often integrated with these visits by children. In addition to providing some structure to the visits, the goal is to teach parenting skills. These seminars may remediate existing family problems; ''it is easy to romanticize the situation of women prisoners and their children. Some of these women neglected or abused their children before they went to prison . . .'' (McGowan and Blumenthal, 1976:134). But these parenting sessions are also designed to strengthen family bonds and provide women with the confidence needed to successfully rejoin their children after release. (See Harris, 1988, on parenting skills and rehabilitation.)

Other innovative programs centered around the problems mothers face in raising children are survival skills training, job training and education in preparation for release, and even some independent-living programs (Chapman, 1980:133–137). Indeed the problems of mother-child relationships provide a basis for rehabilitative services which are not geared to the inmate's criminal history. In other words, reform efforts need not focus any condemnation on past criminal behaviors (or imply any pathology model of crime causation); rather the emphasis should be on future responsibilities, i.e., child-care issues mothers will face upon return to society.

The provisions for the needs of mothers in prison and their children have been slow and piecemeal. By seeking to reduce the anxiety and helplessness engendered by parent-child separation, the programs described above represent a "normalization" emphasis in women's corrections. Much remains to be done on the outside. For example, children who are placed in foster care because their mother (or father) is incarcerated face significant challenges. But the problems are also acute for the inmate who remains helpless in these situations. A few states are attempting to reduce these problems, but much needs to be done in this area (see Reilly, 1992).

Conclusion

This article has detailed some aspects of life in prison for women. As mentioned at the outset, the numbers of inmates being admitted to these institutions are increasing substantially. One of the major reasons for these increases, though its discussion is beyond the scope of this article, is the rise in drug use among women (Hammett, et al., 1994). This trend also has serious implications regarding the need to address HIV/AIDS in women's institutions. Mark Blumberg and Denny Langston's article in this same volume addresses this issue as it relates to corrections in general.

Ironically, after years of neglect, the increasing numbers of women being incarcerated and the broader concerns related to drug use and HIV/AIDS may cause women's correctional institutions to become the center of significant legal and social reform in the overall American correctional system.

References

Balkan, Sheila, Ronald J. Berger and Janet Schmidt. 1980. *Crime and Deviance in America*. Belmont, CA: Wadsworth.

Baunach, Phillis Jo. 1982. "You can't be a mother and be in prison . . . can you? Impacts of mother-child separation." In B. R. Price and N. J. Sokoloff (eds.), *The Criminal Justice System and Women*. New York: Clark Boardman.

———.1985. *Mothers in Prison*. New Brunswick, NJ: Transaction Books.

Bowker, Lee H. 1977. *Prison Subcultures*. Lexington, MA: D. C. Heath.

Burkhart, Kathryn Watterson. 1976. *Women in Prison*. New York: Popular Library Edition.

Carlen, Pat. 1982. "Papa's discipline: An analysis of disciplinary modes in The Scottish Women's Prison." *Sociological Review*, 30:97–124.

———. 1994. "Why study women's imprisonment? Or anyone else's?" *British Journal of Criminology*, 34:131–39.

Chapman, Jane Roberts. 1980. *Economic Realities and the Female Offender*. Lexington, MA: D. C. Heath.

Fletcher, Beverly R., Lynda Dixon Shaver and Dreama G. Moon (eds.). 1993. *Women Prisoners: A Forgotten Population*. Westport, CT: Praeger Publishers.

Fox, James G. 1975. "Women in crisis." In Hans Toch (ed.), *Men in Crisis*. Chicago: Aldine.

———. 1982. *Organizational and Racial Conflict in Maximum-Security Prisons*. Lexington, MA: D. C. Heath.

———. 1988. "Women in prison: A case study in the social reality of stress." In R. Johnson and H. Toch (eds.), *The Pains of Imprisonment*. Beverly Hills: Sage, 1982. Reprint, Prospect Heights, IL: Waveland Press.

Freedman, Estelle B. 1981. *Their Sisters' Keepers: Women's Prison Reform in America, 1830–1930*. Ann Arbor: University of Michigan Press.

Giallombardo, Rose. 1966. *Society of Women*. New York: John Wiley.

———. 1974. *The Social World of Imprisoned Girls*. New York: John Wiley.

Gibson, Helen E. 1976. "Women's prisons: Laboratories for penal reform." In L. Crites (ed.), *The Female Offender*. Lexington, MA: D. C. Heath.

Glick, Ruth M. and Virginia V. Neto. 1977. *National Study of Women's Correctional Programs*. Washington, DC: National Institute of Law Enforcement and Criminal Justice.

Hammett, Theodore M., Lynne Harrold, Michael Gross, and Joel Epstein. 1994. *HIV/AIDS in Correctional Facilities*. Washington, DC: U.S. Department of Justice.

Harris, Jean. 1988. *They Always Call Us Ladies*. New York: Macmillan.

Heffernan, Esther. 1972. *Making It in Prison: The Square, the Cool and the Life*. New York: John Wiley.

Holt, Karen E. 1982. "Nine Months to life—the law and the pregnant inmate." *Journal of Family Law*, 20:523–43.

Kruttschnitt, Candace. 1983. "Race Relations and the Female Inmate." *Crime and Delinquency*, 29(4): 577–92.

Lambiotte, Joellen. 1980. "Sex role differentiation in a co-correctional setting." In J. O. Smykla (ed.), *Coed Prison*. New York: Human Sciences Press.

Mawby, R. I. 1982. "Women in prison: A British study." *Crime and Delinquency*, 28:24–39.

McGowan, Brenda G., and Karen L. Blumenthal. 1976. "Children of women prisoners: A forgotten minority." in L. Crites (ed.), *The Female Offender*. Lexington, MA: D. C. Heath.

McGurrin, Mary Catherine. 1993. "Pregnant inmates' right to health care." *New England Journal of Criminal and Civil Confinement*, 20:163–94.

McHugh, Gordon A. 1980. "Protection of the rights of pregnant women in prisons and detention facilities." *New England Journal of Prison Law*, 6:231–63.

Neto, Virginia V. 1981. "Expanding horizons: Work and training for female offenders." *Corrections Today* (November/December): 66–72.

Otis, Margaret. 1913. "A perversion not commonly noted." *Journal of Abnormal Psychology*, 8:112–14.

Propper, Alice M. 1981. *Prison Homosexuality*. Lexington, MA: D. C. Heath.

Reilly, Shannon A. 1992. "Incarcerated mothers and the foster care system in Massachusetts: Working together to preserve parental rights." *New England Journal of Criminal and Civil Confinement*, 18:147–81.

Resnik, Judith. 1983. "Should prisoners be classified by sex?" In J. W. Doig (ed.), *Criminal Corrections*. Lexington, MA: D. C. Heath.

Resnik, Judith and Nancy Shaw. 1981. "Prisoners of their sex: Health problems of incarcerated women." *Prison Law Monitor*, 3:57, 68–83.

Simon, Rita J. 1975. *The Contemporary Woman and Crime*. Washington, DC: National Institute of Mental Health.

Ward, David A., and Gene G. Kassebaum. 1965. *Women's Prison: Sex and Social Structure*. Chicago: Aldine.

9

The Victimization of Prisoners by Staff Members

Lee H. Bowker

The documentation on staff-prisoner victimization in America's prisons is extensive but shallow. Most of this material describes victimization in prisons for men, with a smaller amount of documentation for institutions containing delinquent boys and very little information on staff-prisoner victimization in institutions for females. The treatment of the subject is superficial in that incidents tend to be mentioned only in passing (or as part of a polemical piece of writing), and they are not presented or analyzed in any great detail. Like other prison victimization reports, they tend to be recorded factually and not related to any general theoretical framework. Another general problem with documentation on staff-prisoner victimization is that the quality of the reporting of incidents is often difficult to determine. Reports are almost always limited to the views of one of the participants or observers, with no corroboration from others. Even when reports are written by social scientists, they usually consist of second- and third-person accounts derived from interviews rather than direct observation by the scientists.

Source: Reprinted by permission of the publisher from Chapter Seven by Lee H. Bowker, *Prison Victimization*, 101-127. Copyright 1980 by Elsevier Science Publishing Co., Inc.

Material on the victimization of prisoners by staff members is also beset by definitional problems. How does one separate the victimization of prisoners by individual staff members from the "fair" application of institutional policies by correctional officers?

This problem is particularly severe when dealing with historical material for which institutional standards of appropriate treatment are not available. Victimization is generally thought of as consisting of acts committed by individuals and groups that go beyond the conditions imposed upon prisoners by official institutional policies and state laws. In the modern prison, this definitional problem is not such a serious one because the official policies of the state and federal correctional systems are generally quite humane. Excessively victimizing behavior by staff members is usually clearly against the regulations of the institution. This is not the same as saying that offenders against these institutional regulations will be punished. In many correctional systems, it is probable that a careful staff member can engage in extensive victimizing behavior toward prisoners before he or she will be officially reprimanded for it. Even then, it is extremely unlikely that a staff member will ever be terminated for such behavior.

Definitional problems still exist in those jurisdictions that continue to use physically harsh means of punishing prisoners, and also in any correctional institutions where "goon squads" are used. The goon squads are groups of physically powerful correctional officers who "enjoy a good fight" and who are called upon to rush to any area of the prison where it is felt that muscle power will restore the status quo. If a prisoner is ripping up things in his cell and refuses to be quiet, the goon squad may be called and three or four of these correctional officers will forcibly quiet him, administering a number of damaging blows to the head and body. If there is a fight between two prisoners, the goon squad may break it up. Should a prisoner refuse to report to the hospital when he is ordered to do so, he may be dragged from his cell and deposited in the hospital waiting room. Mentally ill prisoners who are acting out are almost always initially dealt with by goon squads rather than by qualified therapeutic personnel or even by orderlies under the direction of such personnel. It is difficult to draw the line between the necessary application of force where human life or the social order are extensively threatened, and the misuse of violence by goon squad members.

Aside from goon squads and the few states that officially permit physically harsh means of punishment, we can define the behavior of a correctional officer as victimizing or nonvictimizing by comparing questionable incidents with the body of official regulations and policies that is usually summarized in a handbook distributed to all correctional officers. If the behavior goes beyond the regulations and policies, then it is victimizing. If it does not, then it is difficult to accuse the officer of being an aggressor in all but the most extreme cases.

However clear we may be able to make the definition of victimization by line staff members, there is no way to create a similarly precise definition for wardens and other top-level correctional administrators. When they implement a policy or regulation that is victimizing or potentially victimizing, they must take responsibility for having created a definition of the situation within which correctional officers may carry out what amounts to victimizing behavior as they perform their duties in conformance with institutional regulations. Few of these regulations are proclaimed by correctional administrators simply out of sadism. Instead, these administrators balance one evil against another, and decide to implement a potentially victimizing regulation because they feel that this regultion will solve more problems than it creates. This means that, except for cases at the periphery of reasonable judgment, we cannot easily judge an administrative action to be victimizing unless we know the rationale behind that action and have some objective set of data about conditions in the institution that informed the administrative decision. Since this kind of information is almost never available, we are left with a murky situation in which administrative responsibility for prisoner victimization can usually be assigned in only the most tentative fashion. With these qualifications in mind, we will proceed to examine the documentation on staff-prisoner victimization in correctional institutions.

Physical Victimization

However unpleasant prisons may be today, historical materials make it clear that they were infinitely worse in the past. Clemmer tells us that it was once common for correctional officers to assault prisoners with clubs and their fists, but by the late 1930s, perhaps in response to a new state law, the frequency of these attacks had declined to the point at which they occurred "only rarely."[1] Conley shows how the emphasis on custody and industrial productivity encouraged brutality and corruption in the Oklahoma prison system from the early 1900s through the 1960s. In addition to the usual beatings, officers used deliberate tortures such as forcing the men to eat in the hot sun during the summer when shade was nearby and handcuffing prisoners to the bars in their cells (with knotted rags in their mouths) so that when their legs collapsed, their body was suspended only by the handcuffs. When wardens ordered that physical victimization of prisoners by correctional officers be suspended, these officers adapted by moving to techniques of psychological victimization.[2]

The decrease in brutality by correctional officers that Clemmer describes as having occurred in Illinois in the 1930s did not reach some southern prisons until the 1970s. The mistreatment of prisoners in the Arkansas prison system has been documented in books such as *Killing Time, Life in the Arkansas Penitentiary*[3] and *Inside Prison U.S.A.*[4] The latter includes a description of the infamous "Tucker telephone," as well as blow-by-blow accounts of beatings. In the Tucker telephone, a naked prisoner was strapped to a table and electrodes were attached to his big toe and his penis. Electrical charges were then sent through his body which, in "long distance calls," were timed to cease just before the prisoner became unconscious. Murton and Hyams state that in some cases, "the sustained current not only caused the inmate to lose consciousness but resulted in irreparable damage to his testicles. Some men were literally driven out of their minds."[5] In testimony under oath, a 15-year-old prisoner accused the superintendent of an Arkansas institution of kicking and hitting him in the back and stomach while another staff member held him on the ground. The superintendent did not confirm this allegation, but he admitted driving a truck at 40 miles per hour with three prisoners draped over the hood and then jamming on the brakes to catapult them to the ground as a unique method of punishment.[6]

Reports from Louisiana,[7] Mississippi,[8] Virginia[9] and Florida[10] confirm that the habitual mistreatment of prisoners is not limited to the Arkansas prison system. The brutalization of prisoners by correctional officers outside of the south seems to be less extensive and also less statistically innovative. Some of the incidents reported from northern prisons make little sense, such as the prisoner who was killed by the use of chemical gassing weapons when he was locked in a solitary security cell[11] or the three prisoners who were handcuffed to overhead pipes as punishment for being too "noisy" during sleeping hours.[12] Most of the incidents reported from these facilities seem to be associated with unusual occurrences such as prison riots, protests and punitive transfers. These incidents all involve some sort of prisoner challenge to the authority of prison staff members, and the challenge is sometimes met with violence as a way of reestablishing administrative authority. For example, prisoners being transferred from one Ohio penitentiary to another after a period of considerable unrest alleged severe guard brutality. One prisoner asserted that he was handcuffed and chained, taken into a bus, and then beaten on the head by a correctional officer with a blackjack and left unconscious. Another prisoner alleged that while handcuffed, he was dragged into the bus where he suffered kicks and other blows about the back, legs, hips and groin. The worst incident described by the prisoners told the story of a prisoner who first had Mace sprayed in his face while he was still in his cell, and then was beaten with chains, blackjacks and fists by five correctional officers who then spit on him, slammed his head against the cell door, and took him to the bus, where he was subjected to further assault.[13]

When 500 prisoners at the Pendleton Reformatory in Indiana refused to return to their cells on a winter day in 1972, the correctional officers used tear gas and shotguns to force them back. None of the prisoners was shot because the shotguns were discharged into the air rather than at the prisoners. This change in policy was probably due to an earlier incident at the Reformatory in which "46 men [prisoners] were wounded, many critically, from shots in the head, in the back, through the chest, in the legs, feet, thigh, through the groin, in the side — in fact some who tried to throw up their hands in the traditional gesture of surrender had their hands shattered and are minus fingers."[14] In a related incident, a group of black prisoners refused to return to their cells, and one black prisoner raised his hand in the black power salute. A guard was heard to say, "That one is mine!" and the young man was fatally riddled with five bullets. Testimony before the United States Senate later revealed that approximately 50% of the correctional officers involved in the incident belonged to the Ku Klux Klan.[15]

Excessive violence used during a prisoner altercation may not be legitimate, but it is understandable. There are few parents who have not gone too far in punishing their children when they were angry. A more serious problem occurs when prisoners are brutalized for an extended period of time after a riot as punishment for having participated. A classic example of this occurred after the disaster at Attica in New York. Correctional administrators, in violation of a court order, refused to admit a group of doctors and lawyers to the prison as observers on the pretext that they needed to have an opportunity to assess the prison's condition. During the time that the observers were deliberately excluded, extreme violence occurred, involving the vanquished prisoners. The Second Circuit Federal Court of Appeals finally issued an injunction against further reprisals and physical abuse and found that in the four days beginning with the recapture of Attica, the state troopers and correctional personnel struck, prodded and assaulted injured prisoners, some of whom were on stretchers. Other prisoners were stripped naked and then forced to run between lines of correctional officers who beat them with clubs, spat upon them, burned them with matches, and poked them in the genitals — among other things.[16]

The Attica reprisals are well documented, but Toch is generally skeptical of other prisoner reports of organized brutality by correctional officers. He takes a different approach, looking at official records of officer-prisoner violence in New York State for the year 1973. A total of 386 incidents were recorded in the official file, and these involved 547 prisoners and 1,288 employees. The relative number of officers and prisoners in these incidents is meaningful in itself in that it indicates the more than two-to-one odds that prisoners face in these altercations. One might argue that with odds such as these, there is little excuse for causing excessive injury to the prisoners. In fact, there were no injuries at all in one-third of the reports. The most common action cited was a "hold," which included such maneuvers as half-nelsons, pulls and choking. Toch believes that correctional officer violence is routinely justified by formulas similar to those used to justify police brutality, and that it is really based on correctional officer subcultural norms favoring violence against prisoners. These norms develop because of the pervasive fear of prisoners that is part of the correctional officer subculture. This same subcultural phenomenon makes it almost impossible to convince a correctional officer to testify against one of his fellow employees, so corroborating testimony is rarely obtained in investigations of officer brutality, except from other prisoners. Toch also links officer violence to official regulations that forbid the forming of meaningful inter-personal relationships between officers and prisoners. Such regulations leave officers with only naked force as a way of enforcing order and also create what Toch characterizes as a "trench warfare climate" in prisons.[17] Whether one concentrates on the day-to-day routinized violence or the extreme brutality that is sometimes associated with prison disturbances and transfers, the conclusion is the same. It is that although most correctional officers in most prisons do not engage in any form of brutality and are only concerned with defending themselves against attack, there are enough officers who have values and beliefs that favor brutality and enough incidents that seem to require some sort of a show of force by officers so that there is a steady stream of minor unnecessary or excessive acts of violence in America's prisons, punctuated by occasional acts in which officers go far beyond any reasonable standard of the application of necessary force.

If an officer who favors the brutalization of prisoners is careful, he or she can limit the application of excessive force to incidents that fit the prison's definition of the appropriate use of force to maintain prison discipline or prevent escapes. Complaints lodged against such a correctional officer will invariably be dismissed by the warden who will rule that the violence was appropriately applied within institutional regulations. In fact, it may be claimed that had officers not used violence in the incident, they would have been delinquent in the performance of stated duties and subject to dismissal. This kind of rationale also makes it difficult for a prisoner to receive a fair hearing in court, where the warden's testimony carries considerable weight with judges and juries. As an example of this, I was close to a case in which a mentally ill prisoner was climbing a fence separating two prison yards and was fatally shot in the head by a prison officer who had commanded him to stop. The officer, who was stationed in a tower, probably was unaware of the mental condition of the prisoner and might not have taken that into account in any case. More importantly, he did not need to shoot the prisoner, as going from one prison yard to another does not constitute a risk of escape. Since the prisoner was unarmed, a shot in the leg rather than the head would have been more than sufficient even had he been climbing a fence on the boundary of the prison compound. The warden chose to ignore these arguments and immediately supported the action of the officer, saying that it was appropriate and required by institutional regulations. The local officials outside of the prison also accepted the judgment of the warden and declined prosecution in the case. There is nothing more serious than murder, and if this can be so easily justified by correctional officials one can appreciate the wide variety of possibly victimizing acts that are similarly justified annually in the United States.

The Involvement of Correctional Officers in Sexual Aggression

There are three ways that correctional officers can be involved in sexual aggression against prisoners. The first is to carry out the aggression themselves. This is occasionally hinted at, but has been well documented only for isolated cases that involved female and adolescent male victims. The second type of involvement is for correctional officers to permit a sexual attack in their presence and then to enjoy the spectacle. Although occasionally mentioned in passing, the best example of this sort of behavior in the literature comes from an institution for the retarded rather than from a prison.[18] The final form of correctional officer involvement in sexual attacks on prisoners is passive participation by deliberately failing to carry out one's custodial responsibilities. In this behavior, the officer does not adequately control an area or deliberately stays away from a site in which it is known that sexual assaults regularly occur. Although seemingly less severe than the first two forms of staff participation in sexual assaults, this third type is the most important because its occurrence is much more common than the first two types. As Sagarin and MacNamara conclude, prison rapes hardly seem possible "without the connivance, or at least deliberate inattention, of prison authorities.[19]

Cole[20] and Wooden[21] cite numerous examples of sexual assaults on juveniles by correctional officers. Boys and girls may be forced to submit to sexual advances by threats of violence or they may be manipulated to cooperate by promises of favors. Bartollas et al. quote a youthful prisoner:

> He had intercourse with me about every two weeks. I did not want to do it, but he talked about getting me out of [here] faster and I wanted to get out because I had been here a long time. I think the reason I did it was I just came back from AWOL and I thought I had a long time to go so I thought I would get out of here.[22]

These authors also show how a staff member can subtly approach the topic of participation in sexual relations with a prisoner so that they can not be quoted as having made a direct overture or threat. Another prisoner that they interviewed told them how a staff member began to talk to him about people they knew in common and then switched to the prisoner's homosexuality in what appeared at first to be an attempt to help him. Then the staff member began to talk about the sexual acts that he enjoyed himself and linked that to sexual acts that the prisoner enjoyed. At this point it was clear to the prisoner that he was being manipulated into committing homosexual acts although the staff member had not made a specific quotable overture.[23]

The occasional reports of sexual assaults carried out against girls and women by jailers, sheriffs, deputies and other correctional officials[24] were taken more seriously after the national publicity given to the case of Joanne Little.[25] Like many other county jails and understaffed correctional facilities, the Beaufort County Jail in North Carolina employed no female staff members to care for its occasional female prisoners. The autopsy report of the Beaufort County Medical Examiner made clear that the 62-year-old jailer had been killed by Ms. Little while he was forcing her to engage in sexual relations with him. Little stabbed him seven times with an icepick and then escaped, only to turn herself in to the police at a later date.[26] It is unlikely that Little was the first prisoner to be sexually approached by this jailer. Unfortunately, professional standards in rural local jails are so variable and documentation so completely lacking that it is impossible to make even "a ball park estimate" of the national incidence of this form of sexual victimization.

The only documented case of a correctional staff member forcing prisoners to engage in sexual behavior with one another is contained in Cole's book, *Our Children's Keepers*. He quotes a 15-year-old boy as saying that two counselors forced a friend of his to go into another room and have sexual intercourse with a known homosexual prisoner. When the friend refused to do so, he was taken into another room and beaten. The counselors then came out and brought in the homosexual prisoner, following which the two prisoners had sexual relations for the amusement of the counselors. In the words of the observer, "They get a kick out of somebody going through it — then they make fun of him in front of everybody else."[27] We cannot give too much credence to this report in view of the way in which it was obtained. It is included here merely as an example of how such events may occur in correctional institutions.

The contribution to sexual assaults between prisoners that is made by correctional officers who fail to carry out adequately their duties is legendary. There are relatively few prisons that are so poorly constructed and so greatly understaffed that it is absolutely impossible for staff members to keep prisoners under sufficient surveillance to prohibit sexual aggression. When Davis asked 26 correctional employees to take polygraph tests, 25 refused, presumably because they felt they were guilty of failing to carry out their assigned duties in situations that led directly to the sexual assault of prisoners in documented cases. Davis describes sexual assaults that were made possible because the officers in charge did not adequately patrol their areas. It is easy for skeptics to dismiss many of the reports of correctional officer complicity in prisoner sexual assaults, but the kind of documentation provided by Davis convinces us of this complicity beyond the shadow of a doubt. In one incident, a prisoner was reported as having screamed for over an hour while he was being gang-raped in his cell within hearing distance of a correctional officer who not only ignored the screams but who laughed at the victim afterward. Prisoners who reported this incident passed polygraph examinations while the accused officer refused to take the test.[28]

Extreme examples of officer involvement in inmate sexual behavior include a southern institution in which a prisoner could buy a homosexual partner from a correctional officer or even from the deputy warden[29] and the use of homosexual prisoners as "gifts" from staff members to prisoner leaders who helped them keep the institution quiet.[30] One ex-prisoner claims to have been presented to "an entire wing of the prison, as a bonus to the convicts for their good behavior. In this wing, any prisoner who wanted his services, at any time and for any purposes, was given it; the guards opened doors, passed him from one cell to another, provided lubricants, permitted an orgy of simultaneous oral and anal entry, and even arranged privacy."[31]

It is easy to see why some authors place heavy blame on correctional officers for their contribution to prison sexual assaults.[32] The only objective observer who defends them is Lockwood, who feels that the combination of sexually aggressive prisoners, overcrowded conditions, management and program needs that require prisoners to intermingle, and legal limitations imposed by the courts creates a situation in which the ability of correctional officers to prevent sexual victimization is sharply attenuated.[33]

Brutality in Children's Institutions

Professional standards in institutions for delinquent youth appear to be much more variable than professional standards in state correctional systems for adults. Although there are many exemplary institutions in which not even the slightest hint of staff brutality would ever be tolerated, these exist close by other institutions in which a wide range of staff aggression toward prisoners is not only tolerated but encouraged. It is impossible to estimate accurately a national rate of staff-prisoner victimization in juvenile institutions, but the impression one gets from reading the literature is that this form of victimization is probably more prevalent in juvenile institutions than in adult institutions. Cole tells about a staff member in a Louisiana institution who assaulted prisoners with a hosepipe and big sticks. The staff member combined the beatings with economic victimization when he extracted a portion of all the gifts received by prisoners through the mail.[34] Quoting descriptions of beatings derived from accounts collected by James,[35] Chase concludes that there are more American children being mistreated in institutions than in their homes.[36] The severity of this indictment is accentuated by the most recent report on American child abuse, which presents 507,494 incidents of child abuse reported to official agencies in 1977, a reporting rate of 2.3 cases per 1,000 population.[37]

The John Howard Association's report on the Illinois Youth Centers at St. Charles and Geneva provides rare detail on the physical abuse of youngsters by staff members. Of 46 youths between the ages of 14 and 19 whom they interviewed at St. Charles, 23 stated that they had been slapped, kicked, punched, had their arms twisted or were struck with an object by a staff member. About half of the youths stated that they had witnessed staff members committing such acts against other youngsters. Many of the staff members also admitted the use of extensive corporal punishment, and there were several staff members who were consistently named as physical abusers of children. One staff member admitted striking youngsters on different occasions with a stick, a fishing pole and his hands. These situations did not involve the use of necessary restraint to subdue a youth who was attacking a staff member or another youth. Instead, it was a matter of general brutality when staff members were in bad moods.[38] This kind of grutuitous punishment differs in degree, but not in kind, from the vicious brutality suffered by youngsters in reformatories more than a century ago.[39]

Reports of beating of institutionalized children are from all parts of the nation, from the deep south[40] to the relatively well-funded institutions that are found in Massachusetts. A Harvard student posing as a delinquent at a Massachusetts institution observed an incident in which a youngster's hair was used to mop up urine from the floor.[41] Feld showed that staff brutality was higher in custody-oriented institutions than in treatment-oriented institutions. The former institutions were characterized by acts such as choking and physical beatings, whereas the more benign treatment-oriented staff members limited themselves to beatings with a plastic baseball bat and other minor physical punishments.[42]

The most detailed analysis of staff-prisoner victimization in juvenile institutions was carried out by Bartollas et al. in their study of an Ohio reformatory. A number of forms of staff-prisoner victimization at this institution were actually supported by the informal staff normative code, a code analogous to the convict code among the prisoners. The "acceptable" forms of staff exploitation were psychological and social in nature, although physical victimization was not supported by the staff normative code. For example, direct physical brutality was defined as unacceptable when a leader was intoxicated, upset because of a personal problem, using weapons against the youth or deliberately trying to seriously injure a youngster. It was also unacceptable to encourage directly (as opposed to passively) the victimization of one prisoner by another, to aid escapes (which led to increased punishment for the escapee when he was caught), and to sexually exploit the boys for one's own pleasure. The tie-in of homosexual gratification to rewards such as cigarettes, protection from peers, or promise of early release was defined as particularly offensive behavior under the staff normative code and was dealt with informally by staff members whenever a rumor about sexual exploitation was substantiated. Informal sanctions usually led to the resignation of the offending staff member.[43]

Psychological Victimization

We have already mentioned Conley's observation that correctional officers in the Oklahoma State Penitentiary who were temporarily forbidden to physically brutalize prisoners switched to psychological forms of victimization. For example, officers conducting shakedowns would deliberately break open little boxes that contained a prisoner's personal trinkets instead of asking him for the key. They would also harass the prisoners by "making noise in the cell house so they couldn't sleep, refusing personal requests, failing to respond to an inmate's call for help if he was ill or a victim of an assault, and otherwise constantly hounding the individuals."[44] These forms of psychological victimization can be perpetrated on individual prisoners who have been marked for special mistreatment or on all prisoners as a matter of personal policy.

The author once observed the classic example of psychological victimization in which the sergeant placed letters to a prisoner where the prisoner could see them but not reach them, and then claimed that there were no letters for that prisoner. The prisoner became quite agitated as a result and eventually developed considerable paranoia about his mail. In each incident, the officer tormented him throughout the day and then gave him the letters in the evening saying that he had just discovered them. Eventually, the prisoner lost control completely and was cited for a disciplinary infraction, which may well have been the officer's goal in the manipulation. A more elegant form of the game is described by Heise as "The Therapeutic 'No.'" In this game, staff members deliberately say "no" to a prisoner who has come with a legitimate request in an attempt to force an explosive or angry response.[45]

A very sophisticated form of the psychological victimization of prisoners by staff members occurs when correctional officers use their special knowledge of the outside world to heighten prisoner anxieties about their loved ones, their release date or other subjects of paramount importance. An example of this, reported from a women's institution, involved a prisoner whose son was in foster care while she was incarcerated. The officer she worked for would wait until she was within hearing distance and then begin a conversation with a second correctional officer about how commonly foster children were mistreated. These discussions went on endlessly, concentrating on subjects such as starvation, corporal punishment and sexual victimization. The prisoner was not allowed to speak, nor could she report the incidents to the administration. How could she prove that the officers were deliberately practicing psychological victimization against her? These incidents, along with the mishandling of a medical condition by the prison physician, almost agitated her enough to attempt an escape.[46]

Staff members are also privy to another source of potentially victimizing information about prisoners — the data in their central files. Information in these files contains not only the complete criminal records of prisoners but also material from social investigations, institutional reports and other items revealing the most intimate details of their lives — details that are often irrelevant to any criminal prosecution. It is common in some institutions for correctional officers to uncover this material to embarrass prisoners. Homosexual behavior, low-status crimes such as sexual offenses against minors, self-destructive acts and bouts with mental illness are examples of the kinds of subjects that officers sometimes extract from central files to use against prisoners. This method of psychological victimization is not confined to correctional institutions, for Goffman also observed it in a mental hospital.[47] A variation on the game occurs when officers pass on derogatory labels that have been affixed to unlucky prisoners by their colleagues in crime, such as "rat," "snitch," and "punk."[48]

The number of forms that psychological victimization of prisoners by staff members can take is almost limitless. New examples are constantly being reported in the literature or revealed in testimony given in the nation's courts. In Nevada, a warden put a pistol to the neck of a prisoner and said, "Move or I'll kill you," when it was not necessary for him to do so because the deputy warden was already walking the prisoner down the corridor to solitary confinement.[49] An officer in a California penitentiary who had been asked for help by a prisoner who was coughing blood gave him a note that said, "Yell for help when the blood is an inch thick, all over the floor, and don't call before that."[50] It is likely that if the officer had judged the prisoner's condition to be serious, he would have summoned medical help. The psychological victimization in this incident occurs because the officer deliberately pretends that he will never summon help while the prisoner is alive. An injunction was granted in New York State against the assignment of male guards at a women's prison, which occurred as a result of testimony that these officers deliberately came into shower rooms to watch the women as they were naked and also deliberately watched them when they were on the toilet.[51] In one of the most gruesome incidents revealed in a Senate subcommittee hearing, an Ohio correctional officer collected pet cats from the prisoners and then "dashed their brains out in sight of the whole prison population."[52] Being deprived of their children, prisoners often invest fatherly and motherly emotion in their pets so that this act of brutality symbolized multiple infanticide to many of the prisoners who could not avoid seeing it.

In the history of prisons in America, groups of prisoners sometimes mutilated themselves in protest against mistreatment by staff members. The mass cuttings of heel tendons described by Keve[53] are no longer common on the American prison scene. Likewise, the self-mutilations accomplished by Peruvian prisoners as a result of severe beatings administered by criminal justice personnel are not replicated in this country.[54] Today, self-destructive behavior by prisoners is much more likely to be an individual act than an act of group protest. Mattick is probably correct that self-destructive behavior is declining as a percentage of all prison violence.[55] The highest rate of self-mutilations known in contemporary American prisons occurred at Angola Prison in Louisiana in a ten-month period in 1974. A total of 107 self-mutilation cases were heard by the disciplinary board during this period, an average of about ten per month.[56] The despair felt by prisoners who damaged themselves has been well documented in the literature.[57] This has been linked to physical victimization by correctional officers,[58] but there has been little recognition in the literature of the ways in which psychological victimization by prison officers can also contribute to suicidal and other self-damaging acts. One occasionally hears comments to the effect that psychologically disturbed and inadequate prisoners are more likely to be "picked on" by staff members than well-adjusted, highly prisonized inmates. In institutions where this is true, the deliberate mistreatment by staff members of prisoners who are already highly disturbed may be sufficient to precipitate self-destructive incidents.

Occasions in which prisoners harm themselves primarily because of psychological victimization by correctional officers are probably relatively rare in the United States. A more common contribution to prisoner self-destruction that is made by correctional officers is the lack of sensitivity to the needs of prisoners who are approaching potentially self-destructive personal crises. Because correctional officers are usually poorly trained in interpersonal relations, most of them neither recognize nor are sufficiently motivated to assist prisoners undergoing psychological breakdowns. For every officer who sadistically torments such prisoners, there are hundred who fail to give adequate support or to call in qualified medical personnel in a situation that is gradually deteriorating. This is not a matter of victimization at the individual level but is instead a reflection of policies and funding priorities in state legislatures and other funding bodies.

Economic Victimization

Prisoner officers and other staff members in correctional institutions may be involved in economic victimization of a very direct sort, such as eating a prisoner's food or wearing his or her clothing. Most institutions guard against this sort of direct economic victimization. It is probably more common for prisoner officers to victimize economically their charges *indirectly* by being involved in contraband operations and loansharking. For example, the director of the Omaha Urban League alleged in 1974 that prisoner officers were regularly bringing in drugs and reaping profits from the drug traffic in a midwestern penitentiary.[59] The warden of the federal penitentiary in Atlanta said that nothing could be done to halt the alleged staff corruption in that institution unless the culprits were actually caught in the act. At the same hearing, one of his prisoners testified that 95% of all marijuana in the prison was provided by staff members.[60] A Tampa newspaper, investigating the homosexual attack and murder of a 19-year-old prisoner, mentioned that the prisoners who assaulted the victim were middlemen for a loan racket run by the officer who was supervising the area in which the prisoner was raped and killed. Testimony revealed that the victim had been subjected to sexual assault before his death as punishment because the correctional officer believed that he was "snitching" on him for selling ham from the kitchen for private profit. In addition to the assault by prisoners, it was alleged that the victim had been beaten by several correctional officers four days before he died and had begged to be placed in the isolation unit but that his request was denied.[61]

When a staff member is involved in a sub rosa economic system of the prison, it is possible to "burn" prisoners with impunity because they cannot possibly report the crime to the administration without revealing their own involvement in the illegal activity. If the prisoner is a member of a powerful gang or clique, pressures can be brought to bear on correctional officers to keep them from this sort of economic victimization. On the other hand, sophisticated officers are careful never to burn any prisoner who has this kind of backing. Instead, they victimize only the isolated prisoners who enlist their help in sub rosa economic transactions. Such a prisoner, who gives an officer some money to smuggle out of the prison for his wife, may find out that the officer has pocketed it instead of delivering it, or perhaps that a portion of it was subtracted as an additional payment for delivery beyond the amount already agreed upon.

The definition of victimization becomes contorted out of all recognition in the case of the officer who regularly participates in sub rosa smuggling activities with prisoners but who keeps his record clean by occasionally reporting unsophisticated prisoners to the administration for attempting to bribe him. Victimization in this instance consists of enforcing the regulations that the officer should *have been enforcing* in a setting in which the regulations were habitually ignored. One officer who allegedly charged up to $300 a trip to "pack" contraband in and out of the prison made enough money over his career to establish an independent business in the free community. This "horse" (a slang term for prison officers who smuggle contraband into the institution) was probably able "to stay in business" for such a long time because he only "packed" for powerful, trustworthy prisoners and systematically wrote infraction tickets on every other prisoner who approached him.

We cannot leave the subject of the economic victimization of prisoners by staff members without mentioning drug testing, industrial victimization and the suppression of prisoner unions. These topics do not fit our definition of victimization because they refer to institutional policy and, in some cases, enacted law. Many prison industries are operated under less than safe conditions in order to maximize productivity. Once a major problem in America's prisons,[62] this lingers on today in industrial programs that continue to use equipment that is antiquated and unsafe.

The testing of dangerous drugs by prisoners, which has been rapidly declining in recent years, is another form of institutional victimization that is outside our technical definition. Beginning with a 1904 study of bubonic plague by Colonel R.P. Strong,[63] prisoners were paid a pittance (if anything) but offered minor administrative favors in return for participating in highly dangerous experiments. Even these small rewards were more than sufficient motivation to recruit prisoners for medical- and drug-testing experiments because the prisoners were artificially economically disadvantaged by polices and laws that forbade them to be paid more than a few cents an hour. Was it really necessary to apply radiation to the testicles of prisoners so that later they would become sterile? Prisoners, whom I know personally, were involved in such an experiment, claiming they were not adequately informed of the consequences at the time that they agreed to participate. Some of them would now like to lead normal married lives and have children, but their criminal records largely rule out adoption and their participation in the radiation experiment leaves them unable to conceive their own children. In an excellent treatment of the subject, Meyer shows how the pharmaceutical companies and the general public have benefited over the years from low-cost prisoner experiments. The victimizing nature of these experiments has been given credence by their abolition under contemporary federal standards for drug-testing experiments.[64]

The substandard wages that are generally paid to men and women working in prison industries are also economically victimizing, although such wages do not constitute victimization under our definition of the subject. However, technical victimization creeps into this situation when prisoners attempt to organize unions, following the model that is accepted in free society, and they are prevented from doing so when administrative actions such as punitive ransfers, punitive segregation and unjust parole board "flops" (parole board decisions to increase sentence length) are used to suppress the formation of prisoner unions.[65] Although prisoner unions are permitted in some European nations (such as KRUM, organized in Sweden in 1966), the only way for prisoner unions to survive in the United States is if they have a power base outside of the institution. The San Francisco-based Prisoners' Union, which was co-founded by John Irwin, is an example of this kind of an organization. Whether it will have any significant national impact remains to be seen.

Social Victimization

The most blatant form of social victimization carried out against prisoners by correctional officers is racial discrimination. Two other forms of victimization that are essentially social in nature are the non-performance of stated duties and the deliberate handing over of supervisory responsibilities to prisoners who then use their staff-sanctioned power to abuse others. Reports of correctional officer discrimination against black prisoners abound in the literature.[66] These reports include evidence of discrimination in job assignments[67] and disciplinary hearings.[68] Racial discrimination becomes mixed with religious discrimination when groups such as the Black Muslims are denied their religious rights.[69] Carroll describes an incident in which kissing between a prisoner and a visitor, which was officially prohibited but always permitted for uniracial couples, resulted in the abrupt termination of a visit when a black prisoner kissed his white visitor.[70] Carroll also observed correctional officers admitting white visitors to inmate organizations without searches, but systematically searching visitors to black organizations and conducting bodily postvisit searches of black prisoners three times as often as similar searches of white prisoners.[71] All of these reports pale in comparison with the allegations of virulent racism by correctional officers at Soledad prison in California.[72]

When a staff member turns over supervisory activities to a prisoner, all of the other prisoners in that jurisdiction are subject to a potential victimization. We have already seen some examples of sexual victimization that occurred because of this form of staff behavior. I cite only two additional examples here. Testimony in a federal court alleged that a prisoner in a Texas institution had been set up as a "prison enforcer" for which he was rewarded with special privileges such as a homosexual in his cell to service his sexual needs and the authority to assault other prisoners at any time in the service of maintaining institutional order.[73] The other example comes from the juvenile institution studied by Bartollas et al. Staff members in this institution often catered to the needs of "heavy" (physically powerful) prisoners in return for their cooperation in running the reformatory. These favored prisoners were permitted to unlock the doors of their fellow prisoners with the staff's keys. This gave the "heavies" license to victimize other prisoners in return for their allegiance to staff members.[74]

The social victimization of prisoners as a class of individuals occurs when correctional officers and other staff members neglect to carry out their stated duties. Bartollas and his associates described staff members who stayed in their offices, perhaps taking naps, thus leaving the weaker prisoners open to all sorts of victimization by their peers.

Other staff members discriminated directly against scapegoats by giving them all the menial work details in the cottage, seldom talking with them, or permitted other youths to victimize them openly in the presence of staff.[75]

Prisoners are beginning to realize that they can file legal actions against correctional staff members who refrain from carrying out their duties in ways that lead to prisoner victimization. A recent issue of *Corrections Compendium* reports several such cases filed under 42 U.S.C. 1983. One of the complainants had suffered sexual abuse and alleged a history of incidents over a period of two years because of inadequate supervision by institutional staff members. The other alleged that one prisoner had been killed and another injured by a fire that broke out in an Arkansas jail while the sheriff had gone to a basketball game, leaving the jail unattended.[76] There is increasing recognition that such actions by correctional staff members constitute a serious form of victimization.

Two theoretical explanations for the victimization of prisoners by correctional officers have been advanced in the literature. These are the total institutions theory and the role theory. Actually there is very little difference between these two approaches. Total institutions theory looks at institutions as a whole and emphasizes the similarities between prisons, mental hospitals and other total institutions. In contrast, role theory emphasizes the role played by correctional officers and argues that citizens can be rapidly socialized to play the role of correctional officer.

The creation of total institutions theory is generally credited to Goffman in his book, *Asylums*, in which he discusses social and psychological assaults upon inmates by staff members. In Goffman's conception, the psychological victimization of inmates by staff members is part of the overall process of mortification, in which the inmates' attachment to civilian life is stripped away. The exasperating thing about much of the unnecessary psychological victimization that goes on is that the staff justifies the victimization in terms of institutional needs.[77] Following this same line of analysis, Hartmann has identified the existence of the staff role of the "key jingler" for persons who deliberately use power in a manner that is debilitating to the inmates. These individuals are concerned with "throwing their weight around" rather than promoting the welfare of the inmates under their control.[78]

The maximum security prison is conceptualized as a miniature totalitarian state by Burns. The six basic features of a totalitarian regime — totalitarian ideology, a single party typically led by one person, a terroristic police, a communications monopoly, a weapons monopoly and a centrally directed economy — are systematically applied to maximum security prisons in Burns' analysis. In this model, staff members who are in a position of great authority will be sorely tempted to practice brutality, blackmail, bribery and favoritism. Terroristic police practices are part of the social control mechanism for keeping inmates in line.[79] If Burns' conception of the maximum security prison as a totalitarian regime is correct, then we would expect that those correctional officers who are better integrated with the culture of the prison and more socially involved in it would be more brutal and totalitarian than those officers who exist at the periphery of the staff subculture. An exploratory investigation by Shoemaker and Hillery suggests that this may be true in some institutions. However, the correlations they found were significant in only one of three institutions (and that was a boarding school rather than a maximum security prison),[80] so their evidence does not lend more than minimal support to the theory advanced by Burns.

Role theory as applied to the victimization of prisoners by officers received support from the Stanford Prison Experiment conducted by Haney et al.[81] In this experiment, college students who had been authenticated as psychologically normal were paid to role-play guards and inmates in a pseudoprison in the basement of a Stanford building. Everyone involved was aware of the fact that the experiment was artificial, although it was very well staged. Commenting on this experiment, Zimbardo says:

> At the end of six days we had to close down our mock prison because what we saw was frightening. It was no longer apparent to most of the subjects (or to us) where reality ended and the roles began. The majority had indeed become prisoners or guards, no longer able to clearly differentiate between role-playing and self. There were dramatic changes in virtually every aspect of their behavior, thinking, and feeling. In less than a week the experience of imprisonment undid (temporarily) a lifetime of learning: human values were suspended, self-concepts were challenged and the ugliest, most base, pathological side of human nature surfaced. We were horrified because we saw some boys (guards) treat others as if they were despicable animals, taking pleasure in cruelty, while other boys (prisoners) became servile, dehumanized robots who thought only of escape, of their own individual survival and of their mounting hatred for the guards.[82]

In the Stanford experiment, approximately one-third of the staff members became tyrannical in their arbitrary use of power over the inmates. They developed creative ways of breaking the spirit of the prisoners who were in their charge. Although the other two-thirds of the staff members were not tyrannical, there was never a case in which one of them interfered with a command given by any of the tyrannical guards. They never even tried to pressure the other staff members into behaving more reasonably. The experiment was called off because of the possibility that some of the subjects were being severely damaged by their experiences. Three of them had had to be released in the first four days because they had severe situational traumatic reactions, such as confusion in thinking, severe depression and hysterical crying.

This experiment devastates the constitutional sadism theory of staff brutality, which is, in any case, not represented in the serious literature on staff-inmate victimization. The realization that any normal human being can take on the negative characteristics commonly associated with the worst of prison officers leads us to look more carefully at how roles are structured in the prison situation. A study of mine shows that even civilian volunteers who become quasistaff members of a correctional institution can engage in types of behavior that are psychologically victimizing. In a volunteer program administered by me in which all but two of the staff members were volunteers from the external community, there were many cases of power-tripping and sexual enticement by the staff members, with power-tripping being primarily engaged in by males, and sexual enticement by females, although the reverse was true in some cases. The power-tripper enjoys a feeling of control over the lives of prisoners and manipulates them in therapy groups and in administrative situations so as to make them more dependent and more anxious than they would otherwise be. Power-trippers are sure that inmates should do what they are told, and they imply that they have a great deal more power over the inmates' release date than is actually the case.

Sexual enticement occurs when the volunteer staff member dresses, talks and acts in a sexually suggestive way while within the prison. Pseudoromances are encouraged in which the prisoners are led to believe that the staff members have a real interest in them, while the staff members in actuality are merely gratifying themselves by being admired and sought after. When the relationship goes too far, the prisoners are often subjected to disciplinary actions because the victimizing staff member claims that it was "all the prisoner's fault." In addition, some prisoners become so emotionally involved that when the relationship falls apart, they become suicidal. Others come looking for thier "lovers" when they are released from prison, only to find out that these staff members have no intention of following up on the promises they made while the prisoners were safe behind bars.[83]

Is the role of the prison guard so compulsive that a certain percentage of the people who play it will be invariably motivated to abuse prisoners in one way or another. The comments by Zimbardo and my experiences say yes, and this idea is also consistent with a report by Jacobs and Kraft, that suggests the possibility that racial differences among guards are suppressed by the "master status" of the prison officer.[84] However, an obscure publication on correctional institutions in Wisconsin offers contrary evidence. This report by Ross describes what happened during a 16-day period when members of the Wisconsin State Employees Union went on strike and National Guard Units took over the administration of the prisons. The National Guardsmen were in the prisons for more than twice the period of time of Zimbardo's experiment, yet they were not institutionalized by the experience. Instead of becoming brutal and mistreating the inmates, they treated them like decent human beings. They relaxed the disciplinary regime and at the same time reduced the number of incidents of violence among inmates.[85]

It is probable that the reason the National Guardsmen's behavior did not deteriorate during their time as correctional officers was that they never conceived of themselves as playing the role of prison officers. They had a different role to play—the role of National Guardsmen acting in an emergency. In addition, they had a network of relations with each other that existed before they had entered the prison and that strengthened their resistance to the negative process of institutionalization. With these kinds of social supports, it is possible that the National Guardsmen could have had tours of duty of one or two years in length without ever adopting the more negative aspects of the role of the prison officer. International studies of prison camps in which the prisoners are able to live rather normal lives under the supervision of military units also offer some evidence in support of the idea that the military role can take precedence over the prison officer role and minimize the appeal of engaging in behavior that is at least psychologically victimizing if not physically brutal.

Notes

1. Donald Clemmer, *The Prison Community* (New York: Holt, Rinehart and Winston, 1940), p. 204.
2. John A. Conley, "A History of the Oklahoma Penal System, 1907-1967," Ph.D. dissertation, Michigan State University, 1977.
3. Bruce Jackson, *Killing Time, Life in the Arkansas Penitentiary* (Ithaca, NY: Cornell University Press, 1977).
4. Tom Murton and Joe Hyams, *Inside Prison, U.S.A.* (New York: Grove Press, 1969).
5. Ibid., p. 7.
6. Prison brutality revealed during the federal hearing, *The Freeworld Times* 1 (January 1972): 2.
7. Fear, Angola's punishment camp terrorizes prisoners, *Southern Coalition Report on Jails and Prisons* 5 (Spring 1978): 3.

8 Stephen Gettinger, Mississippi: Has come a long way but it had a long way to come, *Corrections Magazine* 5 (June 1979): 8; *Corrections Digest* 4 (December 12, 1973): 3.

9 Philip J. Hirschkop and Michael A. Millemann, The prison life of Leroy Jones, in Burton M. Atkins and Henry R. Glick (Eds.), *Prisons, Protest, and Politics* (Englewood Cliffs, NJ: Prentice-Hall, 1972), pp. 55-59.

10 Jessica Mitford, *Kind and Usual Punishment* (New York: Random House, 1971), pp. 41-42.

11 Oklahoma prison guards indicted for inmate gassing incident, *Corrections Digest* 6 (February 5, 1975): 2.

12 Federal jury convicts prison guards of brutality, *Corrections Digest* 5 (March 6, 1974): 2-3.

13 'Dedicated' with violence, *The Freeworld Times* 1 (August 1972): 8-9.

14 Rioters killed, *The Freeworld Times* 1 (February 1972): 6,9.

15 Ibid., p. 6.

16 Mitford (1971), p. 290.

17 Hans Toch, *Police, Prisons, and the Problem of Violence* (Washington, DC: U.S. Government Printing Office, 1977), pp. 65-67.

18 Robert Bogdan and Steven J. Taylor, *Introduction to Qualitative Research Methods* (New York: Wiley, 1975).

19 Edward Sagarin and Donal E. J. MacNamara, The homosexual as a crime victim, *International Journal of Criminology and Penology* 3 (1975): 21.

20 Larry Cole, *Our Children's Keepers: Inside America's Kid Prisons* (New York: Grossman, 1972).

21 Kenneth Wooden, *Weeping in the Playtime of Others: America's Incarcerated Children* (New York: McGraw-Hill, 1976).

22 Clemens Bartollas, Stuart J. Miller and Simon Dinitz, *Juvenile Victimization: The Institutional Paradox* (New York: Wiley, 1976), p. 214.

23 Ibid., p. 214.

24 Gene Kassebaum, Sex in prison, violence, homosexuality, and intimidation are everyday occurrences, *Sexual Behavior* 2 (January 1972): 39-45.

25 The case of Joanne Little, *Crime and Social Justice* 3 (Summer 1975): 42-45. For a more recent case, see Women press for change at Tutwiler, *Southern Coalition Report on Jails and Prisons* 5 (Fall 1978): 3.

26 Woman's killing of jailer raises inmate abuse questions, *Corrections Digest* 5 (December 11, 1974): 11-12.

27 Cole (1972), p. 8.

28 Alan J. Davis, Sexual assaults in the Philadelphia prison system and sheriff's vans, *Trans-Action* 6 (December 1968): 11.

29 Jack Griswold, Mike Misenheimer and Art Powers, *An Eye for an Eye* (New York: Holt, Rinehart and Winston, 1970), pp. 42-43, cited in Anthony M. Scacco Jr., *Rape in Prison* (Springfield, IL: C.C. Thomas, 1975), p. 32.

30 Sagarin and MacNamara (1975).

31 Ibid., pp. 21-22.

32 See, for example, Davis (1968) and Scacco (1975).

33 Daniel Lockwood, *Prison Sexual Violence* (New York: Elsevier, 1980), p. 140.

34 Cole (1972), p. 64.

35 Howard James, Children in trouble, *Christian Science Monitor* (April 5, 12, 19, 26, and May 10, 24, 1969), cited in Naomi F. Chase, *A Child Is Being Beaten* (New York: McGraw-Hill, 1976), pp. 154, 160.

36 Chase (1976), p. 151.

37 National Analysis of Official Child Abuse and Neglect Reporting (Washington, DC: Government Printing Office, 1969).

[38] John Howard Association, *Illinois Youth Centers at St. Charles and Geneva* (Chicago: John Howard Association, 1974).

[39] See, for example, Cliff Judge and Roma Emmerson, Some children at risk in Victoria in the 19th century, *Medical Journal of Australia* 1 (1974): 490-495.

[40] John Vodicka, Louisiana warden indicted for beatings of juveniles, *Southern Coalition Report on Jails and Prisons* 5 (Summer 1978): 1.

[41] Wooden (1976), p. 108.

[42] Barry C. Feld, *Neutralizing Inmate Violence* (Cambridge, MA: Ballinger, 1977).

[43] Bartollas et al. (1976).

[44] Conley (1977), p. 237.

[45] Robert E. Heise, *Prison Games* (Fort Worth: privately published, 1976).

[46] Kenneth Dimick, *Ladies in Waiting Behind Prison Walls* (Muncie, IN: Accelerated Development, 1977), pp. 46-47.

[47] Erving Goffman, *Asylums* (Garden City, NY: Doubleday, 1961).

[48] Heise (1976).

[49] *Corrections Digest* 3 (November 1, 1972), pp. 11-12.

[50] Mitford (1971), p. 148.

[51] Injunction granted against assignment of male guards at Bedford Hills, *Corrections Compendium* 2 (October 1977), p. 3.

[52] Mitford (1971), pp. 268-269.

[53] Paul W. Keve, *Prison Life and Human Worth* (Minneapolis: University of Minnesota Press, 1974).

[54] H. H. A. Cooper, Self-mutilation by Peruvian prisoners, *International Journal of Offender Therapy* 15 (1971): 180-188.

[55] Hans Mattick, The prosaic sources of prison violence, in Jackwell Susman, *Crime and Justice, 1971-1972* (New York: A.M.S. Press, 1974): 179-187.

[56] A. Astrachan, Profile/Louisiana, *Corrections Magazine* 2 (September-October 1975): 9-14.

[57] See, for example, R. S. Esparza, Attempted and committed suicide in county jails, in Bruce Danto (Ed.), *Jailhouse Blues* (Orchard Lake, MI: Epic Publications, 1973), pp. 27-46; James L. Claghorn and Dan R. Beto, Self-mutilation in a prison hospital, *Corrective Psychiatry and Journal of Social Therapy* 13 (1967): 133-141; Robert Johnson, *Culture and Crisis in Confinement* (Lexington, MA: D. C. Heath, 1976); Hans Toch, *Men in Crisis* (Chicago: Aldine, 1975); *Living in Prison: The Ecology of Survival* (New York: Free Press, 1977).

[58] R. J. Wicks, Suicide prevention — A brief for corrections officers, *Federal Probation* 36 (September 1972): 29-31.

[59] Nebraska prisoners speak-out, *The Freeworld Times* 3 (January-February 1974): 7.

[60] Danger, death, corruption at Atlanta federal prison detailed in Senate testimony, *Corrections Digest* 9 (October 6, 1978): 3-4.

[61] Inmate death linked to guard rackets, *The Freeworld Times* 2 (May 1973): 15.

[62] See Conley (1977) for historical examples of excessive industrial accidents caused by deliberate administrative inattention to matters of safety.

[63] Gilbert F. McMahon, The normal prisoner in medical research, *Journal of Clinical Pharmacology* 71 (February-March 1972): 72.

[64] Peter B. Meyer, *Drug Experiments on Prisoners, Ethical, Economic, or Exploitative?* (Lexington, MA: D. C. Heath, 1976).

[65] C. Ronald Huff, Unionization behind the walls, *Criminology* 12 (1974): 175-193; Prisoners' union: A challenge for state corrections, *State Government* 48 (1975): 145-149.

[66] Haywood Burns, The black prisoner as victim, in Michele G. Hermann and Marilyn G. Haft (Eds.), *Prisoners' Rights Sourcebook* (New York: Clark Boardman, 1973), pp. 25-31.

[67] Ronald Goldfarb, *Jails: The Ultimate Ghetto of the Criminal Justice System* (Garden City, NY: Doubleday, 1976), p. 405.

[68] Erik O. Wright, *The Politics of Punishment: A Critical Analysis of Prisons in America* (New York: Harper & Row, 1973), p. 127.

[69] James B. Jacobs, *Stateville: The Penitentiary in Mass Society* (Chicago: University of Chicago Press, 1977), p. 59.

[70] Leo Carroll, *Hacks, Blacks, and Cons* (Copyright © 1974) reissued 1988 by Waveland Press, Inc., Prospect Heights, IL), pp. 123-124.

[71] Ibid., pp. 127-128.

[72] George Jackson, *Soledad Brother: The Prison Letters of George Jackson* (New York: Bantam, 1970).

[73] This week: Texas prison faces federal court test, *Corrections Digest* 9 (October 6, 1978): 2-3.

[74] Bartollas et al. (1976), pp. 208-209.

[75] Ibid., pp. 207-209.

[76] Sheriff may be liable for acts of his subordinates, and Leaving prisoners unattended can lead to civil rights violation, *Corrections Compendium* 2 (June 1978): 5.

[77] Goffman (1961).

[78] Carl Hartman, The key jingler, *Community Mental Health Journal* 5 (1969): 199-205.

[79] Henry Burns, Jr., A miniature totalitarian state: Maximum security prison, *Canadian Journal of Criminology and Corrections* 11 (July 1969): 153-164.

[80] Donald J. Shoemaker and George A. Hillery, Jr., "Violence and Commitment in Custodial Settings," paper presented at the annual meeting of the American Sociological Association, 1978.

[81] Craig Haney, Curtis Banks and Philip Zimbardo, Interpersonal dynamics in a simulated prison, in Robert G. Leger and John R. Stratton (Eds.), *The Sociology of Corrections* (New York: Wiley, 1977), pp. 65-92.

[82] Philip Zimbardo, Pathology of imprisonment, *Society* 9 (6) (1972): 4.

[83] Lee H. Bowker, Volunteers in correctional settings: Benefits, problems, and solutions, in *Proceedings of the American Correctional Association* (Washington, DC: American Correctional Association, 1973), pp. 298-303.

[84] James B. Jacobs and Lawrence J. Kraft, Integrating the keepers: A comparison of black and white prison guards in Illinois, *Social Problems* 25 (1978): 304-318.

[85] Beth Ross, *Changing of the Guard: Citizen Soldiers in Wisconsin Correctional Institutions* (Madison: League of Women Voters of Wisconsin, 1979).

10

Prison Guards and Snitches
Social Control in a Maximum Security Institution

James W. Marquart
Julian B. Roebuck

In prison vernacular "rats," "snitches," "stool pigeons," "stoolies," or finks refer to inmates who "cooperate" with or discretely furnish information to staff members. By and large, the popular imagery and folk-beliefs surrounding these inmates are particularly negative. Typically, prison movies present "rats," as the weakest, most despicable and pitiful creatures in the prisoner society. "Rats" are usually depicted as outcasts or isolates that undermine the solidarity of the cons by breaking the inmate "code" of silence (see Sykes, 1958). Whenever a "rat" appears in a movie scene, groups of inmates stop

Source: Prepared especially for *The Dilemmas of Corrections*. Some of the substantive findings herein are discussed in an article, "Prison Guards and Snitches: Deviance Within a Total Institution" (*British Journal of Criminology*).

talking, disband, or mumble obscenities.[1] Some prison reseachers, like McCleery (1960), contend that uncovering snitches is an obsession for the majority of inmates. This may be true in many correctional institutions because "rats" are often the victims of "accidents" or savage reprisals from other prisoners, as evidenced by the New Mexico prison riot in 1980. The inmates in many other prisons have developed an inmate society, enabling them to define, label, and punish "rats" as deviants.

The sociology of confinement, especially prison role research, has for decades noted the negative perception of "rats" by the other inmates (see Bowker, 1977). Yet, despite the fascination with and knowledge of "rats," prison researchers (unlike police researchers) have offered little systematic research on snitches.[2] Johnson (1961) and Wilmer (1965) are the only prison investigators who have examined informing, but their work focuses on the types and personal attributes of "rats" rather than informing as a mechanism of social control. Perhaps the best descriptions of the exchange relationships between staff members and stool pigeons come from former inmates (see Bettelheim, 1943; Solzhenitsyn, 1975; and Charriere, 1970). Nevertheless, little is known about how officials use inmate-intelligence as a management strategy.

This paper examines· a southwestern state penitentiary control system wherein a network of "paid" inmate informants functioned as surrogate guards. Although known "rats" may be typically loathed and disparaged by the staff and captives in most institutions, the "rats" in the prison under study were hated, but also envied, feared, and respected. No stigma was attached to their deviant role. We focus on the snitch recruitment process, the types of intelligence gathered, the informers' payoff and the use of this intelligence to maintain social order — in short the dynamics of this guard-surrogate guard society.

Setting and Method of Study

The data were collected at the Johnson Unit[3], a maximum security recidivist prison within the Texas Department of Corrections (TDC), that housed nearly 3200 inmates over the age of twenty-five (47% black, 36% white, and 17% hispanic). Many of these hard-core offenders had been convicted of violent crimes. Johnson had a system-wide reputation· for tight disciplinary control, and inmate trouble-makers from other TDC prisons were sent there for punishment. Structurally, the prison had eighteen inside cell blocks (or tanks) and twelve dormitories branching out from a single central hall — a telephone pole design. The Hall, the main thoroughfare of the prison, was a corridor almost one quarter of a mile long, measuring sixteen feet wide by twelve feet high.

The data for this paper are derived from field research conducted from June 1981 through January 1983. The first author entered Johnson as a guard, a role which enabled him to observe and analyze first-hand the social control system. A number of established field techniques were used: participant observation, key informants, formal and informal interviews, and the examination of prison and inmate documents and records. The investigator directly observed and participated in the daily routine of prison events (work, school, meals, sick call, cell and body searches, counts, etc.) as well as various unexpected events (fights, stabbings, suicide attempts, drug trafficking). He also observed and examined officer/officer and officer/inmate (snitch) interaction patterns, inmate/officer transactions, leadership behavior, rule violations, disciplinary hearings, and the administration of punishment. With time, he established rapport with guards and inmates, gaining the reputation of a "good officer." (He was even promoted to sergeant in November 1982).

During the fieldwork, the observer developed, as did most ranking guards, a cadre of "rats" and channelled their information to supervisors (sergeants, lieutenants, captains, majors). These inmates routinely brought him information about prisoners (e.g., weapons, gambling, stealing) and even other officers (e.g., sleeping on the job, drug smuggling, having sex with inmates). The vast majority of snitches were shared, but the "rats" dealt primarily with officers who had the reputation of using good judgment (not overreacting, keeping cool) when handling sensitive information. Enmeshed in the intelligence network, the researcher frequently discussed these matters with the officers and "rats."

The Snitch System

Johnson employed 240 officers and housed nearly 3,200 inmates. One guard was generally assigned to supervise four cell-blocks totalling 400 prisoners. Obviously this situation obviated individual inmate supervision. Therefore, to facilitate control and order, staff members enlisted the "official" aid of the inmate elites as informers and surrogate guards. These snitches, called building tenders (BTs) and turnkeys, in turn cultivated their own inmate snitches. Johnson was managed via a complex information network facilitating a proactive as well as a reactive form of prisoner management. These surrogate guards acted with considerable authority.

Structure and Work Role

The BT system involved four levels of inmates. The top of the hierarchy consisted of the "head" building tenders. In 1981, each of the eighteen cell blocks had one building tender designated by the staff as the "head" BT. These BTs were responsible for all inmate behavior that occurred in "their" particular block. Block "ownership" was recognized by inmates and staff members alike who referred informally but meaningfully, for example, to "Watson's tank" or "Robinson's tank." Head BTs were the block's representatives to the staff and were held accountable for any problems that occurred therein. Besides procuring information (described in the next section), head BTs mediated problems (e.g., lover's quarrels, petty stealing, gambling, fighting, dirty or loud cell partners) within the living areas. They listened to and weighed each inmate's version of an argument or altercation. In most cases, the head BT warned the quarrelers to "get along with each other" or "quit all the grab-assing around." In some cases, they even let two antagonists settle their differences in a "supervised" fistfight. However, those inmates who could not or would not get along with the others were usually beaten and then moved to another cell block. BTs unofficially and routinely settled the mundane problems of prison life in the blocks without the staff's knowledge but with their tacit approval (see Marquart and Crouch, 1983).[4]

The second level of the system consisted of the rank and file building tenders. In every block (or dormitory), there were generally between three and five inmates assigned as BTs, totalling nearly 150 in the prison. BTs "worked the tank" and maintained control in the living areas by tabulating the daily counts, delivering messages to other inmates for the staff, getting the other inmates up for work, procuring information, and protecting the officers from attacks by the ordinary inmates. BTs also socialized new inmates into the system; that is, they educated them to "keep the noise down, go to work when you are called, mind your own business, stop "grab assing around," and tell us [BTs] when you have a problem." BTs broke up fights, issued orders to the other inmates, protected weak inmates from exploitation, protected the officers, and passed on information to the head BT and staff members.

Finally, the BTs unofficially disciplined erring inmates. For example, if an inmate was found stealing another's property, he was apt to receive a slap across the face, a punch in the stomach, or both. If the erring inmate continued to steal, he was summarily beaten and, with the staff's approval, moved to another cell block. The BTs were "on call" twenty-four hours a day and the head BT assigned the others to shifts (morning, evening, and night). It was an unwritten rule that cell block guards were not to order the BTs to sweep the floors, wash windows, or perform other menial tasks. Those officers who violated this "rule" were informed on and frequently disciplined (e.g., reassigned to gun towers, never assigned to that particular block again). This further underscores the building tenders' proprietorship of the tanks as well as their ability and power to curtail the lower ranking guards' authority and behavior.

The third level consisted of inmate runners or strikers. Runners were selected and assigned to work in the blocks by BTs on the basis of their loyalty, work ability, and willingness to act as informants. They also worked at regular jobs throughout the prison (e.g., laundry, shops, kitchen). Runners performed the janitorial work of the block such as sweeping, cleaning windows, and dispensing supplies to the cells. More importantly, runners, who were also called hitmen, served as the physical back-up for the BTs by assisting in breaking up fights and quelling minor disturbances. As a reward for their services, runners enjoyed more mobility and privileges within the block than the other inmates (but less than the BTs). Many runners were also friends or acquaintances of the BTs in the free world, and some were their consensual homosexual partners. Some blocks had three or four runners, while others had seven, eight, or even nine. Altogether, there were approximately 175 to 200 runners.

The fourth level of the BT system consisted of turnkeys, numbering 17 in 1981. The Hall contained seven large metal barred doors, riot barricades that were manned by turnkeys in six hour shifts. Turnkeys shut and locked these doors during fights or disturbances to localize and prevent disturbances from escalating or moving throughout the Hall. These inmates actually carried the keys (on long leather straps) which locked and unlocked the barricades. Every morning, turnkeys came to the central picket (a room containing all the keys for the prison and riot gear) and picked up keys for "their" barricades. Turnkeys routinely broke up fights, provided assistance to the BTs, and physically protected the officers from the ordinary inmates. These doorkeepers passed along information to the BTs about anything they heard while "working a gate." When off duty they lived in the blocks where they assisted the BTs in the everyday management of inmates. Turnkeys occupied a status level equal to that of the BTs.

Selection of BTs and Turnkeys

As "managers" of the living areas and Hall, these inmate-agents obviously performed a dangerous task for the staff. Vastly outnumbered, BTs and turnkeys ruled with little opposition from the ordinary inmates. In fact, most of the ordinary inmates feared their "overseers" because of their status and physical dominance. They were formally selected by the staff to perform an official job within the living areas. Unwritten but "official" departmental policy existed on the appointment of inmates to BT and turnkey positions. The staff at Johnson (and other Texas prisons) recommended certain inmates as BTs/turnkeys to the Classification Committee (a panel of four TDC officials all with prison security backgrounds).[5] This committee then reviewed the inmate records and made the final selections. Recommendations to the Classification Committee from the staff were not always honored and less than half of those recommended were selected for BT/turnkey jobs. One supervisor, an active participant in the recruitment process at Johnson, expressed a typical preference:

> I've got a personal bias. I happen to like murderers and armed robbers. They have a great deal of esteem in the inmate social system, so its not likely that they'll have as much problem as some other inmate because of their esteem, and they tend to be more aggressive and a more dynamic kind of individual. A lot of inmates steer clear of them and avoid problems just because of the reputation they have and their aggressiveness. They tend to be aggressive, you know, not passive.

The BTs and turnkeys were physically and mentally superior inmates, "natural leaders" among their peers. All were articulate and had physical presence, poise, and self-confidence. Generally, they were more violent, prisonized, and criminally sophisticated than the ordinary inmates. Of the eighteen head BTs, eight were in prison for armed robbery, five for murder (one was an enforcer and contract-style killer), one for attempted murder, one for rape, one for drug trafficking, and two for burglary. Their average age was thirty-nine and they were serving an average prison sentence of thirty-two years. Of the seventeen turnkeys, three were murderers, three were armed robbers, six were burglars, two were drug traffickers, one was a rapist and one was doing time for aggravated assault. Their average age was thirty-one and they were serving an average sentence of twenty-two years. All were physically strong, rugged, prison-wise, and physically imposing. BTs and turnkeys were older than most prisoners and often they were violent recidivists similar to the inmate leaders noted by Clemmer (1940) and Schrag (1954). In contrast, the average TDC inmate in 1981 had been given a twenty-one year sentence and was between twenty-two and twenty-seven years old. Almost half (48%) were property offenders or petty thieves.

Information Acquisition

The most important means of controlling inmates' behavior in the cell blocks was the presence of BTs. These inmate-agents, while carrying out their other duties, spent most of their time sitting around the entrance to the block talking with other inmates, especially the runners. Conversations with and observations of other prisoners enabled the BTs to gather a variety of intelligence about inmates' moods, problems, daily behaviors, friends, enemies, homosexual encounters, misbehaviors, plans, plots and overall demeanor.

The runners, who worked throughout the prison had more contact with the ordinary inmates than did the BTs. This contact facilitated eavesdropping and the extracting of information. For example, while mopping the runs (walkways on each tier), runners talked to and observed the inmates already in their cells. At work, these inmates listened to, watched, talked to, and interacted with the others. Runners secured and relayed to the BTs information on work strikes, loan-sharking, stealing of state property, distilling liquor, tatooing, homosexual acts, and escape and revenge plans.

Information Sources in the Cell Blocks

Though informing was expected from runners, they were not formally instructed to inform. A head BT explains this situation:

> You don't pick these people and tell them now you've got to go in there and tell me what's going on inside the dayroom [a TV and recreation area in each living area]. By becoming a runner it is expected that you will tell what's going on; it's an unspoken rule that you will inform on the rest of the people in here. If you hear something you are going to come to me with it.

With the runners' information, the BTs penetrated the tank social system. Ordinary prisoners knew they were under constant surveillance and thus were amenable to the prisoner social control system — a system based on inmate intelligence reports, regimentation, strict rules, and certain punishments. For example, when the BTs found out that two or more inmates were "cliquing up" for any purpose, they immediately told the staff who disbanded the group through cell changes.

Atomized and lacking solidarity, the ordinary inmates "ratted" on each other, especially when they felt the need for protection. Ordinary inmates rarely, if ever, sought out the staff to solve a block problem because this brought punishment from the BTs. Instead they sought the counsel and help of the BTs, the power block they were forced to deal with. From the ordinary inmates, the BTs learned about a variety of things such as gambling pools, illicit sex, petty thievery, tatooing para-phernalia, liquor making, weapons, and numerous other forms of contraband, misbehavior, and planned misbehavior (e.g., plots of revenge, possible attacks on an overbearing guard). This knowledge enabled the guards to take a proactive stance, thereby preventing rule violations. Not all block residents were informers. Those who snitched did so for several reasons.

Like anyone else, prisoners react negatively to certain repugnant behaviors and situations. Most were followers and refrained from taking action themselves. Citizens often call the police, for example, about a neighbor's barking dog or loud stereo rather than complain directly to the neighbor. Inmates took similar action. They told the BTs about various illegalities (especially those that threatened them in any way) because they knew the problem would be resolved in the block without involving themselves or attracting official intervention. The BTs usually took swift action when resolving problems. For example, one inmate told the BTs in his block that his cell mate was making sexual advances to him. After investigating the claims, the BTs solved this problem by beating the sexually aggressive inmate and, with staff approval, moving him to another block. In another cell block, an inmate told the head BT that his cell partner was scaring him by turning off the cell's light bulb. The BT struck the pranking inmate on the head with a pipe and threatened to have him moved to another block. The prankster "got his message."

Inmates were not always straightforward and sometimes informed for revenge. For example, some inmates informed on those they desired to see the BTs punish and/or move to another cell block. Some inmates "planted" contraband in their enemies' cell and then "tipped off" the BTs. Some inmates gave the BTs false information about other inmates, a variety of snitching called "dropping salt" or "crossing out." However, revenge-informing was restricted because the BTs were especially aware of this maneuver—and severely punished the disclosed instigator. Those who gave spurious information of any kind (or who deceived the BTs in any way) played a dangerous game. If discovered, they were beaten. The BTs (like the guards) weighed and checked the informer's information, considered his motive, and noted the relationship between him and the one informed upon before taking action.

Some ordinary inmates reported illegalities to the BTs in return for favors and to get on their good sides. For example, when an inmate told the BTs about someone who was fashioning a weapon, he expected something in return. Favors assumed many forms such as selection as a runner or maybe even a job recommendation. BTs often recommended "helpful" inmates to the staff for jobs in the garment factory, shops, laundry, or showrooms—and these allies served as additional snitches.

A number of ordinary inmates "ratted" on other inmates as a sort of game playing device. They planned a scenario, informed, and then sat back and enjoyed the action and reaction. Several inmates told me that this kind of game playing relieved their boredom at others' expense. The BTs received most of their information from regular legitimate snitches. However, in some cases when the regular channels did not suffice, they resorted to threats and the terrorization of ordinary inmates to gather information.

BTs, like guards, could not be everywhere at once and therefore relied on stool pigeons. For example, BTs could not observe homosexuality in the cells, but their snitches could. Bob, a head BT, sums up the situation: "The tanks are run through an information system. Whether this information comes from runners or even other inmates, this is how trouble is kept down." The BTs' snitching system was officially recognized as part of the prisoner control system whereas their snitches' behavior was informal, though expected.

Information Gathered Outside the Block

Runners and ordinary inmates worked throughout the prison and routinely informed the BTs about activities in the work areas, school, hospital, laundry, dining rooms, and showerrooms. Gary, a head BT, described this activity:

> We [BTs] all have our people, but we don't fuck with each other's people. If you walk down the Hall and hear somebody say "he's one of mine" that means that that particular inmate owes some type of allegiance to a particular BT. The reason he owes that allegiance or loyalty is perhaps he [a BT] got him a job someplace, got him out of the field and into the Garment Factory. These people are loyal to me. I put them there not for me but for the Man [the warden] and they tell me what's going on in that particular place. If you don't help me then I'll bust you. I got Bruce the job in the Issue Room [clothing and supply room]. I own Bruce because I got him that job. He tells me if clothing is being stolen or if inmates are trying to get more than they deserve.

Misbehavior, plots, and plans were not confined solely to the living areas and the BTs had extended "ears" in all areas where inmates interacted. Consequently, they kept abreast of developments everywhere and relatively little happened without their knowledge.

Turnkeys were not isolated from this spy network because they too had snitches. The turnkeys worked in the prison corridor and therefore gathered much information about illegal behavior outside the cell blocks. They acquired information about weapons, drugs, or other contraband being passed in the Hall, a vital area in the prison because large numbers of inmates were in constant movement there from one point to another. The turnkeys had to keep a constant vigil in the Hall to keep out unauthorized inmates and to maintain order in a very fluid and potentially explosive situation. The Hall was divided into the north and south ends and inmates who lived on the north end were forbidden to walk to the south end and vice versa. No inmates were permitted in the Hall who were not enroute to an official designation. Turnkeys generally knew in which end of the building inmates lived and vigorously watched for "trespassers." Holding down the illegal inmate Hall traffic suppressed contraband peddling as well as general disorder.

Efficiency of the System

At first glance, this snitching system appears cumbersome and inadequate because (apparently) BTs' and Turnkeys' snitches could end up snitching on one another and the guards, creating an amorphous situation without accuracy, consistency, or legitimacy. However, the system worked effectively because the BTs and turnkeys, for the most part, knew "whose snitch was whose." Loyalty to key individuals and reciprocity were the key conditions underpinning the snitch system. BTs and turnkeys interacted amongst themselves and generally knew whose "people" were working where, and their grapevine facilitated the necessary communication. Some snitches were "shared" or owed allegiance to several BTs (or turnkeys). The snitches did not owe their allegiance to the guards or to the BTs as a group, but rather to a particular BT or the BTs who ran their cell block or who were in close supervisory contact with them. When a BT's snitch was "busted," he was expected to intervene with the staff to help his snitch get off or obtain light punishment. The snitches were not completely immune from the rules, but they had an edge over other inmates in circumventing certain rules and in receiving lighter punishments when caught in rule breaking.

Types of Information

The major organizational role of the BTs and turnkeys was to gather information on ordinary inmates' behavior, but they did not report every rule violation and violator. They screened all information and passed to the staff only intelligence about actual or potentially serious rule infractions. As Jerry, a head BT, says:

> Look, we don't tell the Man [Warden] about everything that goes on in the tanks. That makes it look bad if I'm running down to the Major's office[6] and telling somebody, old so and so, he's playing his radio too loud, or so and so, he's got an antenna that goes from his cell up to the window. That shows the Man up there that I don't have

control of that tank and I can't let that happen. That makes me look bad.

The BTs handled "misdemeanors" or petty rule violations themselves in the blocks. The BTs and turnkeys regularly informed the staff about five types of serious rule violations, commonly called "Major's Office Business."

"Major's Office Business"

First and foremost, the Bts and turnkeys were constantly on guard to detect escape plans because TDC considered escape the most serious of all violations. For example, one night when the first author was on duty, a cell block officer found several saw marks on the bars of a cell's air vent which provided access to the cell house plumbing area and ceiling fans. Should an inmate stop the fan, he could conceivably climb to the roof and perhaps escape. When a shift supervisor arrived to examine the marks, the block's Bts were assembled and asked about the situation. They knew of no hacksaw blades in the block and doubted that the two suspected inmates were the types to be preparing for an escape. They suggested that the cell's previous occupants were the most likely culprits. In any event, the BTs assisted several officers (including the researcher) in searching the inmates' belongings for escape tools. Nothing was found and everyone was allowed to go back to bed.

Second, BTs informed the staff about ordinary inmates' homosexual behavior. The staff considered this behavior serious because it frequently led to envy, fights, lover's quarrels, retaliation, stabbings, as well as to the buying and selling of "punks." Homosexuality also went against the legal and moral rules of the prison system. The guards, a moralistic conservative group, despised homosexuality and punished it severely, officially or otherwise. BTs were very adept at discovering this form of illicit behavior. For example, one night while I was on the third shift (9:45 to 5:45 a.m.), the head BT on 13-block informed a captain that one well-known homosexual (or "bitch") had entered the wrong cell on the second tier. I accompanied the shift supervisor and head BT as they slowly crept along the walkway and caught the inmates "in the act." Both were charged and punished. The BTs made sure the inmates entered their own cells and not someone else's, thus also keeping stealing to a minimum.

Third, the inmate-agents told the staff about inmates who strong-armed weaker-inmates into paying protection, engaging in homosexual acts, or surrendering their property. Extortion or strong-arming was considered serious because of the potential for violence and the prison's legal obligation to protect inmates from exploitation and physical harm. In most cases, these problems were handled informally within the blocks (i.e., a warning). If the behavior persisted, the offending inmate was generally beaten up ("tuned up") and reported to the staff. Staff members usually gave the erring inmate a few slaps across the face or kicks in the buttocks and transferred him to another cell block.

Fourth, BTs and turnkeys informed the staff about drug trafficking. The introduction of drugs into the population was extremely difficult but occasionally small quantities were smuggled inside. Again, the inmate-agents kept this activity to a minimum and assisted the staff in making "drug busts." For example, one head BT and a turnkey briefed the staff about an inmate who worked outside the prison compound (farm operation) and who was supplying marijuana cigarettes to a certain block. Plans were devised to catch the inmate with his supplies. As he came in from work the next day, another guard and the investigator detained and searched him. Although no marijuana was found, it was later reported to us that the "dealer" quit trafficking because he knew he was being watched.

The BTs and turnkeys also told ranking staff members about guards who brought in drugs. In fact, one head BT was notorious for convincing (or entrapping) officers, especially new recruits, to smuggle narcotics into the institution. If the officer agreed, and some did, the staff was informed, and plans were made to catch the unsuspecting officer. Officers caught bringing in drugs (or any other contraband such as pornography) to the inmates were immediately dismissed. The BTs in one block even assisted the staff in apprehending an officer who was homosexually involved with an inmate. This officer was promptly terminated.

Last, the BTs and turnkeys informed staff members about inmates who manufactured, possessed, or sold weapons, especially knives. Inmates with weapons obviously placed the officers and their inmate-agents in physical jeopardy. One day, John, the head BT on 18-block, came to the Major's Office and told the captain about a knife in the eighth cell on the first row of "his" block. Two officers, two BTs, and the researcher searched the cell and found a knife wedged in between the first bunk and the cell wall. The owner of the weapon received a disciplinary hearing, spent fifteen days in solitary confinement, and was then moved to another cell block. It was common for the BTs to help the guards search suspected inmates' cells because they knew the tricks and places that inmates used to conceal weapons. Many officers learned how to search cells from the BTs. On another occasion a turnkey told the first author that an inmate, who had just exited a dining hall, was carrying a knife in his ankle cast. The cast was searched and a small homemade knife was found. The turnkey later revealed to the investigator that one of his snitches spotted the inmate putting the "shank" in his cast just prior to leaving the block for the dining hall.

Routing of Information

The actual passage of information did not always follow a formal chain of command. Though runners and ordinary inmates "reported" directly to the BTs and turnkeys, these latter inmates relayed information only to those ranking officers (sergeants, lieutenants, captains, majors, wardens) with whom they had developed a personal relationship. Some guards were trusted by few if any inmate-snitches and were essentially left out of the informer process. Others who had displayed sufficient consistency and common sense in handling sensitive information were trusted, respected, and admired by the inmate elites. Inmate-agents actively sought alliances with these officers. Indeed, only a "man" could be trusted with confidential information. Such officers were briefed each day about events on and off their work shifts. Some of these inmate-agents were so loyal to a particular staff member that they refused to "deal" with other officers in that particular staff member's absence.

Staff members who had a cadre of inmate-agents "working" for them were in a better position to anticipate and control problems in the prison. Somewhat ironically, therefore, inmates were in a position to confer status on officers and even to affect indirectly their promotions. Some officers often gave their favorite BT or turnkey special jobs generally performed only by staff members. These jobs included stake outs, shadowing, or entrapping a suspected inmate or officer to gather evidence about rule violations or plans of wrongdoing. These special assignments brought the staff member and inmate together in an even tighter, symbiotic relationship, leading sometimes to mutual trust and friendship. Some of these snitches were so fanatical in their loyalty that they openly stated they would kill another inmate if so ordered by "their" officer.

An Open System of Informing

Unlike "rats" in prison movies, BTs and turnkeys did not hide the fact that they were snitches. It was not uncommon to see some of these inmate-agents point out the misdeeds of another inmate to a guard in the presence of other inmates. It was quite common to see Bts and turnkeys "escort" their officer "friends" as companions and bodyguards while these guards were making their rounds. While accompanying "his" officer, the inmate-agent openly informed the staff member about what was "going on" in a particular cell block or work area. The "betrayer-betrayed" relationship was not hidden and when the guards searched an inmate's cell or body, the suspected inmate knew full well in most cases who had "tipped off" the staff. One could argue that the BTs and turnkeys were not "rats" because they officially, voluntarily, and openly worked for the staff. Following this reasoning, the only "real" snitches were the BTs' and turnkeys' informers who were ordinary inmates. These inmates were mildly stigmatized by other inmates, but rarely punished because all inmates feared the BTs' presence and wrath.

Although informing occurred throughout the prison, the Major's Office was the official focal point of such activity. This office, located directly off the main corridor, was the place BTs-turnkeys conducted their "business;" that is, turned in intelligence reports and discussed plans of action. This site was divided into two rooms; the front part (off the Hall) housed the inmate bookkeepers and the back room contained two desks for the major and captains. Disciplinary court was convened in the back room where such punishments as slapping, punching, kicking, stomping, and blackjacking were administered.

The staff and their "inmate-guards" socialized here as well as conducted the daily "convict business." Throughout the day, BTs and turnkeys came in to visit their bookkeeper friends and mingle with the ranking guards. Together, in this office area, the guards and their inmate-agents drank coffee, smoked, discussed the point spreads for sporting events, joked, chatted, engineered practical jokes, roughhoused, and ate food from the prison canteen. Whenever a captain, major, or warden entered, these inmates (sometimes there were eight or nine) would, if sitting, stand and say "hello sir." However, all was not fun and games. These inmates also kept the staff abreast of what was "going on," especially in terms of Major's Office business. All day, a steady stream of these inmate-agents filed in and out. BTs and turnkeys entered this office at will. However, the Major's Office was off-limits to the ordinary inmates except for official reasons. It was a status symbol for the "rats" to hang around this office and interact with the guards.

The Informer's Payoff

Skolnick (1966: 124), in his account of police informants, maintains that "the informer-informed relationship is a matter of exchange in which each party seeks to gain something from the other in return for certain desired commodities." Similarly, BTs and turnkeys expected to receive rewards for the information they proferred beyond a sense of accomplishment for a job well done.

In addition to status and influence, BTs and turnkeys also enjoyed a number of privileges which flowed from and defined their position. Some of these privileges appear relatively minor, yet they loomed large in a prison setting. The privileges included such scarce resources as specially pressed clothes and green quilted jackets. Ordinary inmates, meanwhile, wore white, ill-fitting coats. Some BTs possessed aquariums and such pets as cats, owls, rabbits, and turtles. BT cell block doors were rarely closed, permitting BTs to move freely about the block and to receive "visits" in their cells from friends and homosexuals. The latter were not threatened or forced to engage in sexual behavior; they voluntarily moved in to share the benefits. Head BTs roamed the halls and spent considerable time in and around the Major's Office.

Furthermore, BTs were able to eat whenever they desired and often ate two or three times in one meal period. Part of this special freedom stemmed from the fact that BTs and turnkeys were on call 24 hours a day. Nonetheless it was viewed by them and others as a special privilege. These inmate-agents were permitted to carry weapons with which to protect themselves and the guard force. These weapons, usually kept concealed, included wooden clubs, knives, pipes, blackjacks, "fistloads," and hammers. A special privilege was relative immunity from discipline. For example, if a fight occurred between a BT (or turnkey) and another inmate, the non-BT might receive several nights in solitary or ten days in cell restriction; the BT might receive a reprimand or, more likely, no punishment at all. This differential treatment reflected the understanding that the BT was probably "taking care of business." The BTs also used their influence to persuade the staff to "go lightly" on their runners who faced disciplinary cases for "helping the Man." In short, the BTs and turnkeys did "soft" time. Because of their position and privileges, the BTs-turnkeys were hated, but also feared, envied and respected by the other prisoners.

On an interpersonal level, many of the BT-turnkey-officer relationships transcended a simple quid pro quo of exchange of favors for instrumental purposes. That is, upper level staff members called their favorite BTs and turnkeys by their first names. Sometimes, they even took the word of a head BT over that of a cell block officer. In this way, the status differential between the staff members and their inmate-agents was decreased. As one supervisor put it:

> Look, these guys [BTs-turnkeys] are going to be here a while and they get to know the cons better than us. I can't depend on some of these officers, you know how they are, they're late, they're lazy, they want extra days off, or just don't show up. Hell, you've got to rely on them [BTs and turnkeys].

This preferential treatment of a subset of inmates caused frustration and low morale among many low ranking officers, contributing to a high turnover rate among the guard staff, especially weak guards.[7]

Inmates, Information, and Social Control

The prison staff's primary duty is to maintain social order and prevent escapes. Although Johnson's barb-wire fences, lights, alarm system, perimeter patrol car, and rural isolation reduced the possibility of escapes and mass disorder, routine control and order were achieved proactively by penetrating and dividng the inmate population. Walls, fences, and alarms were the last line of defense as well as symbolic forms of social control. Moreover, the staff's guns, tear gas, and riot gear were also an end of the line means of control and were infrequently utilized. The prison guards, like police officers, rarely employed weapons to achieve order.

The day-to-day maintenance of order at Johnson depended on the co-optation of inmate elites, a snitching system, and the terrorization of the ordinary inmates. The constant surveillance and terrorization of ordinary inmates prevented them from acquiring the solidarity necessary for self-protection and the cohesion needed for organized resistance. Although the ordinary inmates were atomized, they lived in a regimented and predictable environment. The staff's power, authority, and presence permeated the institution.

The role and identify of the inmate-agents was not hidden and they did not suffer from role strain or spoiled identities. Even though the ordinary inmates surreptitiously called the BTs-turnkeys "dogs" among themselves, they avoided physical confrontations with the "dogs" at all costs. They lacked the influence, prestige, power and organization necessary to stigmatize the BTs'-turnkeys' status or define their roles as deviant (see Lofland, 1969). To compound deviancy, one must be caught committing an inappropriate act, and snitching by the BTs and turnkeys was not considered inappropriate (see Matza, 1969: 148-9). At Johnson, informing was a means to enhance one's status and well-being. The inmate-agents were pro-staff and openly sided with and protected the guards. As one building tender stated: "I'm proud to work for the Man [Warden] because I know who butters my bread." They rationalized away their snitching behavior by denigrating and dehumanizing the ordinary inmates, referring to them as "scum" and "born losers." Ordinary inmate-snitches were looked down upon but rarely punished.

The guard staff used this snitch system to penetrate the inmate population and thereby act proactively to reduce the likelihood of such breaches of prison security as escapes, murders, rapes, narcotic rings, mob violence, loansharking, protection rackets, excessive stealing, and racial disruption. The officers, protected by the elites, were rarely derogated or attacked and never taken hostage or murdered. The staff was rarely caught off guard. This totalitarian system virtually destroyed any chances among the ordinary inmates (as individuals or groups) to unite or engage in collective dissent, protests, or violence. Those ordinary inmates who were docile and went along with the system were generally protected and left alone. This proactive system was so successful that only two inmate murders and one riot occurred from 1972 through 1982.

The aggressive use of co-opted snitches was not, however, without problems. Ordinary inmates under this system were non-persons who lived in continuous fear, loneliness, isolation, and tension. They never knew when they might be searched or, for that matter, disciplined on the basis of another inmate's accusation. BTs and turnkeys were not above occasionally falsely accusing "insubordinate" inmates of wrongdoing. The staff routinely backed up their allies. Some "unruly" inmates were "set up" by the BTs (e.g., having a knife thrown in their cell while they were at work) and then reported to the staff. Every ordinary inmate was suspect and even lower ranking guards were sometimes terminated solely on the word of a head BT. Furthermore, a federal judge, as part of the class action civil suit *Ruiz v. Estelle (1980)*, stated that this form of prisoner control at TDS was corrupt and deviant in terms of progressive penology. The snitch system at Johnson is now defunct and the staff no longer uses BTs and turnkeys (see Marquart, 1984).

Conclusion

This paper examined the structure and workings of an informer-privilege system within a penitentiary for older recidivists. At Johnson, the official informers, called BTs and turnkeys, worked for and openly cooperated with the staff. These snitches, the most aggressive, older, and criminally sophisticated prisoners, were not deviants or outcasts. In turn, they cultivated additional snitches and, with the staff's help, placed these allies in jobs or positions throughout the institution. Ordinary inmate behavior as well as that of lower ranking guards was under constant scrutiny. Therefore, the staff knew almost everything that occurred within the institution, permitting proactive control and thereby preventing in many instances, violent acts, group disturbances, and escapes.

The ordinary inmates considered the inmate-guards "rats." However, they lacked the influence, prestige, and power to define and label them as such—to impute deviancy to the BT-turnkey role. Selection as a BT or turnkey was not assignment to a deviant category, but rather to an elite corp of pro-staff inmates. Within this system, the only deviants were the unruly ordinary inmates and weak lower ranking guards. Both of these groups were stigmatized and labelled deviant by the staff and their inmate-agents within the prison. From the standpoint of progressive penologists and reform-minded citizens, this entire system would be considered deviant, inhumane, and morally corrupt. Although the system described in this paper may be unusual, it remains to be seen if and how other prison staffs co-opt elite inmates to help maintain social order. Past prison research has demonstrated some informal alliances between prison staffs and inmate elites. However, the form of this alliance may vary widely from prison to prison.

Notes

[1]Perhaps the epitome of the hatred of "rats" was in the movie "Stalag 17" (1952) wherein William Holden was falsely accused of being a "plant" in a German POW camp during World War II.

[2]The use of informants in police work, especially in vice and narcotic operations has been well-documented (see Greeno, 1960; Skolnick, 1966; Westley, 1970).

[3]Johnson is a pseudonym.

[4]For a more thorough analysis of the BT/turnkey system see Marquart (1983).

[5]The exact format or guidelines used by the Classification Committee is not known. However, this committee was composed primarily of security personnel and these members probably exerted the greatest voice in the selection process.

[6]The Major's Office is simply an office area where the ranking guards (sergeants, lieutenants, captains, majors and wardens) conducted disciplinary hearings and other forms of prison "business."

[7]Weak guards were easily bullied by the inmates, could not or would not enforce order, failed to break up fights, failed to fight inmates, and were basically ignored and laughed at by the other guards and inmates.

References

Bettelheim, B.
　　1943　　"Individual and mass behavior in extreme situations." Journal of
　　　　　　Abnormal and Social Psychology.
Charriere, H.
　　1970　　Papillon. New York: Basic Books.
Clemmer, D.C.
　　1940　　The Prison Community. New York: Holt, Rinehart and Winston.
Greeno, E.
　　1960　　War on the Underworld. London: John Long.

Johnson, E.H.
1961   "Sociology of Confinement: Assimilation and the prison 'rat.'"
         The Journal of Criminal Law Criminology, and Police Science. 51:
         528-533.
Lofland, J.
1969   Deviance and Identity. Englewood Cliffs, NJ: Prentice Hall.
Marquart, J.W.
1984   The Impact of Court-Ordered Reform in a Texas Penitentiary: The
         Unanticipated Consequences of Legal Intervention. Paper pre-
         sented at the Southern Sociological Society Annual meetings in
         Knoxville (April).
Marquart, J.W. and B.M. Crouch
1983   Coopting the Kept: Using Inmates for Social Control in a Southern
         Prison. Paper presented before the American Society of Crimin-
         ologists Annual meetings in Toronto.
Matza, D.
1969   Becoming Deviant. Englewood Cliffs, NJ: Prentice Hall.
McCleery, R.
1960   "Communication patterns as bases of systems of authority." in
         Theoretical Studies in Social Organizations of the Prison. New
         York: Social Science Research Council.
Ruiz v. Estelle, 503 F. Supp. 1265 (S.D. Texas) 1980.
Schrag, C.
1954   "Leadership among prison inmates," American Sociological
         Review. 19: 37-42.
Skolnick, J.H.
1966   Justice Without Trial: Law Enforcement in Democratic Society.
Solzhenitsyn, A.I.
1975   The Gulag Archipelago II. New York: Harper and Row.
Sykes, G.
1958   The Society of Captives. Princeton, N.J.: Princeton University Press.
Westley, W.
1970   Violence and the Police. Cambridge, MA: MIT Press.
Wilmer, H.A.
1965   "The role of a 'rat' in prison." Federal Probation 29 (March): 44-49.

11

Doing Research in Prison
The Strengths and Weaknesses of Full Participation as a Guard

James W. Marquart

The dominant mode of prison guard research is survey methodology, and in the past decade guards have been polled on such numerous topics as role stress (Poole and Regoli 1980), turnover (Jacobs and Grear 1977), role conflict (Hepburn and Albonetti 1980), occupational socialization (Crouch and Alpert 1982), and race relations and the guard culture (Jacobs and Kraft 1978). These inquiries have contributed greatly to the literature on guards and their role within prison organizations. Questionnaire data, however, are collected from a "distance" and fail to penetrate the inner or backstage prison behavioral settings. On the other hand, some investigators (e.g., Sykes 1958; Carroll 1974; Jacobs and Retsky 1975) have collected qualitative data on guards, but they entered the setting in the typical observer role as nonparticipants or "outsiders-as-researchers." These prison methodologies offer only a restricted or limited view of guards and their organizational role. Specifically prison researchers, unlike those who have become police officers to study police work (see Van Maanen 1973), have avoided full participation as a means to study guards and prisons.

Source: *Justice Quarterly*, Vol. 3 No. 1, March 1986. © Academy of Criminal Justice Sciences

In the spring of 1981, I became a prison guard to examine the official and unofficial methods of prisoner control and discipline in a large maximum security penitentiary within the Texas prison system. I worked as a researcher-guard for nineteen months (June 1981 through January 1983) and collected ethnographic materials while working, participating, and observing in a variety of locations and activities (e.g., cell blocks, dormitories, visitation areas, recreation periods, dining halls, shower rooms, solitary confinement, disciplinary hearings, and hospital). I eventually obtained unlimited access to the unwritten and more sensitive aspects of guard work, ·prisoner control, and the guard culture.

The activities of entering the prison, negotiating a research role, establishing field relations, studying social control and order, and exiting the field were not the clear and orderly processes so often described in ethnographic reports. Instead, immersion in the prison scene placed some unusual demands on me as an observer (and person) not generally experienced by other more "traditional" qualitative researchers (see also Styles 1979; Van Maanen 1982). Complete participation is a viable research role, yet there are some pitfalls. This article addresses the strengths, weaknesses, and ethical implications of the researcher-guard role and full participation as a prison methodology.

Becoming an Outside-Insider

My first experience with Texas prisons was in the summer of 1979 when I participated in a project evaluating guard training, supervision, and turnover throughout the Texas prison system. During the research, I met a warden who in turn made arrangements for me to visit the Eastham Unit*—a maximum security facility housing 3200 prisoners over the age of twenty-five who had been incarcerated more than three times. My first visit was spent touring the institution with the warden, meeting various ranking guards, observing disciplinary court, and driving around the prison's 14,000-acre agricultural operation. The warden informed me at the end of the tour that I was welcome to visit Eastham.

For the next year and a half I went to Eastham almost every other month, with each trip lasting five to eight hours. I had complete freedom to walk unescorted throughout the compound and converse with guards at work and with inmates while they ate, worked, spent recreation time in the gym, or lounged in their cells. I often followed an officer for several hours to observe his work routine. During these trips, I met several "old time" convicts who described in detail the rich folklore surrounding

*All names in this article are pseudonyms.

Texas prisons. Moreover, each time I visited Eastham, my guard and inmate contacts pressed me to work as a guard to see the "real" penitentiary. I avoided their suggestions, explaining that I wanted to remain impartial, free to roam the prison. Actually, my real reason was outright fear of the prisoners. Yet I knew they were correct and after assessing my research goals, I realized full participation would foster the necessary inside perspective to examine prisoner control. In April 1981, the warden arranged for me to begin work in June 1981.

I entered Eastham without a clearly-defined role (cf., Jacobs 1977). Although the warden, a few guards, and several inmates knew I was a graduate student in sociology, they did not know the exact details of my research plans. The Texas prison system was at this time embroiled in the bitterly contested prison reform case of *Ruiz v. Estelle* (1980).[1] This suit alleged, among other things, that guard brutality was rampant and that the building tender system (using dominant/aggressive inmates to control other inmates) was abusive. Eastham was a target unit in the case. One of my research goals was to observe and analyze the building tender system (see Marquart and Crouch 1984).[2] I felt, however, that if I revealed my aims to the security staff they would not allow me to work as a guard or even conduct research. Therefore, I kept the specifics of the project vague and told the warden of my interest in guards, guard work, and the ways in which various court orders have affected the staff's ability to maintain control and order. Moreover, my presence as a researcher-guard was not officially announced to the prison community. I had no official letter from the director of the prison system or the warden identifying me as a researcher. I was to be treated as any other employee, which was reflected in my first shift assignment—the third shift (9:45 P.M.–5:45 A.M.).

I never at any time misrepresented my identity. I "passed" as a sociology doctoral student who was tired of the books and sought real prison experience. If asked about my personal or educational background, I gave true information in order to prevent suspicion and rumor. But this strategy was not enough of an explanation and precipitated several rumors. The prison grapevine had it that I was an F.B.I. agent or an official from the Department of Justice "placed" at Eastham to investigate and report on prison operations. Some inmates thought I was a writer and followed me for hours detailing their life of crime and violence, hoping I would write their life histories. I was also tagged as Mr. Estelle's (then, the director of the prison system) son, a rumor that lasted throughout the research. I also foolishly contributed to these rumors when I was seen photographing the prison compound. Like most prison field observers (Giallombardo 1966; Carroll 1974; Jacobs 1974), I had to prove constantly that I was not a spy or government agent.

I relied on two contacts, both of whom eventually became trusted informants and friends, to facilitate my acceptance and quell rumors. One was PP, a high ranking guard and Ph.D. student at a nearby university. We had met during an earlier visit and shared our research interests. He was well-respected by the guards and prisoners and introduced me to the two most politically powerful inmates at Eastham. I told them of my background and interest in Texas prisons. They agreed to be interviewed only because they said "PP told us to." In addition, I met MM, an older, politically powerful prisoner who introduced me to other important prisoners. These latter contacts in turn introduced me to others and soon I developed (through snowball sampling) an extensive network of inmate informants. As for the guards, I befriended several workmates who became allies and informants. PP's and MM's assistance enhanced my status tremendously; however, their endorsement did not ensure immediate acceptance or totally eliminate doubt about "what I was really up to." Many guards and inmates respected my willingness to work as a guard, but they did not regard me as reputable. In their eyes, I was an untested novice who had to earn their favor before being accepted, respected, and able to collect data.

Character Development and Data Collection

Maximum security prisons are rife with fear, conflict, paranoia, racial animosities, and intense factionalism. Building rapport and establishing trust in the context of a research role is difficult and time-consuming. Prison researchers are on center stage and their behavior is constantly scrutinized by officers and inmates who look for clues (or cues) that reveal the observer's character and intentions. I followed a careful strategy in establishing field relations.

Three Factors Leading to Acceptance

First, I kept a low profile and concentrated on working hard to establish a reputation as a reliable employee. In this institution, following orders without hesitation was an important value within the guard subculture. I accepted without complaint difficult and boring work assignments, broke up inmate fights, and wrote disciplinary reports on several inmates. My eagerness so impressed my supervisors that I was promoted to Hall "Boss" (inmates referred to the guards as "boss" or "bossman"). Hall bosses were regarded by the guards and prisoners alike as the cream of the non-ranking officers. Obtaining one of these positions was also viewed as a promotion by the officers, his peers, supervisors, and prisoners. Moreover, all line staff sought to become one of these officers because they were free from cell block duty and worked closely with ranking guards which aided in rank-obtaining promotions. Among the three shifts, there were around 25 hall officers, the majority of whom were white. With this advancement, I became quickly and deeply involved in the guard world and I was an ally of the building tenders, who taught me the official and unofficial means of prisoner control.

Second, I began weightlifting and boxing in the prison gym with several prisoners. One inmate, WW, was my "teacher" and we worked out daily, played basketball, jogged, as well as trained on the "heavy bag." Others loaned me their body-building magazines and books, and gave assorted advice on how to weight train. These inmates were weightlifting experts and I used their suggestions. I soon won their trust because I listened and never questioned their knowledge, but instead let them tell me what to do—a reversal of their normally subordinate status. By deferring to them, I demonstrated my acceptance of their expertise and this fostered a bond that established a high degree of rapport. While we exercised, they described how the guards recruited snitches, used unofficial force to punish and control inmates, and told me which officers were respected and why. Moreover, weightlifting and boxing (especially in prison) were prized masculine activities and my eagerness to learn enhanced my status among the prisoners. In fact, many prisoners based their respect for other inmates and officers on their ability to exhibit superior strength (mental and physical) or compulsive masculinity (see Toby 1966).

The third and most important factor which established my credibility and earned the guards' and prisoners' respect was an occurrence on December 15, 1981. This event and my subsequent behavior solidified my reputation as a "good" officer (i.e., not afraid of the inmates, firm but fair) and a "true" insider. At approximately 11:25 P.M., another hall officer and I went to 1-block (a solitary confinement area) to help several other hall officers search inmate Friar's property which was in a large canvas sack. He had been placed in solitary confinement earlier that day for assaulting an officer. Friar, who weighed nearly 300 pounds, stood in the Hall (central corridor in the prison) waiting for us to inventory his property. I ordered him to take his property out of the sack. He remained motionless. I then said, "unsack it." He lifted the bag and spilled the contents on the floor, threw the sack in the air, and then punched me in the forehead nearly knocking me unconscious. I was forced to defend myself. With the help of two other hall officers, Friar was finally subdued and quartered in solitary confinement. I required medical attention for a large knot on my forehead.

Early the next morning, I was standing near the Commissary (prison store) when Supervisor L approached me and said:

L: "Hey, there's the raging bull. Tell us what happened. What happened?"

I then retold the story to his delight. The following morning another ranking guard pointed at me and yelled "Hey, there's Bruiser." Then he came over and started shadow boxing with me. That evening two second shift hall officers, who had previously avoided me, also asked me about the incident. After finishing the story, these officers stated they would help me with anything they could.

The fact that I had been assaulted and had defended myself in front of several officers and building tenders raised my esteem and established my reputation. The willingness to fight inmates was an important trait rewarded by the ranking guards (see Marquart and Roebuck 1984). Due to this "fortunate" event, I earned the necessary credibility to establish rapport with the prison participants and allay their previous suspicions of me. I passed the ultimate test—fighting an inmate even though in self-defense—and was now a trustworthy member of the guard subculture. I had character, or the "balls" or "nuts," to stand up for and defend myself. The significance of this fight is underscored in the following conversation, which occurred months later with LC, a politically powerful black prisoner:

LC: "Well, I didn't trust you until that deal you had down there on 1-block with Friar. I heard you got hit and defended yourself and took care of business. After that I was more willing to talk to you than before. I trust you now, otherwise, I wouldn't talk to you."

I entered Eastham as a guard to discover "how things really operated," but this was not a ticket to obtaining good data. As an outsider-insider, I had to prove myself through hard work and by standing up to the inmates. More important, I had to share and actually experience the traumas, risks, violence, and dangers of the prison environment. My presence and acceptance depended on how well I negotiated these daily realities. Although the Friar incident ultimately secured my acceptance, I continually had to demonstrate loyalty to the guards and building tenders. Few research roles are ever finalized (complete acceptance) and this situation heightens the fieldworker's awareness of the necessity to constantly guard against overconfidence in matters of acceptance (Lofland 1971). Consequently, when the situation rose, I broke up fights, hauled bleeding self-mutilators or attempted suicides to the prison hospital, and utilized legitimate force in subduing inmates (e.g., in dining halls, shower rooms, cells). I even wrestled with and took a knife away from an inmate who slashed open his own stomach out of despair.

Insider Status and Data Collection

Hard work, often involving "dirty work," and the willingness to use official force enabled me to recruit informants among the guards and inmates, particularly the building tenders. I quickly made friends with several officers, told them my research interests, and they willingly agreed to work as surrogate observers, describing events or incidents on the other shifts (see Scott 1965). I also interviewed officers in their homes, in bars, or on the job. From these interviews and countless conversations, data was obtained on, for example, morale, the staff's recruitment of snitches, and when and where the guards used unofficial force (beatings) to subdue, control, and terrorize "unruly" inmates. These home interviews were tape-recorded while those on the job were written down and reconstructed later.

From my inmate informants, I collected data on how the guards officially recruited and coopted the most dominant and aggressive inmates to become building tenders. Because of my guard role, I closely associated with these inmate elites and nearly a dozen were key informants. They showed me how they made liquor or "pruno," stole food from the prison kitchen, made knives, and sold tattoo patterns and machines. These latter activities were clearly illegal but I kept their trafficking confidential; this too demonstrated my trustworthiness. The ability to "keep one's mouth shut" was a highly prized asset and I quickly internalized this important value. I also made sure that all interviewees were told that their conversations were confidential and off the record. The gathering of information, however, was not one-sided and I reciprocated when and wherever possible (see Wax: 1971). I often helped inmates obtain job or cell changes, new uniforms or shoes, or hospital appointments. I also periodically bought my key inmate informants sodas, cigars, candy, or coffee. After exiting the field, I wrote letters of recommendation to the parole board for five prisoners, all of whom are now free citizens.

Building rapport and earning trust in the prison community was initially difficult but my actions eventually secured my acceptance. Like Jacobs (1974), once I was regarded as an insider, I had little trouble making the necessary contacts to obtain information. However, with my ability to establish trust came the problem of deep involvement in the guard subculture. I tried to balance my roles, to be both a sociologist studying prisoner control and a legitimate member of the prisoner control apparatus. The participative or outside-inside role is emotionally and physically taxing because the researcher, in any scene or setting, must in essence wear "two hats." One persistent problem, to be discussed below, was that the guard role often superseded my sociological interests.

Problems of the Participative Research Role

As a researcher-guard or outside-insider, I was able to collect data on activities concealed from most other prison researchers (e.g., beatings, verbal intimidation, the use of snitches). I was a member of good standing in the setting and I used this position to my advantage, especially in actually experiencing the daily feelings, mood shifts, and emotions of the prison participants. The participative research role was not problem-free and three major difficulties were encountered throughout the fieldwork.

Occupational Pressures

I spent my first three months working cell blocks and this assignment severely restricted my ability to make contacts or ask questions. In the fourth month, I was promoted to hall "boss," which afforded the needed mobility to traverse the prison compound. Yet at certain times of the day my work duties (e.g., counting, searching cells, monitoring inmate traffic to and from meals, showers, and work) tied me down for several hours. Prison is a structured world and the work role demanded that I do the same things each day at the same time. To manage this role conflict, I scheduled my "free" time to interview, gather records, and review ideas or data with informants. This does not mean that I did not collect data while actually working. On the contrary: I observed, interviewed, listened to, and conversed with inmates and guards wherever and whenever I could. But as a guard, it was necessary to be security conscious first and a researcher second—a problem inherent in the participative prison research role. This strain would also pose problems for investigators who become police officers or hospital orderlies—the official work role in these cases must supersede, when the situation arises, research interests.

I also collected data off-duty while exercising with several inmates in the prison gym. Once rapport was established, they eventually became key informants and I used these recreation periods to interview, reformulate ideas, or simply discuss our personal lives. I was extremely close to these inmates, who provided a rich data source. As for the officers, we sometimes spent after-hours playing football, swimming, target shooting, drinking beer and shooting pool, eating pizza, and relaxing. I listened to and participated in their conversations about guard work, fights they had with inmates (or other officers), their supervisors, other guards, troublesome inmates, or the Texas prison system. I made mental notes of their comments and reconstructed these conversations later. I even had several key officer informants tape record their thoughts about work, prisoner control, careers, or other prison-related subjects. Not only did these off-duty sessions provide data, but they enabled me to form lasting and meaningful friendships.

Clearly, the most difficult problem in being an outside-insider was role conflict. During the first few months on the "job," I had little difficulty remaining a uniformed sociologist. However, I slowly adopted the guard perspective due to my participation and deep involvement in the guard world. I laughed while guards teased and taunted inmate homosexuals, nodded approvingly when others described how they ripped apart an inmate's cell during a search, and kept a straight face when supervisors threatened to kill inmates. I also remained silent when observing guards and building tenders beat and physically injure inmates. Where and when possible, I defended the system and guards to naive outsiders. I explained to them that guards were the "good guys" and that prisons were necessary to isolate social predators. In many respects I was an apologist for the guards (see Manning 1972).

I was a guard forced to confront the enormous pressures of occupational socialization; this is the major drawback of full participation. I was expected to think, act, and talk like a guard. It was a personal battle to refrain from "going native," especially after the promotion to sergeant in November, 1982. Three factors helped me to adjust and maintain some role stability and distance. First, I left the prison on my designated days off. I worked seven days and then was off three days, which were spent debriefing in my dissertation advisor's office, with friends, and with other faculty members. Maintaining non-guard associations were critical in remaining objective. Second, I never insulted or fought inmates for fun. Many new guards displayed bravado ("John Wayne syndrome"), acting and talking tough to the inmates. I completely avoided this fronting behavior because I knew prison was too dangerous a place to act tough. Some guards paid the price both physically and mentally when an inmate called their bluff. Finally, I made extensive field notes about this role conflict and kept myself aware of how "deeply" I was moving into the guard subculture. In short, I was extremely sensitive to this problem and forced myself not to lose all objectivity.

Reactivity

The concept of reactivity specifies the proclivity of the research subjects to alter their behavior as a consequence of the researcher's presence (Vidich 1970). Because of his or her presence, a researcher does not observe the subjects' true behavior—a problem endemic to participant observation. Did the guards and prisoners alter their behavior in my presence? I entered Eastham with the full knowledge and approval of several high ranking prison officials. Even though I was known to some of the subjects beforehand, the majority had no idea who I was and treated me as another guard. However, some of the prison participants regarded me as a possible undercover agent investigating Eastham for the Department of Justice. Rumors were also spread about my "intentions" and several guards avoided me.

To negate these suspicions, I embarked on a strategy of earning the guards' trust to combat their false impressions of me and to minimize reactivity. I made it a point to work hard and share the emotional highs and lows of institutional life. In addition, it took nearly eight months of careful interaction, laying low, and "passing" various character tests to prove I was trustworthy. Most fieldworkers do not have this amount of time to invest in character development. After eight months, I was considered to be a "good" officer and this reputation facilitated data collection.

I also observed a great deal of backstage behavior. For example, I witnessed fifty incidents in which guards beat inmates (some were severely injured) and all of these guards were well aware of my identity as a researcher. Had ranking staff members been afraid or leery of my presence, they would have assigned me to isolated duty posts. Instead, they viewed me as a loyal member of the subculture. To them, I was an employee and they did not have time to alter their behavior in my presence when breaking up brawls, fighting inmates in cells, disciplining inmates, searching cells or inmates, rushing attempted suicides or self-mutilators to the prison hospital, or stopping knife fights among inmates. These behaviors were spontaneous and occurred in similar fashion with or without my presence. Other researchers have noted that once respondents have accepted you (in whatever role) they tend to act as if you were one of them or as if you were not on the scene (see Skolnick 1966).

The vast majority of the inmates considered me to be "just another guard." Some initially told me that they, like some guards, were hesitant to talk with me. The support of third parties allayed some of their apprehensions but my reputation as a fair officer won their confidence, enabling me to secure key informants. Most of my inmate allies were building tenders who occupied positions of power and status within the prisoner society. They candidly answered questions and trusted me because I expressed a true interest in their welfare. Most importantly, I kept everything they said strictly confidential.

Although I cultivated the friendship of a number of inmate elites, I had great difficulty interviewing the "run of the mill" inmates. My uniform was a barrier that limited access to these prisoners and I never completely resolved this problem. I was able to get close to only ten "ordinary" inmate informants who described, from their perspective, snitching, homosexuality, staff use of force, rules and regulations, and verbal threats from the guards. To obtain this information, I often interviewed them in their cells, shower rooms, or on their way to and from meals. The insider role "slotted" me in the prison social structure and almost completely curtailed any contact with Hispanic inmates (c.f., Davidson 1974). For cultural reasons and because of their minority status, these inmates generally stayed away from other inmates and avoided almost all contact (e.g., saying hello, talking about sports, asking questions about various rules) with the staff. For many Hispanic inmates, voluntary interaction with guards was viewed as "ratting" and something to be avoided. Therefore, my contacts with these and most other ordinary inmates were primarily official.

Coping with Violence

Maximum security prisons are conflict-ridden societies where violence or the threat of it is a daily reality. As an outside-insider, I saw, took part in, and was personally affected by the inescapable presence of violence. Full participation brought me face-to-face with actual fear and terror, emotions most field observers never encounter (c.f., Van Maanen 1982). It is difficult for me to describe how I felt when I saw officers punch, kick, and knock inmates senseless with riot clubs as they screamed and begged for mercy. On several occasions I assisted guards in restraining inmates while medics sutured their wounds without any anesthetic. These incidents were shocking experiences. I also observed building tenders throw inmates head first into the bars and "blackjack" others who failed to report for work, remained too long in the dining hall, or cheered for the Houston Oilers instead of the Dallas Cowboys. One brawl involving four building tenders and one inmate so unnerved me that I almost quit. This event was so disturbing that I could not even write about it until several weeks later.

I knew prisons were violent, but only through the writings and experiences of other people. I learned to cope with the ever-present violence and tension by accepting it as an element of this milieu. Violence in prison is banal and everyone must learn to cope with it or else retreat from the situation. For officers, retreat often resulted in quitting and for inmates, in isolation. My particular coping strategy was indifference, the route of most prison participants. If people got hurt, especially inmates, I maintained a cold detachment. However, inwardly I was hurt because human suffering appalled me. In the end, I coped and survived as well as I could (see Jacobs 1974).

Moral and Ethical Dilemmas of Full Participation

All fieldworkers run the risk, due to their presence, of obtaining "guilty knowledge" (see Van Maanen 1982). Because of my insider status, I was privy and party to discrediting information about the nature of guard work and prisoner control. I was firmly entrenched In the prison world—and this may raise some complaints from other researchers. There are ethical dilemmas surrounding this methodology which stem primarily from the observation of numerous violations, not only civil but legal as well. I observed the following incident but had a guard participant tape record his own description.

> I was sitting at the Searcher's desk and Rick (convict) and I were talking and here comes Joe (convict) from 8-block. Joe thinks he knows kung-fu, hell he got his ass beat about four months ago. He comes down the Hall and he had on a tank top, his pants were tied up with a shoe lace, gym shoes on, and he had all his property in a large sack. As he neared us, Rick said "Well, Joe's fixing to go crazy again today." He came up to us and Rick asked him what was going on and Joe said they (staff) were fucking with him by not letting him have a recreation card. I told him "Well take your stuff and go over there to the Major's office" and there he went. Officer A went over and stood in front of Joe, so did Officer B who was beside Joe, Officer C was in back of A, and two convicts stood next to Officer A. Inmate James, an inmate who we "tuned up" in the hospital several days before, stood about ten feet away. All of a sudden Joe took a swing at Officer A. A and B tackled Joe. I ran over there and grabbed Joe's left leg while a convict had his right leg and we began kicking his legs and genitals. Hell, I tried to break his leg. At the same time B was using his security keys, four large bronze keys, like a knife. The security keys have these points on their ends where they fit into the locks. Well, B was jamming these keys into Joe's head. Joe was bleeding all over the place. Then all of a sudden another brawl broke out right next to us. Inmate James threw a punch at Officer D as he came out of the Major's office to see what was going on. James saw Joe getting beat and he decided to help Joe out. I left Joe to help Officer D. By the time I got there (about two seconds), Officer D and about six convicts (building tenders) were beating the shit out of James. Officer D was beating James with a blackjack. Man, you could hear that crunch noise every time he hit him. At the same time a convict was hitting him in the stomach and chest and face. These other inmates were kicking him and stomping him at the same time. It was a wild melee, just like being in war. I got in there and grabbed James by the hair and Officer D began hitting him, no love taps. He was trying to beat his brains out and yelling "you mother fucker, you think you're bad, you ain't bad, you mother fucker, son of a bitch, you hit me and I'll bust your fucking skull." I think we

beat on him alone for ten minutes. I punched him In the face and head. Then Officer D yelled "take him (James) to the hospital." Plus we punched and stomped him at the same time. At the hospital, Officer D began punching James in the face. I held his head so D could hit him. Then D worked James over again with a blackjack. We then stripped James and threw him on a bed. D yelled at James "I'm going to kill you by the time you get off this unit." Then D began hitting him in the shins and genitals with a night stick. Finally we stopped and let the medics take over. James had to leave via the ambulance. Joe required some stitches and was subsequently put in solitary.

This brutal episode was frightening and certainly went beyond any departmental regulation concerning the proper use of force to subdue an inmate. No civil suits were ever filed against the officers and the incident was "closed." My field notes contain the identities of all the actors. Like Van Maanen (1982) in his police fieldwork, I witnessed many illegalities at Eastham but "did not see them." To block or neutralize the moral predicament of seeing "too much," I kept quiet and simply observed. In fact, I could not "tell all" because this would have violated the implicit research bargain assumed by the officials when I entered the situation—an agreement not to use information to injure the subjects. I could not stop the violence and perhaps no one ever will. During the project, the Texas prison system came under a sweeping court order (*Ruiz v. Estelle*) to end guard and building tender brutality. I was contacted by an attorney in the Special Master's Office, who knew of my background, to testify against the Texas Department of Corrections. I told the lawyer that I had nothing to say. I believed my materials were confidential and even envisioned going to jail for contempt of court. Fortunately, this never happened.

I rationalized the violence as being a part of prison life and as something a full participant would in all likelihood have to face. Complete involvement or immersion means just that, and like it or not the insider must sometimes come to grips with various difficult and trying situations (see Styles 1979). Direct observation is unpredictable and the researcher has little control over the strange and unusual events in the setting. There are no formal standards for doing this research and therein lies the problem of full participation. In some cases, getting too close to the data might force the observer to compromise his or her values and morals in order to remain a trusted member. In the end, ethics are purely situational and no research method is completely safe for the researcher and the subjects (Humphreys 1970).

A Reversal of Research Roles: Is It Possible?

I returned to Eastham in September 1984 under the sponsorship of the National Science Foundation[3] to collect data on the impact of the *Ruiz v. Estelle* decision on prisoner control, order maintenance, and violence, among other things. For nearly four months, I was granted complete access to the prison. Prior to my arrival, the warden circulated a document among the guard staff clearly identifying my research role. I also wrote several inmates to alert them of my arrival date and full research aims. In this research, I entered the prison in the traditional fieldwork role of outsider, not as an insider or prison guard. Further, I openly carried a tape-recorder, notepads, and sometimes a camera, symbols to legitimize my presence and research role within the institution.

Given this new set of circumstances, I was curious about how I would be treated by the prisoners and guards and how it would affect my ability to collect data. My first week was spent reestablishing ties and reminiscing with friends (guards and inmates) as well as further clarifying my role and research purposes. To my good fortune, many of my previous informants were still at the prison and all agreed to assist in the research. Their cooperation was primarily due to the reputation that I had established while working as a guard. This time I was able to develop contacts among the general inmate population, including Hispanic inmates. The majority of the prisoners knew of my previous official role and many asked whether or not I was a guard. I responded truthfully to all queries about my background and only one inmate (a prison gang chieftain) declined to be interviewed. In addition, I had countless inmates (and officers too) stop and ask me when they were going to be interviewed.

My previous research role as a guard in no way hampered the research process. More to the point, my involvement as a guard actually enhanced my position as a participant observer. My reputation as a fair and trustworthy officer was the critical factor in the relative ease in reaffirming contacts and rapport. I was not subjected to the character tests or loyalty checks that I had experienced as a researcher-guard. I had been a credible person in the past and this was sufficient proof for the subjects. In the new research, the participative research role proved to be an asset that paved the way for data collection. Researchers who favor full participation must develop good working relations with their subjects because, if future research is planned in any research role, the problems associated with access, rapport, and data collection will be greatly reduced.

Conclusions

The research process is filled with our own biases and preconceptions which influence the groups or settings that we study and how we study them (Styles 1979). The question "to participate or not?" presents the investigator with a profound moral decision. Indeed, there are strengths and weaknesses associated with both the outside and inside research roles. I am not arguing that one way is superior to another; this is a value judgment that depends on what one wants to study (Becker 1978). Both are important methodologies that should be carefully evaluated before entering the field. I chose to study the prison setting in the participative role. By studying prisoner control as a guard, I collected some unique data but observed much wrongdoing. Yet this is the necessary risk in full participative field research; I took this risk when I made the decision to become a guard. In a positive light, involvement enabled me to experience face-to-face the totality of prison life. In addition, the insider role promotes a firsthand view of the institution and whether or not policies are being complied with or circumvented. Prison reform and prisoner control have historically been intense political and social issues. For this reason, an insider's knowledge can be extremely useful to officials or administrators.

When a researcher decides to participate as a prison guard, several issues must be weighed beforehand. First, the participative role restricts access to some events and can lead to biased sampling. That is, the participant-researcher cannot continuously be on the scene. Further, the fact that he or she is "slotted" in an official role hinders the researcher's ability to make contacts with some prisoner groups. Second, full participation is extremely time consuming due to the special problems of building rapport and earning respect. I "had" to suffer a physical attack before I was regarded as "alright." Third, this methodology can create complex ethical issues for the researcher. The problem of personal commitments versus social issues can become overwhelming and affect the research process. Finally, full participation breeds questions about reactivity. The direct observer must document how and in what ways, if any, his or her presence affects the scene and validity of the data.

As in any form of research, there are a variety of costs and benefits. By studying prisons from the inside, we can learn how desperately we need new theories and techniques to understand these institutions adequately. If we can obtain this information, then we can provide informed input into new policies and procedures, thus making a genuine contribution to reform.

References

Abbott, J. H. (1981), *In the Belly of the Beast*. New York: Random House.

Becker, H. S. (1978), "Practitioners of Vice and Crime." In N. K. Denzin (ed.), *Sociological Methods: A Sourcebook*. New York: McGraw-Hill.

Bettelheim, B. (1943), "Individuals and Mass Behavior in Extreme Situations." *Journal of Abnormal and Social Psychology* 38:417–452.

Bulmer, M. (1982), "When Is Disguise Justified? Alternatives to Covert Participant Observation." *Qualitative Sociology* 4:251–264.

Carroll, L. (1974), *Hacks, Blacks and Cons: Race Relations in a Maximum Security Prison*. Lexington MA: Lexington Books. Reprint, Prospect Heights, IL: Waveland Press, 1988.

Charriere, H. (1970), *Papillion*. New York: Basic Books.

Clemmer, D. C. (1940), *The Prison Community*. New York: Holt, Rinehart and Winston.

Crouch, B. M. and G. Alpert (1982), "Sex and Occupational Socialization Among Prison Guards: A Longitudinal Study." *Criminal Justice & Behavior* 9(2):159–176.

Davidson, R. T. (1974), *Chicano Prisoners: Key to San Ouentin*. New York: Holt, Rinehart, and Winston.

Giallombardo, R. (1966), *Society of Women: A Study of Women's Prison*. New York: John Wiley.

Hepburn, J. R. and C. Albonetti (1980), "Role Conflict in Correctional Institutions." *Criminology* 17(4):445–459.

Humphreys, L. (1970), *Tearoom Trade*. Chicago: Aldine.

Irwin, J. (1970), *The Felon*. Englewood Cliffs, NJ: Prentice-Hall.

Jacobs, J. (1974), "Participant Observation in Prison." *Urban Life and Culture* 3(2):221–240.

———. (1977), *Stateville: The Penitentiary in Mass Society*. Chicago: University of Chicago Press.

Jacobs, J. and M. Grear (1977), "Dropouts and Rejects: An Analysis of the Prison Guard's Revolving Door." *Criminal Justice Review* 2(2):57–70.

Jacobs, J. and L. Kraft (1978), "Race Relations and the Guard Subculture." *Social Problems* 25(3):304–318.

Jacobs, J. and H. Retsky (1975), "Prison Guard." *Urban Life* 4(1):5–29.

Lofland, J. A. (1971), *Analyzing Social Settings*. Belmont, CA: Wadsworth.

Manning, P. K. (1972), "Observing the Police: Deviants, Respectables, and the Law." In J. Douglas (ed.). *Research on Deviance*. New York: Random House.

Marquart, J. W. and B. M. Crouch (1983), "Coopting the Kept: Using Inmates for Social Control in a Southern Prison." Paper presented at the American Society of Criminologists annual meetings, Toronto.

Marquart, J. W. and J. B. Roebuck (1984), "The Use of Physical Force by Prison Guards: Individuals, Situations, and Organizations." Paper to be presented at American Sociological Assoc. Meetings in San Antonio (August).

Poole, E. and R. Regoli (1980), "Role Stress, Custody Orientation and Disciplinary Actions." *Criminology* 18:215–227.

Roebuck, J. (1965), *Criminal Typology*. Springfield, IL: Charles C Thomas.

Ruiz v. Estelle, 503 F. Supp. 1265 (S.D. Texas) 1980.

Scott, W. R. (1965), "Field Methods in the Study of Organizations." In J. G. March (ed.), *Handbook of Organizations*. Chicago: Rand McNally Co.

Schutz, A. (1944), "The Stranger: An Essay In Social Psychology." *American Journal of Sociology* 49:499–507.

Simmel, G. (1908), *Sociology*. Leipzig: Dunker and Humblot.

Skolnick, J. H. (1966), *Justice Without Trial: Law Enforcement in Democratic Society*. New York: Macmillan.

Solzhenitsyn, A. L. (1973), *The Gulag Archipelago*. New York: Harper and Row.

_____ (1975), *The Gulag Archipelago II*. New York: Harper and Row.

Styles, J. (1979), "Outsider/Insider: Researching Gay Baths." *Urban Life* 8:135–152.

Sykes, G. (1958), *The Society of Captives*. Princeton: Princeton University Press.

Thomas, J. (1979), "Some Aspects of Negotiated Order, Loose Coupling and Mesostructure in Maximum Security Prisons." *Symbolic Interaction* 4:213–231.

Toby, J. (1966), "Violence and the Masculine Ideal: Some Qualitative Data." *ANNALS* 364 (March):19–27.

Van Maanen, J. (1973), "Observations on the Making of Policemen." *Human Organization* 32:407–418.

_____ (1982), "Fieldwork on the Beat." In J. Van Maanen et al. (eds.), *Varieties of Qualitative Research*. Beverly Hills: Sage Publications.

Vidich, A. (1970), "Participation Observation and the Collection and Interpretation of Data." In W. J. Filstead (ed.), *Qualitative Methodology: Firsthand Involvement With the Social World*. Chicago: Markham.

Wax, R. H. (1971), *Doing Fieldwork: Warnings and Advice*. Chicago: University of Chicago Press.

Webb and Morris (1978), *Prison Guards: The Culture and Perspective of an Occupational Group*. Coker Books.

Notes

[1] This prison reform case, the most sweeping in penal history, was a massive class action suit filed against the Texas Department of Corrections. A federal judge ruled that many TDC operations were unconstitutional and that wholesale organizational changes (e.g., health care, inmate housing) be instituted to remedy the situation.

[2] Building tenders (BTs) were the physically and mentally superior inmates officially recruited and coopted (given special privileges) by the guard staff to control the inmates in the living areas. BTs had a pro-staff orientation and worked hand-in-hand with the guards to control the other prisoners.

[3] This research was supported by the Law and Social Science Program, NSF (SES-8410925).

12

Guard Work in Transition
Ben M. Crouch

Prior to the 1970s, two conceptions of prison guards prevailed. First, the popular media pictured guards as brutal or dull white males dividing their time between manning towers and harassing inmates. Second, the social science conception cast guards as non-entities, mere background contributors to the inmates' "pains of imprisonment." In both, guards and guard work are simple and seemingly inconsequential to prison dynamics. Just the opposite is true, however. Guards make up approximately two-thirds of any prison staff, have the closest and most influential interaction with inmates, and can significantly influence the success of prison policies. Although media portrayals of guards have changed little over time, corrections researchers have come to recognize that guards constitute a significant presence behind the walls (see Crouch, 1980).

My purpose in this chapter is to examine the guard role and work environment, especially as they have been affected by fundamental transitions in institutional corrections over the past three decades or so. I begin by identifying the changes which seem most to affect guard work. Then I examine some of the more significant problems guards face on

Source: Prepared especially for *The Dilemmas of Corrections*.

the job, problems often exacerbated by rapid change. And finally, I consider how prison personnel accommodate an altered work environment.

Guard Work in Context

Contemporary accounts of prison guards frequently depict guards as relatively isolated workers in a tense and uncertain environment. Some observers even invoke an incarceration imagery, characterizing guards as "imprisoned" (Lombardo, 1981) or as "society's professional prisoners" (Wicks, 1980); men who feel "rejected, shunned and even despised" (Jacobs and Zimmer, 1983:145).

This sense of embattlement among guards became especially apparent as external pressures and reforms rocked the prison world (Irwin, 1980). The most consequential changes for guards have been: (1) an emphasis on rehabilitation, (2) changes in the size and composition of inmate populations, and (3) judicial intervention. Since these changes serve as the backdrop for the following discussion of guards, each will be considered briefly.

The reemergence of rehabilitation as a major prison goal in the late 1950s had direct implications for guards. The introduction of rehabilitation meant prison workers were to reform as well as control inmates. For security staff this often led to role conflict and to conflict with treatment personnel. Although studies purporting to show that correctional treatment programs were generally ineffective eventually led to a deemphasis on rehabilitation, the initial push toward treatment fostered a greater concern for humane treatment of inmates. Consequently, prison officers felt pressured somehow to combine treatment with custody.

The second broad change affecting guard work involved shifts in the size and composition of inmate populations. Prison populations surged in the early 1970s and again in the late 1970s; the latest upward trend continues into the 1990s. Population growth strains prison personnel as well as housing and support services. Consequently, officers must supervise and control many more inmates on a very tight daily schedule. As the growth of inmate populations outstrips the hiring of new officers, the existing staff may find itself spread too thin. At the same time, changes in the composition of prison populations exacerbate the overcrowding situation. As corrections officials divert less serious offenders to community corrections programs, those who actually do time are more apt to be violent as well as young and from a minority group (Toch, 1976). Such population shifts add tensions to guard work.

The third, and perhaps most consequential, change in the prison environment has been court intervention to guarantee the civil rights of inmates (see Alpert, Crouch and Huff, 1984). Prior to the mid-1960s, judges adhered to a "hands off" policy, accepting the notion that convicted felons lost their rights. At that time, changes in legal philosophy and case law led to a much greater willingness by judges to hear prisoner petitions. As judicial activism increased, prisoners gained for the first time a source of relief apart from their keepers (see Haas, 1977; 1981). Court decrees to reform unconstitutional practices and conditions altered standards of prisoner care and custody, and, in turn, changed traditional power relations between the keepers and the kept (Crouch and Marquart, 1989).

Problems On The Line

These and related changes have increased problems guards face in relating to inmates, administrators, and co-workers. In the following sections, I will examine six of these problems in some detail: (1) role conflict and ambiguity, (2) danger on the job, (3) loss of control, (4) stress, (5) racial and sexual integration of guard forces, and (6) deviant behavior on the job.

Role Conflict and Ambiguity

While officers have generally accepted the legitimacy of prisoner rehabilitation as a prison objective, they have often had trouble combining treatment expectations with custody routines. Specifically, the juxtaposition of security and rehabilitation can create role conflict for guards.

Role conflict among guards is particularly likely when prison administrators rapidly introduce treatment objectives, as Carroll's (1974) analysis of the Eastern Correctional Institution (ECI) illustrated. After years of operation as a custody-oriented prison, a new manager took over at ECI and called for a strong commitment to treatment goals. Guards saw this shift in emphasis as jeopardizing security and prisoner control. In turn, they experienced considerable role ambiguity and conflict in trying to meet both traditional custody demands and new, ill-defined treatment demands. Role conflict is also likely if officers take the title "correctional officer" quite literally and try, through some form of social work, to reform inmates. This orientation ensures some level of role conflict for security officers since the realities of their job limit the extent to which guards can actually treat or reform prisoners. If they remain in security, these officers will likely reduce role conflict by adopting a modest definition of treatment. They may move from trying to change lives to helping prisoners each day in situation-specific ways.

Danger

While prisons have always been potentially dangerous places to work, prisoner assaults on staff were relatively infrequent three decades ago. Then, prisoners were apparently more accepting of the prison status quo, more willing to accept both their time in prison and the authority of their keepers. But as reforms altered the prison world and as prisoner aggressiveness and gangs grew, risks to officers grew as well. Through the 1970s, evidence from several state prisons indicated that the proportion of altercations involving guards and prisoners increased, with assaults on staff becoming more deliberate and even status-conferring for some prisoners (Toch, 1976).

Although being taken hostage in an escape attempt or riot is certainly less likely than being assaulted by an inmate, it is nevertheless a source of danger for officers. A 1974 escape attempt in a Texas prison provides an illustration. To force prison officials to free them, three inmates took 11 people hostage, including several women teachers and one uniformed officer. The correctional officer hostage was singled out for special attention during the 11 days of negotiation. Several times one of the three rebels placed a gun barrel to the head of the officer and squeezed the trigger, letting the hammer fall on what only the inmate knew to be an empty chamber. The officer assumed each time he was about to die (House, 1975).

Being held hostage in a riot situation may be even more dangerous, if only for the number of inmates involved. Officers taken hostage in a riot are at risk at three points. The first is when prisoners take over parts of the prison and attempt to subdue or eliminate opposition from officers. The second point is when prisoners gain control over the building or cell block area and of the officers who have not gotten away in the takeover. Officers taken hostage at best may be blindfolded, herded about and threatened and, at worst, physically abused or even killed. During the Santa Fe prison riot in February, 1980, for example, one young officer was repeatedly sodomized, an experience that has left long-term psychological scars. Finally, officer hostages are at risk if the authorities retake the institution by force, as occurred during the Attica riot in September, 1971. Regardless of the circumstances, being a hostage is a traumatic event, and survivors may suffer prolonged anxiety along with loss of sleep, appetite, and sexual potency (Donovan, 1983).

Fear and uncertainty are daily realities for many guards. They see inmate-inmate violence and know that it could be directed at them. It is thus not surprising that guards in New York (Lombardo, 1981:114) and Illinois (Jacobs, 1981:45) named danger as the major disadvantage or source of dissatisfaction on the job.

How do officers deal with danger? Some simply leave. The possibility of injury certainly contributes to the high turnover among guards, especially those in the lower ranks. Most, however, adjust in some other manner, perhaps by having a private plan for staying out of harm's way. An informant in the Texas system told me, for example, that all the officers on one of the more tense prison units had identified a hiding place to be used "when it came down." Others may rely on their relations with particular inmates. Just prior to the Santa Fe riot, friendly inmates told several officers and treatment staff to "be sick" and not show up the day before the riot. Probably the most common method of handling fear, however, is to deny it, to present to self and others a "manly" front.

Loss of Control

During the 1960s, prisons were politically and legally isolated from the societal mainstream. Officials frequently operated according to self-determined and unquestioned policies which made guarding and doing time predictable, if not always constitutional. The subordinate status of prisoners was clearly defined, and role expectations were unequivocal. Officers maintained dominance over inmates by whatever means they found practical and were typically supported by their superiors. But as political, social, and legal activists criticized prison conditions and operations, inmates gained power relative to their keepers. Media attention and litigation especially called into question or eliminated many traditional methods of inmate control and punishment. While most officers today probably would not favor a wholesale return to the control devices and strategies of the past, most feel that inmates have too much freedom and that guards have lost much authority and control (Hepburn, 1983).

Guards have been concerned not only about diminished control, but about reduced support from prison administrators as well. This sense of being forsaken by the "front office" stems in part from court intervention. As the number of suits grew and the range of issues subject to litigation widened, administrators readily complied with court rulings, sometimes even welcoming court intervention as a means of improving prison conditions (Haas and Champagne, 1976). Administrative sensitivity to inmate plaintiffs, however, convinced many line officers that their administrators were more interested in inmates than in them. The frequent turnover of administrators in many prisons also undermined guard-administrator relations. That is, to protect their jobs administrators sometimes became more attuned to political and judicial pressures than to the frustrations of their staffs. This situation limited front-office support for guards and, in turn, eroded guard confidence in their own authority in dealing with prisoners. A New York officer's statement reflects the frustration of having limited support in a hostile work setting (Lombardo, 1981:122):

> With our job today we really don't have authority like we used to. You're restricted. The state doesn't back you if something happens. They don't want to know right from wrong. Now when there's a mob situation, you just stand there and observe. Years ago you would disperse them, persuade them to move. Today they're hesitant. We just let things boil longer and things develop into confrontations.

Guards have reacted to this apparent erosion of authority and control in several ways. One reaction is alienation (Poole and Regoli, 1981), the feeling that traditional norms are no longer appropriate or acceptable and that control over one's work has diminished. To combat alienation and restructure their work setting, guards may become more punitive and thus more likely to invoke disciplinary procedures against inmates (Poole and Regoli, 1980a). Other officers may adopt a very cynical attitude toward their work and the prison organization generally, especially if they believe that they do not have the support of the front office (Poole and Regoli, 1980b).

Most officers, however, probably try to disguise the toll taken by the job and make the best of what is often a frustrating situation. Though not immune to the pressures of the workplace, these officers project a tough, steady image which precludes sharing frustrations with either co-workers or family members. Some of these officers may be particularly vulnerable to stress.

Stress

The problems just examined—role conflict, danger, and diminished control—may produce considerable stress for front-line prison officers (Cullen, et al., 1985; Robinson, Porporino and Simourd, 1996). Stress as experienced by correctional workers has received considerable research attention in recent years on the assumption that current prison conditions exacerbate it. If inordinate stress is present within a guard force, it can be costly to both individual officers and to the institution. Among officers it can promote heart attacks, hypertension, ulcers, and hypoglycemia (Dahl, 1980). Organizational costs of stress include reduced work efficiency as officers become more negative, caustic, and inclined to perform "by the book." At the same time, increases in sick leave and resultant overtime pay can be very expensive.

Stress among correctional officers has several sources. An immediate stressor is the perception that the workplace is increasingly dangerous and that guards cannot lawfully retaliate in kind to violence by inmates. Long-term stress is particularly likely when the following conditions are present: (1) contradictory goals, objectives, and limited support from superiors; (2) role ambiguity, (3) uncooperative consumers of the worker's service; (4) felt vulnerability; and (5) inability to leave the job (Brodsky, 1977). Work on correctional stress suggests that a particularly significant source of stress among guards is a kind of "double bind" (Cheek and Miller, 1982). Specifically, officers want to respond to both intractable inmates and overcrowding by "putting the lid on," by "cracking down." Yet their superiors, fearing litigation, call for officers to limit their control efforts, to be "loose." The bind is further felt by officers when they realize that to maintain control, rules must be bent. Officers who do bend rules may find administrators unwilling to support them. Not surprisingly, stress is most likely among line officers with the closest interaction with prisoners in maximum-security or more custody oriented facilities (Van Voorhis, Cullen, Link, and Wolfe, 1991). However, while stress is a reality in prison work, it may be misleading to portray all or even most officers as under high, job-related stress. Saylor and Wright (1992) found, for example, in their study of over 3,300 officers in the federal prison system that only about 15 percent reported being troubled by job-related stress.

Integration of the Guards

Guarding in prison has traditionally been the occupational domain of white males. Security forces have included black officers, but they have been relatively few in number, even where the inmate population has been predominantly black. Women officers in men's prisons have been even more rare. Despite some resistance, however, the proportion of black and women officers has grown in recent years. The result has been increasingly heterogeneous and fragmented guard forces.

Racial integration. By the late 1950s, blacks and other minorities began to enter guard work in greater numbers than ever before. The civil rights movement which opened prisons to black employment coincided with a growing need for correctional manpower. As courts required prison administrators to increase the ratio of officers to inmates, many officials found it necessary to look beyond the local, white manpower pools from which they had traditionally drawn officers. Pressure from inmate groups also prompted administrators to hire more minority officers (Jacobs and Kraft, 1978).

Veteran white officers have been at best suspicious of this growing contingent of black officers. In Illinois the "old guard" felt that this "new breed" of typically non-white, urban guards was more pro-inmate and less trustworthy (Irwin, 1977). Not surprisingly, black officers have seen race and racism as barriers to recruitment, co-worker relations, and promotion (Beard, 1975).

Racism is particularly pernicious when it has an institutional character. Institutional racism exists when almost no minority officers hold upper-level security positions and few can qualify for those posts. Such a situation existed in New York in 1972 (Jacobs and Zimmer, 1983:146). When only two black officers made the sergeant's list in the New York Department of Corrections, a group of minority officers challenged the department's promotion process. Subsequent litigation led to a nondiscriminatory promotional system and a racial quota for promotions. White officers then sued, claiming reverse discrimination. An appellate court ultimately struck down the quota system but found the original examination to be valid. Such confrontations may not be characteristic of race relations among officers in all prisons, nor is race as divisive among officers as it is among inmates. Nevertheless, it remains a significant and complex factor in guard relations on and off the job (Britton, 1997).

Sexual integration. Though still a fairly small minority, the number of women guards in adult male prisons has grown considerably (Jurik, 1985). In state and federal prisons they constitute 6 and 18 percent, respectively (Morton, 1981; Ingram, 1980). These women are usually in the lower ranks of the guard hierarchy.

Title VII of the 1964 Civil Rights Act removed legal barriers to the employment of women officers, but their entry has been resisted by both prison administrators and male officers. Indeed, they have probably been more resistant to female officers than to minority male officers. After all, the latter at least meet the size and gender criteria guards have long believed to be unquestionable requisites for the job. Just to get hired, would-be women officers have had to overcome through litigation the argument that being male is a "bona fide occupational qualification for working in male institutions" (Alpert, 1984).

Yet getting hired is only the first step; women still have to perform the tasks guard work requires. Traditional objections to women guards have involved their ability to relate to, supervise, and control male prisoners. One matter regularly at issue in litigation, and relevant to the women officers' success on the job, is inmate privacy (Jacobs, 1983). Women can apparently learn, however, to deal effectively with situations where they are in close proximity to inmates. One female officer, for example, stated: "I've stood at a cell door and talked to a man using the toilet. I just looked the other way. When they're in the shower, they might wave their thing at you. You just ignore it" (Potter, 1980:33).

Although some inmates may not mind being supervised in shower or toilet activities by officers of the opposite gender (Kissel and Katsampes, 1980:220), it is troublesome for many inmates. At the same time many officers feel their work assignments should not be influenced by the gender of the inmates they supervise. In short, prisons and courts wrestle with the conflict between privacy rights claims by inmates and equal employment opportunity rights claims by some security personnel. Many prisoners, both male and female, object to being observed engaging in highly personal activities by officers of the opposite gender (Crouch and Alpert, 1991). Yet, officers feel that being kept from working the full range of security assignments to protect inmate privacy may impair their experience, and thus, their advancement on the job. For example, female officers in male prisons resent not getting the same assignments as their male co-workers, including supervising housing and shower units and conducting the body searches. Courts have generally held that the employment rights of officers should prevail over inmate privacy rights so long as there is no abuse. At the same time, except for emergencies, officers should conduct strip and body cavity searches only on inmates of their same gender (Bennett, 1995).

Another question raised about women guards concerns their ability to establish personal authority in dealing with inmates and thereby maintain order. Again, women appear to perform well. Inmates report women officers are generally no more easily conned or manipulated than men (Petersen, 1982:451). Moreover, women officers do not promote prisoner aggression or violence through their sexuality or presumed greater vulnerability to being taken hostage. Indeed, women officers may even facilitate order by bringing about a more relaxed and normal atmosphere (Potter, 1980). The only shortcoming women appear to have is handling violence once it is initiated; inmates as well as male officers prefer males in such situations (Petersen, 1982). This does not mean that women officers shrink from the aggressiveness of inmates. Indeed, recent evidence suggests that they are as aggressive in dealing with unruly inmates as male officers (Jenne and Kersting, 1996). Women officers thus appear to be as capable as their male counterparts on the job. For individual women officers, the initial difficulties with inmates tend to wane with time; gender apparently becomes less of an issue as female officers and inmates become used to each other.

Although it too may improve with time, the most persistent problem women officers appear to face is non-acceptance by their male coworkers. Women working in male prisons enter a masculine world and encounter a more specific occupational subculture; they must accommodate the normative expectations of both (Crouch, 1985). General masculine norms demand toughness, confidence, and aggressiveness, while the guard subculture proscribes being friendly to inmates, getting conned, snitching on other officers (solidarity), and trusting the "front-office" (Bowker, 1982:176–184). If women are generally less physically aggressive, less apt to take formal action, more nurturing, and have a higher need to affiliate (Petersen, 1982), then they will contravene both sets of norms. To the extent these norms prevail among their male counterparts, women officers in men's prisons are going to be at a disadvantage.

While racism and sexism on the part of white, male officers accounts for some of the conflict which has accompanied the racial and gender integration of guard forces, they are not the only reason. Some conflict derives from a somewhat different orientation which many black and female officers bring to the job. For example, black officers may be more treatment oriented, more open to prisoners (Van Voorhis, Cullen, Link and Wolfe, 1991; Britton, 1997). Similarly, female officers are less likely than male officers to project a traditional custodial orientation in their work, one reason they may experience more stress on the job than their male counterparts (Walters, 1992). Recent research has examined the relative significance of race and gender for shaping work orientations. The question asked is whether the tendencies black and female employees bring to prison work are the primary influences on their work orientations or whether their orientations are over time more significantly defined by the prison work environment itself. Results suggest that both prior attitudes and the work environment are important in determining how minorities and women experience guard work, although these officers may experience more stress, fear and job dissatisfaction than their white, male counterparts (Van Voorhis, Cullen, Link and Wolfe, 1991:494). This prospect makes organizational support and the quality of supervision especially important as guard forces continue to diversify.

Deviant Behavior on the Job

Guard deviance is the failure to comply with laws and the legal policies of the prison administration. So defined, the range of deviance can be broad. A study of security employee offenses within the Florida Department of Corrections (1981) between 1967 and 1980 suggested an illustrative, though certainly not exhaustive, list of deviant acts: (1) introduction of or trafficking in contraband; (2) grand theft; (3) warehouse sabotage; (4) homosexual relations with inmates; (5) bartering with inmates; (6) inappropriate use of force; (7) horseplay leading to injury of inmates; (8) assisting in an escape; and (9) theft of .38 caliber revolvers. Such acts have an important impact on institutional safety, inmate control, and the economic efficiency of the prison organization.

One of the few studies to address systematically the distribution of guard deviance is by McCarthy (1981). He examined 122 cases of serious misconduct referred to the Internal Affairs Unit of one prison system during the period from October, 1978 to December, 1979. McCarthy found that misuse of authority by guards accounted for 44 percent of the offenses, theft (over $50) accounted for another 20 percent, and embezzlement and trafficking in contraband accounted for 16 percent each; miscellaneous offenses accounted for the remainder.

Officers abuse their authority when they use their position for personal gain, such as accepting gratuities to secure privileges for prisoners. For example, an officer managing a work release program solicited a fee from an inmate for finding him a job. Another officer asked an inmate to pay him for transfer to a less secure facility. Similarly, officers may solicit payoffs from inmates to foster or overlook illicit activities. This would include "selling" the rights or franchises to illicit businesses such as drugs, gambling, or prostitution within the prison. In one case reported by McCarthy, an officer told an inmate he would leave a gate open for an escape if the inmate would pay him $6000. Extortion is an even more blatant misuse of authority. The personal gain here is typically money or a percentage of illicit profit. One female inmate, however, alleged that a male supervisor threatened to place her on restriction if she did not grant him sexual favors. A final misuse of authority noted by McCarthy is mismanagement, usually involving illicit skimming or other profiteering from the work area, warehouse, or industry the employee supervises.

These examples of guard deviance are probably best understood in individual rather than organizational terms. Theft, extortion, and homosexuality appear to stem from "bad guards"—individuals who either brought their penchant for misconduct into the prison with them or developed it essentially on their own in response to an opportunity to exploit a work situation. Other types of officer deviance, however, stem more from the expectations of prisoners, peers, and superiors about how the job is to be done. This latter type of deviance may be more pernicious than theft since it may undermine prison order and/or promote widespread unjust treatment of inmates. Three types of deviance stem primarily from organizational factors: corruption of authority, questionable disciplinary actions, and patterned guard violence.

Corruption of authority. As Sykes (1958) noted in an early study, the authority of prison custodians may easily be corrupted or eroded due to two fundamental realities of guard work. First, guards lack total power. Since they cannot completely impose their will upon inmates, some negotiation is always required. Secondly, guards must work in close, daily proximity to inmates, and thus come to know at least some of them as individuals. Together these two occupational realities can compromise an officer's authority in several ways.

Yielding to cultural pressures to be a "good guy," the officer may begin to interact with inmates on a personal basis, joking or working out with them. Interaction leading to such a relationship may often be initiated by an inmate who astutely picks out a likely officer, observes his moods, and then offers him support and a sympathetic ear. The officer over time comes to depend on this support, expect it and, in turn, feels obligated to the inmate. The result can be not only loss of authority but the officer's trafficking in contraband at the inmate's request or demand. As reforms lead to larger, more diverse guard forces and break down informal controls within the guard subculture, such acts may increase dramatically (see Crouch and Marquart, 1989).

Authority may also be corrupted if the officer, being overly busy or perhaps just lazy, permits an inmate to carry out some of the officer's own duties. In time the officer may discover that his control in the work area has slipped away. Finally, an officer may lose authority by engaging in trade-offs with powerful inmates under his supervision; they ensure order on his cell block, and he grants them special privileges. In addition to cell block order, the officer gets a good rating from his superiors. But here, as in each of these circumstances of authority corruption, the officer may find that when he seeks to invoke his authority over these "special" inmates, his authority may be severely eroded. As Sykes puts it, authority, like virtue, is difficult to retrieve after it has been lost.

Deviance in formal disciplinary actions. The misuse of authority in the formal disciplining of inmates for rule violations is another broad area of guard deviance. Prisons have unique and extensive sets of rules, all ostensibly designed to protect or maintain inmates, officers, and the general order. This plethora of rules means that it is extremely difficult for inmates to avoid violating some minor rule daily and that officers have many opportunities to put inmates on report. Yet in practice officers actually use their authority to formally sanction inmates in a very selective manner.

This selective sanctioning involves two types of deviance: (1) nonenforcement of prison rules when a violation has clearly occurred, and (2) enforcement for personal reasons. First, officers overlook much inmate misconduct, especially of a minor nature. They may not "write him up" because the rule violated seems inappropriate in a given setting, because of personal relations with the violator, or because the cost of invoking sanctions seems too high in terms of the resultant inmate hostility. Second, officers may engage in selective sanctioning to establish or confront their personal authority in dealing with particular inmates. That is, formal disciplinary actions are often not just impersonal, even-handed applications of organizational rules but means of communicating a message to inmates, of establishing an officer's reputation as one deserving respect (Crouch and Marquart, 1980). Technically, the practice of selective sanctioning is deviant; the organizational rules presumably have a purpose, and officer failure to enforce them violates that purpose. Although officially deviant, the practice is nonetheless not only widespread but normative in terms of the informal expectations of inmates, officers, and administrators. Indeed, some selective sanctioning is necessary and even functional for the smooth operation of prisons.

Selective sanctioning becomes much more significantly deviant, however, when officers use the formal disciplinary process to discriminate systematically against a category of inmates (Flanagan, 1983). One question is whether the fact that black inmates have a disproportionately higher rate of prison rule infractions than whites demonstrates discrimination against black inmates in the disciplinary process. Evidence on this question is mixed, although most points to at least some degree of discrimination by officers. White officers constitute the bulk of most guard forces and often do not like non-whites (Irwin, 1980:125): Typically from rural backgrounds, these officers not only often misunderstand the perspective and culture of minority prisoners but feel superior to them. These attitudes make non-whites more likely to be written up and formally sanctioned. Indeed, Held, Levine, and Swartz (1979) report that in those infraction categories where guards do not have to substantiate their charges with evidence (i.e., "disrespect" by inmate), blacks are significantly overrepresented. Apparently, unencumbered by the need to produce evidence, guards give discriminatory tendencies freer rein. In a study of race and severity of prison discipline, however, I found that a generally prejudiced and overwhelmingly white guard force did not give minority inmates more severe punishments than white inmates for comparable infractions (Crouch, 1983). Clearly, the extent of this type of deviance by officers, its consequences, and the conditions under which it exists require further research.

Patterned guard violence. A final area of officer deviance involves physical punishment of inmates instead of or in addition to, formal, legal disciplinary action. Because prisons can be violent places, physical control of inmates by officers is sometimes necessary as in the case of self-defense or of an unbalanced inmate who needs restraint. The problem emerges when officers employ physical force unnecessarily and excessively.

The use of force as a control mechanism may be so routine in some prison settings that abuse of inmates reflects organizational expectations and is best understood in those terms. Punitive violence by guards may not only be encouraged by the informal guard subculture but tacitly supported by the administration. Marquart (1986) reports, for example, that in one prison the willingness to fight an inmate reflected positively on an officer's manhood; those who exhibited this behavior were rewarded, sometimes with promotion. In the prison Marquart investigated, physical punishment of inmates was institutionalized to the point that guards understood two levels of action, the "tune up" and the "overhaul." A "tune up" involved slapping an inmate around for a persistent bad attitude or a minor transgression. An "overhaul" was more serious, often prompted by an inmate striking or merely attempting to strike an officer; here the objective was to hurt the inmate severely.

Officers may also use excessive violence during a riot situation, especially during its quelling and immediately thereafter. The obvious motivation for collective guard violence in such situations is a desire to punish inmates and to ensure that the riot is not repeated. There may, however, be a less obvious motivation, namely a desire to redress lost occupational esteem. In his analysis of the unauthorized participation by guards in the retaking of the Attica prison in 1971, Stotland (1980) argues that guards at Attica, for many of the reasons discussed above, felt a reduced importance on the job. Their excessive violence in the retaking of the prison and the harsh treatment of inmates in the riot's aftermath were efforts to recapture their own self-esteem.

The extent of staff violence is difficult to determine. Some evidence, however, suggests that guard brutality in prisons has diminished these last two to three decades (Toch, 1976). May (1981:33), for example, reports that in Connecticut, the prison ombudsman handled 1,062 inmate complaints in a three-year period in the early 1970s, and only 15 involved the appropriate use of force by guards. The primary reason for less physical coercion is that in more recent years, prison staff behavior has received much closer scrutiny from the courts and media.

Regaining Control

Prison security forces are much more diverse than they were two or three decades ago. Officers of different sexes, races, and backgrounds work together. Differences in organizational goals or in personal orientations to the job lead some to be institutional cops and others to be overtly concerned with prisoner welfare. Even at the same prison, solidarity within the officer force may be more apparent than real. Despite this diversity, however, officers who experience the problems considered above tend in time to reflect similar attitudes and perspectives on the job (Crouch and Alpert, 1982; Jacobs and Kraft, 1978). One of the most commonly shared perceptions among officers is that they have less control both over prisoners and over their jobs, and, as a result, feel dissatisfied.

While there are many means through which officers may regain some measure of control on the job and, in the process, improve their morale, three seem particularly significant: unionization, professionalization, and bureaucratization. Each represents a restructuring of prison relations and has a different potential for improving the officers' lot.

Unionization

Concerned about their loss of power on the job, guards have increasingly expressed their general dissatisfaction through sick-outs, slow-downs, strikes, and a heightened push toward unionization (Irwin, 1980:221). The most formal of these actions, the unionization movement, is relatively new. While a few states have had unionized guard forces for decades, most correctional staffs which have turned to collective bargaining began to do so only during the 1970s (Flanagan, van Alstyne and Gottfredson, 1982:138–39). Prior to this, officers saw little need for unionization, feeling comfortable with their relations with prisoners and especially with prison managers. Reforms, however, created a rift between officers and those managers. Feeling forsaken by the front office, under judicial, media and even legislative scrutiny, many officers turned to the apparent power of unions.

But while union pressure can help improve wages and working conditions, limit management arbitrariness, and promote management-union interaction, there are limitations on the extent to which unions can improve control or morale. In a study of the New York guard union, Jacobs and Zimmer (1983) found that while collective bargaining helped with problems of wages, benefits, and some specific grievances, it was not able to address the most fundamental problems facing officers in New York and elsewhere—loss of control, loss of status, and racial tension. At the same time, guard unions may limit job mobility by stressing seniority and by generally preserving and extending the status quo (Wynne, 1978).

Thus, as an occupational strategy for accommodating current and anticipated changes in institutional corrections, unionization may not be sufficient. It may be that more fundamental changes in guard work will be called for in the future than unionization may foster or permit.

Professionalization

Whereas unionization is initiated primarily by the officers themselves, professionalization must be initiated and supported by prison administrators. Professionalization connotes, among other things, the hiring of better educated people, more sophisticated and protracted training, and the enlargement or diversification of the guard role. Its goal is to improve staff qualifications so that officers can project a humane treatment orientation, can reduce prison tensions, and can experience greater occupational self-esteem by having more control over decision making. Unfortunately, professionalization efforts have not been especially productive in achieving these objectives.

A number of factors limit the professionalizing of guard forces (Jurik and Musheno, 1986). First, despite much rhetorical support for creating a professional force, there is still public, legislative, and even administrative opposition to professionalizing programs and expenditures, as they might appear to "coddle" prisoners. Thus, formal efforts to expand the job beyond custodial duties are often thwarted. Second, resources are typically insufficient to attract many skilled people to corrections work through high salaries or to develop the sophisticated pre- and in-service training that professionalization requires. A third barrier, beyond informal resistance from "custody-oriented" staff and administrators, is the fact that the formal, para-military organization of prison security is structurally incompatible with professional autonomy. Guard force hierarchies have been, and largely remain, uninterested in input from the bottom, preferring tight control of information flow and of the actions of rank-and-file officers. Thus, when well-trained and professionally-oriented officers do find their way to the cell blocks, they are often particularly frustrated and dissatisfied.

Litigated reform may also limit the on-the-job autonomy which professionalism requires. Court intervention into prison operations typically occurs when policies and practices in some way abuse prisoners. Since guards put those policies into practice, it is the guards and their supervisors that the courts have been particularly keen to monitor. To ensure that guards act legally, the prison administration, following court directives, carefully spells out what officers can or must do. This accountability to strict, imposed rules limits autonomy and the enlargement of the officer role. When litigated reforms restrict guard actions, low morale is a predictable by-product (Crouch and Marquart, 1989).

Bureaucratization

Reforms of the past twenty-five years have left prison organizations more specialized, centralized, and formalized—in short, more bureaucratic. The fundamental objective of this trend has been to restructure prison organizations and operations so they will be more constitutional and humane. As suggested above, reform very often involves redirecting and then closely controlling guards to ensure their compliance with new policies. The most effective type of staff control is bureaucratization, and it has significantly altered traditional guard work. Specialization reduces the scope of line officers' influence on prisoners' lives, centralization shifts power from supervisors and wardens to top administrators, and formalization proliferates rules and the paperwork to hold officers accountable to them. That prisoners seem to gain freedoms and that courts and top administrators seem bent on taking away officers' discretion is disheartening to officers.

Yet, bureaucratization, which seems to have so tied the hands of officers, has actually become a tangible means for regaining control, if not satisfaction. That is, many guards have learned to use the rules and not to fight them. In time, the new, more formal guidelines for doing work become routine; guards become accustomed to new ways of relating to prisoners and to superiors. In the process, officers discover that even if they have relatively less discretion, they can still control prisoners by holding them to the "letter of the rule" or by using the initially abhorred rules and paperwork to punish, deprive, or harass inmates (Crouch and Marquart, 1989).

Prison Guards in the 1990s

In the 1990s, the fear of crime and violence has made citizens willing to support an unprecedented prison construction program in this country. For example, in March 1993 Texas voters turned down the issuance of $750 million in general obligation bonds to build new schools; eight months later the voters approved $1 billion in general obligation bonds to build new prisons. This growth translates into a growth in prison jobs as well. To staff these new prisons Texas plans to hire over 11,000 new correctional officers. In addition to the growth in state prisons, the growing number of private correctional facilities has created a new and largely unresearched security environment for officers (Stolz, 1997).

Wherever they work, prison officers across the country do not face the same demands on the job as their predecessors.

Through the 1970s and 1980s state prison guards frequently claimed they had lost the ability to control prisoners and to maintain order. But this was more lament than an accurate description of guard work. Guards today do have control; they just use somewhat different means. Recognizing that the arbitrary and abusive control techniques of the "old days" are taboo, officers have learned to use strict rule enforcement and the threat of long-term lockdown in an "administrative segregation" cell—methods that are technically in accord with due process—to deal with problem prisoners. Bolstering this bureaucratic order is the fact that officers may have less to fear from prisoners who would attack them through the courts. In the 1980s, numerous Supreme Court decisions curtailed the availability of judicial relief for prisoners, thus making it more difficult for inmates to bring suits against their keepers (Haas and Alpert, 1989).

But if officers today have control over prisoners, they are still frequently frustrated and dissatisfied. A major reason is the loss of traditional intrinsic rewards on the job, both from relationships with prisoners below and administrators above. Until the 1960s and in some prisons through the 1970s, guards enjoyed unquestioned dominance and related to prisoners in a very paternalistic manner. At the same time, relatively small, all-male and largely white security forces could sustain considerable subcultural solidarity, bolstered by support from powerful, sometimes charismatic, administrators. These aspects of guard work were intrinsic rewards which helped to compensate for low pay and the "dirty work" the job often entails. Yet, these aspects of guard work have been eroded, primarily by the prisoners' rights movement and by other humanitarian reforms of the last two decades. Among other things, reforms extended the rights of prisoners, made guard forces larger and more heterogeneous, and attenuated traditional front-office support, especially for questionable guard actions. Many officers thus feel they have lost some major sources of job status and self-esteem—clear dominance over prisoners, broad discretion on the job, inclusion in a closed masculine subculture, and loyalty rewarded by administrative support—that in the past provided gratification on the job.

This analysis suggests a peculiar problem facing prison security forces in the 1990s. In the turmoil of American prisons from the late 1960s through the 1980s, guards have frequently felt powerless and dissatisfied. While unionization and professionalization have generally failed to redress these grievances, bureaucratization, somewhat ironically, has at least provided legal means of prisoner control. But none of these has been able to offer career officers much in the way of job status and satisfaction. In today's more structured prison environment, guards lack the trappings of professionalism and are not often expected to contribute either to treatment or to policy. Predictably, some officers respond by simply going through the motions, by just "putting in their eight." There are many officers, however, who despite endemic problems and frustrations, are able on their own to find meaning on the job and to carry out their tasks with dedication and humanity.

References

Alpert, G. 1984. "The Needs of the Judiciary and Misapplications of Social Research: The Case of Female Guards in Men's Prisons." *Criminology* 22 (August): 441–56.

Alpert, G., B. Crouch and C. Huff. 1984. "Prison Reform by Decree: The Unintended Consequences of *Ruiz v. Estelle*." *The Justice System Journal* 9 (Winter): 291–305.

Beard, E. 1975. *Final Report: The Recruitment and Retention of Minority Correctional Employees Research Project*. Washington, DC: Institute for Urban Affairs and Research, Howard University.

Bennett, K. 1995. "Constitutional Issues in Cross-Gender Searches and Visual Observations of Nude Inmates by Opposite-Sex Officers: A Battle Between and Within the Sexes." *The Prison Journal* 75 (March): 90-112.

Bowker, L. 1982. *Corrections: The Science and the Art*. New York: Macmillan.

Britton, D. M. 1997. "Perceptions of the Work Environment Among Correctional Officers: Do Race and Sex Matter?" *Criminology* 35 (1): 85-105.

Brodsky, C. M. 1977. "Long-term Work Stress in Teachers and Prison Guards." *Journal of Occupational Medicine* 19 (February): 133–38.

Carroll, L. 1974. *Hacks, Blacks and Cons*. Prospect Heights, IL: Waveland Press (reissued 1988 with changes).

Cheek, F. and M. Miller. 1982. "Reducing Staff and Inmate Stress." *Corrections Today* (October): 721–78.

Crouch, B. (ed.). 1980. *The Keepers*. Springfield, IL: Charles C Thomas.

_____. 1983. "Inmate Deviance and Formal Prison Discipline: The Relevance of Minority Status to Punishment Severity." *Sociological Focus* 18 (August): 221–34.

_____. 1985. "Pandora's Box: Women Guards in Men's Prisons." *Journal of Criminal Justice* 13: 535–48.

Crouch, B. and G. Alpert. 1982. "Sex and Occupational Socialization: A Longitudinal Study of Prison Guards." *Criminal Justice and Behavior* 2 (June): 159–76.

Crouch, B. and G. Alpert. 1991. "Cross-Sex Guarding, Personal Privacy and Institutional Security: Perceptions of Jail Inmates and Staff." *Criminal Justice and Behavior* 18 (September): 304-317.

Crouch, B. and J. Marquart. 1980. "On Becoming a Prison Guard," pp. 63–109, in B. Crouch (ed.), *The Keepers: Prison Guards and Contemporary Corrections*. Springfield, IL: Charles C Thomas.

———. 1989. *An Appeal to Justice: Litigated Reform of Texas Prisons*. Austin: University of Texas Press.

Cullen, F. T., et al. 1985. "The Social Correlates of Correctional Officer Stress." *Justice Quarterly* 2(December): 505–34.

Dahl, J. J. 1980. "Occupational Stress in Corrections," pp. 207–22, in *Proceedings of the 110th Annual Congress of Corrections*. College Park, MD: American Correctional Association.

Donovan, E. 1983. "Responding to the Prison Employee-Hostage as a Crime Victim," pp. 17–24, in *Correctional Officers: Power, Pressure and Responsibility*. College Park, MD: American Correctional Association.

Flanagan, T. 1983. "Correlates of Institutional Misconduct Among State Prisoners." *Criminology* 21(February): 29–39.

Flanagan, T., D. van Alstyne and M. Gottfredson (eds.). 1982. *Sourcebook of Criminal Justice Statistics—1981*. Washington, DC: U.S. Department of Justice, Bureau of Justice Statistics.

Florida Department of Corrections. 1981. "Response to the Findings and Recommendations of the Ad Hoc Subcommittee of the House Committee on Corrections, Probation and Parole."

Haas, K. C. 1977. "Judicial Politics and Correctional Reform: An Analysis of the Decline of the 'Hands-off' Doctrine." *Detroit College of Law Review* (Winter): 795–831.

———. 1981. "The 'New Federalism' and Prisoners' Rights: State Supreme Courts in Comparative Perspective." *Western Political Quarterly* 34 (December): 552–71.

Haas, K. C. and G. Alpert. 1989. "American Prisoners and the Right of Access to the Courts," in L. I. Goodstein and D. L. McKenzie (eds.), *The American Prison: Issues in Research and Policy*. New York: Plenum.

Haas, K. C. and A. Champagne. 1976. "The Impact of *Johnson v. Avery* on Prison Administration." *Tennessee Law Review* 43 (Winter): 275–306.

Held, B., D. Levine and V. Swartz. 1979. "Interpersonal Aspects of Dangerousness." *Criminal Justice and Behavior* 1 (March): 45–58.

Hepburn, J. 1983. "The Prison Control Structure and Its Effects on Work Attitudes: A Study of the Attitudes of Prison Guards." Paper presented at the American Society of Criminology meeting, Denver.

House, A. 1975. *The Corrosco Tragedy*. Waco: The Texian Press.

Ingram, G. 1980. "The Role of Women in Male Federal Correctional Institutions," pp. 275–81, in the *Proceedings of the 110th Congress of Corrections*. College Park, MD: American Correctional Association.

Irwin, J. 1977. "The Changing Social Structure of the Men's Correctional Prison," pp. 21–40, in D. Greenberg (ed.), *Corrections and Punishment*. Beverly Hills: Sage.

———. 1980. *Prisons in Turmoil*. Boston: Little, Brown.

Jacobs, J. 1981. "What Prison Guards Think: A Profile of the Prison Force," pp. 1–53, in R. Ross (ed.), *Prison Guard/Correctional Officers: Uses and Abuses of the Human Resources of Prisons*. Toronto: Butterworth.

_____. 1983. *New Perspectives in Prisons and Imprisonment*. Ithaca: Cornell University Press.

Jacobs, J., and L. Kraft. 1978. "Integrating the Keepers: A Comparison of Black and White Prison Guards in Illinois." *Social Problems* 5: 304–18.

Jacobs, J., and L. Zimmer. 1983. "Collective Bargaining and Labor Unrest," pp. 145–59, in J. Jacobs (ed.), *New Perspectives in Prisons and Imprisonment*. Ithaca: Cornell University Press.

Jenne, D. L., and R. C. Kersting. 1996. "Aggression and Female Correctional Officers in Male Prisons." *The Prison Journal* 76 (December): 442-460.

Jurik, N. 1985. "An Officer and a Lady: Organizational Barriers to Women Working as Correctional Officers in Men's Prisons." *Social Problems* 32 (April): 375–88.

Jurik, N., and M. Musheno. 1986. "The Internal Crisis of Corrections: Professionalization and the Work Environment." *Justice Quarterly* 3 (December): 457–80.

Kissel, P. and P. Katsampes. 1980. "Impact of Women Corrections Officers on the Functioning of Institutions Housing Male Inmates." *Journal of Offender Counseling Services and Rehabilitation* 4 (Spring): 213–31.

Lombardo, L. 1981. *Guards Imprisoned*. New York: Elsevier.

McCarthy, B. 1981. "Patterns of Prison Corruption." Paper presented at the American Society of Criminology annual meeting, Philadelphia.

Marquart, J. 1986. "Prison Guards and the Use of Physical Coercion as a Mechanism of Social Control." *Criminology* 24:347–66.

Marquart, J., and B. Crouch. 1984. "Coopting the Kept: Using Inmates for Social Order in a Southern Prison." *Justice Quarterly* 1 (December): 491–509.

May, E. 1981. "Prison Guards in America—The Inside Story," pp. 19–40, in R. Ross (ed.), *Prison Guard/Correctional Officer: The Use and Abuse of the Human Resources of Prisons*. Toronto: Butterworth.

Morton, J. 1981. "Women in Correctional Employment: Where Are They Now and Where Are They Headed?" pp. 7–15, in *Women in Corrections*. College Park, MD: American Correctional Association.

Petersen, C. 1982. "Doing Time with the Boys: An Analysis of Women Correctional Officers in All-Male Facilities," pp. 437–60, in B. Price and N. Sokoloff (eds.), *The Criminal Justice System and Women*. New York: Clark Boardman.

Poole, E., and R. Regoli. 1980a. "Role Stress, Custody Orientation and Disciplinary Actions: A Study of Prison Guards." *Criminology* 18 (August): 215–26.

_____. 1980b. "Work Relations and Cynicism Among Prison Guards." *Criminal Justice and Behavior* 7 (September): 303–14.

_____. 1981. "Alienation in Prison: An Examination of Work Relations Among Prison Guards." *Criminology* 19 (August): 251–70.

Potter, J. 1980. "Should Women Guards Work in Prisons for Men?" *Corrections Magazine* 5 (October): 30–38.

Robinson, D., F. J. Porporino, and L. Simourd. 1996. "Do Different Goups Vary on Attitudes and Work Adjustments in Corrections?" *Federal Probation* 60 (3): 45-53.

Saylor, W. G., and K. N. Wright. 1992. "Status, Longevity, and Perceptions of the Work Environment among Federal Prison Employees." *Journal of Offender Rehabilitation* 1 (314): 133–60.

Stolz, B. A. 1997. "Privatizing Corrections: Changing the Corrections Policy-Making Subgovernment." *The Prison Journal* 77 (1): 91-111.

Stotland, E. 1980. "Self-Esteem and Violence by Guards and State Troopers at Attica," pp. 291–301 in B. Crouch (ed.), *The Keepers.* Springfield, IL: Charles C Thomas.

Sykes, G. 1958. "The Corruption of Authority and Rehabilitation." *Social Forces* 34 (March): 257–62.

Toch, H. 1976. *Peacekeeping: Police, Prisons and Violence.* Lexington: Lexington Books.

Van Voorhis, P., F. T. Cullen, B. G. Link, and N. T. Wolfe. 1991. "The Impact of Race and Gender on Correctional Officers' Orientation to the Integrated Environment." *Journal of Research in Crime and Delinquency* 28 (4) (November): 472–500.

Walters, S. 1992. "Attitudinal and Demographic Differences between Male and Female Corrections Officers: A Study of Three Midwestern Prisons." *Journal of Offender Rehabilitation* 18 (1/2): 173–89.

Wicks, R. J. 1980. *Guard: Society's Professional Prisoner.* Houston: Gulf.

Wynne, J. M., Jr. 1978. *Prison Employer Unionism: The Impact on Correctional Administration and Programs.* National Institute of Law Enforcement and Criminal Justice.

Part III

The Courts and Corrections

Introduction

Prior to the 1960s, the vast majority of courts refused to hear cases in which prisoners complained of cruel punishments or harsh conditions of confinement. In declining jurisdiction over litigation involving prisons, the courts relied upon a policy generally referred to as the "hands-off doctrine." This approach to inmate lawsuits reflected the views that a convicted prisoner was a "slave of the state" without enforceable rights and that the courts lacked the authority and expertise to intervene in correctional affairs. In practice, the hands-off doctrine made it virtually impossible for prisoners to seek judicial relief from alleged mistreatment at the hands of prison officials.

In the 1960s, many federal courts and a few state courts began to relax their traditional hands-off attitude toward the legal rights of prisoners, and the early 1970s were years of growth and development in prison litigation. Federal court decisions enlarged the scope of the prisoners' right of access to the courts and expanded (but did not totally recognize) inmate rights to religious freedom, uncensored mail correspondence, decent medical care, and procedural due process during prison disciplinary hearings. Although most cases were decided in favor of prison authorities, prisoners nevertheless won significant victories protecting them from arbitrary beatings and tortures, contaminated and nutritionally inadequate food, poor sanitation, severe overcrowding, and prolonged confinement in isolation cells which were covered with the bodily wastes of previous cell inhabitants and which were lacking light, ventilation, and any means of maintaining bodily cleanliness.

These victories for prisoners, however, have now given way to what legal scholars are calling a "modified hands-off doctrine." Since 1976, the Supreme Court has sanctioned strict limitations on prisoners' rights to visitation, free speech, and freedom of expression. The Court has minimized due process protections when prisoners are disciplined or transferred to more punitive facilities, and it has imposed a series of troublesome and time-consuming procedural obstacles to the access of state prisoners to federal courts.

Such setbacks have tempered earlier enthusiasm over the role courts can play in bringing about correctional reform. This is not to say that recent decisions should be read as the death knell for prison litigation. Rather, it seems likely that prisoners' rights have reached a status quo that is likely to remain static for the next decade or so. Moreover, a good case can be made that federal court decisions on behalf of prisoners during the past 30 years have spurred more improvements in American corrections than all other types of reform efforts over the preceding 200 years. The selections in Part III are intended to give students a broad perspective of what the judiciary has and has not accomplished in the area of penal reform.

In the first article in this section, Frank Johnson, a man who served for many years as a federal district judge in Alabama, graphically details the brutal and degrading conditions that existed in Alabama's prisons in the 1970s. He does so to explain his controversial prisoners' rights decisions mandating broad improvements in staffing, physical facilities, medical care, rehabilitation programs, inmate classification, and many other aspects of Alabama prison management. Judge Johnson argues that the intolerability of life in Alabama's prisons had reached such a critical state that it was his constitutional duty to take measures to defend prisoners from barbaric and inhumane conditions. He makes a convincing case that concerns about excessive judicial activism and the increasing volume of prison litigation must never prevent the courts from preserving the rights of prisoners or any other minority group that must resort to the courts to secure protection against abuses perpetrated or tolerated by the executive and legislative branches of government.

Legal scholars generally recognize the right of access to the courts as the most important constitutional protection accorded prisoners, primarily because it is the right upon which all other rights turn. Without the right of access, prisoners would have no way to vindicate other constitutional rights, such as their right to freedom of religion and their right to be protected against cruel and unusual punishments. As a federal court declared in 1966, "A right of access to the courts [is] of incalculable importance to the protection of other precious rights" [*Coleman v. Peyton*, 302 F.2d 905, 907 (4th Cir. 1966)]. In "American Prisoners and the Right of Access to the Courts: A Vanishing Concept of Protection," Ken Haas and Geoffrey Alpert, the editors of this volume, analyze trends in this area of law. They demonstrate that the U.S. Supreme Court has made it increasingly difficult for prisoners to seek judicial redress of their grievances, and they discuss the implications of this state of affairs for correctional practitioners and researchers.

There have been two noteworthy developments in this area of law since the third edition of *The Dilemmas of Corrections*. First, in *Lewis v. Casey*, decided in 1996, the U.S. Supreme Court narrowed the scope of the prisoner's right of access to the courts in a way that gives prison officials more breathing room in establishing a constitutionally permissible system of providing legal assistance to prisoners. Previously, as discussed in the Haas-Alpert chapter, the Court held in *Bounds v. Smith* (1977) that prison officials must provide inmates with an adequate law library or adequate assistance from people trained in the law. Since *Bounds* there has been a great deal of confusion and litigation on questions involving the adequacy of particular prison law libraries and legal services programs.

These kinds of questions are still with us, but the *Lewis v. Casey* decision settled one lingering issue. By a five-to-four vote, the Court held that an inmate alleging a violation of *Bounds* must show that shortcomings in the prison's library or assistance program caused him "actual injury"—that these shortcomings hindered or stymied his efforts to pursue a legitimate legal claim. Writing for the majority, Justice Scalia announced that an inmate no longer would be permitted to bring a right-of-access claim simply by demonstrating that his prison's law library or legal services program is deficient "in some theoretical sense." The inmate must also show that these deficiencies obstructed his efforts to file a legal claim. Justice Scalia added that prisoners could satisfy the actual-injury requirement only when they bring a "nonfrivolous" or "arguable" claim that either challenges the conditions of their confinement or attacks their sentences, directly or collaterally. The impairment of any other kind of legal action, Justice Scalia stressed, "is simply one of the incidental (and perfectly constitutional) consequences of conviction and incarceration."

Another important development is the 1996 passage of the Prison Litigation Reform Act (PLRA). This law requires, among other things, that before a prisoner can file a civil rights suit in a federal court, he must exhaust all available administrative remedies including any inmate grievance system the prison may have. Moreover, an inmate who sues in federal court will now have to show that he suffered a physical injury in order to recover monetary damages for mental or emotional injury suffered while in custody.

The PLRA also contains its own "three strikes and you're out" provision. It prohibits a prisoner from filing an *in forma pauperis* petition (a petition to allow an indigent litigant to proceed with his case when the court determines that he lacks the funds to pay the filing fee) if he has previously filed three or more federal petitions that were dismissed as frivolous or malicious, or for failing to state a claim for which relief can be granted. Additionally, the PLRA provides for sanctions, including the possible loss of previously earned "good-time" credits, to be imposed on federal prisoners who are found to have presented false evidence in a lawsuit or to have filed suit for malicious purposes.

The combined effects of *Lewis v. Casey* and the PLRA will be significant in the years to come. Since *Lewis* was announced on June 24, 1996, federal and state courts have dismissed dozens of inmate right-of-access claims for failure to meet the "actual injury" requirement. Similarly, the PLRA, since its passage on April 26, 1996, has resulted in the dismissal of many inmate lawsuits that would have been considered in the past. *Lewis* and the PLRA are in line with the trends discussed in the Haas-Alpert chapter; we have come to the end of an era in which prisoners' rights of access were gradually expanded. It is important to remember, however, that *Bounds v. Smith* and the other key decisions discussed in this chapter remain substantially intact. It is still correct to say that "a right of access to the courts is one of the rights a prisoner clearly retains" [*Coleman v. Peyton*, 302 F. 2d 905, 907 (4th Cir. 1966)].

The Supreme Court's declining solicitude toward the rights of prisoners in various areas of correctional law was compellingly demonstrated during the Court's 1988-89 term. All six prisoners' rights cases decided in that term were resolved in favor of correctional officials and against prisoners. Our next selection offers a brief review of two particularly important cases from that term. "The Supreme Court's Retreat From the Protection of Prisoners' Rights" is adapted from the *Correctional Law Reporter*, a bi-monthly journal edited and published by

William C. Collins and Fred Cohen, two of the nation's leading authorities on prison law.

The two cases highlighted here expand the authority of prison officials to place limits on the inmate's right to receive correspondence (*Thornburgh v. Abbott*) and visitors (*Kentucky v. Thompson*). The holdings in these cases and the Court's willingness to defer to the judgments of correctional administrators indicate that judicial involvement in correctional affairs will continue to diminish in the foreseeable future.

Despite the Supreme Court's retreat from the protection of prisoners' rights, lawsuits arising from prison disciplinary hearings remain common. William C. Collins offers readers an insightful analysis of judicial activity in this sphere of law in "Disciplinary Hearings: Something Old, Something New, but Always Something." The years 1985 and 1986 were especially noteworthy in terms of Supreme Court and lower court treatment of prison discipline issues, and Collins shows how courts continue to struggle with issues left unsettled by the Supreme Court's landmark decision of *Wolff v. McDonnell* (1974).

A 1995 Supreme Court decision has added to the confusion. In *Sandin v. Connor*, the Court held that a state prisoner in Hawaii who had been given 30 days in segregated confinement for an alleged disciplinary infraction could not bring a *Wolff*-type lawsuit challenging the constitutionality of his disciplinary hearing. A five-to-four majority reasoned that 30 days in the Hawaii segregation unit did not impose an "atypical and significant hardship" on this inmate, in part, because he was serving a sentence of 30 years to life in a maximum-security prison.

According to Chief Justice Rehnquist's majority opinion, the inmate's 30-day punishment was "within the range of confinement to be normally expected" while serving such a sentence. The Chief Justice added that prisoner complaints that are nothing more than complaints about "the ordinary incidents of prison life" should not be accorded constitutional status by federal judges. *Sandin v. Connor* did not overrule *Wolff v. McDonnell*. However, *Sandin* does make it somewhat harder for prisoners to bring constitutional challenges against prison disciplinary proceedings or against transfer and classification decisions made by correctional officials. The main result will be still more confusion as lower courts decide on a case-by-case basis whether or not an inmate's grievance involves an "atypical and significant hardship."

Prison law is often perplexing and ambiguous. As in all areas of law, the Supreme Court simply cannot hear enough cases to clarify all of the corollary principles that may derive from its major decisions. The emotionally charged issues that are often present in major prisoners' rights cases and the difficulties inherent in writing majority opinions that must represent a compromise among the differing viewpoints of individual justices add considerably to the likelihood that the Supreme Court's corrections law decisions will be inexact and uncertain. Our next article—another contribution by William C. Collins—provides an excellent overview of the confusion generated by the Supreme Court's prison law decisions. In "The Eighth Amendment in Prison: Does the Supreme Court Know Where It Is Going?" Collins tries to make sense out of the Supreme Court's recent efforts to determine what constitutes a "cruel and unusual" punishment in the prison context. This is a relatively new and interesting area of law, and readers will almost surely conclude that the answer to the question in the article's title is "no."

Our final two selections in Part III assess the impact of prison litigation. First, Geoffrey Alpert, Ben Crouch, and Ronald Huff investigate the latent or unintended consequences of *Ruiz v. Estelle* (1980)—a case in which a federal district judge declared the operations of the Texas prison system to be in violation of the Eighth Amendment and entered an extensive remedial order affecting virtually every aspect of Texas prison management. Applying "rising expectations" theory to their analysis of events immediately following the *Ruiz* decision, Alpert, Crouch, and Huff contend that while mandating many desirable changes, the remedial decree set in motion a chain of events that led to at least a temporary increase in prison disturbances and riots. In 1982, a federal appeals court affirmed the district court's finding of unconstitutional prison conditions, but modified some of the relief, particularly the orders relating to overcrowding. However, much of the original decree remains in effect, and only time will tell whether the *Ruiz* decision will result in a long-term reduction of violence and meaningful improvements in institutional conditions.

More positive findings concerning the impact of court decisions on inmate behavior have been reported elsewhere. For example, some of the studies cited in chapter 14 of this book show that improved prison legal assistance programs mandated by court decisions have promoted values conducive to rehabilitation by convincing inmates that they are being treated fairly. The finding that legal aid programs can be rehabilitative may surprise some readers. However, by reducing the tensions that inevitably accompany unresolved legal problems and by decreasing feelings of vulnerability and powerlessness, litigation can sometimes have a beneficial effect upon a prisoner's mental health. A dramatic example of this phenomenon is provided in the final selection in Part III. Richard Korn's "Litigation Can Be Therapeutic" tells the fascinating story of Bobby Hardwick's legal struggles against the Georgia prison system. Bobby Hardwick's victory over his keepers in the courtroom was remarkable, but even more remarkable was his triumph over mental illness.

13

The Constitution and the Federal District Judge

Frank M. Johnson

Modern American society depends upon our judicial system to play a critical role in maintaining the balance between governmental powers and individual rights. The increasing concern paid by our courts toward the functioning of government and its agencies has received much comment[1] and some criticism[2] recently. As governmental institutions at all levels have assumed a greater role in providing public services, courts increasingly have been confronted with the unavoidable duty of determining whether those services meet basic constitutional requirements. Time and again citizens have brought to the federal courts, and those courts reluctantly have decided, such basic questions as how and when to make available equal quality public education to all our children; how to guarantee all citizens an opportunity to serve on juries, to vote, and to have their votes counted equally; under what minimal living conditions criminal offenders may be incarcerated; and what minimum standards of care and treatment state institutions must provide the mentally ill and mentally retarded who have been involuntarily committed to the custody of the state.

Source: Published originally in 54 Texas L. Rev. 903, (1976). Copyright © 1976 by the *Texas Law Review*. Reprinted by permission of the *Texas Law Review*.

The reluctance with which courts and judges have undertaken the complex task of deciding such questions has at least three important sources. First, one of the founding principles of our Government,[3] a principle derived from the French philosophers of the eighteenth century, is that the powers of government should be separate and distinct, lest all the awesome power of government unite as one force unchecked in its exercise. The drafters of our Constitution formulated the doctrine of separation of powers to promote the independence of each branch of government in its sphere of operation. To the extent that courts respond to requests to look to the future and to change existing conditions by making new rules, however, they become subject to the charge of usurping authority from the legislative or executive branch.

Second, our Constitution and laws have strictly limited the power of the federal judiciary to participate in what are essentially political affairs. The tenth amendment[4] reserves any power not delegated to the United States to the individual states or to the people. Reflecting the distrust of centralized government expressed by this amendment, courts and citizens alike since the Nation's beginning have regarded certain governmental functions as primarily, if not exclusively, state responsibilities. Among these are public education;[5] maintenance of state and local penal institutions;[6] domestic relations;[7] and provision for the poor, homeless, aged, and infirm.[8] A further limitation on the role of federal courts with respect to other governmental bodies lies in the creation and maintenance of these courts as courts of limited jurisdiction.

Last, federal judges properly hesitate to make decisions either that require the exercise of political judgment[9] or that necessitate expertise they lack.[10] Judges are professionally trained in the law—not in sociology, education, medicine, penology, or public administration. In an ideal society, elected officials would make all decisions relating to the allocation of resources; experts trained in corrections would make all penological decisions; physicians would make all medical decisions; scientists would make all technological decisions; and educators would make all educational decisions. Too often, however, we have failed to achieve this ideal system. Many times, those persons to whom we have entrusted these responsibilities have acted or failed to act in ways that do not fall within the bounds of discretion permitted by the Constitution and the laws. When such transgressions are properly and formally brought before a court—and increasingly before federal courts—it becomes the responsibility of the judiciary to ensure that the Constitution and laws of the United States remain, in fact as well as in theory, the supreme law of the land.

On far too many occasions the intransigent and unremitting opposition of state officials who have neglected or refused to correct unconstitutional or unlawful state policies and practices has necessitated federal intervention to enforce the law. Courts in all sections of the Nation have expended and continue to expend untold resources in repeated litigation brought to compel local school officials to follow a rule of law first announced by the Supreme Court almost twenty-two years ago.[11] In addition to deciding scores of school cases, federal courts in Alabama alone have ordered the desegregation of mental institutions,[12] penal facilities,[13] public parks,[14] city buses,[15] interstate and intrastate buses and bus terminals,[16] airport terminals,[17] and public libraries and museums.[18] Although I refer to Alabma and specific cases litigated in the federal courts of Alabama, I do not intend to suggest that similar problems do not exist in many of our other states.

The history of public school desegregation has been a story of repeated intervention by the courts to overcome not only the threats and violence of extremists attempting to block school desegregation[19] but also the numerous attempts by local and state officials to thwart the orderly, efficient, and lawful resolution of this complicated social problem.[20] Desegregation is not the only area of state responsibility in which Alabama officials have forfeited their decisionmaking powers by such a dereliction of duty as to require judicial intervention. Having found Alabama's legislative apportionment plan unconstitutional,[21] the District Court for the Middle District of Alabama waited ten years for State officials to carry out the duty properly imposed upon them by the Constitution and expressly set out in the court's order. The continued refusal of those officials to comply left the court no choice but to assume that duty itself and to impose its own reapportionment plan.[22] State officers by their inaction have also handed over to the courts property tax assessment plans;[23] standards for the care and treatment of mentally ill and mentally retarded persons committed to the State's custody;[24] and the procedures by which such persons are committed.[25]

Some of these cases are extremely troublesome and time consuming for all concerned. I speak in particular of those lawsuits challenging the operation of state institutions for the custody and control of citizens who cannot or will not function at a safe and self-sustaining capacity in a free society. Ordinarily these cases proceed as class actions seeking to determine the rights of large numbers of people. As a result, the courts' decisions necessarily have wide-ranging effect and momentous importance, whether they grant or deny the relief sought.

A shocking example of a failure of state officials to discharge their duty was forcefully presented in a lawsuit tried before me in 1972, *Newman v. Alabama*,[26] which challenged the constitutional sufficiency of medical care available to prisoners in the Alabama penal system.

The evidence in that case convincingly demonstrated that correctional officers on occasion intentionally denied inmates the right to examination by a physician or to treatment by trained medical personnel, and that they routinely withheld medicine and other treatments prescribed by physicians. Further evidence showed that untrained inmates served as ward attendants and X-ray, laboratory, and dental technicians; rags were used as bandages; ambulance oxygen tanks remained empty for long periods of time; and unsupervised inmates without formal training pulled teeth, gave injections, sutured, and performed minor surgery. In fact, death resulting from gross neglect and totally inadequate treatment was not unusual.

A nineteen-year-old with an extremely high fever who was diagnosed as having acute pneumonia was left unsupervised and allowed to take cold showers at will for two days before his death. A quadriplegic with bedsores infested with maggots was bathed and had his bandages changed only once in the month before his death. An inmate who could not eat received no nourishment for the three days prior to his death even though intravenous feeding had been ordered by a doctor. A geriatric inmate who had suffered a stroke was made to sit each day on a wooden bench so that he would not soil his bed; he frequently fell onto the floor; his legs became swollen from a lack of circulation, necessitating the amputation of a leg the day before his death.[27]

Based on the virtually uncontradicted evidence presented at trial, the district court entered a comprehensive order designed to remedy each specific abuse proved at trial and to establish additional safeguards so that the medical program in Alabama prisons would never again regress to its past level of inadequacy.[28] The State was ordered to bring the general hospital at the Medical and Diagnostic Center (now Kilby Corrections Facility) up to the minimum standards required of hospitals by the United States Department of Health, Education, and Welfare for participation in the medicare program.[29] The court also directed the Alabama State Board of Health to inspect regularly for general sanitation all the medical and food processing facilities in the prison system.[30] Finally, the court decreed that all inmates receive physical examinations by physicians at regular intervals of not more than two years.[31]

One of the most comprehensive orders that I have entered concerning the operation and management of state institutions relates to the facilities maintained by the Alabama Department of Mental Health for the mentally ill and mentally retarded. Plaintiffs in *Wyatt v. Stickney*[32] brought a class action on behalf of all patients involuntarily confined at Bryce Hospital, the State's largest mental hospital, to establish the minimum standards of care and treatment to which the civilly committed are entitled under the Constitution. Patients at Searcy

Hospital in southern Alabama and residents at the Partlow State School and Hospital in Tuscaloosa joined the action as plaintiffs, thereby compelling a comprehensive inquiry into the entire Alabama mental health and retardation treatment and habilitation program.

At trial plaintiffs produced evidence showing that Bryce Hospital, build in the 1850's, was grossly overcrowded, housing more than 5000 patients.[33] Of these 5000 people ostensibly committed to Bryce for treatment of mental illness, about 1600 — almost one-third — were geriatrics neither needing nor receiving any treatment for mental illness. Another 1000 or more of the patients at Bryce were mentally retarded rather than mentally ill. A totally inadequate staff, only a small percentage professionally trained, served these 5000 patients. The hospital employed only six staff members qualified to deal with mental patients — three medical doctors with psychiatric training, one Ph.D. psychologist, and two social workers with master's degrees in social work. The evidence indicated that the general living conditions and lack of individualized treatment programs were as intolerable and deplorable as Alabama's rank of fiftieth among the states in per patient expenditures[34] would suggest. For example, the hospital spent less than fifty cents per patient each day for food.[35]

The evidence concerning Partlow State School and Hospital for the retarded proved even more shocking than the evidence relating to the mental hospitals. The extremely dangerous conditions compelled the court to issue an interim emergency order[36] requiring Partlow officials to take immediate steps to protect the lives and safety of the residents. The Associate Commissioner for Mental Retardation for the Alabama Department of Mental Health testified that Partlow was sixty percent overcrowded; that the school, although it had not, could immediately discharge at least 300 residents; *and that seventy percent of the residents should never have been committed at all.*[37] The conclusion that there was no opportunity for habilitation for its residents was inescapable. Indeed, the evidence reflected that one resident was scalded to death when a fellow resident hosed water from one of the bath facilities on him; another died as a result of the insertion of a running water hose into his rectum by a working resident who was cleaning him; one died when soapy water was forced into his mouth; another died of a self-administered overdose of inadequately stored drugs; and authorities restrained another resident in a straitjacket for *nine years* to prevent him from sucking his hands and fingers. Witnesses described the Partlow facilities as barbaric and primitive;[38] some residents had no place to sit to eat meals, and coffee cans served as toilets in some areas of the institution.

With the exception of the interim emergency order designed to eliminate hazardous conditions at Partlow, the court at first declined to devise specific steps to improve existing conditions in Alabama's mental health and retardation facilties. Instead, it directed the Department of Mental Health to design its own plan for upgrading the system to meet constitutional standards.[39] Only after two deadlines had passed without any signs of acceptable progress did the court itself, relying upon the proposals of counsel for all parties and amici curiae, define the minimal constitutional standards of care, treatment, and habilitation[40] for which the case of *Wyatt v. Stickney* has become generally known.

During the past several years conditions at the Partlow State School for the retarded have improved markedly. It was pleasing to read in a Montgomery newspaper that members of the State Mental Health Board (the *Wyatt* defendants) recently met at Partlow and agreed that "what they saw was a different world" compared to four years ago; that "things are now unbelievably better," with most students "out in the sunshine on playground swings or tossing softballs [,]...responding to a kind word or touch with smiles and squeals of delight"; and that "enrollment has been nearly cut in half, down from 2,300 to just under 1,300 while the staff has tripled from 600 to 1,800."[41]

Persons incarcerated in state and local prison and jail facilities around the Nation increasingly have attacked the conditions of their confinement as unconstitutional. In recent years, federal courts in Alabama,[42] Arkansas,[43], Florida,[44] Maryland,[45] Massachusetts,[46] and Mississippi,[47] among others, have been forced to declare that the constitutional rights of inmates are denied by the mere fact of their confinement in institutions that inflict intolerable and inhuman living conditions. In Texas a federal judge has held unconstitutional the detention of juveniles in certain facilities maintained by the Texas Youth Council because of the extreme brutality and indifference experienced in these institutions.[48] In fashioning appropriate remedies in these cases, the courts have exhibited sensitivity to the real but not the imagined limitations imposed on correctional officials forced to operate penal facilities with the meager sums appropriated by legislators who see few or no political rewards in supporting constitutional treatment of prisoners. Some courts have ordered that entire institutions be closed and abandoned;[49] others have required substantial improvements in facilities and services as a precondition to their continued operation.[50]

Knowing firsthand the considerable time, energy, and thought that must precede any decision affecting mental hospital or prison conditions, I seriously doubt that any judge relishes his involvement in such a controversy or enters a decree unless the law clearly makes it his duty to do so. The Fifth Circuit adheres to the well-settled rule that federal courts do not sit to supervise state prisons or to interfere with their internal operation and administration.[51] The American system of justice, however, equally acknowledges that inmates do not lose all constitutional rights and privileges when they are confined following conviction of criminal offenses.[52]

James v. Wallace,[53] a recent class action tried before me objecting to conditions in Alabama's state penal facilities, presents another graphic example of how a state's irresponsibility in carrying out an essential governmental function necessitated federal judicial intervention to restore constitutional rights to citizens whose rights were systematically disregarded and denied. Preserving prisoners' rights is no less vital than safeguarding the liberties of school children, black citizens, women, and others who have found it necessary to resort to the courts to secure their constitutional rights.[54] The *James* trial began last August following extensive pretrial discovery, which included more than 1000 facts stipulated to by all parties and filed with the court. At the close of the defendants' case, the lead counsel for the Governor and the State Board of Corrections acknowledged in open court that "the overwhelming majority of the evidence...shows that an Eighth Amendment violation has and is now occurring to inmates in the Alabama prison system."[55]

Plaintiffs in *James* demonstrated the intolerability of life in Alabama's prisons by proof of both general living conditions and commonplace incidents. Fighting, assault, extortion, theft, and homosexual rape are everyday occurrences in all four main institutions. A mentally retarded twenty-year-old inmate, after testifying that doctors had told him he had the mind of a five-year-old, told in open court how four inmates raped him on his first night in an Alabama prison.[56]

The evidence showed that most prisoners found it necessary to carry some form of homemade or contraband weapon merely for self-protection. One prisoner testified that he would rather be caught with a weapon by a prison guard than be caught without one by another prisoner.[57] Seriously dilapidated physical facilities have created generally unsanitary and hazardous living conditions in Alabama's prisons. Roaches, flies, mosquitoes, and other vermin overrun the institutions. One living area in Draper prison housing over 200 men contained one functioning toilet.

A United States public health officer, testifying as an expert witness after having inspected the four major prisons, pronounced the facilities wholly unfit for human habitation according to virtually every criterion used for evaluation by public health inspectors. He testified that as a public health officer, he would recommend the closing of any similar facilities under his jurisdiction because they presented an imminent danger to the health of the exposed individuals.[58] Moreover, all the parties to the lawsuit agreed that severe overcrowding and understaffing aggravated all these other difficulties. At the time of trial over 3500 prisoners resided in facilities designed for no more than 2300. The Commissioner of the Alabama Board of Corrections testified that although the prison system required a minimum staff of 692 correctional officers, it then employed 383.[59] Correctional experts testified that such an overflow of prisoners, coupled with the shortage of supervisory personnel, precludes any meaningful control over the institutions by the responsible officials. The facts bore out that conclusion. Prison guards simply refused to enter some dormitories at night,[60] and one warden testified that he would not enter a certain dormitory at his institution without at least four guards by his side.

Understaffing and lack of funds have deprived nearly all the inmates who are confined twenty-four hours a day of meaningful activity; usually they lie around idle. Most live in dormitories or barracks that afford them neither privacy nor security for their personal possessions. The defendants stipulated that over half of the prison population possessed no skills, and that in the first quarter of 1975 the average entering inmate could not read at the sixth-grade level. The few vocational training and basic education programs offered can accommodate only a tiny fraction of the inmates, and the entry requirements for the programs are highly restrictive. Alabama prisons do not have a working classification system, an essential ingredient of any properly operated penal system. A functioning classification system enables officials to segregate for treatment and for the protection of other prisoners not able or willing to function in any social setting. Currently, mentally disturbed inmates receive no special care or therapy, and are housed and treated like the general prison population. Consequently, violent and aggressive prisoners live together with those who are weak, passive, or otherwise easily victimized. For example, when the twenty-year-old inmate I spoke of earlier reported the rape to prison officials, the warden of the institution told him that he, the warden, could do nothing about it.

Since the final order in *James,* new reports have revealed other instances of what at best constitute questionable management practices. A committee of the Alabama Legislature investigating prison operations disclosed that financial records reflect the use of prison funds to purchase cases of caviar, evidently consumed in the course of entertaining legislators.[61] The committee also questioned a recent transaction in which the Alabama Board of Corrections approved the bartering of fifty-two head of beef cattle owned by the Board in exchange for three Tennessee walking horses. The Commissioner of Corrections publicly explained that the horses were acquired for breeding purposes.[62] It later developed that the horses obtained for breeding purposes were geldings.[63]

Based on the overwhelming and generally undisputed evidence presented at trial, the court granted immediate partial relief to plaintiffs in the form of two interim orders,[64] which remain in effect. One order enjoined the State from accepting additional prisoners, except escapees and parole violators, until each State prison facility decreases its population to its design capacity. The second ruling banned the use of isolation and segregation cells that fail to meet minimum standards. Before this order, as many as six inmates were confined in four-by-eight foot cells with no beds, no lighting, no running water, and a hole in the floor for a toilet that only a guard outside could flush.

The final opinion and order entered in *James* in January 1976 established a broad range of minimum standards[65] designed to remedy the broad range of constitutional deprivations proven at trial and conceded to exist by the State's lawyers. The standards govern staffing; classification of prisoners; mental and physical health care; physical facilities; protection of inmates; and educational, vocational, recreational, and work programs.

The fourteenth amendment,[66] which generates much of the litigation discussed above, forbids a state to "deprive any person of life, liberty or property, without due process of law" or to "deny to any person within its jurisdiction the equal protection of the laws."[67] The Supreme Court has interpreted the due process clause to require that the states fulfill most of the obligations toward citizens that the Bill of Rights imposes on the federal government.[68] Each state in all its dealings with its people must recognize and preserve their guaranteed freedoms. Nevertheless, state officials have frequently raised the tenth amendments's reservation of powers to the states as a defense to the exercise of federal jurisdiction over actions alleging state violations of constitutional rights. While the tenth amendment clearly preserves for the states a wide and important sphere of power, it does not permit any state to frustrate or to ignore the mandates of the Constitution. *The tenth amendment does not relieve the states of a single obligation imposed upon them by the Constitution of the United States.* Surely the concept of states' rights has never purported to allow states to abdicate their responsibility to protect their citizens from criminal acts and inhumane conditions. I find it sad and ironic that citizens of Alabama held in "protective custody" by Alabama had to obtain federal court orders to protect themselves from violent crimes and barbaric conditions.

The cornerstone of our American legal system rests on recognition of the Constitution as the supreme law of the land,[69] and the paramount duty of the federal judiciary is to uphold that law.[70] Thus, when a state fails to meet constitutionally mandated requirements, it is the solemn duty of the courts to assure compliance with the Constitution. One writer has termed the habit adopted by some states of neglecting their responsibilities until faced with a federal court order "the Alabama Federal Intervention Syndrome," characterizing it as

> the tendency of many state officials to punt their problems with constituencies to the federal courts. Many federal judges have grown accustomed to allowing state officials to make political speeches as a prelude to receiving the order of the district court. This role requires the federal courts to serve as a buffer between the state officials and their constituencies, raising the familiar criticism that state officials rely upon the federal courts to impose needed reforms rather than accomplishing them themselves.[71]

As long as those state officials entrusted with the responsibility for fair and equitable governance completely disregard that responsibility, the judiciary must and will stand ready to intervene on behalf of the deprived. Judge Richard T. Rives of the Court of Appeals for the Fifth Circuit, in joining a three-judge panel that struck down attempts by state officials to frustrate the registration of black voters, eloquently expressed the reluctance with which the vast majority of federal judges approach intervention in state affairs:

> I look forward to the day when the State and its political sub-divisions will again take up their mantle of responsibility, treating all of their citizens equally, and thereby relieve the federal Government of the necessity of intervening in their affairs. Until that day arrives, the responsibility for this intervention must rest with those who through their ineptitude and public disservice have forced it.[72]

We in the judiciary await the day when the Alabama Federal Intervention Syndrome, in that State and elsewhere, will become a relic of the past. To reclaim responsibilities passed by default to the judiciary — most often the federal judiciary — and to find solutions for ever-changing challenges, the states must preserve their ability to respond flexibly, creatively, and with due regard for the rights of all. State officials must confront their governmental responsibilities with the diligence and honesty that their constituencies deserve. When lawful rights are being denied, only the exercise of conscientious, responsible leadership, which is usually long on work and short on complimentary news headlines, can avoid judicial intervention. The most fitting Bicentennial observance I can conceive would be for all government officials to take up the constitutional mantle and diligently strive to protect the basic human rights recognized by the founders of our Republic two hundred years ago.

Notes

[1]See, e.g., L. Levy, *Judgments* 33-57 (1972); Mason, *Judicial Activism: Old and New*, 55 *Va. L. Rev.* 385, 394-426 (1969).

[2]See, e.g., Griswold, *The Judicial Process*, 31 *Fed. B.J.* 309, 321-25 (1972).

[3]See *The Federalist* Nos. 47, 48 (J. Madison).

[4]*U.S. Const.* amend. X.

[5]Cumming v. Richmond County Bd. of Educ., 175 U.S. 528, 545 (1899); Crews v. Cloncs, 432 F.2d 1259, 1265 (7th Cir. 1970).

[6]Hoag v. New Jersey, 356 U.S. 464 (1958); Threatt v. North Carolina, 221 F. Supp. 858, 860 (W.D.N.C. 1963).

[7]Ohio *ex rel.* Popovici v. Agler, 280 U.S. 379, 383 (1930); Morris v. Morris, 273 F.2d 678, 682 (7th Cir. 1960); Ainscow v. Alexander, 28 Del. Ch. 545, 550, 39 A.2d 54, 56 (Super, Ct. 1944).

[8]Adkins v. Curtis, 259 Ala. 311, 315, 66 So. 2d 455, 458 (1953); Beck v. Buena Park Hotel Corp., 30 Ill. 2d 343, 346, 196 N.E.2d 686, 688 (1964); Collins v. State bd. of Social Welfare, 248 Iowa 369, 375, 81 N.W.2d 4, 7 (1957).

[9]See, e.g., Marbury v. Madison, 5 U.S. (1 Cranch) 137, 170 (1803).

[10]See, e.g., Brotherhood of Locomotive Firemen v. Chicago, R.I. & P.R.R., 393 U.S. 129, 136-37 (1968).

[11]Brown v. Board of Educ., 347 U.S. 484 (1954).

[12]Marable v. Mental Health Bd., 297 F. Supp. 291 (M.D. Ala. 1969).

[13]Washington v. Lee, 263 F. Supp. 327 (M.D. Ala. 1966), *aff'd*, 390 U.S. 333 (1968).

[14]Gilmore v. City of Montgomery, 176 F. Supp. 776 (M.D. Ala. 1959), *modified*, 277 F.2d 364 (5th Cir. 1960), *rev'd in part*, 417 U.S. 556 (1974).

[15]Browder v. Gayle, 142 F. Supp. 707 (M.D. Ala.), *aff'd*, 352 U.S. 903 (1956).

[16]Lewis v. Greyhound Corp., 199 F. Supp. 210 (M.D. Ala. 1961).

[17]United States v. City of Montgomery, 201 F. Supp. 590 (M.D. Ala. 1962).

[18]Cobb v. Library Bd., 207 F. Supp. 88Q (M.D. Ala. 1962).

[19]United States v. United Klans of America, 290 F. Supp. 181 (M.D. Ala. 1968).

[20]Harris v. Board of Educ., 259 F. Supp. 167 (M.D. Ala. 1966); Lee v. Board of Educ., 231 F. Supp. 743 (M.D. Ala. 1964).

[21]Sims v. Frink, 208 F. Supp. 431 (M.D. Ala. 1962), *aff'd sub nom.* Reynolds v. Sims, 377 U.S. 533 (1964).

[22]Sims v. Amos, 336 F. Supp. 924 (M.D. Ala.), *aff'd*, 409 U.S. 942 (1972).

[23]Weissinger v. Boswell, 330 F Supp. 615 (M.D. Ala. 1971) (per curiam).

[24]Wyatt v. Stickney, 324 F. Supp. 781 (M.D. Ala. 1971), *enforced*, 344 F. Supp. 373 (M.D. Ala. 1972) (mentally ill) *and* 344 F. Supp. 387 (M.D. Ala. 1972), *modified sub nom.* Wyatt v. Aderholt, 503 F.2d 1305 (5th Cir. 1974) (mentally retarded).

[25]Lynch v. Baxley, 386 F. Supp. 378 (M.D. Ala. 1974).

[26]349 F. Supp. 278 (M.D. Ala. 1972), *aff'd in part*, 503 F.2d 1320 (5th Cir. 1974), *cert. denied*, 421 U.S. 948 (1975).

[27]*Id.* at 285.

[28]*Id.* at 286-88.

[29]*Id.* at 286.

[30]*Id.* at 287.

[31]*Id.*

[32]325 F. Supp. 781 (M.D. Ala. 1971), *enforced,* 344 F. Supp. 373 (M.D. Ala. 1972) *and* 344 F. Supp. 387 (M.D. Ala. 1972), *modified sub nom.* Wyatt v. Aderholt, 503 F.2d 1305 (5th Cir. 1974) (affirming constitutional "right to treatment").

[33]*Id.* at 782.

[34]*Id.* at 784.

[35]Wyatt v. Aderholt, 503 F.2d 1305, 1310 (5th Cir. 1974).

[36]Wyatt v. Stickney, Civil No. 3195-N (M.D. Ala., Mar. 2, 1972) (emergency order). This order preceded the final order.

[37]Wyatt v. Aderholt, 503 F.2d 1305, 1310 (5th Cir. 1974).

[38]See Wyatt v. Stickney, 344 F. Supp. 387, 391 n.7 (M.D. Ala. 1972).

[39]Wyatt v. Stickney, 325 F. Supp. 781, 785-86 (M.D. Ala. 1971).

[40]344 F. Supp. at 395-409 (Partlow State School); 344 F. Supp. at 379-86 (Bryce Hospital).

[41]Reese, *Things Unbelievably Better at Partlow, Director Says,* Alabama Journal, Feb. 20, 1976, at 13, cols. 3-4.

[42]McCray V. Sullivan, Civil. No. 5620-69-H (S.D. Ala., Feb. 10, 1976); James v. Wallace, 406 F. Supp. 318 (M.D. Ala. 1976).

[43]Holt v. Sarver, 309 F. Supp. 362 (E.D. Ark. 1970), *aff'd,* 442 F.2d 304 (8th Cir. 1971).

[44]Costello v. Wainwright, 397 F. Supp. 20 (M.D. Fla. 1975), *aff'd,* 525 F.2d 1239, *rehearing in banc granted,* 528 F.2d 1381 (Mar. 3, 1976) (No. 75-2392).

[45]Collins v. Schoonfield, 344 F. Supp. 257 (D. Md. 1972).

[46]Inmates of Suffolk County Jail v. Eisenstadt, 360 F. Supp. 676 (D. Mass. 1973), *aff'd,* 494 F. 2d 1196 (1st Cir.) *cert. denied,* 419 U.S. 977 (1974).

[47]Gates v. Collier, 349 F. Supp. 881 (N.D. Miss. 1972), *aff'd,* 501 F.2d 1291 (5th Cir. 1974).

[48]Morales v. Turman, 383 F. Supp. 53 (E.D. Tex. 1974).

[49]*Id.*

[50]James v. Wallace, 406 F. Supp. 318 (M.D. Ala. 1976); Costello v. Wainwright, 397 F. Supp. 20 (M.D. Fla. 1975), *aff'd,* 525 F.2d 1239 (5th Cir. 1976).

[51]Novak v. Beto, 453 F.2d 661, 671 (5th Cir. 1971); Newman v. Alabama, 349 F. Supp. 278, 280 (M.D. Ala. 1972), *aff'd in part,* 503 F.2d 1320 (5th Cir. 1974), *cert. denied,* 421 U.S. 948 (1975).

[52]Washington v. Lee, 263 F. Supp. 327, 331 (M.D. Ala. 1966), *aff'd per curiam,* 390 U.S. 333 (1968).

[53]406 F. Supp. 318 (M.D. Ala. 1976).

[54]Recently courts have recognized that prisoners retain all their constitutional rights except those necessarily diminished as an incident of incarceration. See Pell v. Procunier, 417 U.S. 817, 822 (1973); Jackson v. Godwin, 400 F.2d 529, 532 (5th Cir. 1968); James v. Wallace, 406 F. Supp. 318, 328 (M.D. Ala. 1976).

[55]Record, vol. II, at 357. The eighth amendment prohibits "cruel and unusual punishments." *U.S. Const.* amend. VIII.

[56]406 F. Supp. at 325.

[57]*Id.*

[58]*Id.* at 323-24.

[59]*Id.* at 325.

[60]*Id.*

[61]Montgomery Advertiser, Feb. 6, 1976, at 1, cols. 5-8.

[62]*Id.*

[63]Alabama Journal, Feb. 6, 1976, at 13, cols. 5-6.

[64]406 F. Supp. at 322, 327.

[65]*Id.* at 332-35.

[66]*U.S. Const.* amend. XIV.

[67]*Id.*

[68]Duncan v. Louisiana, 391 U.S. 145 (1968).

[69]See *U.S. Const.* art VI, §2.

[70]See Mitchum v. Foster, 407 U.S. 225, 238-39 (1972); Zwickler v. Koota, 389 U.S. 241, 248 (1967); England v. Louisiana State Bd. of Medical Examiners, 375 U.S. 411, 415 (1964).

[71]McCormack, *The Expansion of Federal Question Jurisdiction and the Prisoner Complaint Caseload,* 1975 Wis. L. Rev. 523, 536 (footnotes omitted).

[72]Dent v. Duncan, 360 F.2d 333, 337-38 (5th Cir. 1966).

14

American Prisoners and the Right of Access to the Courts
A Vanishing Concept of Protection

Kenneth C. Haas
Geoffrey P. Alpert

Introduction

In 1987, Americans celebrated the 200th anniversary of the United States Constitution. It is from this document that our basic rights and responsibilities have been developed. These rights, however, have never been distributed equally to all segments of the population. For example, the rights enumerated in the Constitution have never been fully extended to those who are incarcerated. Although the rights of free citizens have been generally preserved during this 200-year period, the history of prisoners' rights is a history of indifference and neglect.

Source: From *The American Prison: Issues in Research and Policy*, edited by Lynne Goodstein and Doris Layton MacKenzie (Plenum Publishing Corporation, 1989). Reprinted by permission of the publisher.

Prisoners have always been the forgotten Americans in the United States Constitution. The original document of 1787 affirmed the fundamental right of habeas corpus (the right to challenge the legality of one's confinement) but did not specifically mention prisoners. Two years later, the Bill of Rights—the first 10 amendments to the Constitution—provided safeguards for those accused of crime. However, it would take nearly two centuries for the Bill of Rights to emerge as a major weapon in securing rights for those already convicted of crimes. And it would take the courts equally as long to recognize that "a right of access to the courts is one of the rights a prisoner clearly retains" (*Coleman* v. *Peyton*, 1966: 907).

The purposes of this chapter are to examine the prisoner's right of access to the courts and to comment on how changes in this area of law may affect research on prisons and on the role of the courts in spurring prison reform. The right of access is the most important of all prisoners' rights because it is the right upon which all other rights turn. Without it, prisoners would have no way to appeal their convictions or to vindicate their rights in such areas of law as the First Amendment's protections of speech, religion, and peaceable assembly; the Eighth Amendment's ban on cruel and unusual punishments; and the right to Fifth and Fourteenth Amendment due process in prison disciplinary proceedings.

We will explore the right of access by examining the two major types of cases that make up this body of law. First, we will focus on cases that involve the constitutionality of various prison policies that allegedly interfere with inmate efforts to seek judicial relief. Second, we will analyze recent trends in cases dealing with the availability of judicial remedies frequently sought by prisoners. These cases involve procedural and jurisdictional questions that can either make judicial remedies easier to obtain or place severe restrictions on the right of access.

Prison Policies and Practices Affecting the Right of Access to the Courts

U.S. Supreme Court Decisions

Until the past 20 years, federal and state courts followed a policy of declining jurisdiction in nearly all suits brought by prisoners. Generally known as the "hands-off" doctrine, this policy reflected the traditional view of the prisoner as a "slave of the state" (*Ruffin* v. *Commonwealth*, 1871: 796) without enforceable rights. As a practical matter, the judiciary's extreme reluctance to become involved in the internal operations of prisons made it virtually impossible for prisoners to seek judicial relief from alleged mistreatment and needlessly harsh conditions of confinement (Haas, 1977). Generally, the courts based their refusals to hear prisoner complaints on one or more of five rationales:

1. The separation of powers doctrine
2. The low level of judicial expertise in penology
3. The fear that judicial intervention would undermine prison discipline
4. The fear that opening the courthouse doors to prisoners would result in a deluge of inmate litigation
5. The view that considerations of federalism and comity should preclude consideration of the claims of state prisoners by federal courts (Haas, 1977).

A strict version of the hands-off doctrine prevailed among most courts until the late 1960s and early 1970s. Nevertheless, it was in 1941—a time when the hands-off doctrine remained strong—that the U.S. Supreme Court first recognized that the due process clauses of the Fifth and Fourteenth Amendments guarantee all Americans—even prisoners—the right of access to the courts. In the case of *Ex Parte Hull*, the Court struck down a Michigan prison regulation that required inmates to submit all their legal petitions to prison officials for approval. Whenever prison authorities felt that inmate petitions were frivolous, inaccurate, or poorly written, they would refuse to mail them to the courts. The Supreme Court held that this procedure amounted to an impermissible denial of the fundamental right of access to the courts. In no uncertain terms, the Justices told prison officials: "Whether a petition for a writ of habeas corpus addressed to a federal court is properly drawn and what allegations it must contain are questions for that court alone to determine" (*Hull* at 549).

Despite the *Hull* ruling, most courts remained extremely reluctant to interfere with prison policies restricting inmate access to the courts. In the 1950s and 1960s, many courts approved such prison practices as refusing to allow prisoners to purchase law books, prohibiting correspondence with law book publishers, allowing the confiscation of an inmate's legal documents found in another inmate's cell, refusing to permit a prisoner to type his or her own legal papers, and censoring or withholding legal correspondence between prisoners and attorneys (Edwards, 1968). Moreover, even when prison regulations were more accommodating to the right of access, ignorance, illiteracy, and poverty kept prisoners with arguably meritorious claims from filing their complaints.

Like their counterparts of yesteryear, today's prisoners often discover that legal barriers and personal handicaps can make court access very difficult. The right to a state-supplied attorney does not extend to inmate actions attacking prison conditions or to discretionary appeals of a criminal conviction (*Ross* v. *Moffitt*, 1974). Prisoners lack the money to hire attorneys, and they rarely possess the literacy needed to write and interest attorneys who might take a case without fee. As a result, the large majority of cases brought by prisoners originate from either the petitioning prisoner or from a "jailhouse lawyer" or "writ-writer" — a prisoner who claims to have expertise in law and prepares legal documents for fellow inmates. Thus it is not surprising that the first major right of access case after *Hull* involved the limitations that prison officials could place on jailhouse lawyers.

In *Johnson* v. *Avery* (1969), the Supreme Court invalidated prison regulations that prohibited jailhouse lawyers from helping other prisoners with their legal problems. The Court conceded that jailhouse lawyers may burden the courts with frivolous complaints and undermine prison discipline by establishing their own power structure and taking unfair advantage of gullible prisoners (*Johnson* at 488). Nevertheless, the Justices declared that these concerns were outweighed by the importance of insuring that prisoners have reasonable access to the courts and "the fundamental importance of the writ of habeas corpus in our constitutional scheme" (*Johnson* at 485). Because most prisoners possess neither the necessary funds to hire their attorneys nor the necessary educational background to write their own appeals, their only recourse in most cases, reasoned the Justices, was to seek the help of a jailhouse lawyer (*Johnson* at 488-490). Consequently, the High Court concluded that prison officials could no longer enforce no-assistance rules unless the prison itself provided some type of legal services program that was reasonably effective in assisting prisoners with their petitions for post-conviction relief (*Johnson* at 490).

At first glance, the *Johnson* holding may seem to be rather narrow. However, the *Johnson* precedent, more than any other decision, paved the way for more effective efforts by prisoners seeking access to the courts. In the aftermath of *Johnson*, it became increasingly difficult to escape the logic that if inmates have the right to the assistance of another inmate in the preparation of legal documents, they cannot be absolutely restrained from acquiring the requisite legal materials and due process protection needed to assist in the preparation of petitions or to acquire an attorney or some other type of competent assistance to help them seek an appropriate and speedy judicial remedy (see Haas, 1982: 728).

However, the *Johnson* decision lacked precision. It provided prison officials with only the basic parameters of the right of access. Since 1969, the Supreme Court has resolved several important issues left unsettled by *Johnson*. In *Younger* v. *Gilmore* (1971), the Court affirmed a lower court ruling that required prison officials to provide inmates with a law library that contained a sufficient collection of books and materials to assure that prisoners were able to file petitions that demonstrate at least some legal proficiency. Three years later, the Court struck down a California prison policy that barred law students and legal paraprofessionals from working with prisoners (*Procunier* v. *Martinez*, 1974: 419-422). Also in 1974, the Justices invalidated a Nebraska regulation stating that prisoners could seek legal assistance only from a single "inmate legal adviser" who was appointed by the warden and who was permitted to provide assistance only in preparing habeas corpus petitions (*Wolff* v. *McDonnell*, 1974: 577-580). Finally, in *Bounds* v. *Smith* (1977), the Court held that even when prison policies allow jailhouse lawyers to operate, prison officials nevertheless must provide prisoners with either an adequate law library or adequate assistance from persons trained in the law.

Like the *Johnson* opinion, the *Bounds* opinion was far from specific in explaining what it would take to provide "adequate" legal services and materials for prisoners. The *Bounds* Court simply noted:

> While adequate law libraries are one constitutionally acceptable method to assure meaningful access to the courts, our decision here . . . does not foreclose alternative means to achieve that goal. . . . Among the alternatives are the training of inmates as paralegal assistants to work under lawyers' supervision, the use of paraprofessionals and law students, either as volunteers or in formal clinical programs, the organization of volunteer attorneys through bar associations or other groups, the hiring of lawyers on a part-time consultant basis, and the use of full-time staff attorneys, working either in new prison legal assistance organizations or as part of public defender or legal services offices. (*Bounds* at 828)

Thus there is still confusion after *Bounds* as to what prison officials must do to guarantee inmates meaningful access to the courts. Questions involving the adequacy of particular prison law libraries or legal services programs must be answered by the state and federal courts on a case-by-case basis. In states with small, homogenous prison populations, it may be sufficient to provide adequate law libraries and access to materials with some quasi-professional help. But in large, multilingual prison populations that are found in larger states, licensed attorneys may be necessary to guarantee access to the courts (Note, 1983; Alpert and Huff, 1981). A federal district court in Florida adopted that view in 1982 (*Hooks* v. *Wainwright*), holding that the state's plan to provide prisoners with law libraries staffed by inmate law clerks and librarians was insufficient to guarantee prisoners access to the courts. Accordingly, the court ordered the Florida Department of Corrections to provide some form of attorney assistance as part of its legal services plan.

However, on appeal, this decision was reversed by the Eleventh Circuit Court of Appeals (*Hooks* v. *Wainwright*, 1985). The court of appeals held that the lower court had interpreted *Bounds* too broadly and that attorneys were not required. In other words, a combination of law libraries and inmate law clerks will meet the *Bounds* mandate. The Ninth Circuit also approved the use of inmate law clerks rather than lawyers (*Lindquist* v. *Idaho Board of Corrections*, 1985) but indicated that the clerks must have received at least some sort of organized training.

Thus the issue of what must be done for illiterate inmates remains unsettled. But at a minimum, it appears that most courts will require both an adequate law library and assistance from persons who have some demonstrable understanding of the legal process. We now look at some of the available programs that provide legal services to inmates in state prisons, and we assess the impact of such programs.

Prison Legal Assistance Programs and Their Impact

Two frequently found types of prison legal aid programs are (1) institutionally supported networks of jailhouse lawyers, and (2) resident counsel programs staffed by actual attorneys. Among the states that have institutionalized the jailhouse lawyer as a source of legal assistance to other prisoners are Nebraska and Pennsylvania (Bluth, 1972; Rudovsky, Bronstein, and Koren, 1983). Although the participating jailhouse lawyers are not permitted to collect fees or special favors for their work, they are commonly awarded "good time" credits that earn them earlier release from prison. Under the Pennsylvania system, a group of writ-writers offers free legal services to other prisoners, with work credit, supplies, and office space provided by prison officials. There is no definite answer as to whether or not such writ-writer programs are truly successful in meeting the complex legal needs of prisoners. But many legal scholars believe that to be effective, jailhouse lawyers should be supervised by an attorney who can make sure that the writ-writers are capable of competent work and do not encourage frivolous or repetitious suits (Gobert and Cohen, 1981: 31).

The second type of legal assistance program, resident counsel, may be designed to include jailhouse lawyers and law students or paralegals under the supervision of lawyers at the prison (Alpert and Huff, 1981: 339). Early examples of such programs can be found in Washington, Texas, and Massachusetts. These programs, and others like them, provide legal assistance in non-fee-generating cases through the use of licensed attorneys and trained paralegals. It seems likely that resident counsel programs are generally superior to jailhouse lawyer-run programs in providing competent and comprehensive legal assistance to prisoners. Attorneys with some background in prison law are usually familiar with the technical aspects of drafting pleas and practical matters of legal strategy.

As to possible disadvantages, resident counsel programs can be very costly, depending upon the number of attorneys required. Moreover, problems may develop in the relationships among attorneys and correctional officials. On the other hand, the fact that these lawyers are state employees may cause inmates to stay away from the service— seeing it as a "cop-out to the man" or as a token program designed merely to co-opt prisoners. If inmates fail to use state-funded attorneys for these or other reasons, access to the court has not been provided.

What affects the use of resident counsel programs by prisoners? In a study of such a program in the state of Washington, 120 out of 198 surveyed prisoners (61%) acknowledged that they had legal problems (Alpert, 1976). Ninety-one out of the 120 (76%) sought recourse to the legal aid project. Twenty-nine prisoners who had legal problems decided not to use the project. Out of these 29, five (17%) stated that they were retaining private counsel, 4 (14%) just "didn't give a damn," and 20 (69%) said that state funding discouraged their use of the Legal Services Project. Of those using the service, 63% felt that the project served the prisoners, whereas 37% felt it served the needs and goals of the state.

Research on resident counsel programs in Texas and Massachusetts also found that most of the inmate clients had positive attitudes toward the service (Alpert, 1980: 14-15). The research showed that for inmates in Texas

> participation in the legal aid project is a significant factor in producing positive changes in prisonization and in prisoners' attitudes toward police, lawyers, law and the judicial system. . . . A second significant finding which moves beyond attitudinal changes concerns the number of institutional infractions committed by members of our cohorts. The finding that users of legal aid experience fewer convictions for institutional infractions is significant in that it uses a behavioral measure as an independent variable. Providing legal services to prisoners is one step to reduce

tension and anxiety, and reduce hostility among inmates. (Alpert, 1978: 44, 46-47)

The assertion that prison legal service programs can effectively reduce institutional tensions may seem surprising. However, this is a conclusion with which correctional administrators overwhelmingly concur. Two nationwide surveys of prison officials found that a large majority of the respondents believe that the inmate legal assistance programs mandated by court decisions have led to a decrease in disciplinary problems and have facilitated rehabilitation efforts. For example, Cardarelli and Finkelstein (1974) reported that over 80% of a large sample of state corrections commissioners, prison wardens, and treatment directors agreed that legal services provide a safety valve for inmate grievances, reduce inmate power structures and tensions from unresolved legal problems, and contribute to rehabilitation by showing the inmate that he or she is being treated fairly.

A second nationwide survey of prison officials (Haas and Champagne, 1976) disclosed that the prison systems that had hired attorneys to supervise legal aid programs had experienced a marked decline in problems with jailhouse lawyers and in friction between staff and inmates concerning alleged violations of rights. This study concluded that legal services programs supervised by attorneys help to maintain an atmosphere of discipline by undermining the power of the more unscrupulous jailhouse lawyers and by providing inmates with an outlet for their grievances and frustrations. Clearly, this is one area of correctional law that has contributed measurably to positive changes in American prisons.

Procedural and Jurisdictional Obstacles to Inmate Access

Section 1983 of the Civil Rights Act of 1871

We have just shown that over the past 20 years, the U.S. Supreme Court has broadened the prisoner's right of access to the courts by striking down prison regulations barring the activities of jailhouse lawyers and by requiring prison officials to establish reasonably adequate law libraries and/or legal assistance programs. However, it is important to understand that the right of access also encompasses questions involving judicial policies affecting the availability of the various judicial remedies sought by prisoners. Cases dealing with procedural and jurisdictional issues are of great importance because such cases can either limit or expand the availability of judicial relief for prisoners. And in this area of law, prisoners have not fared very well in recent years, for the Supreme Court has made it increasingly difficult for prisoners to secure full judicial review of their grievances.

Because over 90% of America's nearly 700,000 state and federal prisoners are housed in state prisons (Bureau of Justice Statistics, 1989), the large majority of lawsuits attacking allegedly unconstitutional prison practices are brought by state prisoners. Most of these suits are filed in federal court under Section 1983 of the Civil Rights Act of 1871 (hereinafter Section 1983). Although some state courts are more inclined to support civil rights and liberties than they were in the past (see generally Tarr and Porter, 1987), state prisoners generally believe that federal judges, as a group, are more sympathetic to their claims than are state judges. Indeed, research on comparative judicial behavior suggests that prisoners are correct in this regard. State courts that have been quite vigorous in protecting the rights of other minority groups generally have been less vigilant than the federal courts in safeguarding the rights of prisoners (Haas, 1981).

This state of affairs may change as an increasing number of President Reagan's appointees assume their duties on the federal bench. But there are important institutional and structural factors that militate against change. For example, whereas all federal judges enjoy lifetime appointments, the majority of the nation's state trial and appellate judges must stand in periodic elections and thus are more susceptible to public sentiments against prisoners. Moreover, federal court rules and procedures in such critical areas as pleading, fact finding, immunities, attorneys' fees, pretrial discovery, and class actions are more hospitable to prisoners' cases than the rules used by most state courts (Neuborne, 1981).

Section 1983 has been by far the most effective device for redressing the grievances of state prisoners (see generally Turner, 1979). Originally passed in an effort to combat the Ku Klux Klan in the aftermath of the Civil War, Section 1983 provides that any person acting under color of state or local law who violates the federal constitutional or statutory rights of another "shall be liable to the party injured in an action at law, suit in equity, or other proper proceeding for redress." Under Section 1983, state prisoners may challenge violations of their First Amendment freedoms of speech, religion, and association, or, for that matter, unconstitutional prison policies that deny or restrict their right of access to the courts. Most inmate Section 1983 cases, however, focus on allegedly unconstitutional conditions of confinement, covering such issues as privacy, unsanitary conditions, inadequate medical and dental care, overcrowding, nutritionally inadequate food, lack of exercise opportunities, inadequate heating, ventilation, and lighting, and unprovoked physical attacks by prison staff. Due process violations also are frequently litigated under Section 1983. Such cases may involve the rights of prisoners in disciplinary hearings, reclassification proceedings, interprison transfers, and parole eligibility hearings. Section 1983 actions also are commonly brought by probationers and parolees who claim that they were denied constitutionally mandated protections before or during revocation proceedings.

Monroe v. *Pape* (1961) and Its Progeny

Section 1983 was rarely invoked by prisoners or anyone else for nearly a century. But in a landmark 1961 case (*Monroe* v. *Pape*), the U.S. Supreme Court interpreted Section 1983 as giving federal courts original jurisdiction over any claims alleging violations of federal constitutional rights by state or local officials. This meant that petitioners suing state or local officials would not have to worry about the delays and expense involved in meeting the traditional requirement of exhausting all state judicial remedies before bringing suit in a federal court. They could instead bypass the state courts and go directly to the federal court with their Section 1983 claims. Three years later (*Cooper* v. *Pate*, 1964), the High Court made it clear that state prisoners could bring allegations of unconstitutional prison policies and conditions against state correctional employees under the provisions of Section 1983, thus creating a readily available and effective judicial remedy for prison abuses.

To be sure, there are other statutes, state and federal, under which prisoners can file legal claims. These include the federal Habeas Corpus Statute, the federal Tort Claims Act, state habeas corpus statutes, and state tort claims acts. However, for a variety of reasons, state prisoners and their attorneys prefer Section 1983 as the fastest and potentially most advantageous device for advancing claims against prison officials (see generally Manville, 1983: 163-220). Section 1983, for example, clearly is an appropriate vehicle for challenges to a prisoner's conditions of confinement. By contrast, many state habeas corpus statutes allow prisoners to challenge the legality of their conviction but not to challenge the conditions of confinement. Whereas Section 1983 is phrased in terms that permit the awarding of both compensatory and punitive damages to a victorious plaintiff, most state tort claims acts do not provide for punitive damages. The federal Habeas Corpus Act allows no monetary damages of any kind and strictly requires the exhaustion of all state remedies. The federal Tort Claims Act can be a useful remedy for some kinds of suits, but the Tort Claims Act does not allow prisoners to sue governmental bodies for assault and battery claims or other intentional (as opposed to negligent) torts.

Because Section 1983 is the major device by which state prisoners seek to protect their rights to fair treatment and humane conditions, any new laws or court decisions that limit the usefulness of Section 1983 pose a major threat to prisoners. And, indeed, from the perspective of prisoners and the advocates of prison reform, there have been disturbing signs that Section 1983 may not survive into the twenty-first century. In a series of recent cases, the U.S. Supreme court has begun to diminish the effectiveness of Section 1983 as a means by which to combat violations of inmate rights.

Space limitations preclude a discussion of all of the Supreme Court decisions that have affected the use of Section 1983 by state prisoners (see generally Nahmod, 1986). Furthermore, it should be noted that a few of the Court's decisions have benefited inmate Section 1983 litigants. For example, inmates in city and county jails have profited from recent decisions establishing that local municipalities can be sued for compensatory damages under Section 1983 (*Monell* v. *Department of Social Services*, 1978) and that municipalities are unprotected by any kind of qualified immunity (*Owen* v. *City of Independence*, 1980).

The High Court also upheld the traditional scope of Section 1983 liability in a case involving a young inmate who suffered a night of rape and torture because a guard needlessly placed him in a cell with two prisoners known to have violent tendencies (*Smith* v. *Wade*, 1983). By a 5-4 vote, the Court affirmed that a prison employee may be held liable for punitive damages in a Section 1983 action alleging violations of the Eighth Amendment's cruel and unusual punishment clause. The *Wade* Court also determined that a Section 1983 plaintiff with Eighth Amendment claims is entitled to punitive damages if he or she can show that the defendant acted with reckless or callous disregard for the plaintiff's health or safety. The plaintiff, in other words, does not have to show that the defendant acted with malicious intent to injure the plaintiff, a more demanding standard.

Despite these victories for prisoners, most of the Supreme Court's jurisdictional pronouncements have sent a clear signal to the lower federal courts to cut back the availability of Section 1983 relief for state prisoners. For example, in 1973, the Court's decision in *Preiser* v. *Rodriguez* placed significant limitations on inmate use of Section 1983. *Preiser* established that whenever a state prisoner files a claim that, if successful, would result in a reduction in the length of his or her sentence (for example, a due process challenge to the fairness of a prison disciplinary committee's decision to take away an inmate's "good time" or early release credits), the prisoner can no longer sue under Section 1983. Instead, he or she will have to file the suit as a habeas corpus action, thus necessitating the time-consuming and often futile exhaustion of all state judicial and administrative remedies.

The *Preiser* majority conceded that the "broad language" of Section 1983 made it applicable to actions in which prisoners challenge prison practices that may unfairly lengthen their sentences (*Preiser* at 488-489). Nevertheless, the majority Justices held that the history of habeas corpus, the specific wording of the federal Habeas Corpus Statute, and the importance of allowing state courts the first opportunity to correct unfair state prison practices justified their decision to declare habeas corpus to be the sole remedy for state prisoners challenging the length of their confinement (*Preiser* at 477-490). In dissent, Justice Brennan asserted that the majority's effort to distinguish between prisoner challenges to prison practices affecting the conditions of confinement (where Section 1983 can be used) and prison practices affecting the duration of confinement (where habeas corpus, with its exhaustion requirement, must be used) was historically incorrect, analytically unsound, and certain to create unnecessary confusion that would inevitably thwart the fair and prompt resolution of legitimate inmate grievances (*Preiser* at 506-511).

More recent decisions have also narrowed the scope of liability under Section 1983. The Supreme Court has declared that states are not considered "persons" subject to suit under Section 1983 (*Quern v. Jordan*, 1979) and that local governments cannot be sued for punitive damages in Section 1983 cases (*City of Newport v. Fact Concerts*, 1981). State legislators have long enjoyed absolute immunity from Section 1983 liability (*Tenney v. Brandhove*, 1951), and the Court has made it clear that prison officials are protected by the affirmative defense of qualified or "good faith" immunity (*Procunier v. Navarette*, 1978).

In 1980, Congress passed legislation intended to curtail the use of Section 1983 by state prisoners. Section 1997e of the Civil Rights of Institutionalized Persons Act (hereinafter Section 1997e) requires state prisoners to exhaust state *administrative* remedies before they can file a section 1983 suit in a federal court. This requirement, however, applies only when either the attorney general of the United States or the federal court in which the suit is filed has certified that the state administrative remedy — some kind of inmate grievance system — meets minimally accepted standards of fairness. Section 1997e further states that a federal court must continue the case for no more than 90 days in order to require exhaustion of the administrative remedy.

In *Patsy* v. *Florida Board of Regents* (1982), the Supreme Court held that nonprisoner Section 1983 plaintiffs cannot be required to exhaust state administrative remedies. However, the Justices bestowed their approval on Section 1997e's special filing requirements for prisoners, noting that it was reasonable to carve out an exception to the general no-exhaustion rule in order to relieve the burden of inmate complaints on the federal courts (*Patsy* at 509). It can be argued that a 90-day delay is not unreasonable and that Section 1997e may have the beneficial effect of motivating state prison administrators to improve their internal grievance systems (see McCoy, 1981). Nevertheless, prisoners can only find it unsettling to be singled out as the only class of Section 1983 litigants who cannot proceed directly to a federal court to seek relief from possible violations of their constitutionally protected rights.

From *Parratt* (1981) to *Daniels-Davidson* (1986)

In *Parratt* v. *Taylor* (1981), the Supreme Court announced the first of a series of decisions that have considerably weakened Section 1983 as a vehicle by which state prisoners can go to federal court to challenge prison policies. *Parratt* involved a Section 1983 suit brought by a Nebraska prisoner seeking $23.50 from prison employees for their alleged negligence in failing to follow the normal prison procedure for receiving mailed packages and thereby losing a mail-order hobby kit for which he had paid $23.50. The lower courts had determined that the loss of the prisoner's property was properly construed as a violation of the due process clause of the Fourteenth Amendment and thus was cognizable in a Section 1983 suit.

The Supreme Court, however, disagreed, holding that when a plaintiff asserted the loss of property because of the negligent action of a state employee, the existence of a state postdeprivation remedy precludes a Section 1983 claim based on the due process clause. In this case, according to Justice Rehnquist's majority opinion, the prisoner must bring his suit under the Nebraska Tort Claims Act—a state law that Justice Rehnquist conceded to be less efficacious than Section 1983 in that it contained no provisions for trial by jury or for punitive damages (*Parratt* at 543-544). Nevertheless, in Justice Rehnquist's view, a state remedy that may not be as advantageous as Section 1983 but that can potentially compensate a prospective Section 1983 plaintiff for his or her losses is "sufficient to satisfy the requirements of due process" (*Parratt* at 544). Therefore, the negligent conduct that had led to the loss of the prisoner's property had occurred with due process of law—the possibility of postdeprivation relief in the state courts—and was not actionable in the federal courts under Section 1983 (*Parratt* at 543-544).

Legal commentators were quick to point out that the implications of *Parratt* were ominous for state prisoners (see, for example, Friedman, 1982; Blum, 1984), and they turned out to be absolutely correct. Three years later, the logic of *Parratt* was extended to *intentional* deprivations of property. In *Hudson* v. *Palmer* (1984), a state prisoner in Virginia brought a Section 1983 action against a prison guard who allegedly had conducted a "shakedown" search of the prisoner's cell and had intentionally destroyed his *noncontraband* personal property including legal papers, a letter from his wife, and a picture of his baby. The suit was based on two legal theories: (1) the assertion that prisoners retain some reasonable expectation of privacy in their cells and are thus constitutionally entitled to some minimal Fourth Amendment protections against unreasonable searches and seizures (i.e., the right to be present during cell searches); and (2) the contention that the guard's intentional destruction of the inmate's personal property should be actionable as a due process claim in federal court under Section 1983 regardless of whether an adequate state postdeprivation remedy was available.

In an opinion authored by Chief Justice Burger, the *Palmer* Court decided both of the previously mentioned issues in favor of the guard and against the prisoner. First, a 5-4 majority held that prisoners possess absolutely no recognizable expectations of privacy in their cells (*Palmer* at 529-530). Therefore, according to the majority, prisoners enjoy no Fourth Amendment protection against arbitrary searches or unjustified confiscation of their personal property, even if the sole purpose of the search and seizure is to harass the inmate (*Palmer* at 529-530).

Second, the Court voted unanimously to apply the reasoning behind *Parratt* v. *Taylor* to intentional deprivations of property by state employees. Pointing out that the destruction of the prisoner's property was a random, unauthorized act by a state employee rather than an established state procedure (in which case Section 1983 arguably could still be used), Chief Justice Burger argued that predeprivation due process was "impractical" because the state court "cannot predict when the loss will occur" (*Palmer* at 532). Therefore, according to the Chief Justice, the underlying rationale of *Parratt* must be applied to intentional deprivations of property because there is "no logical distinction between negligent and intentional deprivations of property insofar as the 'practicality' of affording predeprivation due process is concerned" (*Palmer* at 533).

Perhaps the weakest aspect of the Chief Justice's majority opinion is his failure to offer any explanation as to why prisoners who suffer unjustified, egregious, and humiliating property losses at the hands of state employees must use the arguably less efficacious state postdeprivation remedy rather than the federal postdeprivation remedy — Section 1983 — that Congress has established as the means by which to redress wrongs committed by state employees. Nevertheless, the result of *Palmer* is that when the state provides an "adequate" postdeprivation remedy by which abused prisoners can seek compensation for their losses, they are barred from seeking compensation under Section 1983 in a federal court — even if they lose their state court lawsuit. Chief Justice Burger acknowledged that under the Virginia Tort Claims Act, a prisoner "might not be able to recover . . . the full amount he might receive in a Section 1983 action" (*Palmer* at 535). However, the Chief Justice embraced Justice Rehnquist's *Parratt* argument that a state remedy need not be as efficacious as Section 1983 in order to satisfy the due process requirements of the Fourteenth Amendment (*Palmer* at 535).

In the aftermath of *Palmer*, one legal commentator accused the Supreme Court of "reviving the era of near total deference to prison administrators" (Leading Cases, 1984). Others speculated that the outlook for inmate litigants could become even worse if the rationale of *Parratt* and *Palmer* were to be applied to deprivations of liberty as well as to deprivations of property (Levinson, 1986). But this is precisely what the High Court did in two cases decided in January 1986 — *Daniels v. Williams* and *Davidson v. Cannon*.

In *Daniels*, a county jail inmate had slipped on a pillow negligently left on the stairs by a guard. The inmate then brought a Section 1983 suit seeking compensation for his alleged back and ankle injuries on the grounds that the guard's negligence had deprived him of his *liberty* interest under the Fourteenth Amendment to be free from bodily injury caused by government employees. Writing for a unanimous Court, Justice Rehnquist (who would be confirmed as Chief Justice later in 1986), argued that the Fourteenth Amendment's guarantee that no state shall "deprive any person of life, liberty, or property, without due process of law" was originally intended to apply only to *intentional* deprivations of life, liberty, or property by government officials (*Daniels* at 331). Justice Rehnquist offered no evidence to support the contention that the 1868 Congress that enacted the Fourteenth Amendment held such a narrow view of the due process clause. However, he asserted that the history of the Supreme Court's handling of due process cases supported his argument:

> No decision of this Court before *Parratt* supported the view that negligent conduct by a state official, even though causing injury,

constitutes a deprivation under the due process clause. (*Daniels* at 331)

The practical impact of Justice Rehnquist's extraordinarily brief examination of the history of the Fourteenth Amendment was devastating for state prisoners and local jail inmates. In one swift stroke, Justice Rehnquist overruled the one aspect of *Parratt* that had allowed prisoners any legal recourse when they had suffered losses at the hands of negligent state or local officials:

> Upon reflection, we . . . overrule *Parratt* to the extent that it states that mere lack of due care by a state official may 'deprive' an individual of life, liberty, or property under the Fourteenth Amendment. (*Daniels* at 330-331)

Thus state prisoners are not only barred from bringing negligence claims to federal courts under Section 1983; as a result of *Daniels*, they are not even constitutionally entitled to an adequate state postdeprivation remedy when they have suffered losses of life, liberty, or property at the hands of negligent state or local employees. In other words, under *Daniels*, negligent acts, however stupid or harmful, can never violate the Fourteenth Amendment. If the state has not enacted some kind of tort claim act under which the victim of negligent conduct can seek redress (and this was indeed the plight of plaintiff Roy Daniels), he or she simply will have no right to go to any court — state or federal — to seek relief.

One of the nation's leading authorities on tort law described *Daniels* as "novel," "far-reaching," and as a "reinterpretation of the Fourteenth Amendment" (Mead, 1986: 27). But the damage done to the prisoner's right of access to the courts is perhaps best demonstrated by showing how the *Daniels* precedent was applied to the facts of *Davidson* v. *Cannon* (1986). Whereas *Daniels* was a simple slip-and-fall case that could arguably be called "insipid," *Davidson* involved egregious and inexcusable negligence on the part of state prison officials. After another prisoner had threatened him, Robert Davidson, the plaintiff, reported the threats both orally and in writing to the appropriate prison officials. His written request for protection found its way to the assistant superintendent of the prison who read it and sent it to the cellblock's corrections sergeant on December 19, 1980. But the sergeant, though informed of the note's contents and the identity of the threatening prisoner, forgot about the note and left it on his desk unread when he left the prison some 8 hours later. Because both the assistant superintendent and the sergeant did not work on December 20 or 21, the guards on duty knew nothing about the threat. On December 21, the inmate who had threatened Robert Davidson attacked him with a fork, breaking his nose and inflicting severe wounds to his face, neck, head, and body.

Without question, the facts of Robert Davidson's case are far more compelling than those of Roy Daniels' case. Surely Justice Rehnquist could not conclude that judicial willingness to consider Robert Davidson's claims "would trivialize the centuries-old principle of due process of law" (*Daniels* at 332). But in a four-page majority opinion, Justice Rehnquist, in effect, did just that. This was nothing more than a simple case of negligence, declared Justice Rehnquist, and therefore "the principles enunciated in *Daniels* [are] controlling here" (*Davidson* at 347-348)

It is notable that three justices dissented in *Davidson*. The three dissenters—Justices Blackmun, Marshall, and Brennan—expressed the belief that the conduct of the prison officials in *Davidson* arguably reached the level of *deliberate* or *reckless indifference* to the prisoner's safety (*Davidson* at 349-360). Thus they would have remanded the case to the lower courts to consider whether the actions of the prison officials should be treated as a "reckless indifference" claim under the Eighth Amendment's cruel and unusual punishment clause as in *Smith v. Wade* (1983). In Justice Blackmun's words:

> When the state incarcerated Daniels, it left intact his own faculties for avoiding a slip and a fall. But the state prevented Davidson from defending himself, and therefore assumed some responsibility to protect him from the dangers to which he was exposed. In these circumstances, I feel that Davidson was deprived of liberty by the negligence of prison officials. Moreover, the acts of the state officials in this case may well have risen to the level of recklessness. I therefore dissent. (*Davidson* at 350)

For prisoners and the supporters of prison reform, the implications of *Daniels* and *Davidson* are foreboding. The Supreme Court's next step could very well be to decide that *intentional* deprivations of *liberty* can no longer be litigated in federal courts when state remedies are available. For that matter, the Court may eventually go even further and apply the logic of *Daniels* to intentional deprivations of liberty, thus allowing the states to decide whether or not to provide remedies for such violations. Also in doubt is the continued vitality of *Smith v. Wade* (1983). Few legal scholars would be surprised if the Court were to hold that Eighth Amendment claims of reckless indifference to state prisoners' health or safety can no longer be brought under Section 1983 to the federal courts when adequate state remedies are available.

As a result of the Supreme Court's narrowing of Section 1983 jurisdiction, prisoners increasingly find themselves in a classic "Catch

22'' situation. In *Johnson* v. *Avery* (1969), *Bounds* v. *Smith* (1977), and other cases, inmates won the right to challenge prison policies that violate their right of access to the courts and other substantive constitutional rights. But these hard-earned rights are rapidly becoming "rights without remedies" because of Supreme Court decisions that establish formidable and inflexible procedural and jurisdictional barriers to bringing suit in a federal or state court.

Implications for Research on the Courts and Corrections

Since *Monroe* v. *Pape* (1961), American prisoners have been transformed from "slaves of the state" to individuals with significant constitutional rights. The courts agreed to consider the complaints of prisoners only after years of neglect and the failure of prison administrators to manage their institutions appropriately. One consequence of the judiciary's willingness to review prison conditions was the raising of the iron curtain that had been drawn between the courts and prisoners. For a window in time, the pendulum was swinging toward the advantage of those who were incarcerated. As the previous analysis has demonstrated, the pendulum has reached its most advanced degree and is now moving rapidly in the opposite direction, toward the return of what can be termed a "modified hands-off doctrine." In particular, the Supreme Court's recent decisions curtailing the availability of Section 1983 relief for state prisoners have, in effect, closed the federal (and, in some cases, the state) courthouse doors to prisoners who may have verifiable and meritorious claims.

The major justification for this trend is that inmate petitions — especially Section 1983 filings — are placing increasing burdens on the time and resources of judges and correctional officials. Several Supreme Court justices, notably Chief Justice Rehnquist and Justice O'Connor, have charged that inmate Section 1983 suits waste scarce judicial resources and create financial hardships for state and local governments (see *Monell* v. *Department of Social Services* (1978) at 724 (Rehnquist, J., dissenting; O'Connor, 1981: 808-815). Even judges who are generally more sympathetic to the need for federal protection of civil rights through Section 1983 have expressed concerns about the burdens that Section 1983 imposes on the federal courts (Coffin, 1971; Friendly, 1973: 87-107).

These concerns suggest that it is important to conduct a great deal more research on the financial and social costs of inmate Section 1983 claims and other types of lawsuits brought by prisoners. Is there really a deluge of prison litigation? Is the Section 1983 caseload a problem of crisis dimensions for court personnel and correctional employees? Or is it possible that the so-called flood of litigation is a largely illusory problem, created by the hyperbole of those who are simply hostile to prisoners as a class of litigants?

To answer the preceding questions will require increasingly sophisticated research on how the courts process prisoner petitions and how correctional personnel respond to inmate complaints. So far, the few empirical studies of how Section 1983 cases are handled by the federal courts tend to undermine the assertion that these cases are overburdening the federal docket (see, for example Bailey, 1975; Eisenberg, 1982; McCoy, 1981; Turner, 1979). It is especially interesting that most of these studies have indicated that the burden on the federal courts may be exaggerated by those who advocate limits on inmate Section 1983 cases. For example, Turner (1979: 637) discovered that "a large proportion of [Section 1983] cases are screened out and summarily dismissed before they get under way, . . . court appearances and trials are rare, and . . . prisoner cases are not particularly complex as compared to other types of federal litigation."

On the other hand, Roger Hanson (1987: 224) recently pointed out that the burdens of screening and disposing of Section 1983 cases especially the typically inarticulate *pro se* complaints drafted by inmates without benefit of counsel should not be underestimated. His study of four federal district courts revealed that the major workload of a majority of Section 1983 cases falls not on federal judges, but "on the shoulders of federal magistrates and *pro se* law clerks" (1987: 224). Moreover, Hanson stresses that we do not know and thus need more research on such important factors as:

(1) The cost to state attorneys general (or private counsel) in defending state officials.
(2) The cost to federal magistrates and their staff in the time spent handling cases through the pretrial stages.
(3) The time spent by federal district court judges and their staff in preparing for and conducting trials.
(4) The time spent by federal circuit court judges and their staff in hearing appeals.
(5) The administrative costs to the federal district and circuit courts in the maintenance and processing of court documents.
(6) The costs in time and money to correctional officials in attending hearings, preparing answers, submitting to depositions, and transporting inmates to and from the courthouse. (1987: 225)

Even without additional research on the costs of prisoner litigation, it would not be premature to conclude that the costs are indeed significant. This is not to say that the costs necessarily outweigh the benefits. Some of the benefits are precious and priceless. For example, there is no way to put a dollar value on the importance of upholding the principle that all Americans — even those who have shown no respect for the law — are entitled to humane treatment, fundamental fairness, and due process of law. But if these values could be preserved while decreasing the social and economic costs of inmate litigation, everybody would benefit.

This intuitively appealing idea suggests the desirability of developing and refining inmate grievance systems that can resolve inmate complaints in a fair and prompt manner while reducing the caseloads of the federal and state courts. It was presumably with this intention that Congress passed the Civil Rights of Institutionalized Persons Act in May, 1980. This Act, discussed earlier, was designed specifically to reduce the Section 1983 caseload. It allows prison officials who have had their institutional grievance systems approved by either the United States Attorney General's Office or the federal court of jurisdiction to delay Section 1983 cases for up to 90 days in order to attempt to resolve inmate grievances internally. In other words, the Act provides for a period of negotiation in which a determination of the accuracy and importance of the allegations can be made, and a fair and just resolution can be negotiated.

Unfortunately, the states have shown an unwillingness to request certification for inmate grievance procedures and a reluctance to take advantage of the provisions of the Act. Only four states — Virginia, Wyoming, Iowa, and Louisiana — have certified grievance mechanisms in place, and only Virginia has had a certified procedure in place long enough to allow study of the effects of the Institutionalized Persons Act. Preliminary research by Hanson (1987: 227) indicates that "Virginia has experienced a substantial decrease in filing rates after gaining certification whereas adjoining states in the same federal circuit that have not been certified have experienced much smaller changes in litigation rates." This suggests that there is a compelling need for additional research on the effectiveness of certified grievance procedures and on how internal grievance systems generally affect the rights of both prisoners and correctional staff. Among the questions that need to be answered are:

1. What kinds of grievance systems are most effective in resolving inmate complaints?

2. Are certain kinds of grievance systems more effective than others in reducing Section 1983 litigation?

3. Is inmate participation (in a decisional capacity) in a grievance system helpful or counterproductive in settling disputes?

4. Can grievance systems offer fair compensation to prisoners who have suffered losses that are no longer compensable in the courts as a result of *Daniels, Davidson,* and other Supreme Court decisions?

5. Do grievance systems reduce—or merely postpone—frivolous and nonmeritorious Section 1983 suits?

6. How satisfied are prisoners and correctional staff with various kinds of grievance procedures?

Answers to these and other questions about the impact of internal grievance mechanisms on the courts and on the prisons may encourage the states to establish new and better dispute resolution procedures. However, it would be naive to be overly optimistic about this possibility. As Christopher Smith (1986: 149) warned, "[r]elying on the states for the development of remedies means [that the] implementation of protections for prisoners' rights is placed squarely in the hands of the elected legislatures and governors who fostered the unconstitutional prison conditions in the first place."

Thus it remains vitally important to continue earlier research on the realities of American prison conditions (see, e.g., Bowker, 1980; Toch, 1977) and to carry out new research on how these conditions affect the character, content, and number of suits filed by prisoners. In addition, it will be necessary to update earlier studies focusing on the impact of court decisions on prison policies and practices (Alpert, 1978; Haas and Champagne, 1976). Accordingly, our initial research agenda includes the following:

1. Comparative and longitudinal analyses of the conditions under which prisoners seek and are either provided or denied access to the courts.

2. Comparative and longitudinal analyses of how prisoners achieve access to the courts by type of prison and jurisdiction.

3. Studies on how the provision of legal assistance affects the attitudes and behavior of prisoners and staff.

4. Studies on how specific court decisions affect the attitudes and behavior of prisoners and staff.

The changing scope of the prisoner's right of access to the courts over the past century has reflected evolving judicial philosophies about the meaning of justice, the limits of punishment, and the proper role of the courts in a free society. It is our hope that a philosophy of humanitarianism, informed by carefully crafted and skillfully executed research, will shape correctional policies and provide guidance for the courts of the future.

References

Alpert, G. P. Prisoners' right of access to courts: planning for legal aid. *Washington Law Review*, 1976, 51, 653-675.

Alpert, G. P. *Legal rights of prisoners*. Lexington, MA: Lexington Books, 1978.

Alpert, G. P. Prisoners and their rights: An introduction. In G.P. Alpert (Ed.), *Legal rights of prisoners*. Beverly Hills, CA: Sage Publications, 1980.

Alpert, G. P., and Huff, C. R. Prisoners, the law and public policy: planning for legal aid. *New England Journal on Prison Law*, 1981, 7, 307-340.

Bailey, W. S. The realities of prisoners' cases under U.S.C. Section 1983: A statistical survey in the northern district of Illinois. *Loyola University of Chicago Law Journal*, 1975, 6, 527-559.

Blum, K. M. The implications of *Parratt v. Taylor* for Section 1983 litigation. *The Urban Lawyer*, 1984, 16, 363-386.

Bluth, W. Legal services for inmates: Coopting the jailhouse lawyer. *Capital University Law Review*, 1972, 1, 59-81.

Bowker, L. H. *Prison victimization*. New York: Elsevier, 1980.

Bureau of Justice Statistics. *Prisoners in 1988*. Washington, DC: U.S. Government Printing Office, 1989.

Cardarelli, A., and Finkelstein, M. M. Correctional administrators assess the adequacy and impact of prison legal services programs in the United States. *Journal of Criminal Law and Criminology*, 1974, 65, 91-102.

Coffin, F. M. Justice and workability: Un essai. *Suffolk University Law Review*, 1971, 5, 567-587.

Edwards, J. A. The prisoner's right of access to the courts. *California Western Law Review*, 1968, 4, 99-114.

Eisenberg, J. Section 1983: Doctrinal foundations and an empirical study. *Cornell Law Review*, 1982, 67, 482-556.

Friedman, L. *Parratt v. Taylor*: Closing the door on Section 1983. *Hastings Constitutional Law Quarterly*. 1982, 9, 545-578.

Friendly, H. I. *Federal jurisdiction: A general view*, New York: Columbia University Press, 1973.

Gobert, J. L., and Cohen, N. I. *Rights of prisoners*. Colorado Springs: Shepard's/McGraw-Hill, 1981.

Haas, K. C. Judicial politics and correctional reform: An analysis of the decline of the "hands-off" doctrine. *Detroit College of Law Review*, 1977, 4, 796-831.

Haas, K. C. The "new federalism" and prisoners' rights: State supreme courts in comparative perspective. *Western Political Quarterly*, 1981, *34*, 552-571.

Haas, K. C. The comparative study of state and federal judicial behavior revisited. *Journal of Politics*, 1982, 44, 721-746.

Haas, K. C., and Champagne, A. The impact of *Johnson v. Avery* on prison administration. *Tennessee Law Review*, 1976, *43*, 275-306.

Hanson, R. A. What should be done when prisoners want to take the state to court? *Judicature*, 1987, *70*, 223-227.

Leading cases of the 1983 term. *Harvard Law Review*, 1984, *98*, 151-165.

Levinson, R. B. Due process challenges to governmental actions: The meaning of *Parratt* and *Hudson*. *The Urban Lawyer*, 1986, *18*, 189-208.

Manville, D. E. *Prisoners' self-help litigation manual*. New York: Oceana Publications, 1983.

McCoy, C. The impact of Section 1983 litigation on policymaking in corrections. *Federal Probation*, 1981, *45*, 17-23.

Mead, S. M. Evolution of the "species of tort liability" created by 42 U.S.C. Section 1983: Can the constitutional tort be saved from extinction? *Fordham Law Review*, 1986, *55*, 1-62.

Nahmod, S. *Civil rights and civil liberties litigation*. Colorado Springs: Shepard's/McGraw-Hill, 1986.

Neuborne, B. Toward procedural parity in constitutional litigation. *William and Mary Law Review*, 1981, *22*, 725-787.

Note. A prisoner's constitutional right to attorney assistance. *Columbia Law Review*, 1983, *83*, 1279-1319.

O'Connor, S. D. Trends in the relationship between the federal and state courts from the perspective of a state court judge. *William and Mary Law Review*, 1981, *22*, 801-819.

Rudovsky, D., Bronstein, A. I., and Koren, E. I. *The rights of prisoners*. New York: Bantam, 1983.

Smith, C. E. Federal judges' role in prisoner litigation: What's necessary? What's proper? *Judicature*, 1986, *70*, 141-150.

Tarr, G. A., and Porter, M. C. State constitutionalism and state constitutional law. *Publius*, 1987, *17*, 1-12.

Toch, H. *Living in prison: The ecology of prison survival*. New York: The Free Press, 1977.

Turner, W. B. When prisoners sue: A study of prisoner Section 1983 suits in the federal courts. *Harvard Law Review*, 1979, *92*, 610-663.

Cases

Bounds v. Smith, 430 U.S. 817 (1977).

City of Newport v. Fact Concerts, 453 U.S. 247 (1981).

Coleman v. Peyton, 302 F.2d 905 (4th Cir. 1966).

Cooper v. Pate, 378 U.S. 546 (1964).

Daniels v. Williams, 474 U.S. 327 (1986).

Davidson v. Cannon, 474 U.S. 344 (1986).

Ex parte Hull, 312 U.S. 546 (1941).

Hooks v. Wainwright, 536 F. Supp. 1330 (M.D. Fla. 1982), rev'd, 775 F.2d 1433 (11th Cir. 1985).

Hudson v. Palmer, 468 U.S. 517 (1984).

Johnson v. Avery, 393 U.S. 483 (1969).

Lindquist v. Idaho Board of Corrections, 776 F.2d 851 (9th Cir. 1985).

Monell v. Department of Social Services, 436 U.S. 658 (1978).

Monroe v. Pape, 365 U.S. 167 (1961).

Owen v. City of Independence, 445 U.S. 622 (1980).

Parratt v. Taylor, 451 U.S. 527 (1981).

Patsy v. Florida Board of Regents, 457 U.S. 496 (1982).

Preiser v. Rodriguez, 411 U.S. 475 (1973).

Procunier v. Martinez, 416 U.S. 396, 419-422 (1974).

Procunier v. Navarette, 434 U.S. 555 (1978).

Quern v. Jordan, 440 U.S. 332 (1979).

Ross v Moffitt, 417 U.S. 600 (1974).

Ruffin v. Commonwealth, 62 Va. (21 Gratt.) 790 (1871).

Smith v. Wade, 461 U.S. 30 (1983)

Tenney v. Brandhove, 341 U.S. 367 (1951).

Wolff v. McDonnell, 418 U.S. 539, 577-580 (1974).

Younger v. Gilmore, 404 U.S. 15 (1971).

15

The Supreme Court's Retreat From the Protection of Prisoners' Rights

Two Major Cases From the Court's 1988-89 Term

Correctional Law Reporter

Rules for Publication and Letter Rejection Eased, Early Precedent Overruled

Thornburgh v. Abbott
109 S.Ct. 1874 (1989)

With this decision, the Supreme Court has taken perhaps its most dramatically conservative shift since it began deciding prisoners' rights cases in the early 1970s.

The issue in the case was one of censorship under the First Amendment: under what circumstances could a prison or jail censor or reject publications coming to an inmate from the outside? Specifically under attack was a comprehensive set of regulations of the federal Bureau of Prisons.

Source: *Correctional Law Reporter*, Vol. 1, No. 3 (August 1989), pp. 37-41. Reprinted with the permission of the co-editors, William C. Collins and Fred Cohen.

The Court of Appeals for the District of Columbia had thrown out substantial portions of the rules on the grounds they allowed rejection of a publication which didn't go so far as to "encourage" a breach of security or some impairment of rehabilitation. (The regulations at issue are reproduced in their entirety at the end of this article). The appeals court thus held that publication which merely depicted or described such things as escapes from prison could not be rejected, 824 F.2d at 1166.

The Court of Appeals decision seemed on solid ground since it relied on one of the earliest Supreme Court prisoners' rights cases, and the first case which dealt directly with First Amendment rights, *Procunier v. Martinez*, 416 U.S.396 (1974).

The Supreme Court reversed, upheld the regulations, and (surprisingly) rejected *Martinez* as a basis for evaluating the case. The Court simply overruled a substantial part of *Martinez*. Instead of *Martinez*, the Court said the 1987 case of *Turner v. Safley*, 482 U.S. 78, provides the basis for reviewing challenges to publication denials:

> In sum, we hold that *Turner's* reasonableness standard is to be applied to the regulations at issue in this case, and that those regulations are facially valid under that standard, 109 S.Ct. at 1884.

The Court went on to extend the *Turner* reasonableness test (under which the proper inquiry is whether the challenged regulations are "reasonably related to legitimate penological interests") to review of incoming correspondence of all sorts, not just publications. The *Martinez* standard (which requires a greater showing of need on the part of prison officials) was held to apply only to outgoing correspondence, which the Court felt presents a security concern of a "categorically lesser magnitude" than material entering the prison, 109 S.Ct. at 1881.

The Court also held that when a portion of a particular publication or letter is properly rejected, the *entire document* may be rejected. Correctional officials do not have to cut and paste materials. This part of the case, which also reversed the lower court, should bring a sigh of relief from staff involved in handling of inmate mail.

What is startling about the decision in *Abbott* is the Court's specific overruling of its earlier decision in *Martinez* when, even in the judgment of Justice Blackmun who wrote the majority opinion, the Court could have simply interpreted *Martinez* to reach the result the majority wanted.

Abbott then marks a major milestone in correctional law not only for its specific holding but, perhaps even more significantly, because it is the first time the Court has had the opportunity to review one of its own precedents in this field and, some would say, gut that precedent almost entirely.

What then does *Abbott* mean for those running prisons or jails?

Most obviously, it lowers the requirements which must be met in order to reject a publication. Although the majority of the Court believes the *Turner* standard is not "toothless," 109 S.Ct. at 1882, one must question the sharpness of the teeth the test possesses and whether the new standard is strong enough to overturn the rejection of almost any sort of publication even remotely connected with security or rehabilitation, at least where the inmate has access to other, alternative sources of reading material. Unfortunately, the test may encourage or allow rejection of material which in fact presents no meaningful threat to security.

By lowering the legal requirements for rejection of materials, the case may also suggest agencies review and revise the policies and procedures or regulations under which they presently operate, since odds are that those regulations were adopted to meet a more demanding legal standard than now prevails. (Again, the BOP regulations challenged and upheld in *Abbott* are offered as a model. Note that all the Court did in *Abbott* was to approve these rules *as written*. The *Abbott* case has gone back to the lower courts to see if the actual censorship decisions made by the BOP and attacked in the case were made properly under the new testa adopted by the Court.)

By rejecting *Martinez* as the foundation for reviewing publication and incoming correspondence rejection claims, *Abbott* implicitly reverses virtually every existing case in this area, since virtually all of those cases relied on *Martinez*. Thus the law of publication censorship in corrections begins anew, as of May 15, 1989, the date of the *Abbott* opinion.

Abbott may allow (but clearly doesn't require) the censorship of many publications which have been coming into many prisons and jails for years. But the administrator who begins censoring and rejecting publications with a vengeance, perhaps trying to test the limits of the *Abbott* decision, invites a shift of this type of litigation into state court and before judges not nearly as conservative as those now making up a majority of the Supreme Court. Prudence would suggest that before every publication which "depicts or describes" escapes, criminal activity, or other possible security breaches is rejected (which would include most editions of the daily newspaper and even many editions of *Reader's Digest*), a realistic examination be made of what publications currently are allowed in facilities around the country and what problems in fact are created by them.

Due Process Doesn't Protect Visiting—
Plus Blueprint To Avoid Creating Liberty Interests

Kentucky v. *Thompson*
109 S.Ct. 1904 (1989)

While *Thompson* will be known as the "visiting case," its far greater significance lies in the area of Due Process and the confusing concept of "state created liberty interests." This article will discuss both the visiting and Due Process aspects of the decision. First, visiting:

The six Justice majority said:

> "Respondents do not argue—nor can it seriously be contended, in light of our prior cases—that an inmate's interest in unfettered visitation is guaranteed directly by the Due Process Clause," 109 S.Ct. at 1909.

So visiting isn't inherently protected by the Fourteenth Amendment. But in a concurring opinion Justice Kennedy warns:

> "Nothing in the Court's opinion forecloses the claim that a prison regulation permanently forbidding all visits to some or all prisoners implicates the protections of the Due Process Clause in a way that the precise and individualized restrictions at issue here do not," 109 S.Ct. at 1911.

In other words, *Thompson* does *not* say a prison or jail could ban visits altogether for some or all inmates. Such complete bans would face serious constitutional challenge.

Next, State Created Liberty Interests
And How To Avoid Them

What the opinion *does* say is that the Fourteenth Amendment (Due Process) does not inherently require some sort of hearing as part of the decision to ban or terminate visiting for a particular inmate or visitor in a particular situation.

After this point, the opinion becomes considerably more complex and significantly more important, for what it says goes far beyond questions of just visiting.

Although the Fourteenth Amendment doesn't inherently require some sort of a hearing as part of the visiting denial process, state rules and regulations could be written in such a way as to create Due Process protections. This is the concept of *state created* liberty interests.[1] The Court in *Thompson* decided that two sets of visiting rules used by

Kentucky (one applicable just to the Reformatory) did not create liberty
interests. Thus, in the pessimistic words of Justice Marshall's dissent:

> "Corrections authorities at the . . . Reformatory are free to deny
> prisoners visits from parents, spouses, children, clergy members,
> and close friends for any reason whatsoever, or for no reason at all.
> Prisoners will not even be entitled to learn the reason, if any, why
> a visitor has been turned away," 109 S.Ct. at 1911.

Justice Marshall's rhetoric aside, his point is accurate: by interpreting
Kentucky's rules as not creating a liberty interest, the majority opinion
removes a constitutional protection for the visiting denial decision AND
provides a model for writing other institution rules in ways which do
not create liberty interests.

The state created liberty interest concept says, in essence, that
whenever an agency imposes a limitation on its own discretion in making
some type of decision-making through rules, policies, etc., it creates a
"liberty interest" which in turn means that some from of due process
must accompany the decision to assure that proper grounds exist for
making the decision. Thus rules which say the institution "shall" place
someone in administrative segregation "only" upon finding the person
is a threat to security, an escape risk, or meets some other specific
condition, create a liberty interest. The liberty interest then demands
that some level of Due Process accompany the decision, even if the
amount of process due may be slight. If the same rule said the institution
"may" put someone in administrative segregation whenever it is felt
appropriate, no liberty interest would be created.

Without Due Process Protections, Will Decisions Be Made Properly?

The goal of procedural due process is to enhance the quality of the
decision being made by trying to assure (through procedures) that facts
exist to warrant making the decisions and that the decisions are
something the agency is legally authorized to make.

Due process then is the court's way of preventing abuse of agency
power. For the agency, other means may exist to reach this goal, through
various forms of supervision, audits, and other reviews of decisions. The
effect of *Thompson* is to put the burden on the institution administration
to assure that such supervisory techniques, in whatever form, are used
to assure that decisions, such as those denying visits are made fairly,
with good reason.

The dissent notes the virtually universal agreement among correctional professionals that visiting is important for inmates and that visits shouldn't be denied without "good cause shown," 109 S.Ct. at 1912. The *Thompson* opinion may open the legal door to allow denial of visits without good cause. The challenge for correctional leaders then is, through enforced policy, to prevent this from taking place.

Notes

¹ The Fourteenth Amendment prohibits deprivations of "life, liberty or property without Due Process of law." Thus if an individual has an "interest" in life, liberty, or property, that interest is protected by Due Process. Through the language of its rules, the state can create a liberty interest.

Appendix

Mail Censorship Regulations Approved By Supreme Court In *Abbott*,
from 28 CFR Ch. V, Subpart F, Sec. 540.70,
et seqs (7-1-88 ed.)

Subpart F—Incoming Publications

Authority: 5 U.S.C. 301; 18 U.S.C. 4001, 4042, 4081, 4082, 5006-5024, 5039; 28 U.S.C. 509, 510; 28 CFR 0.95-0.99.
540.70 Purpose and scope.

(a) The Bureau of Prisons permits an inmate to subscribe to or to receive publications without prior approval and has established procedures to determine if an incoming publication is detrimental to the security, discipline, or good order of the institution or if it might facilitate criminal activity. The term publication, as used in this rule, means a book (for example, novel, instructional manual), or a single issue of a magazine or newspaper, plus such other materials addressed to a specific inmate as advertising brochures, flyers, and catalogues.

(b) The Warden may designate staff to review and where appropriate to approve all incoming publications in accordance with the provisions of this rule. Only the Warden may reject an incoming publication.

[44 FR 38260, June 29, 1979, as amended at 47 FR 55129, Dec. 7, 1982]
540.71 Procedures.

(a) An inmate may receive hardcover publications and newspapers only from the publisher, from a book club, or from a bookstore. An inmate may receive other softcover material (for example, paperback books, newspaper clippings, or magazines) from any source. The Warden may have all incoming publications inspected for contraband.

(b) The Warden may reject a publication only if it is determined detrimental to the security, good order, or discipline of the institution or if it might facilitate criminal activity. The Warden may not reject a publication solely because its content is religious, philosophical, political, social or sexual, or because its content is unpopular or repugnant. Publications which may be rejected by a Warden include but are not limited to publications which meet one of the following criteria.

(1) It depicts or describes procedures for the construction or use of weapons, ammunition, bombs or incendiary devices;

(2) It depicts, encourages, or describes methods of escape from correctional facilities, or contains blueprints, drawings or similar descriptions of Bureau of Prisons institutions;

(3) It depicts or describes procedures for the brewing of alcoholic beverages, or the manufacture of drugs;

(4) It is written in code;

(5) It depicts. describes or encourages activities which may lead to the use of physical violence or group disruption;

(6) It encourages or instructs in the commission of criminal activity;

(7) It is sexually explicit material which by its nature or content poses a threat to the security, good order, or discipline of the institution, or facilitates criminal activity.

(c) The Warden may not establish an excluded list of publications. This means the Warden shall review the individual publication prior to the rejection of that publication. Rejection of several issues of a subscription publication is not sufficient reason to reject the subscription publication in its entirety.

(d) Where a publication is found unacceptable, the Warden shall promptly advise the inmate in writing of the decision and the reasons for it. The notice must contain reference to the specific article(s) or material(s) considered objectionable. The Warden shall permit the inmate an opportunity to review this material for purposes of filing an appeal under the Administrative Remedy Procedure unless such review may provide the inmate with information of a nature which is deemed to pose a threat or detriment to the security, good order or discipline of the institution or to encourage or instruct in criminal activity.

(e) The Warden shall provide the publisher or sender of an unacceptable publication a copy of the rejection letter. The Warden shall advise the publisher or sender that he may obtain an independent review of the rejection by writing to the Regional Director within 15 days of receipt of the rejection letter. The Warden shall return the rejected publication to the publisher or sender of the material unless the inmate indicates an intent to file an appeal under the Administrative Remedy Procedure, in which case the Warden shall retain the rejected material at the institution for review. In case of appeal, if the rejection is sustained, the rejected publication shall be returned when appeal or legal use is completed.

(f) The Warden may set limits locally (for fire, sanitation or housekeeping reasons) on the number or volume of publications an inmate may receive or retain in his quarters. The Warden may authorize an inmate additional storage space for storage of legal materials in accordance with the Bureau of Prisons procedures on personal property of inmates.

[44 FR 38260, June 29, 1979, as amended at 47 FR 55130, Dec. 7, 1982: 50 FR 411, Jan. 3, 1985]

16

Disciplinary Hearings
Something Old, Something New,
But Always Something

William C. Collins

Judicial activity in the area of prison discipline remains active at the Supreme Court level as well as in the lower courts. In the last two years, (1985-1986), the Supreme Court has decided three cases involving prison disciplinary issues. At the lower court level the rights clearly established in 1974 with the Supreme Court's landmark decision of *Wolff* v. *McDonnell*, 94 S.Ct. 2963 remain the subject of continuing litigation. In *Wolff*, the Court held that the due process clause of the Fourteenth Amendment obligates prison officials to give a prisoner accused of serious misconduct the opportunity to appear before an impartial prison hearing board to rebut the charges against him. The prisoner must be given written notification of the charges against him at least 24 hours prior to his appearance before the hearing tribunal. The prisoner also may present documentary evidence and call witnesses in his defense at the hearing unless this jeopardizes institutional safety or other

Source: Reprinted from William C. Collins, *Correctional Law 1986*, 39–46. Reprinted with the permission of the author.

correctional goals. Further, the prisoner is entitled to the assistance of a "counsel substitute" (either a fellow prisoner, if permitted, or a staff member) when the inmate is illiterate or the issues are unusually complex. Finally, *Wolff* requires the hearing board to provide the prisoner with a written statement of the evidence supporting its decision and the reasons for any disciplinary action taken. It is equally important to note that the *Wolff* Court held that inmates are not entitled to retained or appointed counsel and that they have no constitutional right to confront or cross-examine hostile witnesses (although the hearing board has the discretion to permit confrontation and cross-examination).

Since *Wolff*, the courts have continued to struggle with questions such as what restrictions should apply when information from anonymous informants is used in a disciplinary hearing and how much due process must be afforded for minor infractions. While there will always be litigation about prison disciplinary proceedings, much current litigation could have been avoided by closer adherence to rules and procedures which have been in effect for years.

Supreme Court: Judicial Review of the Evidence, Reasons for Denying Witnesses, and No Judicial Immunity

Sufficiency of the Evidence

Federal courts usually are not interested in whether an inmate was guilty or innocent of a disciplinary infraction. Instead the courts are interested in whether proper procedures were followed.

This trend received a sharp boost from the Supreme Court in *Superintendent v. Hill*,[1] a 1985 case in which the Court decided how much evidence is required by the Fourteenth Amendment to support a finding of guilty. The answer? "Some Evidence." The Court's precise holding:

> We conclude that where good time credits constitute a protected interest, a decision to revoke such credits must be supported by some evidence," 105 S.Ct. at 2770.

What the Court was saying becomes clearer when one examines other statements from the opinion and when one considers the facts of the case, which the Court found sufficient to support a guilty finding from a disciplinary hearing in a Massachusetts hearing.

> "We hold that the requirements of due process are satisfied if some evidence supports the decision. . . to revoke good time credits. This standard is met if 'there was some evidence from which the conclusion of the administrative tribunal could be deduced. . .' (citation

omitted). Ascertaining whether this standard is satisfied does not require examination of the entire record, independent assessment of the credibility of witnesses, or weighing of the evidence. Instead, the relevant question is whether there is any evidence in the record that could support the conclusion reached by the disciplinary hoard," 105 S.Ct. at 2774.

In other words, a court reviewing the evidence in a disciplinary hearing under the Fourteenth Amendment will not be able to weigh the evidence. Once the court finds there is some evidence which, if believed, would support a conclusion of guilt, due process is satisfied.

The evidence in the case was described by the Supreme Court as "meager," but still was sufficient. An officer reported he had heard an inmate twice say in a loud voice "What's going on?" Upon investigating, the officer found another inmate lying bleeding. Dirt was strewn about, suggesting a scuffle had occurred. Three inmates, including the two inmates who were respondents in the case at the Supreme Court, were seen jogging away down a walkway. Testimony was given at the hearing supporting that the inmate had been beaten. Both inmates denied beating anyone and the victim stated in writing that the two had not beaten him. There was no direct evidence linking the two inmates with the beating.

One of the more significant aspects of *Superintendent* may be its clear statement that credibility will not be an issue for review under the Fourteenth Amendment. Thus hearings which boil down to swearing contests between staff and inmate ("He did it." "No I didn't, I was asleep in my cell when it happened.") should not be subject to federal court review.

The results in this case should be taken with a grain of salt. They apply only to Fourteenth Amendment reviews of evidence in disciplinary hearings. They do not necessarily apply to reviews conducted under applicable state laws or constitutional provisions. It is entirely possible that stiffer review standards will be imposed under these criteria. It is certainly likely that "sufficiency of the evidence" issues will be presented to state courts, since clearly the federal Constitution is no longer an attractive source of review for inmates.

Reasons For Denying Witnesses

In *Wolff* in 1974, the Court held that an inmate in a disciplinary hearing has the right to call witnesses unless "unduly hazardous to institutional safety or correctional goals."[2] The issue before the Court 11 years later in *Ponte v. Real*[3] was "when must the institution tell the inmate its reasons for denying witnesses in a given case?"

Although the reasonable time to state such reasons would be at the hearing, when the reasons are fresh in the minds of the hearing committee and when they can be reviewed by other institution officials, the Supreme Court held that due process does not require that reasons for denying a witness be given at that time. Instead, the Court held that the reasons need not be given until the inmate challenges the denial in court. In other words, nowhere in the administrative process (in the hearing, during any administrative appeals, etc.) must the reasons for denying a witness be given. Only if the inmate pursues the denial by filing a lawsuit must the reasons be stated.

While there may be situations where it is necessary to not state a reason for denying a requested witness in a hearing before the inmate who called him, it does not appear wise to postpone stating the reason in any or all administrative contexts in favor of waiting to see if the inmate files a lawsuit over the question. This delay creates several potential problems: It invites more litigation and court involvement in the disciplinary process. It increases the likelihood that the hearing committee members may not remember why the denial was made, or even that the members may no longer work for the institution. It means that there is no administrative review of denial decisions, even though these decisions are obviously of constitutional significance.

The more prudent practice would be to require, by administrative rule, that the committee state its reason for denying inmate witnesses at the hearing, in writing. If there are security-related justifications for not telling the inmate the reason, then a record still should be made which then could be reviewed either in the context of an inmate appeal of the decision or independently of the appeal process, simply as a regular administrative review of the disciplinary process.

In its opinion in *Ponte* the Court also noted that in judicial reviews of denial decisions, the reviewing court should examine the reasons in chambers, away from the inmate, "if prison security orother paramount interests appear to require" such examination.[4]

While it has always appeared that disciplinary hearing officers should have the inherent right to limit witnesses for other that security reasons, simply as a part of running an orderly hearing, there has remained some question about this power since *Wolff* spoke only in security and "correctional goal" terms. This uncertainty probably has been laid to rest by a comment in Justice Marshall's dissent in *Ponte*. In calling for a requirement that reasons be given at the hearing, Justice Marshall states:

"To include (in the statement of reasons for the final decision in the hearing) a brief explanation of the reasons for refusing to hear a witness, such as why proffered testimony is "irrelevant" or "cumulative" could not credibly be said to burden disciplinary boards in any meaningful way. . .," 105 S.Ct. at 2207.

This statement recognizes that "correctional goals" include the goal of running efficient disciplinary hearings, with some ability to control the inmate who may request an inordinate number of witnesses, or demand to call witnesses who clearly could not offer information relevant to the question of guilt or innocence. This ability was applied and upheld in a 1985 Virginia case.[5] The inmate requested to call witnesses, but the request was denied on the basis that there was only one witness who had already been interviewed in the investigation and whose testimony would have made no difference to the outcome of the hearing. The Court agreed with this result.

Hearing Officers Ain't Judges. Hold Onto Your Pocketbooks. Maybe.

In a 1986 case, *Cleavinger* v. *Saxner*,[6] the Court rejected an argument that prison disciplinary hearing officers should enjoy a quasi-judicial (absolute) immunity. Instead, the Court limited the hearing officers to only qualified immunity, the same enjoyed by other government officials. Had the case gone the other way, hearing committee members would have been completely immune from having to pay damages in Civil Rights cases, even though their actions in the hearing may have violated the rights of the inmate.

Complete immunity could have provided some comfort to hearing officers, because the area of rights with which such officers are concerned are, for the most part, clearly established. As such, their violation subjects a defendant to liability for damages. For example, damages of $25 per day for each day an inmate was held in segregation following a constitutionally defective disciplinary hearing were imposed in one case, along with $78 for the inmate's loss of pay. Total bill: $1203 actual damages, plus a small sum for nominal damages, and an unspecified amount of attorneys' fees.[7]

Lower Court Activity: Review of Clearly Established Rights Means Potential Damages

The primary issues in lower court litigation which arise out of the disciplinary process are those relating to the application of existing rights which were originally stated by the Supreme Court in *Wolff*. However, some issues seen with some regularity in the lower courts still have not reached the Supreme Court.

Do It Right or Pay the Price.

The likelihood that any violation of an inmate's rights in the disciplinary process will result in damages of some amount, along with whatever injunctive relief the court may feel appropriate (expungement of records, etc.), makes it even more important that hearings are conducted in accordance with applicable rules. This means that staff conducting the hearing and involved in the hearing process should be trained to know inmate due process rights, know applicable state/institution rules and policies, and know how to conduct a hearing.

It still seems that correctional staff often do not have an understanding of the importance courts place on procedural rights. Instead, staff tends to focus on what is perceived as probable guilt and on expediency. The guiltier an inmate appears to be, the less important are the procedural due process rights which are part of the disciplinary process, in the minds of at least some staff. In the case cited in footnote 7, the inmate was charged with possessing marijuana which was found in his cell. The inmate denied possessing the marijuana, and offered information from other inmates suggesting it had been left by a prior occupant of the cell known only as "Bo." The inmate asked the officer appointed to assist him in the hearing to search records to see when the cell had last been searched and to find Bo and take a statement. The officer did not check the records. Limited investigation by the hearing committee did not identify Bo and the committee chair finally indicated:

> "Alright. I am not going to try to identify the inmate and. . .(even) if we could identify him, which is doubtful, then we'd have to take the time and the expense to track him down; and, like I say, it is very,very doubtful that the man would admit to making such a statement, anyway, even if he did make it."[8]

The court concluded that the help from the staff assistant was inadequate in light of the failure to carry out the inmate's requests which were, under the facts of the case, reasonable on their face. These problems were continued by the actions of the hearing committee in refusing to pursue the inmate's requests and totally rejecting the inmate's defense, without affording the inmate the opportunity to fully prepare the defense.

Experienced correctional staff reading the facts above may quickly come to the conclusion that the defense was one commonly contrived by inmates in whose cell contraband is found and that to pursue the claim of the inmate would have indeed been a waste of time and money. A reviewing court cannot and will not make these assumptions, particularly when they are used to deny the inmate due process rights.

Participants in the hearing process — investigators, staff appointed to assist the inmate and most certainly the hearing committee itself — must be sure that the required procedural steps are taken. To ignore them for expediency reasons or because "everybody knows the inmate is guilty" only invites the result in the New York case: damages, expungement of the records, and prohibitions against any further disciplinary action based on the original incident.

The chair of the hearing committee is in a particularly important position by being able to check that rights are properly afforded and to correct any errors which may have crept into the process, even if this means starting the hearing process over again. Knowledge of what rights the inmate has and knowledge of how to conduct a hearing, particularly how to make a solid record, can avoid a great deal of litigation. Cases which are filed should be far easier to defend when they challenge hearings presided over by officers who (to reverse the usual complaint) "know more about the rules than the inmates do."

Any appellate review of the hearing process also must be sensitive to violations of procedural rights if the appellate process is to play a litigation prevention function.

The rights of inmates in the disciplinary process are not that long or complex. One need not be a judge to understand or apply the rights in question. Virtually every correctional system in the country has rules and regulations which comply with the rights the courts have defined. The problem then is simply assuring that these rights are followed in the disciplinary process and that any mistakes that might be made are identified and corrected at the earliest possible opportunity. Proper training and review of the disciplinary process should result in few, if any, errors getting to court.

Use of Anonymous Informants.

Under what circumstances and in accordance with what procedural protections may information from an informant whose identity is not disclosed to the inmate be used against the inmate in a disciplinary hearing? Several courts have addressed this issue over several years. While the results are not all identical, the use of anonymous testimony has uniformly been approved. Indeed, the Supreme Court in *Wolff*, by refusing to impose a right to confront and cross-examine witnesses in a prison disciplinary hearing implicitly recognized and approved the use of anonymous testimony. Where the courts have differed is on the question of what steps must the institution go through to establish the reliability and credibility of the missing witness.

Late in 1985 the 7th Circuit addressed the anonymous witness issue in a case coming from the federal prison at Marion.[9] Anonymous informants had implicated inmate Mendoza in the stabbing death of another inmate. Mendoza sought to overturn the results of the disciplinary hearing (where he was found guilty of murder and lost one year of good time and was given disciplinary segregation for 60 days) for various reasons, all relating to the use of informant testimony.

The court quickly ruled that use of informant testimony was generally acceptable and the hearing committee has discretion to decide whether to reveal the names of witnesses. However, the committee must make a determination as to the reliability of the informant and that determination is subject to review by the court. The committee need not state in any public record what the factual basis is for its determination (citing to *Ponte*, the court emphasized that the reasons need not be presented to anyone prior to litigation. Obviously, the reasons should be set down somewhere prior to going to court, if the reasons are to be recalled in any detail).

The court's review may be "in camera," i.e., in chambers and in the presence of only the judge. Even the inmates' counsel may be excluded. The court said that judicial review must give a good deal of deference to the decisions of the committee. A reference to *Superintendent* v. *Hill* suggests that if the review by the court shows some evidence on which the committee could have based a finding of reliability, the committee's decision must be upheld.

Even if a stricter standard than "some evidence" is required to uphold the decision to withhold the informant's identity from the inmate, the decision of the 7th Circuit is notable for its approval of "in camera" examination of the documentation which is used to support the committee's decision. The court approved a review by the judge alone, allowing what the dissent criticizes as a "secret trial,"[10]

In a later case, the 7th Circuit approved a process for using anonymous inmate testimony in disciplinary hearings:[11]

- The report of an investigative officer (if such an officer was involved) had to be under oath.
- Guilt normally would have to be based on more than one reliable confidential source or one source plus other corroborating factual evidence. A single confidential source could suffice if

peculiar circumstances existed convincing the committee that the informant must be reliable.

- Informant reliability must be established. Past reliability as well as other (unspecified) factors will suffice to establish reliability. These should be given to the committee. Staff had an affirmative duty to determine if there was any basis for the informant providing false information.

- All confidential information coming to the committee must be in writing, stating facts and the manner in which the informant arrived at knowledge of those facts.

- The chair of the committee, at least, must know the identity of the informant. The entire committee must know the substance of the informant information. The record of the hearing should state the basis for the committee's finding that the information given by the informant was reliable. (Note, this means the committee must decide both that the informant is reliable and the specific information provided is also reliable.)

- The committee must at least incorporate the informant's statements into the record by reference. Normally the hearing report should document the finding of reliability. Where this information cannot be shared with the inmate, a separate report should be prepared.

A process which allows the hearing committee to rely on a third party's conclusion about informant reliability may exceed the limits of due process. From the perspective of being able to defend committee decisions in court, clearly the better procedure is for the committee to receive sufficient information (which can be heard outside the presence of the inmate) to allow the committee to decide for itself that the informant is generally reliable and the specific information being provided is believable. The more specific, factual information the committee has, the more defensible its decisions will be.

Must the Reporting Officer be Present?

The disciplinary process begins with a report prepared by an officer, often indicating that the officer was a witness to an infraction by the inmate. Must the officer be present at the hearing, or may simply the written report by introduced as evidence? Relying on *Wolff's* statement that inmates do not have the right to confront and cross-examine witnesses, the inmate does not have a right to have the officer present.[12]

But there is a catch to this issue. While the inmate lacks the right to confront and cross-examine a witness against him, the inmate does have a limited right to call witnesses. What then if the inmate chooses to call the reporting officer as a witness? Then the refusal to call the witness must be based on the conclusion that calling the witness would be "unduly hazardous to institutional safety or correctional goals."[13] Unless it appears the inmate has no purpose in calling the officer except for harassment, refusals should be limited to grounds of "undue hazard . . ."

Assistants Should be of Assistance.

In the *Wolff* decision, the Supreme Court held that inmates do not have the right to counsel in disciplinary hearings, but also noted that when an illiterate inmate is involved in a hearing or the issues are so complex that the inmate can't reasonably be expected to collect and present information for a defense, the inmate should be allowed to have the assistance of a fellow inmate or designated staff member to assist in preparation for the hearing.

While the illiteracy test is relatively objective, the complexity test may depend on the circumstances. For instance, the otherwise intelligent inmate probably cannot adequately prepare for a hearing if locked in pre-hearing detention pending the hearing. However, this same inmate may be quite capable of presenting information at the hearing, assuming someone has gathered it for him.

It is not clear if the role of the assistant is that of an advocate or something more neutral. Caselaw does not address this issue to any degree, although it appears that many states see the role as non-adversarial. Given that the Supreme Court in *Wolff* chose not to require counsel in disciplinary hearings because they would increase the adversary cast of the proceedings, it would appear that a non-adversarial role is consistent with *Wolff*.

A couple of recent cases suggest the problems with assistants is not defining the role as adversarial or non-adversarial, but is somewhat more basic: simply having it recognized that the assistance must be meaningful in quality and quantity to meet the requirement of *Wolff*. An apparent lackadaisical attitude on the part of one appointed assistant contributed to a violation of a New York inmate's rights, see footnote 7. In another case, a summary judgment in favor of the institution was reversed by a court of appeals in part because the record showed the inmate had been given all of five minutes to confer with a fellow inmate allowed to assist in a disciplinary hearing.[14]

Where an inmate is permitted assistance from either staff or inmate, the hearing committee should assure itself that there has been sufficient contact between the two and that the assistant has done what the inmate requested, or has at least made a good faith attempt to fulfill the inmate's requests. Where there are problems apparent to the committee, steps should be taken to remedy the problems, including temporarily recessing the hearing. Similarly, any appellate review should be sensitive to this issue and be ready to remand cases back for new hearings when there is doubt about the adequacy of the assistance provided an inmate.

Is *Wolff* The Last Word in Disciplinary Due Process?

After the decision in *Wolff* v. *McDonnell* in 1974, it appeared that the question of how much process was due an inmate in a disciplinary hearing was settled. Although the bulk of the opinion in *Wolff* focuses on the loss of good time as the sanction which triggered the due process protections required in the opinion, most people interpreted the holding as also applying to other serious sanctions, including disciplinary segregation. The result is that most disciplinary rules are broken into major and minor categories, with very minor sanctions being attached to the latter category.

A recent Supreme Court decision concerning due process and administrative segregation raises the question as to whether the line between major and minor disciplinary proceedings must be drawn where it is or whether stiffer sanctions could be included for so-called "minor" infractions without requiring the full *Wolff* due process procedures.

Whether due process is required in most prison contexts depends on whether a "state-created liberty interest" exists.[15] In other words, due process protections may not be inherently required by the Fourteenth Amendment in a given context (i.e., the decision to place someone in administrative segregation), but the state, by the way it writes its statutes, rules, or policies, can create a liberty interest which then is protected by some level of due process under the Fourteenth Amendment. The state creates a liberty interest when it chooses to voluntarily place limits on circumstances under which it will exercise its discretion. A rule which says that a specific action will be taken by the institution (such as placing someone in administrative segregation) will take place only upon a finding of certain facts or conditions (e.g., a finding that the individual is a threat to the security of the institution) creates a liberty interest. A rule which does not impose such limits ("an inmate may be placed in administrative segregation in the discretion of the superintendent") does not.

Applying this somewhat confusing concept to the administrative segregation placement decision, the Supreme Court in the *Hewitt* case decided that placing someone in administrative segregation under the state regulations involved in *Hewitt* did require limited due process protections. Even though the Court assumed conditions in administrative segregation were no different than conditions in disciplinary segregation, the Court chose not to require *Wolff* protections. Instead, the Court required only an informal, non-adversary review:

> An inmate must merely receive some notice of the charges against him and an opportunity to present his views to the prison officials charged with deciding whether to transfer him to administrative segregation. Ordinarily, a written statement by the inmate will accomplish this purpose, although prison administrators may find it more useful to permit oral presentations in cases where they believe a written statement would be ineffective.[16]

In other words, no in-person hearing, no limited right to call witnesses, no limited right to assistance are required. Only a notice and an opportunity to respond in writing. Although the Court did not specify that the decision maker had to be impartial, this can be assumed.

The reasons the Court differentiated the administrative segregation procedures from disciplinary procedures largely had to do with the judgmental, predictive nature of the administrative segregation decision, as contrasted with the relatively factual nature of the disciplinary decision.

It is common for prison discipline to have two levels, with minor infractions being handled with less than *Wolff* due process. But these minor proceedings are truly minor, with very limited sanctions available. Does the result in *Hewitt* suggest that the level of minor infractions could be raised, with more severe sanctions still available with process less than that required by *Wolff*? Can *Wolff* be limited to only those situation where good time is at stake? At least one court has recently recognized that "the process due may decrease as the severity of the punishment decreases," without suggesting where *Wolff* due process leaves off and something less may begin.[17]

Before administrators leap to amend disciplinary codes, it must be emphasized that the hypothesis suggested above has little or no specific caselaw to support it, other than the general sort of comment quoted above. Therefore, the hypothesis may be nothing more than idle legal speculation.

Even assuming the legal risk is worth taking, there is a question as to whether any change would be worth it administratively. A procedurally simpler disciplinary process would probably save some time and money. It could also reduce liability exposure. Various questions would have to be addressed in developing such a system. For instance, what infractions would be included in which level? Could a "minor" infraction be referred to the "major" committee to allow a sterner sanction and if so, according to what standards?

Would the actual fairness of the expanded minor procedure decrease as the inmate's procedural protections were decreased? Certainly inmates and many observers of prison administration would perceive a decrease in fairness.

Such a restructuring, which perhaps could limit *Wolff* requirements to those cases where time loss was involved, should only be undertaken after close consultation with counsel both as to the probable legality of such a change and as to how such a change could be initiated with minimal liability exposure. For instance, it can be assumed such a change would be challenged in court. But if the revised process were allowed to run during the pendency of the challenge, the institution could be faced with having to undo easily two years or more worth of disciplinary infractions should the rules be found unconstitutional.

Comment

Due process and prison disciplinary systems have come a long way from the days when the thought of imposing some sort of procedural requirements on the process threatened life as we knew it. But there are still a significant number of lawsuits arising from prison disciplinary hearings, which usually allege that the hearing committee failed to follow the institution's own rules and in so doing violated a mandate of *Wolff* or some other court decision. Many of these suits can be avoided — or at least won easily — if those involved in the hearing process paid greater attention both to following applicable rules and to understanding more about what the rules are intended to produce: a hearing process which is fair both to the inmate and the institution.

Notes

[1] 105 S.Ct. 2769 (1985).
[2] 418 U.S. at 566.
[3] 105 S.Ct. 2192.
[4] 105 S.Ct. at 2197.

[5] *Cook v. Robinson*, 612 F. Supp. 187 (D.Va., 1985).

[6] 106 S.Ct. 496 (1986).

[7] *Pino v. Dalshiem*, 605 F. Supp. 1305 (S.D. N.Y., 1984).

[8] 605 F. Supp. at 1312.

[9] *Mendoza v. Miller*, 779 F.2d 1287 (7th Cir., 1985).

[10] 779 F.2d at 1304, n. 9.

[11] *McCollum v. Williford*, 793 F.2d 903, 907, n. 3(7th Cir., 1986). *McCollum* and *Mendoza* are the latest in a series of anonymous witnesses cases the 7th Circuit has been dealing with over the last several years, all coming from Marion. Given the attention the 7th Circuit has been giving to this issue, the results in these cases probably deserve special attention. Other circuits have consistently approved use of informant testimony where the committee makes a determination as to the reliability of the informant, although these opinions are not as exhaustive as those of the 7th Circuit in the Marion series of cases, *Helms v. Hewitt*, 655 F.2d 487 (3rd Cir., 1981), *Smith v. Rabalais*, 659 F.2d 539 (5th Cir., 1981), *Kyle v. Hanberry*, 677 F.2d 1386 (11th Cir., 1982).

[12] *Harrison v. Pyle*, 612 F. Supp. 850 (D. Nev., 1985).

[13] *Ponte v. Real*, 105 S.Ct. at 2197.

[14] *Grandison v. Cuyler*, 774 F.2d (3rd Cir., 1985).

[15] *Hewitt v. Helms*, 459 U.S. 460, 103 S.Ct. 864, 74 L.Ed.2d 675 (1983).

[16] 103 S.Ct. at 874.

[17] *Gibbs v. King*, 779 F.2d 1040, 1044 (5th Cir., 1986).

17

The Eighth Amendment in Prison
Does The Supreme Court Know Where It Is Going?
William C. Collins

> Excessive bail shall not be required, nor excessive fines imposed, nor cruel and unusual punishment inflicted.
> —Amendment VIII, U.S. Constitution

The Eighth Amendment is the font of a great deal of momentous litigation in corrections over the last third of the Twentieth Century. The Eighth Amendment protects incarcerated offenders from the excess use of force by officers and affords the basis for challenging various conditions of confinement when those conditions present actual or serious threats of harm to inmates. As early as 1962, a federal district court found two years of isolation in solitary confinement for violation of minor prison rules to be cruel and unusual punishment[1]

The effects of Eighth Amendment litigation on correctional institutions and operations have been dramatic. Millions of dollars have been spent by agencies defending Eighth Amendment cases, and more than that has been spent in remedying Eighth Amendment violations. For instance, bringing the Louisiana prisons into compliance with the United

Source: Prepared especially for *The Dilemmas of Corrections*.

States Constitution required an initial supplemental operating appropriation of over $18,000,000 and over $105 million in capital outlays.[2] An inmate now can be relatively assured of having at least minimal levels of medical care because of the Supreme Court's decision in *Estelle v. Gamble*, which said that the Eighth Amendment was violated by "deliberate indifference to serious medical needs."[3] John Midgely, an attorney who has spent most of his career representing inmates, notes the improvements in the quality of medical care as one of "the most important case-spurred developments in corrections" over the last twenty years.[4]

While the impact of Eighth Amendment litigation on corrections is obvious, the Supreme Court has had a difficult time trying to decide exactly what "no cruel and unusual punishments inflicted" means in the context of a correctional institution. While most of the attention over the years has been on the meaning of cruel and unusual punishment, the Court's more recent Eighth Amendment prison cases focus largely on the meaning of "inflicted."[5] Leading up to *Farmer* was a series of earlier Supreme Court decisions which increasingly examined whether the defendant's state of mind was a relevant inquiry in Eighth Amendment litigation and, if so, what that state of mind must be in order to cross the threshold of the Eighth Amendment.

The reasonableness of examining a defendant's state of mind is understandable in some types of Eighth Amendment cases which involve the actions of one or two individual correctional officials against a single inmate. Examples of this type of case would include inadequate or improper medical care or use of force. But where a case challenges systemic deficiencies, such as the overall medical system or excessive levels of danger in the institution, inquiries into the state of mind of individual defendants seem considerably less important than simply assessing the quality of the system under attack.

First Application of Eighth Amendment In Prison Context

The phrase "cruel and unusual punishments" is inherently vague. The Supreme Court did not have to try to define the phrase in the context of a prison case until its decision in 1976 in *Estelle*, although the meaning of the phrase had been explored in a variety of other contexts.

Estelle was essentially a medical malpractice case, litigated at a constitutional level. An inmate complained that various Texas prison officials, ranging from the chief medical officer of the prison to the Director of the Department of Corrections, had not provided adequate medical care for back injuries sustained when a bale of cotton fell on the inmate or for the inmate's blood pressure and heart problems. The inmate had been seen by medical staff for these problems a number of times, and the inmate's contention was that they should have done more in the way of both diagnosis and treatment.

In *Estelle*, Justice Marshall noted the Amendment prohibited punishments which "involve torture or a lingering death."[6] He also noted the Amendment addressed more than just "physically barbarous punishments."[7] The Amendment embodies "broad and idealistic concepts of dignity, civilized standards, humanity, and decency."[8] It prohibits punishments which are incompatible with "the evolving standards of decency that mark the progress of a maturing society"[9] or punishments which "involve the unnecessary and wanton infliction of pain."[10] Other courts in the early days of Eighth Amendment prison litigation used a "shocking to the conscience" test to define the boundaries of the Eighth Amendment.[11]

In *Estelle*, the Court noted that prisoners are dependent on institution officials for their medical care, and if care is not provided, the result in the worst case could be "torture or a lingering death,"[12] i.e., a violation of the Eighth Amendment of the most traditional form.

The Court was unwilling to say that an accident, even if it produces severe anguish, could amount to the wanton and unnecessary infliction of pain. It was also limited by an earlier death penalty case in which it had ruled that the Eighth Amendment did not prevent a second execution attempt where an accident had botched the initial attempt. The Court also felt that the "conscience of mankind" would not be offended as a result of a simple accident, i.e., negligence.

This reasoning led the Court to the conclusion that "deliberate indifference to serious medical needs of prisoners constitutes the unnecessary and wanton infliction of pain" in violation of the Eighth Amendment.[13] Perhaps dreading the aspect of constitutionalizing the tort of medical malpractice for inmates, the *Estelle* opinion makes it clear that simple negligence will not state a claim for relief.

The phrase "deliberate indifference" was new to Supreme Court jurisprudence, but the phrase, or similar terms, had been developed by various lower courts in their attempts to judge inmate claims about constitutionally inadequate medical care.[14] Justice Marshall did not try to define the meaning of deliberate indifference, other than to indicate it meant something worse than simple negligence.

Applying its newly minted test to the facts of the case, the Court held that Mr. Gamble stated no claim for relief under the Eighth Amendment, because he had been seen many times by medical staff, who had prescribed various medications and actions for these conditions. Disagreements over the efficacy of these actions could not amount to deliberate indifference, although they might amount to negligence.

Justice Stevens dissented. One of his areas of disagreement with the majority was over their adoption of a state of mind component for an Eighth Amendment violation. To Justice Blackmun, a defendant's motivations were irrelevant. The sole key to an Eighth Amendment violation, in his mind, should be "the character of the punishment," i.e., what happened to the inmate.[15] Looking at the Court's subsequent attempts to live with its deliberate indifference requirement suggests the wisdom of Justice Blackmun's position.

Interestingly, after arguing against a state of mind requirement, Justice Stevens seems to read one back into his version of the Eighth Amendment: "Of course, not every instance of improper health care violates the Eighth Amendment. Like the rest of us, prisoners must take the risk that a competent, diligent physician will make an error. Such an error may give rise to a tort claim, but not necessarily to a constitutional claim."[16] If the error had very serious consequences, would it create a constitutional claim?

Deliberate indifference became a major aspect of medical cases with facts similar to Estelle, i.e., complaints from individual inmates about the care which they received. From experience, the author of this article can say that a common defense in such cases, usually successful, was to demonstrate that medical staff had seen the complaining inmate a number of times and had prescribed various sorts of treatment. Faced with such a response, lower courts would rarely get into evaluating the adequacy of the treatment prescribed. Simply the fact that the inmate was seen and some treatment given usually was enough to show officials were not deliberately indifferent.

Deliberate indifference also became a major part of failure to protect cases, where a single inmate might allege that officials had failed to protect him from an assault by other inmates.[17]

State of Mind Overlooked

If the state of mind prong of an Eighth Amendment case was alive and well in cases involving a single inmate, it was overlooked virtually entirely in conditions of confinement cases.

Although conditions of confinement litigation was rampant during the 1970s, the first such case which was based on the Eighth Amendment did not reach the Supreme Court until 1981.[18] In the absence of Supreme Court guidance on conditions of confinement analysis, lower courts did not hesitate to blaze their own trail into the thicket of cruel and unusual punishment and prison conditions. Without going into detail about the results of many of these early cases or the specific theories courts used, suffice it to say that these courts focused on the conditions, not the state of mind of the defendants.[19] Some courts asked whether institutions were adequately providing life's basic human needs for the inmate: "If the State furnishes its prisoners with reasonably adequate food, clothing, shelter, sanitation, medical care, and personal safety, so as to avoid the imposition of cruel and unusual punishment, that ends its obligations under Amendment Eight."[20] Others focused more narrowly on overcrowding and the amount of cell space available to inmates.[21] The crowding approach reached its zenith in cases where a federal court held that double celling inmates in cells designed to hold only a single inmate was unconstitutional.[22]

It was this case, *Chapman v. Rhodes*, which provided the Supreme Court with its next opportunity to examine the contours of the Eighth Amendment. *Rhodes* involved the Southern Ohio Correctional Facility at Lucasville, a maximum security prison which was less than a decade old when the district court found it unconstitutionally overcrowded. But for the overcrowding, the rest of the institution was apparently not in bad shape. The physical plant was, to the district court, "top-flight, first-class."[23] Heating and ventilation were adequate. Dayrooms were available to the inmates, as were various rehabilitative and recreational programs. Violence in the institution had not increased beyond the increases in population. In short, the primary problem in Lucasville was that it held 2300 inmates in an institution designed to hold just over 1600.

If the corrections establishment had wanted the perfect conditions of confinement case to take to the Supreme Court, *Rhodes v. Chapman* was probably it, since the institution did not present any of the dramatic, appalling problems of filth and neglect which characterized many of the early conditions cases.

Applying a contemporary standards of decency approach, the District Court used various studies recommending approximately 55 square feet of cell space per inmate to define contemporary standards, and found Lucasville to violate the Eighth Amendment because of the crowding, and despite the other generally acceptable conditions.[24]

The Supreme Court reversed.[25] Writing for the five member majority, Justice Powell delivered the opinion of the Court. His opinion emphasized that conditions must involve "the wanton and unnecessary infliction of pain" before they become unconstitutional.[26] He cited other cases which spoke of conditions depriving the inmates of "the minimal civilized measure of life's necessities,"[27] which, he said, "could be cruel and unusual punishment under the contemporary standard of decency standard that we recognized in" *Estelle*.[28] The crowding alone, which was of importance to the District Court, could not overcome the other favorable conditions.

Justice Brennan wrote a concurring opinion, joined by Justices

Blackmun and Stevens, in which he was even more succinct: "In determining when prison conditions pass beyond legitimate punishment and become cruel and unusual, the 'touchstone is *the effect upon the imprisoned.*'"[29]

While the majority opinion cites *Estelle*, neither it nor Justice Brennan's concurrence makes the slightest suggestion that the state of mind of the defendants was a critical key to evaluating conditions of confinement. "When the 'cumulative impact of the conditions of incarceration threatens the physical, mental, and emotional health and well-being of the inmates and/or creates a probability of recidivism and future incarceration,' the court must conclude that the conditions violate the Constitution."[30]

The legacy of *Rhodes* then was that crowding alone cannot be the measure of the constitutionality of a prison because crowding does not necessarily indicate what the effects of the conditions are on the inmate. After *Rhodes*, the focal points in conditions cases became how bad conditions and their effects had to be before they violated the Eighth Amendment, what conditions were relevant, and how various conditions should be weighed in relation to one another. The state of mind of defendants was irrelevant in answering these questions.

Many lower courts applied a "totality of conditions" approach, cumulating the effects of various poor conditions together.[31] This approach had at least the implicit blessing of the Supreme Court because in *Rhodes* the majority opinion in dicta noted that "conditions other than those in *Gamble* (medical care) and *Hutto* (various poor conditions) *alone or in combination may*" violate the Eighth Amendment.[32]

Unless courts defined what conditions were relevant to the "totality," almost every conceivable complaint inmates might have about institution life became an issue in the trial, part of the legal Mulligan stew which was the end product of an unrestricted totality approach to a conditions case. The Ninth Circuit rejected the totality approach and at the same time defined what conditions were relevant in *Hoptowit v. Ray*.[33] Echoing *Newman*, the "basic human needs" of food, clothing, shelter, sanitation, medical care, and personal safety were what was important. Each of these areas should be analyzed independently of the others. In other words, if the problems with the food service were not so bad as to be cruel and unusual punishment, they could not be carried over and combined with problems related to cellhouse sanitation. This decision foreshadowed part of the Supreme Court's decision in *Wilson v. Seiter*.[34] Regardless of the position they took about the totality of conditions, *Hoptowit* and other post-*Rhodes* decisions all looked at conditions and their effect on the inmates. If conditions were bad enough, the facility was unconstitutional.

Prison Riot Reintroduces State of Mind Requirement

At this point, it is necessary to digress from surveying the Supreme Court's Eighth Amendment conditions of confinement cases to discuss the Court's first Eighth Amendment review of a use of force incident, *Whitley v. Albers.*[35]

Just as *Rhodes* involved a set of facts favorable to the correctional defendants, so did *Whitley.* The results of the decision were also favorable to correctional administrators, not to inmates. *Whitley* was similar to *Estelle* in that it involved injuries inflicted on one inmate by one staff member and did not involve questions about systemic problems.

Whitley arose out of a riot/hostage incident at the Oregon State Penitentiary in Salem. Prison staff were negotiating with inmates who had taken over a cell block and were holding hostages, whom they threatened to kill. After consideration of alternatives, the decision was made to rush the cell block. Under the guise of continuing negotiations, staff persuaded inmates to open the door of the cell block they held. Staff rushed in. Albers, the plaintiff, tried to flee up a flight of stairs. Because the hostages were held upstairs, staff had been instructed to shoot at any inmate attempting to get upstairs. Thus, a shot was fired, hitting Albers in the back of the leg and inflicting what turned out to be a fairly serious injury.

The Supreme Court found no fault with the shooting, saying that infliction of pain under these circumstances would violate the Eighth Amendment only if done "unnecessarily and wantonly." In a riot situation, not even deliberate indifference on the part of officials would be enough to violate the Eighth Amendment. To be "wanton" under these circumstances, the Court said that force would have to be used "maliciously and sadistically, for the very purpose of causing harm." If used in good faith to maintain order and restore discipline, the force would not violate the Eighth Amendment. To the Court, the extra leeway for officials which the malicious and sadistic standard afforded over the somewhat more demanding deliberate indifference approach was necessary because in the context of a prison disturbance, officials must make decisions "in haste, under pressure, and frequently without the luxury of a second chance," and these decisions must be balanced against "competing institutional concerns for the safety of prison staff and other inmates."[36] This language led most observers to read *Whitley* as being limited to emergency situations, such as riots. As a further indication of this intent, Justice Marshall's dissent objected to a riot providing justification for lessening "the constraints imposed on the prison authorities by the Eighth Amendment."[37]

So while *Whitley* reintroduced the question of officials' state of mind in Eighth Amendment litigation, it appeared to do so in a very limited context, i.e., emergencies. Accordingly, most observers did not foresee extension of the *Whitley* standard or the state of mind concept beyond the facts of *Whitley*.

Deliberate Indifference

Five years after *Whitley* and a decade after *Rhodes*, the Supreme Court considered another Eighth Amendment prison conditions case, *Wilson v. Seiter*.[38] It is with *Wilson* that Supreme Court Eighth Amendment jurisprudence regarding prisons begins to become confusing.

Pearly Wilson, an inmate in an Ohio prison, protested a variety of conditions, including crowding; noise; lack of storage space; improper heating, cooling, and ventilation; inadequate restrooms; unsanitary dining facilities and food preparation; and housing with mentally and physically ill inmates.

Despite the complex facts in the typical conditions case, *Wilson* was surprisingly decided on summary judgment, without a trial. On appeal, the Sixth Circuit said that several of Mr. Wilson's issues simply did not rise to the level of cruel and unusual punishment, even if he could prove what he alleged. Then the court said that for the other issues where the allegations involved conditions potentially serious enough to present an Eighth Amendment question, a state of mind requirement borrowed from *Whitley* and described as "obduracy and wantonness" also applied.[39] Because defendants' affidavits said they were trying to improve conditions and the plaintiff's responses did not contest this, the court said the plaintiff failed to raise a question as to the state of mind of the defendants. Thus, his Eighth Amendment claim failed, even though arguably some of the conditions were bad enough to potentially be cruel and unusual.

The Supreme Court accepted review and affirmed that the state of mind of prison officials is a critical element for a finding of cruel and unusual punishment in a prison conditions case.

> If the pain inflicted is not formally meted out *as punishment* by the statute or the sentencing judge, some mental element must be attributed to the inflicting officer before it can qualify, 111 S.Ct. at 2325, emphasis in original.

The majority rejected the suggestion that *Rhodes* approved an Eighth Amendment test for conditions concerned only with conditions, and not the state of mind of prison officials. They argued that *Whitley* embraced a state of mind requirement and that *Rhodes* simply didn't present the issue of an official's state of mind, so no comment about this component of cruel and unusual punishment was necessary in *Rhodes*. It is difficult, if not impossible, to read *Rhodes* as dealing with only one half of an Eighth Amendment equation. At least until *Whitley* reintroduced the state of mind issue, I am not aware of a lower court conditions case which stated that officials' state of mind was an inquiry in an Eighth Amendment conditions case which had equal importance to the inquiry as to the adequacy of the conditions.

To the truly prescient observer, the Court's concern over who inflicts punishment and the state of mind of defendants might have been foreshadowed in the Court's first conditions of confinement case, *Bell v. Wolfish*.[40] *Bell* was not an Eighth Amendment case because it involved federal pretrial detainees. For this group of inmates, quality of conditions are analyzed under the Fifth Amendment's due process clause. The Court said that detainees may not be "punished" by conditions of confinement; only when conditions can be said to amount to punishment do they violate the Fifth Amendment. In defining what would amount to punishment in the jail setting, the Court clearly looked at the purpose behind a particular disability imposed on a detainee (such as double celling, which was one of the key issues in *Bell*), thus suggesting the relevance of the state of mind of the defendant.[41]

Having planted its feet on the state of mind question, the Court went on to disagree with the Sixth Circuit's reliance on *Whitley* as defining the *correct* state of mind requirement. While an official's actions or inactions must be "wanton" to violate the Eighth Amendment, the Court explained that what is wanton in one context is not wanton in another. The *Whitley* definition of wantonness "does not apply to prison conditions cases."[42] Instead, the deliberate indifference form of wantonness from *Estelle* properly is applied in a conditions case. The reason for the difference is due to the "constraints facing the *official*."[43] The Court did not explain what sorts of constraints justify a lesser or greater definition of wantonness, except to conclude that medical care is a condition of confinement and, therefore, other conditions of confinement should be judged under the same deliberate indifference standard as medical issues.

Wilson also addressed the totality of conditions means of analysis, denying that the "alone or in combination" statement in *Rhodes*, quoted earlier, was intended to approve a totality approach.[44] Only when two or more conditions have a "mutually enforcing effect that produces the deprivation of a single, identifiable human need such as food, warmth, or exercise" can their impact be considered cumulatively.[45]

Four Justices dissented in *Wilson*, arguing against the state of mind requirement. The dissenting Justices contended that only the objective severity of the punishment should be a relevant Eighth Amendment inquiry and that the subjective intent of governing officials simply has no place in the equation.

The most telling deficiency in requiring a state of mind showing as part of a conditions case is that it raises the possibility of what might be called the "pure of heart" defense. Prison officials may be able to show that they are aware of problems and are making reasonable, but unsuccessful, efforts to correct them and thus they are not deliberately indifferent. This in fact was the result in *Rhodes*. The failure to address the defendant's showing of good intentions and efforts to improve the institution (the "pure of heart" defense) precluded the plaintiffs from litigating the severity of the conditions themselves.

A pure of heart defense can readily be imagined when deficiencies can be traced to a lack of funding from the legislature. The result of the lack of funding (perhaps combined with dramatic population increases which an institution administrator also cannot control) may be abysmal conditions but as long as officials who are subject to suit under 42 USC Section 1983 can show they are doing the best they can with what they are given, they should be able to defeat an Eighth Amendment conditions challenge.

The state itself (and hence the legislature) is not subject to suit under Section 1983 because Section 1983 only allows suits against persons and the state is not considered a "person" under the law.[46] Suing a defendant such as a warden or director of corrections in their "official capacity" for injunctive relief permits a civil rights case essentially to be brought against the state. However, if the official capacity defendant is acting without deliberate indifference, what then? Will the failures of the legislature somehow be imputed to the named defendant? *Wilson* does not suggest the answer to this question.

An official capacity defendant typically inherits a lawsuit begun during the tenure of a predecessor, but may a new official capacity defendant who moves to try to correct deficiencies created in a prior era successfully assert that he is not deliberately indifferent?

The prospect of such a pure of heart defense was raised in *Wilson*, but the majority brushed it aside as not being an issue in the case. The Court also noted that other officials have not tried to use the lack of funds as a defense to *Estelle* cases.[47] The failure of officials to use a lack of funds defense in a medical case may have been a result of many courts emphatically stating that lack of funds was not a defense to inadequate conditions.[48] The defense wasn't regularly offered because it was futile.

Under the *Wilson* majority's rigid insistence that someone must *inflict* a cruel and unusual punishment before there can be a violation of the Eighth Amendment, it appears that in the final analysis bad conditions can escape Eighth Amendment scrutiny if defendant officials are not deliberately indifferent to those conditions.

To the author's knowledge, the pure of heart defense has yet to be asserted in a post-*Wilson* case in a way which prevents a court from addressing conditions which are bad enough to meet the objective prong of the Eighth Amendment. However, the possibility of such an occurrence is so obviously possible that it is disturbing that the majority in *Wilson* would dismiss it so lightly.

After *Wilson*, it was clear that for all kinds of Eighth Amendment issues arising from prison conditions or practices, the plaintiff must surmount two hurdles. The first, objective, barrier relates to the seriousness of the conditions or practices and the effect they have on the plaintiff. The second, subjective, barrier relates to the state of mind of the defendant. Where suppression of an insurrection was the issue, a malicious and sadistic state of mind must be shown. Where conditions were at issue, the somewhat less culpable state of deliberate indifference must be established.

There were still some gaps left in the Court's approach to Eighth Amendment prison cases. What test should apply to uses of force outside the riot situation? And what in fact is "deliberate indifference"? For instance, could an official be found to be deliberately indifferent for poor conditions or practices which a reasonable prison administrator should have known about, but which the defendant official in fact did not know of?

"Malicious and Sadistic" State of Mind

A year after *Wilson*, the nonemergent use of force case arrived at the Court. Whereas *Rhodes* and *Whitley* came with facts generally favorable to the defendants, *Hudson v. McMillian*[49] did not.

In *McMillian*, an inmate was simply beaten by two officers at the state penitentiary in Angola, Louisiana. There was no emergency. There was no suggestion that this was an appropriate use of force which had gotten out of hand or that the District Court (which awarded the plaintiff $800 in damages) had misapplied the law to a valid use of force. Mr. Hudson, the inmate, was being escorted in shackles from his cell to the prison segregation unit following an argument with an officer. Along the way, that officer and another punched and kicked Hudson several times. A supervisor watching was quoted as telling the officers "not to have too much fun."[50]

Hudson suffered minor injuries as a result of the beating. The extent of these injuries became the reason the case went to the Supreme Court. The Fifth Circuit Court of Appeals had reversed the judgment for Hudson, saying that as part of an Eighth Amendment excess force case an inmate *had* to prove he sustained a significant injury. If there was no significant injury, there was no Eighth Amendment claim, despite how unreasonable or unnecessary the force might have been.[51]

The Supreme Court reversed the "no harm, no foul" approach of the Fifth Circuit, holding that significant injuries are not a *sine qua non* of a valid claim although the extent of an inmate's injuries are relevant in an Eighth Amendment excess force case.

In deciding what is not required in a use of force claim, the Court had to discuss what is required, which led once again to a revisiting of the ever-shifting state of mind requirement. How would the Court define "wanton" in a beating case, where there was no emergency and no need for hasty, pressure-laden decisions with the safety of both staff and inmates riding on the outcome? The answer was that the Court did not treat *McMillian* as a *beating* case! Instead, it treated the case as a "guards use force to keep order" issue:

> Many of the concerns underlying our holding in *Whitley* arise whenever guards use force to keep order. Whether the prison disturbance is a riot or a lesser disruption, corrections officers must balance the need "to maintain or restore discipline" through force against the risk of injury to inmates. Both situations may require prison officials to act quickly and decisively, 112 S.Ct. at 998–999.

While this quotation makes sense in many force situations, Justice O'Connor's majority opinion did not explain why prison officials must act quickly and decisively in deciding to beat a shackled inmate who is offering no resistance. In essence, the Court ignored the aberrational abuse of force in *McMillian* in order to write an opinion dealing with more normal uses of force where facts typically suggest some force was appropriate and the lawsuit turns on whether what started out as a proper use of force somewhere along the line got out of hand.

The larger holding of *McMillian*, therefore, is that the *Whitley* "malicious and sadistic" definition of wantonness, created to deal with prison disturbance situations, governs all Eighth Amendment use of force cases. At least some lower courts had already extended the test even beyond use of force situations.[52]

Justice O'Connor indicated five factors which courts should consider in deciding whether officials applied force in a "good faith effort to maintain or restore discipline or maliciously and sadistically to cause harm":[53]

1. The "need for the application of force"
2. The relation between the "need and the amount of force actually used"
3. The extent of injuries arising from the incident
4. The threat "reasonably perceived by responsible officials"
5. Efforts to "temper the severity of a forceful response"[54]

After being so clear in *Wilson* that the Eighth Amendment has both objective and subjective components which must be considered independently of one another, Justice O'Connor's listing of factors relevant to the general question of whether force was wanton and unnecessary appears to blend the objective and subjective components of an Eighth Amendment violation into a single "totality of conditions" type of evaluation, where weaknesses of either component (effect of force or motivation for it) may be overcome by strengths of the other. This is contrary to the message from *Wilson*. For instance, the lack of serious injury (weak objective component) can arguably be compensated for if a plaintiff can show clearly improper motivations by defendants (strong subjective component). Likewise, it would appear that serious injuries could tip the scale in favor of a plaintiff where officials' motivations were unclear.

McMillian provided Justice Thomas with his first opportunity to address the meaning of cruel and unusual punishment in the prison setting. Joined by Justice Scalia, he staked out the extreme position that the Eighth Amendment simply did not apply to prison conditions or practices issues, since he did not think prison conditions or practices could amount to "punishment" in the legal sense.

McMillian extended *Whitley* far beyond what first appeared to be its riot/disturbance limits, clarifying somewhat the sorts of "constraints" on officials which justify a looser standard of review. The constraints appear to be problems attendant to the use of force, especially in an emergency. But is *McMillian* the outer limits of the "malicious and sadistic" standard, or are there additional "constraints" of significance? At least one court of appeals has extended the malicious and sadistic state of mind standard even beyond the use of force situation. In *LeMaire v. Maass*,[55] an extraordinarily dangerous and notorious inmate complained of a variety of quite extreme restrictions which had been placed on him by officials at the Oregon State Penitentiary. The Court felt that because the restrictions were imposed following proper due process proceedings and because they related to security and discipline, their imposition must be evaluated through the "malicious and sadistic" test from *Whitley*, not a deliberate indifference approach.[56] *LeMaire* then appears to say that restrictions on living conditions (such as placing inmates in constantly illuminated quiet cells, removal of clothing, or prolonged denial of outdoor exercise opportunities), if imposed on the basis of at least extreme security needs, should be reviewed under the most forgiving state of mind requirement the Supreme Court has yet announced.

If security based restrictions justify the least rigorous state of mind review, but nonsecurity areas such as medical care justify the somewhat more demanding deliberate indifference level of review, how should security based restrictions which impact medical care be reviewed? For instance, what if maintaining what the warden in good faith feels is an adequate security department results in budget cuts and a corresponding reduction in service to the medical department? Ah, what webs we weave . . .

Threat of Future Harm

The Court next visited the Eighth Amendment in a prison context in 1993 with its decision, *Helling v. McKinney*.[57] In holding that an inmate states an Eighth Amendment claim by alleging officials are deliberately indifferent to serious future health needs by unreasonably exposing him to second-hand cigarette smoke, the Court really only addressed the application of the principles set out in earlier cases. *Helling* amounts to recognition by the Supreme Court that the threat of future harm, if serious enough, can meet the requirements of the objective component of an Eighth Amendment violation. For those who have litigated in area of conditions of confinement, this is not a new or startling principle.[58] The "nobody is dead yet" defense to serious threats of harm has rarely, if ever, been accepted by lower courts. The important questions under a "threat of future harm" charge are, how serious must the threat be? and how is it proven? *Helling* speaks of "sufficiently imminent dangers," and an "unreasonable risk of serious harm."[59] It notes that scientific and statistical inquiries regarding the seriousness question will be likely and then adds that a court must also consider whether "society considers the risk that the prisoner complains of to be so grave that it violates contemporary standards of decency to expose *anyone* unwillingly to such a risk."[60]

Justices Thomas and Scalia repeated their concerns about the limits of the Eighth Amendment first stated in their dissent in *McMillian*. No other Justice seemed inclined to join them in their restrictive interpretation as to the scope of the Eighth Amendment.

Actual Knowledge Requirement

Having adopted "deliberate indifference" as defining the forbidden state of mind of officials in at least some types of Eighth Amendment prison cases in 1977, the Court in 1994 finally had the opportunity to try to define the term in *Farmer v. Brennan*.[61] Earlier cases had given only the outer boundaries of what deliberate indifference was not: it was more than negligence (*Estelle*), but less than purposeful or knowing conduct (*Wilson*).

Lower courts had generally defined deliberate indifference as a form of reckless behavior, but split over whether the civil or criminal definition of recklessness applied. The difference between the two, which provided the critical issue in *Farmer*, was whether an official could be deliberately indifferent based on what the official knew or *should have known* (the civil law approach to recklessness) or whether actual knowledge must be shown (the criminal approach).

The Supreme Court opted for the criminal law approach, holding that "... an official's failure to alleviate a significant risk that he should have perceived but did not, while no cause for commendation, cannot under our cases be condemned as the infliction of punishment."[62]

Farmer involved the rape of a preoperative transsexual shortly after his placement in the general population of a federal penitentiary. The man had silicone breast implants and the habit of wearing his shirt off one shoulder, among other mannerisms. The lower courts had dismissed the case because the offender had not complained about his placement and, unless officials actually knew of a danger, they could not be deliberately indifferent to it.

The Supreme Court agreed that actual knowledge was necessary, but reversed because it felt that the requisite knowledge could be shown by ways other than through the inmate's specific complaint.

In adopting an actual knowledge requirement, Justice Souter, writing for eight other Justices, indicated that since it is officials who "inflict punishment" for Eighth Amendment purposes, an official who does not know of a given situation cannot be said to be inflicting punishment through its occurrence or continuation.[63]

In those instances where deliberate indifference defines the subjective component of cruel and unusual punishment, the plaintiff must prove a defendant knows of a "substantial risk of serious harm and disregards that risk by failing to take reasonable measures to abate it."[64] Where the higher "malicious and sadistic" test applies, "purposeful or knowing" conduct is needed.[65]

Proving actual knowledge can be accomplished, said Justice Souter, "through the usual ways, including inference from circumstantial evidence."[66] Proof through inference comes close to a "should have known" result, but the majority opinion makes it clear that inferences are not conclusive and can be disproven by officials. (Watch for future litigation exploring the shifting burdens of proof here.)

Proving that high-ranking officials in an institution, such as the warden, had actual knowledge of serious systemic problems probably will be less difficult than proving knowledge of problems of individual inmates. Even where an inmate raises a problem through a formal grievance, will "knowledge" of the problem actually reach the warden, if authority to respond to grievances has been delegated, or if the grievance report which comes to the warden's desk has a finding of fact contrary to the inmate's allegations? For instance, if the institution's version of the facts (shown at trial to be incorrect) surrounding an inmate's complaint about being denied medical care is that the inmate received all the care needed, can the warden still say "I didn't know about the problem, because my staff told me it didn't exist"? Can a warden avoid possible liability by delegating decisions so as to avoid acquiring knowledge about problems?

Summary

The path followed by the Supreme Court's Eighth Amendment prison cases is not an easy one to follow. It began with a glorified medical malpractice case, where the state of mind of a defendant is an inherent part of the litigation. It moved to a conditions case where any fair reading of the opinion indicates that it is the effect of conditions, not the motivations of the defendants, which makes or breaks a claim of cruel and unusual punishment. The next stop was a prison riot case, where arguably there is a strong need to judge facts in light of the potentially life-threatening exigencies of the moment and not permit a court to second-guess an official too closely. To respond to this need for extra leeway for officials, an extremely tolerant state of mind requirement reappeared. Now the Court apparently felt it was irrevocably stuck with a state of mind requirement in all Eighth Amendment prison situations. The result was *Wilson* and a recognition that in theory good intentions and efforts alone can overcome prison conditions which may even amount to "torture or a lingering death." Perhaps out of an excessive desire to limit court scrutiny of force cases, the Court then applied its very tolerant riot case state of mind requirement in nothing more than a simple beating case. And in its most recent statement, the Court said that an official's lack of knowledge about a problem can be a successful defense in an Eighth Amendment case, even if the defendant's lack of knowledge reflects deliberate indifference to what is occurring in the institution.

Reading the Supreme Court's attempts to develop a consistent approach to Eighth Amendment prison cases creates the impression that the Court began without a clear idea of where it was going and of the variety of factual ways Eighth Amendment issues would come before it. Only after the Court was several years into prison Eighth Amendment cases did it realize that Eighth Amendment case law, at least at the lower court level, was going in different directions, probably in response to very different factual situations under which Eighth Amendment claims can arise. In medical cases (or perhaps from a larger perspective, cases involving one inmate and one injury) the state of mind requirement from *Estelle* fits fairly easily. However, for conditions cases, lower courts were focusing solely on the conditions themselves. The Court's own decisions contributed to these different approaches, despite the Court's later efforts to explain how some of its decisions were misread by others.

Once the Court recognized its cases might be headed in somewhat different directions, it felt compelled to develop a single analytical scheme, but one which is still applied differently in different contexts. The most troublesome and potentially problematic aspect of this single analytical scheme, with its objective and subjective components, is the Court's insistence that punishment must be inflicted by some identifiable individual before it is subject to Eighth Amendment scrutiny. Having insisted that a state of mind determination is an integral part of any Eighth Amendment evaluation and apparently one which is separate from evaluation of the nature of the punishment (the objective component), the Court blurs the separation in its force case and sets up two different state of mind scales, depending on whether the case involves an emergency, or a use of force, or (perhaps) security. A close examination of the seamless web of the Court's Eighth Amendment decisions reveals a few knots holding things together and, one suspects, a few threads that are still dangling, waiting to be attached to something.

Who would have thought, in the early days of Eighth Amendment litigation, when the courts were doing so much to force prison administrators, corrections agencies, and state legislatures to upgrade prison conditions, that the interpretation of the word "inflicted" would emerge as being of equal or greater importance in understanding the Eighth Amendment as the interpretation of the Amendment's heart, "cruel and unusual punishment"?

Notes

[1] *Fulwood v. Clemmer*, 206 F. Supp. 370 (D.D.C., 1962).

[2] 452 U.S. at 357.

[3] 420 U.S. 97 (1976).

[4] VI *Correctional Law Reporter* 2 (June, 1994).

[5] *Farmer v. Brennan*, 114 S.Ct. _____, 62 LW 4446 (1994).

[6] 429 U.S. at 102.

[7] *Ibid.*

[8] Citation omitted.

[9] As much of the American populace becomes increasingly frustrated with the criminal justice system's apparent inability to reduce crime, as shown by the recently expressed sentiment of many in favor of adopting caning as a form of punishment, one must wonder which way America's standards of decency are evolving. Flaying the flesh from the bodies of graffiti writers or other nuisance offenders may satisfy certain urges, but the Supreme Court probably would find such torturous punishments to be cruel and unusual.

[10] *Ibid.*, citation omitted.

[11] *Sostre v. McGinnis*, 442 F.2d 178 (2d Cir., 1971).

[12] 420 U.S. at 103.

[13] 429 U.S. at 104.

[14] 429 U.S. at 106, fn. 14.

[15] 429 U.S. 116.

[16] 429 U.S. at 116, n. 13.

[17] *Thomas v. Booker*, 762 F.2d 654 (8th Cir., 1985).

[18] *Rhodes v. Chapman*, 452 U.S. 337 (1981). *Bell v. Wolfish*, 441 U.S. 520 (1979) also dealt with conditions of confinement, especially crowding. However, because *Bell* involved federal pretrial detainees, the case was analyzed under the Fifth Amendment, not the Eighth.

[19] *Burks v. Walsh*, 461 F. Supp. 4545 (W.D. Missouri, 1978).

[20] *Newman v. Alabama*, 559 F.2d 283, 291 (5th Cir., 1977).

[21] *Battle v. Anderson*, 546 F.2d 388 (10th Cir., 1977).

[22] *Chapman v. Rhodes*, 434 F. Supp. 1007 (S.D. Ohio, 1977).

[23] 452 U.S. at 341.

[24] 452 U.S. at 343.

[25] The handwriting was on the judicial wall for the one-man, one-cell concept since Justice Rehnquist's opinion in *Bell*. There, he indicated that no such concept was "lurking in the Due Process Clause" to protect pretrial detainees. If a right to a single cell did survive Supreme Court scrutiny for detainees, it was not likely to pass for convicted felons.

[26] 452 U.S. at 346.

[27] *Ibid.*

[28] *Ibid.*

[29] 452 U.S. at 364, citation omitted, emphasis added.

[30] 45 U.S. at 364, Brennan, concurring, citation omitted.

[31] *Walker v. Mintzes*, 771 F.2d 920 (6th Cir., 1985).

[32] 452 U.S. at 347, emphasis added.

[33] 682 F.2d 1237 (9th Cir., 1982).

[34] 111 S.Ct. 2321 (1991).

[35] 475 U.S. 312 (1986).

[36] 475 U.S. at 320.

[37] 475 U.S. at 328.

[38] 111 S.Ct. 2321 (1991).

[39] *Wilson v. Seiter*, 893 F.2d 861, 866 (6th Cir., 1990).

[40] 441 U.S. 520 (1979).

[41] 441 U.S. at 538.

[42] 111 S.Ct. at 2326.

[43] *Ibid.* (emphasis in original).

[44] 111 S.Ct. at 2327.

[45] *Ibid.*

[46] *Quern v. Jordan*, 440 U.S. 332 (1979).

[47] 111 S.Ct. at 2326.

[48] *Smith v. Sullivan*, 553 F.2d 373 (5th Cir., 1977), *Rodriguez v. Jiminez*, 409 F. Supp. 582 (D.P.R., 1976).

[49] 112 S.Ct. 995 (1992).

[50] 112 S.Ct. at 997.

[51] 929 F.2d at 1015.

[52] See discussion of *LeMaire v. Maass*, 12 F.3d 1444 (9th Cir., 1994), infra.

[53] 112 S.Ct. at 999.

[54] *Ibid.*

[55] 12 F.3d 1444 (9th Cir., 1994).

[56] 12 F.3d at 1453.

[57] 113 S.Ct. 2475 (1993).

[58] See *Gates v. Collier*, 501 F.2d 1291 (5th Cir., 1974).

[59] 113 S.Ct. at 2481.

[60] 113 S.Ct. at 2482, emphasis in original.

[63] 114 S.Ct. _____, 62 LW 4446 (1994).

[62] 62 LW at 4449.

[63] 62 LW at 4451.

[64] 62 LW at 4452.

[65] 62 LW at 4449.

[66] 62 LW at 4451.

18

Prison Reform by Judicial Decree

The Unintended Consequences of *Ruiz v. Estelle*

Geoffrey P. Alpert
Ben M. Crouch
C. Ronald Huff

Introduction

The history of the world is in part a history of revolutions. As societies evolved from simple, agrarian, and homogeneous to complex, industrial and heterogeneous, the level of social conflict (violence, rebellion, and revolution) increased markedly. One major theoretical perspective which has been formulated to explain collective responses by those seeking relief or freedom is the theory of rising expectations. James Davies (1962), in an influential article, outlined such a theory as

Source: *The Justice System Journal*, Vol. 9, No. 3 (1984), 291-305. Reprinted with the permission of the publisher.

applied to revolutions, and we believe that his ideas and propositions may usefully be extended to the phenomena of prison riots — not at the "grand theory" level, but at least as a useful framework for understanding many prison disturbances.

To summarize briefly, Davies (1962) argued that two ideas set forth in the writings of Marx and Engels and Tocqueville have explanatory and predictive value when juxtaposed and placed in proper temporal sequence. Marx and Engels (1959) noted that progressive social degradation could reach a point of despair, with revolution likely to follow. In a modifying statement, they added that even an increase of benefits, when disproportionate to the increased enjoyments of the capitalists, must be included as a precondition of unrest. This same conclusion was reached by Tocqueville (1955) in his study of the French Revolution. Both theoretical statements emphasize that the loss of something already gained will trigger dissatisfaction, and it is a state of mind (*relative* deprivation), rather than a tangible level of deprivation, which serves as a catalyst for rioting. In light of these observations, it is interesting to note that the National Advisory Commission on Criminal Justice Standards and Goals (1976: 19-20) found that: "... (M)ass violence and terrorism more frequently occur during a time of improvement than during social deterioration. They appear to be stimulated by rising expectations, or, more specifically, by the disappointment in them." Similarly, Gurr (1970) advocated a "relative deprivation" theory of civil strife.[1]

Historically, the courts were reluctant to intervene in prison policy and management.[2] However, such intervention has grown significantly during the past three decades (Alpert and Huff, 1981).[3] Such intervention, especially mandated changes in basic institutional policies and practices (Baker, Blotky, Clemens, and Dillard, 1973), has formalized and legitimated prison conflict. The implementation of court-ordered change has virtually assured us that prisoners will eagerly anticipate improvements in the general conditions of confinement and in many specific areas, such as personal living space, medical care, access to the courts, and working conditions. In addition, court orders have provided prison administrators with unparalleled power if such orders are reversed on appeal or if only lip-service is paid to the mandates. This creation of a "win-loss" situation for one side could end up as a "no-win" situation for the prisons and for society.

Research Questions and Sources of Data

The central purpose of this study is to describe the consequences, both intended and unintended, of court-ordered reform in a major case

(*Ruiz v. Estelle*, 1980) affecting an entire state prison system (Texas). Our purpose here is not to provide "just another case study," but rather to assess the applicability of rising expectations theory in understanding the dynamics of prison conflict, riots, and disturbances.

In the correctional context, the theory of rising expectations must, of course, be adapted in order to serve as a framework for analyzing such impact. We are mindful that our study focuses on a micro, rather than macro (societal revolutions) level. Nonetheless, the *Ruiz* case provides us an opportunity to seek answers to the following research questions:

1. What, if any, observable impact did the decision have on the behavior of inmates (individual and collective)?
2. What, if any, observable impact did the decision have on the behavior of management and line staff?
3. What were the consequences of *Ruiz* on the social control system which had been established in the Texas prisons?
4. What policy and management implications may be derived from this research?

These questions are as sensitive as they are important. Where the prison environment is relatively unstable, collecting data to address these issues is particularly problematic. Consequently, for the analysis presented here we have relied on several sources of information. Reliance on multiple sources was also advantageous because that strategy permitted us to check one source against another. Our sources included:

1. newspaper accounts, particularly over the three years following the court order;
2. official Texas Department of Corrections (TDC) information releases;
3. information from periodic reports on compliance and resistance of the TDC;
4. our collective knowledge of prisoner behavior based on prior research and extant literature in the field; and
5. informal interviews with key actors in the system (management, correctional officers, and inmates).[4]

Texas: A Case Study

The Texas Department of Corrections is both a typical and an atypical example of the impact of court-ordered change. It is typical in that it is only one of many state prison systems which have experienced change and uncertainty due to judicial decisions over the past decade (Bowker, 1982: 282-289; Gettinger, 1977). This commonality makes Texas a useful case study. At the same time, Texas is atypical. That is, this prison system had, until the *Ruiz* case, a history of stability inside and a remarkable degree of insularity from external social and political forces. The TDC's insularity and stability also enhance its value as the locus of this case study, because major changes can be attributed more confidently to the court decision, rather than to other variables operating at the same time.

Procedural History of the Ruiz *Case.* The *Ruiz* case was almost nine years old by the time Federal District Judge William Wayne Justice handed down his decision in a memorandum opinion which consumed 248 legal-sized pages (Cohen, 1981). The civil action was initiated in June 1972, when David Ruiz filed suit against the director of the TDC, pursuant to 42 U.S.C. 1983, seeking declaratory and injunctive relief for alleged constitutional violations. The *Ruiz* case subsequently was consolidated with the suits of seven other TDC inmates into a single civil action, *Ruiz v. Estelle* (1980). The case eventually evolved into a class action, and damage issues were considered for all TDC inmates. After more than three years of pre-trial issues, the case finally reached the trial stage. Finally, after 159 days of trial (October 1978 to September 1979), the testimony of 349 witnesses, and the presentation of 1,565 exhibits, the Court issued its opinion.

The Opinion. Judge Justice found the TDC in violation of inmates' constitutional rights in six major areas: (1) overcrowding; (2) security; (3) fire safety; (4) medical care; (5) discipline; and (6) access to the courts. The order granted relief in each of these areas and included, *inter alia,* the following (*Ruiz v. Estelle,* 1980):

1. The TDC must end the practice of putting three inmates in one cell, end the practice of routinely housing two inmates in 45 and 60 square foot cells, and reduce the overcrowding in dormitories;
2. The TDC must end guard brutality, increase the number of guards, improve the selection and training procedures for guards, and eliminate the building-tender system;
3. The TDC must improve its methods of fire safety, its water supply, plumbing, wastewater, and solid waste disposal;
4. The TDC must increase its medical staff, restrict inmates performing medical and pharmacological functions, improve unit infirmaries, substantially renovate the main prison hospital, establish diagnostic and sick-call procedures that eliminate non-medical interferences with medical care, and improve the pharmaceutical operations;
5. The TDC must provide all inmates accused of disciplinary infractions with notice of charges, consider literacy and mental capacity and provide representation for those unable

to represent themselves, inform inmates of their right to call witnesses, and have sufficient evidence before ordering a "lock-up"; and

6. The TDC must desist blocking prisoners' access to the courts.

The order called for a meeting of attorneys from both sides to work out compromises on some issues and to determine a timetable for change on others. When this attempt at negotiation failed, Judge Justice, in March 1981, ordered the TDC to effect the changes ordered by the opinion and announced that he would appoint a special master to oversee the implementation of the decree.[5]

The TDC Prior to Ruiz. According to the theory of rising expectations, either a disproportionate increase or a decrease in benefits can lead to unrest, as can the real or imagined loss of something already gained. Because one must understand the "baseline" historical conditions which existed before one can assess the impact of change, it is therefore necessary to characterize briefly the philosophy and organizational structure of the TDC prior to *Ruiz* so that the impact and consequences of the court order may be more clear.

Traditional TDC philosophy consisted of three major tenets: (1) an emphasis on inmate control at all times; (2) strong support of the conventional work ethic; and (3) the efficient use of human and material resources. Every aspect of TDC's extensive operations reflected these principles. The prison's agricultural program illustrates the extent to which these principles have been integrated in practice. TDC has long required all inmates to work and, at least during the early part of their sentences, all inmates participate in some aspect of the TDC's extensive (100,000 acre) agricultural program. The TDC's rationale for this has been as follows: first, it provides a critical and direct introduction to the work ethic; second, it introduces inmates to the TDC's officer-inmate relationship (Crouch, 1980); and third, it makes use of this inmate labor to reduce the costs of incarceration. Over the past three decades, adherence to this philosophy has created a controversial prison system seen by some as a "paragon of prisons" and by others as a "slave plantation" (*Corrections Magazine,* 1978).

Organizationally, the structure of the TDC has reflected each tenet of this basic philosophy, especially the emphasis on inmate control. The TDC's tradition of stability and relatively low rates of violence (Sylvester *et al.,* 1977) stem largely from the effectiveness of (1) mid-level security personnel and (2) "building tenders" (inmates who work closely with custody officials to maintain order). Mid-level officers (those holding the rank of lieutenant, captain, major, or warden) without exception entered the security hierarchy at the bottom (there is no lateral entry)—in many cases more than twenty years ago—and have risen through the ranks. Because there is considerable turnover at the lowest ranks, these mid-level officers, by virtue of rank and experience, are the control mainstays of the relatively isolated TDC prison units. Their commitment to the traditional definition of inmate subordination and control stems both from the rural, east Texas background of most of these men[6] and from the TDC's preference for promoting to mid-level security positions those men who develop reputations for effective personal control over prisoners (Crouch and Marquart, 1980).

The building tender system officially employs inmates to keep the cellblocks clean and to aid officers with such menial tasks as helping with the count. Unofficially, building tenders actually represent an extension of the security and control machinery directed by the guards.[7] Building tenders administer sanctions to fellow inmates both with and without the knowledge of the authorities (Gettinger and Krajick, 1978; Marquart and Crouch, 1982). Mid-level officers and building tenders have in common the desire and the ability to enforce the TDC's general philosophy—especially inmate control. The extent to which this philosophy has been implemented is reflected in the title of one account of the TDC: "They Keep You In, They Keep You Busy, and They Keep You From Getting Killed" (Krajick, 1978). Although some inmates and outside observers view the TDC as a neocolonial slave system, the official intent of the TDC's philosophy of inmate control is perhaps best summed up in the comments of an inmate who did time in two other state prison systems before being committed to the TDC (Krajick, 1978: 21).

> Everything here is predictable. You know what to expect. You don't have to worry about getting stabbed or raped by other inmates, or what's going to happen from one day to the next, because it's the administration that's totally in control. After a short time here, you realize that if you go to your cell, go to mess, wash up, go to work quietly, all will go well. It's almost more like the service than the penitentiary, except for the bars.

The Impact of the Decree

It did not surprise us to learn that the weight of the federal judiciary rests heavily on the TDC and that its employees are afraid of losing a great deal of the power and influence they have gained over the years. The TDC's power and influence have benefitted from rapid growth in the inmate population (it has risen from 16,000 in 1975 to about 37,000 in 1983, for example) and a corresponding increase in the size of the organization and its budget (Bureau of Justice Statistics, 1983; *Corrections Magazine*, 1978). This shift has also affected the general conditions of confinement and overcrowding. Lawsuits have been filed and won, and these have, to some extent, altered the TDC's operations. The *Ruiz* case did not fall upon a pristine system; however, because of the nature of the *Ruiz* order, the legal complexities involved, and the massive media coverage, *Ruiz v. Estelle* (1980) brought about a concrete realization, by inmates and staff alike, that changes in the status quo were not far away. It is our contention that *Ruiz*, while mandating many desirable improvements in the administration of the TDC, has also set in motion a chain of events that has undermined the traditional stability, safety, and regularity within the TDC and has created a serious crisis of control, with all of the usual dysfunctions which accompany anomic social conditions. Such unanticipated consequences often follow interventions aimed at reforming established social institutions and systems. It is likely that any prison system in which significant change is anticipated will experience major problems of social control. In Texas the contrast, and the effects, are most dramatic.

Impact on Inmates and Guards. An initial and crucial impact of the court order was a generalized sense of rising expectations among inmates. One correctional officer observed: "....They think it's an emancipation proclamation. They expect (Judge) Justice to pull up in his long, black Cadillac, open the gates and turn 'em all loose" (Crouch, 1981b). Although clearly an exaggeration and oversimplification revealing his own emotional reaction to the court order as much as anything else, this officer's comment concerning heightened inmate expectations is supported by other sources. According to our sources inside the TDC and its prisons,[8] many inmates sensed that the conditions of their total subordination were about to be improved measurably. Heightened inmate expectations of improvement, along with notions that official control would diminish, led to increased conflict between guards and inmates. This discord manifested itself in three specific ways. First, guards reported an increase in verbal and physical abuse from inmates. Feeling less constrained by traditional rules and control mechanisms, many inmates were more willing to voice resentment to orders and, in some cases, to disobey them. Second, there was an increase in lawsuits filed by inmates alleging official misconduct. Legal services attorneys reported an increase in requests for assistance, while guards reported that more investigators were asking more questions than ever before. A building captain who had been employed by the TDC for nine years stated that he had talked to more U.S. Department of Justice personnel in the prior year than in all the previous years since he had joined the TDC (Crouch, 1981a). Finally, there was a marked increase in the number of disturbances and riots. During the *Ruiz* trial, the TDC experienced a number of minor inmate disturbances, some of which were intended to demonstrate inmate solidarity for the cause being litigated.[9]

The *Ruiz* order, requiring massive changes, was finalized in March 1981, and as required, each inmate received a copy of the order via the prison newsletter, *The Echo*. This notification was viewed by inmates as evidence of concrete and significant changes, further escalating among inmates the expectation that change would be rapid. Inmate emotions and excitement seemed to be on display in collective violence, with 11 riots taking place between June and November, 1981. In just six months, there were twice as many riots as had occurred in the preceding eight years![10]

Increases in control problems are further reflected in a report recently released by the TDC (*Houston Chronicle*, 1983), which showed that in the first six months of 1983 there had been 13 escape attempts, as compared with only two during the same period in 1982. Moreover, in the early months of 1983, four TDC inmates had been killed by other prisoners, the greatest number in nearly a decade. Finally, the number of offenses committed within TDC prisons increased by 17% over the previous year. The elevated level of prison disturbances appears to be linked to the court order and its effects on the social system of the TDC.

The court order prompted two important changes in life at the TDC. First, the inmates began challenging their status quo and reaching for more freedom. Second, the ruling markedly altered traditional TDC control mechanisms. Because of the shroud of uncertainty, officers were less likely to enforce some rules and to carry out their duties, and a growing number of experienced officers resigned, apparently deciding that they wanted no part of the direction in which the "new TDC" was being moved by the federal court.

Rapid Change and Organizational Anomie. Although TDC's unrest appears to have been stimulated by the rising inmate expectations created by judicial alteration of the old status quo, several related factors exacerbate that unrest. Foremost among these is the serious problem of overcrowding. TDC houses approximately 37,000 prisoners and vies with California as the nation's largest prison system. Another important factor is the loss of information once provided by those elite inmates who worked as building tenders, floormen, or turnkeys. Most TDC officials agree that the demotion of once powerful convicts has caused a significant reduction in both the amount and the quality of information coming to officers about activities within the inmate population. Finally, to comply with the court order and to fill many of the jobs formerly held by inmates, the TDC must increase the number of uniformed security personnel.

The need to increase personnel creates, in turn, at least two conditions which may further diminish the TDC's traditional control and stability. First, although the TDC unit wardens actually removed inmates from old positions and, where necessary, regained control of keys during May and June, 1982, it will take considerable time to find, hire, and train sufficient officers to fill those positions vacated by inmates and those vacancies attributable to normal attrition and resignations. Meanwhile, the TDC continues to be understaffed and its officers have less information than was formerly available to them.

Second, when large numbers of new officers must be hired at one time, the limited selectivity dictated by the available labor pool, along with the often abbreviated training which accompanies wholesale infusion of personnel into an organization in crisis, may create as many problems with "officer control" as with inmate control. There is fairly widespread concern within the TDC about the quality of the current (and probably future) new officers. Where mid-level officers have only marginal trust in line personnel, not only will there be uncertainty among the ranks, but the critical informal socialization process may be hampered as well.

In short, the *Ruiz* decision set in motion an interrelated chain of events which has had the unintended consequence of creating a crisis of control within the Texas prison system. The decision caused the expectations of inmates to rise rapidly, created uncertainty among TDC staff, and, in the new environment characterized mainly by anomie, inmate/guard conflict rose markedly and rioting occurred at a rate which appears to be linked to the court's decision and its effects on the prison system.

Policy and Management Implications

A central thesis of this article has been that externally-imposed reform may induce both intended and unintended consequences. Our focus has not been on the social desirability of the specific reforms ordered by the Court; rather, we have been concerned with an analysis of the effects of the court's order on the Texas prison system. Our primary conclusion is that the *Ruiz* decision led to a number of unanticipated consequences, many of which were dysfunctional. We further argue that one of the mechanisms by which this unanticipated change occurred was through the rising expectations of inmates, linked closely with the organizational anomie which prevailed after the decision. The collective violence which seems to have been associated with the decision (or, more precisely, with the conditions which followed the decision) suggests that serious crisis of control did in fact ensue.

Perhaps the most important implication flowing from this study is the obvious need for greater coordination and cooperation in implementing judicial decrees in complex organizations such as prisons and prison systems. Those familiar with the extant research and theory on complex organizations will undoubtedly find it surprising that so little attention is paid to the implementation of a far-reaching court order after nearly nine years of considering evidence in the case. Likewise, in the *Ruiz* decision there is every indication that the federal judge was fully aware that the TDC had a strongly established set of policies and management practices, not to mention a clear stratification of management, staff, and inmates (perhaps the clearest in the Western world!). It was, in fact, many of those policies and practices which served as the focal point for the decision. Therefore, it would seem self-evident that the iimplementation of change in such a system should be informed by organizational theory. However, this seldom has occurred in the history of institutional legal reform, and it certainly did not occur in *Ruiz*.

As we have argued, serious organizational conflict, including collective violence, can result from externally-induced reform which has certain effects on the social structure of and personal relationships within the organization targeted for change. Therefore, to minimize the possibility of such problems, judges should seek to understand complex organizations in general and the particular organization they seek to reform. Because organizations share some characteristics in common, knowledge of organizational theory and research would greatly benefit judges seeking to restructure or reform them in certain ways. However, every organization is also unique in some ways, and more detailed information is necessary to assess the probable impact of court orders on each one. It is likely, from our point of view, that the same judicial decree would have differential effects across organizations. We further assert that the implementation strategy best suited to each case should be identified only after careful analysis of the organization has been completed.

Although the need for evaluation of court-ordered reform is great (Huff and Alpert, 1982), we can say with reasonable certainty that those judges who understand complex organizations and their behavior are much more likely to formulate and implement successful decrees. (This, of course, presumes a view of legal reform as a substantive, rather than merely symbolic, activity). As another observer has commented: "...If a remedy is to be effective, then a judge designing relief must take into account the nature of the organizations whose policies and processes he seeks to alter" (Note, 1980: 513).

Introducing change in a prison or prison system inherently is more difficult and more risky than changing most other types of organizations. Issues of personal safety (both inside and outside the walls) must be considered carfully and given great weight in formulating an implementation strategy. With respect to the TDC, for example, many policy and management issues were raised in the *Ruiz* case and the judge, finding many of them objectionable, ordered them changed and hired a special master to ensure that change occurred, without giving careful consideration to the functions served by each policy or practice and how these functions might be effectively addressed in a more constitutionally acceptable manner.

One of the most pervasive problems which characterizes the implementation of judicial decrees in prison systems has to do with intergovernmental relations. Specifically, because prisons are part of the executive branch of government, judicial decrees requiring change must be viewed within the perspective of judicial and executive governmental relations. As such, cooperation is often less than satisfactory. In *Ruiz*, of course, this was complicated by the fact that the case involved state/federal, as well as judicial and executive conflicts. Duffee (1980) has provided a useful discussion of the problems of managing change in corrections and the additional difficulties posed by intergovernmental conflict. One of the major problems, of course, is that those responsible for implementing the change are seldom involved in its formulation, and thus have little or no sense of "ownership" in the change to be effected. A participatory model of formulating and implementing change should be considered whenever possible, even though special structural barriers to such a model may exist. Certainly insofar as determining specific strategy for implementing change, it is desirable to involve management whenever possible (and management, in turn, should involve staff whenever possible). The judiciary should identify specific targets to be met (e.g., a shift from reliance on inmate building tenders to greater security staff) and then work closely with the organization, as well as objective experts, in formulating specific strategies and timetables for implementing change.

Greater knowledge of complex organizations would enable judges to structure institutional reform in much more effective ways. As judges juxtaposed their legal reform goals with each organization's mission, goals, current power structure, and other factors, they would have a much greater chance of identifying implementation strategies that could work. Consider, for example, the applicability of the following observation when applied to the *Ruiz* case (note, 1980:524):

> ...(C)hanging tasks is even more difficult when the reward system is closely intertwined with task performance, that is, when employees accustomed to being rewarded for performing certain tasks have those tasks changed as a result of court action. Courts must induce organizational actors to perform the tasks necessary for compliance with the court order. Usually, judges will be most effective when the

actors perceive that compliance will not diminish their professional
rewards.

Our study of the impact of *Ruiz* on the TDC has demonstrated that an
almost purely adversarial climate evolved around the case, with the
judge, the TDC, and the special master involved in open conflict just as
much as the inmates and the guards. Under such circumstances, it is
little wonder that the fragile social system of the prison erupted in
violent conflict.

In conclusion, we believe that judges, prison managers, and all
students of organizational behavior can learn a great deal from the
difficulties which have surrounded the implementation of the *Ruiz*
decision. Judges must become more familiar with complex organizations if they are to improve their record of decree implementation, and
prison managers should be more closely involved in designing implementation strategy. Greater weight must be given to the prevention of
dysfunctional, unintended consequences such as collective violence.
The incremental introduction of change, carefully based on organizational analysis and knowledge of organizational behavior, would
represent a more productive approach to decree implementation.

Notes

[1]See Piven and Cloward (1979: 1-40) for a useful discussion of the structuring of
protest, including a critique of relative deprivation theory.

[2]Historically, the control of prisons and prisoners was left up to the administrator. Only limited activities were subject to external review. The role of the
judiciary in corrections was confined to the interpretation of statutes and
limited review of administrative actions. Prior to the early 1960s, any attempt at
intervention by the judiciary which might go beyond these narrow bounds was
met with severe objections. The "hands-off" doctrine established by the
Supreme Court in *Banning v. Looney* (1954) effectively curtailed the viability of
litigation initiated by inmates and directed at prison officials. This historic
reticence to intervene has been based on three principles: (1) the separation of
powers doctrine; (2) the low level of penological expertise among the judiciary;
and (3) the fear that judicial intervention would undermine prison administrators and their methods of discipline.

[3]Since the 1960s, the judiciary has gone beyond its traditional role and has
become increasingly willing to intervene in cases involving prisons and
prisoners (Rudovsky *et al.*, 1983). This shift in juridical theory was encouraged
by the Supreme Court in *Monroe v. Pape* (1961), which held that the 1871 Civil
Rights Act, 42 U.S.C., 1983, vested federal courts with the jurisdiction to hear
cases involving parties alleging that they were deprived of their constitutional
rights. Although the availability of recourse to the federal courts was created in
Monroe v. Pape (1961), many circuits remained reluctant to hear civil rights
cases brought by state prisoners, citing federalism and comity. It was not until

Cooper v. Pate (1964) that prisoners were able to enjoy fully the protections of 1983. This trend in civil rights protections continued to expand during the late 1960s and 1970s (Alpert, 1980; Alpert and Huff, 1981; Calhoun, 1977; Haas and Champagne, 1976; Turner, 1979). These rulings, decisions, and orders continue to have an unparalleled impact on prison policy and management throughout the United States.

[4]One of the authors has for the past decade conducted research within the TDC, focusing especially on security personnel and the problem of order maintenance in general (see Crouch, 1980). The contacts made and maintained over this period of time on many different TDC units regularly provided information (via informal interviews) on change in the system. Approximately forty interviews were conducted with a wide range of respondents on the impact of the court order. Much additional information came from J.W. Marquart who, as a graduate sociology student and TDC prison guard, contributed valuable interview data and participant observation documentation of inmate and official perceptions of and reactions to *Ruiz* (see Marquart and Crouch, 1982).

[5]Mr. Vincent Nathan was appointed as special master. The role of special master in institutional reform litigation is complex and not, in general, well understood. Two articles which provide thoughtful analyses of this role are Nathan (1979) and Levinson (1982).

[6]Prison officers in many states typically have rural backgrounds, usually due in part to the rural location of prison sites. Jacobs (1977) and March (1978) are among those who have contributed useful discussions to the literature on prison guards. In Texas, a large proportion of mid-level officers, especially, have rural backgrounds (Crouch, 1977). Having grown up in a setting where respect for authority (saying "sir" comes naturally) and hard work are highly valued facilitates socialization into the TDC, because these values are very consistent with the TDC's philosophy.

[7]Limited evidence available to us suggests that building tenders are typically selected on the basis of long sentences, toughness, and the ability to control other inmates.

[8]This conclusion rests primarily on observations of inmate behavior (see note 4) and staff interviews. Virtually all respondents believed that inmates perceived a rise in their own status and power relative to that of their keepers.

[9]Although very difficult to document precisely, guard informants agreed that inmate responsiveness to work orders, as well as inmate productivity, became problematic as the trial and resultant court order became widely known.

[10]The TDC experienced only six major riots from 1973 to 1981.

Cases

Banning v. Looney, 348 U.S. 859 (1954).

Cooper v. Pate, 378 U.S. 546 (1964).

Monroe v. Pape, 365 U.S. 167 (1961).

Ruiz v. Estelle, 503 F.Supp. 1265 (S.D. Tex. 1980); 679 F2d 1115 (5th Cir. 1980); cert. denied, 103 S.Ct. 452 (1983); *Modified on reh'g*, 688 F2d 266 (5th Cir. 1982); cert. denied, 103 S.Ct. 1438 (1983).

References

Alpert, Geoffrey P. (1977) "Collective Violence Behind Bars," in M. Riedel and P.A. Vales (eds.) *Treating the Offender: Problems and Issues*. New York: Praeger. (1980) *Legal Rights of Prisoners*. Lexington, MA: D.C. Heath.

Alpert, Geoffrey P. and C. Ronald Huff (1981) "Prisoners, the Law, and Public Policy: Planning for Legal Aid," 7 *New England Journal on Prison Law* 307.

American Correctional Association (1981) *Riots and Disturbances in Correctional Institutions*. College Park, MD: American Correctional Association.

Baker, Donald P., Randolph Blotky, Keith Clemens, and Michael Dillard (1973) "Judicial Intervention in Corrections: The California Experience — An Empirical Study," 20 *UCLA Law Review* 452.

Bowker, Lee H. (1982) *Corrections: The Science and the Art*. New York: Macmillan.

Bureau of Justice Statistics (1983) "Prisoners at Midyear 1983," *BJS Bulletin*. Washington, DC: U.S. Department of Justice, Bureau of Justice Statistics.

Calhoun, Emily (1977) "The Supreme Court and the Constitutional Rights of Prisoners: A Reappraisal," 4 *Hastings Constitutional Law Quarterly* 219.

Cohen, Fred (1981) "The Texas Prison Conditions Case: Ruiz v. Estelle," 17 *Criminal Law Bulletin* 252.

Corrections Magazine (1978) Volume 4, front cover.

Crouch, Ben M. (1977) "A Profile of the Typical Correctional Officer in the Eastham, Ellis, Ferguson, and Huntsville Units," *Technical Note #5 Research and Development Division*. Huntsville, TX: Texas Department of Corrections.

_____ (1980) "The Book vs. the Boot: Two Styles of Guarding in a Southern Prison," in Ben M. Crouch (ed.) *The Keepers: Prison Guards in Contemporary Corrections*. Springfield, IL: Charles C Thomas.

Crouch, Ben M. and James W. Marquart (1980) "On Becoming a Prison Guard," in Ben M. Crouch (ed.) *The Keepers: Prison Guards in Contemporary Corrections*. Springfield, IL: Charles C Thomas.

_____ (1981a) Field notes, interview with building captain, Eastham Unit.

_____ (1981b) Field notes, interview with correctional officer, Ferguson Unit.

Davies, James C. (1962) "Toward a Theory of Revolution," 27 *American Sociological Review* 5.

Duffee, David (1980) *Correctional Management: Change and Control in Correctional Organizations*. Reissued 1986 by Waveland Press, Inc. Prospect Heights, IL.

Garson, G. David (1972a) "The Disruption of Prison Administration: An Investigation of Alternative Theories of the Relationship Among Administrators, Reformers, and Involuntary Social Service Clients," 6 *Law and Society Review* 531.

_____ (1972b) "Force Versus Restraint in Prison Riots," 8 *Crime and Delinquency* 411.

Gettinger, Steve (1977) "Cruel and Unusual Prisons," 3 *Corrections Magazine* 3.

Gettinger, Steve and Kevin Krajick (1978) "Are 'Building Tenders' the Key to Control?" 4 *Corrections Magazine* 22.

Gurr, T. Robert (1970) *Why Men Rebel*. Princeton: Princeton University Press.

Haas, Kenneth C. and Anthony Champagne (1976) "The Impact of *Johnson v. Avery* on Prison Administration," 43 *Tennessee Law Review* 275.

Heaps, William (1970) *Riots, U.S.A., 1765-1970.* New York: Seabury Press.

Houston Chronicle (1983) "Violence Peaks at 9-year High," July 6, 1983.

Huff, C. Ronald (1983) "Prison Violence: Sociological and Public Policy Implications," (in Hebrew) 11 *Crime and Social Deviance* 65.

Huff, C. Ronald and Geoffrey P. Alpert (1982) "Organizational Compliance with Court-Ordered Reform," in Merry Morash (ed.) *Implementing Criminal Justice Policies.* Beverly Hills, CA: Sage Publications.

Jacobs, James B. (1977) "Macrosociology and Imprisonment," in David Greenberg (ed.) *Corrections and Punishment.* Beverly Hills, CA: Sage Publications.

Krajick, Kevin (1978) "They Keep You In, They Keep You Busy, and They Keep You From Getting Killed," 4 *Corrections Magazine* 4.

Levinson, Marc R. (1982) "Special Masters: Engineers of Court-Ordered Reform," 8 *Corrections Magazine* 7.

March, Ray (1978) *Alabama Bound: Forty-Five Years Inside a Prison System.* University, AL: The University of Alabama Press.

Marquart, James W. and Ben M. Crouch (1982) "Cooptation of the Kept: Maintaining Order in a Southern Prison,": Paper presented at the 1982 meeting of the American Society of Criminology, Toronto, Ontario, Canada.

Marx, Karl and Frederick Engels (1959) "Manifesto of the Communist Party," in L.S. Feuer (ed.) *Marx and Engels: Basic Writings on Politics and Philosophy.* Garden City, NY: Doubleday.

McKay, Robert B. (1983) "Prison Riots," in Sanford H. Kadish (ed.) *Encyclopedia of Crime and Justice.* New York: Free Press.

Nathan, Vincent M. (1979) "The Use of Masters in Institutional Reform Litigation," 10 *The University of Toledo Law Review* 419.

National Advisory Commission on Criminal Justice Standards and Goals (1976) *Disorders and Terrorism.* Washington, DC: Government Printing Office.

Note (1980) "Judicial Intervention and Organizational Theory: Changing Bureaucratic Behavior and Policy," 8 *The Yale Law Journal* 513.

Piven, Francis F. and Richard A. Cloward (1979) *Poor People's Movements.* New York: Random House.

Rudovsky, David, Alvin Bronstein, and Edward Koren (1983) *The Rights of Prisoners.* New York: Bantam Books.

Sylvester, Sawyer, John Reed and David Nelson (1977) *Prison Homicide.* New York: Spectrum Publications.

Tocqueville, Alexis de (1955) *The Old Regime and the French Revolution.* Garden City, NY: Doubleday.

Turner, William B. (1979) "When Prisoners Sue: A Study of Prisoners' Section 1983 Suits in the Federal Courts," 42 *Harvard Law Review* 610.

19

Litigation Can Be Therapeutic

Richard R. Korn

Soviet psychiatrists claim to have discovered certain forms of delusion not yet recognized by Western medicine. One of these is "litigation mania," in which a patient continually claims that his confinement is a violation of his civil rights. American psychiatry has generally rejected "litigation mania" as a diagnosis. But, in one case at least, psychiatric and correctional authorities had no problem with it at all. In prisoner Bobby Hardwick they found a patient who fitted the Soviet diagnosis perfectly.

On January 22, 1970, a Georgia psychiatrist found Hardwick, a newly admitted 39-year-old inmate serving a ten-year sentence for armed robbery, to be suffering from paranoid schizophrenia with hallucinations and delusions of persecution. Hardwick spent the next eight years being shuttled back and forth from solitary cells in prison to solitary rooms in mental hospitals. All the while he deluged authorities with complaints about his treatment. Although Hardwick's attacks on the Georgia penal system were purely literary—he presented no behavioral threat—the prison authorities finally lost patience with him, and in 1974 he was transferred from Reidsville

Source: *Corrections Magazine*, Vol. 7, No. 5 (October 1981), inside cover, 45-48. Reprinted with the permission of the publisher.

prison to a unit for "incorrigibles and security risks" located in H-House of the Georgia Diagnostic and Classification Center (GDCC) at Jackson.

In setting forth his reasons for requesting Hardwick's removal, Reidsville Warden Joseph Hopper unwittingly paraphrased the essential elements of the "litigation mania" diagnosis: "He has written so many writs that it has taken an extra, separate file to hold his legal papers. He has continuously complained about mistreatment. Hardwick has chosen an antisocial path....Therefore it is recommended that he be transferred to GDCC to participate in their behavior modification program in the hope that this will change his devious trend."

Hardwick's new location, a solitary confinement block, did not modify his litigious behavior. In August 1974 he filed suit in the U.S. District Court of Georgia, claiming several violations of his constitutional rights. Named as defendant in the suit was Dr. Allen Ault, who had participated in the design of the H-House program. Dr. Ault was, at the time the suit was filed, commissioner of the Department of Offender Rehabilitation.

Late in 1975 Judge Wilbur T. Owens, Jr. consolidated Hardwick's suit with 25 other cases which had been filed at Hardwick's instigation. The trial in the case of *Hardwick vs. Ault* was set for March 1977, at which point I was called in as an expert witness by the ACLU of Georgia. Given the relative positions and reputations of the two litigants, the outcome hardly seemed in doubt.

But on Jan. 12, 1978, Judge Owens shattered expectations. In a landmark decision, the judge ruled that the totality of conditions in H-House were in violation of the 8th and 14th Amendments. The word of a certified psychotic had prevailed over the diagnosis of his keepers. But something even more remarkable had happend. Throughout the lengthy preparation for the trial, the state's psychiatrists had continued to monitor Hardwick's mental condition. During the same period they also checked frequently on the mental health of his fellow litigants, who were not all mentally ill. After four years in solitary confinement in H-House, the condition of most of the other plaintiffs had deteriorated. But Hardwick, whose diagnosis of schizophrenia had predated his entry to H-House, was clearly getting better in a situation in which normal prisoners were getting worse. Each new report confirmed the trend. By 1978, at the moment of his victory, Hardwick was unmistakably sane. Today he is out of prison and running a successful business in the Southwest.

Under what conditions was Hardwick living during his four year struggle? In his decision, Judge Owens described life in H-House with numbing specificity: "Inmates are kept in their small individual cells almost all the time....The typical prisoner...is out of his cell only slightly over six hours per week. Prisoners...are constantly subject to severe security measures. In addition to being constantly under surveillance...they are strip searched for any movement out of H-2. During the search two correctional officers keep 'stun guns' trained on the prisoner. The prisoners are fed by the guards who deliver the food in carts while another guard watches with a stun gun. No guard ever goes alone down on the range in front of the prisoners. Almost all of the prison staff's communication with inmates occurs through the porthole in the top of the cell."

The "porthole in the top of the cell" is one of the stranger features of isolation in H-House. It allows prison officials to see and hear without being seen or heard. Prior to his confinement there, Hardwick had already been described as "hearing voices." In H-House, being watched by invisible onlookers and talked to by disembodied voices was part of the program. The porthole was reached by an overhead catwalk. Judge Owens described its use: "The catwalk allows guards to monitor constantly...and because [they] follow no set routine the surveillance through the hole in the ceiling...is always unexpected. The catwalk is used...for nearly all communications with prisoners in H-2. Thus the fate of an H-2 inmate is determined in large part by his conversations with people talking to him through a metal grate. Other than through this grate the H-House inmate has very little contact with other human beings."

But by far the most stressful impact of H-House was the sheer duration of the time spent there. "Punishment in H-House is disproportionate in the sense that it has no proportion with respect to time..." wrote Judge Owens. "Because the passage of time is in part a function of space and activity, time truly appears to slow down for the inmate in H-House. This slowing of time is made worse by the indefiniteness of the duration. Without hope or promise as to when the punishment will end, H-House inflicts considerable mental anguish. This anguish was described and testified to by almost everyone who had contact with H-House, including guards, prison counselors, and prison administrators."

Summarizing his assessment of conditions in H-House, Judge Owens concluded: "There can be little doubt that H-House constitutes punishment beyond the original, ordinary incarceration of inmates in the Georgia prison system....Long periods of lock-up in a confined space, limited contact with others, continued and unexpected surveillance and limited exercise eventually take a serious toll on the mental health of the inmates."

Judge Owens' decision was a stinging rebuke to the state's attempt to redefine traditional solitary confinement as a modern form of behavioral treatment. But Hardwick's apparent recovery during the course of his attempts to fight his confinement is an even more fundamental affront to classical psychiatric theory. According to accepted therapeutic doctrine, a paranoid person ought not to be encouraged to believe that his delusions of persecution are valid. Moreover, those who seek to help a paranoid person are supposed to help him realize that his problems are internal rather than environmental, and that his task is to change himself, not his circumstances.

As a former prison psychologist and director of treatment at the New Jersey State Prison at Trenton (1952-1955) I at one time accepted these principles, without question. And I saw it as my professional responsibility to do what I could to dissuade inmates from evading responsibility by merely blaming their environment. One of my duties at the state prison was to monitor the condition of inmates confined to indefinite administrative segregation. As I watched inmate after inmate succumb to the rigors of unrelieved solitary confinement, I described with clinical detachment their struggles to preserve their sanity by fighting back. One of my observations was to be strikingly appropriate to Hardwick 30 years later:

> At the outset the segregated offender typically occupies himself with an ambitious program of protest. Intensive legal activity frequently characterizes this period; the offender busies himself with the search for an effective way to combine the expression of his resentment with a method of obtaining his release. Following the failure of legal appeals, there are attempts to deluge all manner of public officials with a lengthy recital of complaints. As a matter of sound correctional administration, these complaints should be fully and routinely investigated. In addition to providing a precaution against actual injustice, the investigation of unfounded complaints serves a therapeutic purpose. Once again the inmate is provided a demonstration of the failure of his manipulative techniques.

What had not occurred to me, of course, was that indefinite solitary confinement was in itself an injustice, made all the more intolerable by the official belief or pretense that it was for the inmates' own good.

Why, then, did Hardwick not break down under it? One thing was clear not only to me but to others who had observed and interviewed him prior to the trial: Hardwick had recovered his wits even before his legal success. Is it conceivable that it was his struggle, rather than its positive outcome, that was decisive? Or is it possible that Hardwick was never psychotic in the first place?

As an expert witness I was privy to Hardwick's psychiatric reports, which became part of the public record of the trial. I have obtained his permission to reproduce relevant portions of the reports here. Hardwick was first seen by a psychiatrist, Dr. Julius Ehik, in January

1970, shortly after his admission as a new inmate. Dr. Ehik reported: "This inmate...will not eat and has not eaten anything for the past three days. He also will not let anybody come close to him and will beg not to be touched. He thinks that he is in the service. He has conversations with a Captain Whitehead who is, according to him, telling him things to do, and keeps him locked up. He stated that he won't eat because he had been told that the food is poison, and that they were trying to get rid of him....From my brief contact with this prisoner, it would appear to me that he is acutely psychotic, that he is paranoid and is hallucinating."

Hardwick's next psychiatric examination took place in September 1974, soon after he had been transferred to H-House. The report, made by another psychiatrist, Dr. J.F. Casey, reflects an unmistakeable concern and sensitivity: "He seems to be hallucinating at the time of the interview. From time to time he would turn his head as if listening to someone, and then when he was asked about this would be very suspicious and insisted that I had heard the same thing that he had heard....He tells at great length of this conspiracy which is not definitely organized other than that it is against him primarily because he is a highly intelligent person and since he is black 'they' whom he would never identify resent his being as intelligent as he is and are taking various steps to suppress him. These steps include his being sent out of the Army and then arrested and having been sent to prison in order to put him away so that he couldn't participate in the take-over of the world which he insists is going to occur in any event....During the interview he tells about hidden microphones in the examining room with us.

"This is a 30-year-old black inmate who is obviously quite hallucinated and delusional and apparently has been for some time. I feel he is suffering from schizophrenia of a paranoid type with relatively little deterioration."

At no point in his assessment does the psychiatrist note the fact that Hardwick is living in a solitary confinement cell where his contact with other human beings is largely limited to communication with their disembodied voices. This omission is consistent with the conventional view that paranoid schizophrenia can best be understood as an internal problem. This same lack of reference to the patient's environment characterizes the psychiatric reports about Hardwick's fellow inmates in H-House. The second point to be stressed is this: While the condition of most of his colleagues was deteriorating, Hardwick's was apparently improving.

Hardwick next saw Dr. Casey two years later, in March 1976. By this time Hardwick was deeply involved in organizing his massive class action suit. He had enlisted the aid of the ACLU of Georgia, and he was in frequent contact with some of the most prestigious attorneys in the state. And he had earned a respect approaching awe by his fellow sufferers. When speaking to him or about him, they rarely used his name. They called him "Lawyer."

In his report of his 1976 interview, Dr. Casey noted an impressive change in Hardwick: "This inmate appears considerably improved from a mental point of view over what he was when last seen. He seems to have fewer ideas of a typical paranoid nature. Some are still with him but not nearly to the extent they were present on the previous exam....Emotionally he is certainly not depressed. He doesn't appear flattened emotionally as when last seen....At the present time he denies any actual hallucinations, which is in some contrast to the previous time when he didn't actually admit it but his nonverbal communication certainly would intimate so. When informed that he thought previously he had had hidden mikes in the room he was quite doubtful and couldn't remember this and it was obvious that he didn't believe it."

By the time I interviewed Hardwick prior to the trial in 1977, a year after his last examination, there was no evidence whatever of any symptomatology. He was resilient, cheerful, without hostility, and his conversation crackled with wit and good humor. When I first saw him I had not yet read his psychiatric reports. When I saw them I was amazed. My impression of his excellent mental health was shared by all those who worked with him and by those who watched and heard his testimony. One reporter, Marcia Kunstel, wrote: "After watching Bobby Hardwick testify in a confident, contained manner before a federal judge, it was hard to believe a psychiatrist characterized him as 'delusional, schizophrenic, paranoid and definitely psychotic' only a few years ago."

Conventional psychiatric theory does not have an explanation for Hardwick. According to classical psychiatric doctrine, paranoids remain ill by continuing to blame their environment for their troubles. Their only hope for improvement is to begin to realize that their problems are internal. In a situation well calculated to drive sane people mad, Hardwick had, to all intents and purposes, made himself well. He accomplished this feat in a way that violated every canon of psychiatric treatment. Instead of permitting people to persuade him that his beliefs were delusional, he had succeeded in persuading others that they were valid. This alone should have been enough to confirm and exacerbate his illness. Instead of submitting to his circumstances, he had attacked them. Worse, he had attacked them successfully, which according to accepted doctrine amounts to little more than shifting the burden of his madness onto the world.

Conventional psychiatric theory does have the beginning of an explanation for Hardwick's "symptomatic" improvement. The noted psychiatrist Silvano Arieti has written: "There are persons who, because of unusual circumstances...or because of their ability to organize, succeed in changing and manipulating their environment according to their bizarre wishes, and therefore have no need to develop *overt* paranoid symptoms. These are cases of 'acted out' or 'externalized' psychoses. For instance, people like Nero or Hitler were able to alter the environment in accordance with their wishes, no matter how bizarre these wishes were. As long as they were able to do so on a realistic level, they had no need to become psychotic in a clinical or legal sense."

Dr. Arieti's concept presents some internal difficulties. Is an idea still "bizarre" after many people finally come to believe it? Was Hardwick's wish to change his circumstances irrational? His psychiatrists thought so, but many other rational people, including a federal judge, did not agree. These people found H-House rather bizarre. They found it hard to accept a treatment program which somehow managed to fulfill almost every condition of paranoia itself, including conversations with invisible people who appeared and disappeared unexpectedly.

Some years ago the late psychiatrist J.L. Moreno, creator of psychodrama and sociometry, recalled his frustrating work as a young resident in the disturbed wards of the main mental hospital in Vienna. One of Moreno's patients was a former bank clerk who was convinced that he was actually a general being held in captivity as a prisoner of war. Another was an elderly lady who was positive that the ragged doll she constantly clutched to herself was actually her infant.

After spending his day in the wards, fruitlessly trying to convince his patients to give up their delusions, Moreno would gratefully descend into the streets of Vienna. On his way home he would pass young boys playing at being soldiers, and young girls pushing their toy baby carriages and talking with great seriousness about their "children." Moreno then posed for himself a question: Why are the adult fantasists in the hospital wards thought to be insane, while children acting out fantasies in the street are considered normal? And why were the children willing and able to put their fantasies aside when they returned home, while the adults in the wards were not?

Moreno pushed his questioning one step further. Why, he asked, do people, adults and children alike, need to have fantasies in the first place? Why isn't "reality" enough? His answer to his first question provided a clue to the second. Peole obviously need to relieve themselves with dreams and fantasies when their reality frustrates their inner needs, or violates their inner sense of who they actually are and need to be. Later studies of dream deprivation would confirm Moreno's insight. Waking up experimental subjects when they are about to start dreaming is seriously disturbing. It follows that the ability to indulge in dreams and fantasies, and to believe in them at some level, is essential for coping with stresses of a refractory and frustrating reality. In effect, to be denied the relief and release of dreaming is to be crippled in one's ability to cope on any level.

An indulgent adult world gives children permission to act out their fantasies in play. Children grant each other's fantasies the essential element of credibility by confirming them in vivid and convincing role-playing. A little boy who needs to act out a fantasy of power can mobilize other children to confirm him as a "general" by taking the role of his soldiers. Having satisfied his inner need by expressing it in emotionally authentic action, the boy can relinquish it. He can content himself with playing ordinary soldier to another child's "general," or he can go back to his assigned role of little boy.

Unlike a child, an unhappy adult is not given permission to suspend an accepted but frustrating social identity by acting out his fantasies in the real world. Nor, unless he is a Hitler or a Nero, will he ordinarily find other adults who are willing to confirm his secret self by acting out the counterpart roles of his fantasy with him.

The tragedy of conventional mental hospital treatment is that it intensifies the process that compelled the individual to take on his compensatory fantasy role in the first place. It was to counteract a treatment process that essentially mimicked the disease that Moreno created his system of psychodramatic therapy. Recognizing the metaphorical validity of the patient's fantasies, he also understood that one can relinquish an essential wish only after one has fulfilled it on some psychologically authentic level. So he encouraged his clients to confirm each other's aspirational identities as children do, in dramatic action.

Inmates of prisons and mental hospitals have been drastically "disconfirmed" by their social environments. Like children, their identities are subject to the definitions of others; they are in the clutch of circumstances they cannot control. They have few good choices. To accept their dependency is to accept their neutralization as self-directing human beings. To act out against their circumstances, to try to transform them or to escape from them, is to risk further restriction and neutralization.

All of these conditions are exacerbated in indefinite solitary confinement. There the choices are even more bleak. Inmates can resist by violence. They can retreat into a world of fantasy from which they may not emerge. They can sink into vegetative apathy, or permit themselves to be tranquilized into a state of mindlessness. They can try to escape by self-destruction. The high rates of assault, self-inflicted injury, suicide and psychosis testify to the prevalence of these doomed attempts to transcend the horrors of immobility, isolation and sensory and social deprivation in prolonged solitary confinement.

Litigation offers a striking promise of a better alternative. By persuading outsiders to acknowledge their terrible circumstances, prisoners can obtain confirmation that their difficulties are not merely "internal." By enlisting the aid of these outsiders — attorneys, expert witnesses, judges — they can participate in an attempt to change their circumstances, or to procure their release from them. Whether they are successful or not, the activity of litigation offers an alternative to self-destructive acceptance of a pathological environment, or equally self-destructive violence against it.

There may well be other advantages. Litigation changes the offender's relationship to the law. As a predator, the offender looked at the law and its agents as enemies to be defied or evaded. By definition, the successful criminal is a successful law-breaker. In turning to litigation as his last hope, the offender must enlist the law as his friend. If he is serious, he must take the role of the law, and he must look at himself and his pleadings with a critical eye for their defects. In effect, he must, for perhaps the first time, look at himself as a judge and jury might look at him. The chance exists that he may internalize these attitudes as criteria for his future conduct.

Psychotic or not, Hardwick seems to have succeeded in doing all these things. If he was truly delusional, he was delusional only when he was unable to do anything about his situation in fact. One may not need to feel that he must save the whole world if he can save at least his part of it. The moment Hardwick began to use the law on his behalf, and on behalf of his fellow prisoners, his grander projects were less and less necessary or useful. What was useful now were his powers of observation, his rationality, his ability to persuade. These abilities are preeminently the abilities of a sane human being.

Hardwick was, of course, an exception to the rule. As a result of Judge Owens' court order, H-House was closed and its inmates dispersed in the general prison population. It is now Georgia's death row, and is the subject of a new inmate/ACLU lawsuit charging that confinement there constitutes cruel and unusual punishment.

Part IV

The Rehabilitation Debate
What Works?

Introduction

For most of the past 200 years, the dominant purposes of corrections have gradually moved from a strictly punitive philosophy toward the ideal of rehabilitation. This rehabilitative ideal—the belief that criminal offenders can be reformed and taught to live socially productive, crime-free lives—became a major goal of correctional policy in the 1950s and 1960s. By the early 1970s, however, the public's increasing fear of crime and widespread perceptions that both crime rates and recidivism rates were rising led many to view rehabilitation programs as well-intentioned but misguided efforts that simply do not work.

The critics of rehabilitation were bolstered by Robert Martinson's 1974 article in *The Public Interest*, "What Works? Questions and Answers About Prison Reform." In that highly publicized piece and in a subsequent book, *The Effectiveness of Correctional Treatment*, Martinson and his colleagues Douglas Lipton and Judith Wilks assembled evidence pointing to the conclusion that "nothing or almost nothing works" in criminal rehabilitation. Martinson and his colleagues reviewed over 200 evaluative studies of correctional treatment programs such as vocational training, education programs, work opportunities, group counseling, individual counseling, and psychotherapy. All of the studies were done between 1945 and 1967, and Martinson's review convinced him that "with few and isolated exceptions, the rehabilitative efforts that have been reported so far have had no appreciable effect on recidivism."

Martinson's conclusions were highly compatible with the "get tough" approach to the crime problem increasingly embraced by Americans and their elected representatives. Indeed, the contention that "nothing works" is still widely promulgated by many federal and state criminal justice officials. However, a growing number of correctional scholars and practitioners have come forward to refute the assertion that treatment programs are ineffective. The defenders of rehabilitation argue that prison treatment programs rarely have been given a fair and fully funded opportunity to produce positive results. The cost of prison rehabilitation projects amounts to less than 5 percent of the billion of dollars spent annually on state and federal prison operations. The vast majority of correctional employees do nothing in the way of treatment; they merely guard prisoners. When supported by reasonable budgets and carried out by well-trained staff, treatment efforts, say the supporters of rehabilitation, will prove successful in reforming criminal behavior. Up to now, it is asserted, many correctional officials have mastered the rhetoric of rehabilitation programs while actually using such programs to suppress inmate dissent and maintain the punitive practices of the past.

The advocates of rehabilitation also criticized Martinson's methods of evaluating the findings of earlier correctional treatment studies. For example, Martinson was chastised for limiting his review to studies done in the 1945-to-1967 time period, thereby ignoring the more optimistic findings of studies that were done in the 1967-to-1974 time period. In an influential 1975 article, "Martinson Revisited," published in the *Journal of Research in Crime and Delinquency*, Ted Palmer criticized Martinson for refusing to judge a treatment program as successful unless it had generated almost exclusively positive results. Palmer's reassessment of the studies included in the Martinson survey indicated that nearly half of them had yielded at least "partly positive results." According to Palmer, the effectiveness of correctional treatment depends upon a variety of factors, including the type of offender, the type of rehabilitation program, and the skills brought to the task by staff members. Thus, although no single method of treatment will benefit all offenders, some offenders will respond positively to some types of treatment programs.

In the late 1970s, Martinson published several articles (see, for example, "Save Parole Supervision" in Part V of this book) recognizing that certain correctional programs had demonstrated measurable success in curbing recidivism rates. Today, the debate over the efficacy of rehabilitation is by no means finished. However, there seems to be an emerging consensus among scholars that we should redirect our efforts toward developing better research methods that may help us discover which, if any, treatment strategies will work best for which types of offenders and under what conditions. For that matter, it has been pointed out, perhaps most eloquently in Francis Cullen and Karen Gilbert's book, *Reaffirming Rehabilitation* (1982), that there are other reasons why it would be a mistake to abandon rehabilitation as a goal of our correctional system. Most importantly, even if rehabilitation programs do not change most criminals into model citizens, the ideal of rehabilitation can serve as a valuable resource for those who are striving to improve conditions and increase humanitarianism in America's prisons.

The possibility that "[c]orrectional intervention can operate in a framework of humane interaction" is among the ideas discussed by Ted Palmer in "The 'Effectiveness' Issue Today: An Overview," the first selection of Part IV. Palmer shows that the combatants who took extreme positions for and against correctional treatment programs in the 1960s and 1970s have been replaced by two somewhat more moderate "camps." On the one hand, a relatively "sanguine" camp of scholars believes that many treatment efforts have proved successful with various offender populations and thus should be refined and expanded. On the other hand, a more "skeptical" camp of researchers contends that although a small number of treatment projects may have achieved slight reductions of recidivism, rehabilitation programs have failed to demonstrate enough potency to deserve to play a major role in the future of corrections.

The next two selections in Part IV represent positions taken by the "sanguine" and "skeptical" camps, respectively. Embracing an optimistic outlook, Paul Gendreau and Robert Ross argue that there no longer can be any serious doubt that many criminal offenders are capable of learning new attitudes and acquiring new behaviors. They believe that the most important questions still to be answered in the rehabilitation debate concern why some programs work and some do not. Their analysis of how successful treatment programs differ from unsuccessful programs contains valuable advice for anyone interested in working with juvenile or adult offenders.

In the first edition of his highly influential 1975 book, *Thinking About Crime*, political scientist James Q. Wilson took a very pessimistic view of correctional rehabilitation programs:

> It requires not merely optimistic but heroic assumptions about the nature of man to lead one to suppose that a person, finally sentenced after (in most cases) many brushes with the law, and having devoted a good part of his youth and young adulthood to misbehavior of every sort, should, by either the solemnity of prison or the skillfulness of a counselor, come to see the error of his ways and to experience a transformation of his character (p. 190).

By 1980, Wilson, though not ready to jump on the rehabilitation bandwagon, was willing to acknowledge the possibility that certain offenders ("amenables") may become less criminal in response to certain rehabilitation programs. In "'What Works?' Revisited: New Findings on Criminal Rehabilitation," reprinted from the Fall 1980 issue of *The Public Interest*, Wilson also points out that some treatment programs may contribute to an increase in law breaking among certain offenders ("nonamenables"). The rehabilitation debate, he cautions, is more complex than earlier commentators may have realized, and no clear answers can be expected until researchers utilize more sensitive and realistic measures of the success or failure of treatment programs.

This is just what is done in our next selection. In "Evaluating Correctional Boot Camp Programs: Issues and Concerns," Angela R. Gover, Gaylene J. F. Styve, and Doris Layton MacKenzie take a close look at a correctional program that has been widely publicized as a way to respond to the needs of young offenders. Prison "boot camps," technically called "shock incarceration," have been praised as cost-effective and successful alternatives to other punishments, especially by politicians who subscribe to the "get tough" ideology of criminal justice. Students of correctional history, however, are well aware that the "boot camp" bandwagon may turn out to be an example of the so-called "panacea phenomenon"—the tendency to embrace and exaggerate the effectiveness of simplistic, "cure-all" approaches to correctional rehabilitation that do not prove to be especially effective upon closer examination.

In his 1982 book, *Scared Straight and the Panacea Phenomenon*, James Finckenauer skillfully debunked the dramatic and exaggerated claims of success for "Scared Straight" or "Juvenile Awareness" programs in which juvenile offenders are brought to a prison where they meet with hardened, long-term prisoners who tell them prison horror stories and counsel them to lead a "straight" life. While such programs may be helpful for some youngsters (for example, those who do not already have an extensive history of delinquency) as part of a larger treatment effort, there is no evidence that serious young offenders can be turned around simply by "Scared Straight" or similar short-term programs.

Will prison boot camps prove to be more successful than previous efforts to rehabilitate offenders? According to Gover, Styve, and Mac-Kenzie, the verdict is still out. After describing the various kinds of adult- and juvenile-offender boot camp programs that have emerged in recent years, Gover, Styve, and MacKenzie review the research literature on the effectiveness of these programs. Overall, they find no evidence that these programs constitute a major breakthrough in correctional rehabilitation. On the other hand, there are some intriguing findings. For example, boot camp prison inmates generally reported that they felt the program helped them and that they were now more optimistic about the future. Moreover, there is some evidence that boot camp programs that emphasize rehabilitation programming (i.e. counseling, drug treatment, education programs, etc.) and intensive post-release supervision may prove helpful for some inmates. On the whole, however, boot camp graduates do not have significantly lower recidivism rates than do general population inmates. Gover, Styve, and MacKenzie conclude that more research is necessary to determine precisely what components, if any, can make boot camp prisons more effective in reducing prison crowding and recidivism rates. They conclude by suggesting a research model that may prove particularly helpful in this regard.

The next two selections in Part IV focus on what may very well be the most pressing need in correctional rehabilitation programs for offenders with drug problems. Many of those behind bars are there because (1) they committed a drug-related crime (i.e. possession, distribution, sale, possession with intent to distribute, etc.) or (2) they were under the influence of alcohol or some other drug when they committed a serious crime. It stands to reason that freeing these prisoners from their dependency on drugs is an essential first step if they are to have any real chance to live law-abiding lives. In the first of these two selections, Professor Jim Inciardi, Director of the Center for Drug and Alcohol Studies at the University of Delaware, reports on the therapeutic community ("TC") concept as applied in a promising program for drug-involved offenders in Delaware. Professor Inciardi describes the three-stage TC model that he and his staff have developed for Delaware prisons, and he notes that preliminary evaluations of the program's effectiveness are quite promising.

If newer models of corrections-based drug abuse treatment eventually prove to be successful, the beneficiaries will be thousands of people like Bill Giddens—the subject of our next article. Like many "junkies" and "crackheads" who prey on the weak to finance their craving for illicit drugs, Giddens was "a one-man crime wave." But in "The Detoxing of Prisoner 88A0802," Peter Kerr, a reporter for *The New York Times*, tells us how Giddens made it through a drug-treatment program in a New York State prison. The New York program is similar to the Delaware program in that it involves rigorous therapy programs administered first in a prison-based therapeutic community and then in a residential therapeutic community outside the prison. The story of Bill Giddens is inspiring; six months after his release from the residential facility, the man who had robbed more than 200 people was still drug free and crime free. The apparent detoxing of Bill Giddens and the promising preliminary data from Delaware are quite encouraging, to say the least. However, Peter Kerr poses two questions that will not be answerable until more research is done:

> Can six months, a year, two years of treatment undo decades of antisocial behavior? How will the best of the inmates in [drug abuse treatment] fare, once they are alone, in poor neighborhoods, where unemployment is above 20 percent, where old friends are addicts, and crime and drugs still seem, to so many, to be the only way out?

Similar questions will have to be answered with respect to all of the ongoing efforts to rehabilitate criminal offenders, and this certainly applies to the ideas offered in the final selection in Part IV. In "Factories with Fences," Warren E. Burger, who retired as chief justice of the United States Supreme Court in 1986, advocated a much greater emphasis on work programs in American penology. Prisons, he argued, should be converted into "places of education and training and into factories and shops for the production of goods." Most readers will probably agree that Mr. Burger made a persuasive case that programs emphasizing vocational training and meaningful work experiences can only have a positive impact on prisoners.

20

The "Effectiveness" Issue Today
An Overview
Ted Palmer

In 1974, a wide-ranging debate regarding the effectiveness of rehabilitation was launched by Robert Martinson's assertion that nothing
or almost nothing works. [18] Since then, rebuttals and counter-
rebuttals have been exchanged and, in the process, some light has been
shed though considerable heat and haze remain. This process has been
difficult but necessary; and, though "sides" are still sharply drawn,
the justice system may soon reap some benefits from the exchange.
What, then, is the current status of this debate, and what are its
emerging trends?

The overview that follows derives primarily from several major
works conducted during 1966-1980. Chief among these are reviews and
evaluations by: Adams; Bailey; Empey; Gendreau and Ross; Greenberg;
Lipton, Martinson, and Wilks (LMW); Martinson; the National
Academy of Sciences Panel; Palmer; Romig; Wilson; Wright and Dixon.
[1; 3; 6; 7; 10; 14; 18; 20; 21; 23; 24; 26; 27] These efforts focused on
experimental studies of juvenile and adult offenders in institutional as

Source: *Federal Probation*, Vol. 47, No. 2 (June 1983), 3-10.

well as community settings. Each such category of offender and setting was well-represented in the studies reviewed, as were the major, traditional, rehabilitation methods (individual and group counseling; vocational and educational training; etc.); other, less common interventions were also included. Most such methods were implemented under non-voluntary conditions and — in the case of institutional programs — in an indeterminate-sentence context. Though the studies which were reviewed related to minor as well as serious or multiple offenders, the present overview will emphasize the implications of those reviews for the latter individuals. Throughout, the central question will be: Does rehabilitation work?

To address this question we will focus on programs that were judged successful or unsuccessful because — whatever else they did or did not accomplish with their target group — they either did or did not reduce recidivism. Use of recidivism is consistent with our view that the ultimate goal of rehabilitation is increased public protection. Clearly, rehabilitation efforts may also produce successful or desireable outcomes with respect to attitude-change, skill development, and various aspects of community adjustment, and these as well as other outcomes often do — but often do not — relate to recidivism. Nevertheless, for present purposes, the central criterion of success or effectiveness will be the reduction of illegal behavior — arrests, convictions, and related actions. This criterion was also used in the reviews mentioned above.

As discussed in this overview, rehabilitation or habilitation includes a wide range of interventions whose principal as well as ultimate goal is the increased protection of society. This, the *socially centered* goal of rehabilitation, is achieved when the offender's behavior is modified so that it conforms to the law. It is promoted but not in itself achieved by modifying given attitudes, by strengthening the offender as an individual, by reducing various external pressures and increasing given supports or opportunities, and/or by helping him or her become more satisfied and self-fulfilled within the context of society's values. Attitude-change, increased coping ability, etc., comprise the secondary or *offender-centered* goal of rehabilitation. Though this goal has absolute value in itself, it is — from the perspective of the overall justice system and this system's function in society — chiefly a "means" to the socially centered "end" of public protection. [20]

Before proceeding, let us briefly indicate what we mean by the phrase "rehabilitation program or approach." The following is not a formal, exhaustive identification of rehabilitation or habilitation; however, for present purposes, it will suffice.

The primary and secondary goals of rehabilitation are achieved by focusing on such factors and conditions as the offender's present adjustment techniques, his interests and skills, his limitations, and/or his life-circumstances, in ways that affect his future behavior and adjustment. Rehabilitation efforts are thus focused on particular factors or conditions and are directed toward particular future events. Insofar as they involve specific components or inputs (e.g., counseling or skill-development) that are organized, interrelated, and otherwise planned so as to generate changes in those factors and conditions (e.g., skills or life-circumstances) that may in turn help generate the desired future events, those efforts can be called rehabilitation programs or approaches. Such efforts—"interventions"—may involve what has been called treatment, external control, or both. Under some conditions, what has been called punishment may be considered an adjunct approach to rehabilitation.[1] However, methods such as electroshock treatment, psycho-surgery, etc., are not included under rehabilitation despite the factors or conditions on which they may focus and despite the specific effects—e.g., reduced illegal behavior—they may produce or be designed to produce.[2]

We now turn to the overview of "effectiveness."

Current Status of "Effectiveness"

Martinson's conclusion that "nothing works," which was widely accepted during the middle and later 1970's, is increasingly seen as a faulty synthesis of the findings from recidivism studies previously described by Lipton, Martinson, and Wilks. [14, 18] Palmer's critique of Martinson's method of synthesizing those findings showed that the latter's conclusion was valid only in the following sense: No single, broadly categorized treatment method, e.g., group counseling or vocational training (each of which, of course, has many variations[3]), is guaranteed to reduce the recidivism of its target group. [21] The critique ("Martinson Revisited") showed that several group counseling programs (in effect, variations or types of group counseling) did reduce recidivism either for the target group as a whole or for various subgroups within the total target group. This was observed in high-quality and acceptable-quality research studies alike. Because of this and subsequent critiques, Martinson, in 1978 and 1979 explicitly repudiated his highly pessimistic conclusion that nothing or almost nothing works. Instead, he recognized the difference between evaluative statements concerning individual programs and those relating to groups of programs, i.e., broadly categorized methods. [2; 8; 17; 20]

Though extreme pessimism no longer prevails regarding the effectiveness of rehabilitation or habilitation programs, the pendulum is by no means swinging rapidly toward the opposite extreme. Nor is it even approaching the rather optimistic position that most treatment efforts (broadly categorized or not) have substantially reduced recidivism with many or perhaps most offenders, even in certain settings only (e.g., institutions). Moreover, what might be considered today's officially sanctioned position—that taken by the National Academy of Sciences in 1979—is very guarded: No single correctional program (and, therefore, no broadly categorized method) has been unequivocally proven to reduce the recidivism of its target group; that is, using very strict standards of evidence, none has been shown to work beyond almost all doubt. At any rate, none can be guaranteed to work. [24]

Despite its extreme scientific caution and stringent methodological standards, the NAS Panel indicated the following (these views were based on what it acknowledged as the "suggestions...concerning successful rehabilitative efforts" that were reported by *LMW*, and partly on the above and subsequent critiques):

1. A few approaches may perhaps be working for some subgroups within the total target group; however, the quality and especially quantity of evidence do not allow for definite conclusions regarding the subgroup-success of these approaches.

2. Though no specific approaches have been proven to work, neither have they been disproven; instead, it is simply unclear which approaches have and have not been "given a fair trial." [24]

3. Many programs might have proven effective if they had been better implemented, if they had operated more intensively (i.e., had more treatment-input per client), etc.

In sum, the NAS Panel's position was very guarded and carefully qualified, but contained some glimmers of hope. In 1981, the Panel reaffirmed its position and further discussed these glimmers. [15]

The Panel's marked caution seemed to closely parallel the position taken by Empey in 1978, both as to the "inconclusive" nature of most research studies and the extreme difficulty of scientifically sorting-out precisely what works. [6] (That is, sorting-out is difficult even when good-quality research designs exist and certainly when program operations are only sketchily described.) Yet Empey was less restrictive than the Panel in one respect. He apparently did not believe that the results from all research studies which, methodologically, had been somewhat less than flawless but which were still relatively strong, should be discounted as a basis for correctional policy recommendations. Rather than insist that the results from any given study be demonstrated with almost absolute certainty, e.g., beyond the shadow of a doubt, he seemed to accept what amounted to a preponderance-of-evidence standard in this regard. As a result, he believed that some programs, though probably not many, *had* been adequately shown to be successful with serious offenders; at least, they seemed promising enough to have positive policy implications.

Beyond this, Empey—like the NAS Panel after him—believed that some programs might have produced better results if they had been directed, not at the full range of offenders, but at certain subgroups only. This view reflected the already existing "differential intervention" position, summarized below.

Several researchers and scholars—chiefly Palmer and Warren; Romig; Gendreau and Ross—have expressed a more sanguine view than that offered by the NAS Panel, by Greenberg, and, more recently, by Conrad [4; 7; 10; 23; 24; 25]. To be sure, these individuals, like the Panel and Conrad, believe that *much* criminal justice research has been mediocre and that *most* rehabilitation efforts have probably been unsuccessful thus far, relative to their overall target group. Nevertheless, they believe that many programs, often well-researched programs by *LMW's* detailed standards and those of others, have been shown to work with specified offenders (subgroups) under specific conditions. Their view—with the partial exception of Romig's—is generally known as the differential intervention (DI) position.[4,5] This view, which mainly grew from the early efforts of Warren, et al., in California's Community Treatment Project [25] goes beyond another well-known view—that which focuses on "amenability" alone.

In contrast to DI (see below), what might be termed the basic treatment-amenability (BTA) position only minimally distinguishes among types of offenders. The BTA position generally asserts that (1) certain offenders (e.g., the "bright, verbal, and anxious") will respond to many treatment approaches, presumably under most conditions or settings, and (2) most remaining offenders will respond to few if any approaches, again, regardless of conditions or settings. In contrast, the differential intervention view suggests that some offenders (BTA's amenables included) will respond positively to given approaches under very similar conditions; other combinations of offender, approach, setting—and resulting outcome—are also implied. Finally, DI also suggests that many offenders who in the BTA view are generally described as nonamenables may in fact respond positively to certain approaches under particular conditions, e.g., close structuring within institutional settings. [7; 20; 25]

> In short, overly simplified, DI asserts that certain categories of offenders (e.g., the Conflicted) but not others (e.g., the Power Oriented) will respond positively to certain approaches only, at least under specified conditions—and that the opposite may occur in response to other approaches or conditions. There are no all-around amenables and nonamenables, even though some individuals do usually perform better than others.

Thus, compared with BTA, the DI view is both more and less "optimistic" about so-called amenables; it is more optimistic about offenders who are often considered non-amenables, as well.

The "basic treatment amenability" and "differential intervention" positions have both been supported by Glaser, Adams, and others. [1; 8] The *amenability* view has, in addition, recently been supported by Wilson, a long-time critic of rehabilitation who also accepts the NAS Panel's overall caution regarding the validity of research findings to date. [26] All in all, there is increasing agreement among researchers, academicians, and practitioners as to which offenders are most likely to respond positively to standard—and, to a lesser extent, more specialized—rehabilitation approaches. *DI* has further been supported by Jesness, Hunt, Quay and Parsons, Megargee, et al., Wright and Dixon, and others. [11; 12; 13; 19; 22; 27] By 1979, Martinson himself was essentially supporting differential intervention:

> ...no treatment program now used in criminal justice is inherently either substantially helpful or harmful. The critical fact seems to be the *conditions* under which the program is delivered. For example, our results indicate that a widely-used program, such as formal education, is detrimental when given to juvenile sentenced offenders in a group home, but is beneficial (decreases reprocessing rates) when given to juveniles in juvenile prisons. Such startling results are found again and again in our [recent] study for treatment programs as diverse as individual psychotherapy, group counseling, intensive supervision, and what we have called "individual/help" (aid, advice, counseling). [17]

Finally, as indicated, both Empey and the Panel believe there may be something to this view.

In sum, both the BTA and DI positions have received moderate but clearly growing support within the justice system community; quantitatively, this applies to their empirical support as well. Nevertheless, as the Panel indicated, this evidence—while suggestive—is neither overwhelming nor entirely consistent.[9; 24]

Whether *many* programs or only a *small percentage* of programs have reduced recidivism is unclear. (Here, it makes little difference whether numbers or percentages are considered. However, by "many" we mean at least 30% of the sample-of-programs reviewed by such authors as *LMW*, Bailey, and Adams, respectively—recognizing that many programs were included in more than one such sample.) The many-programs position is found not just among reviewers who have questioned the effectiveness of rehabilitation efforts. The small-percentage view—with no specific percentage or percentage-range having been stated—is that implied by the Panel, by Empey, and by Greenberg.[7] Though the truth (objective reality) may well lie between these positions, the available evidence favors the former—assuming that "small" means less than 15 percent. More specifically, direct counts (Bailey's included, e.g., for "experimental studies") suggest that — conservatively — at least 20-25 percent of all experimental programs reviewed have reduced recidivism for their total target groups, while at least an additional 10-15 percent have done so for one or more subgroups only. [1; 3; 20; 21] However, the exact percentages may not be too important. What may matter in the long-run is whether knowledge has been and can be gathered regarding the nature of (1) those programs which work and (2) offenders whom those programs apparently serve best. Such information could make it possible to reproduce, improve, and more efficiently utilize those and similar programs, and to discard whatever approaches seem to accomplish little for the preponderance of their clients. In this way, the percentage of successful programs could increase — whether from today's small or more substantial level.

Long-range considerations aside, percentages — or at least terms such as "most," "many," and "few" — have nevertheless played a large and often confounding role in the effectiveness literature. For instance, DI proponents believe that many individuals who consider rehabilitation programs ineffective consistently overlook or ignore a basic fact, whether or not recidivism is involved as the sole outcome-measure: Although *most* programs have probably not worked well and *most* research was probably not done well, this still leaves numerous programs — i.e., from among the several hundred that were experimentally studied — that did work well or moderately well, that were researched satisfactorily, or both. Moreover, even if only 10 percent of those several hundred were found to work, this would still leave "many."

> In short, proponents feel that, by overlooking this fact, these effectiveness-critics erroneously conclude or at least imply that since most programs — literally hundreds of programs — have not done well, rehabilitation efforts are obviously a failure and claims of effectiveness can be dismissed. Yet, in context, most is far from *all*.

DI proponents also believe that the dozens of programs mentioned above have, collectively, provided not only very strong evidence that *something*, in fact several things, work, but substantial converging evidence as to *what* works for many offenders. Thus, given these numerous positive-outcome programs, they consider it immaterial that the *general* quality of research-to-date, and even program-implementation-to-date, may have been far from satisfactory, or perhaps even lamentable. Meanwhile, however, effectiveness-critics suggest that DI and perhaps BTA proponents greatly exaggerate the importance or implications of what they, the critics, consider the *few* programs that may possibly have worked. In any event, effectiveness critics usually emphasize the atypical — and, by implication, the probably-difficult-to-replicate—nature of these few. [4]

Apart from *how many* programs reduce recidivism, there is the question of how sizable that reduction is. *LMW* indicated that although some programs did indeed work, "corrections has not yet found satisfactory ways to reduce recidivism by significant amounts." [14] They neither defined significant nor presented a percentage-reduction figure. In addition, Martinson, in 1976, suggested that the reduction in question was probably trivial—meaning, 5-to-15 percent. [16] (In 1979, however, he stated: "...contrary to my previous position, some treatments *do* have appreciable effect on recidivism." [17] The NAS Panel was silent on this point, and, at present, only one percentage-reduction figure seems to exist. Focusing on all programs reported in *LMW* which reduced recidivism by at least 10 percent,[8] Palmer found an average reduction of 32 percent, the mean followup being 19 months; from a public-protection as well as cost perspective, even half this figure might often be considered important. [20] At any rate, since this is the only available figure, it is perhaps best to conclude that little is presently known regarding the average recidivism-reduction of positive-outcome studies—i.e., of *all* such studies (not just *LMW's*), and using varying definitions of success. Nevertheless, we suspect that the average reduction is substantial, e.g., over 20 percent. (The problem of defining successful programs is independent of the fact that *LMW* and Martinson may have made their estimates by combining successful and unsuccessful programs. At any rate, much depends on how success is operationally defined.)

The following question is closely related to the issue of percentage reduction in recidivism. For what percentage of the total target group, i.e., all offenders combined, have programs been "appropriate"? That is—in terms of the presently considered criterion—how often have they reduced recidivism? Here, no specific answer is known, and no average figure exists. Despite this absence of information, certain principles and related implications can be stated: Clearly, if a program and all its offender-subgroups are matched, the percentage reduction that may result will be larger than if unmatched, in this case "inappropriate," subgroups are included. To date, few programs or even major program components have been designed for defined offender subgroups only—more specifically, for only those individuals who would presumably or theoretically be matched to those particular approaches. However, where program/offender matching *has* been used—as in California Youth Authority institutions during the 1960's—it has shown considerable promise. [12] Of course, the ideal program would perhaps be one that is flexible enough or contains enough relevant components to successfully work with *all* major subgroups, even though that program might not quite maximize the percentage reduction in recidivism for all its offenders combined.

Such programs — in effect, near-panaceas — are nowhere on today's horizon; in fact, as indicated, the NAS Panel believes that no approach has been decisively shown to work even for *specific subgroups*. To be sure, the Panel's view with respect to demonstrated subgroup success is shared by neither differential intervention nor treatment-amenability proponents. Yet, despite this disagreement, both sets of individuals agree as to the existence of two major preconditions to effective rehabilitation or habilitation:

1. Single-modality approaches may be too narrowly focused to deal with the complex or multiple problems of most serious offenders. Instead, combinations-of-methods, e.g., vocational training *and* individual counseling, may be required.
2. Program input may have to be considerably greater ("More intense") than it has typically been — that is, if, as in (1) above, one wishes to generate lasting behavioral or other forms of change in most serious offenders.

These preconditions would apply regardless of the program components or specific input involved, provided, of course, that the latter do bear on the particular offenders' problems. As indicated, the Panel believed that — with improved research designs — many approaches might have been shown to work if they had met pre-conditions such as these.

This agreement among otherwise differing observers is important, particularly in light of their further agreement regarding the value (or, in the case of the Panel, the directly implied value) of matching offenders with programs. Together, these preconditions/principles suggest that concentrated efforts, and perhaps greater individualization than in the past, are needed in order to effect substantial change in serious offenders. These suggestions may comprise some of the more constructive or at least potentially constructive products of the effectiveness-debate thus far. At any rate, they would have policy implications regardless of *how many* programs have been successful, and exactly *how* successful they have been.

Finally, it should be added that differential intervention proponents largely agree among themselves on two additional points (here, the Panel took no public stand):

1. Some offenders probably require, not so much the standard rehabilitation inputs such as counseling, vocational training, etc. They may require — primarily, or perhaps on an equal footing — external controls, heavy structuring, and, with respect to community programs, considerable surveillance.

2. Staff characteristics and staff/offender matching are probably major factors in successfully implementing given approaches, at least for many offenders.

Though the evidence for these points is neither overwhelming (quantitatively) nor entirely consistent, it is by no means insubstantial and has grown considerably in the past several years. At any rate, the present author would add a different and perhaps broader point, one that focuses on likely preconditions to effective rehabilitation and applies across the board:

3. Fairness or fair treatment by the justice system, and humane interactions overall, can help create a tolerable, believable, sometimes supportive atmosphere for involvement and decision-making by offenders, especially but not exclusively in institutions.

Yet the following might be kept in mind. Fair treatment, etc., like just deserts and standardized dispositions by themselves, do not supply the direction, do not arouse the motivation, and do not provide the feedback or personal reward that probably must exist before realistic, satisfying decisions are generated and maintained by those individuals. That is, unlike many rehabilitation efforts, they do not address the specifics of the offenders' future—their concrete needs and opportunities within an often demanding environment. Nor do they address the often complex task of motivating or realistically helping them come to grips with that environment and, in many cases, with themselves. Thus, for many offenders, fairness and humane interactions without programmed assistance can be empty, in a sense blind, and programs without fairness can be futile, even pathetic. [20]

Review and Conclusion

An unsettled atmosphere exists regarding the effectiveness of rehabilitation or habilitation. Neither the global optimism of the 1960's nor the extreme pessimism of the middle and later 1970's seem justified, and neither view in fact prevails. Two slightly more moderate "camps" have replaced them, and a sizable but not entirely unbridged gap exists between these two.

Within the "skeptical" camp, some individuals believe it is clear—based on what they consider enough adequately conducted research—that relatively few rehabilitation programs work; moreover, those which work probably reduce recidivism by fairly small amounts. These individuals feel that rehabilitation, while not a total loss, therefore holds little promise and should be given a minor role. The remaining individuals within this group believe that *very little* is clear: Because of (1) minor or major research flaws in almost all studies, (2) poorly implemented programs, or (3) both, we don't really know whether given approaches do or do not—can or cannot—work, for their target groups as a whole. In this respect, rehabilitation has not been "given a fair trial." Though some approaches may possibly have worked for at least some offenders, the picture is again unclear because the findings are neither ironclad for any one study nor entirely consistent across various studies. These individuals believe that rehabilitation may well have promise—and a major role—but that no specific approaches can be recommended right now, at least not widely.

The more "sanguine" camp agrees that most programs have not been particularly effective thus far, certainly with their overall target groups. However, it believes that many programs and approaches have been shown—with reasonable scientific assurance—to work for specified portions of their target group. Some such proponents believe that certain offenders ("amenables") will respond positively to many approaches under a wide range of conditions and that many or most remaining offenders will probably respond to very few. Other proponents partly accept this view but believe that almost all offenders will respond positively, neutrally, or negatively depending on the *specific* approach and the external conditions or setting. The objective evidence, while neither vast in quantity nor flawless in quality, tends to support the latters' position while not negating the formers'. Both groups believe that successful programs often reduce recidivism by substantial amounts; they also feel that various approaches can be recommended right now for some offender-groups, even though these recommendations would reflect knowledge that is still largely "atheoretical" or at least not systematically and explicitly linked to a carefully defined set of underlying mechanisms and principles which have themselves been largely validated or seem quite plausible. Moreover, whether few or many programs have worked thus far (however those terms are defined), those and similar programs can perhaps be built upon and the remaining programs or approaches can eventually be discarded. In addition, whether recidivism reductions are considered moderately large or relatively small within typical programs to date, those reductions—like the percentage of successful programs itself—can probably be increased through program/offender matching in future rehabilitation efforts.

The differences between the more skeptical and more sanguine individuals are complex and can only partly be traced to technical factors such as differing units of analysis,[9] differing standards of evidence, differing approaches to synthesizing as well as generalizing various findings from within and across studies, etc. They seem to be partly experiential and philosophical as well. For the most part, these differences — especially the latter two — will probably long remain, even though the former (the technically centered) will doubtlessly be narrowed quite a bit. Beyond this, disagreement exists as to when the results from a given study or *group* of studies should be used for various types and levels of policy recommendation, espeically if those results are positive. At a more basic yet related level, disagreement has clearly emerged as to what constitutes an adequately or well-researched study, one whose findings — whether positive or negative — can be considered valid and somewhat generalizable.

Given such differences and disagreements, it is significant that certain areas of agreement nonetheless exist. Basically, many "skeptics" and "sanguines" seem to believe that, to be effective with serious or multiple offenders, rehabilitation programs must be broader-based and more intensive than in the past. That is, given the often complex and interrelated problems, limitations, and attitudes of most such offenders, future programs will often have to use "multiple modality" approaches, e.g., simultaneous or successive combinations of vocational training, individual counseling, and perhaps others. Moreover, to achieve substantial rather than minimal impact, such approaches will have to be provided on a more intensive basis. One final area of agreement exists or is at least implied: program/offender matching. Here, a program's resources — multiple or otherwise, intensively provided or not — are organized and distributed according to the needs, interests, and limitations of the offender subgroups that are present; they are not applied to the *total* offender group in an indiscriminate, across-the-board manner. Taken together, these areas of agreement suggest that future programs should be more carefully adapted to the life circumstances and personal/interpersonal characteristics of offenders. This view has policy implications regardless of the exact content of those as well as present programs.

The truth regarding "effectiveness" may lie between the skeptical and more sanguine views — in fact, it probably does. Yet, however the effectiveness issue may finally devolve, the future of rehabilitation or habilitation programs will be neither dim nor dull; for one thing, not only direction but considerable room for improvement already exists. In any event, the above areas of agreement may reflect one important part of that truth, and future.

And regarding that future, three last points. First, rehabilitation need not be wedded to a medical model; it can proceed on the assumption that offenders, like nonoffenders, have positive potential which they can, should, and usually wish to use. Offenders need not be viewed as defective; and, like most nonoffenders, the vast majority are quite capable of recognizing the potential relevance to their lives of various forms of assistance, e.g., vocational training. To assume that offenders lack this ability or can seldom exercise or sustain it is to consider them defective or highly indifferent indeed — no less so, perhaps, than in a "medical model" itself. Along a related line, the fact that some or perhaps many offenders often play "treatment games" within or outside institutions does not mean that the majority do so or that they do so most of the time. [20]

Secondly, rehabilitation need not be linked to indeterminate sentencing; it can be implemented for — and by — offenders under conditions of determinate sentencing, with or without written contracts.

Finally, rehabilitation or correctional intervention need not demean its participants or interfere with given reform movements. It can disassociate itself from the more questionable or undesirable practices of the past and can be integrated with numerous justice system concerns and legitimate strivings of the present and future. Correctional intervention can operate in a framework of humane interaction and exchange despite the unavoidable need, outside and inside the system, for some degree of social control. By building on its past *successes*, be these "many" or "few," it can eventually regain its place and recognition (this time on more solid grounds) as one more useful tool — another option for society and offenders alike. [5; 20]

Notes

[1]Though punishment — temporary confinement, withdrawal-of-privileges, added restrictions, etc. — may well affect future behavior and adjustment, it is not part of a rehabilitation effort if used as an end in itself or as a means to such ends as revenge. However, if used in the context of focused, directed, and organized activities such as the above, e.g., if occasionally used to bolster given components by gaining the individual's attention, it may be considered part of rehabilitation. Nevertheless, the distinguishing features of most rehabilitation programs are those which have been designed to (1) change/modify the offender mainly through positive incentives and rewards, subtle and otherwise, or to (2) change/modify his life-circumstances and social opportunities by various pragmatic means.

[2]Perhaps arbitrarily, we are including only those methods whose "humaneness" is not open to serious, certainly widespread, question. At any rate, we are focusing on methods that basically utilize, develop, or redirect the powers and mechanisms of the individual's mind, not reduce, physically traumatize, disorganize, or devastate them, whether or not by mechanical means; the former may be called positive treatment programs (PTP's), the latter, drastic or traumatic rehabilitation approaches (DRA's). We are also excluding various methods — not infrequently used in other times and/or places — such as: mutilation or dismemberment; sterilization or castration; physical stigmatization (e.g., branding); public humiliation (e.g., via stock and pillory).

[3]That is, each *individual program* which is categorized as, say a "group counseling" *method* represents a variation within the method.

[4]These individuals believe that the conclusions which were drawn from several hundred studies conducted during 1945-1978 (mainly 1960-1975) were justified either in terms of a preponderance-of-evidence standard or, somewhat more strongly, beyond a reasonable doubt; at least, this applied to the conclusions from numerous studies that yielded positive results. In any event, they regard the latter conclusions as scientifically supportable even though the individual study designs were indeed far from flawless and the conclusions were therefore not justified with almost absolute certainty (as the NAS Panel would have preferred), i.e., virtually beyond the *shadow* of a doubt. Moreover, they believe it would be inappropriate and certainly peculiar to dismiss the similar or converging evidence regarding given program approaches and program components that was observed *across* many such positive-outcome studies — studies which they feel had defensible research designs and that involved at least adequate program implementation.

[5]Romig, while accepting this view, believes one should go beyond it — to "truly individualized treatment." [23] Thus, he supports but does not identify with DI per se. (It might be noted that individualization is a relative term.)

[6]Regarding the question of (1) which offenders are usually more amenable than others? and (2) which approaches seem to work for whom? BTA and/or DI proponents and supporters generally believe that results from various studies, i.e., *across* studies, are more consistent than inconsistent and show greater convergence than scatter. At any rate, they believe the consistency and convergence is substantial and revealing, and that it — in some respects, an expression of partial replication — partly compensates for less-than-flawless research designs. On this latter point, "the importance of scientific replication does not negate that of unusually impressive [e.g., virtually flawless] individual studies. However, the latter value can hardly substitute for the former..." Thus, for example, one unusually impressive study which, say, "focused on particular treatment inputs and involved specific operating conditions" would not necessarily be seen, by most DI proponents, as outweighing "several acceptable [or perhaps high-quality] studies which, collectively, may have covered a wider range of treatment inputs and operating conditions."[20]

[7]The reason for substantially differing estimates is somewhat unclear. At any rate, the many programs-estimates generally range from 30% to 55% and were obtained not just from reviews which did, but from others which did not, include the following among their sample-of programs: those for which positive results were reported either for the total target group or only for a major subgroup within the total group. When the latter were included, estimates were only slightly higher than when they were not. An explanation for the differing estimates may partly lie in the fact that the various reviewers seldom focused on an identical or even nearly identical set of programs. Beyond that, they used somewhat different definitions of success.

[8]Included, here, was 42% of *LMW's* pool of positive- and negative-outcome studies combined. These 42% comprised four-fifths of all programs which — based on a behavioral, not just a policy-related index such as revocation or discharge — had reduced recidivism by *any* amount, i.e., by 1% or more. (Again, programs that reduced recidivism by less than 10% — via, by 1-9% — were *not* considerred positive-outcome studies in this as well as in most reviews and

evaluations; if these programs *had* been included in the present analysis, the 32% recidivism-reduction figure would have dropped to 26%). Most of the 42% showed a statistically significant difference (.05 level) between the total target group and its control or comparison group. *LMW* had categorized many studies from within this 42% group as high-quality, not just adequate-quality. [14; 20]
⁹For example, an emphasis on either (1) broadly categorized treatment methods only (in effect, treatment-*types* or types of individual programs—as in Martinson, pre-1978). (2) overall programs, i.e., individual programs, viewed as undifferentiated entities, (3) program components within the overall program, or (4) similar program components or common factors that are found *across* numerous overall programs.

References

[1] Adams, S. "Evaluative research in corrections: status and prospects." *Federal Probation, 38(1)*, (1974): 14-21.

[2] Allinson, R. "Martinson attacks his own earlier work," In: *Criminal Justice Newsletter, 9*, (December, 1978): 4.

[3] Bailey, W. "Correctional outcome: An evaluation of 100 reports." *J. Criminal Law, Criminology, and Police Science.* 57, (1966): 153-160.

[4] Conrad, J. "Research and developments in corrections: A thought experiment," *Federal Probation, 46(2)*, (1982): 66-69.

[5] Cullen, F. and Gilbert, K. *Reaffirming Rehabilitation.* Cincinnati, Ohio: Anderson Publishing Co. 1982.

[6] Empey, L. *American Delinquency: Its Meaning and Construction.* Homewood, Ill.: Dorsey, 1978.

[7] Gendreau, P. and Ross, R. *Effective Correctional Treatment.* Toronto: Butterworths. 1980.

[8] Glaser, D. "Achieving better questions: A half-century's progress in correctional research." *Federal Probation, 39*, (1975): 3-9.

[9] Gottfredson, M., Mitchell-Hersfeld, S., and Flanagan, T. "Another look at the effectiveness of parole supervision." *J. of Research in Crime and Delinquency, 19(2)*, (1982): 277-298.

[10] Greenberg, D. "The correctional effects of corrections: A survey of evaluations." In: Greenberg, D. (ed.) *Corrections and Punishment.* Beverly Hills, Calif.: Sage Publications. 1977. 111-148.

[11] Hunt, D. *Matching Models in Education.* Toronto: Ontario Institute for Studies in Education. 1971.

[12] Jesness, C. *The Preston Typology Study: Final Report.* Sacramento: California Youth Authority. 1969.

[13] Johnson, S. "Differential classification and treatment: The case against us." *The Differential View, 11*, (1982): 7-18.

[14] Lipton, D., Martinson, R., and Wilks, J. *The Effectiveness of Correctional Treatment: A Survey of Treatment Evaluation Studies.* New York: Praeger. 1975.

[15] Martin, S., Sechrest, L., and Redner, R. *New Directions in the Rehabilitation of Criminal Offenders.* Washington, D.C.: The National Academy Press. 1981.

[16] Martinson, R. "California research at the crossroads." *Crime and Delinquency, 22,* (1976): 180-191.

[17] _____. "Symposium on sentencing. Part II." *Hofstra Law Review, 7(2),* Winter, 1979): 243-258.

[18] _____. "What works? — questions and answers about prison reform." *The Public Interest, 35,* (Spring, 1974): 22-54.

[19] Megargee, E., Bohn, M. Jr., Meyer, J. Jr., and Sink, F. *Classifying Criminal Offenders: A New System Based on the MMPI.* Beverly Hills, Calif.: Sage Publishers, Inc. 1979.

[20] Palmer, T. *Correctional Intervention and Research: Current Issues· and Future Prospects.* Lexington, Mass.: Lexington Books, 1978.

[21] _____. "Martinson revisited." *J. of Research in Crime and Delinquency, 12,* (1975): 133-152.

[22] Quay, H. and Parsons, L. *The Differential Behavior Classification of the Juvenile Offender.* Morgantown, West Virginia: Robert F. Kennedy Youth Center. 1970.

[23] Romig, D. *Justice for Our Children.* Lexington, Mass.: Lexington Books. 1978.

[24] Sechrest, L., White, S., and Brown, E. *The Rehabilitation of Criminal Offenders: Problems and Prospects.* Washington, D.C.: The National Academy of Sciences. 1979.

[25] Warren, M. "Classification of offenders as an aid to efficient management and effective treatment." *J. Criminal Law, Criminology, and Police Science, 62,* (1971): 239-258.

[26] Wilson, J. "What works?" revisited: New findings on criminal rehabilitation." *The Public Interest, 61,* (Fall, 1980): 3-17.

[27] Wright, W., and Dixon, M. "Juvenile delinquency prevention: A review of evaluation studies." *J. of Research in Crime and Delinquency, 14(1),* (1977): 35-67.

21

Correctional Treatment
Some Recommendations for Effective Intervention
Paul Gendreau
Robert R. Ross

Martinson's well-publicized conclusion that in correctional rehabilitation "almost nothing works" (Martinson, 1974) touched off a debate that preoccupied the criminal justice system for more than a decade. Although there were a few dissenters who rejected the validity of Martinson's castigation of correctional treatment programs, there appeared to be a widespread endorsement of the view that treatment of the offender is an ineffective response to delinquent or criminal behavior. Proclamations about the apparent lack of evidence of the efficacy of correctional treatment undoubtedly have had major repercussions throughout the field of criminal justice (cf. Empey, 1979). Correctional managers, faced with dwindling budgets, have been loathe to expend funds on treatment programs which, they were told,

Source: *Juvenile and Family Court Journal*, Vol. 34 (Winter 1983-1984), 31-39.
Reprinted with the permission of the publisher.

had little likelihood of success. Academicians and policy-makers disenchanted with correctional rehabilitation models or "medical" models which, they were told, had failed to live up to their extravagant promises, became enamoured with alternative models. Radical nonintervention (Schur, 1973), justice-as-fairness (Fogel, 1979), and deterrence (Tullock, 1974) along with a succession of others attracted loyal disciples eagerly seeking new panaceas. Perhaps the most significant effect of the "nothing works" proclamation was the promotion of a pervasive cynicism and feeling of hopelessness among correctional workers who were reminded again and again that their efforts at offender rehabilitation were of no value.

A further consequence of Martinson's "almost nothing works" assertion was that it motivated some researchers to reexamine the evidence for and against treatment effectiveness. Notable among these researchers was Ted Palmer (1975: 1978) who rejected Martinson's broad indictment of correctional programs by reference to evidence that Martinson himself had reported (and disregarded). Many of the programs that Martinson had reviewed actually were quite successful! Palmer's "revelation" was given short shrift in the debate on treatment effectiveness which unfortunately deteriorated into polemic and name-calling, becoming little concerned with more substantive matters, and less objective (Gendreau & Ross, 1979).

Recently, however, there appears to be a growing recognition that the "almost nothing works" credo is invalid. The evidence continues to mount that some programs *do* work and work well (Andrews, 1980: Gendreau & Ross, 1979, Peters, 1981). Even the most vociferous and persuasive proponent of the anti-treatment camp, Martinson recently acknowledged publicly that he could have been in error in his conclusion that correctional treatment was impotent (cf. Serrill, 1975; Martinson & Wilks, 1977). In our recent review of the published literature between 1973 and 1979 we found convincing evidence that some correctional programs significantly reduce recidivism (Gendreau & Ross, 1979). A number of these programs have been presented with additional follow-up data in a recent book (Ross & Gendreau, 1980).

In our view, the debate on correctional effectiveness should no longer focus on *whether* treatment programs are effective. That should now be viewed as an overly simplistic question. A more meaningful question which should now be addressed is *which* programs work. Equally important, questions should be asked about *why* some programs work and some do not.

The question of which programs work was addressed in previous publications which identified a substantial number of effective treatment programs (Gendreau & Ross, 1979; Ross & Gendreau, 1980). In this paper, we present a preliminary answer to the second question by discussing the characteristics of effective programs and suggesting some of the reasons why other programs fail.

It is not yet possible to speak with absolute assuredness about the essential ingredients of effective correctional programs but our examination of successful programs does suggest some guidelines which may help managers and policy-makers in the field of delinquency.

Effective Programs

Evaluation

The first characteristic of an effective program is not really a characteristic of the program per se, but of the evaluation of the program. Most of the recent successful programs we identified, were conducted in methodologically impressive research. Of the studies, 33 percent employed true experimental designs with random assignment of subjects. Twenty-three percent employed a variety of baseline comparisons. Twenty-five percent used matched comparison groups. Clearly there has been a major improvement in the quality of research on the outcome of correction intervention. Hackler's (1972, p. 346) "well-known law" of delinquency program research asserts that "the more carefully you evaluate a program, the greater the probability that it will show little effect" is simply incorrect. The quality of program evaluation in the correctional treatment area is now in many cases far superior to the evaluation of other correctional approaches including deterrence (Gendreau & Ross, 1981).

Magnitude and Persistence of Effects

The effectiveness of programs has been demonstrated in a wide variety of correctional areas with both juvenile and adult offenders. Whereas the majority are community-based, remarkably successful programs have also been conducted in various institutional settings. The type of offenders involved range from pre-delinquents to sophisticated hard-core offenders and recidivistic adult criminal heroin addicts. Major reductions in recidivism have been demonstrated ranging in well controlled studies from 30-60 percent (e.g., Alexander & Parsons, 1973; Chandler, 1973; Lee & Haynes, 1980; Phillips et al., 1973; Ross & McKay, 1976; Walter & Mills, 1979). These are by no means short-term effects. Substantial beneficial results have been reported in follow-ups as much as three to 15 years after treatment! (e.g., Blakely, Davidson, & Saylor, 1980; Sarason, 1978; Shore & Massimo, 1979).

Program Conceptualization

The successful programs appear to share a number of characteristics that distinguish them from their less successful counterparts. We found no evidence of the effectiveness of programs which were derived from the medical (disease) or the clinical sociology model of criminology. Rather the majority of successful programs were based on a social learning model of criminal conduct (cf. Bandura, 1979; Nettler, 1978; Nietzel, 1979). In some instances, the intervention was in accord with specific assumptions of Differential Association Theory (Andrews, 1980; Burgess & Akers, 1966), developed not from assumptions about delinquents' psychopathology, but from assumptions about their clients' cognitive or social skills. Most attempted to broaden their social perceptions or their repertoire of adaptive behaviors rather than attempting to cure some underlying emotional disorder.

Program Types

Disappointing, of course, to panacea-seekers is the fact that no one therapeutic modality can be associated with success. The intervention techniques of successful programs vary greatly. They include family therapy, contingency contracting, behavioral counseling, role-playing and modeling, vocational and social skills training, interpersonal cognitive problem-solving training, and peer-oriented behavioral programs. All effective programs are, in fact, multi-facetted. The superiority of any one technique is yet to be demonstrated.

Program Components

Although the identification of the essential parameters of successful intervention is still in its infancy, much has been learned from some of the successful intervention research programs. In particular, the studies of Andrews & Kiessling (1980, p. 445, 446) are exemplary in this regard. They examined factors associated with effective supervision and counseling of probationers and identified five sets of conditions which influence the outcome of intervention: (a) authority — where rules and or formal legal sanctions are clearly spelled out; (b) anti-criminal modeling and reinforcement — where the development of pro-social and anti-criminal attitudes, cognitions and behaviors are engendered and reinforced by appropriate modeling of pro-social behavior; (c) problem-solving — the client is assisted in coping with personal or social difficulties, particularly in the instances where they relate to fostering attitudes which have led him to experience pro-social behavior; (d) use of community resources; (e) quality of interpersonal relationship — an effective relationship consists of empathy, and the establishment of open communication and trust.

Our examination of successful programs suggests that each incorporates at least some of the factors identified by Andrews & Kiesling. As would be expected, there does exist considerable variation among successful programs in terms of the factors they emphasize. For example, Platt, Perry, & Metzger (1980) focussed on interpersonal problem-solving, whereas Lee & Haynes (1980) stressed the quality of interpersonal relationships and Ross & McKay (1976) emphasized an anti-criminal modeling and reinforcement approach.

Unsuccessful Programs

As we develop our knowledge about the types of programs that have a reasonable guarantee of success we also are acquiring insight as to the characteristics of programs and practices which are likely to fail.

Andrews (1979) has critically reviewed the studies of counseling programs in the correctional area. He found that counseling procedures which depend primarily on open communication "friendship" models, are non-directional, or involve self-help groups in which the offenders themselves are in charge of the program, typically have either had negligible effects or actually increase illegal behavior. A number of studies support this conclusion (e.g., Craft, Stephenson, & Granger, 1964; Fenton, 1960; Grant & Grant, 1959; Kassebaum, Ward, & Wilner, 1971). One implication of this observation is that with offender populations, trust, positive regard, warmth and empathy, though they may be necessary are simply not sufficient in themselves to effect change. Anti-criminal program components (verbalizations, contracting or modeling, etc.) must be an integral part of the successful intervention, or else the "good relationship" will be less than effective. The Ross & McKay (1976) study illustrates this point. Their program clearly communicated respect and trust for their institutionalized chronic delinquents and utilized a peer therapist procedure. However, central to the intervention and a key to its success was a programmatic structure which was deliberately established to yield pressure towards pro-social behavior rather than anti-social behavior. The delinquents were directed towards responsible behavior which persuaded them that they were, in fact, pro-social individuals. Attempts to replicate this program by providing only the peer self-help aspects of the program were dramatically unsuccessful (Ross & McKay, 1979).

Behavior modification programs have enjoyed both impressive success and dramatic failure in corrections. The differences between those which have "worked" and those which have not are relatively clear. Reviews of this literature (Ross & McKay, 1978; Emery &

Marholin, 1977) pointed out that many programs should never have been expected to succeed because they really never operationalized behavioral principles in their practices. They were operant conditioning programs in name only. Others completely distorted or bastardized the behavioral principles or attempted to change behaviors which had little relevance to the clients' anti-social or delinquent behavior. Ross & McKay's (1978) review revealed that unsuccessful programs had the following features: (a) they were imposed on the offenders who were never involved in the development of the program; (b) the target behavior; (c) they failed to neutralize or utilize in a positive way the offenders' peer group. The successful behavior modification programs behavior; (c) they failed to neutralize or utilize in a positive way the offenders peer group. The successful behavior modification programs (cf. Hoefler, 1975; Davidson & Robinson 1975) avoided or minimized these negative elements.

As we noted earlier, programs based on a "medical-model" disease conception of anti-social behavior (cf. Balch, 1975) have not been fruitful. Whether the disease is some form of psychopathology or biological deficit (e.g., extra chromosomes), we have not found one well controlled positive report (Ross & Gendreau, 1980), although Hippchen (1976), among others, states that alleviating nutritional chemical deficiencies of delinquents, reduces anti-social behavior. Unfortunately, studies purporting to support this view (e.g., Von Hilsheimer, Philpott, Buckely & Klotz, 1977) have been lacking in adequate controls.

Intervention programs based on a deterrence model were once proclaimed quite frequently (cf. Martinson, 1976) to be the "cureall" for combating crime but the most recent evidence has provided a very sobering experience for deterrence proponents. Although there is the occasional study attesting to effective deterrence on a large societal scale for the short-term (Gendreau & Surridge, 1978) or for a certain crime in a specific area (Schnelle, Kirchner, McRae, McNees, Eck, Snodgrass, Casey, & Uselton, 1978), there are many more studies showing mixed, if not negligible effects (cf. Blumstein, Cohen, & Nagin, 1978; Gendreau & Ross, 1981). Moreover, some studies indicate that deterrence programs were associated with increased offending (Critelli & Crawford, Jr., 1980; Erickson, 1977; Hart, 1978). The lack of evidence of effective deterrence may not entirely reflect the inadequacy of the deterrence model per se but shortcomings in its application. Attempts at applying the deterrence model have generally been so poorly conceptualized that no firm conclusions about the efficacy of deterrence could be reached (cf. Zimring, 1978). Moreover, there are profound and, perhaps, unresolvable methodological problems in deterrence research (cf. Gendreau & Ross, 1981) mitigating against finding easy, simplistic answers in the near future. Nevertheless, deterrence research should not be abandoned as there may be payoffs in considering how specific deterrence and treatment techniques can interact to produce effective intervention. The Hayes (1973) and Walter & Mills (1979) studies are two examples of this type of approach to intervention.

Confronting the Issues

Our review of the treatment research literature has confirmed that there are programs which can and have reduced recidivism and some which have not and probably cannot. However, we are not naive enough to assume that correctional agents and agencies will rush to replicate these successful programs nor will there be a marked modification of correctional policy in light of this recent positive evidence. There are any number of reasons for this despairing reality, one of these being that we are far from being an experimenting society (cf. Campbell, 1969; Tavris, 1975) at least in the criminal justice system. We seem neither to learn from our successes or failures, which is one characteristic we appear to share with the offenders we deal with—the failure to profit from experience. As we have documented previously (cf. Gendreau & Ross, 1981; Ross & McKay, 1978) pana-ceaphalia and negativism run rampant throughout the field. Fads are too enthusiastically embraced.

These characteristics are not, of course, indigenous to the criminal justice system; elements of this kind of thinking can be found in other applied fields where ready answers to complex problems have not been forthcoming. Likely, as the criminal justice system matures these characteristics will gradually extinguish. However, presently there are four issues that we feel are particularly crucial and must be urgently addressed. Failure to take a comprehensive view of the behavioral literature, the lack of therapeutic integrity, the neglect of differential treatment, and the failure to assess and examine the system itself can only lead to negative consequences.

Comprehensive View of the Literature

While the study of criminology purports to be a multi-disciplinary endeavor, in actual fact, the proponents of various positions have rarely taken the broad, well-informed view. The debate over rehabilitation centered on literature published before 1967 and various reviews (purportedly to settle the issue) have been highly selective and/or ignored large bodies of relevant material (Gendreau & Ross, 1979, p. 464-465). As Andrews (1980) incisively noted, the popularity of clinical sociology (Cressey, 1955) has never undergone any kind of thorough scrutiny whatsoever, as proponents of the model failed to test their assumptions and remained blind to the behavioral evolution that occurred outside their discipline. We have reported on a similar phenomenon occurring amongst deterrence proponents who have virtually ignored the fact that weaknesses in their model and theory building are in part due to a profound ignorance of basic experimental psychology (e.g., Carroll, 1978; Walters & Grusic, 1977) that directly touches upon their concerns.

In our opinion, the long term consequences of failing to take an informed view has led to some of the barren theorizing that has characterized the criminal justice field. Only by ignoring the relevant literature, could one comfortably arrive at the policy positions characterized by the radical criminology, or radical non-intervention (Schur, 1973) or just desert models (Fogel, 1979). The former demands a wrenching radical change in Western society; the second (in some cases) suggests programs that have a good chance of increasing recidivism (Andrews, 1980, p. 449) and the latter theory besides demanding "justice-as-fairness" sounds the cheerful note that outside of killing people we cannot stop people from committing crimes (e.g., Fox, 1974).

Therapeutic Integrity

The major issue in service delivery has centered about the lack of quality and intensity of the service delivery systems developed to date. For example, "to what extent do treatment personnel actually adhere to the principles and employ the techniques of therapy they purport to provide? To what extent are the treatment staff competent? How hard do they work? How much is treatment diluted in the correctional environment so that it becomes treatment in name only?" (Gendreau & Ross, 1979, p. 467). As Quay (1977) and Sechrest et al. (1979) have reported, the above questions are rarely answered positively in delinquency intervention research.

This sort of problem, unfortunately, is not one of history. It still occurs. In the recent review of behavioral contracting programs with delinquents, Peters (1981) reported that "the single most important contributing factor to the success or failure of the programs is that quantity and quality of supervision provided to the therapists as they implement the programs..."

Differential Treatment

The potential of treatment programs has also been dismissed by those who naively require that in order for program effectiveness to be established, it must be demonstrated across-the-board with *all* offenders. It seems reasonable to think that in correctional programming, as in every other human enterprise, the effect of an action will depend upon the individual to whom the action is applied and the situation in which it occurs. A program which is effective with some offenders may not be so with other offenders. There are no cure-alls nor should we expect there ever will be. Thankfully, the failure to consider differential treatment effects is becoming less common in the delinquency literature (cf. Glaser, 1975; Warren, 1977). The majority of the effective programs examine individual differences and their interactions with treatment variables. They are crucial to assessing the value of employment programs (e.g., Andrews & Kiessling, 1980; Andrews, Wormith, Daigle-Zinn, Kennedy & Nelson, 1980: Jessness, 1975) and community-based and family therapy programs (e.g., Alexander, Barton, Schiavo & Parsons, 1976; O'Donnell & Fo, 1976).

Differential tretment is not a mere "will of the wisp" phenomenon as Martinson (1976) argued.

System Variables

Chaneles (1976) has noted that a very small percentage of correctional budgets are spent on offender programs. Berk & Rossi (1976) have pointed out that so many bureaucratic and political constraints have been placed on programs that their potential effectiveness is often neutralized. A great deal of the criticism of treatment programs should more properly be directed to criticizing the failure of program managers to attend to how system variables impinge on the program to influence its impact. There have been a few individual accounts (e.g., Rappaport, Seidman & Davidson, 1979; Reppuci, Sarata, Saunders, McArthur & Michlin, 1973) of how program policies in and of themselves can affect outcome. But we need more concentrated efforts at systems analysis linking (a) setting factors — the physical and social structure of the program, (b) process and content of intervention, (c) intermediate targets, e.g., attitude change and (d) recidivism and cost-benefit (e.g., Andrews & Kiessling, 1980, p. 443). We need to examine how variables affecting the implementation of service systems affect outcome.

Finally, correctional administrators have sensed for a long time that political expediencies often prevent the network of social service systems from functioning harmoniously so as to deliver services efficiently (e.g., McDougall, 1976). The extent to which this has happened has been ignored. Even in correctional and social service systems reported to be affluent and progressive, the system operates inefficiently in service delivery. Very often few offenders and their families recieve services outside of the criminal justice system (Gendreau, Madden & Leipciger, 1979). A few successful intervention programs have bridged this gap (See Gendreau & Ross, 1979, p. 488), but in most cases the services are simply not there or are not oriented towards offenders (Peters, 1981)—a reality that has escaped proponents of the advocacy-broker model and "leave the children alone" approach (Dell'Apa, Adams, Jorgenson & Sigurdson, 1976) of service delivery.

The systems and operations research must be drastically increased if any of our successful programs are to be entrenched and we are to even remotely approximate our claims as the experimenting society.

Conclusion

There are correctional programs that are effective. They can be distinguished from unsuccessful programs. There are perfectly good reasons why, in spite of our knowledge of what kinds of programs work, only limited success has been achieved to date, and it is within our means to be constructive in this regard. Admittedly, there are crime problems that go beyond the pale of what is possible given our current acceptance of what is possible given our current acceptance of what we construe to be moral and ethical correctional intervention (Gendreau & Ross, 1980, p. 25). Nevertheless, the majority of offender problems are well within bounds of our means to implement programs that work.

References

Alexander, J.F., Barton, C., Schiavo, R.S., and Parsons, B.V. Systems—Behavioral Intervention with Families Behavior and Outcome. *Journal of Consulting—Clinical Psychology*, 1976, 44, 656-664.

Alexander, J.F. and Parsons, R.J. Short-term Behavioral Intervention with Delinquent Families: Impact on Family Process and Recidivism. *Journal of Abnormal Psychology*, 1973, 81, 219-225.

Andrews, D.A. The Friendship Model of Voluntary Action and Controlled Evaluations of Correctional Practices: Notes on Relationships with Behavior Theory and Criminology. Toronto: Ministry of Correctional Services, 1979.

Andrews, D.A. Some Experimental Investigations of the Principles of Differential Association Through Deliberate Manipulations of the Structure of Service Systems. *American Sociological Review*, 1980, 45, 448-462.

Andrews, D.A. and Kiessling, J.J. Program Structure and Effective Correctional Practices: A Summary of the CAVIC Research. In R.R. Ross and P. Gendreau (eds.) *Effective Correctional Treatment*. Toronto: Butterworths, 1980.

Andrews, D.A., Wormith, J.S., Daigle-Zinn, W.J., Kennedy, D.J., and Nelson, S. Low and High Functioning Volunteers in Group Counseling with Anxious and Non-Anxious Prisoners: The Effects of Interpersonal Skills on Group Process and Attitude Change. *Canadian Journal or Criminology*, 1980, 22, 443-456.

Balch, R.W. The Medical Model of Delinquency: Theoretical, Practical, and Ethical Implications. *Crime and Delinquency*, 1975, 21, 116-129.

Bandura, A. The Social Learning Perspective: Mechanisms of Aggression. In H. Toch (ed.) *Psychology of Crime and Justice* (Copyright (c) 1979) reissued 1986 Waveland Press, Inc., Prospect Heights, IL.

Berk, R.A. and Rossi, P.H. Doing Good or Worse: Evaluation Research Politically Re-examined. *Social Problems*, 1976, 23, 337-349.

Blakely, C.H., Davidson, W.S., Saylor, C.A., and Robinson, M.J. Kentfields, Rehabilitation Program: Ten Years Later. In R.R. Ross and P. Gendreau (eds.) *Effective Correctional Treatment*. Toronto: Butterworths, 1980.

Blumstein, A., Cohen, J., and Nagin, D. (eds.) *Deterrence and Incapacitation: Estimating the Effects of Criminal Sanctions on Crime Rates*. Washington, DC: *National Academy of Sciences*, 1978.

Burgess, R.L. and Akers, R.L. A Differential Association-Reinforcement Theory of Criminal Behavior. *Social Problems*, 1966, 14, 128-147.

Campbell, D.T. Reforms as Experiments. *American Psychologist*, 1969, 24, 409-428.

Carroll, J.S. A Psychological Approach to Deterrence: The Evaluation of Crime Opportunities. *Journal of Personality and Social Psychology*, 1978, 36, 1512-1520.

Chandler, M.J. Egocentrism and Antisocial Behavior: The Assessment and Training of Social Perspective-Taking Skills. *Developmental Psychology*, 1973, 9, 326-333.

Chaneles, S. Prisoners can be Rehabilitated Now. *Psychology Today*, 1976, 10, 129-133.

Cratt, M., Stephenson, G., and Granger, C.A. A Controlled Trial of Authoritarian and Self-governing Regimes with Adolescent Psychopaths. *American Journal of Orthopsychiatry*, 1964, 34, 543-554.

Cressey, D.R. Changing Criminals: The Application of the Theory of Differential Association. *American Journal of Sociology*, 1955, 61, 116-120.

Critelli, J.W. and Crawford, R.F. The Effectiveness of Court-Ordered Punishment: Fines Versus Punishment. *Criminal Justice and Behavior*, 1980, 7, 465-470.

Davidson, W.D. and Robinson, M.J. Community Psychology and Behavior Modification: A Community-Based Program for the Prevention of Delinquency. *Corrective and social Psychiatry*, 1975, 21, 1-12.

Dell'Apa, F., Adams, W.T., Jorgenson, J.D.D. and Sigurdson, H.R. Advocacy, Brokerage, Community: The ABC's of Probation and Parole. *Federal Probation*, 1976, 40, 37-44.

Emery, R.E. and Marholin II, D. An Applied Behavior Analysis of Delinquency: The Irrelevancy of Relevant Behavior. *American Psychologist*, 1977, 32, 860-873.

Empey, I.T. From Optimism to Despair: New Doctrines in Juvenile Justice. In C.A. Murry and I.A. Cox, Jr. *Beyond Probation: Juvenile Corrections and the Chronic Delinquent*. Beverly Hills, CA: Sage, 1979.

Erickson, M.L., Gibbs, J.P. and Jensen, G.F. The Deterrence Doctrine and the Perceived Certainty of Legal Punishments. *American Sociological Review*, 1977, 42, 305-317.

Fenton, N. Group Counselling in Correctional Practice. *Canadian Journal of Corrections*, 1960, 2, 229-239.

Fogel, D. *We Are the Living Proof: The Justice Model for Corrections*. Cincinnati: Anderson, 1979.

Fox, S.J. The Reform of Juvenile Justice: The Child's Right to Punishment. *Juvenile Justice*, 1974, 25, 2-9.

Gendreau, P. and Andrews, D.A. *Psychological Consultant*. New York: Grune & Stratton, 1979.

Gendreau, P., Madden, P., and Leipciger, M. *Norms and Recidivism* Rates for Social History and Institutional Experience of First Incarcerate: Implications for Programming. *Canadian Journal of Criminology*, 1979, 21, 416-441.

Gendreau, P., and Ross, R.R. Effective Correctional Treatment: Bibliotherapy for Cynics. *Crime and Delinquency*, 1979, 25, 463-489.

Gendreau, P., and Ross, R.R. Effective Corrections Treatment: Bibliotherapy for Cynics. In R.R. Ross and P. Gendreau (eds.) *Effective Correctional Treatment*. Toronto: Butterworths, 1980.

Gendreau, P., and Ross, R.R. Correctional Potency: Treatment and Deterrence on Trial. In R. Roesch and R. Corrado (eds.) *Evaluation Research and Policy in Criminal Justice*. Beverly Hills: Sage, 1981.

Gendreau, P., and Ross, R.R. Prescriptions for Successful Intervention. Manuscript under review, 1981.

Gendreau, P., and Ross, R.R. Getting Serious about the Deterrence of Offenders: Problems and prospects. Manuscript under review, 1981.

Gendreau, P., and Surridge, C.T. Controlling Gun Crimes: The Jamaican Experience. *International Journal of Criminology and Penology*, 1978, 6, 43-60.

Glaser, D. Achieving Better Questions: A Half-century's Progression in Correctional Research. *Federal Probation*, 1975, 39, 3-9.

Grant, J.D., and Grant, M.Q. A Group Dynamics Approach to the Treatment of Non-Conformists in the Navy. *Annals of the American Academy of Political and Social Science*, 1959, 322, 126-135.

Hackler, J.C. *The Prevention of Youthful Crime: The Great Stumble Forward*. Toronto: Methuen, 1978.

Hart, R.J. Crime and Punishment in the Army. *Journal of Personality and Social Psychology*, 1978, 36, 1456-1471.

Hayes, S.N. Contingency Management in a Municipally-Administered Antiabuse Program for Alcoholics. *Journal of Behavior Therapy and Experimental Psychiatry*, 1973, 4, 31-32.

Hippchen, L.J. Biomedical Approaches to Offender Rehabilitation. *Offender Rehabilitation*, 1976, 17, 115-123.

Hoetler, S.A., and Bornstein, Ph. H. Achievement Place: An Evaluative Review. *Criminal Justice and Behavior*, 1975, 2, 146-168.

Jeffrey, R., and Woolpert, S. Work Furlough as an Alternative to Incarceration: An assessment of its Effects on Recidivism and Social Cost. *Journal of Criminal Law and Criminology*, 1974, 65, 405-415.

Jessness, C.F. Comparative Effectiveness of Behavior Modification and Transactional Analysis Programs for Delinquents. *Journals of Consulting and Clinical Psychology*, 1975, 43, 758-779.

Kassebaum, G., Ward, D., and Wilner, D. *Prison Treatment and Parole Survival: An Empirical Assessment.* New York: Wiley, 1971.

Lee, R., and Haynes, N.M. Project CREST and the Dual-Treatment Approach to Delinquency: Methods and Research Summarized. In R.R. Ross and P. Gendreau (eds.) *Effective Correctional Treatment.* Toronto: Butterworths, 1980.

Martinson, R. "What works? Questions and Answers About Prison Reform. *The Public Interest,* 1974, 35, 22-54.

Martinson, R. California Research at the Crossroads. *Crime Delinquency,* 1976, 22, 180-191.

Martinson, R.,and Wilks, J. Save Parole Supervision. *Federal Probation,* 1977, 41, 23-27.

McDougall, E.C. Corrections has not been tried. *Criminal Justice Review,* 1976, 1, 63-76.

Nettler, G. *Explaining Crime.* New York: McGraw-Hill, 1978.

Nietzel, M.T. *Crime and Its Modification: A Social Learning Perspective.* New York: Pergamon, 1979.

O'Donnell, C.R., and Fo, W.S.O. The Buddy System: Mediator-Target Locus of Control and Behavioral Outcome. *American Journal of Community Psychology,* 1976, 4, 161-166.

Phillips, E.L., Phillips, R.A., Fixsen, D.L., and Wolf, M.W. Behavior Shaping Works for Delinquents. *Psychology Today,* 1973, 6, 75-79.

Palmer, T. Martinson revisited. *Journal of Research in Crime and Delinquency,* 1975, 12, 133-152.

Palmer, T. *Correctional Intervention and Research.* Lexington, MA: Heath, 1978.

Peters, R. Deviant Behavioral Contracting with Conduct Problem Youth: A Review and Critical Analysis. Department of Psychology, Queen's University, Kingston, Ontario, 1981.

Platt, J.J., Perry, G.M., and Metzger, D.S. The Evaluation of a Heroin Addiction Treatment Program Within a Correctional Environment. In R.R. Ross and P. Gendreau (eds.) *Effective Correctional Treatment.* Toronto: Butterworths, 1980.

Quay, H.C. The Three Faces of Evaluation: What Can Be Expected to Work. *Criminal Justice and Behavior,* 1977, 4, 341-354.

Rappeport, J., Seidman, E., and Davidson II, W.S. Demonstration Research and Manifest Versus True Adoption: The Natural History of a Research Project. In R.F. Munoz, L.R. Snowden, and J.G. Kelly (eds.) *Social Psychological Research and Community Settings.* San Francisco: Jossey-Bass, 1979.

Repucci, N.D., Sarata, B.P., Saunders, J.T., McArthur, A.V., and Michlin, L.M. We Bombed in Mountville: Lessons Learned in Consultation to a Correctional Facility for Adolescent Offenders. In I.I. Goldenberg (ed.) *The Helping Professions in the World of Action.* Boston: D.C. Heath, 1973.

Ross, R.R. and Gendreau, P. *Effective Correctional Treatment.* Toronto: Butterworths, 1980.

Ross, R.R. and McKay, H.B. A Study of Institutional Treatment Programs. *International Journal of Offender Therapy and Comparative Criminology,* 1976, 20, 165-173.

Ross, R.R. and McKay, B. Treatment in Corrections: Requiem for a Panacea. *Canadian Journal of Criminology*, 1978, 120, 279-295.

Ross, R.R. and McKay, B. *Self-Mutilation*. Boston: Lexington, 1979.

Sarason, I.G. A Cognitive Social Learning Approach to Juvenile Delinquency. In R.D. Hare and D. Schalling (eds.) *Psychopathic Behaviour Approaches to Research*. New York: Wiley, 1978.

Schnelle, J.F., Kirchner, R.E., McRaie, J.E., McNees, M.P., Eck, R.H., Snotdgrass, S., Casey, J.D., and Uselton, P.H. Police Evaluation Research: An Experimental and Cost-Benefit Analysis of a Helicopter Patrol in a High Crime Area. *Journal of Applied Behavior Analysis*, 1978, 11, 11-21.

Schur, E.M. *Radical Nonintervention: Re-thinking the Delinquency Problem*. Englewood Cliffs: Prentice-Hall, 1973.

Sechrest, L., West, S.G., Phillips, M.A., Redner, R., and Yeaton, W. Some Neglected Problems in Evaluation Research: Strength is Integrity of Treatments. In L. Sechrest, S.G. West, M.A. Phillips, R. Redner and W. Yeaton, *Evaluation Studies Annual Review* (Vol. 4). Beverly Hills: Sage, 1979.

Sechrest, L., White, S.O., and Brown, G.D. (eds.) *The Rehabilitation of Criminal Offenders*. Washington, DC: National Academy of Sciences, 1979.

Serrill, M.S. Is Rehabilitation Dead? *Corrections Magazine*, 1975, 11, 3-12, 21-26.

Shore, M.F. and Massimo, J.L. Fifteen Years After Treatment: A Follow-up Study of Comprehensive Vocationally-oriented Psychotherapy. *American Journal of Orthopsychiatry*, 1979, 49, 240-245.

Tayris, C. The Experimenting Society: To Find Programs That Work, Government Must Measure its Failures. *Psychology Today*, 1975, 9, 47-56.

Tullock, G. Does Punishment Deter Crime: *Public Interest*, 1974, 35, 103-111.

Von Hilsheimer, G., Philpott, W., Buckley, W., and Klotz, S.D. Correcting the Incorrigible: A Report on 229 Incorrigible Adolescents. *American Laboratory*, 1977, 101, 197-218.

Walter, T.L., and Mills, C.M. A Behavioral-Employment Intervention Program for Reducing Juvenile Delinquency. In J.S. Stumphauzer (ed.) *Progress in Behavior Therapy with Delinquents*. Springfield, IL: Thomas, 1979.

Walters, G.C., and Grusec, J.E. *Punishment*. San Francisco: Freeman & Co., 1977.

Warren, M.Q. Correctional Treatment and Coercion: The Differential Effectiveness Perspective. *Criminal Justice and Behavior*, 1977, 4, 355-376.

Zimring, F.G. Policy Experiments in General Deterrence: 1970-75. In A. Blumstein, J. Cohen, and D. Ngain (eds.) *Deterrence and Incapacitation: Estimating the Effects of Criminal Sanctions on Crime Rates*. Washington, DC: National Academy of Sciences, 1978.

22

"What Works?" Revisited
New Findings on
Criminal Rehabilitation
James Q. Wilson

Few articles appearing in this magazine have been as widely reprinted or as frequently cited as Robert Martinson's "What Works? —Questions and Answers About Prison Reform," published in 1974. Its major conclusion has become familiar to almost everyone even casually interested in crime control programs: "*With few and isolated exceptions, the rehabilitative efforts that have been reported so far have had no appreciable effect on recidivism.*" For politicians as well as for scholars, the message seemed clear — nothing works. In fact, the article was careful to point out that there were, scattered through the 231 studies that were reviewed by Martinson and his co-workers, hints of *some* reductions in criminality for *some* kinds of offenders under *some* circumstances. But these hints did not constitute, even generously interpreted, a clear and consistent pattern of success on which a public policy might be based.

Source: Reprinted with permission of the author from *The Public Interest*, No. 61 (Fall 1980), 3-17, © 1980 by National Affairs, Inc.

There was little new in the 1974 article. In 1967, R.G. Hood had published in Europe a review that concluded that different ways of treating offenders generally led to similar, and not very encouraging, results. A year earlier, Walter C. Bailey published in this country a survey of 100 evaluations of correctional treatment programs that led him to the judgement that "evidence supporting the efficacy of correctional treatment is slight, inconsistent, and of questionable reliability." Indeed, such gloomy findings go back at least 30 years. In 1951, Edwin Powers and Helen Witmer reported on the results of the ambitious Cambridge-Somerville Youth Study, begun in 1939 as an effort to prevent delinquency by an intensive counselling program. Despite high hopes, they had to conclude that, by any measure, boys randomly assigned to counselling were as likely as similar boys left on their own to run afoul of the law.

Unlike these earlier studies, the Martinson article—based on a massive volume he had prepared in collaboration with Douglas Lipton and Judith Wilks—created a sensation. Partly it was the times: It appeared in the early 1970's, after the optimism of the Great Society had been dashed and the enthusiasms of the 1960's had moderated, but when politicians were still searching desperately for some response to the widespread public fear of street crime. Martinson did not discover that rehabilitation was of little value in dealing with crime so much as he administered a highly visible *coup de grace*. By bringing out into the open the long-standing scholarly skepticism about most rehabilitation programs, he prepared the way for a revival of an interest in the deterrent, incapacitative, and retributive purposes of the criminal justice system.

But it was not just the times. During the 1960's, there had developed in California a remarkable concentration of talent and energy devoted to finding and testing rehabilitation programs, especially ones designed to treat delinquents in the community. Marguerite Q. Warren, Ted Palmer, and others not only used advanced psychological testing to classify delinquents by personality type and employed skilled counsellors to provide intensive community supervision, they randomly assigned delinquents to the treatment and control groups in order to insure the best possible scientific evaluation of the results.

At first, these results were encouraging, so much so that the President's Commission on Law Enforcement and Administration of Justice, in its 1967 report to Lyndon Johnson, endorsed the Community Treatment Program (CTP) of the California Youth Authority, describing it as having reduced delinquency (as measured by parole revocation) from 52 percent among youth who were incarcerated before release to 28 percent among those given intensive counselling in the community.

The Martinson article was particularly critical of these claims. In their re-analysis of the California data, Lipton, Martinson, and Wilks concluded that Warren and her colleagues had substantially under-counted the number of offenses committed by the youth in the experimental community program. Apparently, probation officers assigned to these delinquents developed such close relations with their charges, and were so eager to see their program succeed, that they failed to report to the authorities a number of offenses committed by the experimentals, whereas youth assigned to the control groups had their offenses reported in the normal way by probation and parole authorities.

California Counterattacks

Given the resources devoted to the California project and the publicity it had received, it is hardly surprising that its leaders counter-attacked. Ted Palmer published in 1975 a rebuttal to the Martinson article, claiming that it overlooked or downplayed a number of success stories in the rehabilitation literature and that in particular it mis-represented the CTP. Palmer conceded that the youth in the experimental program had a number of offenses overlooked by counsellors, but argued that these were largely minor or technical violations, many of which were detected simply because the youth were under closer observation and some of which involved merely the failure to partici-pate regularly in the intensive supervision program. Moreover, the Martinson review ended in 1967; if it had continued through 1973, Palmer said, the differences between experimentals and controls, at least for serious offenses, would have been clear.

Martinson responded vigorously to this challenge, and the battle was joined. In the midst of the verbal pyrotechnics of Palmer and Martinson —they were nothing if not spirited adversaries—a new and, as it turned out, more weighty voice was heard. Paul Lerman, a Rutgers sociologist, published a book-length evaluation of the CTP (as well as of the California probation subsidy program) in which he concluded, after a painstaking analysis of the published data, that "the CTP did not have an impact on youth behavior that differed significantly from the impact of the control program."[1] Moreover, the "community" focus of the experimental program turned out to be somewhat exaggerated— in fact, the great majority of experimental youth were placed in detention at least once and many were detained repeatedly in order to maintain control over them. Indeed, the youth in the experimental "community" program were *more* likely to be sent to detention centers than the control group supervised by regular parole officers. Finally, Lerman found strong evidence that, though the CTP had tried to match experimental and control groups by randomly assigning youth to each, over the many years the program operated the two groups began to differ markedly in their characteristics as persons dropped out of the program for one reason or another. In particular, the experimental group came to be composed disproportionately of persons who were older, had higher IQ's, and were diagnosed as "neurotic" (rather than as "power-oriented"). This intriguing finding, largely buried in an appendix to the Lerman book, raises issues to which we shall return presently.

Lerman had made many of these points earlier, in a 1968 article; he made them more elaborately in the 1975 book. Curiously, Palmer, who continued to protest against the Martinson article, appears to have taken little notice, at least publicly, of the Lerman criticisms. Palmer's book-length attack on Martinson and his reassertion of the claims of the CTP appeared in 1978; there is no mention of Lerman in it.[2]

Enter the National Research Council

While the debate in correctional journals raged, the public view, insofar as one can assess it from editorials, political speeches, and legislative initiatives, was that Martinson was right. Because of this widespread belief that "nothing works," the National Research Council, the applied research arm of the prestigious National Academy of Sciences, created in 1977 a Panel on Research on Rehabilitative Techniques, chaired by Professor Lee Sechrest, then of the Department of Psychology of Florida State University. The Panel was charged with reviewing existing evaluations of rehabilitative efforts to see if they provided a basis for drawing any conclusions about the effectiveness of these efforts. Its first report—on efforts to rehabilitate in correctional institutions—was issued in 1979; a second report, on community rehabilitation, will appear later.

Owing to the importance in the public debate of the review by Lipton, Martinson, and Wilks (LMW), that book was made the focus of the Panel's attention.[3] In addition, the report examined reviews that analyzed studies appearing after 1968, the cutoff date for the LMW review. Among the papers commissioned by the Panel was a detailed re-analysis of a sample of the studies analyzed by LMW, carried out by two scholars not identified with the on-going debate, Stephen Fienberg and Patricia Grambsch.

The conclusion of the Panel is easily stated: By and large, Martinson and his colleagues were right. More exactly, "The Panel concludes that Lipton, Martinson, and Wilks were reasonably accurate and fair in their appraisal of the rehabilitation literature." If they erred at all, it was in being overly generous. They were sometimes guilty of an excessively lenient assessment of the methodology of a given study. Moreover, the evaluations published since 1968 provide little evidence to reverse this verdict. For example, David F. Greenberg's 1977 review of the more recent studies comes to essentially the same conclusion as Martinson. S.R. Brody's survey in England on the institutional treatment of juvenile offenders agrees.

The Panel looked in particular at Palmer's argument that nearly half the studies cited by Martinson showed a rehabilitative effect. The Panel was not persuaded: "Palmer's optimistic view cannot be supported, in large part because his assessment accepts at face value the claim of the original authors about effects they detected, and in too many instances those claims were wrong or were over-interpretations of data...." In any event, "we find little support for the charge that positive findings were overlooked."

The conclusion that Martinson was right does not mean that he or anyone else has proved that "nothing works," only that nobody has proved that "something works." There is always the chance, as the Panel noted, that rehabilitative methods now in use but not tested would, if tested, show a beneficial effect and that new methods yet to be tried will prove efficacious. (One such method will be discussed in a moment.)

Are Some Offenders Amenable to Treatment?

One unresolved issue is whether certain kinds of offenders are more amenable to rehabilitation than others. If this is the case, and if the amenable subjects are mixed together in a treatment group with non-amenable ones, then any reductions in criminality among the former might be masked by increases in criminality among the latter; the average (and misleading) result would be, "no change."

This view has been vigorously advanced by Daniel Glaser, among others. Writing in 1973, a year before the Martinson article appeared, he pointed to evidence from a variety of evaluative studies suggesting that certain kinds of offenders were especially amenable to rehabilitation. They tended to be persons who could easily communicate, who had not found their prior criminal career to be especially rewarding, and who had not been greatly disappointed by their efforts to find legitimate alternatives to crime. The CTP, for example, made explicit use of a psychological classification scheme designed to differentiate among delinquents on the basis of their "interpersonal maturity level" and their particular mode of behavior. One such group was classified as having a relatively high level of maturity, by which is meant the members had an internalized set of standards and some regard for the opinions of others, but displayed as well neurotic tendencies — either feelings of guilt and anxiety or a proclivity to "acting-out." The interpretation of the CTP data by Glaser, Palmer, and others was that these anxious, neurotic, guilt-stricken delinquents benefitted substantially from intensive counselling. Recognizing the criticisms already levelled by Lerman (in his 1968 article) at the CTP, Glaser felt that even allowing for counsellor bias the neurotics did substantially better in the treatment groups than they did when left alone in the control groups. Moreover, Glaser has argued that Lerman himself neglected the long-term effects of treatment on different types of delinquents.

If this is true, then those studies which show no change among treated offenders may include not only some "amenables" who commit less crime *but some non-amendables who actually commit more crimes as a result of the treatment.* And this is exactly what Palmer believed he found in the CTP data. In his 1978 book, he showed the monthly arrest rates for two kinds of offenders — the "conflicted" (by which he apparently means "neurotic") and the "power-oriented" (by which he seems to mean those delinquents who lack an internalized set of conventional standards and either manipulate others or identify with the norms of a deviant group). Neurotic delinquents in the treatment group had a lower monthly arrest rate than neurotics in the control group, both during the early stages of the program and four years after discharge. "Power-oriented" offenders in the treatment groups, on the other hand, had a *higher* arrest rate than the power-oriented controls four years after discharge. Glaser had surmised that this increase in criminality among power-oriented delinquents in the treatment program arises because they learn from it how to manipulate their counsellors, obtain favors, win early release, and generally "con" the system. "Treating" such persons — at least by means of verbal therapy — apparently makes society worse off.

An earlier study by Stuart Adams provides some confirmation for this point of view. In 1961 he described the "Pilot Intensive Counselling Organizations" (PICO) in California, aimed at reducing delinquency among older juvenile offenders. The eligible youth were first classified as "amenable" or "non-amenable" by the persons running the project. (Exactly how they reached these judgments is not clear.) Once classified, they were then randomly assigned to either a treatment or control group. (The treatment consisted of individual counselling sessions, once or twice a week for about nine months, carried on inside a correctional institution). After nearly three years of observation, Adams discovered that the amenable delinquents who had been treated were much less likely than amenable delinquents who had not been treated to be returned to custody. On the other hand, delinquents judged non-amenable who were given counselling did much worse — indeed, they were *more* likely to be returned to jail than the non-amenables who had *not* been treated. *In short, if you are amenable, treatment may make you less criminal; if you are not, treatment can make you more criminal.* Adams found that the delinquents judged to be amenable were "bright, verbal, and anxious." These characteristics are similar to those of the neurotics in the CTP.

This conclusion is consistent with a good deal of evidence about the effects of psychotherapy generally. Changing delinquents is not fundamentally different from changing law-abiding people: "Crime," after all, is not a unique form of behavior; it is simply behavior that is against the law. The illegality of the behavior is no trivial matter, but illegality alone does not differentiate one action from many similar actions. For example, many (perhaps most) offenders tend to do poorly in school, to have emotional problems, to find it difficult to get along with parents and friends, and to drink a good deal of alcohol. They are generally a mess. But poor school work, strained peer relations, emotional stress, and drinking liquor are not illegal.

Psychologists have long argued over whether any form of therapy will help any kind of problem. H.J. Eysenck, in a famous pair of articles published in 1952 and 1965, claimed that there was little evidence that therapy did anybody much good. He was (and is) the Robert Martinson of psychotherapy. Of late, psychologists have questioned the sweeping nature of Eysenck's claim. Mary Lee Smith and Gene V. Glass published in 1977 a comprehensive review of nearly 400 controlled evaluations of therapy and counselling and concluded that the client was often better off being treated than not. However, they noted that the improvements were generally with respect to such matters as "adjustment" (under which heading, of course, one finds most criminal behavior). Smith and Glass also tried to measure what factors made some subjects more amenable to therapy than others. They were able to identify two statistically significant ones: whether the therapist resembled the client, and the IQ of the client. Brighter clients did better than duller ones.

Similarly, if we are to believe Lerman, the brighter (and more neurotic) delinquents remain in the CTP program longer than those with the opposite characteristics; thus, any improvement measured by Palmer in their law-abidingness may result either from their greater receptivity to therapy, or from their tendency over time to outnumber the more delinquent-prone youth, or both.

The possibility that some persons are amenable to criminal rehabilitation is intriguing but it is not yet clear how much to make of it. The National Research Council Panel took note of the issue but remains skeptical that we have any clear understanding of it. The CTP, the major source of claims about amenability, is methodologically flawed. The PICO project did not define amenability with any rigor. Classifying a criminal as "amenable" may only mean that a therapist has a good hunch as to who will cooperate with the program. But if the therapist cannot communicate to others the basis for that hunch or provide a clear explanation of its rationale, it is hard to see how it can be used routinely as the basis for classifying and treating offenders. Moreover, some difficult legal and ethical issues arise. Suppose we are able to differentiate, accurately, amenable from non-amenable offenders. Suppose further that the treatment from which the amenables will benefit is less restrictive, more benign, and shorter in duration than the conventional punishment to which non-amenables will be assigned. Should we allow the criminal justice system to be "nicer" to "amenable" offenders than to non-amenable ones, even though their offenses and prior records may be identical. (Of course, it may also turn out that the rehabilitative program is felt by the recipients to be more onerous than doing "straight time"; the issue, however, remains the same.)

Nevertheless, the possibility of identifying amenable subjects and aiming programs at them that work is sufficiently attractive as to merit intensive new research. Someone has even coined a shorthand term to describe what we now suspect are the amenable subjects of therapy: YAVIN (young, anxious, verbal, intelligent, neurotic).

Recidivism, Rates, and Restrictiveness

The most dramatic new argument in the continuing debate over rehabilitation, however, comes from two authors who do not, at first glance, appear to be writing about rehabilitation at all. Charles A. Murray and Louis A. Cox, Jr., members of a private research organization, were retained to find out what happens to chronic delinquents in Chicago who are confronted by sanctions of varying degrees of restrictiveness.[4]

The Chicago authorities wanted to know if any of the programs offered in that city—ranging from commitment to a conventional juvenile reformatory, to newer programs that left the delinquent in the community or sent him to a wilderness program—changed the rate at which delinquents committed offenses. Such studies have been done many times, usually with the negative results reported by Martinson. But Murray and Cox redefined the outcome measure in a way that seems to make a striking difference. Until now, almost all students of recidivism "rates" or rehabilitation outcomes have measured the success or failure of a person by whether or not he was arrested for a new offense (or was convicted of a new offense, or had his parole revoked) after leaving the institution or completing the therapeutic program. "Success" was an either-or proposition: If you did not (within a stated time period) get into trouble again, you were a success; if you did get into trouble—*even once*—you were a "failure." Though the evaluators of rehabilitation programs typically speak of "recidivism rates," in fact they do not mean "rate" at all—they mean "percent who fail." More accurately, they use "rate" in the sense of "proportion," as in the "birth rate" or the "tax rate." But there is a different meaning of rate: the *frequency* of behavior per unit of time. Even a cursory glance through the studies reviewed by Lipton, Martinson, and Wilks reveals that almost all of them use "recidivism rate" to mean "the proportion who fail."

It was Murray's and Cox's happy thought to use rate in the sense of frequency and to calculate how many arrests per month were charged against a given group of delinquents before and after being exposed to Chicago juvenile treatment programs, and to do so separately for each kind of program involved. They examined three groups of youth.

The first was composed of 317 serious delinquents. They had been arrested an average of 13 times prior to being sent to the Department of Corrections, which was when Murray and Cox first started to track them. They were young—the average age was 16—but active: They had been charged with 14 homicides, 23 rapes, over 300 assaults and 300 auto thefts, nearly 200 armed robberies, and over 700 burglaries. The boys entered the study by having been sentenced by the court to a state correctional institution where they served an average of about ten months. Murray and Cox followed them for (on the average) 17 months after their release.

By the conventional measure of recidivism, the results were typically discouraging—82 percent were rearrested. But the *frequency* with which they were arrested during the follow-up period fell dramatically—the monthly arrest rate (i.e., arrests per month per 100 boys) declined by about *two-thirds*. To be exact, the members of this group of hard-core delinquents were arrested 6.3 times each during the year before being sent away but only 2.9 times each during the 17 months on the street after release.

The second group consisted of 266 delinquents who were eligible to go to a state reformatory but who instead were diverted to one of several less custodial programs run by the Unified Delinquency Intervention Services (UDIS), a Cook County (Chicago) agency created to make available in a coordinated fashion non-institutional, community-based programs for serious delinquents. Though chosen for these presumably more therapeutic programs, the UDIS delinquents had criminal records almost as severe as those sent to the regular reformatories—an average of over 13 arrests per boy, of which eight were for "index" (i.e., serious) offenses, including nine homicides, over 500 burglaries, and over 100 armed robberies. Nonetheless, since these youth were specially selected for the community-based programs, one would expect that in the opinion of probation officers, and probably in fact, they represented somewhat less dangerous, perhaps more amenable delinquents.

Despite the fact the UDIS group may have been thought more amenable to treatment, the reduction in their monthly arrest rates was *less* than it had been for the group sent to the reformatories (about 17 percent less). In general, UDIS did not do as well as the regular Department of Corrections. Even more interesting, Murray and Cox found that *the more restrictive the degree of supervision practiced by UDIS, the greater the reduction in arrest rates.* Youths left in their homes or sent to wilderness camps showed the least reduction (though some reduction nonetheless); those placed in group homes in the community showed a greater reduction; and those put into out-of-town group homes, intensive-care residential programs, or sent to regular reformatories showed the greatest reduction. If this is true, *it implies that how strictly the youth were supervised, rather than what therapeutic programs were available, had the greatest effect on the recidivism rate.*

Ordinarily, we do not refer to the crime-reduction effects of confinement as "rehabilitation." Technically, they are called the results of "special deterrence" ("special" in the sense that the person deterred is the specific individual who is the object of the intervention, and not the general delinquent population). "Rehabilitation" usually refers to interventions that are "nice," benevolent, or well-intended, or that involve the provision of special services. A psychologist might say that rehabilitation involves "positive reinforcements" (such as counselling) rather than "negative reinforcements" (such as incarceration). Indeed, the National Research Council Panel defines rehabilitation as the result of "any planned intervention" that reduces further criminal activity, "whether that reduction is mediated by personality, behavior, abilities, attitudes, values, or other factors," provided only that one excludes the effects of fear or intimidation, the latter being regarded as sources of special deterrence.

Although the distinction has a certain emotional appeal, it makes little sense either scientifically or behaviorally. Scientifically, there is no difference between a positive and negative inducement; behavioral psychologists long ago established that the two kinds of reinforcements have comparable effects. (It is not generally true that rewards will change behavior more than punishments, or vice versa). Behaviorally, it is not clear that a criminal can tell the difference between rehabilitation and special deterrence if each involves a comparable degree of restriction. Rehabilitation can (and usually does) involve a substantial degree of coercion, even of intimidation ("be nice or you won't get out," "talk to the counsellor or stay in your cell," "join the group discussion or run the risk of being locked up"). Behavior-modification therapy can involve the simultaneous use of positive reinforcers ("follow the rules and earn a token") and negative ones ("break the rules and lose a token"). It might help the discussion of offender-oriented programs if the distinction between rehabilitation and special deterrence were collapsed.

Two Questions

The real issue raised by the Murray-Cox study is not, however, what to call the effect they observe, but whether they have actually observed any effect at all. A number of criticisms have been made of it, but two are of special importance. First, does the decline in arrests indicate a decline in actual criminality or merely an increase in skill at avoiding apprehension? Second, if there is an actual decline in criminality, might this not be explained by the maturation of youth—that is, growing out of crime as they become older? Andrew C. Gordon, Richard McCleary, and their colleagues made these and other criticisms in response to a preliminary report of the Murray-Cox findings. In their later, book-length treatment of the Chicago project, Murray and Cox responded.

The second criticism seems the easiest to answer. Murray and Cox were able to show that the decline in rearrest rates existed for all incarcerated serious delinquents regardless of age. As an additional check, the authors examined a third group—nearly 1,500 youth born in Chicago in 1960 and arrested at least once by the Chicago Police Department before their 17th birthdays. Since this group was chosen at random from all arrested youth of the same age, it naturally is made up primarily of less serious offenders. Indeed, only 3 percent of this group was ever referred to UDIS or the Department of Corrections. When the monthly arrest rates for this group were examined, the data showed a more or less steady increase throughout the teenage years. Being arrested or being placed on probation had no apparent effect on subsequent delinquency. By all the tests they used, therefore, the decline in arrest rates for those delinquents given strict supervision cannot be explained by the fact that they were simply getting older.

The other criticism is harder to answer. Strictly speaking, it is impossible to know whether arrest data are a reasonable approximation of the true crime rate. No one argues, of course, that every crime results in an arrest. All that is at issue is whether a more or less constant fraction of all crimes result in arrests. There are two possibilities — either having been arrested before draws police attention to the boy (he is "stigmatized" or "labeled", thus making him *more* likely to be arrested for subsequent crimes, or the arrest and subsequent punishment increases his skills at avoiding detection (the system has served as a "school for criminals"), thus making him *less* likely to be arrested for a given offense.

Now it is obvious that the first of these two possibilities — the "labeling" effect of being arrested — cannot be true, for, we have seen, delinquents who are placed under supervision have their subsequent arrest rates *decline*. If the police "pick on" previously arrested youth, they either do so without making an arrest (by keeping an eye on "troublemakers," for example) or they try harder to arrest them but find the youth are not committing as many crimes as before.

The other possibility — that boys become skilled at avoiding arrest — is impossible to disprove, but Murray and Cox raise some serious questions as to whether this gain in skills, if it occurs at all, could explain the decline in arrest rates. Perhaps their most telling argument is this: One must not only believe that correctional institutions are "schools of crime," one must believe they are such excellent schools that they produce a two-thirds gain in arrest-avoiding skills. This would make reformatories and group homes the most competent educational institutions in the country, since no one has yet shown that conventional schools, with the best available educational technology, can produce comparable gains in learning non-criminal skills. And all this must be accomplished within the ten-month period that is the average length of detention. It is still possible, of course, that the "schools of crime" hypothesis is true, but it requires one to make some heroic assumptions in order to sustain it: that large numbers of boys learn more during ten months in a reformatory than they learn in ten years on the street; that the great majority, despite their statements to the contrary made to interviewers, increase their commitment to crime as a way of life (rather than as an occasionally profitable activity) as a result of incarceration; and that the object of their efforts when back on the street is to employ their sharpened skills at avoiding apprehension while committing relatively unprofitable crimes rather than attacking more profitable (and riskier) targets.

Though Murray and Cox make a persuasive case for the validity of their findings, it cannot be taken as a conclusive study. For one thing, we would like to know what happens to these delinquents over a much longer period. Most studies of rehabilitation suggest that any favorable effects tend to be extinguished by the passage of time (though such extinction usually appears within the first year). We would also like to know more about the kinds of offenses for which these persons were arrested, before and after court intervention (perhaps they change the form of their criminal behavior in important ways). And above all, we would like to see such a study repeated in other settings by other scholars. It may even be possible to do this retrospectively, with data already in existence but never before analyzed using frequency of offending (rather than proportion of failures) as the measure of outcome.

In fact, long before the Murray-Cox study, LaMar T. Empey and Maynard L. Erickson had reported on the Provo Experiment in Utah, an effort to reduce delinquency that was evaluated by arrest rates before and after treatment—the same outcome measure used by Murray and Cox (indeed, the latters' book contains a foreword by Empey). The Provo Experiment was, in principle at least, an even better test of changing recidivism rates than the Chicago project because the former, unlike the latter, randomly assigned delinquent boys to either treatment or control groups and kept detailed records (in addition to before-and-after measures) of what actually happened to the boys in the treatment programs. The experimental program was community-based, but unlike conventional probation or even group homes, involved an intensive level of participation in a supervised group discussion program, absence from which was promptly penalized by being locked up. The program was in time killed by community opposition (many persons thought it excessively punitive, others quarreled over who should pay for it). The four years worth of data which could be gathered, however, indicate that there have been substantial reductions in arrest rates that cannot be explained by maturation or social class differences for all boys. This was true of both those incarcerated and those left in the community, with the greatest reductions occurring among boys in the experimental programs.[5] Though open to criticism, the Provo data provide some support for the view that, if one measures offense *frequency*, some kinds of programs involving fairly high degrees of restrictiveness and supervision may make some difference.

Thoughts for the Future

The Murray-Cox and the Empey-Erickson studies are important, not only because they employ rates rather than proportions as the outcome measure, or even because they suggest that something might work, but also because they suggest that *the study of deterrence and the study of rehabilitation must be merged—that, at least for a given individual, they are the same thing.* Until now, the two issues have been kept separate. It is not hard to understand why: Welfare and probation agencies administer "rehabilitation," the police and wardens administer "deterrence"; advocates of rehabilitation think of themselves as "tender-minded," advocates of deterrence see themselves as "tough-minded"; rehabilitation supposedly cures the "causes" of crime, while deterrence deals only with the temptations to crime; psychologists study rehabilitation, economists study deterrence. If Murray-Cox and Empey-Erickson are correct, these distinctions are artificial, if not entirely empty.

The common core of both perspectives is, or ideally ought to be, an interest in explaining individual differences in the propensity to commit crime, or changes in a single individual's propensity over time. The stimuli confronting an individual can rarely be partitioned neatly into things tending to produce pain and those likely to produce pleasure; most situations in which we place persons, including criminals, contain elements of both. If explaining individual differences is our object, then studying individuals should be our method. Studies that try to measure the effect on whole societies of marginal changes in aggregate factors (such as the probability of being imprisoned, or the unemployment rate) are probably nearing the end of the line — even the formidable statistical methodologies now available are unlikely to overcome the gross deficiencies in data that we shall always face.

Policy makers need not embrace the substantive conclusions of Murray and Cox (though it is hard to see how they could reasonably be ignored) to appreciate the need to encourage local jurisdictions to look at the effect of a given program on the rate of behavior of a given set of offenders. If they do, they may well discover, as Murray and Cox feel they have discovered in Chicago, that for the serious, chronic delinquent, the strategy of minimal intervention — probation, or loosely supervised life in the community — fails to produce any desirable changes (whether one calls those changes deterrence or rehabilitation), whereas tighter, more restrictive forms of supervision (whether in the community or in an institution) may produce some of these desired changes, or at the very least not produce worse delinquency through "labeling" or "stigmatization." It is hard to imagine a reason for not pursuing this line of inquiry.

Notes

[1]Paul Lerman, *Community Treatment and Social Control* (Chicago: University of Chicago Press, 1975), p. 67.
[2]Ted Palmer, *Correctional Intervention and Research* (Lexington, Mass.: D.C. Heath/Lexington Books, 1978).

[3]Douglas Lipton, Robert Martinson, and Judith Wilks, *The Effectiveness of Correctional Treatment: A Survey of Treatment Evaluation Studies* (New York: Praeger, 1975).

[4]Charles A. Murray and Louis A. Cox, Jr., *Beyond Probation: Juvenile Corrections and the Chronic Delinquent* (Beverly Hills, California: Sage Publications, 1979).

[5]LaMar T. Empey and Maynard L. Erickson, *The Provo Experiment* (Lexington, Mass.: D.C. Heath/Lexington Books, 1972).

23

Evaluating Correctional Boot Camp Programs
Issues and Concerns

Angela R. Gover
Gaylene J. F. Styve
Doris Layton MacKenzie

Boot camp prisons require offenders to serve a short term in a prison or jail in a quasi-military program similar to boot camp or basic training in the military. Today, many local and state governments as well as the Federal Bureau of Prisons are using this correctional option for adult as well as juvenile offenders. The programs are characterized by a structured environment that promotes order and discipline. Inmates rise early in the morning and follow an intensive schedule of daily activities. Boot camp advocates expect the regimented environment to instill discipline in youthful offenders.

Components of boot camp programming vary depending on the philosophy of the institution. Some programs may devote nearly five hours per day to military activities such as drill and ceremony, marching, and physical labor. Other programs with more of a rehabilitative focus may devote more time to activities such as counseling, academic educa-

Source: Prepared especially for *The Dilemmas of Corrections*.

tion, or drug treatment. In addition to programming differences, other differences among boot camp models include program capacities, program location, participant eligibility criteria and selection practices, program duration, populations served, and community aftercare components. These differences, especially the emphasis placed on programming components and goals, will have an effect on participants' successful completion of the program. From a research perspective, such diversity among programs makes it difficult to generalize findings from an individual site evaluation to other programs.

This chapter reviews the research on correctional boot camps for adults and juveniles. The research to date has been disappointing to boot camp advocates because there is no evidence that these programs have had long-term impacts on participants. In examining the research, it becomes obvious that we do not have a good grasp of what components of the boot camps are expected to change offenders. Literature reviews and meta-analyses provide some consensus about the components of effective rehabilitation programs. However, there is little available information on whether boot camps incorporate these components into their environments. In this chapter, we present a model that can be used to measure the desired intermediate and long-term outcomes for boot camps.

A Day in the Life of a Boot Camp Inmate

Upon arrival at the boot camp prison, male inmates have their heads shaved (females may be permitted short haircuts) and they are informed of the strict program rules. At all times they are required to address staff as "Sir" or "Ma'am," to request permission to speak, and to refer to themselves as "this inmate." Punishments for minor rule violations are summary and certain, frequently involving physical exercise such as push-ups or running; major rule violations may result in dismissal from the program.

In a typical boot camp prison, the ten- to sixteen-hour day begins with a predawn reveille. Inmates dress quickly and march to an exercise yard where they participate in an hour or two of physical training followed by drill and ceremony. Then they march to breakfast where they are ordered to stand at parade rest while waiting in line and to exercise military movements when the line moves. Inmates are required to stand in front of the table until commanded to sit and are not permitted to make conversation while eating. After breakfast they march to work sites where they participate in hard physical labor that frequently involves community service, such as cleaning state parks or highways. When the six- to eight-hour work day is over, offenders return to the compound where they participate in more exercise and drill. A quick dinner is followed by evening programs consisting of counseling, life skills training, academic education, or drug education and treatment.

Boot camp inmates gradually earn more privileges and responsibilities as their performance and time in the program warrants. A different color hat or uniform may be the outward display of their new prestige. Depending upon the facility, somewhere between 8 and 50 percent will fail to complete the program. For those who successfully complete the program, an elaborate graduation ceremony occurs with visitors and family invited to attend. Frequently awards are given for achievements made during the program. In addition, the inmates often perform the drill and ceremony they have practiced throughout their time in the boot camp.

Different Perspectives on Correctional Boot Camps

Boot camps are controversial for a variety of reasons (MacKenzie and Souryal, 1995a; MacKenzie and Parent, 1992; Meachum, 1990; Morash and Rucker, 1990). Much of the controversy has to do with an instinctive reaction toward the military atmosphere. It is important, however, to separate this instinctive reaction from the debates that occur among people who are more knowledgeable about the programs and corrections in general. Here, there is a much more interesting debate. One perspective exhibited by many knowledgeable correctional experts is a "Machiavellian" point of view (MacKenzie and Souryal, 1995b). These individuals expect little direct benefit from the military atmosphere of the boot camp programs, but are willing to support the concept to achieve two ends: early release for nonviolent offenders and additional funding for treatment programs (both inside and outside prison). In their opinion, the popularity of the boot camps with policy makers and the public allows early release and treatment that would not otherwise be available to these offenders.

Opponents of the boot camp model fear dangers associated with this correctional option. Many psychologists who are experienced in both corrections and behavioral change take this position when examining boot camp programs. They believe that the potential dangers of the military model are too great to compromise for early release or funds for treatment. Furthermore, they argue that boot camps cannot provide a mechanism for treatment because many of the characteristics of the programs (confrontation, punishment instead of reward, etc.) are antithetical to treatment. The confrontational interactions may be particularly damaging for some individuals such as those who have been abused in the past or others who have problems with dependency in relationships. Morash and Rucker (1990) contend that aspects of the boot camps may actually inflict damage on participants. Additionally, boot camp opponents fear that even though some programs may be used as early release mechanisms, most have a serious potential for widening the net (i.e., adding to the overall numbers of offenders in confinement—perhaps drawing more from those who would be subject to probation than from those who would serve prison sentences). The net-widening issue is particularly critical for the newly developing juvenile programs.

There are some additional concerns about using these programs for juveniles. Juveniles may be in a different stage of development. It may be difficult for the juveniles to obey authority figures if they do not believe that such obedience is in their own best interest. They may rail against the injustice of group punishment. Some juveniles, such as those who have been victimized in the past, may have additional problems that make the boot camps a harmful experience for them. An additional fear is that the program will greatly increase the number of juveniles incarcerated due to the fact that they appear to many to be the perfect solution for an unruly and undisciplined juvenile.

Another perspective argues that the military atmosphere is an effective model for changing offenders. Persons who have worked in drug treatment programs—where strict rules, discipline, and confrontational interactions are common—seem to be more comfortable with the military model. Military personnel assert that the leadership model of basic training provides new and appropriate techniques for correctional programming. Of course, many of those responsible for the development and implementation of individual boot camp programs are committed to and believe in the viability of this approach. They argue that the stress created in boot camp may shock the inmates and make them amenable to change and thus take advantage of the treatment and aftercare programs offered. Further, the military atmosphere of boot camp may actually enhance the effectiveness of this treatment by keeping the offenders physically and mentally healthy while enabling them to focus on their education, treatment, and therapy.

So the debate continues. What is clear is that these boot camps are proliferating across the nation, yet we have limited knowledge about their effects on the individuals involved and the impact on correctional systems. The main point may be that we need to identify the beneficial aspects of the camps as well as the potential drawbacks. Certainly, we can assume that the effect of the camps will differ depending upon the needs of the individuals involved. Further, we need detailed information on the specific components of the programs and how these components affect those involved. Lastly, we need to learn what type of boot camp is (or is not) effective for specific types of offenders.

Empirical Research Examining the Effectiveness of Boot Camp Programs

Research examining correctional boot camps focuses on the impact of the programs on: (1) prison crowding and costs; (2) changes made by participants during the time they are in the boot camps; (3) women participants; (4) recidivism and adjustment of the participants when they return to the community; and, (5) juvenile offenders.

Impact on Prison Crowding

Many correctional programs are designed to be intermediate sanctions which are less restrictive than prison but more restrictive than probation (Morris and Tonry, 1990). Because boot camp prisons are commonly considered not to be more restrictive than prison, they are often categorized this way. The problem is that intermediate sanctions may, on the one hand, have a net-widening effect and, on the other, require a greater degree of structured control over the offender's daily activities. The former adds to the cost of corrections due to the increased overall number of offenders, the latter due to the necessary increase in staff time. While boot camps may not involve a significantly smaller degree of control, they may reduce the amount of time that the offender is incarcerated and thus reduce correctional costs.

On the other hand, if offenders who would normally be given probation are being sent to the boot camps then we might expect both the costs and prison crowding to increase. MacKenzie and Piquero (1994) examined the impact of adult boot camps on prison crowding using a statistical model that weighted the impact of factors such as program size, number of dismissals, and recidivism rates. In the models, they varied the percent of the offenders who would have been given sentences of probation or prison. The results indicated that boot camps can reduce prison crowding if they are designed as early release mechanisms for offenders who would have been sent to prison. However, while the programs may have the potential to reduce prison crowding, in actuality they seldom do. For example, in the multi-site evaluation completed by MacKenzie and her colleagues, only two of the five boot camp programs examined appeared to save prison beds (MacKenzie and Piquero, 1994; MacKenzie and Souryal, 1994). In the remaining three states, the boot camp programs appeared to increase the need for prison beds. Thus, the evidence that boot camp prisons reduce crowding and the associated costs is not extremely persuasive.

The Impact of the Programs on the Participants

To date, research examining boot camps has shown very little negative impact from the programs. Offenders have reported being drug free and physically healthy when they leave the boot camps (MacKenzie and Souryal, 1994). Participants have also reported that the program helped them and they were optimistic about the future. This was true of the "enhanced" boot camp programs that emphasized treatment as well as programs that predominantly focused on military training, hard labor, and discipline. Also, when MacKenzie and Souryal (1995a) examined changes in antisocial attitudes they found that participants in the boot camps, as well as the comparison samples of prisoners, became less antisocial. Again, results on the effectiveness of the boot camps are mixed and we are left with questions about the specific components of the camps that lead to positive change. In an exploratory analysis, these authors found some evidence that participants became less antisocial in boot camps that devoted more time to rehabilitation, had higher dismissal rates, and were voluntary (Ibid.).

Women in Boot Camps

The majority of the boot camp participants are male. For this reason, most of the research examining boot camps has focused on male offenders. In a 1992 survey of state prisons, MacKenzie et al. (1996) found thirty-nine boot camps for adults operating in twenty-five states. Only thirteen of these states had female participants who comprised a mere 6.1 percent of the total number of incarcerated boot camp offenders. Most of the female inmates were integrated into programs along with the male participants. Only four states operated separate programs for women.

MacKenzie and Donaldson (1996) studied six boot camps that had female participants. In direct interviews, the women reported difficulties keeping up with the physical demands of the program. They further reported experiencing extensive emotional stress because the majority of the boot camp staff and inmates were male. It is for this reason that some researchers and practitioners argue that it is not appropriate to integrate female boot camp inmates with male inmates and drill instructors as a high proportion of incarcerated women have past histories of abuse by men (MacKenzie et al., 1996). This abuse factor combined with the highly confrontational environment of boot camps is likely to trigger emotions associated with past feelings of mental and physical abuse for many women. Furthermore, when comparing programs that integrated men and women to programs with women only, women in separate programs reported less emotional and physical stress. Therefore, it is important to consider the potential effects of gender integration on program participants during the early stages of program development.

Some of the boot camp programs do offer increased opportunities for therapeutic programming such as drug treatment and parent training. Others offer participants a way to obtain early release. These opportunities may not be available to inmates in regular prison. Therefore, if women are excluded from participation in boot camps they may not have the same chance for similar therapeutic programming or early release.

Previous descriptive studies of women offenders have identified some of their major needs as the following: employment or vocational training to prepare them to support themselves and their children; treatment for substance abuse; domestic violence and sexual assault counseling; and education/training on issues related to family obligations such as parenting, life skills, and community reintegration (American Correctional Association, 1993). MacKenzie and Donaldson (1996) found the characteristics of the female boot camp inmates to be similar to the characteristics of the typical female inmates identified in these earlier studies. Therefore, in their opinion, these characteristics should be programming considerations for boot camps with female populations.

Nearly all of the female inmates interviewed in the MacKenzie and Donaldson study had children for whom they would be financially responsible when returning to the community. Programs with lenient visitation policies would help establish, reunite, and maintain relationships between mothers and their children while they are incarcerated. Also, since a large proportion of female boot camp inmates reported having some type of serious problem associated with drug use, the provision of drug treatment and services is a key component of an effective treatment model. Yet, many of the boot camps did not incorporate components that would address the needs of women offenders. After examining the boot camps, MacKenzie and Donaldson conclude that most boot camps are designed with the male inmates in mind, and women are placed in the camps as an afterthought. Therefore, they suggest all programs be designed for females. Such programs would emphasize parenting skills and responsibilities, or education about spousal abuse. Those developing boot camps should ask themselves why such programs are not appropriate for men.

Recidivism and Community Adjustment
of Adult Boot Camp Releasees

At this point in time there have been no experimental studies examining the impact of boot camps on the community adjustment and recidivism of adult offenders. In a recent report looking at the effectiveness of crime prevention programs, Sherman and colleagues examined both the scientific rigor and the results of the research on the recidivism of boot camp participants (1997). They found few studies reached moderate levels of scientific quality, although some of the research made use of statistical controls to adjust for the original differences between the boot camp releasees and comparison groups. In general, the results demonstrated no significant difference in recidivism between offenders who were sent to the boot camps and those who were given probation or prison sentences. The recidivism rates of offenders who served time in the boot camps were approximately the same as the rates of offenders who had served other sentences such as prison or probation.

After reviewing the results of the adult and juvenile boot camp research, Sherman and colleagues concluded there was no evidence that the military atmosphere, structure, and discipline of correctional boot camps significantly reduced the recidivism of releasees in comparison to other correctional sanctions (1997). However, in some programs where a substantial number of offenders were dismissed from the boot camp prior to completion, the recidivism rates for those who completed the program were significantly lower than the rates for those who were dismissed. Thus, although there is no evidence that the boot camps actually change offenders, there is some indication that the programs can be used to "signal" which offenders will have difficulty completing probation or parole. From this perspective, offenders who remain in the program and complete it are less at risk for recidivism than those who are dismissed (by either voluntarily dropping out or being expelled for misbehavior).

In one exploratory analysis examining program differences and recidivism rates, MacKenzie et al. (1995) found some commonalities among programs where the boot camp releasees had lower recidivism rates than comparison groups on some but not all measures of recidivism. These programs scheduled more than three hours per day for therapeutic activities such as counseling, drug treatment, and education. The programs also required inmates to volunteer for participation and provided some type of community follow-up after release. Since these are components of treatment programs that have been found to be effective, the researchers ended with the question: "Does the military atmosphere add anything above and beyond a short-term, quality prison treatment program?" They were careful to warn the reader that these results are tentative until more research is completed.

In another study, MacKenzie and Brame (1995) found that boot camp releasees adjusted more positively than comparison samples during community supervision in only one of five sites. Thus, both the recidivism studies and the positive adjustment studies suggest that there may be some programs that have positive impacts on participants. However, the specific components that lead to positive change remain unclear.

Correctional Boot Camps for Juveniles

As boot camp programs have moved from adult prisons to local jails and juvenile populations, new issues have arisen (Cronin, 1994; Austin, Jones and Bolyard, 1993). For example, while adult programs could target nonviolent offenders in prison, nonviolent juveniles are much less likely to be incarcerated. Thus, net-widening and the associated costs have become critical issues in the development of juvenile programs. This is particularly relevant given the history of concern with the destructive environment of detention centers for nonviolent juveniles or status offenders. The deceptively seductive idea of providing discipline and structure for disruptive juveniles means there is a real threat that increasingly large numbers of juveniles will be placed in boot camps, regardless of whether it is a suitable alternative sanction. Furthermore, in contrast to adult boot camps, academic and therapeutic programming as well as aftercare are viewed as necessary components in juvenile programs. In fact, besides the military atmosphere, there are questions about how much the boot camp programs actually differ from other residential facilities for juveniles.

The emergence of juvenile boot camps has been a recent and explosive trend. In June of 1995, MacKenzie and Rosay (1996) surveyed state and local juvenile correctional administrators and identified a total of thirty-seven programs operating at that time. Only one of these programs opened prior to 1990 with nearly all of them opening during or after 1993. The passage of the 1994 Crime Act permitted the Department of Justice to allocate a substantial amount of funding for juvenile boot camps; twelve jurisdictions were awarded grants to develop boot camp programs for juveniles and another twelve jurisdictions received funds for the renovation of existing facilities or the construction of new ones. Thus, the number of juveniles in boot camps will most likely continue to increase in the next few years.

The type of juveniles participating in boot camp programs tend to be fairly similar. Unlike adult boot camps, juvenile programs are rarely limited to individuals convicted of their first serious offense and who volunteer. The typical juvenile boot camp inmate was a nonviolent male between the ages of fourteen to eighteen who was placed in the program by a juvenile court judge. However, only about half of the boot camps were solely limited to nonviolent offenders while the other half accepted offenders convicted of violent crimes. Differences among programs can be found in population capacities and program length. The capacities of juvenile boot camps ranged from 12 to 396 and program length ranged from one day to one year.

Almost all boot camps for juveniles emphasized a military atmosphere with drill and ceremony, platoon grouping, and discipline. About half used military titles and uniforms for both staff and juveniles. In addition to the military atmosphere, the majority included physical labor in the daily activities. Youth also engaged in physical fitness, sports activities, and some type of challenge or adventure programming. Overall, juveniles spent between one and ten hours per day in physical training, military drill, and work. In comparison they spent, on average, about six and a half hours in educational classes or counseling. Because of this heavy emphasis on education and counseling, it comes as no surprise that juvenile boot camp administrators rated rehabilitation as a very important goal of their programs. Reducing recidivism was also rated as very important.

In the crime prevention report authored by Sherman et al. (1997), MacKenzie further reviewed the research examining the impact of juvenile boot camps on delinquent recidivism. The quality of these studies was rated as high since juveniles were randomly assigned to the boot camps or comparison groups. Four random assignment studies examining boot camps in California, Alabama, Colorado, and Ohio were located. In three of the sites there were no significant differences between the boot camp youth and the control groups. In one site the youths released from the boot camp recidivated more than those in the control group. The juvenile recidivism research parallels adult boot camp research; there is no evidence demonstrating the effectiveness of these programs in reducing recidivism.

Summary of the Research

This short review of the literature on boot camp programs for juveniles and adults demonstrates that most research has focused on individual programs and the impact of these programs on subsequent criminal activities. The fact that programs differ dramatically in their goals and components is problematic. Thus, knowledge about the effectiveness of one program may be dependent upon very atypical aspects of the program or even a charismatic leader, and not necessarily be related to boot-camp-type characteristics of the program. The research results may show us that one program works but not *why* that program works. To understand why the program works we need to know more about the relationship between the specific components of the program and the impacts on the individuals involved. Questions revolve around the specific conditions of confinement or the environment of the boot camps. How do conditions of a boot camp differ from traditional prisons and detention centers? What are the impacts of these conditions on those involved? If they do indeed differ for juveniles, there are questions about the effectiveness of the camps for certain types of offenders (e.g., higher risk, older, those with a high number of prior commitments). Furthermore, some are fearful that aspects of the camps may be particularly damaging for some individuals such as those with certain past histories (e.g., juveniles who have been physically or sexually abused).

Rehabilitation and Treatment

Today, there is still a debate about the effectiveness of rehabilitation programs for offenders. However, recent literature reviews and meta-analyses demonstrate that rehabilitation programs can effectively change some offenders. According to Andrews et al. (1990), the pattern of research results strongly supports the idea that there are service programs working for some offenders under some circumstances. The important issue is not whether something works but what works for whom. While there has been some debate about whether boot camps can or do incorporate components of successful rehabilitation programs, there has been little empirical research designed to examine this issue.

What is obvious is that some approaches to treatment are better than others. Psychological researchers have emphasized that effective treatment programs must follow some basic principles (Gendreau and Ross, 1987). Treatment must directly address characteristics that can be changed (dynamic factors) and that are directly associated with an individual's criminal behavior (criminogenic factors). There are numerous risk factors associated with criminal activity such as age, gender, and early criminal involvement. However, while predictive of recidivism, these static characteristics cannot be changed in treatment.

Evidence from meta-analyses suggests that effective correctional treatment programs are carefully designed to target the specific characteristics and problems of offenders that can be changed in treatment (dynamic characteristics) and those that are predictive of the individual's future criminal activities (criminogenic characteristics such as antisocial attitudes and behavior, drug use, anger responses) (Lipsey,

1992; Andrews et al., 1990). Programs must also be implemented so they are appropriate for the participating offenders, utilize techniques that are known to work, and provide sufficient contact with other offenders.

Again, there has been little research designed to analyze the specific components of boot camps and to determine which aspects of these programs may successfully address the rehabilitative needs of which types of offenders.

Performance Standards for Correctional Boot Camps

Quality management has been a driving force in recent years in the redesign of private organizations and corporations; these concepts have only recently been applied to public agencies (Jablonski, 1991). Osborne and Gaebler's book *Reinventing Government* (1992) was key in describing how performance standards could be developed for public agencies. In 1993, Congress passed the Government Performance and Results Act (GPRA) with the purpose of improving "the efficiency and effectiveness of federal programs by establishing a system to set goals for program performance and to measure results" (RAND, 1995). The law attempts to improve program management through the process of operationalizing strategic plans and specifying outcome measures, including how they will be evaluated.

There are several lines of research that have moved in the direction of quality management for corrections. For example, Logan (1993) developed quality of confinement indices to compare the performance of private versus public prisons. The Office of Juvenile Justice and Delinquency Prevention, U.S. Department of Justice, has worked to develop methods to measure the conditions of confinement for juveniles. These projects are attempts to quantify aspects of the environments that can be used as indices of the quality of confinement. The next step requires a clear definition and a way to measure the expected relationship between the aspects of confinement and the outcomes to be achieved. Frequently measures of success in corrections (e.g., recidivism) are dependent upon numerous factors (e.g., number of police officers, drug availability, social decay) that are not directly under the control of correctional administrators. Recognizing this, several criminologists have advocated that corrections be evaluated on intermediate outcomes as well as long-term goals.

A substantial body of literature recommends the need to specify the components of correctional programs and their relationships with outcomes. For example, a recent OJJDP (Office of Juvenile Justice and

Delinquency Prevention) publication by Dale Parent on conditions of confinement examined the conditions of juvenile detention and corrections facilities (OJJDP, 1994). Using mail surveys, the Children in Custody Census, and site visits, researchers measured conformity to national professional standards and other selected aspects of conditions. They recommended further study on why facilities vary so dramatically in such factors as control and safety. Furthermore, they suggested that more research be conducted to examine the effects of these conditions on the juveniles both while they are in the facilities and upon release.

Similarly, after completing their evaluation of a wilderness adventure program, Greenwood and Turner (1987) also recommended that future evaluations describe and measure the "program inputs and processes" which can influence the effectiveness of a program. As we argue here, they propose that the general classification of a program as a boot camp or wilderness program does not give a detailed enough description to enable us to identify the components that will produce the desired impact. We need more detailed information about the conditions of confinement and about how these conditions are associated with measures of performance and effectiveness.

Two other lines of work have sparked discussions within the criminal justice community about the need to measure the conditions or components of the environment. The first centers around a recent Bureau of Justice Statistics–Princeton University project, *Performance Measures for the Criminal Justice System*. The second line of work focuses on performance-based standards for corrections. The performance measures working group (DiIulio, 1993) proposed that the use of traditional criminal justice performance measures should be rethought. In particular, DiIulio argues that while rates of crime and recidivism may represent basic goals of public safety, they are not the only, or necessarily the best, measures of what criminal justice institutions do. He advises criminal justice agencies to develop mission statements that include any activities that the agency can reasonably and realistically be expected to fulfill (DiIulio, 1993). In line with this is Logan's (1993) emphasis on evaluating prisons on the day-to-day operations, not on ultimate, utilitarian goals of rehabilitation or crime reduction. Likewise, Petersilia (1993) argues that along with their public safety functions, community corrections should be evaluated on other activities such as the accuracy, completeness, and timeliness of presentence investigations, monitoring of court-ordered sanctions, and how well they do in assisting offenders to change in positive ways. Thus, not only are these researchers emphasizing the need to investigate components or conditions of the environments being studied but also the need to use a wider range of measures to examine effectiveness.

The second focus of much attention in the corrections community has been on the standards used specifically for corrections. Traditionally, these standards have been based on the opinions of experts in the field. Recently, however, there has been a push toward verifying the validity of these standards through the use of data on actual performance (performance-based standards). High rates of conformity with nationally recognized standards does not necessarily mean that all is well. Many of the existing standards specify procedures and processes to be followed, but not outcomes to be achieved (OJJDP, 1994). These performance-based standards would tie the standards to the desired performance or outcomes desired.

A Model to Examine Conditions and Outcomes

As indicated throughout this chapter, boot camp programs differ dramatically. Underlying the programs are some consistent goals that would be expected of any quality corrections program such as safety, therapeutic programming, fairness, and health care. Other goals are more individually related to the boot camps, such as structure and order. Figure 1 presents a model for examining the impact of conditions of confinement for boot camps and other facilities. As shown in the model, it is expected that the conditions of confinement, including all aspects of the environment from safety to therapeutic atmosphere, will have intermediate impacts on both the individual participants and on the institutional climate. Specific conditions will be associated with specific intermediate and long-term outcomes. For example, programs that address family issues and concerns are expected to lead to increased bonds between the offender and the family. Intensive educational programming (as measured by time in class, qualifications of teachers, etc.) is expected to be associated with reduced recidivism, increased employment, and positive adjustment. These intermediate impacts are anticipated to have an influence on long-term outcomes such as recidivism, positive adjustment, drug use, and employment. An intermediate outcome like increased bonds between the offender and family may impact how offenders adjust once they are released from a facility. Furthermore, it is assumed that these outcomes will be mediated by individual differences. For instance, juveniles who have a history of abuse (an individual difference shown in figure 1) may respond very differently to a program like a boot camp that has a high level of confrontational discipline. They may experience increased stress (intermediate outcomes) and actually perform worse on long-term outcome measures such as adjustment in the community and recidivism.

As shown in the figure, it is anticipated that the conditions of confinement will also have an impact on institutional measures such as the number of assaults, misconducts, staff attitudes, escapes, and injuries. Thus, an environment that has a high level of structure and discipline like a boot camp may reduce the number of assaults, escapes, and injuries but not necessarily increase offenders' adjustment once they are released. However, it would be expected that the effects would be mediated by the characteristics of the individuals confined in the institution. In a facility with a large number of high-risk individuals, structure and discipline may be particularly important in reducing such negative occurrences in the institution. However, in an institution with mostly low-risk inmates, structure and discipline may not be as important.

Questions that continually arise with regard to boot camps concern what exactly the participants do, and how these activities differ from traditional prisons and detention centers where these inmates might otherwise be. From previous process evaluations and descriptions of programs, we know that the boot camps differ dramatically from each other. The assumption is also made that the boot camps differ from the more traditional facilities where the inmates might be if the boot camps did not exist. Actually, there is little information to tell us how a boot camp in a particular jurisdiction differs from a prison, detention center, or other program where these offenders might be detained.

While there have been numerous descriptions of boot camp programs, few researchers have tried to quantify aspects of the environment. If aspects of the boot camp were quantified, it would be possible to compare the boot camp experience with that of other facilities. That is, how much time do the inmates spend in education, physical training, and sports? Are offenders more active in the boot camps? Is the environment safer for offenders in the boot camps? If factors such as these were quantified for both environments, aspects of traditional prisons or detention centers where these inmates might otherwise be detained could be compared to the boot camps.

Furthermore, these statistical descriptions of the characteristics of the programs could be used in analyzing the impact of the program on the offenders. The relationships among the conditions (or environment characteristics) and both the recidivism and positive activities of the offenders during community supervision could be examined. For example, if drug treatment available during the boot camp were exactly the same as in another facility then we might expect offenders to be similar in drug use once they are returned to the community. On the other hand, if there are large differences between the environments, it would

Figure 1: Proposed Model for Studying Inpact of Conditions of Confinement on Intermediate and Long-term Outcomes for Correctional Boot Camps and Comparison Facilities.

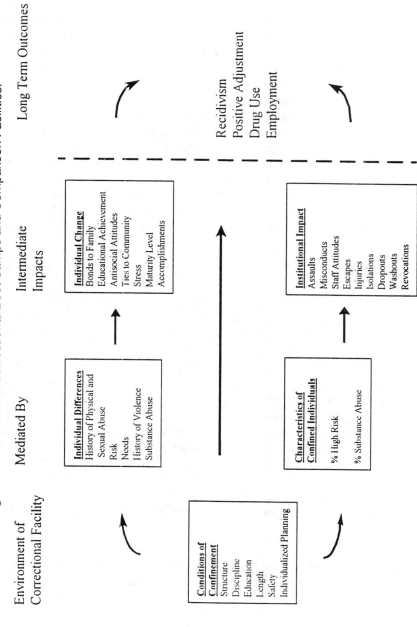

be important to identify what factors from the two environments have an impact on drug use during community supervision.

Another example of an environmental component is safety. An unsafe environment may lead to increased gang activity and future recidivism. The question is whether the environment in the boot camp is safer than a non–boot camp environment (e.g., prison, detention center, training school)? Second, is the boot camp consistently safer or does the level of safety change over time? Finally, is the safety of the environment associated with the behavior of the juveniles once they are released to the community (e.g., recidivism, positive activities)?

Similar questions could be asked about indices measuring the structure of the environment or quality of the programming. Does the boot camp environment have more structure than a non–boot camp environment? Is the therapeutic programming consistent with what has been shown to be effective in literature reviews and meta-analyses? Do these factors change over time? Lastly, how are structure and program quality related to recidivism and positive activities during community supervision?

Summary

There is little research demonstrating the effectiveness of boot camp programs in changing the long-term outcomes of the participants. We argue that, while there is evidence that rehabilitation programs in general may be effective with some offenders, there has been very little research to evaluate which components of successful programs may be present in boot camp environments. Furthermore, the movements toward performance-based standards and total quality management strongly recommend more detailed measurement of both the intermediate and long-term outcomes of boot camps and other facilities. These measures should be directly associated with particular outcomes. Our task becomes one of measuring environmental conditions and examining how the conditions are related to outcomes. Without such information, administrators have no way to decide whether the program they design and administer is meeting the desired objectives.

References

American Correctional Association. 1993. *Female Offenders: Meeting Needs of a Neglected Population*. Laurel, MD: American Correctional Association.

Andrews, D. A., I. Zinger, R. D. Hoge, J. Bonta, P. Gendreau, and F. T. Cullen. 1990. Does correctional treatment work? A clinically-relevant and psychologically-informed meta-analysis. *Criminology*, 28:369–404.

Austin, J., M. Jones, and M. Bolyard. 1993. A survey of jail-operated boot camps and guidelines for their interpretation. In *Correctional Boot Camps: A Tough Intermediate Sanction*. D. L. MacKenzie and E. E. Herbert, eds. Washington, DC: National Institute of Justice.

Cronin, R. C. 1994. Boot Camps for Adult and Juvenile Offenders: Overview and Update. National Institute of Justice Research Report, Washington, DC: National Institute of Justice.

DiIulio, J. J., Jr. 1993. Rethinking the criminal justice system: Toward a new paradigm. In *Performance Measures for the Criminal Justice System*. Washington, DC: U.S. Department of Justice (NCJ-143505).

Gendreau, P. and R. R. Ross. 1987. Revivification of rehabilitation: Evidence from the 1980's. *Justice Quarterly*, 4:349–407.

Greenwood, P. W. and S. Turner. 1987. The VisionQuest Program: An Evaluation. Santa Monica, CA: The RAND Corporation.

Jablonski, J. R. 1991. *Implementing Total Quality Management: An Overview*. San Diego: Pfeiffer.

Lipsey, M. W. 1992. Juvenile delinquency treatment: A meta-analytic inquiry into the variability of effects. In *Meta-Analysis for Explanation: A Casebook*. T. Cook, H. Cooper, D. S. Cordray, H. Hartman, L. V. Hedges, R. Light, T. A. Louis, and F. Mosteller, eds. New York: Russell Sage Foundation.

Logan, C. H. 1993. Criminal justice performance measures for prisons. In *Performance Measures for the Criminal Justice System*. Washington, DC: Department of Justice (NCJ-143505).

MacKenzie, D. L. and R. Brame. 1995. Shock incarceration and positive adjustment during community supervision. *Journal of Quantitative Criminology*, 11:111–142.

MacKenzie, D. L., R. Brame, D. McDowall, and C. Souryal. 1995. Boot camps and recidivism in eight states. *Criminology*, 33:327–357.

MacKenzie, D. L. and H. Donaldson. 1996. Boot camp for women offenders. *Criminal Justice Review*, 21:21–43.

MacKenzie, D. L., L. Elis, S. S. Simpson, and S. B. Skroban. 1996. Boot camps as an alternative for women. In *Correctional Boot Camps: A Tough Intermediate Sanction*. D. L. MacKenzie and E. E. Herbert, eds. Washington, DC: National Institute of Justice.

MacKenzie, D. L. and D. Parent. 1992. Boot camp prisons for young offenders. In *Smart Sentencing: The Emergence of Intermediate Sanctions*. J. N. Byrne, A. J. Lurigio, and J. Petersilia, eds. London: Sage.

MacKenzie, D. L. and A. Piquero. 1994. The impact of shock incarceration programs on prison crowding. *Crime and Delinquency*, 40:222–249.

MacKenzie, D. L. and A. Rosay. 1996. Correctional boot camps for juveniles. In *Juvenile and Adult Boot Camps*. Laurel, MD: American Correctional Association.

MacKenzie, D. L. and C. Souryal. 1994. Multi-Site Evaluation of Shock Incarceration: Executive Summary. Report to the National Institute of Justice. Washington, DC: National Institute of Justice.

MacKenzie, D. L. and C. Souryal. 1995a. Inmates' attitude change during incarceration: A comparison of boot camp with traditional prison. *Justice Quarterly*, 12:325–354.

MacKenzie, D. L. and C. Souryal. 1995b. A "Machiavellian" perspective on the development of boot camp prisons: A debate. *University of Chicago Roundtable*. Chicago: University of Chicago Press.

Meachum, L. M. 1990. Boot camp prisons: Pros and cons. Paper presented at Annual Meeting of American Society of Criminology, Baltimore, MD.

Morash, M. and L. Rucker. 1990. A critical look at the ideal of boot camp as a correctional reform. *Crime and Delinquency*, 36:204–222.

Morris, N. and M. Tonry. 1990. *Between Prison and Probation: Intermediate Punishments in a Rational Sentencing System*. New York: Oxford University Press.

Office of Juvenile Justice and Delinquency Prevention (OJJDP), by Dale Parent. 1994. *Conditions of Confinement: Juvenile Detention and Correctional Facilities*. Washington, DC: OJJDP, U.S. Department of Justice.

Osborne, D. and T. Gaebler. 1992. *Reinventing Government*. New York: Praeger.

Petersilia, J. 1993. Measuring the performance of community corrections. In *Performance Measures for the Criminal Justice System*. Washington, DC: U.S. Department of Justice (NCJ-143505).

RAND. 1995. *Assessment of Fundamental Science Programs in the Context of the Government Performance and Results Act*. Prepared for the Office of Science and Technology Policy. Santa Monica, CA: The RAND Corporation.

Sherman, L. W., D. Gottfredson, D. L. MacKenzie, J. Eck, P. Reuter, and S. Bushway. 1997. *Preventing Crime: What Works, What Doesn't, What's Promising*. A report to the U.S. Congress prepared for the National Institute of Justice (NCJ-165366).

24

Prison-Based Therapeutic Communities
An Effective Modality for
Treating Drug-Involved Offenders
James A. Inciardi

The relationship between drug use and criminal activity has been well documented. For example, follow-up studies of career addicts in Baltimore have found high rates of criminality among heroin users during those periods they are addicted and markedly lower rates during times of non-addiction (Ball et al., 1981; Ball, Shaffer, and Nurco, 1983; Nurco et al., 1985). Street studies conducted in Miami, Florida have demonstrated that the amount of crime drug users commit is considerable, that drug-related crime is at times quite violent, and that the criminality of street drug users is far beyond the control of law enforcement (Inciardi, 1989; Inciardi and Pottieger, 1991; Inciardi and Page, 1991; Inciardi, Horowitz and Pottieger, 1993). Research conducted elsewhere, furthermore, has arrived at similar conclusions (Johnson et al., 1985; Goldstein et al., 1989; Anglin and Hser, 1987). The majority

Prepared especially for *The Dilemmas of Corrections*.

of the research seems to say that although the use of cocaine, heroin, and other drugs does not necessarily initiate criminal careers, it tends to intensify and perpetuate them. That is, street drugs tend to freeze users into patterns of criminality that are more acute, dynamic, unremitting, and enduring than those of other offenders.

A concomitant of drug-related criminality and the "war on drugs" of the 1980s and 1990s has been increased numbers of drug-involved offenders coming to the attention of the criminal justice system. This has been amply demonstrated by the Drug Use Forecasting (DUF) program, sponsored by the National Institute of Justice. In twenty-three major cities throughout the nation, the DUF program routinely conducts urinalyses of samples of arrestees. DUF reports indicate that as many as 60 percent of arrestees test positive for cocaine, and up to 80 percent in some cities test positive for at least one illicit drug (Wish, 1991). Furthermore, it has been reported that perhaps two-thirds of those entering state and federal penitentiaries have histories of substance abuse (see Leukefeld and Tims, 1992). As such, there has been considerable interest in recent years in both providing and improving drug abuse treatment programs in correctional settings.

However, much has been written about the problems of implementing new drug treatment programs in penitentiary settings because despite any arguments to the contrary, the primary task of prisons is custody. The internal order of the prison is maintained by strictly controlling the inmates and regimenting every aspect of their lives. In addition to their loss of freedom and basic liberties, goods and services, heterosexual relationships, and autonomy, they are deprived of their personal identities. Upon entering prison, inmates are stripped of their clothing and most of their personal possessions; and they are examined, inspected, weighed, documented, classified, and given a number. Thus, prison becomes painful, both physically and psychologically (Clemmer 1958; Sykes 1965).

The rigors and frustrations of confinement leave but a few paths open to inmates. They can bind themselves to their fellow captives in ties of mutual aid and loyalty, in opposition to prison officials. They can wage a war against all, seeking their own advantage without reference to the needs and claims of others. Or they can simply withdraw into themselves. Ideally these alternatives exist only in an abstract sense, and most inmates combine characteristics of the first two extremes. Within this balance of extremes an inmate social system emerges and functions, and one of the fundamental elements of this social system is the prison subculture.

Every correctional facility has its subculture, and every prison subculture has its system of norms that influence prisoners' behavior, typically to a far greater extent than the institution's formally prescribed rules. These subcultural norms are informal and unwritten rules, but their violation can evoke sanctions from fellow inmates ranging from simple ostracism to physical violence and death. Many of the rules revolve around relations among inmates and interactions with prison staff, while others reflect preoccupations with being "smart," "tough," and street wise. As such, this prison code often tends to militate against reform in general, and drug rehabilitation in particular, or as one Delaware inmate put it, "people in treatment are faggots" (Inciardi, Lockwood, and Martin 1991).

In addition, there are many other phenomena in the prison environment that make rehabilitation difficult. Not surprisingly, the availability of drugs in prisons is a pervasive problem. Moreover, in addition to the one-on-one violence that seems to be a concomitant of prison life, there is the violence associated with inmate gangs, often formed along racial lines for the purposes of establishing and maintaining status, "turf," and unofficial control over certain sectors of the penitentiary. Within this setting, it would appear that if any drug rehabilitation approach had a chance of succeeding, it would be the therapeutic community.

Therapeutic Communities in Corrections

The therapeutic community (or "TC" as it is most commonly called) is a total treatment environment isolated from the rest of the prison population—separated from the drugs, the violence, and the norms and values that rebuff attempts at rehabilitation. The primary clinical staff of the TC are typically former substance abusers—"recovering addicts"—who themselves were rehabilitated in therapeutic communities. The treatment perspective of the TC is that drug abuse is a disorder of the whole person—that the problem is the *person* and not the drug, that addiction is a *symptom* and not the essence of the disorder. In the TC's view of recovery, the primary goal is to change the negative patterns of behavior, thinking, and feeling that predispose drug use. As such, the overall goal is a responsible drug-free lifestyle (see De Leon and Ziegenfuss 1986; Yablonsky 1989).

Recovery through the TC process depends on positive and negative pressures to change, and this is brought about through a self-help process in which relationships of mutual responsibility to every resident in the program are built. Or as the noted TC researcher Dr. George De Leon once described it:

> The essential dynamic in the TC is mutual self-help. Thus, the day-to-day activities are conducted by the residents themselves. In

their jobs, groups, meetings, recreation, personal, and social time,
it is residents who continually transmit to each other the main
messages and expectations of the community (De Leon 1985).

In addition to individual and group counseling, the TC process has a
system of explicit rewards that reinforce the value of earned achievement. As such, privileges are *earned.* In addition, TCs have their own
specific rules and regulations that guide the behavior of residents and
the management of their facilities. Their purposes are to maintain the
safety and health of the community and to train and teach residents
through the use of discipline. TC rules and regulations are numerous,
the most conspicuous of which are total prohibitions against violence,
theft, and drug use. Violation of these cardinal rules typically results in
immediate expulsion from a TC.

It appears that the first corrections-based TC was established in
1962 in Nevada State Prison as an extension of Charles Dederick's
Synanon program (Pan et al. 1993). Several more appeared during the
latter half of the 1960s. In 1967, the Federal Bureau of Prisons estab-
lished a therapeutic community in its Danbury, Connecticut institution
(Bol and Meyboom 1988). As part of Governor Nelson A. Rockefeller's
Narcotic Addiction Control Commission and its ill-fated civil commit-
ment program for heroin addicts, a small TC program was piloted in
New York's Green Haven Prison, a maximum security facility some
ninety miles north of Manhattan. At about the same time, the New York
City Addiction Services Agency organized TC units in Rikers Island and
Hart Island penitentiaries.

From the early 1970s through the mid-1980s, prison-based TCs
seemed to come and go—in Arkansas, Connecticut, Georgia, Michigan,
Nebraska, New York, Oklahoma, South Carolina, Virginia, the federal
system, and elsewhere. Along with the prison TCs established in the
1960s, almost all were closed, the result of prison crowding, state budget deficits, staff burnout, and changes in prison leadership. In a few
instances, shutdowns were precipitated by inmate residents smuggling
drugs and alcohol into the TC units. In others, custodial officers dis-
trusted TC staff and operations, and deliberately sabotaged the
programs (Camp and Camp 1990; Smith 1977; Toch 1980; Weppner
1983). Not to be forgotten was Robert Martinson's notorious paper,
"What Works? Questions and Answers About Prison Reform," published in *The Public Interest* in the spring of 1974 (Martinson 1974). In
it, Martinson reviewed the literature on hundreds of correctional treatment efforts and concluded that with few and isolated exceptions,
nothing worked! His paper created a sensation and helped to usher in
an "abolish treatment" era, characterized by a "nothing works" philoso-

phy. This did little to help the cause of therapeutic communities in corrections.

In the midst of the distrust and skepticism of the period, however, there seemed to be a few bright spots. Somewhat visible in this behalf was the Stay 'N Out therapeutic community, established in the New York State correctional system in 1974 (Frohling 1989). Having one component in a men's institution and another in a women's facility, Stay 'N Out was the joint effort of state agencies responsible for substance abuse, correctional services, and parole supervision. Program residents came from other state correctional institutions; they had to be at least eighteen years old and have a history of drug abuse, but with no mental illness or sex crime involvement. In addition, each client had to demonstrate positive involvement in prior prison programs.

Stay 'N Out helped define the model structure for prison-based therapeutic communities. Units were established away from the rest of the prison population, staffed with ex-addicts and other personnel capable of providing positive role models. Along with individual counseling, confrontation and support groups played important roles in the therapeutic process. Clients were expected to prove themselves through work and participation in the therapeutic community, achieving greater status and more responsible positions as they succeeded. Strict rules were enforced, however, and penalties were seen as learning opportunities. In various ways, the prosocial values of honesty, responsibility, and accountability were emphasized and reinforced.

Follow-up studies of Stay 'N Out provided evidence that prison-based TC treatment could produce reductions in recidivism rates for both male and female offenders with histories of serious drug use (Wexler and Williams 1986; Wexler, Falkin and Lipton 1990). Of the 1,626 men who spent an optimal 9 to 12 months in the program, for example, 77 percent successfully completed parole. Women who spent that amount of time in the program fared even better, with 92 percent completing parole. Both men and women spending 9 to 12 months in the TC were three times less likely to become recidivists than those spending less time in the program. Along with other TC evaluations (De Leon, Wexler, and Jainchill 1982; De Leon 1984; Field 1989), the Stay 'N Out experience quite clearly suggested that the therapeutic community might be the most appropriate approach for treating drug-involved offenders.

The Staging of Corrections-Based TC Treatment

Based on experiences with correctional systems and populations, with corrections-based drug treatment, and with the evaluation of a whole variety of correctional programs, it would appear that the most appropriate strategy for effective TC intervention with inmates would involve a three-stage process (Inciardi, Lockwood, and Martin 1991). Each stage in this regimen of treatment would correspond to the inmate's changing correctional status—incarceration, work release, and parole (or whatever other form of community-based correction operates in a given jurisdiction).

The *primary stage* should consist of a prison-based therapeutic community designed to facilitate personal growth through the modification of deviant lifestyles and behavior patterns. Segregated from the rest of the penitentiary, recovery from drug abuse and the development of pro-social values in the prison TC would involve essentially the same mechanisms seen in community-based TCs. Therapy in this primary stage should be an ongoing and evolving process. Ideally, it should endure for nine to twelve months, with the potential for the resident to remain longer, if necessary. As such, recruits for the TC should be within eighteen months of their work release date at the time of treatment entry.

It is important that TC treatment for inmates begin *while they are still in the institution,* for a number of reasons. In a prison situation, time is one of the few resources that most inmates have an abundance of. The competing demands of family, work, and the neighborhood peer group are absent. Thus, there is the *time* and opportunity for comprehensive treatment—perhaps for the first time in a drug offender's career. In addition, there are other new opportunities presented—to interact with "recovering addict" role models; to acquire pro-social values and a positive work ethic; and to initiate a process of education, training, and understanding of the addiction cycle.

Since the 1970s, work release has become a widespread correctional practice for felony offenders. It is a form of partial incarceration whereby inmates are permitted to work for pay in the free community but must spend their nonworking hours either in the institution, or more commonly, in a community-based work release facility or "halfway house." Inmates qualified for work release are those approaching their parole eligibility or conditional release dates. Although graduated release of this sort carries the potential for *easing* an inmate's process of community reintegration, there is a negative side, especially for those whose drug involvement served as the key to the penitentiary gate in the first place.

This initial freedom exposes many inmates to groups and behaviors that can easily lead them back to substance abuse, criminal activities, and reincarceration. Even those receiving intensive therapeutic community treatment while in the institution face the prospect of their recovery breaking down. Work release environments in most jurisdictions do little to stem the process of relapse. Since work release populations mirror the institutional populations from which they came, there are still the negative values of the prison culture. In addition, street drugs and street norms tend to abound.

Graduates of prison-based TCs are at a special disadvantage in a traditional work release center since they must live and interact in what is typically an anti-social, nonproductive setting. Without clinical management and proper supervision, their recovery can be severely threatened. Thus, secondary TC treatment is warranted. This *secondary stage* is a "transitional TC"—the therapeutic community work release center.

The program composition of the work release TC should be similar to that of the traditional TC. There should be the "family setting" removed from as many of the external negative influences of the street and inmate cultures as is possible; and there should be the hierarchical system of ranks and job functions, the rules and regulations of the environment, and the complex of therapeutic techniques designed to continue the process of resocialization. However, the clinical regimen in the work release TC must be modified to address the correctional mandate of "work release."

In the *tertiary stage*, clients will have completed work release and will be living in the free community under the supervision of parole or some other surveillance program. Treatment intervention in this stage should involve outpatient counseling and group therapy. Clients should be encouraged to return to the work release TC for refresher/reinforcement sessions, to attend weekly groups, to call on their counselors on a regular basis, and to participate in monthly one-to-one and/or family sessions. They should also be required to spend one day each month at the program, and a weekend retreat every three months.

The TC Continuum in the Delaware Correctional System

This three stage model has been made operational within the Delaware correctional system, and is built around three therapeutic communities—The KEY, B.W.C.I. Village, and CREST Outreach Center.

The KEY is a prison-based therapeutic community for male inmates located at the Multi-Purpose Criminal Justice Facility in Wilmington, Delaware. The KEY represents the primary stage of TC treatment, and was established in 1988 through a Bureau of Justice Assistance grant. In 1990, the state of Delaware took over the funding of the program, expanding it from its original forty beds to seventy. In June of 1993, the state allocated funds for a further expansion of the program to 115 beds.

In general terms, the treatment regimen at The KEY follows a holistic approach. Different types of therapy—behavioral, cognitive, and emotional—are used to address individual treatment needs (Hooper, Lockwood, and Inciardi 1993). Briefly:

1. *Behavioral therapy* fosters positive demeanor and conduct by not accepting antisocial actions. To implement this, behavioral expectations are clearly defined as soon as a new resident is admitted to the program. At that time, the staff's primary focus is on how the resident is to behave. The client works with an orientation manual which he or she is expected to learn thoroughly. Once again, the focus is on behavior as opposed to thoughts and feelings. As the client learns and adjusts to the routines of the therapeutic community, more salient issues are dealt with in the treatment process.

2. *Cognitive therapy* helps individuals recognize errors and fallacies in their thinking. The object is to help the client understand how and why certain cognitive patterns have been developed across time. With this knowledge the client can develop alternative thinking patterns resulting in more realistic decisions about life. Cognitive therapy is accomplished in both group and individual sessions.

3. *Emotional therapy* deals with unresolved conflicts associated with interactions with others and the resulting feelings and behaviors. To facilitate this treatment strategy, a nonthreatening but nurturing manner is required so that clients can gain a better understanding of how they think and feel about themselves as well as others.

A number of techniques are employed to implement these three alternative therapeutic approaches and to motivate individuals to change, including transactional analysis, psychodrama, and branch groups. *Transactional analysis* involves a detailed assessment of the roles that one plays in interactions with others. The ego states affecting behavior are defined in terms of "parent," "adult," and "child." Through group and individual sessions, clients are taught how to recognize which ego state they typically select for certain interactions and the effects of allowing their behavior to be controlled by that ego state.

In the *psychodrama*, individuals relive and explore unresolved personal feelings and thoughts. Through this process, clients are helped to bring to closure unresolved issues which have prevented them from developing more adequate life-coping skills. Group and individual sessions are used as the vehicle for this treatment.

In *branch groups*, clients meet on a routine basis to share both feelings and thoughts about the past and present. In-depth thoughts and feelings are dealt with so that there can be a better understanding of how a person is perceiving his or her world. With this understanding, that person is in a better position to develop more adequate coping skills.

B.W.C.I. Village is a prison-based therapeutic community for women inmates located at the Baylor Women's Correctional Institution in New Castle, Delaware. Like The KEY, B.W.C.I. Village represents the primary stage of TC treatment, and was established during the closing months of 1993 through a Center for Substance Abuse Treatment grant. The Village follows a treatment regimen similar to that at The KEY, but with adaptations designed specifically for women.

Near the end of 1990, the Center for Drug and Alcohol Studies at the University of Delaware was awarded a five-year treatment demonstration grant from the National Institute on Drug Abuse to establish a work release therapeutic community. Known as CREST Outreach Center, it represents the first dedicated work release TC in the nation, and it has been designed to incorporate stages two and three of the treatment process previously outlined.

The treatment regimen at CREST Outreach Center follows a five-phase model over a six-month period. *Phase one* is composed of entry, assessment and evaluation, and orientation, and lasts approximately two weeks. New residents are introduced to the house rules and schedules by older residents. Each new resident is also assigned a primary counselor, who initiates an individual needs assessment. Participation in group therapy is limited during this initial phase, so that new residents can become familiarized with the norms and procedures at CREST.

Phase two emphasizes involvement in the TC community, including such activities as morning meetings, group therapy, one-on-one interaction, confrontation of other residents who are not motivated toward recovery, and the nurturing of the newer people in the environment. During this phase, residents begin to address their own issues related to drug abuse and criminal activity, in both group sessions and during one-on-one interactions. They also begin to take responsibility for their own behaviors by being held accountable for their attitudes and actions in group settings and in informal interactions with residents and staff. Residents are assigned job functions aimed at assuming responsibility and learning acceptable work habits, and they continue to meet with their primary counselors for individual sessions. However, the primary emphasis in phase two is on becoming an active community member through participating in group therapy and fulfilling job responsibilities necessary to facility operations. This phase lasts approximately eight weeks.

Phase three continues the elements of phase two, and stresses role modeling and overseeing the working of the community on a daily basis (with the support and supervision of the clinical staff). During this phase, residents are expected to assume responsibility for themselves and to hold themselves accountable for their attitudes and behaviors. Frequently, residents in this phase will confront each other in group settings. They assume additional job responsibilities by moving into supervisory positions, thus enabling them to serve as positive role models for newer residents. They continue to have individual counseling sessions, and in group sessions they are expected to help facilitate the group process. Phase three lasts for approximately five weeks.

Phase four initiates preparation for gainful employment, including mock interviews, seminars on job seeking, making the best appearance when seeing a potential employer, developing relationships with community agencies, and looking for ways to further educational or vocational abilities. This phase focuses on preparing for re-entry to the community and lasts approximately two weeks. Residents continue to participate in group and individual therapy, and to be responsible for their jobs in the CREST facility. However, additional seminars and group sessions are introduced to address the issues related to finding and maintaining employment and housing as well as returning to the community environment.

Phase five involves "re-entry," which involves becoming gainfully employed in the outside community while continuing to live in the work release facility and serving as a role model for those at earlier stages of treatment. This phase focuses on balancing work and treatment. As such, both becoming employed and maintaining a job are integral aspects of the TC work release program. During this phase, residents continue to participate in house activities, such as seminars and social events. They also take part in group sessions addressing issues of employment and continuing treatment after leaving CREST. In addition, residents begin to prepare to leave CREST. They open a bank account and begin to budget for housing, food, and utilities. At the end of approximately seven weeks, which represents a total of twenty-six weeks at CREST Outreach Center, residents have completed their work release commitment and are free to live and work in the community as program graduates.

The CREST Outreach Center community is comprised of women and men at a variety of stages of treatment. Through this interaction, newer residents are given hope and encouragement for changing their lifestyles and the older residents can assess their own changes and become positive role models. Moreover, beginning in phase two, residents are encouraged to engage family and significant others in the treatment process through family and couples groups led by CREST counselors.

Because the majority of CREST graduates have probation and/or parole stipulations to follow after their period of work release, an *aftercare* component has been developed to ensure that graduates fulfill probation/parole requirements. This represents the tertiary phase of treatment, providing continued treatment services so as to decrease the risk of relapse and recidivism. This aftercare program endures for six months, and requires total abstinence from drug and alcohol use, one two-hour group session per week, individual counseling as scheduled, and urine monitoring. Graduates must return once a month to serve as role models for current CREST clients. Participation in a twelve-step AA (Alcoholics Anonymous) and/or NA (Narcotics Anonymous) program is also encouraged.

Postscript

The Center for Drug and Alcohol Studies at the University of Delaware is currently funded by the National Institute on Drug Abuse to evaluate the relative effectiveness of the prison and work release treatment programs described above. Field follow-ups are being conducted on all KEY and CREST clients, and on a nontreatment/work release comparison group. (The evaluation of B.W.C.I. Village began only recently, and outcome data will be reported after a sufficient number of women clients have been followed up.) A six-month follow-up takes place at the completion of work release, with a second follow-up eighteen months after the client has been released from prison. At those two points, there is HIV and urine testing, as well as an in-depth assessment of drug use and HIV risk behaviors. At this point in time, the six- and eighteen-month follow-ups have been completed on 475 clients, and as illustrated in table 1, all are serious offenders with extensive histories of both drug use and arrest. In terms of outcome, the data appear to be quite promising. As illustrated in figure 1, based on self-reports and urine testing:

- Of those clients in the no-treatment/work release comparison group, only 16 percent were drug-free at the eighteen-month follow-up.

- Of those graduates of The KEY prison-based TC for men who did not attend CREST but went directly to conventional work release, only 22 percent were drug-free at the eighteen-month follow-up.

Table 1
Descriptive Data for 475 Clients with 6 and 18 Month Follow-ups*

	Comparison	KEY	CREST	KEY/CREST
TOTAL # OF CASES	184	38	183	70
Age (Mean)	29.4	31.7	29.1	30.9
Males (%)	82.1	100	77.0	75.4
African-American (%)	67.9	84.2	72.7	85.5
White (%)	29.3	15.8	24.6	11.6
Hispanic (%)	2.7	0.0	2.7	0.0
Age at First Arrest	18.2	14.6	17.3	15.3
Mean # of Arrests	9.3	11.5	9.8	9.1
Mean # of Times in Prison	3.1	3.3	2.9	3.2
Cocaine/Crack (%)	83.2	97.4	86.9	77.9
Heroin/Opiates (%)	17.4	50.0	22.4	41.2
Marijuana (%)	63.0	76.3	72.7	57.4

* Drug use data represent any report of use during the six months prior to entering prison.

- Of those who went to the CREST Outreach Center who had no prior treatment while in the institution, 31 percent were drug-free at the eighteen-month follow-up.
- Of those who received primary treatment at The KEY and transitional treatment and aftercare at CREST Outreach Center, 50 percent were drug-free at the eighteen-month follow-up.

Going further, and as illustrated in figure 2:

- Of those clients in the no-treatment/work release comparison group, only 44 percent were arrest free at the eighteen-month follow-up.
- Of those graduates of The KEY prison-based TC for men who did not attend CREST but went directly to conventional work release, only 41 percent were arrest-free at the eighteen-month follow-up.
- Of those who went to the CREST Outreach Center who had no prior treatment while in the institution, 54 percent were arrest-free at the eighteen-month follow-up.
- Of those who received primary treatment at The KEY and transitional treatment and aftercare at CREST Outreach Center, 76 percent were arrest-free at the eighteen-month follow-up.

Figure 1. Percent Drug-Free Since Release by Self
Report and Urine Test at 6 and 18 Month Follow-up,
Controlling for Other Group Differences[1]

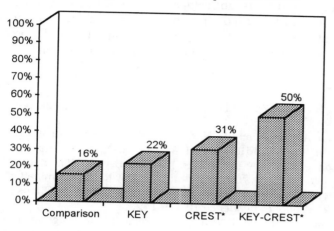

Comparison:
no TC, N=184
KEY:
in-prison TC
only, N=38
CREST:
work-release TC
only, N=183
KEY-CREST:
both TCs, N=70

*Significantly different from comparison group, p<.001
[1]Adjusted percentages from logistic regression using control variables
measuring: gender, race, age, criminal history and previous drug use.
Data as of July, 1997.

Figure 2. Percent Arrest-Free Since Release at 6 and 18
Month Follow-up, Controlling for Other Group Differences[1]

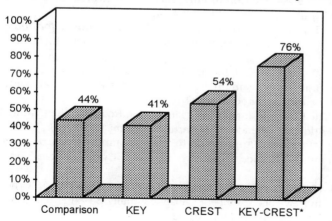

Comparison:
no TC, N=184
KEY:
in-prison TC
only, N=38
CREST:
work-release TC
only, N=183
KEY-CREST:
both TCs, N=70

*Significantly different from comparison group, p<.05
[1]Adjusted percentages from logistic regression using control variables
measuring: gender, race, age, criminal history and previous drug use.
Data as of July, 1997.

These data document that the clients who participated in the full continuum of treatment were more likely to be drug-free and arrest-free at the end of eighteen months than any other group. A forty-two-month follow-up is in progress, and no doubt relapse and arrest rates will be higher. However, it is anticipated that the largest proportions of drug-free and arrest-free clients will continue to be among those who participated in the three-stage KEY-CREST continuum of treatment.

References

Anglin, M. D., and Y. Hser (1987). "Addicted Women and Crime," *Criminology* 25:359–397.

Ball, J. C., L. Rosen, J. A. Flueck, and D. N. Nurco (1981). "The Criminality of Heroin Addicts: When Addicted and When Off Opiates," In *The Drugs-Crime Connection*, J. A. Inciardi (ed.), 39–66 (Beverly Hills: Sage).

Ball, J. C., J. W. Shaffer, and D. N. Nurco (1983). "The Day-to-Day Criminality of Heroin Addicts in Baltimore—A Study in the Continuity of Offense Rates." *Drug and Alcohol Dependence* 12:119-142.

Bol, W. W., and M. L. Meyboom (1988). "Penitentiary-Related Drug Programs in the U.S., Sweden, Switzerland, Austria, and the Federal Republic of Germany," National Institute of Justice, *International Summaries*, Spring.

Camp, G. M., and C. G. Camp (1990). *Preventing and Solving Problems Involved in Operating Therapeutic Communities in a Prison Setting* (South Salem, NY: Criminal Justice Institute).

Clemmer, D. (1958). *The Prison Community* (New York: Rinehart).

De Leon, G. (1984). *The Therapeutic Community: Study of Effectiveness* (Rockville, MD: National Institute on Drug Abuse).

_____. (1985). "The Therapeutic Community: Status and Evolution," *International Journal of the Addictions*, 20:823–844.

De Leon, G., and J. T. Ziegenfuss (1986). *Therapeutic Communities for Addictions: Readings in Theory, Research and Practice* (Springfield, IL: Charles C. Thomas).

De Leon, G., H. K. Wexler, and N. Jainchill (1982). "The Therapeutic Community: Success and Improvement Rates Five Years After Treatment," *International Journal of the Addictions* 17:703–747.

Field, G. (1989). "The Effects of Intensive Treatment on Reducing the Criminal Recidivism of Addicted Offenders," *Federal Probation*, 53:51–56.

Frohling, R. (1989). "Promising Approaches to Drug Treatment in Correctional Settings," Criminal Justice Paper #7. National Conference of State Legislatures.

Goldstein, P. J., H. H. Brownstein, P. J. Ryan, and P. A. Bellucci (1989). "Crack and Homicide in New York City, 1988: A Conceptually Based Event Analysis," *Contemporary Drug Problems* 16:651–687.

Hooper, R. M., D. Lockwood, and J. A. Inciardi (1993). "Treatment Techniques in Corrections-Based Therapeutic Communities," *Prison Journal* 73:290–306.

Inciardi, J. A. (1989). "Trading Sex for Crack Among Juvenile Drug Users: A Research Note," *Contemporary Drug Problems* 16:689–700.

Inciardi, J. A., and A. E. Pottieger (1991). "Kids, Crack, and Crime," *Journal of Drug Issues* 21:257–270.

Inciardi, J. A., and J. B. Page (1991). "Drug Sharing Among Intravenous Drug Users," *AIDS* 5:772–773.

Inciardi, J. A., R. Horowitz, and A. E. Pottieger (1993). *Street Kids, Street Drugs, Street Crime: An Examination of Drug Use and Serious Delinquency in Miami* (Belmont, CA: Wadsworth).

Inciardi, J. A., D. Lockwood, and S. S. Martin (1991). "Therapeutic Communities in Corrections and Work Release: Some Clinical and Policy Considerations," National Institute on Drug Abuse Technical Review Meeting on Therapeutic Community Treatment Research, Bethesda, Maryland, May 16–17.

Johnson, B. D., P. J. Goldstein, E. Preble, J. Schmeidler, D. S. Lipton, B. Spunt, and T. Miller (1985). *Taking Care of Business: The Economics of Crime by Heroin Abusers* (Lexington, MA: Lexington Books).

Leukefeld, C. G., and F. M. Tims (1992). *Drug Abuse Treatment in Prisons and Jails* (Rockville, MD: National Institute on Drug Abuse).

Martinson, R. (1974). "What Works? Questions and Answers About Prison Reform," *The Public Interest* 35:22–54.

Nurco, D. N., J. C. Ball, J. W. Shaffer, and T. Hanlon (1985). "The Criminality of Narcotic Addicts," *Journal of Nervous and Mental Disease* 173:94–102.

Pan, H., F. R. Scarpitti, J. A. Inciardi, and D. Lockwood (1993). "Some Considerations on Therapeutic Communities in Corrections," in *Drug Treatment and Criminal Justice*, James A. Inciardi (ed.), 30-43 (Newbury Park, CA: Sage).

Smith, R. (1977). *Drug Problems in Correctional Institutions* (Washington, DC: Law Enforcement Assistance Administration).

Sykes, G. M. (1965). *The Society of Captives: A Study of a Maximum Security Prison* (New York: Atheneum).

Toch, H. (ed.) (1980). *Therapeutic Communities in Corrections* (New York: Praeger).

Weppner, R. S. (1983). *The Untherapeutic Community: Organizational Behavior in a Failed Addiction Treatment Program* (Lincoln: University of Nebraska Press).

Wexler, H. K., G. P. Falkin, and D. S. Lipton (1990). "Outcome Evaluation of a Prison Therapeutic Community for Substance Abuse Treatment," *Criminal Justice and Behavior* 17:71–92.

Wexler, H. K., and R. Williams (1986). "The Stay 'N Out Therapeutic Community: Prison Treatment for Substance Abusers," *Journal of Psychoactive Drugs* 18:221–229.

Wish, E. D. (1991). "Drug Testing and the Identification of Drug Abusing Criminals," In *Handbook of Drug Control in the United States*, J. A. Inciardi (ed.), 229–244 (Westport, CT: Greenwood Press).

Yablonsky, L. (1989). *The Therapeutic Community: A Successful Approach for Treating Substance Abusers* (New York: Gardner Press).

25

The Detoxing of Prisoner 88A0802

Peter Kerr

The 200 inmates at the Phoenix House Drug treatment unit at the State Medium Security Facility in Marcy, N.Y., are cordoned off from the 1,300 other prisoners by a high chain-link fence topped with barbed wire. When they march out of the treatment zone for meals, stepping smartly in double file, other prisoners glare and mutter "crackheads" and "snitches" at them. They are hated because their life, inside a protected world each day, violates the unwritten laws of prison.

"You *must* have hospital corners," says Bill Giddens, a slender prisoner of 6 foot 2 and 180 pounds. Giddens is touring rows of cubicles separated by chest-high partitions. Men stand attentively next to beds made tight enough to bounce coins off. He walks the shiny waxed floors with heavy socks pulled over his shoes so he will not leave a mark. An assistant with a clipboard trails behind.

"This is the place where you get your pride and quality," Giddens says as he runs his long bony fingers down walls, behind chairs and over hidden flat surfaces. "Dust on a partition divider." The assistant makes a note.

Bill Giddens is an unlikely drill sergeant. One day six years ago the shoe of a police officer pressed down so hard on his face he thought his skull would crack. Cold grains of concrete dug into his cheek. Yet as he lay surrounded by a circle of armed officers, he struggled to reach for one of their revolvers. By the frenzied calculus of a heroin addict, he imagined that he could outgun them all. As happens so often in the Williamsburg section of Brooklyn where Giddens grew up, a crowd gathered to see detectives arrest the young man—one more terrifying figure from the neighborhood who deserved to go prison.

Bill Giddens, like the legions of junkies and crackheads who haunt many communities, had been a one-man crime wave: in two years he had robbed more than 200 people. His was a life of craving and satiation. He knew little of guilt or responsibility. He was the type who long ago led criminal-justice experts to abandon the idea that predatory street criminals could be rehabilitated.

But at drug-treatment programs, like the one at the Marcy prison, in more than a dozen states from California to Connecticut, criminal-justice officials now report enough success to begin to transform their thinking. Two decades ago, they concluded that such programs were just about worthless. Now they are finding that, with the help of new research and revised techniques, prison and post-prison "therapeutic communities," as the programs are called, have significant potential if operated correctly. Inmates can readily obtain drugs somewhere in most prisons, and freeing them of addiction is a momentous event. This is true not only for the individual inmate, but also for society.

A relatively small number of severe addicts commit a high percentage of street crime. By targeting them, these programs may thus have impact. This realization comes just at a time when a rebellion is building against the 1980s approach of lock 'em up and throw away the key—if only because states find they soon have to make room for other prisoners. In April, two well-known Federal judges in New York, Whitman Knapp and Jack B. Weinstein, declared they would no longer preside over drug cases because the Government's emphasis on long imprisonment without treatment, rehabilitation or prevention was a failure. And last month [at the writing of the article], the new Attorney General, Janet Reno, called for revision of the national strategy for coping with drugs and crime. Treatment programs in prisons are to be a principal part of that new approach.

So the question reverberates: This time around, have prison authorities hit on a form of rehabilitation that works?

Prisoners inside the beige walls of Marcy's barracks rise at 5 A.M.

They march half a mile to breakfast and back. Then they stand in a circle, arms around each other's shoulders and chant the Phoenix House philosophy—a kind of prayer for redemption and strength:

> Rise from the ashes of our defeat to take our rightful place in society. Society will accept us, for once we have regained our dignity, we will be society.

At a nearby barracks, an encounter session among another circle of green-clad men is reaching full boil. Inmates are challenging R. B., a former drug dealer in his 20s. R. B. has said he is a good father because he bought his family a respectable home in Queens and pampered his little girl with expensive toys and clothes.

"I indict your butt," shouts one prisoner.

"If I need your help, I'll ask for it," snaps R. B., a thickset black slouched in his chair, his arms folded defiantly. "My kid doesn't know what I do on the street."

It doesn't take much for her to figure out what's going on," says Dana Macklin, a 28-year-old former dealer with a daughter of his own. "Are you aware of this criminal history, what effect is it going to have on your kid?"

"Yeah," barks another inmate, "your best thinking is what got you into jail."

R. B. shakes his head. "My little girl doesn't know what I do."

A deputy director of the program, Manny Rivera, a 52-year-old former prisoner with a rhythmic voice, swept-back hair and dark, lively eyes has been watching.

"Look at this from another point of view." He paces with coffee cup in hand. "What does a young girl, wherever she lives, what does she need from a father? Who is going to tuck her in tonight? Who is going to fluff up the pillow?"

The men's faces are tough. Some are marred by knife wounds. One has the tattoo of a tear under his eye, a sign that he has killed someone.

All are silent.

"Who is going to tell her everything is going to be all right?," Manny says. "What man is going to be there for her? You are not that man now."

R. B.'s eyes are downcast.

"I went to jail the last time when I was 40," Manny says. "I don't want that for you, man. We just want what is best for you."

The theory of therapeutic community is this: to treat addiction, one must change a person's values, thinking, moods, behavior and spirituality. The therapeutic community aims to resocialize people and force them to embrace responsibility, honesty and caring for others. It attempts to teach them to recognize their own feelings and think and speak clearly and honestly.

Some prisoners call what is going on brainwashing, or mind control. For many, however, the therapeutic community is the first family they have ever really had. In fact the prisoners call themselves a family. Other versions of the therapeutic community exist outside of prison, not only for treating drug addiction but also for helping alcoholics and the mentally ill.

As Giddens tells it, it was an excruciating breakthrough to learn to step back, look at himself objectively, and express feelings in full sentences.

"Talking with me before I came here, it was always yes-no, I mean you would of thought you were talking to a mute, I mean, I always thought I would always say the wrong thing." He pauses, looks at my notebook and begins to articulate each word slowly. "I am deeply gratified that I have gotten my communication skills up to par. I guess what I have learned here in treatment is that to feel and know yourself is to be strong. I am not ashamed of who is inside Bill."

Giddens takes me back to his "cube" and, from the back of a cabinet, pulls out six shrunken gray objects, with a year written on each in black magic marker. When he arrived in prison, he got six oranges and on each birthday marked off another year. Today they are private symbols of his wasted years.

"They are dried up, no color, no smell, no juice left in them," Giddens says quietly.

Bill Giddens was born in Brooklyn in 1957 to a single mother who went on and off welfare. By 13, he was drinking wine and smoking marijuana in a local park and, with friends in the ninth grade, he learned to jump out from hidden spots in subway stations, grab people from behind and rob them.

He won a basketball scholarship to North Carolina A.& T., but dropped out of college after three months and returned to the neighborhood. In the years that followed, he drifted from job to job, fathered two children and eventually slipped into heavy drug use. A year-long stint at a state minimum-security prison for car theft, Giddens recalls, had about as much effect as a drop of water on a chunk of wax.

"Nice countryside," he says. "You get pretty much everything you want. I guess I just took to it pretty well."

By 1985 Giddens was shooting up heroin three or four times a day. To support the $90-a-day habit, he says he sometimes robbed as many as two people a day. He often confronted them in elevators or building entryways. They were usually compliant, so he says he did not have to hurt them. It all seemed easy. But one morning when he went out to buy a bottle of orange juice, he was jumped by six policemen and arrested for robbery.

He spent the next five and a half years in some of New York State's toughest prisons. Everyone owned a weapon, be it a knife sharpened from a steel bedpost part or a razor blade tucked between gum and cheek. Drugs were easy to obtain. Giddens learned to trust no one and show no weakness. In Sing Sing, he said, prison society tested a new arrival by having one longtime inmate offer a cigarette. Saying "thank you" with a tone of relief or appreciation betrayed fear and weakness. Within days, the new prisoner was told he was in debt and had to do what the gang commanded. Unless he refused and fought, he would be marked forever as a victim.

Giddens refused to take anything from anyone.

The current national turn back to rehabilitation arises in part from desperation.

With the end of the Reagan-Bush years when the Federal Government frowned on rehabilitating prisoners, courts have ordered more than 40 states to relieve overcrowding. Staggering numbers of young minority men are under the supervision of the criminal justice system (by one study, about one in four black men ages 20 to 29 is in prison, on probation or on parole). Incarceration costs $25,000 a year per prisoner in New York. The present number of prisoners is expected to rise from more than 1.3 million to more than 2 million people by the year 2000; small wonder that many criminal justice experts say the Government must take a new approach.

"The great drug triumph of the Reagan-Bush years—the decline in the number of marijuana and cocaine users—produced few visible social benefits," says a leading authority on drug enforcement, Mark A. R. Kleiman, an associate professor of public policy at the John F. Kennedy School of Government at Harvard. "Hard-core problem users were not the ones who stopped using drugs. But they are where the crime, violence and disorder come from."

The program at Marcy, which has been run by Phoenix House along with the Department of Corrections since 1990, is one of seven in New York State. It chooses prisoners who have no convictions for violent or heinous crimes and are available for release within two years. If they join and succeed at 6 to 12 months of therapy, they can be released for up to one year more of treatment in a residential therapeutic community in Queens. Or the most promising are released to live at home, work and attend therapy sessions at night. In either case, they are required to stay in the program, attending intensive encounter sessions until they have been in treatment for two years. If their behavior turns erratic or they fail a weekly urine test for drugs, they are returned to prison.

The attraction is that if they agree to treatment, they may get out of prison early. But once they enter treatment they cannot choose to leave until it's over.

Arriving at the treatment unit, Bill Giddens recalls, was like passing through the looking glass. When he got off the bus, several inmates grabbed his bags and ran ahead with them into the dormitory. Giddens thought this was a test and was heading for a fight. But inside he found his bags on his bed and the perpetrators smiling, welcoming him aboard.

"I was most worried by the fact that the inmates were in charge," Giddens says. "I thought I would be subject to someone disrespecting me and abusing me and no one there to do anything about it. The next day I saw a circle of men were cursing, screaming."

He says they begun to insult one member viciously. "I see it in his face that this guy wants to jump someone. I say to myself, Bill, stay clear, someone's gonna get hurt. But afterwards, they get up and they hug each other. I say, this is weird stuff. I gotta learn how the game goes so I do not stand out."

Giddens practiced for hours in advance what he would say in meetings. He grew angry when others, particularly younger men or those with worse criminal records, tried to correct him. Slowly he became aware of his rage at a world that treated him as worthless. Even worse, he loathed himself because he believed the world was right.

The idea is that even when prisoners are not attending their intensive therapy sessions, which may be twice a day, they are working together, recording each other's missteps and attempting to rise in a hierarchy by demonstrating empathy, honesty and dedication to work.

A new arrival usually starts at the bottom, sweeping, mopping, cleaning toilets. A first promotion allows him to work as a barber, or a maintenance worker, and beyond that, in more attractive jobs like supply clerk, or the organizer of group meetings. At the top is a ladder of leadership positions, with individuals often rising and falling, depending on how their peers and counselors judge their progress. It all amounts to a 24-hour-a-day floating psychotherapy session, in which men experience a level of scrutiny and intimacy they have never known before.

Over eight months, Giddens began to believe he could change, stay free of drugs and crime and begin to organize a life outside. But he learned that life outside was more complicated than when he left it. The mother of his children had become a crack addict, and last July, his 11-year-old son and his 7-year-old daughter were separated and sent to live with what he believed were insensitive foster families.

He became desperate to retrieve his children: "I felt that they were doing time, for what I have done."

To prepare for life outside, he used his first three-day furlough to wander through department stores and in the legal district of downtown Brooklyn and strike up conversations with sales people, legal secretaries and lawyers. He wanted to practice talking to articulate people. He got in touch with relatives to see if they knew of any kind of menial job. And he met with his children at a city social service center. He promised they would be together sometime soon.

One day after he returned from that furlough, I walked with him to the prison dining hall. Looking up at him as he towered over me, I found my own mind spinning off a bit: I thought both that I liked him and that he scared me.

Soft-spoken, self-effacing, Giddens had the manner of an earnest student. Yet I could also imagine him in a dark subway entrance or in an alleyway, pointing a gun at my head. In my imagination he was demanding my wallet, my watch and my wedding ring. Was this "Raising Arizona," the film in which prison therapy turns ordinary bank robbers into "emotionally integrated" bank robbers, who terrorize the countryside while getting in touch with their feelings?

Can six months, a year, two years of treatment undo decades of antisocial behavior?

How will the best of the inmates in this program fare, once they are alone, in poor neighborhoods, where unemployment is above 20 percent, where old friends are addicts, and crime and drugs still seem, to so many, to be the only way out?

Those same thoughts come to mind as I interview David Jordan, a 25-year-old, short, rotund former crack dealer from Harlem who never finished the ninth grade. Jordan, or Jelly, as they call him, left school to pursue a career as a break dancer on Manhattan sidewalks. He hit it big, appearing in television commercials and touring in concerts. But when work suddenly disappeared, he figured only the drug trade offered him same quick status and money.

"The program says if you stick to it you can do it," Jelly says. "I know I am being trained. The way I speak. The way I present myself. I am starting to feel good about myself. But my people, we don't have much. I am poor. I am poorly educated. When I get outside, I need an income and I feel like if I believe in this too much, am I setting myself up for a fall.

"Sometimes I am faking changes and it's like a war inside me." He adds: "I don't know which side is real. . . . I don't know which side I'm on."

Doubts about rehabilitation took hold in the early 1970s, and were expressed in a seminal article in *The Public Interest* in 1974. It concluded that "with few and isolated exceptions, the rehabilitative efforts that have been reported so far have no appreciable effect on recidivism." From that article, and a book called *The Effectiveness of Correctional Treatment*, by Douglas S. Lipton, Robert Martinson and Judith Wilks, published the following year, the belief that "Nothing works," entered the corrections vocabulary. Much of the financing for rehab efforts disappeared.

But drug-related crime has continued to increase in the last decade, despite increased prison sentences for criminals. Between 1978 and

1992, the number of people behind bars grew from 466,000 to 1,326,000. Of people arrested in the 22 largest cities, the Federal Government has found that 55 to 80 percent test positive for drug use. Meanwhile, studies show that a few heavy users commit a disproportionate share of street crimes. Heavy heroin addicts, known among criminal-justice experts as "predators," for example, commit 10 times as many thefts, 15 times as many robberies, 20 times as many burglaries as offenders who don't use drugs. If such offenders can stay off of drugs, research indicates, their criminal activity drops precipitously.

Yet federal policy during the Reagan-Bush years gave much higher priority to seizing drugs at the borders, fighting drug production overseas and making arrests, than to drug treatment. Justice Department officials who tried to expand treatment programs in prison were rebuffed.

Lipton, one of the authors who once helped promote the "nothing works" theory, now says that the earlier research did not fully explore the potential of therapeutic communities. He says he has found what he regards as surprisingly positive results in a therapeutic community in a state prison on Staten Island with prisoners who on average had been arrested four times. The study of 450 prisoners who started the program between 1977 and 1984 found that 27 percent were rearrested in the three years after they left prison. That compared with a 41 percent rate for those who had no treatment at all. Lipton, a researcher at National Development and Research Institutes, a nonprofit corporation for drug and AIDS research in New York, argues that if prisons target the worst predators, good programs could have a striking impact on street crime. A program in the Oregon State Hospital in Salem showed that 71 percent of the program's graduates were not reincarcerated within three years after release, compared with only 26 percent of inmates who dropped out in less than one month. In addition, studies of graduates of therapeutic communities outside of prisons, where most therapeutic communities operate, show significant reduction in long-term drug use.

Harry K. Wexler, a researcher in the field, says programs often failed in the past because staff workers were poorly trained and treatment did not continue after a prisoner was released.

Critics say some of the current research may be misleading, that, for instance, it may be measuring the behavior of the prisoners who are most likely to succeed. A survey of drug treatment research published by the Federal Institute of Medicine, showed that if one combined the graduates of the Oregon program and those that dropped out in less than one month, the percentage reincarcerated was 36 percent. By comparison, of Oregon parolees who got no treatment 37 percent were reincarcerated.

Others like Mark Kleiman of Harvard agree that therapeutic communities undoubtedly reduce criminal behavior. But how much, they say, is still unclear.

Dr. Mitchell S. Rosenthal, president of Phoenix House, the largest
residential drug treatment organization in the country, also cautions
against rushing over-optimistically to build therapeutic communities.
It takes years, Rosenthal says, to cultivate good programs, which rely
on experienced counselors who are often graduates of the programs
themselves. And after-care programs are essential. Other experts, like
Bruce Carnes, who served in the Bush anti-drug program, ask whether
it is fair to give treatment to criminals when other people not in prison—
teen-agers in housing projects, for example—are turned away because
of limited public funds.

But even if success rates turn out to be low, the arithmetic of treatment
is compelling. Therapeutic communities cost about $2,500 to $5,000 per
inmate per year. In a state where keeping a prisoner behind bars costs
$25,000 a year, treatment pays for itself if just one in five participants
serves just one year less. Operators of the Staten Island program, for
example, say they far surpass that success rate. Besides, there are
immense added savings if any of those prisoners stay off drugs
permanently: Innocent people are not mugged, children and spouses
do not suffer abuse, AIDS transmission by drug users is reduced and
drug-related violence is lessened.

If such thinking seems theoretical, one has only to look at Texas and
Alabama last year. Texas, which has more than a half-million people
in prison or under supervision of probation and parole authorities,
established a program to allow judges to sentence convicts to new
therapeutic communities instead of prisons. Financed by a $1 billion
bond issue, the state intends to create a virtually separate prison system
of treatment, with 14,000 new beds. In Alabama, where the number of
prisoners has risen to 18,000 from 5,000 in 1980, the state has committed
1,000 beds to drug treatment programs and is also designing separate
facilities. Other programs are under way in California, Connecticut,
Colorado, Delaware, Florida, Georgia, Hawaii, Minnesota, New Jersey,
North Carolina, North Dakota, Ohio, Oregon, Pennsylvania, Virginia,
Washington, D.C., Wisconsin, as well as in city and county jails in
Illinois and Arizona.

"Our failures on work release have been cut nearly in half," says Dr.
Merle Friesen, director of treatment for the Alabama Department of
Corrections, referring to temporary release of prisoners for job programs.
"People down here are conservative but they aren't dumb. They know
that addicts are either stealing or they are about to start."

One day last fall, Bill Giddens awoke at 4 A.M. and moved quietly
through the dark, still barracks. He placed a pair of loafers on the chair
in one prisoner's cubicle, a sweater in another, a baseball hat in another.

When the men in unit J-2 awoke, those with the least to wear found gifts from the man who was going home.

Freedom struck Giddens harshly as he stepped off the bus at the Port Authority Terminal in New York. On a subway platform, he saw two large police officers threatening to arrest a small young man. He walked away.

The weeks that followed were hard. He moved in with his mother and brother in a crowded apartment in the projects of Williamsburg. In contrast to prison, where he had worked his way to the top of society, he found himself at the bottom again, begging for work of any kind.

Day after day he walked into stores and offices in Manhattan, hair neatly combed, in a freshly ironed shirt, saying he was looking for a job. Everyone said no. Officials of the foster care system were reluctant to let his children come to live with his mother, because she had already taken in two other children who belonged to another relative who had become a drug addict.

In his old neighborhood he felt isolated. "I saw one guy I used to do stickups with," he says. "He's out there looking bad. No shoes. Hair's nappy. In my whole neighborhood the guys who are alive haven't moved anywhere. But as soon as they talk to me, see my expressions, they know not to say, 'Hey, Bill, let's hang out.'"

One night I took him to dinner in Greenwich Village. Giddens clearly tensed as we ordered from the menu. When a waitress asked him to repeat himself, he seemed crestfallen, as if he had failed a test. Later we walked the streets crowded with shoppers. At a corner, he stared at the passers-by. I asked, "What is it?"

"Sometimes I look around and I say, Bill, are you the only one around here who doesn't have a real job?," he said. "You are 35 years old and you don't have anything and it is your own fault."

After about a month, Giddens had one of his first successes. He made a list of all the women he knew and sent a letter to the only one he could think of who never used drugs and always had a steady job. He had not seen her in 18 years.

She called. Giddens explained that he had been in prison and that he was starting a new life. "Well, why did you call me?" she says. He replied: "Well, to be honest, I went down the list of all the women I knew and you were the pick of the litter." She laughed, and agreed to a date. They have been seeing each other ever since.

After six weeks he found a part-time job as an usher at Broadway theaters run by the Nederlander organization, which paid him between $85 and $185 a week. But then the job disappeared and he was unemployed for more than a month. Later with the help of Phoenix House, he got work at a stapler factory. He got up every day at 5:30 A.M. and rode the subway an hour and a half to work. Three evenings a week he attended therapy sessions and twice a week met with probation officers. Typically he got home at 11 P.M. On a salary of less than $200 a week, he was able to put $10 each Friday into savings. But after seven weeks, that job disappeared as well.

Then he seemed to wobble. His counselors found him a gritty, low-paying job in a recycling plant but he quit without promptly telling them. Not a good sign. They told me I should stop seeing him without a counselor present. They worried that my interviews might be making him think he was a celebrity and that his struggles in half-finished treatment were over.

But at the end of May, after weeks of searching, he found himself a job as an assistant in a recreation program run by a nonprofit agency in Brooklyn, earning $300 a week. No one can guarantee that Bill Giddens will succeed. Some of the men who left Marcy at about the same time have already been sent back. But his counselors, so far, are encouraged. So is he.

"All I want is a good place for my kids to come to after school that they can call home," he said. "When I see my kids they ask, 'Dad, when will we be together?' I just tell them soon, soon. It will be soon."

26

Factories with Fences

Warren E. Burger*

The ancient and honorable American custom of commencement speeches is an innocuous one that has done very little harm to those who are graduating, and it may even have the beneficial consequence of teaching the graduates the virtue of patience. With the problems you are about to confront in the disturbed world of today, you will need patience. And the parents, who are now to be released from paying the high costs of keeping a student in college, are bound to be in such a happy mood that no speech could depress them.

I have no talent or inclination for framing cosmic remarks about the future, and I have never thought that even the most eloquent of speakers could make much out of "handing the torch" to those who have survived the rigors of a university education.

All of my training and experience, as a lawyer and as a judge, is to try to go to the heart of problems and to seek and frame solutions.

I discover, on reading about Pace University, that I am almost as old

*Chief Justice, Supreme Court of the United States.
Source: This address was delivered at the commencement exercises of Pace University on June 11, 1983, at Madison Square Garden, New York. It was first published in the Pace Law Review, Vol. 4, No. 1 (Fall 1983), 1-9. Reprinted with the permission of the publisher.

as the university itself and quite frankly I was astonished to find that you have an enrollment approaching 30,000 men and women. More important than either the age or the size of the university, is how it approaches its task. It is clear that Pace University is in the forefront of institutions that look to the future and to the enormous role that technology will play in our lives in the years ahead. In its systematic anticipation of the needs of the future, Pace University fulfills one of the great obligations of a university. I naturally have a particular affinity for night school graduates. And those who attended your *day* law school have a *special* benefit — they can always call on their more mature friends of the night section for help and advice and guidance!

Now to be serious —

Today I want to discuss with you a grave problem which my generation and those who went before me have failed to solve and as a result, you inherit the consequences of that failure. In one sense we can say that it is a "torch" you are being handed, one that will singe your pocketbooks and affect your lives from now on.

Since I have been a member of the federal judiciary I have thought and spoken on the subject of penal and correctional institutions and those policies and practices that ought to be changed. I see this as part of the administration of justice. People go to prisons only when judges send them there and judges should have a particular concern about the effectiveness of the prisons and the correctional process, even though we have no responsibility for their management. Based on my observations as a judge for more than twenty-five years and from visiting prisons in the United States and in most of the countries of Europe — and in the Soviet Union and The People's Republic of China — I have long believed that we have not gone about the matter in the best way.

This is one of the unresolved problems on your agenda and today I will propose some changes in our approach to prisons. But before doing that, let me suggest why the subject has a special relevance, even a special urgency, right now. Our country is about to embark on a multi-billion dollar prison construction program. At least one billion dollars of construction is already underway. The question I raise is this: are we going to build more "human warehouses" or should we change our thinking and create institutions that are training schools and factories with fences around them where we will first train the inmates and then have them engage in useful production to prepare them for the future and to help pay for their confinement?

One thoughtful scholar of criminal justice described the state of affairs in much harsher terms than I have ever used. Four years ago he wrote this:

> Criminal justice in the United States is in a state of spreading decay.
> ...The direct costs of crime include loss of life and limb, loss of

[earnings],....physical and mental suffering by the victims and their families....[1]

These direct losses, he continued, run into many billions of dollars annually. But indirect losses are vastly more and reach the astonishing figure of 100 billion dollars a year. These indirect costs include higher police budgets, higher private security measures, higher insurance premiums, medical expenses of the victims, and welfare payments to dependents of prisoners and victims. In the immediate future these astounding figures and the great suffering that underlies them can be reduced. This can be done by more effective law enforcement which in turn will produce a demand for more and more prison facilities. But more prisons of the kind we now have will not solve the basic problem. Plainly, if we can divert more people from lives of crime we would benefit those who are diverted and the potential victims. All that we have done in improved law enforcement, in new laws for mandatory minimum sentences, and changes in parole and probation practices has not prevented thirty percent of America's homes from being touched by crime every year.

Twenty years ago I shared with such distinguished penologists as the late James V. Bennett, longtime Director of the Federal Bureau of Prisons, Torsten Eriksson, his counterpart in Sweden, and Dr. George K. Sturrup in Denmark and others, high hopes for rehabilitation programs. These hopes now seem to have been based more on optimism and wishful thinking than on reality. During that period of time we have seen that even the enlightened correctional practices of Sweden and other northern European countries have produced results that, although better than ours, have also fallen short of expectations.

On several occasions I have stated one proposition to which I have adhered to for the twenty-five years that I have worked on this problem and it is this:

> When society places a person behind walls and bars it has an obligation — a moral obligation — to do whatever can reasonably be done to change that person before he or she goes back into the stream of society.

If we had begun twenty-five, thirty-five, or fifty years ago to develop the kinds of correctional programs that are appropriate for an enlightened and civilized society, the word "recidivist" might not have quite as much currency as it does today. This is not simply a matter of compassion for other human beings, it is a hard common sense matter for our own protection and our own pocketbooks.

In just the past ten years the prison population in America has doubled from less than 200,000 inmates to more than 400,000. This reflects, in part, the increase in crime, better law enforcement, and the imposition of longer sentences and more stringent standards of parole and probation. Budgets for law enforcement, for example, like the rates for theft insurance have skyrocketed.

If we accept the idea that the most fundamental obligation of government in a civilized society is the protection of people and homes, then we must have more effective law enforcement, but equally important, we must make fundamental changes in our prison and correctional systems. Just more stone, mortar and steel for walls and bars will not change this melancholy picture. If we are to make progress and at the same time protect the persons and property of people and make streets and homes safe from crime, we must change our approach in dealing with people convicted of crimes. Our system provides more protection and more safeguards for persons accused of crime, more appeals and more reviews than any other country in the world. But once the judicial process has run its course we seem to lose interest. The prisoner and the problem are brushed under the rug.[2]

It is predictable that a person confined in a penal institution for two, five or ten years, and then released, yet still unable to read, write, spell or do simple arithmetic and not trained in any marketable vocational skill, will be vulnerable to returning to a life of crime. And very often the return to crime begins within weeks after release. What job opportunities are there for an unskilled, functional illiterate who has a criminal record? The recidivists who return to our prisons are like automobiles that are called back to Detroit. What business enterprise, whether building automobiles in Detroit or ships in Norfolk, Virginia, or airplanes in Seattle, could continue with the same rate of "recall" of its "products" as our prisons?

The best prisons in the world, the best programs that we can devise will not totally cure this dismal problem for, like disease and war, it is one that the human race has struggled with since the beginning or organized societies. But improvements in our system can be made and the improvements will cost less in the long run than the failure to make them.

I have already said that today one billion dollars in new prison facilities is actually under construction. More than thirty states have authorized construction programs for new prison facilities that over the next ten years will cost as much as ten billion dollars.

If these programs proceed, and we must assume they will, it is imperative that there be new standards that will include the following:

A. Conversion of prisons into places of education and training and into factories and shops for the production of goods.
B. Repeal of statutes which limit the amount of prison industry production or the markets for such goods.

C. Repeal of laws discriminating against the sale or transportation of prison-made goods.

D. The leaders of business and organized labor must cooperate in programs to permit wider use of productive facilities in prisons.

On the affirmative side I have every reason to believe that business and labor leaders will cooperate in more intelligent and more humane prison programs. Of course, prison production programs will compete to some extent with the private sector, but this is not a real problem. With optimum progress in the programs I have outlined, it would be three to five years, or even more, before these changes would have any market impact and even then it will be a very small impact. I cannot believe for one moment that this great country of ours, the most voracious consumer society in the world, will not be able to absorb the production of prison inmates without significant injury to private employment or business. With the most favorable results, the production level of prison inmates would be no more than a tiny drop in the bucket in terms of the Gross National Product. Yet, we find prisons in the United States with limited production facilities which are lying idle because of statutory limitations confining the sale of their products to city and county governments within the state.

Amazingly enough, Congress recently dealt prison industry another blow in the form of a rider to the five percent gas tax, which prohibits the use of prison labor products in federally funded highway projects. This will damage state prison industries which were employing hundreds of prisoners in sign making, and may cost many millions of dollars in unsaleable inventory.

Happily this may be changed. The House of Representatives just passed a bill repealing the highway prohibition and increasing authorization for prison industry projects. It is now up to the Senate.

Prison inmates, by definition, are for the most part maladjusted people. From whatever cause, whether too little discipline or too much; too little security or too much; broken homes or whatever, these people lack self-esteem. They are insecure, they are at war with themselves as well as with society. They do not share the work ethic that made this country great. They did not learn, either at home or in the schools, the moral values that lead people to have respect and concern for the rights of others. But if we place that person in a factory, rather than a "warehouse," whether that factory makes ballpoint pens, hosiery, cases for watches, parts for automobiles, lawnmowers or computers; pay that person reasonable compensation, charge something for room and board, I believe we will have an improved chance to release from prison a person better able to secure gainful employment and to live a normal, productive live. If we do this, we will have a person whose self-esteem will at least have been improved so that there is a better chance that he or she can cope with life.

There are exceptions of course. The destructive arrogance of the psychopath with no concern for the rights of others may well be beyond the reach of any programs that prisons or treatments can provide. Our prison programs must aim chiefly at the others—those who want to change.

There is nothing really new in this concept. It has been applied for years in northern Europe, and in my native state of Minnesota there are important beginnings. Special federal legislation authorized pilot programs for contracts with private companies to produce and ship merchandise in interstate commerce. Even though Minnesota's pilot program involves only a fraction of the inmates it represents a significant new start. In that program prisoners were identified by tests to determine their adaptability for training. After that they were trained and now there are approximately fifty-two prisoners in one section of the Minnesota prison engaged in assembling computers for Control Data Corporation. These prisoners will have a job waiting for them when they leave prison. Is it not reasonable to assume that the temptation to return to a life of crime will be vastly reduced?

On my first visit to Scandinavian prisons twenty-five years ago, I watched prison inmates constructing fishing dories, office furniture, and other products. On my most recent visit six years ago, prisoners in one institution were making components for prefabricated houses, under the supervision of skilled carpenters. Those components could be transported to a building site and assembled by semi-skilled workers under trained supervision. Two years ago in a prison I visited in The People's Republic of China, 1000 inmates made up a complete factory unit producing hosiery and casual sport shoes. Truly that was a factory with a fence around it. In each case, prisoners were learning a trade and paying at least part of the cost of their confinement.

Today the confinement of the 500,000 inmates in American prisons cost the taxpayers of this country, including the innocent victims of crimes, who help pay for it, more than twelve million dollars a day! I will let you convert that into billions. We need not try in one leap to copy fully the Scandinavian model of production in prison factories. We can begin with the production of machine parts for lawnmowers, automobiles, washing machines or refrigerators. This kind of limited beginning would minimize the capital investment for plant and equipment and give prisoners the opportunity to learn relatively simple skills at the outset.

We do not need the help of behavioral scientists to understand that human beings who are taught to produce useful goods for the marketplace, and to be productive are more likely to develop the self-esteem essential to a normal, integrated personality. This kind of program would provide training in skills and work habits, and replace the sense of hopelessness that is the common lot of prison inmates. Prisoners who work and study forty-five to fifty-five hours a week — as you graduates have done — are also less prone to violent prison conduct. Prisoners given a stake in society, and in the future, are more likely to avoid being part of the "recall" process that today sends thousands of repeat offenders back to prisons each year.

One prison in Europe, an institution for incorrigible juvenile offenders from fourteen to eighteen years of age who had been convicted of serious crimes of violence, has on the wall at the entrance to the institution four challenging statements in bold script with letters a foot high. Translated they read approximately this way:

1. You are here because you need help.
2. We are here to help you.
3. We cannot help you unless you cooperate.
4. *If you don't cooperate, we will make you.*

Here is an offer of a compassionate helping hand coupled with the kind of discipline that, if missing in early life in homes and schools that ignored moral values, produces the kind of maladjusted, incorrigible people who are found in prisons. Some voices have been raised saying that prisoners should not be coerced into work and training programs. Depending upon what these speakers mean by "coerced," I might be able to agree. But I would say that every prisoner should be "induced" to cooperate by the same methods that are employed in many other areas. Life is filled with rewards for cooperation and penalties for non-cooperation. Prison sentences are shortened and privileges are given to prisoners who cooperate. What I urge are programs in which the inmate can earn and learn his way to freedom and the opportunity for a new life.

Opportunities for rewards and punishments permeate the lives of all free people and these opportunities should not be denied to prison inmates. At the core of the American private enterprise system is the idea that good performance is rewarded and poor performance is not. So I say we can induce inmates to cooperate in education and in production. A reasonable limit is that they should not be made to study more or work longer hours, for example, than students at Pace University must work to earn a degree! Surely it would not be rational to settle for less. I can hardly believe that anyone would seriously suggest that prisoners should be treated with less discipline than the young men and women in the colleges of America.

With as much as ten billion dollars of prison construction looming, we are at a crossroad, deciding what kind of prisons we are to have. As we brace ourselves for the tax collector's reaching into our pockets for these billions we have a choice: we can continue to have largely "human warehouses" with little or no educational, training or production programs or we can strike out on a new course with constructive, humanizing programs that will in the long run be less costly. The patterns are there in our federal prisons and in states like Minnesota.

It is your future. You make the choice.

Notes

[1]J. Gorecki, *A Theory of Criminal Justice* at xi (1979).

[2]The Federal Bureau of Prisons under the leadership of the late James V. Bennett and now Norman Carlson, the present Director, has performed extremely well, given legislative restraints on production of goods in prisons and archaic attitudes of business and labor. But the Federal Bureau of Prisons deals with barely seven percent of the 400,000 prisoners now confined.

Part V

Corrections in the Community

Introduction

If, as many experts contend, the prison drill only hardens prisoners' antisocial tendencies and teaches them the skills they need to pursue a criminal career, what alternative punishments are available? Many criminologists have criticized the courts for being too lenient with habitually violent felons and too harsh on nonviolent offenders. Over half of the nation's inmates are serving time for nonviolent offenses, and many of these offenders arguably pose little or no threat to society. It is more humane, more effective, and far cheaper, many experts assert, to send nondangerous offenders to halfway houses or work release programs and to require them to perform community services and to reimburse the victims from whom they stole.

The argument that the best way to remedy prison overcrowding is to channel nonviolent offenders into community-based programs is not new. In 1967, the final report of the President's Commission on Law Enforcement and the Administration of Justice advocated a major shift to community correctional programs and far greater funding for proba-

437

tion and parole programs, halfway houses, work release centers, and other alternatives to imprisonment. Prisons, according to the commission, should be used only as a last resort, preceded by many interim options designed to keep men and women as close as possible to their families and jobs—not caged, dehumanized, and deprived of all opportunities to learn self-reliance. Six years later, another president's crime commission—The National Advisory Commission on Criminal Justice Standards and Goals—concluded a sober review of the scandals of incarceration with the recommendation that "[p]risons should be repudiated as useless for any purpose other than locking away persons who are too dangerous to be allowed at large in a free society."

In some states, the challenge of community-based corrections has been taken seriously. Minnesota, Oregon, Kansas and Mississippi, among others, have established community work programs in which offenders are given employment counseling, are assigned to jobs in the community, and are required to make restitution to their victims. For that matter, as of December 31, 1996, 3,180,363 people were on probation and 704,709 were on parole.

Community-based corrections, however, certainly has not succeeded in eliminating the most prominent and distressing features of the U.S. prison system. Prisons cost taxpayers billions of dollars in operating costs each year to achieve a monumental record of failure. They are still underfunded, more overcrowded than ever, and run by an undertrained and underpaid staff who are unable to protect prisoners from other prisoners. Moreover, despite opposition from the supporters of community corrections, billions of dollars in federal, state, and local cell construction is planned over the next decade.

Those who advocate an accelerated campaign of prison construction have argued that although building more prisons is costly, the costs of not building more prisons may also prove expensive. Pointing to studies indicating that some hardened, habitual offenders can be "one-person crime waves" who single-handedly commit well over 100 crimes per year, a 1987 report issued by the National Institute of Justice (Edwin W. Zedlewski, "Making Confinement Decisions") took the position that the costs of building and running prisons may not be too expensive when weighed against the money saved by incapacitating and deterring those who would otherwise commit serious crimes that impose great monetary and social costs on crime victims and on society generally. Supporters of expanded prison construction also contend that community corrections has not been proven to be demonstrably effective in protecting the public and reducing recidivism rates. Indeed, although some community-based programs have been judged to be safe and effective, many evaluative studies have produced inconsistent and contradictory results, in part because of the methodological problems that are widespread throughout all corrections research (see Part IV).

Some detractors of community-based programs have claimed that many such programs actually increase the amount of control, punishment and surveillance to which offenders are subjected. Critics also have warned that expanded community corrections efforts will not necessarily lead to reduced prison populations. For example, in his 1980 book *Prisons in Turmoil*, John Irvin declares that "[i]nstead of dipping into the [prison population], community corrections and other diversion programs receive those who were formerly filtered out of the system through dismissal, reduction of charge, and probation."

With all of the controversy surrounding community-based corrections, it is fitting that the first article in Part V addresses the question of whether community-based corrections can survive in today's political climate. In a thoughtful essay, "Beyond Reintegration: Community Corrections in a Retributive Era," Peter J. Benekos argues that the answer is "yes," but that community corrections is moving in a more punitive direction. Benekos, a professor of criminal justice at Mercyhurst College, points to a growing body of evidence indicating that humanitarian rationales for community-based programs are being replaced by motives that are both more punitive than in the past and rooted in economic rather than therapeutic considerations. Thus, even though we are likely to see an expansion in community corrections programs, the rehabilitative success of these programs may be undermined by an ideology of vengeance and a failure to make intelligent use of effective alternatives to prison.

Interestingly, Professor Benekos refers to a growing tendency by public officials to justify community-based alternatives to prison with "get-tough" rhetoric. But is this always mere rhetoric? And is it really such a bad thing if offenders come to see electronic monitoring, house arrest, intensive probation, and other community programs as tough, unpleasant, and punitive? These are among the questions addressed in our next selection, "Probation in the United States: Practices and Challenges." In this article, Joan Petersilia, a professor of social ecology at the University of California-Irvine and a prolific author on the subject of corrections, examines contemporary U.S. probation practices and services. She points out that probation departments are more extensively engaged with offenders than any other criminal justice agency. Yet it is not clear whether probation actually is effective in reducing crime. Professor Petersilia suggests that today's intensive supervision programs have, in fact, become tougher than traditional probation programs and that this is a positive trend that may help Americans understand that probation can be a suitable sanction for some offenses. Professor Petersilia cites evidence that some community-based sanctions may be perceived by offenders as more punitive than short prison terms. Among other things, this suggests that we need to make probation a priority research area and to take this research into account in designing community-based programs.

Like probation, parole—the practice of supervising released prisoners in the community—is a controversial topic. Over the past 15 years, a growing number of states have either abolished or sharply curtailed the use of parole as a method of granting prisoners a reduction in the length of their sentence. The movement toward the abolition of parole is often justified by reference to the "nothing works" findings reported by Robert Martinson and his colleagues in 1974 and 1975 (see Part IV). It is therefore ironic that in 1977, Martinson and Judith Wilks identified a correctional program that does seem to work. In "Save Parole Supervision," they report the results of a study in which they examined the arrest, conviction, and reimprisonment rates of two statistically comparable groups of released prisoners—those released under parole supervision and those released without parole supervision. Their conclusions: "The evidence seems to indicate that the abolition of parole supervision would result in substantial increases in arrest, conviction, and return to prison."

As noted earlier, community corrections programs have generally failed to win support from politicians and the public. However, our next article offers evidence that this state of affairs may be changing. In "Alternatives to Incarceration: A Conservative Perspective," Charles Colson and Daniel W. Van Ness point out that an increasing number of conservative politicians have announced their support for community-based alternatives to imprisonment. Colson, chairman of the board of Prison Fellowship Ministries, and Van Ness, president of Justice Fellowship (the criminal justice reform arm of Prison Fellowship Ministries), have worked on behalf of correctional reform with public officials across the United States. They argue that the time has come for men and women from every political perspective to support well-run, community-based correctional programs that can benefit offenders, victims, correctional employees, and the taxpaying public. Equally important, Colson and Van Ness offer profiles of specific types of community programs that have been introduced in some states in recent years. As readers will see, there are a number of programs—including intensive probation supervision, house arrest, restitution, and community service—that may prove to be superior to imprisonment in dealing with nonviolent offenders.

The final three selections in Part V provide insights into three types of community-based correctional programs that have been promoted as effective ways to punish criminals without punishing taxpayers. First Joan Petersilia and Susan Turner report the results of an ambitious, nationwide evaluation of intensive supervision probation/parole (ISP). The evaluation reveals what can and cannot be expected of ISP. Petersilia and Turner also offer a research strategy that could be used to determine "whether ISP, a concept that may be sound in theory, might be structured and implemented differently to produce better results."

Second, Annesley K. Schmidt discusses the increasing use of electronic monitoring devices that signal authorities when the wearer— usually a nonviolent offender—attempts to leave a particular location. Although the technique of tracking offenders with bracelets and telephones has been in existence for more than a decade, its use remains controversial. The author reminds us that electronic monitoring cannot prevent crimes and cannot be used as a replacement for appropriate programming and live supervision. Accordingly, she urges careful consideration and proper use of the devices.

The final selection in Part V discusses community-based corrections programs based on the so-called "restorative justice" philosophy. In "Restorative Justice: Including Victims in Community Corrections," Myron Steele and Thomas J. Quinn lament that the criminal justice process all too often ignores the victims of crime. One way to change this situation, they suggest, is to expand and improve victim-offender mediation (also known as victim-offender reconciliation programs). Although such programs are relatively new in the United States, they actually represent a return to the ancient understanding that offenders must settle accounts with the victims of their crimes. Steele and Quinn argue that victim-offender mediation (although certainly not appropriate in all cases) and other programs reflecting the restorative justice philosophy can restore dignity to victims and help the offender "to understand the crime's hurtfulness to the victim, including the victim's physical losses, fear, suspicion, and anger."

27

Beyond Reintegration
Community Corrections in a Retributive Era

Peter J. Benekos

Only a few decades ago community-based corrections was viewed enthusiastically as a humane, logical, and effective approach for working with and changing criminal offenders. As researchers and administrators acknowledged that institutional rehabilitation was limited in its ability to correct offenders, community-based programs, predicated on a new philosophy of reintegration, were advocated as a means to restore the offender to society. The Corrections Task Force of the President's Commission on Law Enforcement and the Administration of Justice endorsed this model and recommended it for the following reasons (1967:7):

> The task of corrections, therefore, includes building or rebuilding solid ties between the offender and the community, integrating or reintegrating the offender into community life—restoring family ties, obtaining employment and education, securing in the large sense a place for the offender in the routine functioning of society. This requires not only efforts directed toward changing the individual offender, which have been almost the exclusive focus of rehabilitation, but also mobilization and change of the community and its institutions.

Source: *Federal Probation*, Vol. 54, No. 1 (March 1990), 52–56.

It is important to note that this conceptualization of community corrections required more than a change in the individual; it required a change in the community.

In O'Leary and Duffee's (1971) discussion of correctional policies, reintegration was operationalized as a policy with high concern for both the offender and the community. The authors observed that these programs were not intended to simply shift offenders from institutional-based programs to community-based ones. Other authors (e.g., Bartollas, 1985:27) have also recognized that with this correctional model, there was an explicit goal to involve the communities in the process of developing reformed and law-abiding citizens. Doeren and Hageman emphasized this when they explained the importance of "community relationships as the key set of variables in determining the degree to which a program is community-based" (1982:14). In their discussion of the concepts and components of this form of corrections, they concluded that: "clearly and unmistakably, then, the goal of community-based corrections is the successful reintegration of the offender into the community" (16).

Even though the literature suggests several social, therapeutic, philosophical, and economic advantages of community-based as compared with institutional-based corrections, Doeren and Hageman offered a cautionary observation (1982:19):

> Community-based corrections is not, and should not, be viewed as a panacea for the massive problems presently being experienced by our correctional system.

In response to their observation, the purpose of this article is to review briefly some recent correctional developments in an effort to examine the status of community corrections and to evaluate the current ideological basis for the renewed interest in community programs.

Developments in Corrections

A number of issues and problems have become commonplace in corrections systems. Accordingly, several authors have delineated and discussed the problems (e.g., Gottfredson and McConville, 1987; Conrad, 1985; Roberg and Webb, 1981; Bartollas, 1985; Clear and O'Leary, 1983; Duffee, 1989; Scott and Hirschi, 1988), and some conclude that these developments are contributing to a growing sense of pessimism about corrections (Roberg and Webb, 1981). While the individual issues are important, the literature suggests that three related developments characterize the state of corrections today and reflect several dimensions of correctional problems: institutional crowding; ideological restatement; and intermediate initiatives.

Institutions

In the criminal justice system today, the word "crisis" has become synonymous with prisons. Over-populated institutions and crowded conditions characterize state and Federal prisons. As early as 1978, former director of the Federal Bureau of Prisons, Norman Carlson, identified overcrowding as the "most pressing problem" in the Federal system (Bartollas, 1981:259). More specifically, a recent Bureau of Justice Statistics report calculated a "continuing space demand of about 1,000 new prison beds every week" (BJS, 1987:56). It is no wonder that the yearly increases in incarcerated inmates explain why corrections is "one of the ten fastest growing occupations" in the United States (Landon, 1989).

The impact of overcrowded institutions on the criminal justice system was discussed in a recent report by the American Bar Association (1988). This committee report also recognized the economic and administrative consequences of court orders often resulting in "closing prisons or providing early release for convicted criminals" (ABA, 1988:5).

This state of corrections has created a demand for space which has generated a reactivity throughout corrections. In an attempt to build out of the problem, new construction has become characteristic of most state systems (Cory and Gettinger, 1984); lured by profit motivation, private entrepreneurs are eager to enter the prison business (Robbins, 1988), and community corrections, viewed as a "cost-effective" alternative to institutions, is receiving renewed public and political attention (Ball, Huff, and Lilly, 1988). These reactive efforts, however, have themselves raised financial, legal, and administrative issues which further contribute to some of the dilemmas confronting corrections.

Several factors may explain this crowding crisis but two explanations are especially relevant to this discussion. First, and somewhat obvious, the space needs are exceeding administrative efforts and the economic capacity to expand existing facilities and/or to construct new prisons. This is in part a situation created by "inadequate funding" which results in "insufficient resources." The recent ABA report addressed this issue (1988:44):

> Legislatures must not only appropriate more for criminal justice but must also adopt a system-wide approach and fund all components of the criminal justice system adequately. Legislation that increases the number of crimes and length of prison sentences without also providing for additional police, prosecution, and defense services, as well as additional prison cells, must be seen as a futile, counterproductive gesture. (emphasis added)

While the demand for prison cells is increasing, the resources are not forthcoming, and, therefore, cost-saving alternatives are becoming more attractive if not necessary. Based on this view, various community placements as well as privatization efforts (with profit incentives) are presenting interesting public and administrative options. These responses, however, suggest economically motivated programs and policy perspectives.

Another explanation for the increasing use of prisons and the crowding problem is that a new public mood toward offenders has resulted in different policies and sentencing practices which have sent more offenders to prison for longer periods of time (Hudson, 1987). This "get tough" response suggests an ideological dimension to the problem and another contemporary theme in corrections.

Ideology

In response to the criticisms and failures of rehabilitative philosophy and policies, both liberals and conservatives have succeeded in establishing a Justice Model era in criminal justice (Cullen and Gilbert, 1982). While the proponents of the model offer propositions for "doing justice" (von Hirsch, 1976), the prevailing ideology of incapacitation, punishment, and deterrence has resulted in get-tough sentencing practices which contribute to rising prison populations (Hudson, 1987). This shift to "just deserts" has facilitated a punitive reaction which has overshadowed and "co-opted" the ideals of the Justice Model and offered the reality of retributive incarceration (Greenberg and Humphries, 1980).

In this model, not only have the basic assumptions of crime and criminality been reformulated, but the purpose and rationale of corrections have also been reconceptualized. Bartollas (1985:74) explains that the focus on punishment has resulted in a repressive approach to corrections. Since offenders make "free-will" decisions to commit crime, they no longer deserve compassion and correction; and since treatment is ineffective and coddling, offenders need "proportionate" punishments which stress incapacitation and signal retaliation and retribution for the harm inflicted upon society.

This oversimplified description indicates that corrections and criminal justice are again characterized by a philosophy which stresses vengeful and retributive practices. In Cohen's (1985) model, the emphasis on imprisonment signals an "exclusionary" era of repressive social control which attempts to banish, expel, and stigmatize the criminal deviant. However, in spite of the predominance of these ideas and practices, it is interesting that a resurrection of community corrections efforts is under way.

Intermediate Sanctions

In the collision between the rhetoric of getting tough and the realities of prison crowding, a "new" generation of community-based corrections is emerging. This third development in corrections is a consequence of the first two: the capacity limits for incarcerative policies.

While retribution, deserts, and exclusion still reflect corrections ideology, "the search for intermediate punishments is an attempt to find mid-range solutions" which meet social and criminal justice needs for controlling and punishing offenders (McCarthy 1987:3). It is important to note, as does McCarthy, that the "growing interest" in these intermediate sanctions, e.g., intensive probation, house arrest, and electronic monitoring, is not *only* based on the need to develop cheaper alternatives to prisons. However, the economic realities cannot be denied (McCarthy, 1987:3):

> In the 1980s, the economic advantages of community corrections have shifted from the status of an ancillary selling point to a principal rationale, prompted by an enormous institutional overcrowding problem that repeatedly forces a choice between new construction and the development and utilization of "alternatives."

This observation brings the three developments into focus and characterizes the state of corrections: In an exclusionary, punitive era, corrections is being strained because it has exceeded the capacity to implement the punishment policies. As a result, economic reality dictates that cost-effective measures must be developed, and this is motivating the development of intermediate sanctions. In order to succeed in this "rediscovery" of community corrections, however, it is necessary to promote and justify these community sanctions as alternatives which are consistent with the prevailing ideology. In other words, these sanctions cannot be viewed by the public as extensions of probation and previous community-based corrections programs because these responses are associated with the rehabilitation era and are generally perceived as failed, "non-punishment" responses (Conrad, 1984:255).

Cooptation of Community Corrections

As a result of the need to create the vision or image of punitive, get-tough sanctions, the promotion of intermediate punishments requires the get-tough rhetoric as rationale for these alternatives. Klein (1988), for example, describes probation as "intermediate punishment with punitive content" (67) and defines community service as "work which is incapacitative" (95). He discusses the role of "community control officers'' (241) and explains alternative sentencing not as "alternatives to incarceration" but as "alternative forms of punishment" (95). Maher and Dufour (1987) also defend the use of community service as the best alternative to prisons since it is a cost-effective way to reduce crowding while still deterring and punishing the offender.

In her discussion of probation "reform," Petersilia explains the necessary transitions in probation rationale and concludes that a new orientation has emerged (1988:167):

> The goal is not offender rehabilitation, but offender control, with public safety the central concern.

She recognizes that the "credibility" of probation is an issue which has resulted in the restructuring of probation services into "quasi-policing" roles. Wooten offers a similar perspective when he observes that (1985:7):

> . . . it is time to openly admit as a profession that we have evolved into performing primarily two tasks; producing presentence investigation reports and minimally monitoring offenders on supervision to the court and parole commission.

An additional example of this punitive rhetoric is presented by Abel and Marsh who develop an extensive argument to support the use of restitution and conclude that this alternative to incarceration "is really a form of punishment" which may be the "best" type of sanction in a modern, industrialized society (Abel and Marsh, 1984:48).

In reviewing these recent trends in corrections, an article in the *Correctional Forum* reflected this need to justify alternatives to prison with tough rhetoric (Leban, 1988:6):

> There is a growing interest in alternatives, if only as a means of relieving overcrowded institutions. Discussion of alternatives, however, is often phrased in terms of punitiveness, to make the idea more acceptable.

One of the consequences of these punitive community alternatives is the need for different and more efficient classification systems which provide relevant information to decision makers and control agents. This requires instruments which are consistent with the shift from rehabilitative needs to risk control needs and can be used to identify high risk offenders for maximum community control. Mackenzie, Posey, and Rapaport (1988) discuss these issues and reflect on the "new" state of corrections in which "prediction" is a salient issue in both research and supervision. Since the goals have changed from rehabilitation to retribution, deterrence, and incapacitation, new classification systems are needed as a means of successfully meeting correctional objectives.

An example of this emphasis on the assessment of risk is the recent revisions to the Pennsylvania Board of Probation and Parole's supervisory classifications (Long, 1988). The Board has adopted a system in which only "risk assessment" is determined (Long, 1988:1):

> It is believed that the changes will provide a more uniform and accurate determination of the grade of supervision and will provide a better management of the clients based on risk.

In discussing these various developments, the authors recognize the changing nature of community corrections. Their observations suggest policies and perspectives in which community programs are not based on reintegrative objectives but on retributive ones. Since corrections is a reactive system (as is criminal justice) it is not surprising that it has again responded to the social, political, and fiscal pressures of the environment (Clear and O'Leary, 1983:4). For community corrections this has created a "conceptual contradiction" in which incapacitative goals have been imposed on community-based programs. As discussed above, this has resulted in efforts to increase the severity of the non-prison penalties in order to create perceptions of punitive, deterrent, and controlling aspects of community-based corrections (Skovron, 1988:193).

These fiscally motivated efforts to make the community pay for institutional crowding are less "mystifying" than an earlier "decarceration" movement which promoted humanitarian rationales for community-based corrections (Scull, 1977). In the 1980s as in the 1960s, economic necessity made alternative social control interventions attractive. While reintegration justified the earlier policies, retribution guides the current efforts. In both movements, however, there has been an expansion of social control (Scull, 1977; Ball and Lilly, 1988).

Cohen, for example, is convinced that simultaneous policies of inclusion and exclusion (characteristic of current developments) are announcements "that the system (of social control) overall is getting larger" (1985:49). In one example of a retributive-era program, electronic monitoring, Ball and Lilly conclude that "social-control entrepreneurs" are motivated by economic self-interest to promote the devices and to use the "imagery of considerable symbolic force" to spread the use of the control technology (Ball and Lilly, 1988:162).

In their discussion of these correctional developments, Shover and Einstadter observe that home incarceration has "substantially increased the control over increased numbers of the population" (1988:205). They also recognize that this recent shift to develop community alternatives has essentially coopted the rationale and objective of community corrections (Ball and Lilly, 1988:205):

What was thought to be a strategy of reintegration has been transformed into a strategy of intrusion and control under the guise of allowing an offender the privilege of remaining in the community.

Their review of the recent community program "reforms" underscores the irony of a transformation of a "correctional strategy arising from a liberal ideology of melioration into one fitting a conservative ideology of efficiency and control" (1988:205).

Discussion

The state of corrections is not healthy: institutional and community systems are being used beyond capacity at the same time that policies of punishment and control have expanded to "startling dimensions" (Harris, 1987a:217). Contrary to political pronouncements and campaign rhetoric, America is not soft on crime. Even though new noninstitutional alternatives are being developed, the ideological underpinnings are not therapeutic and coddling, but punitive and controlling, and the motivation is not humanitarian but economic. Efforts toward correctional reform are characterized by a "popular propensity for punishment."

With this redefinition of community corrections, there is both a sense of urgency and a realization that the future of corrections and improvements in correctional services "will take place in the community" (Conrad, 1984:258). Since "the concept of prison is not open to great change," Conrad concludes that the search for solutions must involve a revised but pragmatic concept of corrections in the community (1984:258). The recent developments in sentencing and corrections indicate this shift, and the practices of electronic monitoring, house arrest, and intensive supervision reflect efforts to make renewed and expanded use of alternatives to prison.

These and other methods of control, however, may already be experiencing problems similar to those characteristic of prisons. Morris, for example, examines the "failure to make effective and intelligent use of non-incarcerative punishments" and is concerned that unless appropriate resources are committed to seriously implementing these alternatives, overuse and misuse will diminish their effectiveness (Morris, 1987:1). In the way that construction costs have frustrated incarcerative control, the failure to allocate resources for non-incarcerative control will serve to again coopt the potential of these "new" forms of corrections.

Community corrections cannot be conceptualized or developed only as a response to prison crowding and punitive motivations. Such reactive efforts will postpone but not prevent the inevitable need "to question and rethink the entire basis of the punishment system'' (Harris, 1987b:35). If, as Schoen (1987) argues, money and economic interests are ultimate determinants of punishment policies, then perhaps Wilkins' recommendation for a ''national punishment budget'' in which punishment is quantified as a ''scarce resource'' would require more accountability and justification for the use of punishment (Wilkins, 1987:81). From another perspective, Harris (1987a) suggests a sentencing policy which presumes community placement and requires that imprisonment be utilized as the alternative sentence.

These observations suggest that as community corrections re-emerges with a new ideology and mission, the prospects of success may be undermined by economic considerations and conflicting visions of the future of community alternatives. ''If the willingness to cede greater and greater power to institutions of social control is a reflection of a desperate society,'' as Harris (1987b:33) believes it is, then community corrections will be defined by punitive and retributive needs, and offender control policies will become more pervasive as control technologies become more developed. From a crisis in prisons to a crisis in communities, corrections will again mirror self-defeating images.

References

American Bar Association. *Criminal Justice in Crisis*. Washington, DC: ABA, 1988.

Abel, Charles F. and Frank H. Marsh. *Punishment and Restitution: A Restitutionary Approach to Crime and the Criminal*. Westport, CT: Greenwood Press, 1984.

Ball, Richard A. and J. Robert Lilly. ''Home Incarceration with Electronic Monitoring.'' In Joseph E. Scott and Travis Hirschi (eds.), *Controversial Issues in Crime and Justice*. Newbury Park, CA: Sage, 1988, pp. 147–165.

Ball, Richard A., C. Ronald Huff and J. Robert Lilly. *House Arrest and Correctional Policy: Doing Time at Home*. Newbury Park, CA: Sage, 1988.

Bartollas, Clemens. *Correctional Treatment: Theory and Practice*. Englewood Cliffs, NJ: Prentice-Hall, 1985.

_____. *Introduction to Corrections*. Englewood Cliffs, NJ: Prentice-Hall, 1981.

Bureau of Justice Statistics Data Report. Washington, DC: U.S. Department of Justice, 1987.

Clear, Todd R. and Vincent O'Leary. *Controlling the Offender in the Community: Reforming the Community-Supervisor Function*. Lexington, MA: Lexington Books, 1983.

Cohen, Stanley. *Visions of Social Control*. UK: Polity Press, 1985.

Conrad, John P. ''The Redefinition of Probation: Drastic Proposals to Solve an Urgent Problem.'' In Patrick D. McAnany, Doug Thomson, and David Fogel (eds.), *Probation and Justice: Reconsideration of Mission*. Cambridge, MA: Oelgeschlager, Gunn and Hain, 1984, pp. 251–273.

Cory, Bruce and Stephen Gettinger. *Time to Build? The Realities of Prison Construction*. New York: Edna McConnell Clark Foundation, 1984.

Cullen, Frances T. and Karen E. Gilbert. *Reaffirming Rehabilitation*. Cincinnati: Anderson, 1982.

Doeren, Stephen E. and Mary J. Hageman. *Community Corrections*. Cincinnati: Anderson, 1982.

Gottfredson, Stephen D. and Sean McConville (eds.). *America's Correctional Crisis*. Westport, CT: Greenwood Press, 1987.

Greenberg, David and Drew Humphries. "The Cooptation of Fixed Sentencing Reform." *Crime and Delinquency*, 26(2), April 1980, pp. 206–225.

Harris, M. Kay. "A Brief for De-escalating Criminal Sanctions." In Stephen D. Gottfredson and Sean McConville (eds.), *America's Correctional Crisis: Prison Populations and Public Policy*. Westport, CT: Greenwood Press, 1987a, pp. 205–220.

———. "Moving into the New Millennium: Toward a Feminist Vision of Justice." *The Prison Journal*, 67(2), Fall-Winter 1987b, pp. 27–38.

Hudson, Barbara. *Justice Through Punishment: A Critique of the 'Justice' Model of Corrections*. New York: St. Martin's Press, 1987.

Klein, Andrew R. *Alternative Sentencing: A Practitioner's Guide*. Cincinnati: Anderson, 1988.

Landen, Mark D. Correspondence from the Chief of Recruitment, Federal Bureau of Prisons. January 3, 1989.

Leban, Janet A. (ed.). "Trends in Corrections During the 1980's Are Likely to Continue into the Next Decade." *Correctional Forum*. Philadelphia: Pennsylvania Prison Society, November, 1988.

Long, Joseph M. (ed.). "Board Adopts New Supervision Grades." *Palaver*. Harrisburg: Pennsylvania Board of Probation and Parole, September 28, 1980.

MacKenzie, Doris, C. Dale Posey, and Karen Rapaport. "A Theoretical Revolution in Corrections." *Criminal Justice and Behavior*, 15(1), March 1988, pp. 125–136.

Maher, Richard J. and Henry E. Dufour. "Experimenting with Community Service: A Punitive Alternative to Imprisonment." *Federal Probation*, 51(3), September 1987, pp. 22–27.

McCarthy, Belinda R. (ed.). *Intermediate Punishments: Intensive Supervision, Home Confinement and Electronic Surveillance*. Monsey, NJ: Criminal Justice Press, 1987.

Morris, Norval. "Alternatives to Imprisonment: Failures and Prospects." *Criminal Justice Research Bulletin*, 3(7), 1987.

O'Leary, Vincent and David Duffee. "Correctional Policy: A Classification of Goals Designed for Change." *Crime and Delinquency*, 16–17, October 1971, pp. 377–385.

Petersilia, Joan. "Probation Reform." In Joseph E. Scott and Travis Hirschi (eds.), *Controversial Issues in Crime and Justice.* Newbury Park, CA: Sage, 1988, pp. 166-179.

President's Commission on Law Enforcement and Administration of Justice. *The Challenge of Crime in a Free Society.* Washington, DC: U.S. Government Printing Office, 1967.

Robbins, Ira P. *The legal Dimensions of Private Incarceration.* Washington, DC: American Bar Association, 1988.

Roberg, Roy R. and Vincent J. Webb. *Critical Issues in Corrections: Problems, Trends and Prospects.* St. Paul, MN: West, 1981.

Schoen, Kenneth F. "Hard Labor Can Save Prison Time." *The Prison Journal,* 67(2), Fall-Winter 1987, pp. 67-70.

Scott, Joseph E. and Travis Hirschi (eds.). *Controversial Issues in Crime and Justice.* Newbury Park, CA: Sage, 1988.

Scull, Andrew. *Decarceration.* Englewood Cliffs, NJ: Prentice-Hall, 1977.

Shover, Neal and Werner J. Einstadter. *Analyzing American Corrections.* Belmont, CA: Wadsworth, 1988.

Skovron, Sandra Evans. "Prison Crowding: The Dilemmas of the Problem and Strategies of Population Control." In Joseph E. Scott and Travis Hirschi (eds.), *Controversial Issues in Crime and Justice.* Newbury Park, CA: Sage, 1988, pp. 183-209.

Von Hirsch, Andrew. *Doing Justice: The Choice of Punishments.* New York: Hill and Wang 1976.

Wilkins, Leslie T. "Future Penal Philosophy and Practice." *The Prison Journal,* 67(2), Fall-Winter 1987, pp. 76-87.

Wooten, Harold B. "It's O.K., Supervision Enthusiasts: You Can Come Home Now!" *Federal Probation,* 49(4), December 1985, pp. 4-7.

28

Probation in the United States
Practices and Challenges
Joan Petersilia

Adult probationers in the United States surged to nearly 3.2 million at the end of 1996, up from almost 2 million in 1985 and 1.1 million in 1980.[1] Today they comprise about 58 percent of all adults under correctional supervision.[2]

To cope with their workload, probation agencies—often the target of intense criticism—receive less than 10 percent of state and local government corrections funding.[3] Probation's funding shortfall often results in lax supervision of serious felons, thereby encouraging offender recidivism and reinforcing the public's soft-on-crime image of probation as permissive, uncaring about crime victims, and committed to a rehabilitative ideal that ignores the reality of violent, predatory criminals. This poor public image leaves probation agencies unable to compete effectively for scarce public funds.

Source: This article is adapted from Professor Petersilia's essay in volume 22 of *Crime and Justice*, edited by Michael Tonry. Copyright 1997 by University of Chicago Press. Reprinted by permission of the publisher.

Although current programs are often seen as inadequate, the *concept* of probation—begun in 1841 (see "Origin and Evolution of Probation")—has great appeal and much unrealized potential. As one judge noted, "Nothing is wrong with probation. It is the *execution* of probation that is wrong."[4]

Exactly *how* would one go about reforming probation? Many judges are monitoring probationers more closely, while others are imposing more punitive and meaningful probation sentences. Some jurisdictions have implemented policies and programs designed to overcome the difficult problem of finding jail and prison capacity to punish probation violators.

Unfortunately, debating the merits of those and other probation-reform strategies is severely limited because so little is known about current probation practices. Assembling what is known about U.S. probation practices so public policy can be better informed is the main purpose of this article—along with offering suggestions on meeting the challenges facing probation agencies.

Origin and Evolution of Probation

Probation: "A court-ordered disposition alternative through which an adjudicated offender is placed under the control, supervision, and care of a probation field staff member in lieu of imprisonment, so long as the probationer meets certain standards of conduct " (American Correctional Association, *Probation and Parole Directory, 1995-1997*).

Probation in the United States began in 1841 with the innovative work of John Augustus, a Boston bootmaker, who was the first to post bail for a man charged with being a common drunk. Thanks to Augustus's persistence, a Boston court gradually accepted the notion that not all offenders required incarceration.

Virtually every basic practice of probation was conceived by Augustus. He developed the ideas of presentence investigation, supervision conditions, social casework, reports to the court, and revocation of probation.

By 1956, all states had adopted adult and juvenile probation laws. Between the 1950s and the 1970s, U.S. probation evolved in relative obscurity. But a number of reports issued in the 1970s brought national attention to the inadequacy of probation services and their organization.

In recent years, probation agencies have struggled—with continued meager resources—to upgrade services and supervision. Important developments have included the widespread adoption of case classification systems and various types of intermediate sanctions (e.g., electronic monitoring and intensive supervision). Those programs have had varied success in reducing recidivism, but evaluations of them have been instructive in terms of future program design.

Probation and Modern Sentencing Practice

Probation departments are more extensively involved with offenders and their cases—often starting at arrest—than any other justice agency. Many who are arrested and all who are convicted come into contact with the probation department. Probation officers interact with many criminal justice agencies and significantly affect a wide spectrum of justice processing decisions, including these:

- Probation officers, in addition to pretrial service agencies, usually perform personal investigations to determine whether defendants will be released on their own recognizance or bail.

- They prepare reports that courts use as the primary source of information to determine whether to divert defendants from formal prosecution. Probation officers supervise diverted offenders and inform courts about whether the diversionary sentence was successfully complied with, thereby influencing the court's decision to proceed or not with formal prosecution.

- They prepare presentence reports containing pertinent information about convicted defendants and their crimes. The information is critically important, for research repeatedly indicates that (1) the judge's knowledge of the defendant is usually limited to what is contained in the presentence report, and (2) the probation officer's recommendation for or against prison correlates strongly with the judge's sentence of probation, prison, or a combination thereof.

- They supervise offenders sentenced to probation, determine which court-ordered probation conditions[5] to enforce and monitor most closely, decide which violations of conditions to bring to the court's attention, and recommend sanctions.

- They affect, through presentence reports, the initial security classification (and eligibility for parole) of offenders sentenced to prison.

More than 2,000 probation agencies in the United States[6] carry out those and other responsibilities. The agencies differ in terms of whether they reside within the executive or judicial branch of government, how they fund services, and whether those services are primarily a state or local function.

According to one study, 52 percent of staff in the typical probation department are line officers; 48 percent are clerical, support staff, and management.[7] Of line probation officers, only about 17 percent supervise adult felons. The remaining line officers supervise juveniles (half of adult probation agencies have that responsibility) or misdemeanant probationers or prepare presentence reports.

Given an estimated 50,000 probation employees in 1994,[8] and given that 23 percent of them (11,500 officers) were supervising about 2.9 million adult probationers, the average caseload that year was 258 adult offenders per line officer. This contrasts with what many believe to be the ideal caseload of 30 adult probationers per line officer.

Of course, offenders are not supervised on "average" caseloads. Rather, probation staffs use a variety of risk and needs classification instruments to identify offenders needing more intensive supervision or services. Although risk instruments can identify offenders who are more likely to reoffend, funds are usually insufficient to implement the levels of supervision predicted by classification instruments.[9] Research findings indicate that, across all sites and felony crimes studied, about 20 percent of adult felony probationers were assigned to caseloads requiring no personal contact.[10]

Probation funding has long been recognized as woefully inadequate. From the beginning, probation has continually been asked to take on greater numbers of probationers and conduct a greater number of presentence investigations despite stable or declining funding. "Apparently, community supervision has been seen as a kind of elastic resource that could handle whatever numbers of offenders the system required it to."[11]

Who Is on Probation?

According to a Bureau of Justice Statistics study of correctional populations in the United States in 1996:[12]

- About 55 percent of all offenders on probation had been convicted of a felony, 26 percent of a misdemeanor. About 17 percent had been convicted of driving while intoxicated, which can be considered either a felony or misdemeanor, and 2 percent for other offenses.
- Women comprised 21 percent of the nation's probationers.
- About 64 percent of adult probationers were white, 35 percent black. Hispanics, who may be of any race, comprised 15 percent of the probation population.
- Southern states generally had the highest per capita ratio of adult

probationers. Texas had the largest probation population, followed by California.

Data from one study suggest that many offenders who are granted felony probation are indistinguishable in terms of their crimes or criminal record from those who are imprisoned (or vice versa).[13]

Another analysis found that 50 percent of probationers did not comply with court-ordered terms of their probation; 50 percent of known violators went to jail or prison for their noncompliance.[14] A more recent analysis indicates that 33 percent of those exiting probation failed to successfully meet the conditions of their supervision.[15] A study of a national sample of felons placed on probation found that on any given day, about 10 to 20 percent of probationers were on abscond status, their whereabouts unknown; no agency actively invested time finding those offenders.[16]

Does Probation Work?

The most common question asked about probation is, "Does it work?" By "work," most mean whether the person granted probation has refrained from further crime or reduced his or her recidivism—that is, the number of rearrests. Recidivism is currently the primary outcome measure for probation, as it is for all corrections programs.

Probationer Recidivism

Summaries of probation effectiveness usually report the recidivism rates of felons as if they represented the total adult probation population, instead of 55 percent[17] of it. Failure to make this distinction between felons and misdemeanants is why profoundly different assessments have been offered as to whether probation "works."

In reality, there are two stories about probationer recidivism rates. Recidivism rates are low for adults on probation for *misdemeanors*—data suggest that three-quarters successfully complete their supervision. However, recidivism rates are high for *felony* probationers, particularly in jurisdictions that use probation extensively, where offenders are serious to begin with, and where supervision is minimal.[18]

Recidivism rates vary greatly from place to place, depending on the seriousness of the underlying population characteristics, length of follow-up, and surveillance provided. A summary of 17 follow-up studies of adult felony probationers found that felony rearrest rates ranged from 12 to 65 percent.[19] Such wide variation in recidivism is not unexpected, given the wide variability in granting probation and monitoring court-ordered conditions. Despite the desirability of predicting offender recidivism, available data and statistical methods are insufficient to do so very accurately at this time.

Other Probation Outcomes

Another way to examine probation effectiveness is to look at the contribution of those on probation to the overall crime problem. Of all persons arrested and charged with felonies in 1992, 17 percent of them were on probation at the time of their arrest.[20]

Practitioners have expressed concern about the use of recidivism as the primary, if not sole, measure of probation's success.[21] The American Probation and Parole Association (APPA), representing U.S. probation officers nationwide, argues that recidivism rates measure just one probation task while ignoring others.[22] APPA has urged its member agencies to collect data on alternative outcomes, such as amount of restitution collected, number of offenders employed, amount of fines/fees collected, hours of community service, number of treatment sessions, percentage of financial obligations collected, enrollment in school, days employed, educational attainment, and number of days drug free.

Some probation departments have begun to report such alternative outcome measures to their constituencies and believe this practice is having a positive impact on staff morale, public image, and funding.[23]

How Can Probation Be Revived?

The public has come to understand that not all criminals can be locked up, and so renewed attention is being focused on probation. Policymakers are asking whether probation departments can implement credible and effective community-based sentencing options. No one advocates the abolition of probation, but many call for its reform. But how should that be done?

Implement Quality Programs for Appropriate Probation Target Groups

Probation needs first to regain the public's trust as a meaningful, credible sanction. During the past decade, many jurisdictions developed "intermediate sanctions," such as house arrest, electronic monitoring, and intensive supervision, as a response to prison crowding. These programs were designed to be community-based sanctions that were tougher than regular probation but less stringent and expensive than prison.[24]

The program models were plausible and could have worked, except for one critical factor: They were usually implemented without creating organizational capacity to ensure compliance with court-ordered conditions. When courts ordered offenders to participate in drug treatment, for example, many probation officers could not ensure compliance because local treatment programs were unavailable.[25]

Over time, what was intended as tougher community corrections in most jurisdictions did not materialize, thereby further tarnishing probation's image. Although most judges still report a willingness to use tougher, community-based programs as alternatives to routine probation or prison, most are skeptical that the programs promised "on paper" will be delivered in practice.[26] As a result, some intermediate sanction programs are beginning to fall into disuse.[27]

However, some communities invested adequate resources in intermediate sanctions and made the necessary treatment and work programs available to offenders.[28] In programs where offenders received *both* surveillance (e.g., drug tests) and participated in relevant treatment, recidivism declined 20 to 30 percent.[29]

Solid empirical evidence shows that recidivism is reduced by ordering offenders into treatment and requiring them to participate.[30] So, the first order of business must be to allocate sufficient resources so that the designed programs (incorporating both surveillance and treatment) can be implemented. The resources will be forthcoming only if the public believes that the programs are both effective and punitive.

Public opinion is often cited by officials as a reason for supporting expanded prison policies. According to officials, the public's "get tough on crime" demands are synonymous with sending more offenders to prison for longer terms.[31] Recent evidence must be publicized showing that many offenders—whose opinions on such matters are critical for deterrence—judge some intermediate sanctions as *more* punishing than prison.[32]

When, for example, nonviolent offenders in Marion County, Oregon, were given the choice of serving a prison term or returning to the community to participate in intensive supervision probation (ISP) programs—which imposed drug testing, mandatory community services, and frequent visits with the probation officer—about one-third chose prison over ISP.[33]

Why should anyone prefer imprisonment to remaining in the community, no matter what the conditions? Some have suggested that prison has lost some of its punitive sting and, hence, its ability to scare and deter. One study found that for drug dealers in California, imprisonment confers a certain elevated "homeboy" status, especially for gang members for whom prison and prison gangs can be an alternative site of loyalty.[34] According to the California Youth Authority, inmates steal state-issued prison clothing for the same reason. Wearing it when they return to the community lets everyone know they have done "hard time."[35]

It is important to publicize these results, particularly to policymakers who say they are imprisoning such a large number of offenders because of the public's desire to get tough on crime. But it is no longer necessary to equate criminal punishment solely with prison. The balance of sanctions between probation and prison can be shifted, and at some level of intensity and length, intermediate punishments can be the more dreaded penalty.

Once probation's political support and organizational capacity are in place, offender groups need to be targeted on the basis of what is known about the effectiveness of various programs. Targeting drug offenders makes the most sense for a number of reasons. Large-scale imprisonment of drug offenders has only recently taken place, and new evidence suggests that the public seems ready to accept different punishment strategies for low-level drug offenders.

The public appears to want tougher sentences for drug traffickers and more treatment for addicts—what legislators have instead given them are long sentences for everyone. Public receptiveness to treatment for addicts is important, because those familiar with delivering treatment say that is where treatment can make the biggest impact. A report by the Institute of Medicine (IOM) of the National Academy of Sciences notes that about one-fifth of the estimated population needing treatment—and two-fifths of those clearly needing it—are under the supervision of the justice system as parolees or probationers.

Because the largest single group of serious drug users in any locality comes through the justice system every day, IOM concludes that the justice system is one of the most important gateways to treatment delivery and should be used more effectively. Research has shown that those under corrections supervision stay in treatment longer, thereby increasing positive treatment outcomes.[36]

On the one hand, good-quality treatment is not cheap. On the other hand, it is an investment that pays for itself immediately in terms of crime and health costs averted. Researchers in California[37] concluded that treatment was very cost beneficial: For every dollar spent on drug and alcohol treatment, California saved $7 in reduced crime and health care costs. The study found that each day of treatment *paid for itself on the day treatment was received*, primarily through an avoidance of crime. The level of criminal activity declined by two-thirds from before treatment to after treatment. The greater the length of time spent in treatment, the greater the reduction in crime.

Of course, there is much more to reforming the probation system than simply targeting low-level drug offenders for effective treatment, but this would be a start. There also needs to be serious reconsideration of probation's underlying mission, administrative structure, and funding base. And a program of basic research to address some of probation's most pressing problems should be funded.

Make Probation a Priority Research Topic

Noted below are a few of the questions that would be highly useful for probation research to address.

What purpose is served by monitoring and revoking probation for persons committing technical violations, and is the benefit worth the cost? If technical violations identify offenders who are "going bad" and likely to commit crime, time could be well spent uncovering such violations and incarcerating those persons. But if technical violators are simply troublesome, but not criminally dangerous, devoting scarce prison resources to this population may not be warranted.

Despite the policy significance of technical violations, little serious research has focused on this issue. As the cost of monitoring and incarcerating technical violators increases, research must examine its crime control significance.

Who is in prison, and is there a group of prisoners who, based on crime and prior criminal records, could safely be supervised in the community? Some contend that many, if not most, prisoners are minor property offenders, low-level drug dealers, or technical violators—ideal candidates for community-based alternatives. Others cite data showing that most prisoners are violent recidivists with few prospects for reform.

Research examining the characteristics of inmates in different states (by age, criminal record, and substance-abuse history) is necessary to clarify this important debate. Also critical are better follow-up studies (ideally, using experimental designs) of offenders who have been sentenced to prison as opposed to various forms of community supervision. By tracking similarly situated offenders who are sentenced differently, researchers will be able to refine recidivism prediction models and begin to estimate more accurately the crime and cost implications of different sentencing models.

How do probation departments and other justice agencies influence one another and, together, influence crime? Decisions made in one justice agency have dramatic workload and cost implications for other agencies and for later decisions (such as probation policy on technical violations). To date, these systemic effects have not been well studied but research examining how various policy initiatives affect criminal justice agencies, individually and collectively, is likely to generate many benefits.

Conclusion

Several steps may be taken to achieve greater crime control over probationers:

- Provide adequate financial resources to deliver treatment programs that have been shown to work.
- Combine *both* treatment and surveillance in probation programs and focus them on appropriate offender subgroups. Current evidence suggests that low-level drug offenders are prime candidates for enhanced probation programs.
- Work to garner more public support by convincing citizens that probation sanctions are punitive and in the long run cost-effective.
- Convince the judiciary that offenders will be held accountable for their behavior.
- Give priority to research addressing probation's most pressing problems.

Over time, probation will demonstrate its effectiveness, in terms of both reducing the human toll that imprisonment exacts on those incarcerated and reserving scarce resources to ensure that truly violent offenders remain in prison.

Notes

1. Bureau of Justice Statistics, *Probation and Parole Population Reached Almost 3.9 Million Last Year*, Press Release, Washington, DC: U.S. Department of Justice, Bureau of Justice Statistics, August 14, 1997. See also Bureau of Justice Statistics, *Correctional Populations in the United States, 1995*, Washington, DC: U.S. Department of Justice, Bureau of Justice Statistics, May 1997.
2. Ibid.
3. Petersilia, Joan, "A Crime Control Rationale for Reinvesting in Community Corrections," *Prison Journal*, 1995, 75(4): 479-496.
4. Judge Burton Roberts, administrative judge of the Bronx Supreme and Criminal Courts. Cited in Klein, Andrew R., *Alternative Sentencing, Intermediate Sanctions, and Probation*, Cincinnati, Ohio: Anderson, 1997:72.
5. The judge's (and probation officer's) required conditions can include standard conditions (reporting to the probation officer and the like), punitive conditions (house arrest, for example) that reflect the seriousness of the crime and increase the burden of probation, and treatment conditions (such as for substance abuse).
6. Abadinsky, Howard, *Probation and Parole: Theory and Practice*, Englewood Cliffs, New Jersey: Prentice-Hall, 1997.

[7] Cunniff, Mark, and Ilene R. Bergsmann, *Managing Felons in the Community: An Administrative Profile of Probation*, Washington, DC: National Association of Criminal Justice Planners, 1990.

[8] Camp, George M., and Camille Camp, *The Corrections Yearbook 1995: Probation and Parole*, South Salem, New York: Criminal Justice Institute, 1995.

[9] Jones, Peter R., "Risk Prediction in Criminal Justice," in *Choosing Correctional Options That Work: Defining the Demand and Evaluating the Supply*, ed. Alan Harland, Thousand Oaks, California: Sage, 1996.

[10] Langan, Patrick A., and Mark A. Cunniff, *Recidivism of Felons on Probation, 1986-89*, Washington, DC: U.S. Department of Justice, Bureau of Justice Statistics, 1992.

[11] Clear, Todd, and Anthony A. Braga, "Community Corrections," in *Crime*, ed. James Q. Wilson and Joan Petersilia, San Francisco: Institute for Contemporary Studies, 1995:423.

[12] Bureau of Justice Statistics, *Nation's Probation and Parole Population Reached Almost 3.9 Million Last Year*, Press Release, Washington, DC: U.S. Department of Justice, Bureau of Justice Statistics, August 14, 1997.

[12] Petersilia, Joan, and Susan Turner, *Prison versus Probation in California: Implications for Crime and Offender Recidivism*, Santa Monica, California: RAND Corporation, 1986.

[14] Langan, Patrick, "Between Prison and Probation: Intermediate Sanctions," *Science*, 1994, 264:791-793.

[15] Bureau of Justice Statistics, *Nation's Probation and Parole Population Reached Almost 3.9 Million Last Year*.

[16] Taxman, Faye S., and James Byrne, "Locating Absconders: Results from a Randomized Field Experiment," *Federal Probation*, 1994, 58(1): 13-23.

[17] Bureau of Justice Statistics, *Nation's Probation and Parole Population Reached Almost 3.9 Million Last Year*.

[18] Petersilia, Joan, Susan Turner, James Kahan, and Joyce Peterson, *Granting Felons Probation: Public Risks and Alternatives*, Santa Monica, California: RAND Corporation, R-3186-NIJ, 1985.

[19] Geerken, Michael, and Hennessey D. Hayes, "Probation and Parole: Public Risk and the Future of Incarceration Alternatives," *Criminology*, 1993, 31(4): 549-564.

[20] Reaves, Brian A., and Pheny Z. Smith, *Felony Defendants in Large Urban Counties, 1992*, Washington, DC: U.S. Department of Justice, Bureau of Justice Statistics, 1995.

[21] Boone, Harry N., and Betsy A. Fulton, *Results-Driven Management: Implementing Performance-Based Measures in Community Corrections*, Lexington, Kentucky: American Probation and Parole Association, 1995.

[22] Ibid.

[23] Griffin, Margaret, "Hunt County, Texas, Puts Performance-Based Measures to Work," *Perspectives*, 1996:9-11.

[24] Tonry, Michael, and Mary Lynch, "Intermediate Sanctions," in *Crime and Justice: A Review of Research*, vol. 20, ed. Michael Tonry, Chicago, Illinois: University of Chicago Press, 1996.

[25] Petersilia, Joan, and Susan Turner, "Intensive Probation and Parole," in *Crime and Justice: A Review of Research*, vol. 17, ed. Michael Tonry, Chicago, Illinois: University of Chicago Press, 1993.

[26] Sigler, Robert, and David Lamb, "Community-Based Alternatives to Prison: How the Public and Court Personnel View Them," *Federal Probation*, 1994, 59(2): 3-9.

[27] Petersilia, "A Crime Control Rationale for Reinvesting in Community Corrections."

[28] Klein, *Alternative Sentencing, Intermediate Sanctions, and Probation*.

[29] Petersilia and Turner, "Intensive Probation and Parole."

30 Gendreau, Paul, "The Principles of Effective Intervention with Offenders," in *Choosing Correctional Options That Work: Defining the Demand and Evaluating the Supply,* ed. Alan Harland, Thousand Oaks, California: Sage, 1996.

31 Bell, Griffin B., and William J. Bennett, *The State of Violent Crime in America,* Washington, DC: Council on Crime in America, 1996.

32 Crouch, Ben, "Is Incarceration Really Worse? Analysis of Offenders' Preferences for Prisons over Probation," *Justice Quarterly,* 1993, 10:67-88; Petersilia, Joan, and Elizabeth Piper Deschenes, "Perceptions of Punishment: Inmates and Staff Rank the Severity of Prison versus Intermediate Sanctions," *Prison Journal,* 1994, 74:306-328; Spelman, William, "The Severity of Intermediate Sanctions," *Journal of Research in Crime and Delinquency,* 1995, 32:107-135; and Wood, Peter B., and Harold G. Grasmick, "Inmates Rank the Severity of Ten Intermediate Sanctions Compared to Prison," *Journal of the Oklahoma Criminal Justice Research Consortium,* 1995, 2:30-42.

33 Petersilia and Deschenes, "Perceptions of Punishment: Inmates and Staff Rank the Severity of Prison versus Intermediate Sanctions."

34 Skolnick, Jerome, "Gangs and Crime Old as Time: But Drugs Change Gang Culture," *Crime and Delinquency in California, 1989,* Sacramento, California: California Department of Justice, Bureau of Criminal Statistics, 1990.

35 Petersilia, Joan, "California's Prison Policy: Causes, Costs, and Consequences," *Prison Journal,* 1992, 72(1): 8-36.

36 Institute of Medicine, Committee for Substance Abuse Coverage Study, "A Study of the Evolution, Effectiveness and Financing of Public and Private Drug Treatment Systems," in *Treating Drug Problems,* vol. 1, ed. D. R. Gerstein and H. J. Harwood, Washington, DC: National Academy Press, 1990.

37 Gerstein, Dean, R. A. Johnson, H. J. Harwood, D. Fountain, N. Suter, and K. Malloy, *Evaluating Recovery Services: The California Drug and Alcohol Treatment Assessment,* Sacramento: State of California, Department of Alcohol and Drug Programs, 1994. The researchers studied a sample of 1,900 treatment participants, followed them up for as long as two years of treatment, and studied participants from all four major treatment modalities (therapeutic communities, social models, outpatient drug-free, and methadone maintenance).

29

Save Parole Supervision

Robert Martinson
Judith Wilks

The increasing attacks on the institution of parole in the United States today fail to distinguish between parole as a method for releasing offenders from (or returning offenders to) imprisonment and parole as a method for supervising offenders in the community. These two distinct functions need to be separately evaluated for an overall assessment of the usefulness of parole and its fairness in our system of criminal justice.

The parole release (and revocation) decision is inseparable from the indeterminate sentence. Decisionmaking is a quasi-judicial process carried on by small groups of appointed officials organized into Parole Boards. Parole supervision, on the other hand, is not dependent on the indeterminate sentence. It is a method for controlling, helping, or keeping track of offenders in the community. For hundreds of thousands of convicted offenders, it is a major institutional alternative to extended periods of imprisonment. The supervision functions of parole are carried on by an extended network of thousands of agents

Source: *Federal Probation*, Vol. 41, No. 3 (September 1977), 23-27.

organized into parole district offices and divisions.

The essential criterion of parole as a quasi-judicial process is simple fairness and equity. Such issues are especially critical when unreviewed discretion involves deprivation of liberty. Many critics have rightly argued that the parole decisionmaking process is lamentably brief for such an important decision, lacking in essential elements of due process, frequently arbitrary and subject to political interference, and based in part on a myth that parole boards have the ability to accurately predict when a particular offender is "ready" for parole.

The usual criterion for assessing parole supervision has been how *effective* it is in reducing the criminal behavior of those under supervision. Such effectiveness need not be gained at the price of unfairness. On the contrary, since the consequence of engaging in criminal behavior is to be reimprisoned, supervision which is effective directly contributes to fairness in the sense that fewer offenders are deprived of their liberty. By preventing or inhibiting criminal behavior, effective parole supervision insures that fewer offenders will be rearrested, convicted, and returned to prison.

Unfortunately, in their haste to restrict or eliminate the Parole Board decision-making function (and the indeterminate sentence on which it rests), some critics propose to throw the baby out with the bath water. Yet there is no reason why a mandatory and definite parole sentence could not be substituted for the present system of parole board discretion and conditional release under threat of revocation for rule-breaking.[1] And those who propose such radical surgery would do well not to speak in the name of the offender for there is grave danger that the overall consequence of abolishment of parole supervision would be to consign larger numbers of offenders to prison.

One critical empirical question that must be answered is: Would the abolition of the present system of parole supervision increase or decrease the rates at which persons released from incarceration would be reprocessed into the criminal justice system? Previous research has not addressed this question. Such research deals primarily with variants of parole supervision within the existing system.[2] Inferences from such research are speculative and do not permit a "...direct comparison of offenders under parole supervision with offenders set entirely free."[3]

Parole has never been a universal method for releasing offenders from incarceration, and therefore in most jurisdictions in the United States some persons are released on parole supervision while others are released at the expiration of their terms, i.e., "set entirely free." Clearly, the most obvious research method, available to researchers since parole was established in the United States, would be controlled comparisons of persons released under parole supervision with comparable persons released directly from imprisonment without parole supervision. This is the method to be used in the present analysis.

The Survey

The data presented in table 1 are taken from a larger survey of criminal justice research. The survey was designed to provide a standard procedure for maximizing the accumulation of existing information so that substantive questions can be answered and decisions taken on matters of public policy. For a description of the research procedure, the classification of documents received, and the variables coded, it is necessary to read the preliminary report.[4] The present substudy illustrates the utility of the procedure adopted.

Two key concepts were employed in collecting, coding, and organizing the data taken from more than 600 recent documents: the "batch" and the "computable recidivism rate."

Batch. —A "batch" is any number of persons at some specifiable location in the criminal justice system for whom a "proper" recidivism rate is computable. A proper recidivism rate must specify what *proportion* of a batch are recidivists. The term "parent batch" refers to a universal set which contains two or more batches. For example, a universal set of, say 1,000 male and female parolees may be broken into one batch of 800 *male* parolees and one batch of 200 *female* parolees. Each of these batches is coded as "exclusive" since together they exhaust the parent batch and have no members in common. All batches in table 1 are exclusive batches with an N of 10 or more.

Recidivism Rate. —The primary unit of analysis in the survey is the computable recidivism rate. Each such rate specifies what proportion of any batch shall be identified as "recidivists" according to whatever operational definition of recidivism is utilized by the researcher. Such an operational definition will normally specify the length of time which the batch was followed up in addition to the criminal justice action (arrest, suspension, conviction, return to prison, and so forth) which led to the decision to classify a particular person as a "recidivist." All such definitions were coded into seven categories. Three of these categories — arrest, conviction, and return to prison with a new conviction — were judged to be appropriate for a comparison of parolees and persons released from incarceration with no supervision ("max out").[5]

The term "system re-processing rate" specifies precisely what is being measured in table 1. An "arrest," for example, is an event that can occur to a person under the jurisdiction of criminal justice, and an arrest *rate* simply reports what proportion of any batch included in table 1 were reported as being reprocessed in this way in the documents coded in the survey.

Each recidivism rate in the survey has been coded with additional items of information. The coding system developed was guided by the primary aim of the accumulation of knowledge based on the existing state of the art in criminal justice research. Codes were designed to maximize the information produced by the standard procedures now used in the body of documents encountered. Many of the items specify critical methodological features of the study, such as whether the batch is a population or a sample, the type of research design utilized, months in followup, months in treatment, the type of population or sample (e.g., "termination" sample), and so forth. Since studies report information on the characteristics of batches in a bewildering variety of ways, a standard attribute code was developed so as to maximize the reporting of such information as educational attainment, current offense, race, class position, family status, and so forth.[6] In addition, it was possible to code a considerable number of batches (and therefore rates) with such information as mean age, months in incarceration, sex, whether the batch consisted primarily of narcotics cases or persons with alcohol problems, and so forth.

Procedure

The procedure adopted was to exhaust the survey data base of all meaningful comparisons between adult offenders released from incarceration to parole supervision and comparable groups of adult offenders not released to parole supervision ("max out"). This was a simle sorting operation with an IBM counter-sorter. From a total pool of 5,804 recidivism rates for batches of adult persons in the United States and Canada released under parole supervision, those rates which fell in the category of "arrest" (N = 235), "conviction" (N = 135), and return to prison with a new conviction" (N = 738) were sorted out. A similar sort for adult max out rates resulted in 44 arrest rates, 26 conviction rates, and 73 return-to-prison-with-new-conviction rates. The total number of rates produced by these initial sorts are found at the bottom of table 1.

The cards were then sorted on the variables which had been coded in the survey making no distinction between items which were primarily methodological (e.g., time in followup) and those which were primarily descriptive of a batch (e.g., mean age, sex, percent property offenders). All code categories for which at least two rates were reported for both parole and max out were located. Mean rates for these code categories were computed, and are presented in table 1.[7]

TABLE 1.—*Mean recidivism rates*

Batch Characteristic	Definition: Arrest Parole		Max Out			Conviction Parole		Max Out			New Prison Sentence Parole		Max Out		
	X	N*	X	N	D°*	X	N	X	N	D	X	N	X	N	D
1. Batch N = 100-499	26.9	84	32.8	12	5.9	20.5	68	25.9	22	5.4	11.0	227	14.7	44	3.7
2. Male	25.2	174	39.5	32	14.3	19.1	85	29.6	21	10.5	11.3	393	14.3	58	3.0
3. % White = 0 to 24.9	20.8	38	31.0	17	10.2	12.8	18	22.8	6	10.0	13.3	24	22.8	6	9.5
4. Total Population	20.8	62	37.7	22	16.9	13.9	31	28.1	25	14.2	9.7	593	14.5	67	4.8
5. Termination Sets	24.4	206	42.1	25	17.7	21.3	79	35.7	17	15.4	10.9	603	14.9	71	4.0
6. After-Only Research Design	25.2	96	42.3	27	17.1	21.8	60	28.9	25	7.1	10.9	581	14.8	73	3.9
7. Research done in 1970's	24.0	178	43.6	42	19.6	18.1	66	28.9	25	10.8	9.8	543	14.8	73	5.0
8. Standard Treatment	27.4	129	43.0	39	15.6	19.3	96	29.9	26	10.6	10.3	584	14.9	72	4.6
9. 7-12 Months Follow-up	24.6	85	43.7	12	19.1	15.6	66	22.8	6	7.2	8.7	250	5.2	15	-3.5
10. 19-24 Months Follow-up	28.4	41	57.5	10	29.1	20.9	11	32.5	5	11.6	11.0	170	11.2	15	.2
11. 25-36 Months Follow-up	28.9	25	49.5	4	20.6	17.8	15	27.5	10	9.7	15.5	79	18.9	16	3.4
12. Measured Only After Treatment	28.3	8	43.4	36	15.1	46.3	11	33.2	15	-13.1	14.9	48	13.9	62	-1.0
13. % Property Offenders 50-74.9	16.6	39	34.5	6	17.9	13.0	70	22.8	6	9.8					
14. % First Offenders 0-24.9	29.5	32	37.5	10	8.0	13.8	14	22.8	6	9.0					
15. Not Primarily Narcotic Users	32.5	5	32.5	5	0	5.9	7	22.8	6	16.9					
16. Not Primarily Alcohol Problems	43.4	9	36.2	6	-7.2	13.7	12	22.8	6	9.1					
17. % White 25-49.9	27.8	39	51.2	9	23.4	44.5	7	30.7	13	-13.8					
18. Mean Age 25-34.9	22.2	51	40.5	25	18.3	20.9	28	23.1	7	2.2					
19. % High School Graduates 0-24.9	25.5	67	41.2	9	15.7	19.8	17	22.8	6	3.0					
20. Measured over Same Time at Risk	22.6	26	44.0	19	21.4	18.7	55	18.9	9	.2					
21. Months Incarcerated = 12-17	17.3	36	40.8	8	23.5	17.5	10	28.2	19	10.7					
22. % From Broken Families 50-74.9	32.3	9	32.5	5	.2	19.3	23	22.8	6	3.5					
23. Comparison Group	28.3	79	42.5	15	14.2						9.9	126	14.5	9	4.6
24. Batch N = 50-99	20.9	53	64.5	4	43.6						12.6	62	15.5	10	2.9
25. Sample	25.9	62	48.1	22	22.2						14.0	145	16.3	11	2.3
26. "E" Group	23.7	84	42.5	5	18.8										
27. % Property Offenders 25-49.9	21.1	29	48.5	10	27.4										
28. Batch N = 10-49	22.8	72	44.1	28	21.3										
29. Primarily Narcotics Users	29.0	20	29.5	6	.5										
30. Mixed Sex Batch	28.6	39	51.7	9	23.1										
31. % From Broken Families 0-24.9	29.3	31	51.2	3	21.9										
32. % High School Graduates 25-49.9	33.5	10	37.0	4	3.5										
33. Lowest Class	34.1	22	45.8	8	11.7										
34. Non-Random Research Design	24.4	93	43.9	17	19.5										
35. 1-6 Months Follow-up	15.5	61	29.5	12	14.0										
36. 13-18 Months Follow-up	30.1	16	32.5	5	2.4										
37. Months Incarcerated = 24-29	29.5	32	31.2	3	1.7										
38. Months Incarcerated = 30-36	36.2	6	59.5	6	23.3										
39. % Property Offenders 0-24.9						20.5	15	30.5	10	10.0					
40. Highest Class						20.8	19	22.8	6	2.0					
41. Batch N = 500+											9.3	378	13.9	18	4.6
42. 37-60 Months Follow-up											13.5	87	18.4	18	4.9
43. 60+ Months Follow-up											14.1	22	25.4	7	11.3
TOTAL	24.5	235	42.9	44	18.4	19.7	135	29.9	26	10.2	10.5	738	14.8	73	4.3

*N = Number of rates   **D = Max Out Mean minus Parole Mean

Discussion

Item 1 can be used to illustrate how the table should be read. For parole, there were 84 recidivism rates where "arrest" was the measurement of recidivism and for which the batch size fell between 100 and 499. The mean of these 84 rates was 26.9. For this same batch size (100-499), there were 12 max out rates, and the mean of these rates was 32.8. The difference between these two means is 5.9.

Reading across the table, for the "conviction" definition the mean rates for parole and max out were 20.5 and 25.9, respectively. For the "return to prison with new conviction" definition these means were 11.0 and 14.7. Turning to a different batch size of 50-99 (item 24), one notes that comparisons could only be made for two of the three definitions. For some variables comparisons were possible for only one definition.

This table presents data in a manner which is similar to the procedure of simultaneously controlling for adulthood, definition of recidivism, place in the criminal justice system (i.e., parole vs. max out), and at least one additional variable. Given the number of rates available, it would have been possible to have controlled for one (or even more) variables in addition to the four specified above. For reasons of time, these additional controls were not attempted.

It is interesting to note that in *74 of the 80 comparisons contained in table 1, the mean of the recidivism rates for parole is lower than for max out.* This is the case whether the final variable controlled is methodological or sociodemographic. For the arrest definition, the differences *in favor of* parole range from a low of 0.2 (item 22) to a high of 43.6 (item 24). For conviction, the differences in favor of parole range from 0.2 (item 20) to 16.9 (item 15). For new prison sentence, the differences in favor of parole range from 0.2 (item 10) to 11.3 (item 43).

In 6 of the 80 comparisons, the mean of the rates for max out is equal to or lower than the mean for parole. These six cases are unsystematically distributed throughout the table. In three instances the final control variable is methodlogical; in three it is sociodemographic. Two cases fall under the arrest definition; two under conviction; and two under return to prison. These six exceptions do not suggest to us any particular set of conditions which might be further explored to discover subgroups of offenders, or contexts, for which max out would be a superior policy for criminal justice.

Data contained in our Preliminary Report provided a starting point for this analysis. This initial data (based on 3,005 rates coded at that time) indicated that the mean of the rates for parole (25.4) was somewhat lower than the mean of the rates for max out (31.6). This six percentage point difference resulted from a comparison which did not further control for the definition of recidivisim, for adult vs. juvenile, or for any of the other variables utilized in table 1. Increasing the total number of rates, and simultaneously controlling for four additional variables has led to the discovery of larger mean differences between parole and max out.[8]

Summary

Those who propose the abolition of parole supervision in this country often speak of "fairness to the offender." It is difficult to detect in table 1 evidence of such fairness. On the contrary. The evidence seems to indicate that the abolition of parole supervision would result in substantial increases in arrest, conviction, and return to prison. Those who wish to eliminate the unfairness of parole board decisionmaking might well concentrate on finding a specific remedy for this problem, a remedy which would not increase the very "unfairness" they deplore. At the very least, the data in table 1 should give pause to those policymakers and legislators who have been operating on the unexamined assumption that parole supervision *makes no difference*. In face of the evidence in table 1 such an assumption is unlikely.

Notes

[1]See J. Wilks and R. Martinson, "Is the Treatment of Criminal Offenders Really Necessary?," *Federal Probation*, March 1976, pp. 3-9.

[2]See, for example, D. Lipton, R. Martinson, and J. Wilks, *The Effectiveness of Correctional Treatment*. New York: Praeger Publishers, 1975, sections on Probation and Parole.

[3]D.T. Stanley, *Prisoners Among Us: The Problem of Parole*, The Brookings Institution, Washington, D.C., 1976, pp. 181-2.

[4]See, R. Martinson and J. Wilks, *Knowledge in Criminal Justice Planning, A Preliminary Report*, October 15, 1976, pp. 58 (processed).

[5]The other four categories were: 100% minus "success" rate; short of arrest (i.e., AWOL, absconding, suspension, and similar); return to prison for technical violation; and return to prison for technical plus new conviction. Three of these categories were eliminated because they cannot happen to max out groups. The fourth — 100% minus "success" rate — was eliminated because of possible problems in interpreting the meaning of the measure.

[6]The proportion in which any attribute was present in a batch was coded as follows: 1 — 0-24.9%; 2 — 25-49%; 3 — 50-74.9%; and 4 — 75-100%.

[7]Multiplying the total number of coding categories (97) by the three definitions gives a total of 291 possible comparisons if sufficient data had been present. Eliminating 39 cases where data were reported as "unknown," 38 cases in which there were less than two rates in a category of either parole or max out, and 134 cases in which no data were reported leaves the 80 comparisons reported in table 1.

[8]This method is an application of standard research procedures. See, for example, P.F. Lazersfeld, "Interpretation of Statistical Relations as a Research Operation," in: *The Language of Social Research* (P.F. Lazersfeld and M. Rosenberg, eds.), Glencoe, Ill.: The Free Press, 1955.

30

Alternatives to Incarceration
A Conservative Perspective

Charles Colson and
Daniel W. Van Ness

In Michigan, conservative Republican legislators Jack Welborn and William Van Regenmorter worked with liberal Democrat Carolyn Cheeks Kilpatrick to pass a Community Corrections Act (CCA). The result: Non-violent offenders will be punished in their communities instead of prison, which will save money and ease the state's prison overcrowding crisis.

In Indiana, Republican State Sen. Ed Pease led a successful legislative effort to establish home detention as a means of easing the pressure of the state's expanding prison population. Russ Pulliam, editorial writer of the conservative Pulliam newspaper chain, voiced support for the legislation as "one step in the right direction for the future of the criminal justice system in Indiana" (*Indianapolis News* Jan. 20,1988). (The bill was included in The Council of State Governments' *Suggested State Legislation*, 1989).

Source: *The Journal of State Government*, Vol. 62 (March/April 1989), 59-64, published by the Council of State Governments. Reprinted by permission of the publisher and the authors.

In Florida, conservative businessman Jack Eckerd and former Federal Bureau of Prisons Director Norm Carlson are leading a campaign for expanded use of house arrest, drug treatment and restitution centers as alternatives to imprisonment for non-violent offenders.

In Alabama, conservative Democratic Rep. Claud Walker is sponsoring a Community Corrections Act aimed at reducing the large percentage of non-violent inmates in state prisons. Alabama Commissioner of Corrections Morris Thigpen and the Alabama Sheriffs Association are backing the bill.

In Arizona, Republican State Sen. Tony West sponsored the Community Punishment Act. The legislation, which recently passed with the support of Arizona Chief Justice Frank Cordon and Maricopa County Chief Presiding Judge B. Michael Dann, will provide communities with state money to establish restitution, community service, victim-offender reconciliation and other non-prison programs for non-dangerous offenders.

Conservatives are often typecast as champions of the "lock 'em up and throw away the key" battle cry of this "get tough on crime" era. Yet, increasingly, all around the country, conservatives of both parties are advocating alternatives to incarceration for non-violent offenders. They may well be the single most potent force for practical, prudent criminal justice reform today.

What's Going On?

No one can deny the crying need for reform in our nation's criminal justice system. In December 1988 there were 627,402 state and federal prisoners in American institutions—twice as many as in 1978 (Department of Justice press release April 23, 1989). The prison population explosion has filled prisons to overflowing. Federal prisons are 73 percent over capacity, while state prisons are on average 20 percent over capacity, according to the Bureau of Justice Statistics (BJS 1988a).

Prison systems in 45 states have been sued because of overcrowding. In 37 states, at least one major institution is under court order or consent decree. In nine of those 37 states, the entire prison system is under court order. Litigation is pending in eight states (National Prison Project 1988).

The future looks no brighter. The National Council of Crime and Delinquency (NCCD 1988a) estimates that U.S. prison populations will increase by an additional 50 percent in the next 10 years.

Although our country is incarcerating more people than ever, violent and property crimes continue to escalate (BJS 1988b). The indiscriminate "get tough" approach is a grand success in filling prisons. But it fails miserably at reducing crime.

Thankfully, many conservatives actively are pushing saner, wiser solutions to crime's stranglehold on our nation and the prison population explosion.

Why conservatives? Based on Justice Fellowship's work with politicians across the United States, it's clear that many see alternatives to incarceration for non-violent offenders as a natural extension of conservative political philosophy. Legislators cite the following principles: Punishment is appropriate; it should serve victims' needs; public safety is essential; local is better, and wise use of limited government resources is needed.

Let's look at each.

Punishment is appropriate. Since the first "penitentiary" was established in 1789, American criminal justice has been predicated on the belief that crime is the result of environmental or psychiatric factors. Criminals were seen as victims and were sent to prison to be rehabilitated.

This human engineering approach has proven a dismal failure. Studies over the last two decades consistently have concluded that three out of four ex-offenders are rearrested within four years of their release from prison (Federal Bureau of Investigation 1975; Petersilia, Turner and Peterson 1986). Far from rehabilitating offenders, prisons seem better suited to train them in the finer arts of crime.

Pursuing false dreams of rehabilitation undermines the principle of personal accountability. No matter how many environmental factors weigh upon the individual, committing a criminal act is a personal choice. By treating victimizers as victims, society robs them of the dignity belonging to moral agents. They are denied the opportunity to "pay the price" and move on with life. C.S. Lewis ([1949] 1983) put it this way, "To be punished, however severely, because we have deserved it, because we 'ought to have known better' is to be treated as a human person made in God's image."

Treatment programs should be available to offenders who would be helped by them—but justice requires that offenders also must be held accountable for their behavior.

The issue should not be *whether* to punish but *how*. The problem is that our society has increasingly equated "punishment" with "prison" and seems unable to conceive of the notion of punishments aside from prison. Prisons are, of course, necessary for violent offenders. But nearly 50 percent of the American prison population is behind bars for non-violent offenses. Many of them would pose little danger to their communities; they are imprisoned solely for punishment.

For the reasons that follow, many conservatives are concluding that society is not well served by punishing non-violent offenders behind bars. Sound alternatives to prison are available. Restitution, community service and intensive supervision probation are tough and effective punishments that limit freedom and place demands for compensation upon offenders.

Punishment should serve victims' needs. While victims suffer most from crime—physically, emotionally and financially (to the tune of $13 billion per year) (BJS 1988c)—victims' interests are represented least. From the moment a crime is committed, through the time the offender is convicted and sent to prison, the victim is virtually ignored by the criminal justice system. As Roberta Roper whose daughter was murdered seven years ago, said, "Crime doesn't pay—but victims do."

This injustice has sparked the growth of victims' rights groups across the United States. In addition to supporting an increased role for victims in the system, many have promoted restitution and other alternatives to incarceration—not to make life easier for offenders but to benefit victims.

For example, the Alabama Victims Compensation Group and Victims of Crime Against Leniency are supporting the Alabama Community Corrections Act because it holds offenders accountable for their crimes and provides for victim assistance officers to help victims secure restitution and compensation. In Maryland, Justice Fellowship worked with the effective and well-respected Stephanie Roper Committee to promote recently passed mandatory restitution legislation.

Victim restitution must become an essential part of criminal punishments. This a matter of simple justice. In an article describing the Sentencing Improvement Act of 1983, U.S. Sens. William Armstrong, R-Colorado, and Sam Nunn, D-Georgia, (1986) recognized the importance of alternative punishments based on restitution: "Because of growing public concern for crime victims, the restitution concept holds great promise of gaining broad public support. . . . Recent surveys indicate that a great percentage of Americans would prefer to have the non-violent offender repay his victim rather than serve time at public expense."

Public safety is essential. Non-violent offenders who might be sentenced to alternative punishments are taking up precious prison space that should be reserved for violent criminals. (As noted, nearly half of all state prisoners were convicted of non-violent crimes. And 34 percent have never committed a violent crime (BJS 1988d).)

But, prisons are so overcrowded that many states rely on early release to reduce prison populations. This means that some dangerous offenders are let out well before they have served their full sentence. This is the irony of the "get tough" response to crime: By indiscriminately sending more people to prison, communities are less safe.

The case of Charlie Street is illustrative. Street was released from Florida's Martin Correctional Institution in the fall of 1988 after serving only half of his sentence for attempted murder. Ten days later, he gunned down two Dade County police officers — a tragedy that could have been avoided if Street had been kept off the streets and in prison where he belonged. As Jack Eckerd wrote in the *Orlando Sentinel* (Dec. 4, 1988), "We must restore sanity to the system, slamming the door and keeping it shut on violent and career criminals like Charlie Street, while expanding alternate punishments for non-violent offenders."

Any discussion of public safety eventually includes the issue of deterrence. The argument that prisons alone deter is defeated by the facts. Swift and certain punishment deters, not harsh punishment that is neither swift nor certain.

Consider the odds. The federal government reports that, out of 100 crimes, 33 will be reported to the police and seven will result in an arrest. Four will end with a conviction, with one offender going to jail, one to prison and two to probation. In other words, for every 100 crimes committed in the United States, one person goes to prison (Colson and Van Ness 1989).

Can we reasonably believe that doubling or tripling the number of people in prison would significantly deter crime? Would a 2 or 3 percent chance of imprisonment actually deter more crime than a 1 percent chance of imprisonment?

Fortunately, experienced criminal justice practitioners know that tough alternative punishments are feared more by convicted offenders than prison. Trial judges in Florida, for example, say that defendants request prison sentences to avoid the state's tough Community Control Program.

Alternatives promote public safety in other ways as well. For example, they keep the non-violent offender out of prison, the ideal training ground for becoming a more accomplished and dangerous criminal. The Rand Corporation found in a 1986 study (Petersilia, Turner and Peterson) that a group of probationers committed fewer new crimes than an identical group of ex-prisoners. The researchers concluded that "imprisonment was associated with a higher probability of recidivism."

A federal study of Georgia's Intensive Probation Supervision program (National Institute of Justice 1987) found that probationers committed fewer new crimes than comparable prisoners and no violent new crimes.

Community safety depends on increased use of community sanctions.

Local is better. Many alternatives to incarceration significantly benefit local communities. Community Corrections Acts, for example, allow communities to tailor programs to meet their own needs, by dealing with non-violent offenders in their own ways. This also means that communities are involved with their own offenders, who will most likely continue to live in the community after serving their sentences.

Local punishments benefit the state as well. Every offender who stays in a local program is one less person taking up scarce prison space at state expense.

Community service performed by offenders can be another important local benefit. Instead of sending offenders to state prisons, some communities reap the benefits of free or low-pay labor for charitable or governmental agencies. Genesee County, New York, has honed this practice into an art form. Since the establishment of the county's widely acclaimed Genesee Justice program in 1981,offenders performed more than 97,000 hours of community service for 118 community agencies, a total value of $389,000 (Genesee County Sheriff's Department 1988).

Wise use of limited government resources. There is no question that states will have to increase their prison capacities. But state governments cannot afford to rely on prison construction as the sole means to solve the overcrowding crisis. It costs an average of $15,900 to keep an inmate in prison for one year (Camp and Camp 1988). In fiscal 1987 alone state and federal governments spent almost $5 billion in new prison construction (American Correctional Association 1988).

This is placing an extraordinary strain on state budgets. Norman Carlson (1988), writing of the situation in Florida, summarizes the dilemma facing many states, "Constructing sufficient prison space is not a viable solution. The tremendous costs involved in building and operating the required number of new prisons would overwhelm the limited resources available in the state treasury and would compete with other high priority needs, such as education, medical care and transportation."

Explaining why he worked so hard for passage of the Michigan Community Corrections Act, Michigan State Rep. William Van Regenmorter (1988) said, "Michigan's prison system has been overcrowded since 1975. (In). . . 1984, the system held about 300 prisoners more than its intended capacity. To combat this problem, the Department of Corrections constructed many new prisons, almost doubling the system's capacity in just three years. The result of this expensive building program? The system was still overcrowded, this time by some 3,000 prisoners!"

And because of the extraordinary increase (141 percent over the last five years) in the corrections budget—due to the massive prison construction program (*Grand Rapids Press* Jan. 2, 1989)—Michigan now faces cuts in social service programs.

New prison construction costs an average of $80,000 per maximum security cell. The total cost of all current or planned prison construction will be $25 billion (NCCD 1988b). States cannot afford to make such budget-busting investments in concrete and steel condominiums with bars.

To reduce overcrowding and avoid bankrupting other key state programs, conservatives argue in favor of investing in alternatives to prison, so that prisons can be reserved for the dangerous offenders who must be locked away from society. Some states are taking initiatives to do so.

Program Profiles

Community Corrections Acts (CCAs). These acts provide a statewide mechanism allowing local governments to design, develop and deliver—and state governments to fund—local correctional tools such as intensive supervision, restitution, community service, and drug and alcohol treatment. Thirteen states now have CCAs.

Tennessee diverted 504 offenders from prison in fiscal 1987-88 at a cost of $7,599 per offender, compared to the state average of $19,710 for incarceration. In addition, offenders sentenced to community corrections paid $59,145 in restitution to victims and performed 76,294 hours of community service. The estimated total savings to the state was $6.1 million (Mike Jones, Tennessee Department of Corrections, telephone interview September 1988).

Virginia diverted 699 felons from its prisons and jails in fiscal 1987-88. As a result, it saved more than $8 million, which does not include savings realized by diverting more than 6,500 local felons and misdemeanants from jails. Diverted offenders performed 229,812 hours of community service and paid $76,870 in restitution (Gwen Cunningham, Virginia Department of Corrections, telephone interview, September 1988).

House arrest confines offenders to their own homes. They are not allowed out except for approved activities such as health care, special religious services, community service or employment, which in turn most often leads to restitution payments to victims (Petersilia 1987). Many jurisdictions are using electronic surveillance measures to ensure compliance.

Florida's Community Control Program is a nationally recognized house arrest program. Established in 1983, Community Control uses community service and restitution sanctions for some 8,000 offenders statewide. The cost to the state is $2,650 per year per offender, which is 80 percent less than the $13,140 cost for imprisonment (Carlson 1989). By reducing prison commitments by 180 people a month, Community Control has proven a valuable weapon in Florida's fight against overcrowding. Because only 9 percent of its offenders commit new crimes, it is also an effective weapon against crime.

Intensive Probation Supervision (IPS). The key to this program's success is low caseloads. Ideally, officers maintain caseloads of 15-25 people—as opposed to the supervision possible when harried officers in "normal" probation programs carry caseloads of between 120 and 300 offenders. In many IPS programs, offenders must make daily contact with their officers. Most intensive supervision programs require offenders to maintain employment or go to school and to abide by a strict curfew. Many also include restitution and community service as sanctions.

Illinois regularly supervises 570 offenders in its IPS program—a ratio of 25 offenders for every two officers. The annual cost per offender is $2,367. Since the program was established in 1984, Illinois has collected approximately $1 million in restitution, taxes, fines and court costs. Its Intensive Probation Supervision participants performed 145,349 hours of public service valued at $489,921. All told, the state saved $7.7 million in the last five years through IPS (Anderson 1988). And prospects look good for expanding the program to more offenders.

Restitution centers are residential facilities designed to house offenders requiring more supervision than regular or intensive supervision probation but less than total confinement in prison. These centers, which are a tightened-up version of "work release" with a focus on restitution, are used in six states as an alternative to imprisonment.

Georgia's restitution centers can house 2,600 offenders yearly. During fiscal 1987, the state collected from offenders $256,817 in restitution, $626,516 in family support, $1.4 million in room and board, $940,274 in fines and court fees and $1.4 million in taxes. The offenders also performed community service worth $266,516. The annual cost per offender was $8,249. Seventy-five percent of the residents successfully complete the program (Larry Anderson, Georgia Department of Corrections, telephone interview, 1988).

Florida's Probation and Restitution Centers can hold 382 offenders, far below the 900 offenders who would have qualified for the program in 1987, according to a 1988 report by the state Office of the Auditor

General. The annual cost per offender is $10,909, which the state partially defrays by collecting average annual fees of $1,900 per offender. Jack Eckerd and Norm Carlson are among those calling for expanded use of these centers in Florida.

Conclusion

No one could deny the severity of America's criminal justice crisis. The time has come for real solutions rather than overheated rhetoric that fuels public passions, reinforces stereotypes about prisons and prisoners and, in the end, results in taxpayers being punished far more than offenders.

Historically, conservatives have been at the forefront of many great movements in the West: the battle for abolition of the slave trade and of slavery, the fight to end industrial abuses in the late 19th century and in efforts to establish public education. We believe the criminal justice arena is one in which conservatives are beginning to lead the way toward measures that will benefit offenders, victims, correctional officials and taxpayers.

Crime is not a partisan issue. Pursuing alternatives to prison for non-violent offenders will take the endurance, creativity and cooperation of men and women from every political perspective. And conservatives, working with moderates and liberals, can play a key role in forging that public consensus for effective criminal justice policy.

References

Administrative Office of the Illinois Courts. 1988. *Illinois Intensive Probation Supervision: Statewide Summary, Quarterly Statistical Report*. Prepared by Gregg Anderson. Springfield: Administrative Office of the Illinois Courts, July.

American Correctional Association. 1988. *1988 Directory: Juvenile and Adult Correctional Departments, Institutions, Agencies — Paroling Authorities*, ed. Anthony P. Travisono. College Park, MD: American Correctional Association.

Armstrong, William L., and Sam Nunn. 1986. "Alternatives to Incarceration: The Sentencing Improvement Act." *Crime and Punishment in Modern America*, ed. Patrick B. McGuigan and Jon S. Pascale, 337-348. Washington DC: Free Congress Research and Education Foundation.

Bureau of Justice Statistics (BJS), Department of Justice. 1988a. *Prisoners in 1987*. Washington DC: GPO, April.

———. 1988b. *Criminal Victimization 1987*. Washington DC: GPO, October.

_____. 1988c. *Report to the Nation on Crime and Justice*. 2d. ed. Washington, DC: GPO.

_____. 1988d. *Profile of State Prison Inmates 1986*. Prepared by Christopher A. Innes. Washington, DC: GPO, January.

Camp, George M., and Camille Graham Camp. 1988. *The Corrections Yearbook 1988*. New York: Criminal Justice Institute.

Carlson, Norman A. 1988. *Findings and Recommendations on Florida's Prison Crisis*. Tallahassee: Florida Prison Crisis Project, March-April.

_____. 1989. *Florida's Prison Crisis*. Tallahassee: Justice Task Force, January.

Colson, Charles, and Daniel W. Van Ness. 1989. *Convicted: New Hope for Ending America's Crime Crisis*. Westchester, IL: Crossway.

Council of State Governments. 1989. *Suggested State Legislation*, Vol. 48. Lexington: Council of State Governments.

Federal Bureau of Investigation. 1975. Crime in the United States 1975. *Crime in the United States 1975: Uniform Crime Reports for the United States*. Washington, DC: GPO.

Genesee County (NY) Sheriff's Department. 1988. *Genesee Justice 1987-88 Annual Report: Community Service/Victim Assistance Program*. Batavia, NY: Genesee County Sheriff's Department.

Lewis, C.S. [1949] 1983. The Humanitarian Theory of Punishment. Reprint, in *God in the Dock: Essays on Theology and Ethics*, ed. Walter Hooper, 287-294. Grand Rapids: William B. Eerdmans.

National Council on Crime and Delinquency (NCCD). 1988a. *Crime and Punishment in the Year 2000: What Kind of Future?* San Francisco: NCCD.

_____. 1988b. *Illusory Savings in the War Against Crime*. San Francisco: NCCD, July.

National Institute of Justice. 1987. *New Dimensions in Probation: Georgia's Experience with Intensive Probation Supervision*. Prepared by Billie S. Erwin and Lawrence A. Bennett. Washington, DC: GPO, January.

National Prison Project. 1988. *Status Report: The Courts and Prisons*. Washington, DC: National Prison Project.

Petersilia, Joan, Susan Turner and Joyce Peterson. 1986. *Prison versus Probation in California: Implications for Crime and Offender Recidivism*. Santa Monica: Rand.

Petersilia, Joan. 1987. *Expanding Options for Criminal Sentencing*. Santa Monica: Rand.

State of Florida Office of the Auditor General. 1988. *Performance Audit of the Department of Corrections Community-Based Facilities Program*. Tallahassee: Office of the Auditor General, March.

Van Regenmorter, William. 1988. "Helping Young Offenders in Michigan." *The Banner*, Nov. 14.

31

Evaluating Intensive Supervision Probation/Parole
Results of a Nationwide Experiment

Joan Petersilia
Susan Turner

Sentencing practices in this country suggest that offenses can be divided into two categories. When the crime is relatively serious, offenders are put behind bars; when it is less so, they are put on probation, often with only perfunctory supervision. This two-fold division disregards the range of severity in crime, and as a result, sentencing can err in one direction or another: either it is too harsh, incarcerating people whose crimes are not serious enough to warrant a sanction this severe, or too lenient, putting on probation people whose crimes call for more severe punishment. This need for more flexible alternatives—punishments that in harshness fall between prison and probation—led many States to experiment with intermediate sanctions, such as intensive supervision probation/parole (ISP).[1]

Intensive supervision probation/parole is a form of release into the community that emphasizes close monitoring of convicted offenders and imposes rigorous conditions on that release. Most ISP's call for:

- Some combination of multiple weekly contacts with a supervising officer.
- Random and unannounced drug testing.
- Stringent enforcement of probation/parole conditions.
- A requirement to participate in relevant treatment, hold a job, and perhaps perform community service.

Source: *National Institute of Justice: Research in Brief*, U.S. Department of Justice, May 1993: 1–11.

483

Interest in ISP's has been generated in part by the increased proportion of serious offenders among the probation population, a group whose needs and problems may not be effectively addressed by routine probation. Another reason for interest in ISP's is the greater flexibility in sentencing options that they permit. They are better able than the traditional alternatives—prison or probation—to fit the punishment to the crime.

The Problem

The population on probation is a particular focus of ISP's. This population has been growing, increasing 5 to 7 percent each year from 1985 to 1990. At the end of 1990, two-thirds of all people who were under correctional supervision were on probation.[2] More importantly, the type of offender on probation has also changed. More of the current probation population consists of people convicted of felonies than misdemeanors.[3]

As a sentencing option, routine probation was neither intended nor structured to handle this type of offender. One reason is that felons are not good risks for routine probation. A recent report by the Bureau of Justice Statistics revealed that 43 percent of felons on State probation were rearrested for another felony within 3 years.[4] This threat to public safety underscores the need for sentencing alternatives. Moreover, the need is even greater in view of budget cuts at probation agencies.

At the other extreme, reliance on imprisonment has limitations. Prison populations have tripled since 1975. States have responded to the increased need with enormous investments in prison construction. Yet the level of violent crime is now substantially higher than it was a decade ago, indicating that the prospect of imprisonment has not had the deterrent effect that investment in prisons hoped to buy.[5] It has also meant that 36 States are currently operating all or part of their correctional systems under court orders or consent decrees to reduce crowding.[6]

The Rationale for ISP's

Since neither prison nor routine probation can fully respond to the current situation, ISP's have increasingly been viewed as an alternative. Indeed, these programs have been hailed by many as the most promising criminal justice innovation in decades. Between 1980 and 1990 every State adopted some form of ISP for adult offenders.[7] The Federal system has not been as aggressive as the States in ISP experiments, although there are a few programs in selected districts.

Types of ISP's

ISP's are usually classified as prison diversion, enhanced probation, and enhanced parole. Each has a different goal.

Diversion is commonly referred to as a "front door" program because its goal is to limit the number of offenders entering prison. Prison diversion programs generally identify lower risk; incoming inmates to participate in an ISP in the community as a substitute for a prison term.

Enhancement programs generally select already sentenced probationers and parolees and subject them to closer supervision in the community than regular probation or parole. People placed in ISP- enhanced probation or enhanced parole programs show evidence of failure under routine supervision or have committed offenses generally deemed to be too serious for supervision on routine caseloads.

A growing number of jurisdictions have come to believe that by providing increased supervision of serious offenders in the community, ISP's can both relieve prison crowding and lessen the risks to public safety that such offenders pose—and all at a cost savings. In addition to these practical considerations, many believe ISP's should be adopted as a matter of principle, to meet the need for greater latitude in sentencing and to achieve the sentencing objective of just deserts.

The practical argument is the one advanced most often. ISP's are believed to be cost-effective, either in the short run or the long run. Prison-diversion programs (see "Types of ISP's") are thought to be able to reduce corrections costs because they presumably cost less than prison. Probation-enhancement programs are believed to prevent crime because the close surveillance they provide should deter recidivism. With lower recidivism, the need for imprisonment is also reduced, since fewer offenders will be reprocessed by the system.

Assumptions about the effect of ISP's on crime control involve comparisons of various types of sanctions. Prison is assumed to provide the strongest, and routine supervision the weakest, crime control. ISP's are a middle ground, with more control than routine supervision but less control than prison. Theoretically, offenders in ISP programs are deterred from committing crimes because they are under surveillance, and they are constrained from committing crimes because the conditions of the program limit their opportunities.

Initial Reactions to ISP's

Some of the enthusiasm for ISP's was generated by early reports from programs like that of the Georgia Department of Corrections, which seemed to bear out many of the assumptions and to produce a number of benefits.[8] Many ISP programs claimed to have saved at least $10,000 a year for each offender who otherwise would have been sentenced to prison.[9] Participants in the Georgia program, which served as the model for programs adopted elsewhere, had low recidivism, maintained employment, made restitution, and paid a monthly supervision fee.

In other places where ISP's were adopted, evaluations produced mixed results, with some sites reporting cost savings (Illinois and New Jersey, for example), while others did not (such as Massachusetts and Wisconsin); and some reporting reduced recidivism (Iowa, for example), while others did not (such as Ohio and Wisconsin).

The ambiguous results of these programs indicate that assumptions about the ability of ISP's to produce practical results—relieve prison crowding, lower costs, and control crime—may not have been well-founded. Reservations have been raised by independent agencies (such as the U.S. General Accounting Office), as well as by a number of scholars, including proponents of the ISP concept.[10] It appears not that the ISP's themselves have failed, but that the objectives set for them may have been overly ambitious, raising expectations they have been unable to meet.

The evidence seems better able to support the argument based on principle. That is, because ISP's are more punitive than routine probation and parole and because they provide for greater surveillance, they may be able to achieve the goal of permitting needed flexibility in sentencing.

The Demonstration Project

To test the relative effectiveness of ISP's and traditional sanctions, NIJ evaluated a demonstration project sponsored by the Bureau of Justice Assistance (BJA). The demonstration, which involved 14 programs in 9 States, ran from 1986 to 1991 and involved about 2,000 offenders. NIJ commissioned the RAND Corporation to evaluate the programs in a project supported by the Institute as well as BJA.

The participating jurisdictions (see exhibit 1) were asked to design an ISP program and were given wide latitude in doing so. Only two sites (Marion County, Oregon, and Milwaukee, Wisconsin) selected prison diversion programs, in which lower risk offenders who would have entered prison were diverted into the community. All others chose either probation enhancement or parole enhancement programs for the more serious offenders who were then under community supervision.

The offenders whom the jurisdictions chose to target had to meet only two criteria: they had to be adults and they could not be currently convicted of a violent crime. Once these criteria were met, the jurisdictions were free to focus on whatever type of offender population they wished: probationers and/or parolees, people currently in jail, or people who were prison bound.

They were also free to tailor their programs to meet local needs. For example, several sites designed their programs specifically for drug offenders. However, for a variety of reasons, the agencies were unable to place many offenders in drug, alcohol, or other such treatment programs. Thus, the ISP's evaluated were not primarily service and treatment programs, but rather were oriented more toward surveillance and supervision. (See "Study Methods.")

Effectiveness of ISP's

The demonstration was intended to answer the question of how participation in an ISP affected offenders' subsequent criminal behavior (that is, its effect on recidivism). The evaluation was intended to bring to light information about cost-effectiveness and extent of offender participation in counseling, work, and training programs. The effect of ISP's on prison crowding was not a study aim, but it has been a major policy interest in all ISP programs. The participating sites had their own objectives and interests. Most wanted to learn whether ISP's are an effective intermediate sanction, in which probation and parole conditions are monitored and enforced more credibly.

Overall, the results revealed what *cannot* be expected of ISP's as much as what *can* be. Most notably, they suggest that the assumptions about

Study Methods[11]

Program Design

All jurisdictions selected by the Bureau of Justice Assistance for participation in the demonstration and evaluation were asked to design and implement an ISP program that was to be funded for 18 to 24 months. The jurisdictions also were required to receive training and technical assistance, both provided by outside consultants.[12] In addition, they took part in the independent evaluation, which required their gathering data about the program.

The population studied consisted of approximately 2,000 adult offenders who were not currently convicted of a violent crime (homicide, rape, robbery, and assault). The vast majority of the offenders were men in their late 20s and early 30s, and most had long criminal records. In other respects, sites varied. Some, for example, chose offenders with more serious prison records than others. The nature of their offenses varied, as did their racial composition. The proportion of offenders in Dallas had served a prison term, while for Contra Costa the figure was only 5 percent.

Because each site was allowed to design its own ISP, no two programs were identical. They adopted whatever components of the general ISP model they wished (such as random urine testing, curfews, electronic monitoring, and treatment referrals).

Close supervision of offenders was one of the few required program components. It consisted of weekly contacts with the officers, unscheduled drug testing, and stricter enforcement of probation/parole conditions.

Random Assignment

The study was conducted as a randomized experiment. Indeed, the study may well be the largest randomized experiment in corrections ever undertaken in the United States. At each site, along with the experimental group, a control group of offenders was set up to serve as a comparison. The offenders in the control group were not part of the program but instead were given a different sanction (either prison or routine probation or parole, for example).[13] After the jurisdictions selected the pool of offenders they deemed eligible for ISP programs, the researchers assigned them randomly to one or the other of the two groups.

Having a control group with which to compare findings ensured that the results were the product of the manipulated variables of the ISP program rather than of differences among the offenders in the two groups. Previous ISP evaluations lacked matching comparison groups.

Data Collection

For each offender, in both the experimental and the control groups, data collection forms were completed by the participating agency in the respective jurisdictions. A *background assessment* recorded demographic information, prior criminal record, drug dependence status, and similar information. The other forms—*6- and 12-month reviews*—recorded probation and parole services received, participation in treatment and work programs, and recidivism during the 1-year followup. Also recorded on this form were the number of drug tests ordered and taken, the types of drugs for which the offender tested positive, and the sanction imposed.

Measuring Program Effects

Separate calculations were devised for estimating costs and for measuring program implementation, the effect of the ISP's on recidivism, and the effect on social adjustment (percentage of offenders who attended counseling, participated in training, were employed, and the like).

the ability of ISP's to meet certain practical goals—reduce prison crowding, save money, and decrease recidivism—may not have been well-founded and that jurisdictions interested in adopting ISP's should define their goals carefully. Other study findings indicate that ISP's were most successful as an intermediate punishment, in providing closer supervision of offenders and in offering a range of sentencing options between prison and routine probation and parole.

The programs were effective as surveillance.   The ISP programs were designed to be much more stringent than routine supervision, and in every site they delivered more contacts and monitoring than did the routine supervision provided in the control groups. Most of the ISP's were significantly higher than the control programs in number of face-to-face contacts with supervisors, telephone and collateral contacts, law enforcement checks, employment monitoring, and drug and alcohol testing. (See exhibit 2 for findings on contacts and drug tests.)

The data reveal no straightforward relationship between contact levels and recidivism; that is, it is not clear whether the surveillance aspect of the ISP had a positive effect on offenders' subsequent behavior. For example, although the average number of face-to-face contacts in Seattle was 3.4 per month and the average in Macon was much higher at 16.1, the percentage of ISP offenders arrested at both sites was about the same—46 percent in Seattle and 42 percent in Macon.

This finding must, however, be qualified by the nature of the data. The ISP programs were "packages" of contacts and services, and for this reason it is difficult to distinguish the specific effect of individual components of a package (such as contact level, drug testing, and electronic monitoring) on recidivism.

Exhibit 2. **Number of Monthly Face-to-Face Contacts and Drug Tests During 1-Year Followup**

	Face-to Face Contacts		Drug Tests	
	ISP	Controls	ISP	Controls
Contra Costa County, California	2.7	0.5*	1.7	0.2*
Los Angeles County, California	4.1	0.6*	0.5	0.2*
Seattle, Washington	3.4	0.8*	0.4	0.1*
Ventura County, California	7.4	3.0*	2.7	1.3*
Atlanta, Georgia	12.5	14.9	4.8	4.9
Macon, Georgia	16.1	17.7	5.8	3.7*
Waycross, Georgia	22.8	22.4	14.2	1.6*
Santa Fe, New Mexico	10.6	2.8*	2.9	1.1*
Des Moines, Iowa	5.8	3.8*	2.8	1.0*
Winchester, Virginia	8.1	1.9*	1.5	0.4*
Dallas, Texas	3.3	1.5*	0.1	0.0*
Houston, Texas	4.0	1.9*	0.7	0.0*
Marion County, Oregon**	12.2	n/a	2.2	n/a
Milwaukee, Wisconsin	8.8	n/a	0.7	n/a
AVERAGE	5.8 [a]	1.6 [b]	1.4 [a]	0.2 [b]

* Indicates that ISP and control are significantly different, p <.05.

** Based on 6-month followup only.

[a] Weighted average of ISP in all sites.
[b] Weighted average of routine probation in Contra Costa, Los Angeles, Seattle; routine probation/parole in Santa Fe, Des Moines, Winchester; routine parole in Dallas and Houston.

The programs were effective as intermediate sanctions. In a sense, this issue is the same as the preceding one if more frequent contacts and drug testing are viewed as punishment. Most of the ISP's had significantly higher levels of the features that curtail freedom.[14] Both coercion and enforced diminution of freedom were higher for most ISP's than for the control group when measured by the criminal justice system response to offenders' technical violations.[15] In fact, the response to this type of violation gives ISP's their greatest punitive value. The rate of technical violations was high, making the resultant coercion and diminution of freedom experienced by the offenders an added punitive sanction as well as creating a public safety benefit.

The General Accounting Office, in its report on intermediate punishments, noted that if judged by a standard of zero risk, all ISP programs fail to protect public safety.[16] However, what most of these programs try to achieve is a more stringent punishment for at least some of the serious offenders who now receive only nominal supervision. Judged by that criterion, virtually all of the sites succeeded. It is also possible that the closer surveillance imposed on ISP participants may increase the probability that they are caught for a larger percentage of the crimes they commit.

To test this effect, researchers conducted interviews with ISP participants in the Contra Costa site to discuss their perceptions of the harshness of the program. The interview findings confirmed that these offenders viewed the likelihood of their being caught for probation violations to be higher than for offenders who were on routine probation. They felt this to be particularly true when the violations involved drugs. In addition, the ISP offenders believed they would be treated more harshly for most types of violations than would their counterparts who were on routine supervision.

Evidence also suggests that some offenders may view ISP's as even more punitive and restrictive of freedom than prison. Among offenders at the Oregon site, 25 percent who were eligible for prison diversion chose not to participate. The reason may be that Oregon's crowded prisons made it unlikely that anyone sentenced to a year would serve the full term, while offenders assigned to ISP's could be certain of a full year of surveillance in the program. As prisons become more crowded and length of sentence served decreases, ISP's may come to seem increasingly punitive to offenders.

The Effect on Recidivism

The major recidivism outcome measures were officially recorded arrests and technical violations. On these measures, the ISP programs were not as successful as on others.

ISP participants were not subsequently arrested less often, did not have a longer time to failure, and were not arrested for less serious offenses than control group members. The findings reveal that in 11 of the 14 sites, arrest rates during the 1-year followup were in fact higher for ISP participants than for the control group (although not significantly so). At the end of the 1-year period, about 37 percent of the ISP participants and 33 percent of control offenders had been arrested. (See exhibit 3.)

These findings should be interpreted with caution, because officially recorded recidivism may not be as accurate an indicator of an individual's criminality as it is a measure of the impact of the ISP program on the criminal justice system. That is, officially recorded recidivism measures enforcement—the system's ability to detect crime and act on it (through arrests).

As noted earlier, with an ISP program, surveillance may be so stringent as to increase the probability that crimes (and technical violations) will be detected and an arrest made. In this way ISP's may increase officially recorded recidivism. Thus, it may be that an ISP offender is committing the same number or fewer crimes than someone on routine supervision, who has a lower probability of being arrested for them. The ISP offender, whose behavior is more closely monitored, may be caught in the enforcement net, while the offender on routine probation or parole may escape it.

Effect of technical violations. If technical violations are interpreted as another measure of recidivism, the findings are also less positive for the ISP's than the controls. An average of 65 percent of the ISP clients had a technical violation compared with 38 percent for the controls. (See exhibit 3). However, technical violations can be interpreted as effects of the program itself rather than as evidence of criminal activity or recidivism. For one thing, the view of technical violations as a proxy for crime commission is only an assumption. Non-compliant behavior such as disregarding curfews, using alcohol and drugs, and missing treatment sessions may not necessarily signal that the ISP participant is going to commit "new" or "real" crimes.

To test the hypothesis that revoking offenders for technical violations prevents arrests for new crimes, the researchers examined the ISP programs in California and Texas. They computed correlations between number of arrests and number of technical violations and found few statistically significant relationships. In other words, offenders who committed technical violations were no more likely to be arrested for new crimes than those who did not commit them. Moreover, when convictions for arrests during the 1-year followup were examined for all sites, the researchers found no difference in the rates of the ISP offenders and the control group.

ISP's were consistently associated with higher rates of technical violations because of the closer supervision given to those in the programs. If stringent conditions are imposed and people's behavior is monitored, they have more opportunities for violations and for being found out than if there are few conditions and few contacts. For example, the requirement of frequent drug testing alone is virtually guaranteed to generate a large number of technical violations. Few of the sites had many low-risk[17] offenders. The higher the risk, the more likely that offenders are involved with drugs. At most of the sites, drug-related technical violations accounted for a large proportion of all technical violations. Offenders under routine supervision were not subjected to such close scrutiny and would not therefore have had as many opportunities to commit technical violations of the conditions of their probation or parole.

Effect of type of ISP program. Because only 2 of the 14 sites implemented prison diversion programs and their programs experienced difficulties, the research remains inconclusive regarding the ability of this type of ISP to relieve prison crowding. (See "The Experience of the Prison Diversion Programs.")

The findings for parole and probation enhancement ISP's suggest that commitments to prison and jail may actually increase under the program. The reason is the large number of technical violations, which lead to a higher percentage of ISP offenders than controls being recommitted to jail and prison. At a minimum, ISP programs attempt to increase the credibility of community-based sanctions by making certain that the conditions ordered by the court, including those considered "technical" in nature, are monitored, enforced, and if violated, punished by imprisonment. Depending on how severely ISP staff and their respective courts choose to treat ISP infractions, commitments to prison and jails may rise precipitously.

Data from the Houston site illustrate this point. The Houston ISP was a parole-enhancement program that targeted people under supervision who had a high probability of returning to prison. ISP participants were not arrested for new crimes more often than the controls (who were on routine parole), but were returned to prison more frequently for more technical violations. Fully 81 percent of the ISP offenders had technical violations, compared with 33 percent of offenders in the control group. As a result, five times as many ISP offenders were returned to prison for technical violations as those on routine supervision (21 percent versus 4 percent), and at the end of the 1-year followup, about 30 percent of ISP participants were in prison, compared with only 18 percent of the control group.[18]

Exhibit 3. **Offender Recidivism During 1-Year Followup**

	Percentage of Offenders With Any Arrest		Percentage of Offender With Technical Violations		Percentage of Offenders Returned to Prison	
	ISP	Controls	ISP	Controls	ISP	Controls
Contra Costa County, California	29	27	64	41*	2	4
Los Angeles County, California	32	30	61	57	26	22
Seattle, Washington	46	36	73	48*	6	5
Ventura County, California	32	53*	70	73	23	28
Atlanta, Georgia	12	04	65	46	23	4
Macon, Georgia	42	38	100	96	8	21
Waycross, Georgia	12	15	38	31	4	0
Santa Fe, New Mexico	48	28	69	62	14	17
Des Moines, Iowa	24	29	59	55	39	23
Winchester, Virginia	25	12	64	36*	14	8
Dallas, Texas	39	30	20	13	28	17
Houston, Texas	44	40	81	33*	35	20*
Marion County, Oregon	33	50	92	58	50	25
Milwaukee, Wisconsin	58	03*	92	17*	35	3*
AVERAGE	37 [a]	33 [b]	65 [a]	38 [b]	24	15

* Indicates that ISP and control are significantly different, p <.05.

[a] Weighted average of ISP in all sites.
[b] Weighted average of routine probation in Contra Costa, Los Angeles, Seattle; routine probation/parole in Santa Fe, Des Moines, Winchester; routine parole in Dallas and Houston.

The Experience of the Prison Diversion Programs

Prison diversion programs in this study did not provide data on the effect of ISP's on prison crowding. Of the two participating sites that implemented prison diversion programs in the demonstration, one had too few eligible offenders to yield usable results. In the other, the use of randomization was overridden by the jurisdiction, thereby foiling its purpose. The selection process at these two sites therefore makes it impossible to state with certainty the effect of ISP's in reducing prison crowding.

The experience of the two sites (Marion County, Oregon, and Milwaukee, Wisconsin) does reveal a number of insights into the issues jurisdictions face when making decisions about selecting convicted offenders for diversion into the community.

Marion County, Oregon

Marion County set eligibility requirements so stringent that few offenders could qualify for the prison diversion ISP. The study's mandated criterion of excluding offenders currently convicted of violent crimes was extended to exclude offenders with any prior record of violence. Examination of the Marion County data revealed that, in addition, a large percent of potential participants who had current burglary convictions were rejected. Although this offense is considered nonviolent, evidently Marion County did not wish to place burglars into ISP programs.

The three criteria—exclusion of violent offenders, people with any history of violence, and convicted burglars—shrank the pool of eligibles considerably. Furthermore, the local Marion County judge imposed the requirement of informed consent from the offender, producing a sample too small to yield statistically reliable results.

Milwaukee, Wisconsin

In Milwaukee, judges and probation/parole officers overrode the researchers' random assignment of offenders into the experimental and control groups. Milwaukee initially had two pools of eligibles: "front-end" cases consisting of high-risk offenders newly convicted of nonviolent felonies, and "back-end" cases consisting of probation or parole violators who were facing revocation. Regardless of the random designation made by the researchers, most front-end cases were sentenced to prison rather than diversion to an ISP. Of the back-end cases, more than half were sent to routine probation or parole.

That only two sites chose prison diversion suggests the level of concern on the part of the criminal justice system about the risks involved in sending convicted offenders into the community. Further evidence of this concern is the response of these two sites in placing additional restrictions on program implementation.[19]

Thus, in Houston, putting people on ISP added more offenders to the prison population than did routine parole. This is interpreted as an effect of the ISP program itself—which tends to generate more technical violations—rather than the result of differences between the ISP experimental and control groups. Any other differences were eliminated through random assignment of offenders to both groups.

Cost Benefits

Are ISP's a cost-saving alternative? Like other questions about ISP's, this too has an ambiguous answer—one that depends on what is being compared to what. Compared with routine probation, ISP's are more costly because they are highly labor intensive. Because supervision is intensive, ISP's require lower caseloads—typically 25 offenders per supervisor or team of supervisors. An increase of only 100 offenders in an ISP would call for hiring and training 4 to 8 new employees.

If the cost of ISP's is compared to that of imprisonment, the opposite is' true. Virtually no one would question the claim that it is more expensive to keep an offender in prison than on probation. The costs per day for imprisonment are much higher per offender than the costs per day for an ISP. Obviously, ISP's cost less than building new prisons.

Length of time under each sanction also has to be taken into consideration when comparing costs of prison and ISP's. The average cost per year per imprisoned offender is $12,000 and per ISP offender only $4,000. However, if the ISP offender would have otherwise served time in prison (had he or she not been placed in an ISP) for a period of only 3 months, the cost would be $3,000—less than the $4,000 it costs for 1 year of an ISP program. In addition, some of the ISP participants spent part of the followup year incarcerated rather than in the ISP program, thus eliminating part of the cost savings of diversion from prison.

Again, it should be kept in mind in interpreting these findings that the ISP programs resulted in more incarcerations and consequently higher costs than routine probation/parole because of the higher number of technical violations. Across the 12 probation/parole enhancement programs, high violation and incarceration rates for ISP offenders drove up the estimated costs, which averaged $7,200 per offender for the year, compared with about $4,700 for the control group on routine supervision.

Results for Treatment

Treatment and service components in the ISP's included drug and alcohol counseling, employment, community service, and payment of restitution. On many of these measures, ISP offenders participated more than did control group members (see exhibit 4); and participation in such programs was found to be correlated with a reduction in recidivism in at least some sites.

When figures from all sites are examined, they reveal that participation in counseling was not high in either the experimental or control groups, but it was higher for ISP offenders. Forty-five percent of ISP offenders received some counseling during the followup period, compared with 22 percent of the controls.

Overall figures indicate that more than half of the ISP participants were employed compared with 43 percent of the offenders who were on routine supervision. In 4 of the 14 sites (Contra Costa, Los Angeles, Seattle, and Winchester), ISP offenders were significantly more likely than controls to be employed.

Participation in community service varied considerably by site. The highest rate (more than two-thirds of offenders) was reported in the three Georgia sites, where community service has historically played a major role in the ISP design. In seven of the ISP programs, 10 percent or fewer offenders participated in community service, and at no site did ISP offenders participate significantly more often than routine supervision offenders.

Although restitution was paid by only a small minority of offenders, the rate was higher among ISP offenders than those on routine supervision (12 percent and 3 percent, respectively, paid some restitution).

Analysis of the programs in California and Texas revealed a relationship between treatment participation and recidivism. A summary score was created for each offender, with one point assigned for participation in any of four treatment or service programs. Analysis revealed that higher levels of program participation were associated with a 10- to 20-percent reduction in recidivism. However, because offenders were not randomly assigned to participate in these activities within the experimental and control groups, it is not possible to determine whether the lower recidivism was the effect of the treatment or of selection bias. In other words, the positive outcomes may be a function not of the treatment but of the type of offender who entered the treatment program. Nevertheless, the results are consistent with literature showing positive outcomes of treatment.

The ISP programs in the demonstration project were by design oriented more toward surveillance than treatment, with funds used largely for staff salaries rather than for treatment service. Sites had to rely on existing treatment programs, which in some communities were quite minimal. This raises the issue of whether participation in treatment would have been higher had more resources been allocated to it.

Exhibit 4. **Representative Program Participation**

	Percentage of Offenders in Any Counseling During 1-Year Followup		Percentage of Offenders With Any Paid Employment During 1-Year Followup	
	ISP	Controls	ISP	Controls
Contra Costa County, California	39	14*	41	26*
Los Angeles County, California	16*	02	45	18*
Seattle, Washington	42	14*	31	08*
Ventura County, California	78	76	80	79
Atlanta, Georgia	48	48	54	65
Macon, Georgia	65	50	85	71
Waycross, Georgia	100	88	92	96
Santa Fe, New Mexico	100	59*	86	79
Des Moines, Iowa	59	41*	76	70
Winchester, Virginia	32	12	89	56*
Dallas, Texas	04	02	37	33
Houston, Texas	55	32*	61	61
Marion County, Oregon	50	n/a	33	n/a
Milwaukee, Wisconsin	54	n/a	54	n/a
AVERAGE	45 [a]	22 [b]	56 [a]	43 [b]

* Indicates that ISP and control are significantly different, p <.05.

[a] Weighted average of all sites.
[b] Weighted average of routine probation in Contra Costa, Los Angeles, Seattle; routine probation/parole in Santa Fe, Des Moines, Winchester; routine parole in Dallas and Houston.

Policy Implications

Jurisdictions that wish to adopt ISP's might want to revise the model represented in the demonstration to create a better "fit" with their particular needs.

Making controls more stringent. ISP contact levels were greater than with routine supervision, but it might be argued that the programs were not "intensive" enough. It appears that more stringent conditions could be required of ISP's. In the demonstration, ISP contact of any type amounted, on average, to a total of less than 2 hours per month per offender (assuming that 20 minutes, on average, was spent per face-to-face contact). The same is true of drug testing—the average for all sites was just over two tests per month. If the amount of time spent in contacts were greater (that is, if conditions were tougher), the result might be less recidivism. Jurisdictions would have to decide how much more restrictive the conditions should be and would have to weigh possible benefits against the probable higher cost.

Increasing treatment. Jurisdictions might want to strengthen the treatment component of ISP's in hopes of a positive behavioral effect that would lower recidivism. As stated earlier, at the California and Texas sites the recidivism of offenders who received any counseling (for drugs or alcohol), held jobs, paid restitution, and did community service was 10 to 20 percent lower than those who did not.

Overall outcomes might have been even more positive had a greater proportion of the offenders participated in treatment.[20] Participation in drug treatment, in particular, might have had a high payoff. In all the sites, about half the offenders were judged drug dependent by their probation or parole officers. Yet ISP staff often reported difficulties obtaining drug treatment for these people, and at some sites a large percentage of all offenders in need of drug treatment went untreated.[21] It comes as no surprise, therefore, that about one-third of all new arrests were drug-related. A high priority for future research would be evaluation of ISP programs in which treatment plays a major role.[22]

Deemphasizing technical violations. Jurisdictions might want to reexamine the assumption of technical violations as a proxy for criminal behavior. Offenders who commit this type of violation constitute a considerable proportion of the prison population. On any given day, about 20 percent of new admissions nationwide consist of parole or probation violators, and the resultant crowding means early release for other offenders.[23]

The experience of the State of Washington in rethinking parole and probation revocations is instructive. There, the State legislature, responding to the heavy flow of technical violations attendant on stringent parole and probation conditions, set new rules. The rules require conditions be set according to the specific offense and the particular offender's past criminal behavior; they effectively bar the imposition of conditions affecting all offenders. In addition, the new rules state that prison cannot be used as a sanction for technical violations; the maximum sentence is 60 days in jail.[24]

No empirical studies have been performed yet, but Washington officials believe that as a result of the new rules, revocations for technical violations have decreased while arrest rates for new crimes have remained roughly the same.[25] If Washington is successful, it may mean that jurisdictions will have more prison space for really serious offenders and therefore increase public safety by decreasing the number of people sent to prison for technical violations of parole and probation.

Handling costs. When considering the issue of affordability, jurisdictions need to keep in mind its relation to program goals. The more constraints a program imposes and/or the more it is service- and treatment-oriented, the higher will be the cost. In Ventura and Houston, for example, stringent conditions and rigorous response to technical violations drove up costs. On the other hand, future evaluations might reveal that the return on investment in programs with these types of emphasis may be lower recidivism.

Judging outcomes. In assessing the success of ISP's (and deciding whether to invest further in them), jurisdictions need to use the same criterion for deciding whether a program is affordable; that is, does it achieve the goals set? One of the study's strongest implications is that jurisdictions need to establish very clearly their intentions for the ISP's they develop and structure the programs accordingly. If jurisdictions are interested primarily in imposing intermediate sanctions, even if the result is not lower recidivism, that goal should be made clear. Otherwise, the public may interpret the recidivism rates as an indication of program failure.

If jurisdictions are primarily interested in reducing recidivism, prison crowding, and system costs, ISP programs as currently structured may not meet all their expectations. These more ''practical'' objectives were set on the basis of overly ambitious assumptions and on the early results of a few programs that received a great deal of attention and perhaps unwarranted enthusiasm. The findings of this evaluation provide further evidence that surveillance-oriented ISP's will have difficulty in fully achieving these objectives.

If jurisdictions target objectives based more on intermediate sanctions principles, ISP's hold promise. By setting this type of objective, they may be able to impose more stringent controls on offenders than are possible without probation and parole, and they may achieve greater flexibility in sentencing decisions by punishments that more closely fit the crimes committed. Developing an array of sentencing options is an important and necessary first step to creating a more comprehensive and graduated sentencing structure. This goal alone can provide the justification for continued development of ISP and other intermediate sanctions.

Is prison diversion viable? The evaluation findings indicate that prison diversion and, by extension, reduction of prison crowding, is particularly difficult to implement. This difficulty is reflected in the decision by only 2 of the 14 sites to adopt this type of program. The criteria these two jurisdictions used to assign offenders to the programs also suggest a measure of reluctance. (See "The Experience of the Prison Diversion Programs.") The experience with prison diversion in this study indicates that the criminal justice system and the general public do not at present seem receptive to this type of ISP. A targeted public and judicial education campaign would be required to overcome that reluctance.

Future Research

The major issue for further research is determining whether ISP, a concept that may be sound in theory, might be structured and implemented differently to produce better results. The experience of the California sites suggests, for example, that certain program components could be manipulated. At these sites, a higher level of offender participation in treatment and service programs was associated with lower recidivism. In Ventura, which had the highest levels of surveillance, arrest rates were lower than among the controls. A revised ISP model could answer these and other questions:

- Would ISP's reduce recidivism if resources were sufficient to obtain treatment drug offenders need?
- Would more intensive surveillance lower recidivism?
- Would more selective conditions of parole and probation lower revocation rates?
- What combination of surveillance and treatment would produce the best results?

The study findings indicate a number of additional areas for research:

The potential of ISP as prison diversion.   The limited number of study sites selecting this option and their restrictions on the programs indicate major concerns about ISP for prison diversion. Researchers may want to examine the nature of the potential pool of eligibles, document the most commonly utilized criteria for ISP eligibility, and depending on the criteria, simulate the prison population that would qualify.

Testing of different offender populations.   The ISP model in this study was tested primarily on drug-involved offenders who had committed serious crimes. Studies have shown that the more experienced the offenders, the lower they rate the risk of being caught and confined.[26] For this reason, models using a population of less serious offenders might result in greater deterrence.

The effects of different ISP components.   The random assignment in this study permitted testing the effect of the entire ISP "package," but made it impossible to test the effect of a particular program component. By extension, it was not possible to determine how changing a component might change the effects. Future research could be designed specifically to test the incremental impact of various ISP conditions (such as drug testing and drug and alcohol treatment) on offender behavior.

Effectiveness over time.   Recent research indicates that a 1-year followup, the time period on which the evaluation of outcomes was based, may not be long enough.[27] Future research might focus on whether longer followup might ultimately result in behavioral differences between ISP offenders and controls.

Technical violations and criminal behavior.   The study revealed that technical violations resulted in many recommitments to prison and jail. As noted earlier, the view that such recommitments prevent crime may be only an assumption. The policy significance of technical violations suggests that research is needed in a number of areas:

- Empirical evidence of the relationship of technical violations to criminal behavior.
- The types of technical conditions currently imposed at sentencing.
- How technical conditions are used by community corrections to manage offenders, encourage rehabilitation, and protect the community.
- Trends in the growth of the technical-violator population and the effect on jails and prisons.
- Innovative programs, policies, and statutes that have emerged to deal with technical violators.

Appropriate outcome measures. Recidivism is a key outcome used in evaluating all types of interventions, and because success in rehabilitation has been far from complete, it is almost the only measure used in corrections.

In reaffirming its commitment to ISP and to its focus on rehabilitation, the American Probation and Parole Association issued a position paper that identifies behavioral change, not recidivism, as the appropriate outcome measure. Such change includes negotiation skills, managing emotions, and enhanced values and attitude shifts.

Given the centrality of recidivism to research and practice, it is essential to examine its appropriateness as a measure for certain interventions. For some programs, recidivism may be one of many measures, but perhaps not the primary one.

These are not the only issues for a future criminal justice research agenda, but they are currently the most pressing for research on the future of intensive supervision probation and parole.

Notes

[1] The results of NIJ-sponsored research into four major types of intermediate sanctions are summarized in Gowdy, Voncile B., *Intermediate Sanctions*. Research in Brief. Washington, DC: U.S. Department of Justice, National Institute of Justice, 1993.

[2] Bureau of Justice Statistics, *Probation and Parole 1990*. Bulletin. Washington, DC: U.S. Department of Justice, Bureau of Justice Statistics, November 1991.

[3] The figure for felonies is 48 percent, and for misdemeanors, it is 31 percent, according to Bureau of Justice Statistics, *Correctional Populations in the United States, 1990*. Washington, DC: U.S. Department of Justice, Bureau of Justice Statistics, July 1992.

[4] Langan, Patrick A., and Mark A. Cuniff. *Recidivism of Felons on Probation, 1986–89*. Special Report. Washington, DC: U.S. Department of Justice, Bureau of Justice Statistics, February 1992.

[5] A discussion of recent findings about the rise in the rate of violent crime despite the increase in the number of people incarcerated is presented in the National Research Council's *Understanding and Preventing Violence*, ed. Albert J. Reiss, Jr., and Jeffrey A. Roth, Washington, DC: National Academy Press, 1993: 292–294.

[6] Macguire, Kathleen, and Timothy J. Flanagan, eds. *Sourcebook of Criminal Justice Statistics—1991*. Washington, DC: U.S. Department of Justice, Bureau of Justice Statistics, 1992.

[7] General Accounting Office. *Intermediate Sanctions: Their Impacts on Prison Crowding, Costs, and Recidivism Are Still Unclear*. Gaithersburg, Maryland: General Accounting Office, 1990.

[8] For descriptions of the Georgia program, see Erwin, Billie S. "Turning Up the Heat on Probationers in Georgia." *Federal Probation*, vol. 50 (1986):2. See also: Petersilia, Joan. *Expanding Options for Criminal Sentencing*. Santa Monica: RAND Corporation, 1987. Byrne, James M., Arthur J. Lurigio, and Christopher Baird. "The Effectiveness of the New Intensive Supervision Programs." *Research in Corrections*, vol. 2 (1989). The results of a National Institute of Justice evaluation of the program are presented in Erwin, Billie S., and Lawrence A. Bennett. *New Dimensions in Probation: Georgia's*

Experience With Intensive Probation Supervision (IPS). Research in Brief. Washington, DC: U.S. Department of Justice, National Institute of Justice, January 1987.

9 Byrne, Lurigio, and Baird, "The Effectiveness of the New Intensive Supervision Programs."

10 General Accounting Office, *Intermediate Sanctions*. See also Morris, Norval, and Michael Tonry. *Between Prison and Probation: Intermediate Punishments in a Rational Sentencing System*. New York: Oxford University Press, 1990.

11 For more information on the experiences of the site in implementing the experiments, see Petersilia, Joan. "Implementing Randomized Experiments: Lessons for BJA's Intensive Supervision Project." *Evaluation Review*, vol. 13, 5.

12 The training component was directed by Rutgers University, the technical assistance by the National Council on Crime and Delinquency.

13 In the Georgia and Ventura sites, the control programs were another form of intensive supervision. References to all ISP's mean all 14 experimental programs. References to ISP enhancement programs mean all experimental ISP's except Milwaukee and Marion, which adopted prison diversion programs. References to routine supervision probation and parole mean the control programs in eight sites: Contra Costa, Los Angeles, Seattle, Santa Fe, Des Moines, Winchester, Dallas, and Houston.

14 This meets the definition of effective sentencing proposed by Morris and Tonry. It involves "the curtailment of freedom either behind walls or in the community, large measures of coercion, and enforced diminutions of freedom." (*Between Prison and Probation*)

15 A violation that does not consist of committing a crime or is not prosecuted as such is usually called a technical violation. It is behavior forbidden by the court order granting probation or parole but not forbidden by legal statute. Examples are failure to observe curfew, abstain from alcohol, or attend treatment sessions.

16 General Accounting Office, *Intermediate Sanctions*.

17 The risk score was constructed from the following variables: drug treatment needs, age at first or current conviction, previous probation terms, previous probation and parole revocations, previous felony convictions, and type of current offense.

18 NIJ has provided support to RAND to evaluate a prison diversion program in Minnesota that promises to furnish more reliable evidence on the impact of this type of sanction.

19 Turner, Susan, and Joan Petersilia. "Focusing on High-Risk Parolees: An Experiment to Reduce Commitments to the Texas Department of Corrections." *Journal of Research in Criminology and Delinquency*, vol. 29, 1 (1992):34–61.

20 Some recent literature gives credibility to this notion. See Anglin, M. Douglas, and Yih-Ing Hser. "Treatment of Drug Abuse." In *Crime and Justice: An Annual Review of Research, Volume 13: Drugs and Crime*. ed. Michael Tonry and James Q. Wilson. Chicago: University of Chicago Press, 1990; and Paul Gendreau and D. A. Andrews. "Tertiary Prevention: What the Meta-Analyses of the Offender Treatment Literature Tell Us About 'What Works.'" *Canadian Journal of Criminology*, vol. 32 (1990):173–184.

21 For a more complete presentation of this finding, see Petersilia, Joan, Susan Turner, and Elizabeth Piper Deschenes. "Intensive Supervision Programs for Drug Offenders." In J. Byrne, A. Lurigio, and J. Petersilia. *Smart Sentencing: The Emergence of Intermediate Sanctions*. Newbury Park, CA: Sage Publications, 1992.

22 NIJ is providing RAND with support for a randomized field experiment, currently being conducted in Maricopa County, Arizona, that will test the impact on probationers of different levels of treatment.

23 Petersilia, Joan, and Susan Turner. "Reducing Prison Admissions: The Potential of Intermediate Sanctions," *The Journal of State Government*, vol. 62 (1989):2.

[24] Washington State Sentencing Guidelines Commission. *Preliminary Evaluation of Washington State's Sentencing Reform Act.* Olympia: Washington State Sentencing Guidelines Commission, 1983.

[25] Greene, Richard. "Who's Punishing Whom?" *Forbes,* vol. 121, 6 (1988):132–133.

[26] Paternoster, R. "The Deterrent Effect of the Perceived Certainty and Severity of Punishment: A Review of the Evidence and Issues." *Justice Quarterly,* 4 (1987).

[27] Anglin, M. D. and W. H. McGlothlin. "Outcomes of Narcotic Addict Treatment in California." In *Drug Abuse Treatment Evaluation: Strategies, Progress, and Prospect,* ed. F. M. Tims and J. P. Ludford. National Institute on Drug Abuse Research Monograph No. 51. Rockville, MD: U.S. Department of Health and Human Services, National Institute on Drug Abuse, 1984.

32

Electronic Monitors
Realistically, What Can Be Expected?
Annesley K. Schmidt

Introduction

The electronic monitoring equipment presently in use in the United States applies telemetry technology to determine whether an offender is present in the required location at the required times. First used on offenders in 1984, it is presently used daily on at least 12,000 probationers, parolees, work releasees, pretrial releasees, and other offenders under correctional supervision in the community (Renzema).

There are two basic types of electronic monitoring devices. "Continuously signalling devices" constantly monitor the presence of an offender at a particular location. "Programmed contact devices" contact the offender periodically to verify his presence.

A "continuously signalling device" has three major parts: A *transmitter* attached to the offender sends out a continuous signal. Transmitters produced by some manufacturers send an altered signal to alert officials if they are tampered with, and others do not. A *receiver-dialer* located in the offender's home is attached to his telephone and detects signals from the transmitter. It reports to the central computer when it stops receiving the signal and when it starts receiving it again. A *central computer* accepts reports from the receiver-dialer over

Source: *Federal Probation*, Vol. 55, No. 2 (June 1991), 47–53.

telephone lines, compares them with the offender's curfew schedule, and alerts correctional officials to any unauthorized absences. The computer also stores information about routine entries and exits of each offender so that reports can be prepared.

"Programmed contact devices" provide an alternative approach. They contact the offender at intervals to verify that he is at the location where he is required to be. These devices all use a computer programmed to telephone the offender during the monitored hours, either randomly or at specifically selected times. The computer is also programmed to prepare reports on the results of the call. However, each manufacturer uses a different method to assure that the offender is the person responding to the call and is in fact at the monitored location as required. One system uses voice verification technology. Another system requires a "wristlet," a black plastic module, which is strapped to the offender's arm. When the computer calls, the wristlet is inserted into a verifier box connected to the telephone to verify that the telephone is answered by the monitored offender. A third system uses visual verification to assure that the telephone is being answered by the offender being monitored.

"Hybrid" equipment, introduced by several manufacturers, functions as a continuously signalling device. However, when the computer notes that the offender appears to have left at an unauthorized time, it functions similarly to a programmed contact device, contacting the offender by telephone and verifying that the person responding is the offender being monitored either by the use of voice verification technology or the insertion of a "wristlet" into a "verifier box" attached to the telephone. If verification does not occur, notification is made that a violation has occurred.

The role of the telephone, in the electronic monitoring of offenders, requires that certain new telephone technologies are not in use on the offender's telephone. For example, "call forwarding," where the telephone will automatically switch the call to another number, and a portable telephone would make it easier for the offender to respond to calls while away from home. Many programs also prohibit "call waiting" since it might interfere with the equipment's effort to call the central computer or for the verifier box to be attached. The program must review the offender's monthly telephone bill to assure that none of the prohibited services have been acquired.

At present, most of the equipment limits participation in monitoring programs to those who have a telephone at home. However, at least one company produces equipment that allows an officer to drive near the offender's house and tune to the frequency of the offender's transmitter and thus to determine if the offender is home without the officer leaving the car or the offender knowing that monitoring has occurred. Other companies are investigating similar approaches.

Offenders are also monitored without electronic verification. One approach uses the automatic equipment to telephone the offender and records the response. With this approach, verification that the person responding is in fact the monitored offender occurs when the recording is played by someone who recognizes the offender's voice. Another simpler, traditional approach has officers knocking on the door of offenders' homes to assure that they are home.

For the past 6 years, I have been watching the development of these electronic monitoring devices. During that time, which dates almost from the beginning of the correctional application of the technology, I have observed the continuing development, refinement, and improvement of the equipment, along with the beginnings, mergers, demise, and growth of manufacturers. There has also been the parallel development of a related service industry. These companies receive the output of the monitoring and respond to each different agency according to predetermined specifications.

While the equipment and service industries have been developing, the users have made strides toward defining appropriate uses for the equipment, as well as determining which uses are inappropriate because the technology does not further the program's goals. Programs have also become clearer in their definition of purpose and therefore in deciding which type of equipment is most suitable and whether, in that particular program context, it makes more sense to handle their own monitoring equipment or contract with a service provider.

I have also tried to stay aware of developments in the field. To accomplish this, I have read the literature about monitors, written papers, visited programs, and interviewed monitored offenders, the officers supervising them, and those directing the programs. In addition, I have heard and participated in discussions with proponents and opponents. Much of what I have read and heard appears accurate and realistic, but some seemed to include exaggeration, distortion, misunderstanding, or wishful thinking.

The development of new technology has led to at least the possibility of a different approach to the supervision of offenders in the community. However, it has been only a short 6 years since the first program began, so there are many questions, the answers to which are yet to be learned. In this context, it is not surprising that some misinterpretations, misconceptions, myths, and misunderstandings have also emerged.

The sources of various perceptions and misconceptions are different depending on the nature of the issue. There are the concerns that arise from philosophical objection to the use of any equipment to monitor the behavior of offenders in the community. Some show a misunderstanding about the functioning of the equipment. Others have arisen when the equipment and the program using it have been "oversold" so that no program could possibly accomplish the goals that have been established with the resources given. This overselling often reflects a misunderstanding about money, the potential economic impact that a monitoring program might have (Byrne).

Philosophical Issues

The development of electronic monitoring has coincided with the increasing discussion of intermediate sanctions. This dialogue examines sanctions that can be applied to criminal behaviors which are less serious than those requiring long-term incarceration, while, at the same time, being more serious than those deserving standard probation. The use of electronic monitors has fitted into this discussion, both when equipment is the sanction and when it is a part of efforts to increase the credibility and viability of probation as a sanction, as can be seen in programs such as intensive supervision.

When electronic monitoring devices are used as a part of correctional supervision in the community, such application may generate controversy. There are some people who feel that monitoring is improper. This point of view is aptly illustrated by the title of a recent paper, "No Soul in the New Machines: Technofallacies in the Electronic Monitoring Movement" (Corbett & Marx). It discusses "fallacies" that can occur in the establishment of programs. Some of the fallacies the authors mention, such as failure to clearly state the program's agenda or purpose, can occur in the establishment of any kind of program, have happened in a few monitoring programs, and should not be permitted to happen in any well-thought-out program of any type. However, it is not a criticism of monitoring programs, in particular, as much as it is a criticism of impulsive program design.

The issues more specific to monitoring programs are related to the purpose of correctional supervision in the community. A recent annual conference and training institute of the American Probation and Parole Association stated the apparent conflict in its title, "Supervision in the 1990s: Surveillance vs. Treatment" (APPA). The descriptive materials about the conference posed a question: "Are the concepts really conflicting or can they be supporting and complementary?" (Ibid, p. 20). The answer to that question must be determined by each agency. In the case of public agencies, the answer is determined by the politicians who chart the agency's course either overtly or through the budget that they provide. That answer, no matter how it is arrived at, will determine whether the use of monitors could make sense in their context.

Electronic monitoring devices are surveillance technology. Therefore, if surveillance is not one purpose of the program, these devices would be inappropriate. By the same token, if surveillance is a purpose of the program, the use of equipment is one way to enhance effort to achieve it, but not the only way. As mentioned earlier, humans knocking on doors would be another way to achieve the surveillance objective.

Another proposition states that monitoring will lead to "net widening." The expression "net widening" is based on an analogy to catching fish in a net. If the net is opened more widely more fish will be caught. Thus, in this context, it refers both to sanctioning those who would not otherwise have been sanctioned and to sanctioning someone more severely than would otherwise have been done. In this case, the concern revolves around hypotheses about what would happen if the program did not exist or what will happen if a program is established. If offenders are being monitored who would otherwise have been incarcerated, the use of the equipment may be seen as a reduction in the severity of the sanction. If, on the other hand, monitors are being used for offenders who might receive probation with little direct supervision, the level of the sanction appears to have been increased, and the question becomes, "Is the community receiving a needed increase in protection?"—a very different issue.

When "net widening" is discussed, the issue has two distinct ends with abundant space in between. At one end is the concern that the use of monitors may increase the level of sanctioning and therefore cause "net widening." At the other end is the argument that presently offenders are being sanctioned at a lesser level than is appropriate because of prison crowding. Therefore, if there is an increase in the level of sanctioning, it is an increase to an appropriate level. Differences among programs make a general resolution of this issue impossible, and specific resolutions must occur in the context of the handling of individual cases by individual programs.

Another issue has been expressed as: Monitors spy on people and reveal their secrets (Marx, 1985 & 1986). We have all seen the spy movie where the olive in the martini is really a transmitter revealing the plans of "the bad guys" to "the good guys" so that the good guys can come and save the day. It seems plausible that such technology is available, but the present electronic monitoring equipment used on offenders does not have that capacity. Whether future equipment will have that capacity is unknown, and, if it does, whether it would be used is dependent on the ethics of those operating the program. Furthermore, some people would contend that an officer, entering an offender's home during a surveillance check, is likely to learn more about the activities in the house and the interaction of the members of the household.

There is equipment on the horizon with the capacity to track the offender. When this becomes available, programs will be able to plot a route for the offender to use when traveling to and from work and learn of deviations from that, as well as know about unauthorized departures from work. This new knowledge may be reassuring to those concerned about detailed monitoring of activities. At the same time, those who question the appropriateness of surveillance will have a further basis for their questions.

When considering these philosophical issues, it needs to be kept in mind that there is a distinction between the equipment and the program that uses it. It is the program that makes and enforces the rules and responds to what it learns from the equipment. The equipment provides information which can be responded to immediately, later, or not at all, with a phone call or a visit, as specified by the program's procedures.

Misunderstandings About the Equipment

Assuming that any potential philosophical misgivings are answered, it is important that the program designers are realistic about what the equipment can and cannot accomplish. For example, as mentioned earlier, equipment that tracks offenders is expected to come onto the market, but it is not presently available. However, the present equipment is often incorrectly assumed to have the capacity to track the offender as he moves around the community.

Since the introduction of the equipment, some have posited: This is new and it's technology, so it must be "good." As the pioneers who first used the equipment learned, the equipment and the computer programs that convert the signal from the equipment into something meaningful, needed to be tried, tested, refined, and modified in the real world. Vast strides have been made in the technology, and its reliability has increased greatly. At the same time, it seems unlikely that it will ever be 100 percent perfect.

A closely related erroneous assumption is: Monitors are technology so they must be an improvement. Any program that acquires monitors will obtain more information about those being supervised than was previously available. Whether or not this new information is an improvement depends on the use to which it is put. If more paper is added to files, and little else is done, then a question can be raised about the value of the information from the equipment. In addition, when the offender learns by experience that violations are of little or no consequence, the credibility of the program is undermined. On the other hand, if violations are responded to, the offender learns that the program means what it says, and greater control is achieved. Thus, the program establishes its credibility with offenders and the public.

Even when the equipment is functioning correctly, it cannot *prevent* violations, as some have hoped. The offender is free to leave any time he decides to do so, and nothing about the equipment will stop him. In addition, the offender can leave as if he were going to work and then go anywhere. Unless the officer happens to check with the place of employment, he'll find out that the offender did not go to work when he sees reduced hours on the pay stub or when the offender is fired. Finally, there is no information about what the offender is doing when he is home which could be anything from something innocuous like watching TV to something as heinous as drug dealing or inflicting physical abuse on another member of the household. The equipment simply provides information showing that the offender is present within range of the receiver-dialer.

Any program has to determine how it will respond to the increase in information, realizing that the additional information may well mean that the program is now aware of failures that would have previously been unknown. This newly acquired information must be responded to by the staff if the program is to maintain its credibility with the offenders and with the public. If the staff is overworked and unable to respond to the information that it now receives, acquiring more information from monitors will only increase the staff frustration and decrease the program's credibility.

Some manufacturers of continuously signalling equipment provide a special feature in the band that holds the transmitter on the offender. When present, the nature of the signal changes when the band is tampered with. At first blush, this tamper-resistant band appears to prevent violations. However, tamper signals may occur when the equipment is twisted or otherwise handled roughly but not actually tampered with. On the other hand, the tamper signal can only be perceived if the offender is within range of the receiver-dialer. Outside that range, it will signal, but there is no way it can be "heard."

Monitoring requires that an offender have a home with a telephone and that he remain there. Some offenders do not have homes, and others have homes without telephones. Secondly, if others in the household are not supportive of the offender's participation in the monitoring program, they can sabotage the offender. For example, if the household contains teenage phone users who are not willing to limit their calls or relinquish the phone to the equipment, the offender cannot successfully participate. Moreover, there are situations when a house is not a home— at least not one for home confinement. This would be especially true if abuse is present.

Money: What Monitors Can Save

Program funders often hope or assume that they can buy equipment and save money directly or indirectly by decreasing staff or, at the very least, not increasing it. First, capital or money is required if the equipment is purchased. But, equipment can be and often is obtained by lease or lease-purchase arrangements which do not require a large initial outlay. Second, the caseloads of monitoring programs are usually about 25 while regular probation programs frequently have caseloads of over 100 offenders. In addition, monitoring programs require substantial labor if reported violations are responded to on a 24-hour, 7-day per week basis. This may have implications for staff, staffing costs, and labor-management agreements if the staff is required to be available during times which have not been traditionally considered to be working hours. Additionally, the outputs of equipment will provide staff with previously unavailable information to which staff now must respond.

The actual cost obviously depends on the type of equipment, the number of units, and whether the equipment is purchased or leased. In addition to staffing, extra costs may be incurred because of telephone charges. The In-House Arrest Work Release Program of the Sheriff's Stockade in Palm Beach County, Florida, charges participants in the voluntary program $9 per day (Garcia, 1986). Within the first 14 months of program operation, the program's investment in equipment had been returned by offender fees. However, if the initial amount invested is more or less, if fees are charged at a lower or higher rate, or not at all, or if the equipment is in use a greater or lesser proportion of the time, then the pay-back period will change. Also, the costs have changed as the competition between the manufacturers has increased. During the same time, staff salaries have increased, and many programs have been established in sites that are not routinely staffed 24 hours a day, 7 days a week. And, most importantly, there are many who do not feel that it is appropriate to charge offenders for their supervision. This philosophical consideration has been the subject of numerous booklets and articles and is mentioned here. Detailed consideration of this point is outside the scope of this article but an important financial and philosophical issue for program designers to consider.

The staff of some agencies has become concerned that monitors will replace people. However, this loses sight of the fact that monitors are just equipment. People are required for a number of purposes by a program that uses monitors. First, people must screen participants and attach the equipment. Once participants are in the program, staff is required to interpret the output from the equipment. Then, based on that interpretation, staff has to respond to the offender. Additionally, there are things only people can do, such as counseling, job placement, and employment verification. Given the smaller caseloads needed to respond to the additional information provided by the monitors, it seems unlikely that programs will be able to replace staff with the equipment, and many have found that more staff is required.

Many jurisdictions have justified the acquisition of electronic monitors with assurances that it will alleviate prison and jail crowding. This view may be optimistic, for a variety of reasons. First, in addition to issues related to what a community can, will, and should be expected to tolerate, it should be reiterated that monitors are technological devices potentially useful in a variety of program contexts. The population selected as the focus of monitoring programs may or may not be one that might otherwise be sent to jail or prison if monitors were not available. Second, consideration needs to be given to the likely impact on the total problem. In a thousand-man jail, the release of 20 monitored inmates would reduce the population by only 2 percent. One hundred monitored inmates would have to be released before the population would be affected by 10 percent. In a smaller jail, more impact would be achieved by a system the size of the typical initial purchase of 20 units, if all units were being used at the same time. In the prison systems of many states with much larger populations, more monitored inmates would have to be released before a significant reduction in population could occur. Furthermore, the cost of a monitoring program cannot be directly compared to per diem costs of incarceration. The largest component of per diem costs is staff salaries. Therefore, until the number of released inmates is large enough to affect staffing of the facility, the only savings achieved are in marginal categories such as food.

Closely related to the assertion that monitors will solve crowding is the assertion that monitors save money because monitoring is less expensive than jail. The arguments seem to rest on faulty mathematics and inappropriate comparisons when comparing the per diem of jail with the per diem costs of monitoring. Jails are labor intensive, with about 80 percent of the costs being staffing. Therefore, unless staffing can be affected or construction becomes unnecessary, the only cost savings are marginal items such as food and medical care. It is also important to note that this comparison is based on the assumption that all monitored offenders would otherwise be in jail. The experience of many programs makes this assumption at least questionable.

All of the assertions made about monitors in the corrections literature and the popular press lead to the assumption that the use of monitors is widespread. However, Marc Renzema's latest 1-day count shows about 12,000 to 14,000 offenders being monitored (Renzema). At the same time, the Bureau of Justice Statistics tells us that there are 2.6 million offenders under supervision in the community (BJS). As can be readily seen, monitors are used on only a very small proportion of offenders.

Some Strategies to Avoid Misunderstandings

During the short period that monitors have been available, experience has taught some of the issues that must be resolved before or during the establishment of a monitoring program. There are myriad decisions which must be made, few of which have known "right" answers. However, if the questions are answered clearly, many myths can be laid to rest and misunderstandings avoided.

The program needs to provide the context in which the equipment is to be used. If that is lacking, there will be the inappropriate situation of "equipment in search of a program." The program needs to be defined in terms of how an offender enters the program, who will make the decision, and on what will the decision be based—risk, need, offender status, etc.; then, how long people will remain in the program.

The program's statement of purposes and objectives should supply a clear rationale for the use of monitors, which means that at least one of the program goals should be offender surveillance and control. If this is not a goal, there seems little reason to use monitoring equipment and little justification for it.

Then, the program needs to determine what type of equipment will be used, keeping in mind both the cost and surveillance implications of the choice. It should be noted that different features are available on different equipment, even equipment of the same type. These choices should be evaluated in terms of how the features relate to goals of the program. The equipment decision should consider the cost and desirability of certain features to determine whether the program wishes to monitor consistently or intermittently; whether tamper-resistance is required or visual inspection for damage will be sufficient; and what the nature and size of the equipment itself is.

If equipment seems appropriate in the context of the program, the next question is financial. What will be purchased? The usual choice is one of two possibilities—equipment or service. Either the agency obtains the equipment and uses its staff to provide the service or the agency contracts for service with a company that will provide both monitoring equipment and monitoring. The equipment may be acquired through a lease, purchase, or lease with an option to purchase.

The equipment is going to provide information which was previously unknown. This will range from simple facts, such as what time the offender left for work or that the offender was late leaving and therefore was probably late for work. The program will also learn that the offender is not at his residence when he is supposed to be. The program needs to anticipate these issues and determine in advance how it will respond. For the simpler issues, responses may be as simple as telephoning the employer to determine that the offender is, in fact, at work. The response to reported violations may vary. It may be by phone or in person, at the time when it first becomes known or during the next workday.

The decisions about response to violation have implications for costs and staff. They must also be made considering what the responsible authorities—usually a court or parole board—are going to require as proof of violations. When planning the response to violations, the program should consider the possibility that false alarms may occur and that equipment may be damaged accidentally or purposely.

Once these decisions, and many others, have been made, it is important that the program plan allow time to test and get acquainted with the equipment and to train staff.

As the program plan is being developed, there are a variety of other issues which need to be considered. All the elements of the criminal justice system need to be involved in the planning so that their issues and agendas can be considered. Cooperation of the courts and probation and parole will likely be required. Additionally, many times, planning also may involve the sheriff, other law enforcement agencies, and others. As with any multi-agency effort, the lines of responsibility must be clear and the cooperation between them developed. For example, if the program is going to monitor the output of the equipment around the clock, then the base is optimally located where 24-hour staffing is already present. This facility might be a jail operated by the sheriff. If the program, on the other hand, is being operated by the probation office, the division of responsibilities and expectations should be clearly specified, preferably in writing. At the same time, at least some elements of the broader community should be involved, such as the press and political action groups concerned about criminal justice issues, such as MADD (Mothers Against Drunk Driving).

The establishment of a monitoring program in some areas has provided an opportunity for the agency to be proactive, reaching out to the public and the press. This contrasts with the reactive posture often assumed by corrections and may lead to the development of relationships with the press which may be useful in other contexts.

In summary, when starting a program, it is important to be *realistic* about why the program is being established and what it is expected to accomplish. In addition, the program needs to be placed in a context that is well thought out, has consistent policies and procedures, and documents events that occur and specific expectations. Above all, monitoring equipment should never be "equipment in search of a program."

References

American Probation and Parole Association. (1988, Spring). *Perspectives*.

Bureau of Justice Statistics. (1988, March). *Report to the nation on crime and justice*. Washington, DC: U.S. Government Printing Office.

Byrne, J. M., Kelly, L., & Guarino-Ghezzi, S. (1988, Spring). Understanding the limits of technology: An examination of the use of electronic monitoring in the criminal justice system. *Perspectives*, pp. 30–37.

Corbett, R. P., Jr., & Marx, G. T. (1990, November). No soul in the new machines: Technofallacies in the electronic monitoring movement. Paper presented at the Annual Meeting of the American Society of Criminology, Baltimore, MD.

Garcia, E.D. In-house arrest work release program. February 16, 1986, xeroxed, six pages, and personal communication.

Marx, G. T. (1986, Winter). I'll be watching you. *Dissent*, pp. 26–34.

———. (1986, May-June). The new surveillance. *Technology Review*, 45, 43–48.

Rensema, M., personal communication, March 29, 1991.

Rensema, M., & Skelton, D. T. (1990, November/December). *The use of electronic monitoring in the United States: 1989 update (NIJ Reports)*, pp. 9–14.

33

Restorative Justice
Including Victims
in Community Corrections

Myron Steele
Thomas J. Quinn

Background

The demographic and caseload trends across the United States portend more cases, piled on top of already overburdened agencies of justice. It is apparent that the adjudication system as it is now structured will continue to be under stress. Although increases in resources are needed, we cannot foresee the resources increasing sufficiently to meet the need without some structural changes. Despite modest increases in funding, despite management innovations, despite a genuine desire to provide a speedy and fair process, there continues to be delay in bringing offenders to justice and a sense of helplessness on the part of the victims.

Source: Prepared especially for *The Dilemmas of Corrections.*

The fault may be the focus of the system itself, which now all but ignores victims, when in fact for many purposes they should be the centerpiece of the process. Somehow "justice and punishment" have become synonymous. Left largely out of the equation is the victim or the community which has been harmed. Without fundamental changes, these problems will be exacerbated in the next century.

Some agencies of justice have begun to respond to the challenge; to try to better meet the expectations of the public with an emerging community-based philosophy—"restorative justice"—as an adjunct to the retributive model. In the restorative model, the victim is the paramount concern and the process geared to making the victim whole, using the offender as the vehicle where possible. In a sense it is a return to ancient cultures, the legal systems which formed the foundation of Western law and viewed crime as an intensely personal event. Although crime breached the common welfare so that the community had an interest and responsibility in addressing the wrong and punishing the offender, the offense was not considered primarily a crime against the state as it is today. The offense was considered principally a violation against the victim and the victim's family. Thus, ancient cultures held offenders and their families responsible to settle accounts with victims and their families as evidenced in ancient legal codes such as the Babylonian Code of Hammurabi (c. 1700 B.C.); the Sumerian Code of Ur-Nammu (c. 2050 B.C.); the Roman Law of the Twelve Tables (449 B.C.); the earliest surviving collection of Germanic tribal laws (the Lex Salica, promulgated by King Clovis soon after his conversion to Christianity in A.D. 496); and, the Laws of Ethelbert in Kent, England (c. A.D. 600). Crime was understood to break the peace, destroying right relationships within a community and creating harmful ones. Justice, then, aimed to restore relationships to wholeness.[1]

The Norman invasion of Britain in 1066 marked the beginning of a "paradigm shift," a turning away from the understanding of crime as a victim-offender conflict within the context of the community. William the Conqueror and his descendants found the legal process an effective tool for centralizing their own political authority. They competed with the church's influence over secular matters and effectively replaced local systems of dispute resolution.[2]

In 1116, William's son, Henry I, issued the Legis Henrici, securing royal jurisdiction over "certain offenses against the king's peace, arson, robbery, murder, false coinage, and crimes of violence."[3] Anything that violated this peace was interpreted as an offense against the king, and offenders were thus subject to royal authority. Under this new approach, the king became the paramount victim, and the actual victim was denied any meaningful place in the justice process.

The purpose of criminal justice underwent a parallel shift. Rather than centering on making the victim whole, the system now focused on upholding the authority of the state. Instead of addressing the past harm, criminal justice became future-oriented, attempting to make offenders and potential offenders law-abiding. Punishment in the forms of fines and corporal punishment took its place. Since these punishments were administered in public (in hopes of deterring would-be criminals), they caused great humiliation as well.[4]

In reaction to the increasingly brutal treatment of offenders, the rehabilitation model and its principal tool, the prison, evolved. Prior to 1790, prisons were used primarily to hold offenders until trial, but the Quakers in Philadelphia converted the local jail into what they called the "penitentiary." They aimed not only to save offenders from dehumanizing punishment, but also to rehabilitate them. Unfortunately, many of the prisoners, completely deprived of contact with their loved ones and the outside world, went mad. The cure proved worse that the disease.

But this did not discourage prison advocates. If isolation did not achieve the goals of repentance and rehabilitation, then perhaps other measures would work. Succeeding generations moved from theories of repentance to theories of hard work, then to discipline and training, and eventually to medical and psychological treatment. But this search for an approach that guaranteed that governments would "graduate" all offenders from their prisons as law-abiding citizens has met with disappointing results. Over the past 20 years, a growing number of criminal justice policy makers have concluded that rehabilitation is simply an impossible goal, a failed policy.[5]

Treatment programs will play an important role in restorative justice, as we will see. While the rehabilitation model has also used treatment programs, its basic flaws have undermined them, producing a wave of disappointment and disillusionment in the last 20 years.

Unfortunately, the failure of the rehabilitation model has not yet led to a rejection of the current paradigm: that crime is only an offense against the state. Instead, it has prompted governments to impose increasingly repressive and punitive sanctions against those who commit crimes. The goal has become incapacitation. The "get tough" model has been no more successful than the rehabilitation model in controlling crime, and it may be contributing to the breakdown of the criminal justice system itself.

Re-emergence of Restorative Justice

Changing the goal of the justice system from rehabilitation to retribution and incapacitation has not solved the crisis in criminal justice, nor will it. Crime is not merely an offense against the state, and justice is more than punishment. Van Ness argues that if we are going to find solutions to this crisis in criminal justice, we will have to start over, beginning with the very foundation.

In the past 15 years proposals have evolved which: 1) define crime as injury to victims, 2) include all parties in the response to crimes, and 3) address the injuries experienced by all parties as well as the legal obligations of offenders. Following is an overview of these new proposals.

In his 1977 paper, "Beyond Restitution: Creative Restitution,"[6] psychologist Albert Eglash identified three types of criminal justice: retributive justice based on punishment, distributive justice based on therapeutic treatment of offenders, and restorative justice. Both the punishment and treatment models, he noted, focus on the actions of offenders, deny the victim's participation in the justice process, and require merely passive participation by the offender. Restorative justice on the other hand focuses on the harmful effects of offenders' actions and actively involves victims and offenders in the process.

Howard Zehr, a pioneer in the victim-offender reconciliation movement, has been a highly influential advocate for a restorative justice paradigm shift. He notes that retributive justice focuses on establishing the guilt of offenders; restorative justice focuses on solving the problems created by crime. Restorative justice requires the participation of all the parties. Furthermore, retributive justice holds offenders accountable for their crimes by punishing them. In restorative justice, said Zehr, offender accountability is defined as "understanding [the] impact of [the offender's] action and helping decide how to make things right.[7] The process empowers the victim to play a meaningful role in determining the outcome.

Victim-offender mediation (also sometimes called victim-offender reconciliation or VORP) began anew in 1974 in a Kitchener, Ontario program, founded by two Mennonite church members (one a probation officer) who were seeking better means of dealing with young criminal offenders. The first program in the United States was in Elkhart, Indiana in 1978, through the leadership of the Mennonite church there, acting along with a local judge, probation officers, and a local community corrections organization. By 1989, there were at least 171 such programs in the United States.[8] A referred case is screened for acceptance; it may be rejected, for example, if there is overt hostility between the parties or there is no need for reconciliation or restitution. If accepted, the case is referred to mediation, which may be conducted by a single mediator or a pair of co-mediators. Mediators usually are trained, unpaid volunteers; in difficult cases a paid staff member may take over the mediation or assist the volunteer.[9]

In the victim-offender mediation meeting, the mediator explains the process and then encourages each party to relate the facts of the crime from his or her point of view. This is meant to help the victim to understand the offender's motivation and the offender to understand the crime's hurtfulness to the victim, including the victim's physical losses, fear, suspicion, and anger.[10] The formal adversarial court system does not allow this level of interaction, this depth of discussion.

Some states have systematically attempted to divert cases from the formal court process. On July 27, 1981, the New York State Legislature unanimously passed Chapter 847, Laws of 1981 establishing the Community Dispute Resolution Centers Program (CDRCP). The program was placed within the Unified Court System under the supervision of the Administrative Judge of the Courts (Judiciary Law, Article 21A). In the first fiscal year, 1981–82, seventeen private not-for-profit agencies serving fifteen counties were awarded grants. Over the course of the next seven years additional agencies were evaluated and awarded grants, and currently, there are dispute resolution centers in all 62 New York counties, which mediate both misdemeanors and felonies.

In fiscal year 1992–93, the Centers served 106,388 people involved in 43,688 cases which were screened as appropriate for direct services by the Centers. Indirect services in the form of assistance, referrals to appropriate resources and other helpful information are also provided by the Centers each day. In 83 percent of the matters that reached to mediation stage, a voluntary agreement was achieved by the parties. The Centers reported $2,543,692 awarded in the form of restitution and mutual agreements to New York State citizens. The average award per case was $680. Forty-seven percent of the referrals to the Centers were from the courts. Forty-four percent of the conflicts involved matters of a criminal nature, 51 percent were civil and 5 percent involved juvenile problems. Two hundred and seven (207) felony cases were mediated.

It took 15 days from intake to final disposition for the average single-hearing dispute resolution case (16,497 cases) and 46 days for the average multiple-hearing case (802 cases). The average time per mediation/ arbitration was one hour and twelve minutes, at an average state cost per individual directly served through the intervention of the mediation program of $26. The Centers are now teaching conflict management skills to young people in many schools across the state.

Tennessee has also recently attempted to institutionalize community-based mediation. The Victim-Offender Mediation Center Act of 1993 makes appropriations to implement this act for fiscal year 1993–1994. Victim-offender mediation centers can meet the needs of Tennessee's citizens by providing forums in which persons may voluntarily participate in the resolution of disputes in an informal and less adversarial atmosphere. A victim-offender mediation center may be created and operated by a corporation organized to resolve disputes, making use of public facilities at free or nominal cost. The grant from the state of Tennessee may not exceed 50 percent of the approved estimated cost of the program.

Public Support for Community Service/Restorative Justice

Despite the "get tough" attitude prevalent in criminal justice policy and practice, there appears to be growing support among the public for repaying the community. Four our of five Minnesotans favor spending on education, job training, and community programs rather than on prisons in order to reduce crime. More than four out of five Minnesotans indicate an interest in participating in a face-to-face meeting with the offender in the presence of a trained mediator to let the offender know how the crime affected them, to discuss their feelings, and to work out a plan for repayment of losses. Nearly three out of four Minnesotans chose restitution as more important than jail time in sentencing for a burglary of their own home. The results were consistent across age, income, gender, race, and education-level subgroups.[11]

A public opinion research project conducted in Hennepin County, Minnesota, in 1991 by Imho Bae of the University of Minnesota found strong public support for restitution as an alternative penalty to incarceration for property offenders. This research also found a significant lack of awareness by criminal justice officials of public support for restitution and found that crime victims seem to be less punitive than non-victims. Bae concludes that his findings imply that citizens perceive crime issues in a broader social context and independently from reports of the mass media.[12]

In 1991, the Public Agenda Foundation completed a study of public attitudes in Delaware. The public felt that alternative penalties were a tough, appropriate punishment that would better serve the community, and that alternatives improve the chances of rehabilitation, a principle that Delawareans believe in deeply. The specific alternative for community service was well-liked because it is seen as a way for offenders simultaneously to learn job skills and internalize the work ethic, thereby improving their chances of rehabilitation. Respondents to the survey also liked the fact that work done by the offenders would benefit the community; they see it as a way for offenders to give something back to society. A number of respondents felt that community service could be a suitable alternative for offenders who are unemployed or otherwise unable to make restitution.[13]

Respected researchers and authors, Norval Morris and Michael Tonry, state in their widely acclaimed book, *Between Prison and Probation,*

"The services performed by those sentenced in this way are welcomed by the recipients of those services and . . . the sentenced offenders prove to be more diligent workers than had been anticipated." They proffer that community service—either alone or as part of a more complex punishment—provides for an appropriate proportionate sanction in a comprehensive continuum of correctional options and is growing in popularity across the United States.[14]

Results of Research and Evaluations

A growing body of research in North America and Europe is finding that the process of mediating conflict between crime victims and offenders provides many benefits to the parties involved, the community, and the justice system. It has also been found that many victims and offenders want to meet, when given the opportunity, and work things out in a manner than is perceived to be fair to both parties.[15]

Preliminary research suggests that "restorative" approaches to justice may serve as effective alternatives to incarceration. Restorative programs often cost far less than prison, hold offenders personally accountable for the pain they have inflicted, and work to repair the economic, psychological, and emotional trauma which crime represents to both the victim and the community.[16]

The first large cross-site evaluation of victim-offender mediation programs to occur in the United States involving multiple data sets, research questions, comparison groups, and multiple quantitative and qualitative techniques of analysis was initiated by the Citizens Council Mediation Services in Minneapolis through a grant from the State Justice Institute in Alexandria, Virginia.[17] It was conducted in cooperation with the School of Social Work at the University of Minnesota with Dr. Mark Umbreit serving as the principal investigator.

Program sites examined worked closely with juvenile courts in Albuquerque, NM; Austin, TX; St. Paul, MN; and Oakland, CA. The results are encouraging. Victim-offender mediation resulted in very high levels of client satisfaction (victims, 79 percent; offenders, 87 percent) and perceptions of fairness (victims, 83 percent; offenders, 89 percent) with the mediation process for both victims and offenders. This is consistent with a number of previous studies. Victim-offender mediation also made a significant contribution to reducing fear and anxiety among crime victims. Prior to mediation, nearly 25 percent of victims were afraid of being victimized again by the same offender. After mediation only 10 percent were afraid of being re-victimized. Juvenile offenders did not perceive victim-offender mediation to be a significantly less demanding response to their criminal behavior than other options available to the court. The use of mediation is consistent with the goal of holding young offenders accountable for their criminal behavior.[18] Considerably fewer and less serious additional crimes were committed within a one-year period by juvenile offenders in victim-offender mediation programs when compared to similar offenders who did not participate in mediation. Consistent with two recent English studies[19] this important finding, however, is not statistically significant because of the small size of program samples.

Victim-offender mediation has a significant impact on the likelihood of offenders successfully completing their restitution obligation to the victim (81 percent) when compared to similar offenders who completed their restitution in a court-administered program (58 percent) without mediation. Many more victims and offenders must have access to mediation if the well-documented potential of victim-offender mediation is to move from the margins to the mainstream of how we understand and respond to crime in modern industrialized societies.

Conclusion

The fear of crime and violence is expected to continue, and the Clinton Administration has supported plans to increase police manpower on the streets. This can only translate to more arrests, and more cases to be placed on the judicial threshold.

This trend will run headlong into the resource limitations which will be required by concerns over the budget deficit. No longer can the courts, nor other agencies of justice, expect to take greater than their share of the modest growth available in the state coffers. The public and their elected officials will demand ever greater efficiency, requiring funda-mental changes in the way justice is dispensed. Fortunately, other trends are surfacing which should help progressive judicial change agents meet the demands of the next century.

David Osborne, in his thought-provoking book, *Reinventing Government*, predicts that the organizations and agencies that survive in this fast changing world will reflect more flexibility, less bureaucracy, more interdisciplinary collaboration, and greater emphasis on solving problems closer to the source. These are precisely the elements of community-based mediation which offer hope for dealing effectively with the anticipated caseload growth, and they are principles which should drive the courts' preparation for the future. A more complete and rapid sorting of cases will be required, and the traditional hierarchical bureaucracy will no longer suffice.

There is also a growing recognition that prisons do not work for all offenders, that other options can be more effective, that offenders in need of treatment should get that treatment as quickly as possible, and that it is time to stop ignoring the victims of crime. As a result, the need for victim-offender mediation and other community-based programs based on the restorative justice philosophy will become increasingly important.

Notes

1. Van Ness, Daniel; Carlson, David L. Jr.; Crawford, Thomas; and Strong, Karen, 1989, *Restorative Justice: Theory*. Washington, DC: Justice Fellowship
2. Berman, Harold, 1983. *Law and Resolution:The Formation of Western Legal Tradition*. Cambridge, MA: Harvard University, as quoted in Van Ness, Ibid.
3. Day, Frank B., and Gallati, Robert R. 1978. *Introduction to Law Enforcement and Criminal Justice*, p. 50. Springfield, IL: Charles C Thomas, as quoted in Van Ness, Ibid.
4. Cullen, Francis T. and Gilbert, Karen E. 1982. *Reaffirming Rehabilitation*. Cincinnati: Anderson Publishing, as quoted in Van Ness, Ibid.
5. Van Ness, Ibid.
6. Eglash, Albert, 1977. "Beyond Restitution: Creative Restitution" in *Restitution in Criminal Justice*, edited by Joe Hudson and Burt Galloway, 91–99. Lexington, MA: Lexington, as quoted in Van Ness, Ibid.
7. Zehr, Howard, 1985. "Retributive Justice, Restorative Justice." *New Perspectives on Crime and Justice: Occasional Papers of the Mennonite Central Committee Canada Victim Offender Ministries Program and the MCC U.S. Office of Criminal Justice*, Vol. 4. Elkhart, IN: MCC U.S. Office of Criminal Justice, as quoted in Van Ness, Ibid.
8. Umbreit, Mark S. 1993. *How to Increase Referrals to Victim Offender Mediation Programs*. Ontario, Canada; The Funds for Dispute Resolution.
9. Hughes, S. P. and Schneider, A.C., 1989. "Victim Offender Mediation: A Survey of Program Characteristics and Perceptions of Effectiveness." *Crime and Delinquency* Vol. 46, No. 2, as quoted in Clarke, below.
10. Clarke, Stevens H. 1993. *Community Justice and Victim-Offender Mediation Programs*, A Working Paper for the National Symposium on Court Connected Dispute Resolution Research, October 15–16, 1993. State Justice Institute.
11. Pranis, Kay and Umbreit, Mark, 1992. "Public Opinion Research Challenges Perception of Widespread Public Demand for Harsher Punishment." Minneapolis, MN: Minnesota Citizens Council.
12. Ibid.
13. Doble, John; Immerwahr, Stephen; and Richardson, Amy, 1991. *Punishing Criminals: The People of Delaware Consider the Options*. New York: Edna McConnell Clark Foundation.
14. Morris, Norval, and Tonry, Michael, 1989. *Between Prison and Probation*. New York: Oxford University Press.
15. Umbreit, Ibid. p. 2.
16. *Pact Institute of Justice* Brochure on "Restorative Justice Resources."
17. Umbreit, Mark, 1992. "Cross-Site Analysis of Victim Offender Mediation," *Victim-Offender Mediation*, Newsletter, Vol.4 No.1, Fall 1992. U.S.Association for Victim-Offender Mediation.
18. Bazamore, 1990, 1992; Schneider, 1985; Schneider Schram, 1986; as quoted in Umbreit, Ibid.
19. Marshall & Merry, 1990; Digman, 1991; as quoted in Umbreit, Ibid.

Part VI

Critical Problems and Issues in Corrections

Introduction

Correctional officials seem to be perpetually plagued by problems and embroiled in controversy. Each day brings a new set of emergencies, ranging from escape plots and suicide attempts to plumbing problems and work stoppages. Correctional administrators and staff have little choice but to respond to the seemingly unending barrage of crises on a day-to-day basis. Consequently, they rarely have the time to reflect soberly on possible solutions to emerging problems or to develop long-term plans to cope with these problems.

Readers of the first five sections of this book certainly are well aware that the problems of contemporary corrections are numerous and intractable. No single text can possibly do justice to all of the issues that need to be addressed as corrections moves into the twenty-first century. Nevertheless, the editors of this text have selected nine articles that examine correctional problems and issues that have emerged as particularly noteworthy in recent years.

First, Hans Toch, the nation's leading authority on the psychological consequences of imprisonment, explores the extreme difficulties prison officials encounter when dealing with inmates who are severely mentally ill. Professor Toch's "The Disturbed Disruptive Inmate: Where Does the Bus Stop?" reviews the prison careers of several "disturbed disruptive" inmates. These prisoners pose unusually severe disciplinary and mental health problems for staff, and they are extremely dangerous to themselves as well as to others. Typically, correctional and mental hospital officials resort to "bus therapy"—a procedure in which troublesome inmates are shuttled back and forth from prisons to mental hospitals. The result is that they rarely, if ever, receive the kind of intensive, specialized, long-term treatment they need.

A relatively new problem faced by prison administrators—and one that is becoming steadily worse—is how to meet the special needs of elderly prisoners. As a result of the increase in crime by older Americans and the long-term effects of the many state mandatory sentencing laws passed in recent years, American prisons now incarcerate a growing number of inmates who are well past the age of 50. *The New York Times* reported in 1997 that U.S. prisons currently house more than 55,000 inmates over 50, a figure that could reach 200,000 by the year 2005. In "Growing Old Behind Bars," Professor Sol Chaneles examines the various kinds of convicts who will make up the geriatric prison population of the future. As Chaneles points out, few of our prisons are prepared to provide health care for this rapidly increasing segment of the prison population.

Another type of offender with special needs is the juvenile female offender. Frequently overlooked by criminal justice researchers and misunderstood by the general public, incarcerated adolescent females are more likely than their male counterparts to be locked up for mere status offenses (running away from home, curfew violations, and other offenses that would not be considered crimes if committed by an adult). Yet they are less likely than incarcerated adolescent males to receive the kind of vocational and educational programming needed for personal growth and economic independence. In "The Forgotten Few: Juvenile Female Offenders," Ilene R. Bergsmann explains how gender bias and stereotyping have led to the inequitable treatment of female juvenile offenders. She concludes by calling for correctional administrators to implement gender-neutral policies that will ensure equitable and effective programs for all juvenile offenders.

Perhaps the most overlooked causes of juvenile delinquency—and future adult criminal behavior—are undiagnosed and/or untreated learning disabilities. Over the past few years, delinquency experts and correction officials have begun to study closely the link between various learning disabilities and delinquent behavior. In "Learning disabilities, Juvenile Delinquency, and Juvenile Corrections, " Albert R. Roberts and Judith A. Waters review this research. They also call for more early-intervention programs and the development of new juvenile correctional programs that can help learning-disabled young offenders avoid becoming adult criminals.

Without doubt one of the most difficult and ominous problems facing prison officials is the threat posed by acquired immune deficiency syndrome (AIDS). AIDS and the human immunodeficiency virus (HIV) that causes it most frequently result from the sharing of infected needles by intravenous drug users and from homosexual contact. The use of illicit drugs is a common aspect of the pre-imprisonment lifestyles of many prisoners. Moreover, homosexual activities and the use of illegal drugs are prevalent in all too many jails and prisons. In "The Impact of HIV/AIDS on Corrections," Mark Blumberg and J. Dennis Laster examine the difficult policy choices faced by correctional administrators who must confront the threat posed by HIV/AIDS. Blumberg and Laster analyze the arguments for and against such policies as mass screening, condom distribution, and segregation of HIV-infected inmates. They make it clear that this is yet another correctional problem with no easy solution.

Even if there are no easy solutions, is it possible that private corporations could do a better—and less costly—job of running prisons and jails than the state and federal governments have done? This is the intuitively appealing idea behind one of the most important recent developments in American corrections—the privatization of corrections. In 1985, privately operated prison facilities housed only 1,345 inmates. Today privately run prisons house over 80,000 inmates across the country. At least 27 states, as well as the U.S. government and some local governments, have entered into contracts with private-sector prison providers. The two largest of these companies, Corrections Corporation of America and the Wackenhut Corrections Corporation, together control approximately 75 percent of America's private prisons.

The emergence of "prisons for profit" has been met with both praise and criticism. Proponents claim that private industry can do a better job of running prisons than can the government, and that prison privatization will save taxpayers millions of dollars annually in incarceration costs. Critics, however, argue that placing responsibility for prisoners in private corporations will inevitably lead to violations of inmates' rights, compromise the health and safety of prisoners, and result in higher recidivism rates in the long run.

In "Prisons for Profit," Eric Bates discusses some of the pros and cons of the prison privatization movement. Bates focuses on the recent performance of the Corrections Corporation of America in Texas, Tennessee, and several other states, and he finds good reason to be skeptical of claims that private prisons are better than public prisons. Many readers will agree that it would be foolish to rush toward further privatization of prisons without a careful and thorough evaluation of the costs and consequences of delegating this responsibility to private companies.

Many of the articles in this book implicitly or explicitly raise issues of the economic costs and benefits of imprisonment and alternatives to imprisonment. But just how much do we know about the economics of corrections? As it turns out, the answer is "not nearly enough." Perhaps the best available analysis of what we know and don't know about the cost-effectiveness of imprisonment is our next selection. In "Does Prison Pay? The Stormy National Debate Over the Cost-Effectiveness of Imprisonment," John J. DiIulio, Jr. and Anne Morrison Piehl discuss Edwin Zedlewski's controversial 1987 study of the costs and benefits of imprisonment (see the introduction to Part V) and they provide an overview of the most important subsequent research in this area. DiIulio and Piehl show that calculating costs and benefits is difficult at best. They argue, however, that cost-benefit analysis is worthwhile and can only help to introduce "a measure of rationality into debates about the future of corrections."

One highly controversial question is whether it is rational, humane, and worthwhile to impose so-called "shaming" or "scarlet letter" punishments on convicted offenders. In recent years, there seems to have been an increase in criminal sentences that are the modern equivalent of such age-old practices as branding adulterers or placing pickpockets in the pillory. Many cities, for example, publish the names of those convicted of patronizing a prostitute in the local newspaper. Convicted drunken drivers sometimes are required to identify themselves as such by placing one or more brightly colored bumper stickers on their car. Sometimes these kinds of punishments are imposed in addition to a jail or prison term, but usually they are meted out as an alternative to jail or prison, typically as a condition of probation.

But are "shaming" punishments truly effective in protecting the public or in preventing the offender from committing additional crimes? According to Douglas Litowitz, the author of our next chapter, the answer is "no." In "The Trouble with 'Scarlet Letter' Punishments," Litowitz, a law professor at Florida State University, argues that punishments that inflict gratuitous humiliation on offenders may satisfy the public appetite for vengeance, but they will also undermine the more important goal of rehabilitating the offender. Professor Litowitz acknowledges that a case can be made that an offender's lack of shame may in some instances be a cause of his criminal behavior. He stresses, however, that we must make a distinction between "reintegrative shaming" and "stigmatizing shaming," and he concludes that today's brand of shaming punishments all too often fall into the latter category.

The final selection in the book is one of the most important. It focuses upon capital punishment—an issue that is not always viewed as a correctional issue. But ask any prison official about this and you will be told in no uncertain terms that the execution of condemned offenders is the lawful responsibility of the department of corrections in each of the thirty-eight states that authorize capital punishment. Moreover, as the people who must actually house death-row inmates and carry out executions, prison staff at all levels typically have insights into the death-penalty debate that most Americans will never share.

In "The Costliest Punishment: A Corrections Administrator Contemplates the Death Penalty," Paul Keve, a former director of corrections departments in Minnesota and Delaware, offers his view of the role of the death penalty in American corrections. Interestingly, Keve indicates that he agrees with DiIulio and Piehl that the figures given for the annual costs of imprisonment are quite misleading. But this is not the case, he argues, when it comes to the costs of the death penalty. He explains why every careful empirical study on the matter has found that the death penalty is considerably more expensive than its closest alternative—life imprisonment without the possibility of parole (see also "Millions Misspent," a Report by The Death Penalty Information Center, Washington, DC: 1992).

Keve, a death-penalty opponent, regards the death penalty as a high cost/no benefit policy, and he contends that the millions of dollars spent annually on death-penalty cases would be better spent "on more social services to prevent violent crimes, more police services, and more services to deal constructively with the needs of victims' families." Keve may or may not change some readers' views on capital punishment, but there is no doubt that readers will not forget that the death penalty, although not intended to "correct" the condemned inmate, is an important issue in corrections.

34

The Disturbed Disruptive Inmate
Where Does the Bus Stop?

Hans Toch

If prisons had yearbooks, there are inmates who would unquestion-ably be voted "least likely to succeed." Among convicts who would qualify for this honor is a long-term New York prisoner who has served 13 peripatetic years of a 20-year sentence. By "peripatetic" I mean that the inmate has been frequently transferred or "shuttled." Ed (as we shall call the prisoner) has experienced 30 institutional moves, a career which, in a prison system, is an index of continued unpopu-larity.

One reason for Ed's singular status becomes clear when one reviews his folder. Ed's disciplinary dossier is horrendously long and variegated. Some of the recorded infractions suggest that Ed may occa-sionally be disoriented ("out of place," "loitering"), and that he has difficulties adjusting to prison routine. Some of the difficulties may

Source: *Journal of Psychiatry and Law* (Fall 1982), 327-349. Reprinted with the permission of the publisher.

appear simple (Ed is "repeatedly late for mess—[he] has been warned but insists on being late"), but others are more obviously complex ("had dirty cell and had burned his blanket and pillow cases"). Ed is responsible for strings of personal attacks against fellow-inmates and sometimes against guards. Some of these incidents are serious (e.g., "attempted to strangle inmate X"). Similarly serious is a series of suicide attempts and self-mutilation efforts, including an episode in which Ed cut his own throat.

Twelve of Ed's transfers—approximately one each year—placed him in a residential mental health setting. The first such transfer occurred straight out of prison reception. At the time, Ed was experiencing what was diagnosed as an "acute depressive reaction." In Ed's case, difficulties arose from the bizarre form his so-called "depressive reactions" tended to take. As an example, Ed's disappointment with a Christmas turkey shipment not only included manifestations of despondency, but (according to an officer's report) "he [Ed] put an edible portion of turkey in the garbage can, poured water over his head at 12:00 midnight and swallowed a cigarette butt instead of a pill." Private rituals such as these create disciplinary incidents; tardiness occurs, for example, because "I have to wash up and kiss [his family's photograph]... because I respect God and my family." Violence has mystifying origins. An officer is assaulted "because he called me wise guy and cocky"; a fight breaks out when Ed insults a group of black inmates whom he has never met, the day after arriving at a new institution for a predictably short stay.

Other incidents are clear psychotic episodes. A report describes Ed "eating feces from the mess hall toilet"; it notes that he has "burned his hands under boiling water from the faucet" the previous day. Another report describes Ed

> screaming without any reason, laughing inappropriately looking at his family pictures and stating that he will kill them, pouring hot water over his body, talking to himself and picking up and moving things back and forth constantly.

Extreme problems arise where such incidents take (as they do) blatantly destructive or self-destructive turns. The same report continues:

> His condition has become quite critical today, when he started putting his hand in an electric fan, putting his hand in the cigarette lighter socket, burning his hands and arms with cigarettes... threatened to stick his finger in an electric socket while having his foot in a pail of water in his cell.

Outbursts oscillate between attacks on others, such as sleeping fellow-inmates, and attacks on self. The rationale is invariably delusional—for instance, "a voice told me"; "I had the urge to get rid of myself because I had the devil in me"; "the officer [whom Ed assaulted] tried to kill my son—tried to nail me to a cross"; or "hear voices that my wife and children are dead."

Ed's dilemma, and that of the system, are eloquently described (under the evaluation heading "adjustment in prison,") by a prison-employed psychiatrist. The psychiatrist writes:

> Instead of discussing this as Ed's adjustment to prison, one might more appropriately consider this as the Department of Correction's (and Mental Health's) adjustment to Ed. The psychotic episodes were successfully handled by providing hospitalization and/or medication and counseling. Long-term rehabilitation has taken a second place with day-to-day handling being the main consideration. Ed has neither the ability nor the inclination to analyze his own problems and has requested transfers when he could not cope with the pressures of prison life. The transfers were effected without any fuss because Ed's desire to move was equalled, if not exceeded by, the institution's desire to get rid of the problem.

No one, however—least of all, Ed—has "gotten rid" of the problem, which we sense may climax in a completed suicide attempt. Ed is not served because he falls between the cracks of management options and because he is a notorious hot potato. More seriously, Ed defies our capacity to understand who and what he is. He is a conceptual Humpty Dumpty separated into two watertight and irreconcilable components, Ed the "mad" component and Ed the "bad" component.

It is paradigmatic that there is increased concern in the prison field about the prevalence of inmate mental health problems. One hears the topic broached in prison staff interactions ranging from superintendents' meetings to conversations with guards. A federal agency (the National Institute of Corrections) reports that "during recent... Advisory Board hearings, the increase in the number of mentally ill and retarded inmates was identified as a major concern of practitioners."[1] Similar alarm today revolves around perceived dramatic increments in prison violence. The impression is that many more inmates have serious adjustment difficulties, and that a "new violence-prone breed" of offender is abroad in the land.

Such staff impressions matter because they coincide with the advent of prison overcrowding, which poses unscheduled stressors for inmates and also decreases services available to them.

But such difficulties are at least familiar, and in theory at least can be responded to by improving and expanding on what we now do. Such is not the case with composite syndromes such as Ed's—syndromes that *combine* mental health and adjustment difficulties. Such syndromes *of necessity* are inappropriately and ineffectively responded to through existing modalities. The composite (disturbed *and* disruptive) inmate falls between available chairs. He does so because standard responses separately address (mental health or management) problems that are obviously linked. Unsurprisingly, inmates who have disciplinary and mental health problems are notoriously refractory to treatment and their careers through the system are biographies of escalating conflict and suffering. Inmates such as Ed are also at present uncharted and not understood. They mystify peers and staff, inspire fear and aversion, and spawn impotence based on a sense of our ignorance. Presumptively, the impotence extends to community settings faced with such persons, not only to criminal justice and mental health settings, but also to neighborhood groups, schools, and families.

As a category, disturbed disruptive inmates (DDIs) have no theoretical standing, and one reason why the combination "disturbed-disruptive" (DD) is a non-concept is because we are often placed in a "forced choice" situation where what someone does must be interpreted as symptomatic of an underlying disturbance or where we must react to it as a responsible exercise of unfettered malevolence. This occurs because symptomatic behavior and premeditated recalcitrance have mutually exclusive implications as to consequence and culpability. Even where the presence of both manifestations is obvious in the same individual, at any given point we may have to categorize one manifestation as relevant and the other as not.

In practice, the disturbed disruptive person tends to be conceptually segmented over time into a "disruptive" person and a "disturbed" person. At one juncture (for instance, when prison staff review the inmate's latest assault on an officer) they must unambiguously class him as disruptive; at a subsequent juncture (such as after the inmate's "voices" have instructed him to hang himself in the disciplinary segregation cell to which his disruptiveness has taken him) they must adjudge him psychotic. To be sure, the segmentation becomes increasingly unstable with chronicity of disturbance and disruptiveness patterns. Such chronicity makes the DD combination obvious, but invites a second "forced choice" involving selection of the pattern to be regarded as primary in classifying the person. With regard to this choice, the uninviting nature of the person's disruptive behavior reliably overwhelms decisions, and inspires caretakers to classify the person so as to make him primarily the client of other caretakers. This tendency is reinforced by the fact that symptoms of disturbance tend to wax and wane over time.

The competition of rival diagnostic efforts (sometimes referred to as "ping ponging") results in a tendency to shuttle the disruptive disturbed person to mental health settings (invoked by caretakers of disruptive inmates) from which he is returned to mainline disciplinary or custodial settings (by caretakers of the disturbed). This procedure is called "bus therapy," and it reveals pressure to make the "bus stops" as brief as decency permits. In *Corrections Magazine*, reporter Wilson notes that

> administrators from mental health and corrections agencies will each maintain in theory that they are best qualified to handle the "mad and bad." But in practice, neither wants to deal with him. The frequent result is a brutalizing series of transfers.... There are, says Rowen [of the AMA] "problems in both camps. Correctional administrators, wanting to get rid of their bad apples, will ship them off to mental health. And the mental health administrators don't want to monkey around with acting-out clients, so they send them back."[2]

Three prison experts, Freeman, Dinitz, and Conrad, conclude that

> neither mental hospitals nor prisons welcome the disturbed and dangerous inmate....The resulting "bus therapy" expresses the reluctance which both kinds of institutions feel in contemplation of the burden of this kind of inmate. Until courts and administrators can establish rules to govern the disposition of such inmates their programming will be punctuated by bus movements which are clearly not intended for their benefit.[3]

Bus therapy obfuscates the disruptive-disturbed syndrome because the inmate who gets on the bus is labeled disturbed and the one who exits (presumptively after "therapy") is adjudicated disruptive. Such judgments are even made before the person gets on the bus. Recently, an *APA Monitor* reporter claimed that he had been told by a forensic mental health administrator that "corrections officials have sought to use psychologists to control — not necessarily help — prisoners. Prison staff have been known to ask mental health care personnel to get troublemakers committed or given medication....And psychologists have been 'obliged' to honor such requests...in order to keep their jobs."[4] The administrator later pointed out that he had been misquoted, but *Corrections Magazine* also tells us that "a common criticism by psychiatrists of prison administrators is that they want the doctors to handle the problem cases, which are not always psychiatric problems."[5] A prominent clinician (Vicky Agee), by contrast, recalls that

> We discovered that Mental Health institutions are for Mentally healthy patients — not rotten patients, who obviously were not psychotic — but had behavior problems. We drove our disturbed delinquents there — they beat us back — with the diagnosis of "manipulation"....[We] tried to outplay Mental Health at the "Name Game." They won, of course — you can't help but win when you hold

> all the cards....Most of the game revolves around the Psychotic versus Character Disorder names....Character disorders (which I think means anybody who intimidates, messes over, or hurts people) particularly do not belong in hospitals, because they are untreatable.[6]

Such charges are not made out of whole cloth, because "games" such as those referred to by Agee are played on the record. Illustrative is a case I have reviewed of a disruptive and disturbed prisoner who was finally committed after having (1) attempted to hang himself twice in one week, and (2) set fire to his mattress and pajamas (while occupying them). This inmate was returned with the diagnosis "Explosive personality disorders — antisocial personality disorders." Later the same inmate was again committed. The report noted that "he hanged himself last night and was unconscious when he was found." The resulting "trip" was short and unproductive. However, the prison superintendent almost immediately returned the inmate, certifying that "it has been reported to me that this...resident's emotional condition is deteriorating. He has remained depressed, despondent and has smeared feces on his body and all over the room. He is reportedly reacting to auditory hallucinations and has had a serious attempt at suicide, by hanging, one hour after his return to prison." Only one week later, the same inmate reappeared with the discharge diagnosis "Antisocial personality disorder 301.70." The following year, he was again institutionalized. This time, the referring staff noted that the inmate was "hearing voices telling him to kill himself — got 'rope' last night but didn't use it. Harassed by other inmates to 'bug out.'" They also reported that

> in the last two days he has made two suicidal attempts by hanging and set his mattress on fire. He says he is responding to voices telling him to kill himself....On examination this morning he was smeared with feces, says that he did this to baptize himself since the water in his toilet was turned off....He has been having difficulty adjusting to the open prison population and has manifested paranoid ideation.

The prison psychiatrist diagnosed the case as one of "paranoid schizophrenia." The hospital psychiatrist (six weeks later) entered "No diagnosis or condition on Axis I; Antisocial personality disorder."

For most inmates the game is played more honestly and with more integrity, without callousness and risk as embodied in the example. The issue often revolves around remission, or the onset and termination of acute psychotic episodes. Discharges certifying "full remission" are often followed within weeks, days, or hours by renewed manifestations of symptoms. The fact is demonstrable, but need not reflect on the validity of diagnoses. Among other things, as was pointed out somewhat bluntly to Wilson by an informant, "the mental health system drugs them up...gets them sufficiently passive, and sends them back to prison, where they don't give them their medication. Then they decide they have 'regressed,' and they send them back to mental health."[7]

The precise proportion of inmates who experience "bus therapy " is unknown. Equally to-be-established is the assumption that disturbed disruptive inmates are disproportionately subject to expeditious shuttling. A disproportion of expedited transfer would be predicted based on (1) the availability to mental health staff of their patient's disciplinary record, which is calculated to inspire caution in any reasonable man; and (2) the tendency, of some DDIs at least, to resist therapeutic ministrations. Less sanguine predictions could be based on the assumption that psychotropic medication levels can be more or less adjusted to neutralize disruptive tendencies. Of course, if medication regimens are deployed as "therapy," it is improbable that lasting change will occur, and shuttling is therefore likely to continue.

Failure to recognize the integrity of the DD cluster not only contaminates the understanding and treatment of DDIs, but also affects our view of disruptive nondisturbed and disturbed nondisruptive inmates. Where such inmates are conceptually merged with DDIs the result contains heterogeneous melanges whose attributes are understandably mystifying. For instance the Mecklenberg Correctional Center, the maxi-maxi-institution of the Virginia Department of Corrections which contains inmates deemed seriously disruptive, records that "twenty-seven percent of disruptive inmates have been previously committed to a mental health facility for treatment. Of these with prior psychiatric commitments, the average inmate has been committed on 2.12 occasions." Another case in point is provided in an Ohio study of intractable inmates by Myers and Levy, in which intractability is defined as "a chronic disciplinary and adjustment problem within the prison."[9] Myers and Levy discovered, among other things, that "the intractable group had a higher frequency of sick calls (about twice as high), with tension as the primary complaint (22%), and tranquilizers as the primary prescribed medication (44%)."[10] They also noted that "the Psychometric Test results shows that the intractable group scored lower on all IQ, grade level, and psychometric aptitude tests," and that "the intractable group had higher scores on the MMPI (Depression) Scale."[11] The psychometric data are particularly revealing. In the distribution of composite IQ scores (Optic and WAIS) the range of scores for the intractable group extended to a bottom score of 52 (compared to low scores of 72 and 77 for the "tractable" group), and the range for revised Beta scores was 47 to 112 for "intractable" inmates and 79 to 121 for the "tractable" group. Such statistics matter a great deal because prison syndromes in which extremely limited intelligence is a prominent feature seem to be disproportionately represented among DDIs.

The admixture of DDIs and disturbed nondisruptive inmates produces problems of similar complexity. One such problem is that diagnoses that (illegitimately) consider disruptiveness as a criterion highlight antisocial (psychopathic, sociopathic) features, which can be discounted as untreatable, and hence as nonpathological. The noninclusion of antisocial personality disturbances helps students such as Monahan and Steadman to arrive at the "cautious conclusion" that "there is no consistent evidence that the true prevalence rate of nonpsychotic mental disorder is higher among inmate populations than among class-matched community populations."[12] Presumptively different exclusion and inclusion criteria permit authorities such as the President's Commission on Mental Health to contrarily infer that "a high percentage of jail and prison inmates (markedly higher than in the nonprison population) are mentally handicapped."[13] This question is among issues that are unlikely to be resolved unless defensible lines are drawn between DDIs and disturbed nondisruptive inmates.

If DDIs are reliably differentiated from other inmates, some but not all of whose attributes they share, patterned differences *within* behavior dimensions—differences in disciplinary careers and mental health histories—not only can emerge, but are likely to do so. We expect different DD cross-fertilizations such that a given act (like sleeping under the bed) can be disruptive (it interferes with the mandatory custodial body count) but can be pathologically tinged (it can be designed to ward off delusional danger), nonpathologically motivated (designed to resist custody), or ambiguously framed (aimed at ameliorating a psychosomatic backache). The disruptive act that is pathologically motivated (for instance, tearing a bedsheet to produce a rope with which to commit suicide) is as unambiguously disruptive (by destroying "state property") as the same act designed for gain (for pulling contraband from a neighbor's cell), but the quality of the disturbed disruptive act held up to scrutiny will meaningfully differ from that of its nondisturbed counterpart.

Some disruptive behavior patterns, such as cycles of extrapunitive and intrapunitive behavior, are probably most unique to DDI syndromes. Burtch and Ericson note that "a classic statement of the commingling of homicidal and suicidal impulses was propounded by Sigmund Freud in *Mourning and Melancholia*."[14] The "commingling" may be less than universal, but may aptly characterize a subgroup of syndromes in the DDI population, such as the inmate Ed.

Studies of disruptiveness in mental hospitals consistently show that chronic patterns are sharply targeted in a minority of patients. One study cited by Smith found that "2 percent of patients accounted for 55 percent of all violent incidents."[15] A Canadian team surveyed 198 patient assaults, and discovered that "13% (N = 18) of the patients committed 61% of the assaults."[16] Clearly, disturbed disruptive patients exist as do DDIs. They exist, however, in small proportions that can be further reduced by chemical straightjacketing to the negligible levels reported in some studies.[17]

The most critical questions obviously revolve around the psychological link between disturbed and disruptive behavior. Where patterns of disturbance and recalcitrance coexist in the same person, the interconnection is an empirically to-be-investigated issue. Continuity of personality presupposes a connection. Common sense warns against assuming a connection. I have noted elsewhere that

> A schizophrenic who assaults people is a psychotic and is violence-prone. Both facts may diminish the person's popularity, but the combination does not make him a violent psychotic. If the patient obeys voices that tell him to kill, our understanding increases by considering this fact, but in most cases, the link between behavior and emotional and cognitive problems is more remote.[18]

The point of the comment is not that psychopathology and disruptiveness are unrelated, but that we cannot explain one by referring to the other. A diagnosis is a shorthand label for the person's disturbed behavior; it is not a summary of his disruptive behavior; this makes it unsurprising, for example, that, as Kozol, Boucher, and Garofalo note, "the terms used in standard psychiatric diagnosis are almost totally irrelevant to the determination of dangerousness."[19] The same caution applies in reverse. Disruptiveness—which invites disapproval and provokes anxiety—can impair diagnosis of pathology rather than illuminating it.

In exploring DD syndromes, the validity of findings is enhanced by approaching pathology and disruptiveness separately, and then determining what links (if any) can be surfaced where (if) patterns intersect. This calls for reliable criteria for independently diagnosing pathology and disruptiveness, inquiry into differences between DD patterns and non-DD patterns of pathology and disruptiveness, subcategorization of disruptiveness patterns in the DD group, and a search for DD patterns linking disturbance patterns to patterns of disruptiveness.

These links matter. If we are to address the problems and behavior of a disturbed disruptive inmate, it matters whether the inmate's disruptiveness is behavior premised on a delusional view of social reality; is a reaction to pressures that are routine for the average inmate but become overwhelming for the handicapped inmate; results from aversive peer reactions to the person's obnoxious symptoms;

represents a last-ditch gesture deployed to secure needed support; is a pathetic form of protest against intolerable dependence or represents a failure of precarious self-controls. Surfacing and categorizing such links—and drawing out possible implications they may have for action—should be a high-priority enterprise. And it is not as difficult a challenge as the resistance to it may imply. A few summary examples follow to show that the task of surfacing pathology—disruptiveness links can often be met simply by carefully reviewing the folder.

Take the case of George (again, not his real name). George is a large inmate (he weighs over 200 pounds) who is serving the 11th year of a 25-year term. His disciplinary record features a profusion of minor violations (mostly refusals to participate in activities or to obey orders). There are also more serious incidents. Many of these involve assorted acts of ponderous destructiveness: there is a profusion of notations such as "put his hand through window," "threw a pail of hot water at reporting officer," "threw a lightbulb and books on gallery, banged on the wall with his fists," "cut a square piece of material out of his state blanket," "destroying state sink," "flooded his section with water... tore a bible into pieces," "damaged cell door," "broke a glass against wall." There are also recorded fights and attacks on fellow-inmates, some pretty ineffectual. (Once, for example, George approached an officer "demanding to have another inmate's cell open so he could get him because he was a rat.") There are also a number of suicide attempts, and several self-protective requests.

Relatively early in his sentence, George drank a large quantity of acid; in explaining his motives, George reported that he was being harassed by fellow-inmates, who made reference to "his crime and time to serve." The incident was classed as a psychotic depressive reaction. In another incident George cut his wrist and requested transfer because "he claims some inmates called him a 'rat.'" He later attempted suicide after he was (completely predictably) passed over by the parole board. There is general agreement in prison about George being "a person of marginal intelligence who has emotional problems," and staff have also discovered that many of George's emotional problems have to do with his inability to digest or handle stress experiences or routine demands. George always withdraws—if he can—from situations that tax him because of their challenge or complexity. If he cannot withdraw, he explodes. He manages simple demands. For example, he likes a "dining hall assignment with strict supervision."

George has been assigned to a special program—a decent therapeutic community—where he remains after two years, generally under medication. Program staff have observed that George is "unable to learn anything except the most concrete concepts, is further unable to synthesize and learn from his experiences and further is generally unable to process logical thinking and subsequently reach productive conclusions.'' Among other things, George "doesn't really understand how to get along with other people on any more than a basic concrete level, involving exchange of goods and services.'' As a result, George

> has been observed on numerous occasions to involve himself in the trade or transfer of material goods with other inmates...with the same predictable results. Usually, he very quickly over-extends himself financially, and when he is unable to withstand the pressure of repaying his financial debt or when he is unable to withstand the pressure of the person to whom he is indebted, he ordinarily acts out in some way,

Once George is bailed out (or once he has survived the consequences of ill-advised chronic trading and gambling), he invariably renews his self-defeating financial career, alternating between contriteness, emotional breakdowns, and dramatic explosions of impotent rage. Given no evidence of change, therapeutic staff understandably feel that their program, which is designed to achieve personal impact, is wasted on George. They consequently demand his transfer as often as they can. Unfortunately, no alternative plausible placement comes to anyone's mind.

Ben has recently left our state prison system after serving four years of a seven-year prison sentence. His disciplinary record is studded with preemptive fights and threats against staff. Three months into Ben's sentence, for example, an entry charges him as follows:

> you were seen with a "large push broom" and you were holding it over your head. You were expounding loud sounds and directed your anger to the employees. You were attempting to incite other inmates to riot and hurt the officers. But before you were able to assault employees, another inmate disarmed you of the broom.

> You were ordered to return to your room but refused. Only after additional officers arrived on the scene did you return to your room. ...You resisted being pat frisked and handcuffed....

Between such emotionally charged prison disturbances, other incidents are recorded that have a different quality. Some are self-destructive incidents (entries such as "threatened to cut up— counseled and released," "fire in cell"), but most are self-insulating incidents — they reflect Ben's reluctance to leave his cell for program involvement (notations such as "did not go to gym," "refused to work," "skipped school").

A few weeks prior to the push-broom incident — two months after Ben's entry into the system — he was seen by a psychiatrist, who observed that Ben was "mildly depressed with vague reference to auditory hallucinations." In the interview transcript, Ben is reported as saying that "he could not take the pressure of population in the block." He expressed fear of the inmates and correction officers around him. But also (insightfully, as it happens) Ben "expressed the desire to be in a set up where there are not too many people around him." Within days, Ben was again observed "depressed, nervous and crying," and *on the day prior to the pushbroom incident* he was referred

> because of an episode of depression during which time he made threats to "kill himself before others do it." *Inquiry...revealed that he was approached by other inmates in homosexual relationships and felt depressed and anxious about this.* (The finding proves crucial.) [Emphasis added.]

One week later, Ben's disciplinary record was reviewed with him, and he observed (again, insightfully) "that he [always] felt depressed prior to getting into trouble." The sequence (feeling of pressure and depression leading to ideas of reference and explosions) was to repeat itself time after time during Ben's prison stay, including in several self-destructive episodes: the first of these occurred after all of Ben's belongings were stolen by fellow-inmates; in the second, officers "confirmed the staff's opinion that Ben was being pressured by Smith and that as a result of this pressure he decompensated to the point where he became extremely paranoid and eventually suicidal."

Like George, Ben is kept afloat in prison through placement in a special ameliorative program, with the evidence suggesting (as staff put it) "that if Ben were to be transferred to general population at this time, he would be unable to cope with the pressures of prison life and as a result he would decompensate to the point where he could no longer function." Unfortunately, even special programs have their pressures. Ben therefore indulges in numerous "sudden violent attacks against individuals who he 'thought' were going to hurt him...though investigation of the incidents failed to reveal any basis in fact to Ben's assumptions that he was being threatened by the man he attacked." Only in complete isolation (keeplock) did Ben's behavior prove exemplary.

In Ben's case, the relationship between his disturbance and disruptiveness is direct; under stress, Ben's tenuous controls give way. As observed by an interviewing psychiatrist, "when Ben is sick, he becomes paranoid and does not get along with people and causes fights."

Dave has served eight years of a life sentence, and he has accumulated a long, variegated, and serious disciplinary record. Dave has on numerous occasions been seen by prison psychiatrists, who have maintained him—very much at his own request—on psychotropic medication, tranquilizers, and sleeping pills. Dave's psychiatric stock in trade are fear, (demonstrable) anxiety, depression, and (alleged) insomnia. These commodities are systematically used to secure medication, favorable program recommendations, and ameliorations of custody. Dave's level of disturbance is real; in the words of a classification analyst, "he obviously has deep psychological, emotional problems;" a psychiatrist notes, "this man is in a constant anxiety state since his admission to the penal system." But equally real is the flagrant manipulation pattern based on Dave's disturbance—particularly, the threatened risk of completing suicide.

Dave's folder is studded with injunctions to custody by mental health staff, such as "I have notified the security person to keep a close watch on Dave because he may try to hurt himself again;" "this man should be considered a definite suicidal risk....I would suggest to treat him gently and avoid punishment at this stage"; "in view of the inmate's past history of [suicidal behavior] and mental disorder, it seems advisable to the writer not to place this man under undue pressure. Otherwise, it is difficult to predict what this man will do. Moreover, I believe he should be given back his kitchen job...one of his major grievances;" and "I feel if at all possible, he should be out of the metal shop, but of course this is up to the assignment board."

There are also notations such as "patient manipulates environment in order to get habit forming drugs"; and "he has been on Dalmane for over 7 years in other institutions and certainly is addicted to it. I feel this man is manipulating to get Dalmane"; and "diagnostic impression: addiction to Valium and Dalmane"; these notations appear in the folder in the later stages of Dave's career.

Because of Dave's combination of pathology and manipulativeness, he is viewed as a test of prison and mental health staff forbearance. His advent at one assignment (the mess hall) is greeted with the entry "the word has spread far and wide that this man is a creep." The document concludes "as long as inmate behaves himself in the mess hall, I have no objection to his being there, of course; but once he starts to act up, I probably will recommend that he see the psychiatrist." This sequence (like others) ends with Dave "acting up," seeing the psychiatrist, and making the best of his chronically bad situation.

My last example, Frank, recently completed a checkered nine-year prison term, including 18 institutional transfers (five to mental health settings) and 80-plus disciplinary infractions. Upon entry into the system a decade ago, Frank initiated an impressive sequence of disruptiveness—incidents such as "throwing food at an officer"; "broke bed—used pieces for weapons—smashed light fixture in cell," alternating with incidents of self-insulation. With respect to the latter, there are report entries such as "he refused to come out of his cell today," and "the Sgt. informed me that Frank was just standing in the center of his cell"; and "he came up to the desk and mumbled something inaudibly...he refused to speak...and he left."

Frank's paradoxic flight-fight pattern has been in evidence, in unabated cycles, for nine years. Frank's explosions are so frequent that they include his diagnostic interviews. During one interview Frank was offered an apple (a generous gesture or a projective test borrowed from Genesis?) and "after receiving the apple from the psychiatrist, he washed it in the sink and then quickly turned around and threw it at the facility psychiatrist. Frank then proceeded promptly to slap the facility psychiatrist about his face." Other interviews move from unresponsiveness and incoherence into towering rages.

Frank's explosions have been punctuated with after-hours yelling, throwing and smashing of objects, and persecutory beliefs freely (and loudly) expressed. Such behavior has contributed to Frank's growing unpopularity among peers, as well as among staff. One forgets that most of Frank's time is occupied with episodes of quiet restlessness, muteness, unresponsiveness, and inactivity (including refusals to eat), and reports of quiet hallucinations (such as Frank "hears voices which tell him, 'Brush your hair.'").

Now Frank is back in the community, and we do not know what he is up to. We do know that only three months prior to Frank's release, he "punched another inmate without provocation;" he also "bangs on the walls while taking a shower and shows sudden mood swings from laughter to hostility and agitation...standing for long periods of time in one place...sloppy, untidy and unkempt in his appearance...was delusional." At the expiration of his sentence (three months later), Frank had to be released. A final entry in Frank's folder reads:

> Frank was discharged (maximum) from prison and did not want to leave the institution. Dr. W., the institutional psychiatrist, tried to talk to the inmate and the inmate struck him in the side of the face, knocking his glasses off. Inmate was requested by Department of Corrections personnel to leave the premises on several occasions. He would leave temporarily and kept returning. Eventually...the inmate was arrested for harassment and given 15 days in [the local] County Jail.

The irony of this scene has to do with Frank's inability to manage not only the prison situation, but its absence.

Frank is admittedly an uninviting client, and so are Ed, George, Ben, and thousands of others who are similarly situated. Such persons are as uninviting when they terrorize school yards and prison yards as when they contaminate neighborhoods or vegetate under medication in hospitals.

The uninvitingness of setting and person, of course, are mutual. We cannot cope with Frank who cannot cope with his world—or at least, with the settings that he disrupts and disturbs. Frank's settings can—within limits—help themselves. They can expel their Franks and Eds and Georges (always with cause and to other settings) or secrete them to neutralize them in inhouse places of exile, for statutory terms. These are holding patterns and they are unstably, warily, and uncomfortably sustained.

The Franks and Georges who find their world inhospitable have no recourse. To Ed, Frank, and their peers, social settings are dumping grounds, variations on inhospitality, always painful, uncongenial, mystifying, irritating, and harsh. The options Frank and his peers have are non-options—to alternately lash out and retreat, to fight without hope of winning, and to flee without hope of surviving.

To escape the dilemma we must face Frank's despair, which requires suspending our concern with Frank's obnoxiousness, with the "management problem" Frank presents. Frank's bus must somehow be made to stop. It must stop long enough so that we can resonate to the bankruptcy that underlies Frank's disruptiveness. This means that we must understand Frank's cornered explosions as well as the self-insulating efforts we conventionally associate with psychological extremity.

Eventually, we must generate new ameliorative settings and restorative settings for Frank and Ed and Ben. We must care for these walking wounded, for men driven to extremes by a despair that transcends and surpasses the range of the familiar—of mental illness in its more passive and congenial manifestations.

Notes

[1]National Institute of Corrections, *NIC Program Plan for the Fiscal Year 1983* (Washington, D.C., July 1982).

[2]R. Wilson, "Who Will Care for the 'Mad and Bad'?" 6 *Corrections Magazine* 5-17, at 8 (1980).

[3]R.A. Freeman, S. Dinitz, and J.P. Conrad, "A Look at the Dangerous Offender and Society's Efforts to Control Him," *American Journal of Correction*, January-February 1977, pp. 25-31, at 30.

[4]D. Reveron, "Mentally Ill—and Behind Bars," *APA Monitor*, March 1982, pp. 10-11.

[5]Wilson, *supra* note 2, at 14.

[6]V.L. Agee, "The Closed Adolescent Treatment Center," *Utah Correctional Association Annual Conference*, September 10, 1981.

[7]Wilson, *supra* note 2, at 8.

[8]Mecklenberg Correctional Center, "Mecklenberg Treatment Program," mimeographed (Boydton, Virginia, December 1, 1981).

[9]L.B. Myers and G.W. Levy, "The Description and Prediction of the Intractable Inmate" (Columbus, Ohio: Battelle, 1973), p. ii; see also, 15 *Journal of Research in Crime and Delinquency* 214-28 (1978).

[10]Myers and Levy, *supra* note 9, at 15 (1973).

[11]*Id.* at 16.

[12]J. Monahan and H.J. Steadman, "Crime and Mental Disorder: an Epidemiological Approach," in *Crime and Justice: An Annual Review of Research,* ed. N. Morris and M.H. Tonry (Chicago: University of Chicago Press, in press).

[13]Wilson, *supra* note 2, at 6.

[14]B.E. Burtch and R.V. Ericson, *The Silent System: An Inquiry into Prisoners Who Commit Suicide* (Toronto, Canada: University of Toronto, 1977), p. 45.

[15]A.C. Smith, "Violence," 134 *British Journal of Psychiatry* 528-29 (1979).

[16]V.L. Quinsey, "Studies in the Reduction of Assaults in a Maximum Security Psychiatric Institution," 25 *Canada's Mental Health* 21-23 (1977).

[17]M.G. Kalogerakis, "The Assaultive Psychiatric Patient," 45 *Psychiatric Quarterly* 372-81 (1971).

[18]H. Toch, "Toward an Interdisciplinary Approach to Criminal Violence," 71 *Journal of Criminal Law and Criminology* 646-53, at 649 (1980).

[19]H.L. Kozol, R.J. Boucher, and F.R. Garofalo, "The Diagnosis and Treatment of Dangerousness," 18 *Crime and Delinquency* 371-92, at 383 (1973).

35

Growing Old Behind Bars

Sol Chaneles

William David Smith is one of the oldest of some 43,000 inmates currently serving time in the federal prison system. He claims to be 84, although prison records say he was born in 1916. On his birthday in April, he received no greeting cards, no telephone calls, no birthday cake. I was his first visitor in a year and we celebrated with cold cheeseburgers and soft drinks from vending machines in the visitors' lounge of the United States Penitentiary in Terre Haute, Indiana.

Smith, who was transferred in June to the Federal Medical Center in Rochester, Minnesota, has spent 22 years in state and federal prisons, in stretches of 8 months to 6 years, for robbery, grand larceny and kidnapping, among other crimes. Like many chronic offenders, he has a positive self-image to go with his long record. The image shows in the stories he tells about himself. "There was this bank job in I-o-way. I spent six months casing it before I made the hit. I knew where city and county cops would be. For the next few months I lived real good and partied every night." He can poke fun at himself, too. "I hit a supermarket for $11,000 and hid the money bag in a wooded area a few miles away. When I went back a few weeks later to pick up the loot, a groundhog had dug a hole and hauled the bag away . . . like a common thief." He takes his greatest pride in what he sees as his ability to outwit

Source: *Psychology Today*, Vol. 21, No. 10 (October 1987), pp. 47, 49, 51. Reprinted with the permission of the publisher.

the law. He laughed when he told me: "If I got caught for everything I did, they'd hang me."

There was even a touch of professional and paternal pride when he described another crime. "My son, my grandson and me robbed a bank near where my son lived just out of Tul-see, Oklahoma. The job went off all right, but there was so many people in the bank who recognized my son. I told him it was dumb to rob a bank in your own hometown. They're both doing time in the federal prison at El Reno."

Despite thinning hair and a quiet, reflective manner of speaking, Smith looks much younger than his age as he stoically lists his infirmities: coronary problems, arthritis in both legs, failing eyesight, most teeth missing and "a touch of diabetes." Inmate number 024-45030 is one of an increasing number of prisoners growing old behind bars.

Several broad social and psychological trends have combined to produce this graying of our prisons. They include: the overall aging of our population, combined with an even faster-rising level of expectations among older people; a "get-tough" policy that has resulted in longer mandatory sentences; and increased normalization of life inside prisons.

Elderly people, in general, are living longer and living better as their income increases faster than that of any other age group. The image of a "tattered coat upon a stick," as Yeats put it, has been replaced by one of vigorous men and women in jogging suits. Detachment, serenity and wisdom are no longer the ultimate virtues for elderly Americans.

Tax reductions, rent control, subsidized senior citizen housing and recreational centers, increased public advocacy, Medicare, pension guarantees and increasing Social Security benefits—all have helped bring the elderly back into the mainstream with a vengeance. They are more physically able to get what they believe they deserve, and more seem willing to use force to get it. Figures on admissions to state prisons, for example, show that, compared to younger people, a much higher percentage of older people are being incarcerated for murder and manslaughter (see table).

Other statistics confirm that older people are committing more serious crimes than in the past. From 1976 to 1985, the arrest rate for rape committed by men over 65 increased 155 percent. For men 60 to 64, the increase was 112 percent. During the same 10 years, the rate of arrests among the same two groups increased 39 percent and 60 percent for all sex offenses, and 30 percent and 33 percent for larceny-theft.

There were nearly 600,000 inmates 18 and over in our federal, state, county and municipal prisons on January 1,1987. According to my estimates, about 10 percent of these were over 50 and facing the prospect of release only when they are well past 60. By the year 2000, if present

Admissions to State Prisons, 1982

AGE AT ADMISSION

Offense	Total	Less than 18 years	18-24 years	25-34 years	35-44 years	45-54 years	55-64 years	65 years and over
All Offenses	100.0%	100.0%	100.0%	100.0%	100.0%	100.0%	100.0%	100.0%
Murder	4.3	4.5	3.1	4.2	6.3	8.8	11.0	18.4
Manslaughter	2.6	1.7	1.6	2.6	4.3	5.1	9.8	16.8
Rape	2.6	3.8	2.4	2.6	2.9	2.9	2.5	1.0
Robbery	17.6	28.4	20.1	17.1	10.9	7.6	4.6	2.6
Assault	6.6	4.8	5.7	6.9	8.1	9.1	9.1	8.7
Burglary	27.2	36.2	34.9	23.2	15.6	11.3	7.3	4.1
Larceny	10.4	8.6	10.5	10.2	11.1	10.7	7.8	3.6
Auto Theft	1.8	2.3	2.1	1.4	1.3	1.5	0.9	2.0
Forgery, Fraud, Embezzlement	6.2	1.4	4.3	7.5	8.6	9.4	7.5	4.1
Drugs	8.0	0.8	5.1	10.5	12.0	9.8	8.0	9.7
Public Order	5.3	2.3	3.1	5.6	8.9	13.7	19.8	17.3
Other Offenses	7.4	4.6	6.4	7.7	9.4	9.4	11.0	11.7
Number of Admissions*	100,814	2,674	44,423	37,209	11,507	3,696	1,109	196

*Includes other sexual assault, other violent offenses, other property offenses, and miscellaneous offenses.

Source: United States Department of Justice, Bureau of Justice Statistics, Special Report: "Prison Admissions and Releases, 1982."

trends continue, the number of long-term prisoners over 50 should be around 125,000, with 40,000 to 50,000 over 65.

Even these figures only hint at the real increase in crime by the elderly. I believe the facts are obscured by a double standard of law enforcement toward older men and women. Except for the most serious crimes, such as murder, police and prosecutors are inclined to overlook offenses by the elderly, especially women. They often don't make arrests, or if they do, the charges are dismissed. There are probably no more than a thousand women over 65 in U.S. prisons.

Even so, more old people are being sent to prison today and more young people under 30 are getting long mandatory sentences that will keep them imprisoned until they are old. This does not mean that we face a tidal wave of crime. Rather, these facts reflect the "get-tough" policy that emerged following the Vietnam years. Public acceptance of the policy has helped overcome resistance to committing large sums for new prisons. At the current rate of construction, about a thousand state and county prisons will be built by the year 2000, at a cost that has been estimated as high as $200,000 a cell. These figures do not include the cost of new federal prison facilities.

The increased number of prisoners of all ages is less a result of more arrests and more convictions than it is of longer sentences and vastly increased use of mandatory minimum sentences. The increased number of older first-time offenders is less a result of any policy to get tough on the elderly than it is of the fact that older people are more active, more prone to taking what they want. Their greater visibility also makes them more prone to arrest and conviction.

A third reason more old people will grow very old in prison and more young people will grow old there is that conditions on the inside have become, over the last decade or so, closer to those on the outside. Although there are a few prisons in which rich, older mobsters and former government officials live a reasonably pleasant life at minimum-security facilities, most prisons are still harsh and often unthinkingly cruel environments. But the horrors of the past have been reduced to some extent by prison reforms and court decisions upholding the rights of prisoners to decent living conditions.

As a result, many social patterns of the free community now continue behind prison walls. The intense stimulus deprivation of the past has often been replaced by informational abundance, especially for older offenders. In many cases, there are uncensored television sets in each cell and current motion pictures available on video.

New Jersey is a proving ground for what is taking place nationally concerning crime by the elderly and the aging of the prison population. The state has responded to the increase in violent crime with a stern get-tough policy: mandatory minimum sentences of 30 to 50 years for some crimes and authorization of hundreds of millions of dollars for new prisons. New Jersey has also developed long-range plans for a sizable geriatric prisoner population, one unlike any seen in the past.

Four kinds of convicts make up this population. The first, such as Smith, is the chronic offender who has grown old during one major sentence or in a steady series of shorter stretches. The second group consists of those under 30 who have been sentenced to long mandatory terms. The characteristics of these prisoners are clear. My research suggests that among those who will be at least 60 to 70 before they are released, 80 percent have led an actively abusive life involving drugs, alcohol and hallucinogens. Many have been intensely promiscuous bisexuals. Most place high value on physical strength, aggressiveness, violence and predatory behavior expressed through gang membership.

One prison official referred to these young inmates, who face a virtual lifetime in prison, as "jiveass, drug-oriented prisoners." Another described them as "jitterbug celebrities proud of their 50-year mandatory minimum." But without the support of drugs, the drug economy and gang crime, their bravado soon turns to depression and anger. They realize that they may never again walk on a city street and that they face abandonment by family and friends. Their rage often turns into exploitative behavior towards elderly prisoners.

Allen Benowitz, age 40, is serving a 30-year sentence for homicide, with, he says, "only 25 more to go, unless I work harder on myself." Benowitz is the third type of geriatric prisoner, the middle-aged man, often a repeater, who probably won't be released until he is very old. By working hard, he means attending group therapy sessions regularly. Through them and countless hours of introspection, he has "finally come to understand who I am and what my potential is. I have mellowed. When I get out I'll know how to use my creative energies."

Benowitz's chief motivation for making himself into a different person is to win favorable parole consideration after his mandatory minimum of 15 years. "That's only 10 more years," he exclaims, with optimism sparkling in his blue eyes. He will not admit to himself that people convicted of homicide are often not paroled after serving the mandatory minimum. But he does all he can by keeping to himself, avoiding trouble with guards and inmates, keeping fit by running and lifting weights and admitting responsibility for his crimes.

Benowitz, at 40, looks considerably older. The only son of Polish-Jewish immigrants, he has been in trouble most of his life. After he was sent to Trenton State Prison five years ago, his wife divorced him. "She just disappeared with our two sons, aged 14 and 12. She must have gone to Texas or someplace like that and changed her name." He assures me that he will soon make an effort to locate his sons and work out a relationship with them.

Sam Malone represents the fourth type of elderly prisoner, the convict who is serving time for his first serious offense, often murder. A youthful 72-year-old black man who was born in Georgia and raised in Newark, New Jersey, Malone has a quick, philosophical turn of mind. He is proud of his accomplishments and ability, eager to describe how much money he saved and invested wisely during a 40-year career in construction. He repeats, obsessively, that he will win his release because he can prove that the prosecutor made a number of serious, reversible errors during his trial. Malone was convicted of shooting and killing a handicapped 84-year-old neighbor in a senior citizens' residence and received a mandatory sentence of 30 years.

The way he describes his life inside echoes what many prison personnel say about old-timers. "Most never get mail or visits," they say. "They are loners who go their own way." "They are usually comfortable in a secure environment, although they are constantly hustled and cheated by younger inmates.''

Malone, a widower for the past eight years, receives only a few letters from his 24 children and grandchildren, most of whom live less than an hour from the prison. He speaks to them occasionally on the telephone. With no real work assignments, he and other elderly inmates are allowed to feel retired, to go about the prison without the restrictions placed on young inmates. Malone keeps up with the news by watching television in his cell and looks forward to better times. "I've lived a good life,'' he says. "I'm relaxed. I'm happy.'' On the wall of his cell he has taped a number of sayings, including his favorite: "I'm doin' bad and don't need help.''

One thing that makes life inside prison go smoothly for older prisoners is having money to spend on themselves and others. Benowitz's mother helps him out. Smith and Malone have savings and Social Security payments to draw on. Benowitz told me that when young prisoners gamble with older ones and lose, they refuse to pay their debts. When the older men lose, the younger ones not only insist on prompt payment but extort much more for late payments. To give themselves better control over their money, Smith and Malone have both arranged to have their benefits sent to friends they can count on outside.

For prisoners over 62 who are receiving Social Security payments, the checks provide a standard of living higher than that enjoyed by nearly all other inmates and bring privileges traditionally enjoyed behind bars only by convicted public officials, business people and mobsters. "With the Social Security,'' Smith says, "I don't have to touch my savings. I usually buy $60 worth of stuff at a time in the commissary. Except for the few cigars I need for myself, I give the rest away in exchange for favors.''

For Malone, the checks are a way to get things that are officially prohibited in prison. "There's a place in one of the blocks we call 'Times Square.' It's run by the young fellows who use most of their time building up their physique. You can buy nearly anything you want there — sex, drugs, booze.''

Although a federal law that took effect in 1984 requires suspension of payments to all new prisoners convicted of a felony, the Social Security Administration doesn't know how many payments have been stopped. While the law is probably being well enforced in federal prisons, it is unlikely that the states are complying fully; they are traditionally reluctant to return money to the federal treasury.

Elderly inmates, such as Smith and Malone, who aren't confined to a wheelchair or bed are expected to participate in such routine activities as going to meals, outdoor recreation, tidying the cell and clean-up tasks.

"Even if," as Texas prison statistician Larry Farnsworth put it, "all it means is sweeping a two-foot square of corridor." But the growing number of elderly inmates who require more-than-average care is causing administrators to consider the need for special facilities.

By the year 2000, the number of people over 65 is expected to increase 21 percent in the general population. In prisons, I estimate the increase will be 50 percent. Many of these 85 and over, the fastest-growing segment of the elderly population, will require complex, round-the clock health care, creating new cost burdens.

According to William Kelsey, health care administrator for Pennsylvania's Department of Corrections, the money spent for prison health services in that state soared from $1.23 million in 1973 to $16.7 million in 1986. Eyeglasses and dentures are provided and even open-heart surgery is performed when needed. Large prisons with infirmaries have set aside a section to care for elderly inmates dying of cancer and inoperable heart conditions. Some of the wards house elderly inmates suffering from Alzheimer's disease and organic brain disorders.

While the federal prison system maintains hospital at Springfield, Missouri, that cares for some elderly inmates, it is not really equipped for gerontological care. No research has been done within the federal prison system to gauge the future requirements of its aging population.

New York State's Commissioner of Correctional Services, Thomas A. Coughlin III, states a position shared by many prison officials: "The elderly prisoners are in fact a minority. In general, healthy inmates over the age of 60 get only what other inmates get — work, visits, recreation — nothing special because of their age."

36

The Forgotten Few
Juvenile Female Offenders

Ilene R. Bergsmann*

Adolescent female offenders have been described as a "specialty item in a mass market" (Grimes, 1983). Generally overlooked and frequently ignored, relegated to a footnote, and perceived as sexually deviant and in need of protection, these young women have received scant attention from members of the juvenile and criminal justice communities.

What about the juvenile female offender? Who pays attention to her special needs? Unfortunately, the courts and law enforcement pay too much attention for the wrong reasons, while litigators, legislators, and juvenile correctional administrators pay too little attention, also for the wrong reasons. During the past 25 years, few research studies, congressional inquiries, or lawsuits have focused on juvenile female offenders. Even when research is conducted on juvenile offenders, the data are not disaggregated by sex. When the Bureau of Justice Statistics provides valuable and much-needed data on juveniles in the justice

*This article was written as part of a U.S. Department of Education, Women's Educational Equity Act Program grant to the Council of Chief State School Officers. The author wishes to thank Glenda Partee of the council and Denis Shumate, superintendent of the Youth Center at Beloit, Kansas, for their helpful comments and suggestions on the article.

Source: *Federal Probation*, Vol. 53, No. 1 (March 1989), 73-78

system, one or two tables at most provide information by gender. *Uniform Crime Reports* data published by the Federal Bureau of Investigation also provide little information by gender.

Class action suits based on parity of programs proven effective for adult women to increase their educational and vocational training opportunities while in prison have not been filed on behalf of young women. Questionable correctional policies and practices are all too frequently the subject of policy debates within departments of youth services while in adult departments of corrections these same procedures have become the subject for litigation (Collins, 1987).

This article addresses the problems of young women in the juvenile justice system, including a description of who the female adolescent offender is, gender bias and stereotyping by correctional educators and administrators, and much-needed policy changes to ensure equitable programs.

Profile of a Juvenile Female Offender

Young women in trouble with the law are typically 16 years old, live in urban ghettos, are high school dropouts, and are victims of sexual and/or physical abuse or exploitation. Most come from single parent families, have experienced foster care placement, lack adequate work and social skills, and are substance abusers. Over half of these adolescent females are black or Hispanic (Bergsmann, 1988; Crawford, 1988; Sarri, 1988).

For youths in secure confinement, property crimes account for nearly 41 percent of all offenses, possession of drugs accounts for nearly 7 percent, status offenses 9 percent, and violent crime 32 percent (Beck, Kline and Greenfield, 1988). Although the number of females in correctional facilities has remained about the same between 1975 and 1985 (17,192 and 17,009, respectively), a shift has occurred between placement in public and private facilities. In 1975, 53 percent of the female youthful offenders were in public institutions; in 1985, only 40 percent were in such institutions (Kline, anticipated 1989).

In a self-report study conducted by the American Correctional Association Task Force on the Female Offender (Crawford, 1988), 62 percent of the juveniles indicated that they were physically abused, 47 percent with 11 or more incidences of abuse. Thirty percent said the abuse began between ages five and nine, another 45 percent said onset occurred between 10 and 14 years of age. In most instances, parents were the primary abusers.

Sexual abuses follow similar but slightly less harsh patterns. Fifty-four percent of the juvenile females were victims of sexual abuse, 40 percent with abuse occurring once or twice, 33 percent with 3 to 10 occurrences. The age of onset of abuse occurred before age 5 in about 16 percent of the youths, from ages 5 to 9 for nearly 33 percent, and from ages 10 to 14 for nearly 40 percent. Fathers, stepfathers, and uncles accounted for nearly 40 percent of the attackers. Other research conducted on the national, state, and local levels show both higher and lower figures than those cited by Crawford. All, however, document the close connection between physical/sexual abuse and running away from home (Geller and Ford-Somma, 1979; Chesney-Lind, 1987).

Although most of the females were not convicted of drug abuse, self-report data indicate that they are frequent users of controlled substances, with alcohol, marijuana, speed, and cocaine the most frequent drugs used (Crawford, 1988).

Sarri predicts that 90 percent of all youthful female offenders will be single heads of households who will spend 80 percent of their income on housing and child care (1988). Yet, a majority of these youths, who have failed to obtain a high school diploma or a GED and are educationally disadvantaged, also suffer from societal biases against women and minorities.

A majority (64 percent) of female juvenile offenders in secure facilities indicate that a member(s) of their family has been incarcerated. Most (80 percent) also report being runaways. Contrary to staff perceptions, over half report growing up with love and acceptance. Typical of most teenagers, over 80 percent say that peers and friends influence them (Crawford, 1988).

Many teen-age female offenders suffer from low self-esteem. Self-report data show that over half have attempted suicide, 64 percent of whom have tried more than once. They express reasons such as being depressed, life is too painful to continue, and no one cares (Crawford, 1988). While offenders are not a precise mirror of young women in society in the depths of their feelings of poor self-worth, studies demonstrate that lack of self-esteem is generally a common problem among young women. In a study begun in 1981 to measure the self-confidence of high school valedictorians, salutatorians, and honor students, males and females in roughly the same percentages believed that they had "far above average" intelligence at graduation. Four years later as college seniors, 25 percent of the males continued to share this opinion while none of the females did (Epperson, 1988). If women with above average intelligence, leadership ability, and the opportunity to achieve higher education experienced feelings of low self-esteem, it is not too difficult to understand how young women from broken homes, urban ghettos, poor schools, and abusive families develop feelings of despair and hopelessness about themselves and their chances for success.

Gender Bias and Stereotyping in the Juvenile Justice System

Differential treatment of females and males prevails in the juvenile justice system. Sexual promiscuity, including immoral conduct, has prevailed for much of the last 100 years as one basis for locking up juvenile females. Girls are expected to conform to traditional roles within the family and society. They should be inconspicuous; passive in their dealings with others and take few, if any, risks; and obedient to their parents, teachers, and elders. Boys, on the other hand, are expected to be rowdy, boisterous, and get into trouble now and then. They should be aggressive, independent, and strive for great achievements. As Chesney-Lind explains, "From sons, defiance of authority is almost normative whereas from daughters it may be seen as an extremely serious offense. And because so much of the adolescent female sex role evolved to control female sexual experimentation so as to guarantee virginity upon marriage, such defiance is virtually always cast in sexual terms" (Chesney-Lind, 1978).

The courts view female adolescents as "more vulnerable and in need of protection than boys" (Grimes, 1983) and thus have used their "discretionary powers in the service of traditional sex roles . . . (while they) appear to be less concerned with the protection of female offenders than the protection of the sexual status quo" (Datesman, Scarpitti and Stephenson in Sarri, 1983). Of all the juveniles who appeared in court in 1984, females represented 45 percent of all status offender cases compared with only 19 percent of all delinquency cases. Of this 45 percent, 62 percent were runaways (Snyder et al., 1987).

While young women comprised 14 percent of all juveniles in custody in 1985, they represented 52 percent of all status offenders (Bureau of Justice Statistics, 1986). *Uniform Crime Reports* data show that 18 percent of all female juvenile arrests are for curfew and loitering violations and running away, yet only 6.4 percent of male juvenile arrests are for these offenses (Federal Bureau of Investigation, 1987). The 1987 Children in Custody survey indicates that the number of female status offenders has increased since 1985 while the number of male status offenders has declined (Allen-Hagen, 1988). Today, less than 2 percent (1.6 percent) of males are held in training schools for the commission of status offenses compared to 9.3 percent of all females (Beck, Kline and Greenfield, 1988).

Parents, law enforcement officers, and school administrators are inextricably linked to young women's contacts with the law. Often parents use the courts as a route to mending family feuds or as a last resort for addressing problems with promiscuous and sexually active daughters. Because judges have similar parental concerns, they tend to react sympathetically. Rarely are the courts employed as a quick fix for sons who exhibit similar sexual behaviors.

Female sexual activity also frequently becomes part of the record that judges and other court officers review, including levels and types of sexual activity and numbers of children, regardless of the offense for which they are being tried. According to several judges in Missouri, such information is almost never found in delinquent male records (Grimes, 1983).

Police contribute to the differential treatment of these adolescent females as well. Not only do they tend to arrest more females for sexual and relational activities than for criminal conduct, they also promote a different set of sanctions for them. Dating back to the 1950s, research has shown that girls were more likely than boys to be: 1) referred to social or welfare agencies rather than being released from custody; 2) placed on informal probation supervision; and 3) placed in secure treatment facilities for the commission of status offenses (Chesney-Lind, 1982). Females arrested for status offenses often remain in detention longer than males, according to a Minnesota study in which 82.9 percent of all status offenders held beyond the statutory limit were females (Osbun and Rode, 1982). And, 12 percent of all status offenders placed in secure detention are females contrasted with 9 percent for males (Snyder et al., 1987).

Self-report data, on the other hand, indicate that males engage in at least the same amount of sexual activity as females but rarely are arrested for such behavior. Adolescent females in self-report studies indicate that their engagement in criminal activity is greater than what court intake records show. If these studies are accurate, the number of females involved in criminal activity would remain below that of males, but the types of offenses for which they would be arrested would be much the same (Geller and Ford-Somma, 1979; Sarri, 1983; Chesney-Lind, 1987). As Chesney-Lind maintains, "... it is reasonable to assume that some bias (either unofficial or official) is present within the juvenile justice system and functions to filter out those young women guilty of criminal offenses while retaining those women suspected of sexual misconduct" (1982).

A third source of referral to juvenile courts is through the school system. In a study conducted in nine public and parochial high schools in the Midwest, 11 percent of all court referrals come from the schools (Sarri, 1983). These youths have become so disruptive that the teaching and administrative staff are no longer able to contain them.

Administrative Disinterest

Like their adult counterparts, adjudicated juvenile females find themselves with few programs and services to meet their needs for developing socialization and life skills and an awareness of the world of work and their role in it. In the community, services are geared to preventing further physical or sexual harm but not to developing vocational and life skills (National Council of Jewish Women, 1984).

In secure confinement, the amount of staff time to work with these adolescents is limited to the average length of stay of 8 months (Bergsmann, 1988). Yet, it is during incarceration that these young women should be acquiring some of the tools they will need for economic independence and personal growth. The barriers to providing equitable treatment of these females come from several sources: 1) the traditional view of young women held by many female and male correctional administrators and staff; 2) the small number of females who, because of their limited population, are housed in co-correctional (co-educational) facilities; 3) limited resources that are mostly channeled to the males who constitute 93 percent of the incarcerated juvenile population; and 4) lack of program and service integration among state and local education, health, labor, and youth services agencies.

When educationally disadvantaged delinquent females enter the juvenile justice system, they also encounter administrative resistance in the provision of appropriate resources and programs to meet their unique needs. Departments of corrections and youth services rarely, if ever, designate a central office position to coordinate female programs and services (Ryan, 1984). Co-educational institutions are often the result of financial/administrative decisions based on the small number of females and the large number of male offenders. Often, the young women are imposed on all-male facilities in which policy and procedure frequently are not written from an equity perspective and where programs and services are more appropriate for males than females.

Workforce Changes in the 1990s

The traditional or stereotypical orientation of many youth services managers towards delinquent women is a great disservice not only to these young women but also to society. Major economic and workforce changes are anticipated during the 1990s, changes that will most certainly impact women and minorities. Consider the major trends for our economic future that the Hudson Institute forecasts for the year 2000: a growing economy, fueled by an increase in service-related jobs over manufacturing; a workforce that is "growing slowly, becoming older, more female and more disadvantaged," as well as minority; and jobs that require higher skill levels than those of today (Johnston, 1987). In other words, highly skilled employees will have greater employment options while the least skilled will face greater joblessness.

The 1990s will see more women and minorities entering the labor pool. Nearly 66 percent of all new workers will be women, many of whom will be poor single heads of households; non-whites will constitute 29 percent of the new workforce. Although women will continue to work in jobs that pay less than those for men, they also will have greater opportunities for high-paying professional and technical positions. And, even with entry-level positions, employers who are facing a shrinking labor pool are beginning to invest time and money in finding and training new workers. Unless women offenders, who are disproportionately minority, receive sufficient education and training to perform the more complex jobs projected for the coming years, our economy will suffer and their poverty, dependence, and criminal activity will escalate (Johnston, 1987; Packer, 1988).

As jobs become more sophisticated, young women offenders, who have minimal occupational skills, will find it increasingly difficult, if not impossible, to become employed in an occupation with more than poverty-level wages. Many are high school dropouts, and nearly 26 percent suffer educational disadvantages, including learning disabilities and emotional problems (Bergsmann, 1988). Their exposure to vocational education is often limited to traditional programs of cosmetology, office skills, and food services. The Department of Labor's statistics on women, especially women and girls who are minorities, are not encouraging. In 1984, the unemployment rate for black female teenagers was almost three times as great as for white female teens, and for Hispanic women unemployment rates were almost 4 percent above the rates of all women (Council of Chief State School Officers, 1986).

Policy Considerations

The inequitable treatment of juvenile female offenders is often exacerbated by the lack of adequate social and life skills programs and pre-vocational and vocational training programs that are critical for these youths in order to achieve economic and emotional self-sufficiency. Recognizing this problem, the American Correctional Association (ACA) has called for both juvenile and adult women offenders to receive programs comparable with those provided to males, as well as services that meet the unique needs of females. Integral to its policy on "Female Offender Services" is the provision for "access to a full range of work and programs designed to expand economic and social roles of women, with emphasis on education; career counseling and exploration of non-traditional as well as traditional vocational training; relevant life skills, including parenting and social and economic assertiveness; and pre-release and work/education release programs" (1986).

The Correctional Education Association (CEA) concurs with the need for appropriate education for women offenders. Its standards, promulgated in 1988, include a mandatory standard on educational equity which states that, "Institutions housing females provide educational programs, services and access to community programs and resources equitable with those provided for males within the system." This means that small numbers and thus high per capita costs of program delivery cannot be used to justify a lack of equitable programs that are defined "in terms of range and relevance of options, quality of offerings, staff qualifications, instructional materials and equipment, and curriculum design." Pennsylvania is the first state to use the standards to assess the status of its educational programs. A program to enforce the standards is being developed to ensure that all participating jurisdictions would be required to provide equitable educational programs for juvenile female offenders.

Troubled and delinquent offenders have often been the stepchildren of the educational system. Today, these offenders fall within the "at-risk" category of youths whose multiple problems have made their odds of educational success difficult at best. Many of these teenagers have failed academically, been chronic truants, and when they do go to school, frequently act out. Unfortunately, when they enter the juvenile justice system, education, one of their greatest needs and surest routes for entering the economic and social mainstream becomes second to security, which takes preference above all else.

A Bill of Educational Rights for incarcerated youth has been called for (Price and Vitolo, 1988) which seeks "to establish minimum standards for protecting their rights and assuring them of an education program designed to meet their needs." Included in this Bill of Educational Rights are the rights to: 1) "... a public education fostering (youth) development as productive members of society" guaranteed by Federal policy that mandates education for all juvenile offenders; 2) a curriculum that "emphasize(s) the core subjects and skills" including basic academics and independent living skills that use a competency-based system for awarding credits; 3) "a thorough educational assessment" that appropriately identifies and addresses different learning styles and needs; 4) education on "affective development" to focus on positive self-esteem and interpersonal relationships; 5) special education services; 6) state-certified instructors to design a curriculum consistent with the community's educational standards; 7) an educational program that meets "recognized community standards leading to a diploma" in order that youths can continue their education on release; and 8) transition services on release to assist with reintegration back to school, entry into a vocational education program, or job placement.

Inherent in this Bill of Educational Rights are many important elements for delinquent female offenders. These youths need academic encouragement, counseling to improve their self-esteem, introduction to the world of work to encourage them to consider high paying careers, vocational education courses, independent living skills, and transition planning and assistance.

Institutions interested in implementing the provisions of the ACA's policy on female offenders, the CEA standards, including the standard on equity, and the provisions of the Bill of Educational Rights could do so by: 1) developing equitable educational opportunities for adolescent females delivered through a continuum of interrelated programs and 2) establishing a collaborative educational program that links youth service staff with employees in the state departments of education, labor, and employment and training both inside and outside the training school.

To achieve pre-vocational, vocational, health, and life skills, a comprehensive, coordinated service delivery system must be in place within the institution and continue through transition back into the community. Such services include testing and evaluation; pre-vocational and vocational training; independent living and social skills; health education, including human sexuality; individual and group counseling; substance abuse programs and pre-release planning, including a network of support in the community.

Underlying any fundamental change in the way these youths perceive themselves is the need to raise their self-esteem. Contributing to many of these girls' involvement in the juvenile justice system is their poor self-esteem, brought on by abuse and/or exploitation at home, poor academic achievement, little assistance from teachers and administrators and minimal school involvement (Finn, Stott and Zarichny, 1988) and the myriad of social and economic problems in which they have grown up. They tend to underestimate their abilities; fail to consider a full range of career opportunities; become pregnant and then a single parent; perform poorly in school; be overly dependent on young men; fear success and assertiveness; and have an excessive need for external approval (Agonito and Moon, no date). Training school staff, not just educators, must work with these young women to enhance self-esteem through academic and vocational education programs that instill self-confidence and staff-offender interactions based on acceptance and approval.

More subtle, but equally compelling, is the need for staff members to be gender neutral in their interactions with all youthful offenders. For example, teachers need to design curricular materials that incorporate women and minorities. They should employ classroom strategies that encourage female participation, e.g., females, especially minority females, need more "wait time" than other students during classroom interaction. In co-correctional facilities, females should be included fairly in all classroom interactions. Finally, testing and counseling programs should avoid career segregation and stereotyping (Sadker and Sadker, 1988).

Conclusion

Little time, and even less effort, has been devoted to the juvenile female offender in the last century. Criminal and juvenile justice administrators pursue problems that are seemingly more pressing, such as crowding, or those that are more vocal, such as litigation. Researchers study juvenile offenders, generalizing their theories of male juveniles to females. Unfortunately, the adolescent female offender has been silent for so long that the few administrators and researchers who do champion her special needs are often unheard and even when heard go unheeded.

The differential treatment of females and males in the juvenile justice system begins with the schools, continues with law enforcement and the courts, and is perpetuated by the correctional system. Many delinquent females are locked up for running away from home as a result of physical and/or sexual abuse or exploitation. Many others suffer from low self-esteem, inequitable treatment in school from teachers and administrators, and inequitable programs during incarceration.

The need for educational equity for these offenders is paramount. Teachers must begin to design curricula with females in mind and interact in a gender-free environment. Law enforcement officers must stop arresting females for running away and for other status offenses. Judges and magistrates must stop treating girls differently from boys in the length of confinement in detention and the length and types of sentences imposed. Correctional educators and other staff must begin to provide equitable programs and services for this adolescent female population. Only then will female juvenile offenders have the opportunity to develop the social and educational/vocational skills to compete in the ever-changing technological world in which we live.

References

Agonito, R. and Moon, M. *Promoting Self-Esteem in Young Women.* Albany, NY: The State Department of Education, Division of Community Relations and Intercultural Relations, no date.

Allen-Hagen, B. *Children in Custody, Public Juvenile Facilities, 1987.* Washington, DC: Department of Justice, Office of Juvenile Justice and Delinquency Prevention, 1988.

American Correctional Association. *Public Policy for Corrections: A Handbook for Decision-Makers.* Laurel, MD: American Correctional Association, 1986, pp. 28-31.

Beck, A., Kline, S., and Greenfield, L. *Survey of Youth in Custody, 1987.* Washington, DC: Department of Justice, Bureau of Justice Statistics, 1988.

Bergsmann, I.R. *State Juvenile Justice Education Survey.* Washington, DC: Council of Chief State School Officers, 1988.

Chesney-Lind, M. "Young Women in the Arms of the Law." In L.H. Bowker (ed.), *Women, Crime and the Criminal Justice System.* Lexington, MA: Lexington Books, 1978, pp. 171-96.

———. "Guilt by Reason of Sex: Young Women and the Juvenile Justice System." In B.P. Price and N.J. Sokoloff (eds.), *Criminal Justice System and the Law.* New York: Clark Boardman Co., Ltd., 1982, pp. 77-103.

———. "Girls' Crime and Women's Place: Toward a Feminist Model of Female Delinquency." Paper presented at the American Society of Criminology, Montreal, Canada, 1987.

Collins, W. *Collins: Correctional Law, 1987.* Olympia, Washington, 1987, pp. 125-133.

Correctional Education Association. *Standards for Adult and Juvenile Correctional Education Programs.* College Park, Maryland, 1988.

Council of Chief State School Officers. *Equity Training for State Education Agency Staff.* Washington, DC: Resource Center on Educational Equity, 1986.

Crawford, J. *Tabulation of a Nationwide Survey of Female Inmates.* Phoenix, AZ: Research Advisory Services, 1988.

Epperson, S.E. "Studies Link Subtle Sex Bias in Schools with Women's Behavior in the Workplace." *Wall Street Journal.* September 16, 1988, p. 27.

Finn, J.D., Stott, M.W.R., Zarichny, K.T. "School Performance of Adolescents in Juvenile Court." *Urban Education*, 23, 1988, pp. 150-161.

Geller, M. and Ford-Somma, L. *Caring for Delinquent Girls: An Examination of New Jersey's Correctional System*. Trenton: New Jersey Law Enforcement Planning Agency, 1979.

Grimes, C. *Girls and the Law*. Washington, DC: Institute for Educational Leadership, 1983.

Johnston, W.B. *Workforce 2000*. Indianapolis, IN: Hudson Institute, 1987, pp. 75-104.

Kline, S. *Children in Custody 1975-1985: Census of Public and Private Juvenile Detention, Correctional, and Shelter Facilities, 1975, 1977, 1979, 1983, 1985*. Washington, DC: Department of Justice, Bureau of Justice Statistics, anticipated 1989.

National Council of Jewish Women. *Adolescent Girls in the Juvenile Justice System*. New York: National Council of Jewish Women, 1984.

Osbun, L.A. and Rode, P.A. *Changing Boundaries of the Juvenile Court: Practice and Policy in Minnesota*. Minneapolis, MN: University of Minnesota, 1982, pp. 33-49.

Packer, A. "Retooling the American Worker." *The Washington Post*, July 10, 1988, p. C3.

Price, T. and Vitolo, R. "The Schooling of Incarcerated Young People." *Education Week*, 27, June 15, 1988, pp. 27, 36.

Ryan, T.A. *State of the Art Analysis of Adult Female Offenders and Institutional Programs*. Columbia, SC: University of South Carolina, 1984, p. 22.

Sadker, M. and Sadker, D. *Equity and Excellence in Educational Reform*. Washington, DC: The American University, 1988, pp. 25-26.

Sarri, R.C. Keynote remarks. Conference on Increasing Educational Equity for Juvenile Female Offenders. Washington, DC: Council of Chief State School Officers, 1988.

_____. "Gender Issues in Juvenile Justice." *Crime and Delinquency*, 29, 1983, pp. 38-97.

Snyder, H.N., Finnegan, T.A., Nimick, E.H., Sickmund, M.H., Sullivan, D.P., and Tierney, N.J. *Juvenile Court Statistics 1984*. Pittsburgh, PA: National Center for Juvenile Justice, 1987.

United States Department of Justice, Federal Bureau of Investigation. *Crime in the United States 1987*. Washington, DC: U.S. Government Printing Office, 1987.

_____. *Children in Custody 1985*. Washington, DC: Bureau of Justice Statistics, 1986.

37

Learning Disabilities, Juvenile Delinquency, and Juvenile Corrections

Albert R. Roberts
Judith A. Waters

In examining the myriad and complex reasons youths engage in delinquent behavior, scholars and professionals in the areas of both education and the justice system seem to have ignored a common problem frequently undiscovered in both children and adults: learning disabilities. Learning disability is a general term used to describe a number of learning problems including an inability to remember newly presented information, trouble mastering spatial orientation factors, difficulty in articulating ideas and information, an inability to attend selectively or focus on tasks, and so forth. Often individuals with these difficulties have trouble interacting in social settings. A common time to detect and begin treating individuals with learning disabilities is during their elementary school years. However, these problems often go unrecognized and untreated by parents, school officials, and counselors, potentially resulting in grave consequences for many youth.

Source: Prepared especially for *The Dilemmas of Corrections*.

Let us consider the story of a twelve-year-old boy named Justin who was brought to the county juvenile detention center after his mother complained that he was on drugs and uncontrollable. The probation officer's predispositional investigation for the court revealed that the mother, who has a history of psychotic episodes, was released from the state hospital just six months earlier. The judge ruled that the boy should live with the same aunt and uncle with whom he resided while his mother was confined in the hospital (Roberts, 1998).

Prior to his exposure to the corrections system, Justin found middle school very troubling. During 7th grade, Justin exhibited school attentional problems, memory recall problems, and reading comprehension problems. He told his uncle that he felt stupid in class, and thought he was a real "dummy." In the past, when assigned a short story to read, Justin would spend an inordinate amount of time reading and rereading paragraphs. It took him so long that he usually forgot the theme and content of what he had just read about. Later that year, Justin basically gave up on schoolwork. He brought home his report card in February with one C, one D, and three F's.

Luckily, Justin's uncle knew a school psychologist in a nearby town who had played chess with Justin in the summer. In April, they met for four hours of diagnostic testing, and the psychologist also met with his teachers. By May, Justin had been diagnosed with attention deficit disorder (ADD), memory based deficits, ineffective word decoding, and weak phonological awareness. The testing also demonstrated that Justin had high intelligence. During 8th and 9th grade, he spent one hour each day after school with a learning disability teacher/tutor. Seven years later, Justin is graduating in the top ten percent of his college senior class. His plans for the future include becoming a high school social studies and special education teacher.

The Effects of Undiagnosed Learning Disabilities

Unfortunately, most learning disabled students do not have a caring and dedicated uncle or parent who knows a competent school psychologist. Needless suffering, school failure, frustration, humiliation, anger and hostility, truancy, passive-aggressive behavior, and low self-esteem occur whenever children and adolescents experience repeated criticism, failure, and disappointments. All too many 5th, 6th, and 7th graders perform inadequately in middle school. The transition from elementary to middle school often results in a developmental crisis, particularly for young students with undetected and undiagnosed learning disabilities. These pre-adolescents have difficulty concentrating and focusing on reading or math assignments, they seem to be easily bored and distracted, and as students, they begin to question their own worth. School problems such as these usually escalate because most middle school teachers have no education or training in special education. For example, the twelve-year-old with attention deficit hyperactivity disorder (ADHD) is typically sent to the office for the slightest infraction such as being two minutes late to class, accidentally dropping his book on the floor, or refusing to pick up the pretzel under the table in the cafeteria. The downward spiral begins. Within two months of entering middle school, a large number of learning disabled students are given repeated in-school detentions followed by suspensions.

Success or failure is rarely predetermined. Motivation, commitment to an education, hard work, and perseverance are the most important factors that separate highly successful individuals from the "burnouts," the "druggies," and the failures. The motivation and productive energy drive of pre-adolescents can either be stimulated so they flourish, or stifled and crushed so they disappear. School teachers and coaches have an important role to play in the futures of these youth. Many pre-adolescents have the potential to become very successful.

These very same individuals may become chronic delinquents and career criminals. We firmly believe that, without at least one appropriate and charismatic role model (e.g., a parent, teacher, or coach), many learning disabled children and youth are doomed to school failure, antisocial behavior, and crime. There is a shortage of appropriate role models in the public and private middle schools and high schools throughout the United States. One important step toward remedying this situation is for colleges and universities to require education majors to study learning disabilities, their diagnosis, and treatment.

The most overlooked causes of juvenile delinquency are undiagnosed and unrecognized learning disabilities. It is well known that a history of conduct problems, school failure, and truancy can lead to dropping out of school as well as juvenile delinquency. In the vast majority of cases, the underlying reason for school failure is a learning disability and the lack of early intervention and treatment plans (Roberts and Waters, 1998).

A Review of the Literature: Linking Learning Disabilities with Juvenile Delinquency

According to the federally funded National Longitudinal Transition Study (Learning Disabilities Association of Pittsburgh [LDA], 1996), over 1.21 million special education students in the public schools have diagnosed learning disabilities; 35 percent of them drop out of high school; 62 percent of learning disabled students were unemployed one year after high school graduation; and 31 percent of learning disabled youths will be arrested three to five years after high school. The scope of the problem is increased when we take into account the fact that over 50 percent of juvenile offenders tested in a national study were diagnosed with serious learning disabilities (LDA, 1996). Several retrospective recidivism studies, and one longitudinal prospective study indicated that learning disabled youth with specific personality characteristics (e.g., impulsiveness and poor judgment) are prone to persistent and chronic delinquency (Waldie and Spreen, 1993). There is a critical need for early diagnosis in all public and private schools throughout the United States. Once learning disabilities are recognized, it is important that students receive learning accommodations including resource room opportunities with learning disability specialists.

Several noteworthy studies have documented a strong connection between delinquency and various learning difficulties: attentional problems, information processing deficits, hyperactivity (ADHD), language deficits, and deficient moral reasoning skills (Brier, 1989, 1994; Hinshaw, 1992; Moffitt, 1990; Sikorski, 1991). These disabilities and deficiencies can lead to many problems typically associated with delinquent behavior: criticism and rejection by teachers, failing grades, aggressive acts, fighting with peers, lack of social problem-solving skills, suspensions and expulsions, and low self-esteem.

Children, pre-adolescents, and adolescents need "bright spots" or successful experiences in their lives. High self-esteem seems to insulate some youths from delinquency involvement. For example, the learning disabled youth who compensates for his failure in math or reading by excelling in basketball or wrestling is less likely to become a violent delinquent or drug dealer than the youth with no "bright spots." Some school-aged children lack basic reading and math skills. They may have only mild learning disabilities by 5th grade. Since most of the 5th, 6th, and 7th grade teachers in the public schools have little knowledge of learning disabilities, it is likely that many children with mild to moderate learning differences in 5th grade and 6th grade will be ignored. As a result, they will experience serious academic failures by 7th or 8th grade. State department of education guidelines should be expanded and amended to include ADD and ADHD accommodations in all public and private schools, alternative schools, and schools in juvenile correctional facilities. School psychologists, guidance counselors, and child study teams in a number of states still frequently misdiagnose and classify 7th or 8th graders (with ADD or ADHD) as being emotionally disturbed.

The two basic theories utilized to account for the linkage between learning disabilities and delinquency are "the school failure rationale" and "the susceptibility theory" (Waldie and Spreen, 1993: 417). The school failure rationale postulates that a sequence exists which begins with poor academic performance contributing significantly first to a negative self-image and then to delinquent behavior. The probability of delinquency is enhanced by two important factors: (1) association with peers who are school dropouts and (2) the desire for success in some endeavor (e.g., dealing drugs or stealing cars). Recently, a resource room teacher told us that one of her fifteen-year-old seriously developmentally disabled students had shared his pride in a new skill that his younger brother had taught him—breaking into locked autos! As further evidence of the school failure rationale, other researchers cited by Waldie and Spreen have reported that remedial programs designed to improve academic skills have actually succeeded in reducing rates of delinquency in youth with learning disabilities. Therefore, those children in schools where there are no remedial programs are at increased risk for criminal behavior.

The susceptibility theory suggests that children with learning disabilities have traits that make them more vulnerable to cues and opportunities for delinquent behavior than individuals without learning disabilities. Among the traits specified are lack of impulse control, inability to predict the consequences of one's actions, irritability, persuasibility, and the tendency toward "acting out" behavior. Research indicates that youth with learning disabilities are less self-satisfied, less flexible, and lower in both social skills and sociability. Boys with learning disabilities have been shown to be more aggressive and hyperactive than similar boys without learning disabilities. In a longitudinal study of sixty-five participants with learning disabilities (forty-seven males and eighteen females), Waldie and Spreen (1993) reported that the major finding was that two factors—lack of impulse control and poor judgment—distinguished youth with persisting records of delinquency from those who did not engage in repeated criminal activity. The researchers also pointed out that school failure and susceptibility are not mutually exclusive theories.

With respect to the self-esteem issue, there is often a dichotomous distribution for youth with histories of criminal behavior and school failure. While some report feelings of low self-esteem, others have irrationally high opinions of their worth and invulnerability.

Preventing Delinquency by Meeting the Needs of Youth with Learning Disabilities

There has been slow but steady progress in expanding educational policies and programs in juvenile justice settings. During the decade of the 1990s we witnessed a major increase in punitive responses to the processing and incarceration of juvenile offenders. Early intervention, learning accommodations, one-on-one tutoring, social skills training, conflict resolution courses, and prevention programs at the middle and high school levels will become increasingly popular as legislators, school administrators, and juvenile correctional administrators begin to realize that the punitive approach does not work. Punishment should only be used as a last resort.

There are no panaceas or quick fixes to the major problems in the juvenile justice system, the schools, and family life. However, there are model juvenile treatment programs, good schools with caring teachers, and parents willing to advocate for their children's basic right to an education in a nurturing and supportive (rather than rejecting and hostile) environment. Children and youth should be educated and given the full range of academic and vocational skills for a world of opportunity. Schools need to be awakened to the fact that *they* have failed, not the students, if they do not provide alternative teaching methods and individualized instruction for students with learning disabilities. All students have strengths and weaknesses. Even the student with moderate to severe ADD and auditory processing delay has important strengths.

One of the first author's former students had a learning disability which he outgrew. He is now a star quarterback on an NFL team. He received A's in his last two criminal justice courses, and his term papers were in the top five percent of the class. Despite his learning disability, he was able to hyperfocus. He spent several days in three different libraries, often skipping dinner, in order to hand in his term papers one week early. By hyperfocusing, he was able to locate timely articles in esoteric journals that other students were unable to find. Students with learning disabilities need choices and options. This student was allowed to select a particular area of study which would help him with his alternative career in the event that he failed to succeed (due to injury or otherwise) in the NFL.

Conclusion

During the past decade, we have learned a great deal about the behavior of youth at risk, particularly that no human being can thrive by neglecting his or her physical, psychological, and social needs. If a youth is to become a healthy, self-sufficient, and productive law-abiding citizen, then society must provide a nurturing environment. The strength of any society can be measured by how it treats its disabled and, perhaps most importantly, how it addresses the future of its children. It is important for us, as professionals and students of the juvenile justice system to plan and promote effective public policies and to implement procedures and programs for ameliorating the damage inflicted by years of neglect, deteriorating school systems, and overcrowded and punitive juvenile justice systems (Roberts, 1998). Teachers have the capability of bringing out either the worst or the best in these students. Although juvenile justice administrators and school principals are far from reaching their goals, steady progress is being made each year. We strongly recommend the planning and development of early intervention programs and comprehensive education programs. Equally important, delinquency researchers and correctional officials must make it a priority to develop and evaluate specialized treatment programs, and modify existing programs, for learning disabled offenders in correctional settings. Without such programs, many promising youth will ultimately become adult offenders.

References

Brier, N. (1989). The relationship between learning disability and delinquency; A review and reappraisal. *Journal of Learning Disabilities*, 22(9): 546–552.

Brier, N. (1994). Targeted treatment for adjudicated youth with learning disabilities: Effects on recidivism. *Journal of Learning Disabilities*, 27(4): 215–222.

Hinshaw, S. P. (1992). Academic underachievement, attention deficits, and aggression: Comorbidity and implications for intervention. *Journal of Consulting and Clinical Psychology*, 60(6): 893–903.

Learning Disabilities Association of Pittsburgh, PA (1996). *LDA Newsbriefs*, 31(1) supplement: 19–39.

Moffitt, T. E. (1990). Juvenile delinquency and attention deficit disorder: Boys' developmental trajectories from age 3 to age 15. *Child Development*, 61:893–910.

Roberts, A. R. (1998). An introduction and overview of juvenile justice. In A.R. Roberts (ed.), *Juvenile Justice: Policies, Programs and Services*. Chicago: Nelson-Hall, pp. 3–20.

Roberts, A. R. and Waters, J. A. (1998). The coming storm: Juvenile violence and justice system responses. In A. R. Roberts (ed.), *Juvenile Justice, Policies, Programs and Services*. Chicago: Nelson-Hall, pp. 54–56.

Sikorski, J. B. (1991). Learning disorders and the juvenile justice system. *Psychiatric Annals*, 21(12): 742–747.

Waldies, K. and Spreen, O. (1993). The relationship between learning disabilities and persisting delinquency. *Journal of Learning Disabilities*, 26(6): 417–423.

38

The Impact of HIV/AIDS on Corrections
Mark Blumberg
J. Dennis Laster

The first cases of Acquired Immunodeficiency Syndrome (AIDS) were identified among gay males in 1981 (Friedland and Klein, 1987). Soon, there were also reports of this disease among intravenous drug users (IVDUs), hemophiliacs, and persons who had sexual contact with these individuals. By 1983, scientists discovered that the Human Immunodeficiency Virus (HIV) was the cause of AIDS. Two years later, a blood test became available to determine whether a person was infected with this virus (Altman, 1987). It is estimated that as many as 800,000 Americans are infected with HIV (Waldholz, 1996a).

In the developed world, HIV/AIDS has primarily infected gay/bisexual males and intravenous drug users. The Centers for Disease Control and Prevention (1996:10) report that since the epidemic began, 82 percent of adult/adolescent AIDS cases in the United States have been diagnosed among members of these risk groups. Heterosexual transmis-

Source: Prepared especially for *The Dilemmas of Corrections*. The authors would like to thank Douglas Heckathorn, who provided valuable assistance and ideas.

sion, on the other hand, has accounted for 9 percent of total AIDS cases. Most of the latter are sex partners of IVDUs. In recent years, the proportion of cases linked to male homosexual activity has declined whereas intravenous drug use has become a more significant risk factor in the transmission of this virus.

HIV is only transmitted in one of three ways: 1) via sexual activity; 2) through contact with infected blood (as often occurs when IVDUs share needles and/or syringes) and; 3) from an infected mother to a newborn infant. The virus is not transmitted through casual everyday contact including such practices as sharing food, eating utensils, telephones or toilets (Lifson, 1988). In fact, medical researchers have carefully examined households and boarding schools where seropositive[1] individuals resided in order to determine exactly how HIV is transmitted. These studies did not find a single case in which the virus was transmitted from one person to another except as a result of sexual activity, injection drug use or the birthing process (Friedland and Klein, 1987). This finding is rather striking when one considers the fact that many of these seropositive individuals did not even know that they were infected and their households did not take the types of infection control measures that are routinely followed in health care settings.

Correctional Institutions

HIV/AIDS is a serious concern for prisons and jails. The number of "high-risk" inmates has increased dramatically in recent years as a result of the "war on drugs." Harlow (1993:5) reports that approximately 25 percent of state prison inmates have a history of intravenous drug use. Many inmates engage in the types of "high-risk" behavior during incarceration that pose a significant danger of viral transmission. Although levels of activity vary among facilities, both illicit sex and drug injection do take place in correctional facilities (Mahon, 1996). Furthermore, tattooing is not uncommon in many facilities (Braithwaite, Hammett, and Mayberry, 1996), and there are reports in the medical literature of HIV infection among prisoners that resulted from this practice (Doll, 1988).

Correctional administrators must confront a variety of complex issues as they struggle to develop policies that are designed to prevent transmission of this virus within the institutional setting. Many of these are issues that the outside society has also faced: whether to conduct mandatory HIV testing, whether infected persons should be placed in segregation, the appropriate content of educational programs designed to reduce the level of "high-risk" behavior (i.e., whether to teach abstinence or "safer sex"), and the question of condom distribution. At the heart of the debate is the following question: Should prisons and jails adhere to the practices of the larger society or is the institutional environment so unique that deviations from these established policies are justified?

This article explores the policy ramifications of various options designed to minimize the impact of the HIV/AIDS epidemic on prisons and jails. After a brief examination of the empirical data regarding the prevalence and transmission of HIV within correctional institutions, the pros and cons of mandatory HIV testing, segregating inmates infected with HIV/AIDS, and condom distribution are explored. This is followed by a discussion of some of the challenges that prisons and jails face as they attempt to provide quality medical care to inmates with HIV/AIDS. Next, there is a review of some of the legal issues that correctional administrators have been forced to confront as a result of the HIV/AIDS crisis. Finally, the article examines the question of whether institutional staff should be concerned about job-related HIV transmission as a result of their employment.

Prevalence and Transmission of HIV
Within Correctional Institutions

According to a Bureau of Justice Statistics report, 24,226 inmates (2.3 percent of the total) were infected with the AIDS virus in 1995. Approximately 20 percent of these individuals had progressed to "full-blown" AIDS (Maruschak, 1997:1). Nationally, the rate of AIDS cases among inmates is almost six times greater than that of the adult U.S. population (Hammett and Widom, 1996:268).

The percentage of seropositive prisoners varies dramatically among jurisdictions. New York has the highest percentage of inmates (13.9) who are infected. In fact, more than one-third of all seropositive inmates in the nation are incarcerated in that state (Maruschak:1). On the other hand, 27 states reported that fewer than 1.0 percent of their inmate population was HIV-positive, and 8 states held 10 or fewer HIV-positive inmates (Maruschak, 1997:3). In general, correctional systems in the Northeast have more AIDS cases because a higher proportion of intravenous drug users in that region are seropositive (Gaiter and Doll, 1996). In the United States, most institutional HIV/AIDS cases have been diagnosed among individuals with a history of intravenous drug use prior to incarceration (Vlahov, 1990).

Several studies have been conducted which seek to determine how frequently HIV is transmitted among prison populations. The most comprehensive study to date found that only 0.3 percent of a sample of Illinois male inmates who had initially been seronegative[2] tested positive after spending one year in prison (Hammett et al., 1994:28). Low rates of seroconversion[3] have also been reported in Maryland (Brewer et al., 1988) and Nevada (Horsburgh et al., 1990). However, even a rate of 0.3 percent per year translates into a 6 percent risk of HIV infection after 20 years of incarceration. Furthermore, young first-time offenders, a small proportion of the prison population, are probably at greatest risk. Therefore, inmates in this vulnerable group probably have good reason to be concerned. In addition, a study conducted in the Florida Department of Corrections found a disturbingly high rate of infection among inmates who had been continuously incarcerated since the beginning of the HIV/AIDS epidemic (Mutter, Grimes, and Labarthe, 1994). This research suggests that "inmates have a substantial risk of contracting HIV infection while incarcerated" (p. 795). However, the Florida study only tested a small proportion of long-term inmates and the sample may have been self-selected (Braithwaite, Hammett, and Mayberry, 1996).

Clearly, much more research is needed on this question. It is known that there are substantial differences between jurisdictions with regard to the rate of seroprevalence[4] among inmates (Hammett et al., 1994:22–23). It is quite likely that there are also differences between facilities with respect to the level of supervision and the frequency with which "high-risk" behaviors occur. At this point, it is clear that institutional transmission of HIV does take place. What remains unknown is how frequently.

Mandatory HIV Screening

In the United States, public health officials have attempted to control the spread of HIV through education, voluntary testing, and counseling of persons who may be at high risk of HIV. With the exception of immigrants, blood donors, and military recruits (Andrus et al., 1989), most testing has been conducted on a voluntary basis. From the beginning of the epidemic, one of the most strongly debated questions has been whether this policy should also be pursued in correctional institutions. Because prisons and jails contain numerous individuals who have demonstrated a capacity to engage in antisocial behavior and homosexual activity (Nacci and Kane, 1983; Wooden and Parker, 1982), there have been frequent calls by correctional officers for the mandatory testing of inmates (Mahaffey and Marcus, 1995).

Advantages. Proponents argue that mass screening is the best way to identify seropositive inmates. Such a policy provides correctional administrators with an opportunity to target education and prevention programs. In addition, infected inmates can be placed under special supervision to ensure that they do not transmit the virus to others. It is also suggested that mass screening will provide a more accurate projection regarding the number of future AIDS cases that will develop in a particular institution. This will enable correctional officials to plan more effectively and to seek an appropriate level of funding to meet future needs. Finally, supporters of mandatory testing assert that institutions must pursue this policy to insure that infected inmates receive appropriate medical treatment that can prolong their lives.

Disadvantages. Critics of mandatory testing do not accept these rationales. They assert that education and prevention programs must be directed toward all inmates, and that all prisoners should be encouraged to refrain from "high-risk" behavior, not just those identified as seropositive. Furthermore, opponents of mass screening decry the practice of segregating infected individuals from the inmate population. Because the current medical technology cannot identify all infectious individuals,[5] any policy that utilizes isolation runs the risk of inadvertently encouraging "high-risk" behavior by creating the false perception that all inmates who remain in the general prison population are uninfected.

The claim that correctional institutions must be able to accurately project the future number of AIDS cases is not disputed. However, anonymous epidemiological screening can satisfactorily achieve this goal. In fact, many correctional systems have utilized this procedure to ascertain the rate of seroprevalence in various institutions within their jurisdiction (Braithwaite, Hammett, and Mayberry, 1996). Blood samples are simply coded in a manner that ensures prison officials cannot learn the names of infected inmates.

Opponents of mandatory screening also agree that early identification of seropositives is important. Recent scientific advances have contributed to a significant reduction in the fatality rate among HIV/AIDS-infected individuals who receive these medications (Okie, 1997). However, opponents do not believe that mandatory testing is necessary to accomplish this goal because inmates with a history of "high-risk" behavior have a medical incentive to learn their antibody status in order to receive treatment. Their case is buttressed by two studies which found that the majority of infected inmates are reached by voluntary testing programs (Andrus et al., 1989; Hoxie et al., 1990).

There are other objections to mandatory testing. One concern is that mass screening will create a class of outcasts within the institution (Whitman, 1990). HIV-infected inmates could be subjected to harassment, discrimination, and perhaps even violence within the prison—and to difficulties in obtaining employment or housing upon release.

Finally, it is argued that such a policy is not a wise expenditure of scarce correctional resources. Critics assert that these funds would be better spent if directed towards HIV/AIDS education or inmate medical care.

Current Policy. During 1994, the Centers for Disease Control and the National Institute of Justice jointly sponsored the eighth annual survey to determine what policies state/federal prison systems and city/county jails are pursuing with respect to HIV (Braithwaite, Hammett, and Mayberry, 1996). It found that sixteen state prison systems[6] and the Federal Bureau of Prisons require all inmates to be screened for HIV.[7] No city/county jail system which responded to the survey followed this policy. The list of systems with mandatory mass screening has remained unchanged since 1990 (Braithwaite, Hammett and Mayberry, 1996; Hammett et al., 1994:49).

Segregation of Inmates with HIV/AIDS

Advantages. Proponents of segregation assert that it is necessary to prevent transmission of HIV within the institution. In making the case for this policy, advocates note that various types of "high-risk" activities occur in correctional institutions. They note that: 1) previous research indicates homosexual activity does take place in prison (Nacci and Kane, 1983; Wooden and Parker, 1982); 2) other sexually transmitted diseases (e.g., rectal gonorrhea) are sometimes transmitted in the correctional setting; 3) tattooing (although prohibited in most institutions) is a very common practice; 4) illicit drug use probably takes place as well in some facilities (Polonsky et al., 1994); and 5) there is a small proportion of inmates who are sexually assaulted during incarceration (Bowker, 1980).

Disadvantages. Civil libertarians are opposed to the practice of segregation except for valid medical reasons or in cases involving protective custody. They argue that because HIV is not spread through casual contact, special housing is not necessary. It is asserted that segregation undermines the basic public health message that HIV is not transmitted except through certain "high-risk" behaviors.

Opponents of this practice also express concern because infected inmates are sometimes placed in substandard living quarters and denied an opportunity to participate in certain work assignments, rehabilitation, and recreation programs—or to be eligible for work release. Furthermore, because these prisoners are excluded from many institutional programs, they frequently also lose the opportunity to earn "good time" credit toward eventual release.

Segregation raises other problems as well. In those jurisdictions that have a large number of infected inmates, this policy would require the development of what is in fact a second corrections system. Officials may be required to duplicate many existing programs. As the number of cases continues to increase, this policy would put further pressure on correctional budgets that are already severely strained.

There is also concern that inmates will be less likely to come forward for voluntary HIV testing if they are placed in segregation as a consequence of a positive result (Hammett et al., 1994:62). Finally, as already noted, a policy of mass screening and segregation could actually be counterproductive by providing inmates in the general prison population with a false sense of security that all HIV/AIDS-infected persons had been placed in isolation.

Clearly, correctional administrators have a responsibility to pursue policies that minimize the transmission of HIV within the institution. However, it is questionable whether a blanket policy of segregation is the best way to accomplish this objective. As an alternative, prison and jail administrators could reduce the incidence of "high-risk" behavior through such steps as increasing supervision of inmates, hiring more correctional officers, implementing intensive educational programs, and imposing harsh penalties for sexual assault (Vald, 1987:238). In addition, the classification process can be used to identify inmates who are likely to engage in predatory behavior as well as those who are likely to be victimized.

Current Policy. According to the various CDC/NIJ surveys of correctional policy, there is a strong trend toward mainstreaming inmates with HIV/AIDS into the general prison population. Between 1985 and 1994, the number of prison systems that segregated persons with AIDS declined from 38 to 4. For asymptomatic seropositives, the corresponding decline was from 8 to 2 (Braithwaite, Hammett, and Mayberry, 1996: Table 5.5). Many systems have been able to successfully reintegrate inmates without serious incident (Hammett et al., 1994:59). In fact, Alabama and Mississippi remain the only systems that continue to isolate all known HIV-infected inmates (Braithwaite, Hammett, and Mayberry, 1996).

Distribution of Condoms

Previous research indicates that sexual activity does take place in correctional institutions. For this reason, some have suggested that administrators have an obligation to make condoms available in order to protect inmates from infection. However, very few jurisdictions have chosen to follow this course of action. Most have taken the view that homosexual behavior is forbidden in prisons and jails and that distribution of condoms would imply tacit approval of this activity. In addition, concern has been expressed that inmates could use these devices to make weapons or hide contraband. Finally, there is the question of whether condoms actually provide significant protection during anal intercourse.

Although condoms are distributed to prison inmates in 18 nations (Mahon, 1996:1215), only six jurisdictions in the United States (Braithwaite, Hammett, and Mayberry, 1996:83–4) have chosen to do so (Mississippi, New York City, Philadelphia, San Francisco, Vermont, and Washington, D.C.). These correctional systems report few problems. Fears that inmates would use these devices to fashion weapons or smuggle contraband appear to be unwarranted. Nonetheless, the number of institutions providing condoms has changed little in recent years. Although many other jurisdictions have considered the possibility of implementing a distribution policy, none have chosen to do so at the current time (Hammett et al., 1994).[8]

It should be noted that not all systems distribute condoms in the same manner (Hammett et al., 1994:46–47). New York City and Vermont limit inmates to one per medical visit. In Mississippi, an unlimited number may be purchased at the canteen. San Francisco makes them available as part of their AIDS educational program. Washington, D.C., has also chosen this policy as well as allowing inmates to obtain condoms at the infirmary. Finally, Philadelphia offers these items during counseling sessions associated with HIV antibody testing.

Correctional Health Care

AIDS has become one of the leading causes of death in the United States. Fortunately, in recent years, a new class of drugs called "protease inhibitors" has been developed. This treatment has reduced the number of deaths from this disease and may change HIV/AIDS from a fatal to a chronic condition. However, it is important to recognize that these drugs are not a cure. Many questions remain unanswered, including whether the virus will eventually become resistant to this medication.

Protease inhibitors are rapidly becoming the standard of care for seropositive individuals in the community. However, prisons and jails face enormous difficulty in trying to provide this treatment. The annual retail cost of providing this medication to one individual is between $12,000 and $16,000 (Waldholz, 1996b:1). Correctional institutions with large numbers of HIV-infected inmates could easily have their entire health care budget consumed by this expense. In addition, persons receiving this treatment must take between 14 and 20 pills each day in accordance with a rigid dosing schedule and often have to adhere to strict dietary restrictions (Waldholz, 1996b). These requirements can pose serious logistical problems for correctional institutions.

Policies vary widely with respect to protease inhibitors. New York City expects to spend $5.4 million in 1998 to provide these drugs. On the other hand, Louisiana reserves this treatment for inmates who were already receiving this medication prior to incarceration (Purdy, 1997). Given the efficacy of these drugs, there is clearly an ethical obligation on the part of medical personnel to provide inmates with this treatment. Whether there is also a legal obligation is uncertain. Although the U.S. Supreme Court has ruled that inmates have a constitutional right to adequate medical care (*Estelle v. Gamble*, 1976), this decision did not grant inmates "unqualified access to health care." Furthermore, lower courts have subsequently interpreted this standard to mean that inmates rarely have a right to the best medical care (Vaughn and Carroll, 1996).

There are other factors that complicate the treatment of seropositive inmates. To date, many of the important advances in the treatment of HIV/AIDS have come from experimental medications. However, many states forbid inmates from participating in experimental trials of new drugs. In those jurisdictions that do allow such trials, few inmates are actually participating (Collins, Baumgartner, and Henry, 1995). Although the rules which prevent prisoners from taking part in experimental research were initially designed to protect incarcerated individuals, it is clear that these policies are now preventing some inmates from receiving potentially beneficial treatments.

Finally, it should be noted that the treatment of HIV/AIDS has become quite complex. Outside the correctional setting, the management of this disease has increasingly become the responsibility of specialists (Purdy, 1997). Unfortunately, many prisons and jails are forced to rely on primary care doctors who may lack the necessary expertise to provide the most up-to-date care. For these reasons, it is not surprising that the level of care varies dramatically among jurisdictions and sometimes even varies between different facilities within the same correctional system. In fact, the best care is often provided by those institutions which are operating under a court order to improve medical care (Purdy, 1997).

Legal Issues

Several issues have been raised in a proliferation of litigation challenging the HIV/AIDS policies of correctional institutions. The many lawsuits have presented a variety of constitutional and statutory claims.

Cases have been brought by infected inmates seeking relief from institutional policies and by uninfected inmates and correctional personnel seeking protection from transmission of the virus. Of particular importance to correctional administrators are those cases which seek to impose civil liability for a failure to prevent infection in the institution.

Lawsuits brought by infected and uninfected inmates based on constitutional challenges to prison policies and procedures have met with little success. Correctional officials have been effective in defending these cases primarily as a result of *Turner v. Safley*, decided by the U.S. Supreme Court in 1987. In *Turner*, the Court pronounced the standard to be applied in cases alleging constitutional claims brought by prisoners. The Court held that institutional policies and procedures are valid if they are "reasonably related to legitimate penological interests" (*Turner* at p. 89). This requirement of reasonableness, as opposed to more stringent standards of substantial or compelling interests, has made it considerably easier for correctional officials to implement policies which restrict prisoners' rights. In applying the *Turner* standard to HIV-related cases, lower courts have consistently upheld prison policies that restrict the rights of both infected and uninfected inmates.

Most of the suits brought by infected inmates allege differential treatment or the denial of privileges. In *Dunn v. White* (1989), mandatory screening of inmates for HIV infection was challenged on grounds that testing constituted an unreasonable search and seizure and was therefore prohibited under the Fourth Amendment. The court upheld the prison's screening policy and, applying the *Turner* standard, concluded that there was a logical connection between mandatory testing and the prison's goal of preventing the spread of AIDS. Mass screening for the purpose of segregating infected prisoners into HIV dormitories has also been upheld under the same rationale (*Harris v. Thigpen*, 1991). Courts have reached similar results in cases where individual inmates have been singled out for testing after an incident that posed a risk of transmission, as in cases of prison rape. A policy of not testing inmates after potential transmission occurrences has likewise been upheld (*Lile v. Tippecanoe County Jail*, 1992).

Prison policies regarding the segregation of HIV positive inmates has been fertile ground for litigation as well. Despite a consistent trend in favor of mainstreaming seropositive prisoners into the general prison population, the courts have taken a "hands-off" position on the issue and left housing policy decisions to prison officials. Whether the institution chooses segregation or mainstreaming, the policy has been upheld. Thus, infected inmates who bring suit to challenge mandatory segregation policies have not been successful. Courts have also upheld segregation policies against constitutional challenges based on the following claims: cruel and unusual punishment under the Eighth Amendment (*Cordero v. Coughlin*, 1984); equal protection under the Fourteenth Amendment (*Moore v. Mabus*, 1992); due process under the Fifth and Fourteenth Amendments (*Harris v. Thigpen*, 1991). The case of *Nolley v. County of Erie* (1991) represents a rare departure from those decisions upholding mandatory segregation of infected prisoners. Nolley, solely on the basis of her status as an HIV positive inmate, was forced into a segregation unit for prisoners who were suicidal or mentally disturbed. Evidence in the case made it clear that she was not placed in the unit to receive medical care or for her safety. The court found merit in Nolley's assertions that her due process and right of privacy protections were violated. *Nolley* is distinguishable from other cases, however, since the institution failed to follow its own policies regarding the placement of seropositive inmates.

Inmates have also brought suit alleging the unauthorized disclosure of their HIV status. This claim is based on the fact that individuals in the free world have a constitutional right to protect their medical records from unauthorized disclosure (Vaughn and Carroll, 1996). However, the courts have ruled that this principle does not apply to incarcerated individuals and that disclosing an inmate's HIV positive condition to correctional personnel and other inmates does not violate the constitutional right of privacy (*Anderson v. Romero*, 1995).

In other areas as well, courts have applied the *Turner* standard and given prison administrators wide discretion in making decisions that impact upon infected inmates. Courts have upheld prison policies against challenges by inmates asserting differential treatment or a denial of privilege in cases involving exclusion from a community work program (*Williams v. Sumner*, 1986) and prohibiting work in prison cafeterias and hospitals (*Farmer v. Moritsugu*, 1990).

Attempts to invoke the protections of federal statutes have also met with limited success. For example, in *Gates v. Rowland* (1994), infected inmates claimed that their exclusion from certain work assignments was in violation of Section 504 of the Rehabilitation Act of 1973. Courts have ruled that seropositive individuals fall under the protection of this act. Section 504 provides that handicapped persons are entitled to a reasonable accommodation of their employment needs and other activities if they are otherwise qualified to perform the work or participate in the activities. The question in *Gates* was how should the Rehabilitation Act be applied to correctional institutions. The court's decision applied the same test to this statutory claim that it has applied to constitutional claims, namely the *Turner* standard. The court found that the exclusion of infected inmates from prison programs, arguably in violation of the

Rehabilitation Act, was permissible since the policy was reasonably related to the prison's goal of promoting the safety of inmates.

Some cases have been brought by uninfected inmates and correctional personnel seeking to require institutions to implement policies to reduce the risk of transmission in the prison environment. These cases have also met with little success. Courts have not recognized a constitutional right that would require correctional authorities to implement policies of mass screening or segregation (Haas, 1993). As previously noted, most prisons have not adopted policies mandating either of these practices.

The risk of institutional transmission is likely to be the source of an increasing number of cases seeking to hold correctional officials civilly liable for the payment of monetary damages. Prison administrators are charged with protecting the inmates in their custody. Although most studies find that HIV is transmitted infrequently in prisons and jails, the possibility that an inmate might be infected as a result of an attack has been described as "perhaps the most explosive legal and moral issue related to HIV/AIDS in correctional facilities" (Braithwaite, Hammett, and Mayberry, 1996). The case of *Billman v. Indiana Department of Corrections* (1995) is illustrative of the types of inmate claims that may prove worrisome to prison authorities. Billman brought suit under 42 U.S.C. Section 1983, the federal civil rights statute that provides monetary damages for violations of federally protected rights by state officials. The plaintiff alleged that he was the victim of cruel and unusual punishment inflicted upon him by prison authorities in violation of his Eighth Amendment rights. The complaint alleged that employees of the prison system placed a seropositive inmate in the same cell with Billman. Although prison staff were alleged to have knowledge of both the inmate's HIV status and his history of sexually assaulting cellmates, they did nothing to warn Billman of the danger. Billman further alleged that he was raped by the inmate and that prison employees did not act to prevent or interrupt the rape. The court assumed that Billman was not infected, but found that the fear of the rape itself and the additional fear of being infected could give rise to damages. While the court did not reach a decision on the merits of Billman's assertions and remanded the case for other reasons, it did identify the standards to be applied in such cases. The court found the applicable test in cruel and unusual punishment cases to be the "deliberate indifference" standard enunciated by the United States Supreme Court in *Farmer v. Brennan* (1994). Thus, inmates seeking to impose civil liability based on the infliction of cruel and unusual punishment must show that prison officials acted with deliberate indifference to a known substantial risk of physical harm. If Billman could prove the allegations of his complaint, there is little doubt that he would recover damages for the injury suffered. Still, inmate plaintiffs in other cases will find the deliberate indifference standard to be an obstacle that is difficult to overcome.

Historically, correctional authorities have been given broad leeway to develop and implement policy within their institutions. The judiciary has taken a passive role and left the day-to-day operations of the prison to its administrators. This reluctance to intervene is clearly evident from a review of HIV/AIDS-related cases.

HIV and the Corrections Officer

Repeated surveys by the National Institute of Justice reveal that not a single corrections officer in the United States has become infected with HIV as a result of his or her occupational duties (Hammett et al., 1994:13). Despite this fact, correctional personnel often express anxiety that their employment places them at increased risk of infection (Mahaffey and Marcus, 1995). In the earlier days of the epidemic, there were reports that certain staff members in some facilities refused to perform assigned tasks (e.g., transporting a seropositive inmate) because they feared infection (Hammett, 1989:106). Although this type of inappropriate response is now quite uncommon, some correctional officers continue to be concerned that the following types of incidents could place them in jeopardy: 1) being bitten or spat upon by an infected prisoner; 2) a needlestick injury (either received inadvertently during a search or as the result of an assault); and 3) coming into contact with infected blood in the course of attempting to terminate a fight among inmates. Examination of the dynamics of HIV transmission suggest that it is highly improbable that any correctional officer will become infected under these circumstances.

Lifson (1988) reports that follow-up investigations of persons bitten by HIV/AIDS-infected individuals revealed no cases in which the virus had been transmitted in this manner. Bites apparently present little risk because it is the assailant and not the victim who comes into contact with blood during the assault. As a consequence, transmission would be highly unlikely unless the perpetrator had blood in his or her mouth.

Spitting incidents pose little danger (Blumberg, 1990) for two reasons: 1) the virus does not pass through intact skin and 2) HIV is not present in sufficient quantity in saliva to transmit the virus. In fact, the Centers for Disease Control and Prevention (1988) no longer recommend that health care workers take universal precautions[9] when contact with saliva is anticipated unless it contains visible blood.

Needlestick injuries do pose a slight risk of HIV transmission. Studies of health care workers who have accidentally pricked themselves with HIV-infected needles indicate that viral transmission occurs in approximately 0.5 percent of the cases (Centers for Disease Control, 1989:5). In other words, infection resulted in about 1 out of every 200 needlesticks where the victim had been exposed to contaminated blood.

Correctional institutions can take a number of steps to further reduce this risk. These should include: 1) implementing a comprehensive HIV/AIDS education and training program; 2) developing policies and procedures which teach officers how to conduct searches in a manner that minimizes their likelihood of injury; and 3) ensuring that correctional staff follow all prescribed infection control guidelines issued by the Centers for Disease Control (1989).

Finally, institutional personnel have expressed anxiety that the virus could be transmitted during actions taken to break up fights. Specifically, the concern is that one of the participants will be seropositive and that blood from this inmate will come in contact with an officer who has an open sore. Under these circumstances, there is a theoretical possibility that transmission could occur. However, more than one decade has passed since the beginning of the AIDS epidemic, and not a single case has been reported in which a person working in a prison or jail became infected in this manner. Clearly, the risk posed by such incidents, especially for those personnel who follow recommended Centers for Disease Control guidelines, is more theoretical than real.

Summary

This article has examined some of the difficult choices that correctional administrators confront as they attempt to develop policies designed to manage the AIDS crisis within prisons and jails. Clearly, the most critical challenge is the prevention of "high-risk" behavior by inmates. However, very few institutions are taking the kind of innovative steps that many public health experts believe are necessary to prevent the transmission of this virus. As previously noted, relatively few jurisdictions are providing inmates with access to condoms. In addition, the San Francisco jail system is the only correctional department in the United States that officially makes bleach available for the purpose of sterilizing drug injection equipment (Braithwaite, Hammett, and Mayberry, 1996:86).[10] Policymakers should seriously consider implementing the types of public health measures that have been widely undertaken outside of corrections (Mahon, 1996). Current policies may result in more incarcerated persons becoming seropositive. Unfortunately, more institutional HIV/AIDS cases will translate into a larger share of correctional budgets being devoted to health care expenses. In addition, because most inmates are eventually released, it will also mean a greater number of HIV-infected persons being returned to the community.

Cases

Anderson v. Romero, 72 F.3d 518 (7th Cir. 1995).
Billman v. Indiana Department of Corrections, 56 F.3d 785 (7th Cir. 1995).
Cordero v. Coughlin, 607 F. Supp. 9 (S.D.N.Y. 1984).
Dunn v. White, 880 F.2d 1188 (10th Cir. 1989), cert. denied, 110 S. Ct. 871 (1990).
Estelle v. Gamble, 429 U.S. 97 (1976).
Farmer v. Brennan, 511 U.S. 825 (1994).
Farmer v. Moritsugu, 742 F. Supp. 525 (W.D. Wis. 1990).
Gates v. Rowland, 39 F.3d 1439 (9th Cir. 1994).
Harris v. Thigpen, 941 F2d. 1495 (11th Cir. 1991).
Lile v. Tippecanoe County Jail, 844 F. Supp. 1301 (N.D. Ind. 1992).
Moore v. Mabus, 976 F.2d 268 (5th 1992).
Nolley v. County of Erie, 776 F. Supp.715 (W.D.N.Y. 1991).
Turner v. Safley, 428 U.S. 78 (1987).
Williams v. Sumner, 648 F. Supp. 510 (D. Nev. 1986).

Notes

[1] This term refers to individuals whose HIV antibody test indicates that they have become infected with the virus, regardless of whether they exhibit symptoms of illness.

[2] This term refers to individuals whose HIV antibody test indicates that they are not infected with the AIDS virus.

[3] Seroconversion refers to a positive HIV antibody test on the part of an individual who was previously not infected with the virus.

[4] This term refers to the proportion of individuals in a specific group who are seropositive.

[5] The HIV antibody test does not detect infection until at least 6 to 12 weeks after exposure to the virus.

[6] These include Alabama, Colorado, Georgia, Idaho, Iowa, Michigan, Mississippi, Missouri, Nebraska, Nevada, New Hampshire, North Dakota, Oklahoma, Rhode Island, Utah, and Wyoming. In addition, nine prison systems (Hammett et al., 1994:51) attempt to screen inmates who are believed to have a history of high-risk behavior (e.g., intravenous drug use).

[7] Mandatory screening can take the form of testing all incoming inmates, all current inmates, or all inmates who are eligible for release.

[8] Braithwaite, Hammett and Mayberry (1996) report that one other jail system discreetly makes condoms available to inmates (p. 84).

[9] Universal precautions means treating all such fluid as if it were infectious, regardless of the source.

[10] These authors note that inmates in some systems may have de facto access to bleach that is made available for other purposes.

References

Altman, Dennis (1987). *Aids in the Mind of America: The Social, Political and Psychological Impact of a New Epidemic.* Garden City, NY: Anchor Books.

Andrus, Jon K., David W. Fling, Catherine Knox, Robert O. McAlister, Michael R. Skeels, Robert E. Conrad, John M. Horan, and Laurence R. Foster (1989). "HIV Testing in Prisoners: Is Mandatory Testing Mandatory?" *American Journal of Public Health.* Vol. 79, No. 7, pp. 840–842.

Blumberg, Mark (1990). "The Transmission of HIV: Exploring Some Misconceptions Related to Criminal Justice," *Criminal Justice Policy Review.* Vol. 4, No. 4, pp. 288–305.

Bowker, Lee H. (1980). *Prison Victimization.* New York: Elsevier.

Braithwaite, Ronald L., Theodore M. Hammett, and Robert M. Mayberry (1996). *Prisons and AIDS: A Public Health Challenge.* San Francisco: Jossey-Bass.

Brewer, T. Fordam, David Vlahov, Ellen Taylor, Drusilla Hall, Alvaro Munoz, and B. Frank Polk (1988). "Transmission of HIV Within a Statewide Prison System," *AIDS.* Vol. 2, No. 5, pp. 363–366.

Centers for Disease Control and Prevention (1996). *HIV/AIDS Surveillance Report.* 8(2).

_____ (1989). "Guidelines for Prevention of Transmission of Human Immunodeficiency Virus and Hepatitis B Virus to Health Care and Public Safety Workers," *Morbidity and Mortality Weekly Report.* Vol. 38, No. S-6 (June 23).

_____ (1988). "Update: Universal Precautions for Prevention of Transmission of HIV, Hepatitis B Virus, and Other Blood-Borne Pathogens in Health Care Settings," *Morbidity and Mortality Weekly Report.* Vol. 37, No. 24 (June 24).

Collins, Abigail, Dana Baumgartner, and Keith Henry (1995). "U.S. Prisoners' Access to Experimental HIV Therapies," *Minnesota Medicine.* Vol. 78: 45–48.

Doll, Donald C. (1988). "Tattooing in Prison and HIV Infection," *The Lancet.* January 2/9: 66–67.

Friedland, Gerald H., and Robert S. Klein (1987). "Transmission of the Human Immunodeficiency Virus," *The New England Journal of Medicine.* Vol. 317, No. 18, pp. 1125–1135.

Gaiter, Juarlyn, and Lynda S. Doll (1996). "Editorial: Improving HIV/AIDS Prevention in Prisons Is Good Public Health Policy," *American Journal of Public Health.* Vol. 86, No. 9, pp. 1201–1203.

Haas, Kenneth C. (1993). "Constitutional Challenges to the Compulsory HIV Testing of Prisoners and the Mandatory Segregation of HIV-Positive Prisoners," *The Prison Journal.* Vol. 73 (September–December).

Hammett, Theodore M. (1989). *1988 Update: AIDS in Correctional Facilities.* National Institute of Justice, Washington, DC (June).

Hammett, Theodore M., Lynne Harold, Michael Gross, and Joel Epstein (1994). *1992 Update: HIV/AIDS in Correctional Facilities.* National Institute of

Justice and Centers for Disease Control and Prevention, Washington, DC (January).

Hammett, Theodore M., and R. Widom (1996). "HIV/AIDS Education and Prevention Programs for Adults in Prisons and Jails and Juveniles in Confinement Facilities—United States, 1994," *MMWR*. Vol. 45, No. 13, pp. 268–271.

Harlow, Caroline Wolf (1993). *HIV in U.S. Prisons and Jails*. Bureau of Justice Statistics, Washington, DC (September).

Horsburgh, C. Robert, Joseph Q. Jarvis, Trudy McArthur, Terri Ignacio, and Patricia Stock (1990). "Seroconversion to Human Immunodeficiency Virus in Prison Inmates," *American Journal of Public Health*. Vol. 80, No. 2, pp. 209–210.

Hoxie, Neil J., James M. Vergeront, Holly R. Frisby, John R. Pfister, Rjurik Golubjatnikov, and Jeffrey P. Davis (1990). "HIV Seroprevalence and the Acceptance of Voluntary HIV Testing Among Newly Incarcerated Male Prison Inmates in Wisconsin," *American Journal of Public Health*. Vol. 80, No. 9, pp. 1129–1131.

Lifson, Alan R. (1988). "Do Alternative Modes for Transmission of the Human Immunodeficiency Virus Exist?", *Journal of the American Medical Association*. Vol. 259, No. 9, pp. 1353–1356.

Mahaffey, Katherine J., and David K. Marcus (1995). "Correctional Officers' Attitudes Toward AIDS," *Criminal Justice and Behavior*. Vol. 22, No. 2, pp. 91–105.

Mahon, Nancy (1996). "New York Inmates' HIV Risk Behaviors: The Implications for Prevention Policy and Programs," *American Journal of Public Health*. Vol. 86, No. 9, pp. 1211–1115.

Maruschak, Laura (1997). "HIV in Prisons and Jails." Bureau of Justice Statistics, Washington, DC (August).

Mutter, Randal C., Richard M. Grimes, and Darwin Labarthe (1994). "Evidence of Intraprison Spread of HIV Infection," *Archives of Internal Medicine*. Vol. 154, pp. 793–795.

Nacci, Peter L., and Thomas R. Kane (1983). "The Incidence of Sex and Sexual Aggression in Federal Prisons," *Federal Probation*. Vol. 47, No. 4 (December), pp. 31–36.

Okie, Susan (1997). "The Downturn in AIDS Deaths," *Washington Post National Weekly Edition*. July 21 and 28, pp. 37.

Polonsky, Sara, Sandra Kerr, Benita Harris, Juarlyn Gaiter, Ronald P. Fichtner, and May G. Kennedy (1994). "HIV Prevention in Prisons and Jails: Obstacles and Opportunities," *Public Health Reports*. Vol. 109, No. 5, pp. 615–625.

Purdy, Matthew (1997). "As AIDS Increases Behind Bars, Costs Dim Promise of New Drugs." *New York Times*. May 26, p. 1.

Vald (1987). "Balanced Response Needed to AIDS in Prison," *National Prison Project Journal*. No. 7 (Spring), pp. 1–5.

Vaughn, Michael S., and Leo Carroll (1996). "Separate and Unequal: Prison versus Free-World Medical Care," paper presented at Annual Meeting of the American Society of Criminology in Chicago, Illinois.

Vlahov, David (1990). "HIV-1 Infection in the Correctional Setting," *Criminal Justice Policy Review*. Vol. 4, No. 4, pp. 306–318.

Waldholz, Michael (1996a). "AIDS Conferees Debate How Early to Offer New Drugs," *Wall Street Journal*. July 12, p. B1.

_____ (1996b). "New AIDS Treatment Raises Tough Question of Who Will Get It," *Wall Street Journal*. July 3, p. 1A.

Whitman, D. (1990) "Inside an AIDS Colony," *U.S. News and World Report*. January 29, pp, 20–26.

Wooden, Wayne S., and Jay Parker (1982). *Men Behind Bars: Sexual Exploitation in Prison*. New York: Plenum Press.

39

Prisons for Profit
Eric Bates

A few hours after midnight one August evening last year, Walter Hazel-wood and Richard Wilson climbed a fence topped with razor wire at the Houston Processing Center, a warehouse built to hold undocumented immigrants awaiting deportation. Once outside, the two prisoners assaulted a guard, stole his car and headed for Dallas.

When prison officials notified the Houston police that the men had escaped, local authorities were shocked. Sure, immigrants had fled the minimum-security facility near the airport a few times before. But Hazelwood and Wilson were not being detained for lacking the papers to prove their citizenship. One was serving time for sexual abuse; the other was convicted of beating and raping an 88-year-old woman. Both men, it turned out, were among some 240 sex offenders from Oregon who had been shipped to the Texas detention center months earlier—and local authorities didn't even know they were there.

The immigration center is owned and operated by Corrections Corporation of America, which manages more private prisons than any other company worldwide. While C.C.A. made nearly $14,000 a day on the out-of-state inmates, the company was quick to point out that it had

Source: Reprinted with permission from the January 5, 1998 issue of *The Nation*. © 1998.

no legal obligation to tell the Houston police or county sheriff about their new neighbors from Oregon. "We designed and built the institution," explained Susan Hart, a company spokeswoman. "It is ours."

Yet like a well-to-do rancher who discovers a couple of valuable head of cattle missing, C.C.A. expected Texas rangers to herd the wayward animals back behind the company's fence. "It's not our function to capture them," Hart told reporters.

Catching the prisoners proved easier, however, than charging them with a crime. When authorities finally apprehended them after eleven days, they discovered they could no more punish the men for escaping than they could lock up a worker for walking off the job. Even in Texas, it seemed, it was not yet a crime to flee a private corporation.

"They have not committed the offense of escape under Texas law," said district attorney John Holmes. "The only reason at all that they're subject to being arrested and were arrested was because during their leaving the facility, they assaulted a guard and took his motor vehicle. *That* we can charge them with, and have."

The state moved quickly to pass legislation making such escapes illegal. But the Texas breakout underscores how the rapid spread of private prisons has created considerable confusion about just what the rules are when a for-profit company like Corrections Corporation seeks to cash in on incarceration. Founded in 1983 with backing from the investors behind Kentucky Fried Chicken, C.C.A. was one of the first companies to push the privatization of public services. The selling point was simple: Private companies could build and run prisons cheaper than the government. Business, after all, would be free of red tape—those inefficient procedures that waste tax dollars on things like open bidding on state contracts and job security for public employees. Unfettered American capitalism would produce a better fetter, saving cash-strapped counties and states millions of dollars each year.

Sooner or later, people realize that "the government can't do anything very well," Thomas Beasley, a co-founder of C.C.A. and a former chairman of the Tennessee Republican Party, said near the start of prison privatization. "At that point, you just sell it like you were selling cars or real estate or hamburgers."

Not everyone is quite so enthusiastic about the prospect of selling human beings like so many pieces of meat. By privatizing prisons, government essentially auctions off inmates—many of them young black men—to the highest bidder. Opponents ranging from the American Civil Liberties Union to the National Sheriffs Association have argued that justice should not be for sale at any price. "The bottom line is a moral one," says Ira Robbins, who wrote a statement for the American Bar

Association opposing private corrections. "Do we want our justice system to be operated by private interests? This is not like privatizing the post office or waste management to provide services to the community. There's something meaningful lost when an inmate looks at a guard's uniform and instead of seeing an emblem that reads 'Federal Bureau of Prisons' or 'State Department of Corrections,' he sees one that says 'Acme Prison Corporation.'"

But such moral concerns have gone largely unheeded in all the excitement over how much money the boys at Acme might save taxpayers. There's only one problem: The evidence suggests that the savings reaped from nearly fifteen years of privatizing prisons are more elusive than an Oregon convict in a Texas warehouse.

In 1996 the General Accounting Office examined the few available reports comparing costs at private and public prisons. Its conclusion: "These studies do not offer substantial evidence that savings have occurred." The most reliable study cited by the G.A.O. found that a C.C.A.-run prison in Tennessee cost only 1 percent less to operate than two comparable state-run prisons. The track record also suggests that private prisons invite political corruption and do little to improve quality, exacerbating the conditions that lead to abuse and violence.

Although private prisons have failed to save much money for taxpayers, they generate enormous profits for the companies that own and operate them. Corrections Corporation ranks among the top five performing companies on the New York Stock Exchange over the past three years. The value of its shares has soared from $50 million when it went public in 1986 to more than $3.5 billion at its peak last October. By carefully selecting the most lucrative prison contracts, slashing labor costs and sticking taxpayers with the bill for expenses like prisoner escapes, C.C.A. has richly confirmed the title of a recent stock analysis by PaineWebber: "Crime pays."

"It's easier for private firms to innovate," says Russell Boraas, who oversees private prisons for the Virginia Department of Corrections. As he inspects a medium-security facility being built by C.C.A. outside the small town of Lawrenceville, Boraas notes that the prison has no guard towers—an "innovation" that saves the company $2.5 million in construction costs and eliminates twenty-five full-time positions. "Think about it," Boraas says, "A state corrections director who eliminates guard towers will lose his job if a prisoner escapes and molests a little old lady. The president of the company won't lose his job, as long as he's making a profit."

Although corrections officials like Boraas initially viewed the drive to privatize prisons with skepticism, many quickly became converts. The crime rate nationwide remains well below what it was twenty-five years ago, but harsher sentencing has packed prisons and jails to the bursting point. There are now 1.8 million Americans behind bars—more than twice as many as a decade ago—and the "get tough" stance has sapped public resources and sparked court orders to improve conditions.

With their promise of big savings, private prisons seemed to offer a solution. Corporate lockups can now hold an estimated 77,500 prisoners, most of them state inmates. Over the next five years, analysts expect the private share of the prison "market" to more than double.

Corrections Corporation is far and away the biggest company in the corrections business, controlling more than half of all inmates in private prisons nationwide. C.C.A. now operates the sixth-largest prison system in the country—and is moving aggressively to expand into the global market with prisons in England, Australia and Puerto Rico. That's good news for investors. *The Cabot Market Letter* compares the company to "a hotel that's always at 100 percent occupancy . . . and booked to the end of the century." C.C.A. started taking reservations during the Reagan Administration, when Beasley founded the firm in Nashville with a former classmate from West Point. Their model was the Hospital Corporation of America, then the nation's largest owner of private hospitals. "This is the home of H.C.A.," Beasley thought at the time. "The synergies are the same."

From the start, those synergies included close ties to politicians who could grant the company lucrative contracts. As former chairman of the state G.O.P., Beasley was a good friend of then-Governor Lamar Alexander. In 1985 Alexander backed a plan to hand over the entire state prison system to the fledgling company for $200 million. Among C.C.A.'s stockholders at the time were the Governor's wife, Honey, and Ned McWherter, the influential Speaker of the state House, who succeeded Alexander as governor.

Although the state legislature eventually rejected the plan as too risky, C.C.A. had established itself as a major player. It had also discovered that knowing the right people can be more important than actually saving taxpayers money. The company won its first bid to run a prison by offering to operate the Silverdale Work Farm near Chattanooga for $21 per inmate per day. At $3 less than the county was spending, it seemed like a good deal—until a crackdown on drunk drivers flooded the work farm with new inmates. Because fixed expenses were unaffected by the surge, each new prisoner cost C.C.A. about $5. But the county, stuck with a contract that required it to pay the company $21 a head, found itself $200,000 over budget. "The work farm became a gold mine," noted John Donahue, a public policy professor at Harvard University.

When the contract came up for renewal in 1986, however, county commissioners voted to stick with Corrections Corporation. Several enjoyed business ties with the company. One commissioner had a pest-control contract with the firm, and later went to work for C.C.A. as a lobbyist. Another did landscaping at the prison, and a third ran the moving company that settled the warden into his new home. C.C.A. also put the son of the county employee responsible for monitoring the Silverdale contract on the payroll at its Nashville headquarters. The following year, the U.S. Justice Department published a research report warning about such conflicts of interest in on-site monitoring—the only mechanism for insuring that prison operators abide by the contract. In addition to being a hidden and costly expense of private prisons, the report cautioned, government monitors could "be co-opted by the contractor's staff. Becoming friendly or even beholden to contract personnel could lead to the State receiving misleading reports."

But even when problems have been reported, officials often downplay them. The Justice Department noted "substantial staff turnover problems" at the Chattanooga prison, for instance, but added that "this apparently did not result in major reductions in service quality." The reason? "This special effort to do a good job," the report concluded, "is probably due to the private organizations finding themselves in the national limelight, and their desire to expand the market."

The same year that federal officials were crediting C.C.A. with "a good job" at the undermanned facility, Rosalind Bradford, a 23-year-old woman being held at Silverdale, died from an undiagnosed complication during pregnancy. A shift supervisor who later sued the company testified that Bradford suffered in agony for at least twelve hours before C.C.A. officials allowed her to be taken to a hospital. "Rosalind Bradford died out there, in my opinion, of criminal neglect," the supervisor said in a deposition.

Inspectors from the British Prison Officers Association who visited the prison that year were similarly shocked by what they witnessed. "We saw evidence of inmates being cruelly treated," the inspectors reported. "Indeed, the warden admitted that noisy and truculent prisoners are gagged with sticky tape, but this had caused a problem when an inmate almost choked to death."

The inspectors were even more blunt when they visited the C.C.A.-run immigration center in Houston, where they found inmates confined to warehouselike dormitories for twenty-three hours a day. The private facility, inspectors concluded, demonstrated "possibly the worst conditions we have ever witnessed in terms of inmate care and supervision."

Reports of inhumane treatment of prisoners, while deeply disturbing, do not by themselves indicate that private prisons are worse than public ones. After all, state and federal lockups have never been known for their considerate attitude toward the people under their watch. Indeed, C.C.A. and other company prisons have drawn many of their wardens and guards from the ranks of public corrections officers. The guards videotaped earlier this year assaulting prisoners with stun guns at a C.C.A. competitor in Texas had been hired despite records of similar abuse when they worked for the state.

Susan Hart, the C.C.A. spokeswoman, insisted that her company would never put such people on the payroll—well, almost never. "It would be inappropriate, for certain positions, [to hire] someone who said, 'Yes, I beat a prisoner to death,'" she told *The Houston Chronicle*. "That would be a red flag for us." She did not specify for which positions the company considers murder an appropriate job qualification.

In fact, C.C.A. employs at least two wardens in Texas who were disciplined for beating prisoners while employed by the state. And David Myers, the president of the company, supervised an assault on inmates who took a guard hostage while Myers was serving as warden of a Texas prison in 1984. Fourteen guards were later found to have used "excessive force," beating subdued and handcuffed prisoners with riot batons.

The real danger of privatization is not some innate inhumanity on the part of its practitioners but rather the added financial incentives that reward inhumanity. The same economic logic that motivates companies to run prisons more efficiently also encourages them to cut corners at the expense of workers, prisoners and the public. Private prisons essentially mirror the cost-cutting practices of health maintenance organizations: Companies receive a guaranteed fee for each prisoner, regardless of the actual costs. Every dime they don't spend on food or medical care or training for guards is a dime they can pocket.

As in most industries, the biggest place to cut prison expenses is personnel. "The bulk of the cost savings enjoyed by C.C.A. is the result of lower labor costs," PaineWebber assures investors. Labor accounts for roughly 70 percent of all prison expenses, and C.C.A. prides itself on getting more from fewer employees. "With only a 36 percent increase in personnel," boasts the latest annual report, "revenues grew 41 percent, operating income grew 98 percent, and net income grew 115 percent."

Like other companies, C.C.A. prefers to design and build its own prisons so it can replace guards right from the start with video cameras and clustered cellblocks that are cheaper to monitor. "The secret to low-cost operations is having the minimum number of officers watching the maximum number of inmates," explains Russell Boraas, the private prison administrator for Virginia. "You can afford to pay damn near anything for construction if it will get you an efficient prison."

At the C.C.A. prison under construction in Lawrenceville, Boraas indicates how the design of the "control room" will enable a guard to simultaneously watch three "pods" of 250 prisoners each. Windows in the elevated room afford an unobstructed view of each cellblock below, and "vision blocks" in the floor are positioned over each entranceway so guards can visually identify anyone being admitted. The high-tech panel at the center of the room can open any door at the flick of a switch. When the prison opens next year, C.C.A. will employ five guards to supervise 750 prisoners during the day, and two guards at night.

Another way to save money on personnel is to leave positions unfilled when they come open. Speaking before a legislative panel in Tennessee in October, Boraas noted that some private prisons in Texas have made up for the low reimbursement rates they receive from the state "by leaving positions vacant a little longer than they should." Some C.C.A. employees admit privately that the company leaves positions open to boost profits. "We're always short," says one guard who asked not to be identified. "They do staff fewer positions—that's one way they save money." The company is growing so quickly, another guard explains, that "we have more slots than we have people to fill them. When they transfer officers to new facilities, we're left with skeletons."

At first glance, visitors to the South Central Correctional Center could be forgiven for mistaking the medium-security prison for a college campus. The main driveway rolls through wooded hills on the outskirts of Clifton, Tennessee, past picnic benches, a fitness track and a horse barn. But just inside the front door, a prominent bulletin board makes clear that the prison means business. At the top are the words "C.C.A. Excellence in Corrections." At the bottom is "Yesterday's Stock Closing," followed by a price.

In addition to employing fewer guards, C.C.A. saves money on labor by replacing the guaranteed pensions earned by workers at state-run prisons with a cheaper—and riskier—stock-ownership plan. Employees get a chance to invest in the company, and the company gets employees devoted to the bottom line. "Being a stockholder yourself, you monitor things closer," says Mark Staggs, standing in the segregation unit, where he oversees prisoners confined for breaking the rules. "You make sure you don't waste money on things like cleaning products. Because it's your money you're spending."

Warden Kevin Myers (not related to C.C.A. president David Myers) also looks for little places to cut costs. "I can save money on purchasing because there's no bureaucracy," he says. "If I see a truckload of white potatoes at a bargain, I can buy them. I'm always negotiating for a lower price."

But what is thriftiness to the warden is just plain miserly to those forced to eat what he dishes out. "Ooowhee! It's pitiful in that kitchen," says Antonio McCraw, who was released from South Central last March after serving three years for armed robbery. "I just thank God I'm out of there. You might get a good meal once a month. The rest was instant potatoes, vegetables out of a can and processed pizzas. C.C.A. don't care whether you eat or not. Sure they may cut corners and do it for less money, but is it healthy?"

The State of Tennessee hoped to answer that question when it turned South Central over to C.C.A. in 1992. The prison was built at roughly the same time as two state-run facilities with similar designs and inmate populations, giving officials a rare opportunity to compare daily operating costs—and quality—under privatization.

The latest state report on violence at the three prisons indicates that South Central is a much more dangerous place than its public counterparts. During the past fiscal year, the C.C.A. prison experienced violent incidents at a rate more than 50 percent higher than state facilities. The company also listed significantly worse rates for contraband, drugs and assaults on staff and prisoners.

"If that doesn't raise some eyebrows and give you some kind of indication of what the future holds, I guess those of us who are concerned just need to be quiet," says John Mark Windle, a state representative who opposes privatization.

Corrections officials note that understaffing can certainly fuel violence, which winds up costing taxpayers more money. The state legislature has heard testimony that employee turnover at South Central is more than twice the level at state prisons, and prisoners report seeing classes of new recruits every month, many of them young and inexperienced. "The turnover rate is important because it shows whether you have experienced guards who stick around and know the prisoners," says inmate Alex Friedmann, seated at a bare table in a visitation room. "If you have a high turnover rate you have less stability. New employees come in; they really don't know what's going on. That leads to conflicts with inmates."

Internal company documents tell a similar story. According to the minutes of an August 1995 meeting of shift supervisors at South Central, chief of security Danny Scott said, "we all know that we have lots of new staff and are constantly in the training mode." He added that "so many employees were totally lost and had never worked in corrections."

A few months later, a company survey of staff members at the prison asked, "What is the reason for the number of people quitting C.C.A.?" Nearly 20 percent of employees cited "treatment by supervisors," and 17 percent listed "money."

Out of earshot of their supervisors, some guards also say the company contributes to violence by skimping on activities for inmates. "We don't give them anything to do," says one officer. "We give them the bare minimum we have to."

Ron Lyons agrees. "There's no meaningful programs here," says Lyons, who served time at state-run prisons before coming to South Central. "I can't get over how many people are just laying around in the pod every day. I would have thought C.C.A. would have known that inmate idleness is one of the biggest problems in prisons—too much time sitting around doing nothing. You definitely realize it's commercialized. It's a business. Their business is to feed you and count you, and that's it."

Given all the penny-pinching, it would seem that C.C.A. should easily be able to demonstrate significant savings at South Central. Instead, a study of costs conducted by the state in 1995 found that the company provided almost no savings compared with its two public rivals. The study—cited by the General Accounting Office as "the most sound and detailed comparison of operational costs"—actually showed that the C.C.A. prison cost *more* to run on a daily basis. Even after the state factored in its long-term expenses, C.C.A. still spent $35.38 a day per prisoner—only 38 cents less than the state average.

The study contradicted what is supposed to be the most compelling rationale for prison privatization: the promise of big savings. But the industry champion dismissed its defeat by insisting, much to the amazement of its challengers, that it hadn't tried very hard to save tax dollars. "When you're in a race and you can win by a few steps, that's what you do," said Doctor R. Crants, who co-founded C.C.A. and now serves as chairman and chief executive officer. "We weren't trying to win by a great deal."

The comment by Crants, as remarkable as it seems, exposes the true nature of privatization. When it comes to savings, the prison industry will beat state spending by as narrow a margin as the state will permit. To a prison company like C.C.A., "savings" are nothing but the share of profits it is required to hand over to the government—another expense that cuts into the bottom line and must therefore be kept to a minimum, like wages or the price of potatoes. At its heart, privatizing prisons is really about privatizing tax dollars, about transforming public money into private profits.

That means companies are actually looking for ways to keep public spending as high as possible, including charging taxpayers for questionable expenses. The New Mexico Corrections Department, for example, has accused C.C.A. of overcharging the state nearly $2 million over the past eight years for operating the women's prison in Grants. The company fee of $95 a day for each innate, it turns out, includes $22 for debt service on the prison.

Last summer, a legislative committee in Tennessee calculated that state prisons contribute nearly $17.8 million each year to state agencies that provide central services like printing, payroll administration and insurance. Since company prisons usually go elsewhere for such services, states that privatize unwittingly lose money they once counted on to help pay fixed expenses.

The "chargebacks," as they are known, came to light last spring when C.C.A. once again proposed taking over the entire Tennessee prison system. This time the company offered to save $100 million a year—a staggering sum, considering that the annual budget for the system is only $270 million.

Like many claims of savings, the C.C.A. offer turned out to be based on false assumptions. Crants, the company chairman and C.E.O., said he derived the estimate from comparing the $32 daily rate the company charges for medium-security prisoners at South Central with the systemwide average of $54. But the state system includes maximum-security prisons that cost much more to operate than South Central. "It's almost like going into a rug store," says State Senator James Kyle, who chaired legislative hearings on privatization. "They're always 20 percent off. But 20 percent off what?"

Yet the sales pitch, however absurd, had the intended effect of getting Kyle and other lawmakers into the store to look around. Once there, the prison companies kept offering them bigger and better deals. Given an opportunity to submit cost estimates anonymously, firms offered fantastic savings ranging from 30 percent to 50 percent. Threatened by the competition, even the state Department of Corrections went bargain basement, offering to slash its own already low cost by $70 million a year. Despite opposition from state employees, legislators indicated after the hearings that they support a move to turn most prisoners over to private companies—a decision that delighted C.C.A. "I was pretty pleased," Crants said afterward. The governor and legislators are wrangling over the details, but both sides have agreed informally to privatize roughly two-thirds of the Tennessee system. A few prisons will be left in the hands of the state, just in case something goes wrong.

Lawmakers didn't have to look far to see how wrong things can go. South Carolina decided last February not to renew a one-year contract with C.C.A. for a juvenile detention center in the state capital. Child advocates reported hearing about horrific abuses at the facility, where some boys say they were hogtied and shackled together. "The bottom line is the staff there were inexperienced," said Robyn Zimmerman of the South Carolina Department of Juvenile Justice. "They were not trained properly."

Once again, though, such stark realities proved less influential than the political connections enjoyed by C.C.A. The chief lobbyist for the company in the Tennessee legislature is married to the Speaker of the state House. Top C.C.A. executives, board members and their spouses have contributed at least $110,000 to state candidates since 1993, including $1,350 to Senator Kyle. And five state officials—including the governor, the House Speaker and the sponsor of the privatization bill— are partners with C.C.A. co-founder Thomas Beasley in several Red Hot & Blue barbecue restaurants in Tennessee.

The political clout extends to the national level as well. On the Republican side, Corrections Corporation employs the services of J. Michael Quinlan, director of the federal Bureau of Prisons under George Bush. On the Democratic side, C.C.A. reserves a seat on its seven-member board for Joseph Johnson, former executive director of the Rainbow Coalition. The Nashville *Tennessean* points to Johnson as evidence that the company "looks like America. . . . Johnson is African-American," the paper observes, "as are 60 percent of C.C.A.'s prisoners."

Johnson played a pivotal behind-the-scenes role earlier this year, using his political connections to help C.C.A. swing a deal to buy a prison from the District of Columbia for $52 million. It was the first time a government sold a prison to a private company, and C.C.A. hopes it won't be the last. Earlier this year, with backing from financial heavyweights like Lehman Brothers and PaineWebber, the company formed C.C.A. Prison Realty Trust to focus solely on buying prisons. The initial stock offering raised $388.5 million from investors to enable C.C.A. to speculate on prisons as real estate.

Why would cities or states sell their prisons to the C.C.A. trust? PaineWebber cites the lure of what it calls "free money." Unlike many public bond initiatives earmarked for specific projects like schools or sewage systems, the broker explains, "the sale of an existing prison would generate proceeds that a politician could then use for initiatives that fit his or her agenda, possibly improving the chances of re-election." Companies building their own prisons certainly receive friendly treatment from officials. Russell Boraas invited companies bidding on a private prison to a meeting and asked what he could do to help. "I said, 'Guys, I know quite a bit about running construction projects, but I don't know much about private prisons. What are you looking for? What can I do to make this user-friendly for you?' They said it would be nice if they could use tax-exempt bond issues for construction, just like the state." So Boraas allowed companies to finance construction with help from taxpayers, and a local Industrial Development Authority eventually aided C.C.A. in getting $58 million in financing to build the prison.

Such deals raise concerns that private prisons may wind up costing taxpayers more in the long run. Although governments remain legally responsible for inmates guarded by public companies, firms have little trouble finding ways to skirt public oversight while pocketing public money. Instead of streamlining the system, hiring corporations to run prisons actually adds a layer of bureaucracy that can increase costs and reduce accountability. Prison companies have been known to jack up prices when their contracts come up for renewal, and some defer maintenance on prisons since they aren't responsible for them once their contract expires.

Even more disturbing, private prisons have the financial incentive—and financial influence—to lobby lawmakers for harsher prison sentences and other "get tough" measures. In the prison industry, after all, locking people up is good for business. "If you really want to save money you can lock prisoners in a box and feed them a slice of bread each day," says Alex Friedmann, the prisoner at South Central. "The real question is, Can you run programs in such a way that people don't commit more crime? That should be the mark of whether privatization is successful in prisons—not whether you keep them locked up but whether you keep them out."

C.C.A. officials dismiss such concerns, confident the current boom will continue of its own accord. "I don't think we have to worry about running out of product," says Kevin Myers, the warden at South Central. "It's unfortunate but true. We don't have to drum up business."

Perhaps—but Corrections Corporation and other company prisons already have enormous power to keep their current prisoners behind bars for longer stretches. Inmates generally lose accumulated credit for "good time" when they are disciplined by guards, giving the C.C.A. stockholders who serve as officers an incentive to crack the whip. A 1992 study by the New Mexico Corrections Department showed that inmates at the women's prison run by C.C.A. lost good time at a rate nearly eight times higher than their male counterparts at a state-run lockup. And every day a prisoner loses is a day of extra income for the company and an extra expense for taxpayers.

Some C.C.A. guards in Tennessee also say privately that they are encouraged to write up prisoners for minor infractions and place them in segregation. Inmates in "seg" not only lose their good time, they also have thirty days added to their sentence—a bonus of nearly $1,000 for the company at some prisons. "We will put 'em in seg in a hurry," says a guard who works at the Davidson County Juvenile Detention Facility in Nashville.

The prison holds 100 youths—"children, really," says the guard—most of them teenage boys. "They may be young, but they understand what's going on," he adds. One day, as a 14-year-old boy was being released after serving his sentence, the guard offered him some friendly advice.

"Stay out of trouble," he said. "I don't want to see you back here."

"Why not?" the kid responded. "That's how you make your money."

40

Does Prison Pay?
The Stormy National Debate Over the Cost-Effectiveness of Imprisonment

John J. DiIulio, Jr.
Anne Morrison Piehl

Today the U.S. prison population is hovering around the 800,000 mark. Before the end of the decade, it will easily surpass one million. Most analysts place the average annual cost per prisoner at $25,000, and the labor-intensive business of penal administration would appear to offer no appreciable economies of scale. Building, staffing, and paying for prisons is the fastest-growing item in most state budgets. Not surprisingly, a debate is raging over the cost-effectiveness of imprisonment. The debate is being waged as a numbers game, with conservatives citing figures to show that "prison pays," and liberals citing figures to insist that it doesn't. So far, partisans appear not to have noticed that the kind of empirical analysis that would justify strong generalizations on either side of the argument has yet to be done.

Given the fledgling state of empirical work, we question the wisdom of the rush to judgment. Our argument, which is based on our analysis of prisoner self-report survey data gathered from the largest scientifically selected sample of prisoners in a single system ever undertaken, moves from a simple benefit-cost analysis of imprisonment. Needless to say, such an analysis addresses many empirical and normative issues weakly

Source: Reprinted by permission of the Brookings Institution from *The Brookings Review*, Fall 1991.

or not at all. But benefit-cost analyses of imprisonment have figured prominently of late in national debates about corrections policy, and many judgments about the efficacy of imprisonment policies rest on implicit estimates of the costs and benefits of imprisonment.

The Zedlewski Controversy

In July of 1987 the National Institute of Justice published a report entitled "Making Confinement Decisions," by NIJ economist Edwin Zedlewski. Essentially, Zedlewski's study was a benefit-cost analysis of imprisonment. He surveyed cost data from several prison systems and estimated that the annual per prisoner cost of confinement was $25,000. Using national crime data and the findings of criminal victimization surveys, he estimated that the typical offender commits 187 crimes a year and that the typical crime exacts $2,300 in property losses or in physical injuries and human suffering. Multiplying these two figures, he calculated that, when on the streets, the typical imprisoned felon was responsible for $430,000 in "social costs" each year. Dividing that figure by $25,000 (his estimate of the annual per prisoner cost of confinement), he concluded that incarceration has a benefit-cost ratio of just over 17. The implications were unequivocal. According to Zedlewski's analysis, putting 1,000 felons behind prison bars costs society $25 million a year. But not putting these same felons behind prison bars costs society about $430 million a year (187,000 crimes times $2,300 per crime).

At least within criminal justice circles, NIJ's reports tend to get noticed, and like any study that bucks the conventional wisdom in a credible (or credible-looking) way, Zedlewski's analysis attracted its share of critical attention. In a 1988 article, "The New Mathematics of Imprisonment," published in the *Journal of the National Council of Crime and Delinquency*, noted penologists Franklin E. Zimring and Gordon Hawkins charged that Zedlewski's analysis was fatally flawed. Zimring and Hawkins argued that Zedlewski had overstated the net benefit of incarceration by inflating the numerator (crimes per offender and social costs per crime) and deflating the denominator (annual per prisoner costs of confinement). They cited several good studies to bolster their charge, including one indicating that the typical offender commits fewer than 20 (as opposed to 187) crimes in a year.

But Zimring and Hawkins did not use their insights into Zedlewski's methodological errors to recalculate the benefit-cost ratio of imprisonment. Instead, they asserted that such measures were inherently unreliable, dismissed Zedlewski's study as "the wrong dog barking up the wrong tree," and concluded by lamenting that, despite sharp escalations in the nation's prison population, many people continue to demand more prisons. They were joined by other critics who, in effect, wanted to have their corrections cake and eat it too. The logic of Zedlewski's fiercest critics was like the logic of nihilists who insist not only that people believe in nothing but in their particular brand of nothing. Metaphorically speaking, one is free to believe that the benefit-cost ballpark doesn't exist, but having taken that position, one cannot logically proclaim anyone to be out in left field (or, in this case, right).

There was, indeed, no shortage of serious methodological and related problems with Zedlewski's analysis. Zedlewski, for example, quoted the results of a survey by the RAND Corporation that "inmates averaged between 187 and 287 crimes per year, exclusive of drug deals." Although he noted that half the inmate population committed fewer than 15 crimes a year, so that the median number of crimes committed was 15, he used the mean (or average) in his analysis. Making this one adjustment (using 15 rather than 187 for the number of crimes averted through incapacitation of a criminal) reduces the benefit-cost ratio to 1.38.

Zedlewski's research also brings up several aggregation issues, both across crimes and across jurisdictions. The RAND survey, of offenders in prisons and jails in California, Michigan, and Texas, contained self-report data on criminal activity, demographics, and criminal records. The survey reported that inmates who committed burglaries averaged between 76 and 118 annually, while lesser thieves reported they averaged between 135 and 202 thefts a year. Although there is substantial variation in offense rates, the general pattern is that the pettier the crime, the more frequent the offense. Zedlewski's use of averages obscured these distinctions and inflated savings estimates.

Also obscured in the big picture drawn by Zedlewski are the differences among jurisdictions. States vary in many ways, including laws and the austerity with which they are enforced, the structure of the prison and jail systems, the generosity of the welfare system, and economic vitality. These differences influence the benefit-cost calculation by affecting the costs of incarcerating individuals and the characteristics of the arrested offenders. States that imprison a high proportion of offenders are likely to gain less at the margin than states known for their liberal attitudes toward imprisonment. Whereas the Zedlewski approach in a sense gives a benefit-cost estimate for the nation, a measure at the state level, which is the decision-making unit, is of more policy relevance.

Beyond Willie Horton

The controversy surrounding Zedlewski's analysis widened with Richard B. Abell's 1989 essay "Beyond Willie Horton: The Battle of the Prison Bulge," published in *Policy Review*, a journal of the Heritage

Foundation. In this article, Abell, an Assistant Attorney General of the United States, repeated Zedlewski's findings. He used anecdotes to put flesh on the reality behind the numbers and to illustrate the potential costs of not imprisoning criminals. For example, Abell recounted the tale of a Michigan prisoner who in 1975 brutally shot and killed two people in a Detroit bar. A plea bargain reduced the killer's two first-degree murder charges to second degree, and he received a 20- to 40-year prison term. But on the day he entered prison he was automatically granted nearly 10 years of "good-time" credits. He kept those credits even though, after dozens of serious disciplinary infractions, his behind-bars behavior was anything but good. His confinement time was further reduced under the terms of state laws designed to relieve prison overcrowding. In 1984, after serving only eight and a half years of his minimum sentence, the killer returned to the streets. Within three months of his early parole, he and a female accomplice—a fugitive who had been serving time in a halfway house—killed again. This time the victims were a young woman, who was shot as she opened her front door, and a local policeman, the father of six children.

Abell's article generated a storm of commentary, especially after an excerpt from it appeared as a featured op-ed essay in the *Wall Street Journal*. In addition to railing against Abell's use of a graph that showed crime rates falling when imprisonment rates go up, many experts challenged his uncritical reliance on Zedlewski's findings and ridiculed his use of "sensationalistic" anecdotes such as the one summarized in the preceding paragraph.

Abell's crime-imprisonment graph was misleading, but not half as much as the critics' assertion that no relationship exists between the probability of being imprisoned and the propensity to commit crime. Based on existing statistical evidence, the relationship between crime rates and imprisonment rates is ambiguous. By the same token, Abell's embrace of Zedlewski's analysis was uncritical, but no more so than the facile rejection of the same by his (and Zedlewski's) critics.

Finally, there was nothing sensationalistic about Abell's account. Policies that effect the release of convicted criminals have consequences, some of them ugly. It is not sensationalism to recount true stories of innocent people whose lives were ruined as a result of these policies. And it is not responsible to bury detailed evidence of the harms caused by these policies alongside their victims. Indeed, the Michigan killer discussed by Abell was atypical in that he had served more time in prison than most murderers now do. After lavishing good-time credits on its prisoners and reducing their sentences to relieve overcrowding, Michigan released thousands of violent criminals who had served less than half of their sentences in confinement, with tragic results for many of the state's citizens. Similar policies and programs have operated with similar results in many jurisdictions.

Still, the public debate over imprisonment policy is not enriched by analyses, systematic or anecdotal, that overdramatize the benefits of keeping criminals behind bars. Weighing in on the other side, in a September 1989 report, the RAND Corporation summarized and endorsed the academic and popular literature critical of Zedlewski's analysis. In a footnote, RAND stressed that Zedlewski had erred in using the mean figure of 187 crimes a year, when the median figure was 15 crimes a year. The report as a whole stressed the need to compare the costs and benefits of imprisonment to the costs and benefits of other correctional sanctions, especially intensively supervised probation programs.

The debate, however, has continued. Zedlewski has defended his research against its critics, and the chief finding of "Making Confinement Decisions" continues to be cited as settled fact in the popular media. In the November 1990 issue of Reader's Digest, for example, Zedlewski's 1987 study was cited to support the argument that "to pen every serious offender will cost billions, but it's money well spent." The entire text of the article was reprinted as a full-page ad in the New York Times on October 17, 1990.

Last December one of us published a report on corrections in Wisconsin that featured an analysis of the benefits and costs of imprisonment in that state. The report, published by the Wisconsin Policy Research Institute, accounted for many of the methodological problems in Zedlewski's analysis, and estimated the benefit-cost ratio to be a little less than 2. Nevertheless, fierce critics of the Zedlewski study, such as the National Council on Crime and Delinquency, charged that the Wisconsin report was meaningless, ignored its qualifications, and caricatured its contents. Meanwhile, individual champions of the Zedlewski study charged that the Wisconsin report understated the net benefits of imprisonment.

Estimating Crime Commission Rates

Hope for rational, nonideological discourse on this important public policy issue nevertheless springs eternal. Reasonable minds can and do differ over how best to conduct cost-benefit analyses of imprisonment policies, how best to interpret the results of such analyses, and how, if at all, to fashion or reorient public policies accordingly. Based on our reanalysis of relevant 1990 survey data from a scientifically selected sample of more than 7 percent of the Wisconsin male prison population, however, extremists on either side of the Zedlewski debate are bound to be disappointed. In Wisconsin, the net benefits of imprisonment are neither as large as Zedlewski's analysis would predict nor as minuscule as Zedlewski's strongest critics would assert.

We follow other analysts, including Zedlewski, in excluding the effects of incarceration on future crime rates through general deterrence, rehabilitation, or further criminalization of the offender. Because the applied research in this field gives us no firm basis for concluding that the net effects of prison time on future criminality are significantly positive or significantly negative, we focus on incapacitation (based on prisoners' self-reported past history)—that is, the number of crimes averted because the offender was kept off the street.

As other researchers have noted, a few offenders seem to be responsible for the majority of crimes committed, while the bulk of offenders commit a few crimes each. To illustrate this, table 1 shows four different ways to measure the number of crimes committed per prisoner per year in Wisconsin. The average (mean) number of crimes per prisoner per year including drug sales is estimated to be 1,834. The mean number of crimes excluding drug sales is 141. The median number of crimes including drug sales is 26. The median number excluding drug sales is 12.

Table 1. Wisconsin Prisoners' Yearly Crime Rate

	INCLUDING DRUG SALES	EXCLUDING DRUG SALES
Average	1,834	141
Median	26	12

Source: Calculations from the 1990 Wisconsin Prisoner Survey.

It is worth noting here that most analysts have omitted drug sales from their calculations of the net benefit of imprisonment. There is no pure methodological reason why drug sales should not be included in such calculations. Drug sales are crimes, and they involve both direct and indirect social costs. Systematic empirical knowledge about the economic and other consequences of drug sales is scarce. Such data as exist—for example, the June 1990 RAND report on drug dealing in Washington, D.C.—do not point clearly in the direction of leaving drug sales out of such calculations. The issue is complicated by individual moral attitudes toward the distribution of illegal drugs. Some people view drug sales as "victimless crimes" and favor drug legalization, while others view drug sales as serious crimes at the root of many other criminal activities and social ills. Either view may affect one's inclination to include drug sales in calculations of the net benefit of imprisonment.

This is not the place to referee the drug debate. We note, however, that a main reason why drug sales are widely viewed as socially harmful is that they are believed to be strongly correlated with other criminal activities. In the analysis that follows, although we will follow previous studies in excluding drug sales, we will focus on several types of criminal activity that have been associated with drug involvement.

Estimating Social Costs of Crime

Estimating prisoners' yearly rates of committing crimes is only the first step in our analysis. The next step is to estimate how much these crimes would cost society were the prisoners free to commit them. Or, to put it another way, our next step is to estimate how much society benefits from protecting itself from these crimes through imprisonment. Analytically, it is a complicated step, but not an impossible one.

The reason for the complexity should be rather obvious: different crimes impose different social costs. Other things being equal, a bank robbery in which someone is killed or seriously injured is more costly to society than a bank robbery in which no one is harmed. But does every burglary impose the same social costs as every other burglary? Is a petty burglary more or less costly to society than an attempted car theft that ends in vandalism? Are either or both of these crimes more or less injurious to society than a routine drug sale? Generally speaking, without being arbitrary it is difficult to rank categories of crimes in terms of their social costs, and difficult to translate these costs into dollar values.

Indeed, it is often difficult even to classify a convicted offender as a "robber," "burglar," or "drug dealer." About one-third of the property offenders we surveyed, for example, acknowledged involvement in more than one category of crime in the four months before their most recent arrest. Among other problems, official information on a prisoner's conviction charge and past criminal record is often contaminated by plea bargaining and the exercise of judicial discretion.

In the face of these difficulties, the analyst has at least two options (apart from throwing in the towel). One option is to come up with a single estimate of the social cost per crime. In previous studies, many analysts (ourselves included) have done just that. As noted above, Zedlewski used an estimate of social costs per crime of $2,300. Others have argued for and used both higher and lower estimates. While not totally without merit, the single estimate approach results in grossly oversimplified calculations and does not enable one to specify the net benefit of imprisonment for any given category of offenders. In addition, that approach does not capture the differences in the "crime mix"—that is, the types of crimes most frequently committed—from one jurisdiction to the next.

A second option, and the one we will exercise here, is to restrict the analysis to given types of crimes. The two basic categories of crime are violent crime and property crime. We know enough to make social cost estimates for certain types of property crime (robbery, burglary, auto theft, and fraud, forgery, and petty theft) and for at least one type of violent crime (assault). So we will restrict ourselves to an analysis of the net benefit of imprisonment for these crimes.

Using data drawn from the National Crime Survey and from a study of jury awards in cases involving pain and suffering and time lost from work, Mark A. Cohen has estimated the dollar values of these crimes (table 2). The estimates account for pain and suffering, risk of death, lost wages, and medical costs for psychological injury resulting from the crimes. Still, we acknowledge that further research is needed to refine these measures.

Table 2. Estimates of Social Costs of Selected Crimes

CRIME	SOCIAL COST
Robbery	$ 12,060
Assault	11,518
Burglary	1,314
Auto theft	2,995
Fraud, forgery, petty theft	110

Source: Mark A. Cohen, "Pain, Suffering, and Jury Awards: A Study of the Cost of Crime to Victims," *Law and Society Review*, vol. 22, no. 3 (1988). We have revised Cohen's estimates to account for inflation and transfer of wealth.

The Net Benefit of Imprisonment

To assess the net benefit of incapacitation we must make some assumptions regarding who would be incarcerated if prison capacity were expanded at the margin, say by 100 cells. Some researchers have considered lengthening sentences of those currently convicted, for example, by 10 percent, assuming they would remain as criminally active as they reported having been before their arrest. On the basis of evidence that the *probability* of being punished has more deterrent effect than the *degree of the sanction*, we believe a more practical alternative is to consider sending more offenders to prison. Zedlewski followed the same approach.

We have ranked the respondents to the Wisconsin survey according to their "social costliness" in the months just before arrest (see table 3). For each offender we calculated the total cost of having him on the street for a year, committing crimes at the rate he reported on the survey. For example, we simply multiplied an estimate of the number of robberies he would commit times $12,060, giving us a measure of the cost of robberies he would do. Then we added a similar measure for the impact of his assaults (the number of assaults times $11,518 each), continuing the process for each crime listed in the table. For technical reasons in the way the estimates were constructed, the resulting measure of "social costliness" is probably biased upward somewhat.

Table 3. The Social Cost of Property and Assault Crimes per Offender

OFFENDER	COST
Average (mean)	$ 369,131
Median	46,072
25th percentile	15,768
10th percentile	1,980

Source: Calculations from the 1990 Wisconsin Prisoner Survey.

Table 3 summarizes the statistics for the whole sample. It may be more illustrative, however, to consider the criminal activities of a few actual offenders, shown in table 4. As expected from our earlier observation that a few individuals are responsible for most crimes, the distribution of social costs is seriously skewed—an important fact in interpreting the analysis. Offender A committed robberies at a rate of 151 a year and assaults at the rate of 12 a year, at a social cost of almost $2 million dollars. Offender B committed 3 robberies and 3 assaults a year, at a social cost of $70,734. Offender D is considered the "median" offender; half of those surveyed were more costly than he, half less costly. Actually, there are several inmates who fit this profile, having committed 4 assaults a year. The offender at the 25th percentile cutoff, offender E, committed 12 burglaries with an estimated $15,768 in social costs. Taking a simple average of social costs of all of the property or assault offenders gives a mean value of $369,131.

Because attaching dollar values to criminal acts is much more contentious for such crimes as murder and rape, we do not consider those

Table 4. Sample Criminal Profiles for Wisconsin Prisoners

	ROBBERIES	ASSAULTS	BURGLARIES	AUTO THEFT	OTHER THEFT	SOCIAL COST
A	151	12				$ 1,959,276
B	3	3				70,734
C	3		12			51,948
D		4				46,072
E			12			15,768
F					18	1,980

crimes here. In fact, we would venture that it is impossible to make an argument for incarcerating murderers based on projected social savings. Most murderers are not expected to kill again because their crime was one of passion or the result of drinking or drug use. Arguments for their imprisonment must be based on retribution and deterrence, which are quite valid, though not part of the current discussion.

Table 5 transforms the social costs associated with different prisoners in the Wisconsin study into benefit-cost ratios by dividing the numbers in table 3 by the cost of incarcerating an offender. We use an estimate of $25,000 per prisoner per year, which accounts for cell construction costs and operating expenditures.

It clearly does not "pay" from an economic standpoint to keep the least criminal offenders behind bars. But how do we know which estimate is appropriate to assess current imprisonment policy? First, we need to define which of the current inmates the hypothetical additional 100 prisoners would be most like. To answer this question we need some evidence of how well the criminal justice system sorts out the high-rate, high-cost offenders. This depends on the degree to which police officers make accurate judgments about whom to arrest, how the ardor with which public defenders argue their clients' cases is related to criminality, and judicial decisions regarding the type and severity of sanction imposed. One technique for approaching this issue would be to compare self-reports of those sentenced to probation to those sent to prison to see how well judges and the participating attorneys do.

But even without such information, we can still learn something from the benefit-cost ratios of table 5. Using the mean of the incarcerated population as a proxy for the costliness of the next person imprisoned for a property crime implies that you think the system is unable to do any sorting. If this assumption is true, increasing the number of prison beds is desirable public policy, as nearly $15 in social costs is saved

Table 5. Benefit-Cost Ratios of Incarceration for Selected Types of Offenders

OFFENDER	RATIO
Average (mean)	14.77
Median	1.84
25th percentile	0.63
10th percentile	0.08

for every $1 added to the imprisonment budget. Alternatively, the choice of the median as an admittedly blunt instrument implicitly assumes that the corrections community can ascertain whether an offender is likely to be in the most active half of the detained population, but cannot make a more specific determination based on the type of information to which they generally have access. This measure implies that the scope of corrections is just about right. On the other hand, if the system can precisely sift out the more active and more costly criminals, we are overinvesting in prisons.

In a 1982 RAND Corporation report, Peter Greenwood, with Allan Abrahamse, helped kick off a "selective incapacitation" debate by proposing that it is possible to identify and incarcerate only the very active criminals, thus achieving the same crime rate with a much lower prison population and saving a great deal of taxpayers' money. The upshot of the debate, however, is that it is difficult to precisely identify those offenders with information generally available to the criminal justice system. A believer in the efficacy of selective incapacitation would maintain that we could concentrate on the most hard-core criminals, freeing the lowest quartile of inmates. In future work we will focus on more precise definitions of who the "marginal offender" is and how to assess his likely level of criminal behavior under such sanctions as parole or early release.

Policy Implications

Though one cannot conclude whether or not prison pays at the margin without further evidence on where that margin lies, we venture that the criminal justice system is able to do enough sorting that the margin will fall below the mean but above the 10th percentile. Consider, for example, using the median cost of a property offender as the estimate of the social cost of the crime committed by the marginal offender. The net benefits of imprisonment can then be expressed as follows. Imprisoning an additional felon costs the state $25,000 a year, but letting him freely roam the streets in search of victims costs society $46,072 a year; imprisoning 100 people costs $2.5 million, but leaving these criminals on the streets costs $4.6 million.

The effect of other forms of punishment such as parole, probation, intensive supervision, and electronic monitoring on the ultimate benefit-cost ratio is not even considered here and must be the next step in understanding more fully the economics of corrections.

At this point, we cannot conclude that a meticulous benefit-cost analysis (aided by improved data availability) would result in a ratio much greater than 1. While supporting the view that prison is useful, from an economic standpoint, for a portion of the criminal population, our results challenge the implication of Zedlewski's original work: that every available dollar of public money go into expanding prison capacity.

Even if we find that "prison pays" at the margin, it would not mean that every convicted criminal deserves prison; it would not mean that it is cost-effective to imprison every convicted felon; and it would not mean that it is more cost-effective to imprison offenders than to supervise them intensively in the community. Indeed, community-based intensive supervision programs are among our most promising, proven, and viable corrections options. Recent evidence that these programs do not work as well as had been hoped based on early studies should not divert efforts to improve and experiment with them.

What finding that "prison pays" *would* mean is that we have reason to make a balanced use of correctional sanctions, that imprisonment is not "too expensive," and that an affirmative response to the clear and present need for more prison beds is a necessary if unfortunate social investment that will probably pay dividends over time.

Cautions

Three issues may bias our estimate one way or the other. There is, of course, always the possibility that prisoners in a given survey might exaggerate (or understate) the level of criminal activity, or that the extrapolations built into the calculations might exaggerate or understate the actual level of criminal activity among prisoners in the sample. Yet this is the best we can do at this point. Other prisoner surveys have reported higher median figures, but nothing far out of line with our finding of 12. Our survey mimicked the 1987 RAND Second Inmate Survey to take advantage of its extensive before-and-after testing of the survey instrument for accuracy of responses. At a minimum, our work can be confidently compared with other work that has relied upon similar surveys, such as the RAND Corporation's and Zedlewski's.

Second, one might quarrel with the social costs per crime calculated by Cohen. The use of jury awards is questionable, but probably the closest one can come to capturing public valuation. It is easy to recalculate the benefit-cost ratio using the reader's preferred measure of social costs.

The third consideration, the estimate of annual costs of incapacitation, is also contentious, but probably less so than the first two issues. One might argue that the national per prisoner per year estimate of $25,000 is too low. Few states, however, report spending even that much; Wisconsin's most recent estimate, for example, is under $20,000, and New Jersey reports just over $22,000. Also, Douglas C. McDonald, in the most recent and sophisticated analysis of corrections costs available, places the average per prisoner per year figure at $14,000 for operating costs. Using McDonald's correction for the underestimation of capital and indirect costs results in an approximation of yearly incarceration costs in the $20,000–$25,000 range.

Calculating Conclusions

We cannot currently claim that prison either pays or does not pay at the margin. The evidence is not overwhelming on either side. The often-heard argument that slightly changing the methodology will result in wildly variant answers to the question of the net benefit of incarceration is enough to cause even the most reasonable-minded person to mutter "Garbage in, garbage out." And even if one were to conduct a far more sophisticated study of the same subject, certitude about its findings would still be impossible.

But making imprisonment policy based on implicit assumptions about the criminal characteristics of prisoners is merely a path of lesser intellectual resistance. Getting a rough handle on the net benefit of imprisonment by the type of analysis presented above is a useful way of introducing a measure of rationality into debates about the future of corrections. Both those who insist that prisons are costless panaceas and those who shout that prisons cost "too much" resist such analysis because they prefer to make corrections policy in the dark.

41

The Trouble with "Scarlet Letter" Punishments

Douglas Litowitz

One of the latest trends in criminal sentencing is the imposition of "scarlet letter" punishments,[1] where the defendant must submit to some type of public humiliation. The infamous scarlet letter depicted by 19th-century novelist Nathaniel Hawthorne was a large red "A" emblazoned on the dress of an adulteress. In recent times, the following noteworthy cases have received national attention:

- In Illinois, a man convicted of criminal battery was ordered to post a sign on his driveway stating, "A violent felon lives here. Travel at your own risk."[2]

- In Boston, men caught soliciting prostitutes are sentenced to clean the streets under the district attorney's "Operation John Sweep" program.[3]

- A judge in South Carolina ordered a 15-year-old girl shackled to her mother for a month as punishment for various petty crimes.[4]

- A thief in Texas was sentenced to shovel horse manure,[5] while another was sentenced to carry a sign in front of a bookstore stating, "I stole from this store."[6]

Source: Reprinted by permission of the American Judicature Society from *Judicature*, September–October 1997 (Vol. 81, No. 2).

- In Milwaukee, a convicted drunk driver was offered a reduced jail sentence for agreeing to walk through the business district wearing a sandwich board proclaiming his crime.[7]
- In Houston, a man convicted of domestic violence was forced to publicly apologize at the entrance to City Hall.[8]

Shaming punishments typically arise when a defendant qualifies for a prison term but is sentenced to probation instead. Judges are generally allowed to fashion conditions of probation on a case-by-case basis if the conditions satisfy certain statutorily enumerated goals, such as rehabilitation, protection of the public, restitution, and deterrence.[9] Public humiliation is supposed to satisfy these commitments: It is rehabilitative because it forces an offender to admit his guilt, it protects the public because it announces that the offender is dangerous, it is restitutive because the offender must apologize or perform a public service, and it acts as a deterrent because the ritual of humiliation is so distasteful.

Scarlet letter sentences have attracted support from prosecutors, judges, and conservative groups across the country. For example, columnist George Will has argued that "the sting of shame" is a cost-effective alternative to imprisonment.[10] In response, the American Civil Liberties Union and other liberal groups have argued that public humiliation is mean-spirited and will only make criminals more hardened.[11]

The resurgence of shaming penalties raises two key questions: Will these sentences be upheld by the appellate courts, and will they be more effective than our existing methods of punishment?

On the first question, it appears that shaming sentences will survive legal challenge and will probably gain in popularity over the next several years. On the second, there is very little hard data, so at this point we are left with mere conjecture. But from what is known about criminal psychology, it seems unlikely that shaming penalties will have the intended effect of lessening crime and rehabilitating offenders.

The Legal Challenge

Shaming punishments have been challenged in the appellate courts on three fronts: (1) that they violate the Eighth Amendment ban on cruel and unusual punishment, (2) that they violate the First Amendment by compelling defendants to convey a judicially scripted message (in the form of forced apologies, warning signs, newspaper ads, and sandwich boards), and (3) that shaming punishments are not specifically authorized by state sentencing guidelines and therefore constitute an abuse of judicial discretion. The first two challenges might appear stronger since they have a basis in the Constitution, yet they have proven less successful in the appellate courts.

The Eighth Amendment challenge was rejected by a Florida appellate court in a case where a drunk driver was sentenced to affix a bumper sticker to his car reading "CONVICTED D.U.I.—RESTRICTED LICENSE." The court reasoned that "[t]he mere requirement that a defendant display a 'scarlet letter' as part of his punishment is not necessarily offensive to the Constitution."[12] Since the Supreme Court has ruled that the death penalty is not cruel and unusual punishment, it is doubtful that shaming penalties will be found to violate the Eighth Amendment.

Shaming punishments will also probably withstand the challenge that they are a form of state-compelled speech. The freedom of speech argument might seem convincing in light of the Supreme Court's 1977 ruling that the State of New Hampshire could not compel a Jehovah's Witness to display the state motto ("Live Free or Die") on his license plate.[13] Although one would think that requiring criminals to publish confessions scripted by judges would violate the criminal's right to free speech, state and federal courts have rejected this argument.[14]

The final challenge, that shaming penalties exceed the scope of available sentencing options, has met with mixed success. In April 1997, the Illinois Supreme Court used this rationale to strike a probation condition requiring an offender to place a warning sign in his front yard.[15] The Illinois decision looked favorably upon a 1996 decision of the Tennessee Supreme Court that struck a similar warning sign at the home of a child molester, on the grounds that the sentencing guidelines did not authorize such "breathtaking departures from conventional principles of probation."[16] Similarly, the New York Court of Appeals struck a sentence requiring a drunk driver to carry a special tag on his license plate.[17] On the other hand, the Oregon Supreme Court let stand a sentence requiring an offender to post a warning sign at his home,[18] and the Georgia Court of Appeals upheld a probation condition requiring a drunk driver to wear a fluorescent pink bracelet.[19]

When a court vacates a shaming sentence because it is not authorized under the probation guidelines, the court's decision can be trumped if the legislature amends the probation statute to specifically authorize shaming penalties as a condition of probation. Once this occurs, there will be few remaining grounds for challenging such sentences, leaving us with the all-important question: Assuming that shaming punishments will survive legal challenge in the appellate courts, will they constitute an advancement over existing methods of punishment, such as imprisonment, fines, community service, and home monitoring?

There is no hard data on this question because shaming penalties are a very recent development. However, from what we know about criminal psychology, it seems that shaming punishments will prove almost completely ineffective as a method of punishment in the great majority of cases. To see this point, we must first understand why shaming punishments were abandoned in the 19th century, and why they are inappropriate for contemporary society.

Shaming's Death and Rebirth

In Colonial days, the courts favored primitive methods of punishment such as the whipping post, the pillory, stocks, branding, banishment, the dunking stool, and a device known as the "brank," a metal mask that wrapped around the face of a woman who talked too much.[20] More serious offenses were dealt with by public hanging. While many of these sentences had a physical component, they also had a strong symbolic and psychological element, which explains why they were meted out in a public forum. For example, the stocks physically restricted offenders, but it also immobilized them in a public place where they could be pelted with rotten vegetables and stones. The criminal law of the time possessed a strong religious component and punished activities that are now considered private affairs, such as blasphemy, adultery, failing to observe the Sabbath, and general laziness. Since there was no clear line between church and state, punishments were designed to instill religious precepts and make the offender a good Christian. Little attention was paid to the commitments that motivate punishment today, such as deterrence, rehabilitation, and protection of the public. Although the Colonial shaming rituals seemed primitive and harsh, they were often followed by the reabsorption of the offender back into the community.

In Colonial times, courts did not impose shaming penalties in lieu of prison sentences, since the Colonists had no conception that prolonged imprisonment could itself operate as a criminal punishment. Prison as we know it (as a "house of correction" where people "serve time") was virtually nonexistent until the late 18th century. The Colonial prison was often a co-educational facility for debtors and defendants awaiting trial.[21]

Imprisonment replaced public shaming during the 19th century, probably for two reasons. First, under the increasing influence of the Quakers, there was a growing sense that criminality was not caused by sin, but rather by evil influences in the criminal's environment. Instead of shocking criminals into redemption, the logical approach was to remove criminals from their environment and teach them good habits so that they could return to society. The second notion, derived from the work of Italian criminologist Cesare Beccaria and popularized by various founding fathers, was that flamboyant punishments were not as effective as swift and certain punishments of lesser strength.[22] Gradually, public spectacle was replaced by deprivation of liberty (imprisonment), isolation, rigid work schedules, and education.

Shaming punishments also declined because they seemed inappropriate for an increasingly atomistic, impersonal, secular, and industrial society. Shaming punishments may have been appropriate for close-knit communities united by a common religious faith, where individuals were subordinated to the group and where the government freely intruded into private affairs. However, shaming punishments proved less appropriate for an increasingly diverse American society that placed a premium on individual autonomy and privacy. For example, in the days of *The Scarlet Letter*, the birth of an illegitimate child was deemed a public matter affecting the whole town, hence the punishment was public and involved a strong religious component. Nowadays, we feel that when someone commits a crime, it is a private matter between the perpetrator, the victim, and the criminal justice system. To make a spectacle of punishment in front of perfect strangers seems an invasion of privacy, an affront to individual dignity.

If shaming punishments were long ago relegated to the dustbin of history, why are they being revived in courtrooms across the country? Without doubt, the rebirth of shaming penalties is related to the growing realization among judges that the dominant method of punishment—imprisonment—is expensive and ineffective. Statistics from the Department of Justice indicate that as of July 1994, 1 in 128 Americans was incarcerated on any given day, with 1 in 38 under some form of correctional supervision.[23] The total number of Americans in prison is now twice the number of 1985, and the entire prison population is growing at 8.4 percent annually (doubling every 11 or 12 years).[24] The Sentencing Project has reported that one in three young African-American males is tied up in the criminal justice system, either in prison or jail, or on probation or parole; in Baltimore and Washington, D.C., the figures are closer to 50 percent, a condition akin to a police state.[25] While it is true that every society has its lawbreakers, America now has the highest incarceration rate of any industrial Western nation, with no end in sight. Yet even as we are building more prisons and dealing out harsher sentences, we do not feel any safer.

Accordingly, judges have begun to explore alternatives to imprisonment. Apart from shaming, the two most likely alternatives are fines and community service, but each has serious flaws. Fines can send a powerful message, but a fine resembles a license fee, where an offender pays a fee for the privilege of causing harm. Fines also send the message that a criminal action is not serious enough to warrant jail time, thereby weakening respect for the legal system and eroding the deterrent effect of criminal sentencing. Finally, fines seem to discriminate in favor of wealthy offenders who can better afford a monetary setback.

Community service is a possible sentencing option, but it too has serious drawbacks. Most notably, it carries unwanted positive connotations of charity and philanthropy, especially when the offender is working side-by-side with noncriminal volunteers. Many judges feel that community service does not satisfy the public's sense of retribution—it fails to convey the message that the offender has broken a serious rule and must pay for his actions.

Because of the problems with fines and community service, shaming is being touted as one of the few remaining alternatives to imprisonment. In a prominent article dealing with alternative sentencing, Professor Dan Kahan of the University of Chicago Law School identifies four broad types of shaming sentences:[26]

- *Stigmatizing publicity.* The defendant's crime is communicated to neighbors, for example by publishing a list of "johns" in a local newspaper, or by forcing the defendant to publish his picture with a description of his wrongdoing;

- *Literal stigmatization.* The offender must wear a public badge of humiliation, for example, a sandwich board or T-shirt proclaiming the nature of his crime;

- *Self-debasement.* This requires a publicly degrading physical action, for example by requiring slumlords to spend a night in their own slums, requiring "johns" to clean the streets in bright uniforms, or requiring offenders to shovel horse manure;

- *Contrition.* This requires some form of apology and self-effacement, for example by forcing the offender to publicly apologize and beg forgiveness, or to hold a press conference and admit his wrongdoing.

Professor Kahan thinks that shaming penalties are sometimes appropriate because they are cheaper than imprisonment while conveying the same message of moral outrage. (This element is missing from fines and community service, which convey a somewhat benign message of disapproval.) Shaming, then, would seem an ideal alternative. If it worked as planned, it would be cheaper than prison while having the same deterrent and retributive value, and it also expresses community outrage in a public forum. The problem, however, is that shaming will not work in this way.

Why Shaming Won't Work

The premise behind public shaming is that crime is caused by the offender's lack of shame, so the shaming ritual operates to create this missing sense of shame. Public humiliation is supposed to force the offender to recognize the error of his ways and deter him from future crimes.

But this cuts against everything we know about how shame operates as a human emotion. A sense of shame is not something that the state can create out of thin air—one either has a sense of shame or one does not, and a shaming punishment will not likely create a conscience simply by exposing the criminal to public ridicule. Psychologists have pointed out that a sense of shame arises very gradually, only after one has built up a set of values and aspirations and then subsequently fails to meet these aspirations. A person cannot be shocked into feeling a complex emotion like shame. It is much more likely that a person will respond with reactive emotions like anger, frustration, and rage.

Judges who impose shaming penalties make the false assumption that criminals share the average person's view of the legal system. Since the average person would feel shame at being publicly humiliated for breaking the law and would adjust his or her behavior accordingly, judges presume that criminals will react in the same way. Yet this is wrong—many criminals (especially in urban areas) believe that the legal system is illegitimately biased against them and that they were forced to break the law because of their circumstances. Such people are impervious to public humiliation because they see it as another piece of confirming evidence that the entire system is corrupt and cruel.[27] If these people are to be reached, it cannot be done with new and bizarre punishments, but only by measures taken before the crime is committed, by instilling enough values in the criminal that he or she has a sense of shame in the first place.

Many urban criminals see *themselves* as victims, a point brought out in Eldridge Cleaver's comments about black prisoners:

> One thing that the judges, policemen, and administrators of prisons seem never to have understood, and for which they certainly do not make any allowances, is that Negro convicts, basically, rather than see themselves as criminals and perpetrators of misdeeds, look upon themselves as prisoners of war, the victims of a vicious dog-eat-dog social system that is so heinous as to cancel out their own malefactions.[28]

If one takes Cleaver seriously, prisoners in urban areas are not likely to feel shame at violating the laws of a system that, they feel, has delivered them over to poverty and hopelessness.

Another factor to consider is that lawbreakers tend to carve out exceptions and excuses for their behavior, so even if sentenced to public humiliation, they are not likely to become convinced that they are the problem. Charles Starkweather, one of the most notorious mass killers in American history, told a court psychiatrist that he shot a police officer in "self-defense" because, after all, the police were chasing him![29] This type of attitude can be changed only by education and rehabilitation; public shaming will make such people hold fast to their excuses.

It might be argued that shaming sentences are appropriate for people who are not alienated from the system and are basically law abiding, for those who made a wrong turn and ran afoul of the law, such as the teenager who steals a book at the shopping mall, the insurance salesman who is caught driving after too many drinks, and for the quick-tempered construction worker who gets into a bar brawl.

But if these people are generally law abiding, it is hard to see what we gain from making them submit to *public* humiliation—certainly, some sort of private ritual seems more appropriate. Consider the case of the teenager who steals a book: rather than humiliate him publicly, we might require him to pay a fine or work at the bookstore, in which case he might develop sympathy with the store owners, thereby instilling the values that will prevent him from committing a future crime.

It would seem, then, that shaming penalties will not work on hardened "career criminals" who are totally outside the legal system, and they are superfluous when dealing with first- and second-time offenders. This means that shaming would be appropriate only in a narrow band of cases, and even in those cases such punishments might cause more harm than good.

Creating More Criminals

For one thing, it is entirely possible that shaming punishments would become a badge of distinction among criminals, functioning as a rite of passage into the outlaw world. Since the shaming ritual is purely negative, it conveys the message that the offender is thoroughly contemptible to the core of his being, that he is not a valuable and worthy person. This could result in a type of "labeling disorder," where the offender is branded as an outcast and then forms an identity around this label.

Judging from newspaper accounts of shaming rituals, there is reason to doubt whether shaming penalties will have any positive effect on repeat offenders. For example, *The New York Times* reported that a man who was required to keep a warning sign in his driveway felt that the sign was illegal.[30] Similarly, a child molester who was required to publish a confession in a local newspaper felt that the sentence was a "useless gesture" that did not accomplish anything.[31] And a nationwide television audience watched as the rapist-killer of Polly Klaas stood before a packed California courtroom and, instead of admitting his shameful action, accused Polly's father of molesting her. In these cases, public exposure failed to bring about an attitude of shame and contrition—it only made the offenders more hardened and more alienated from the legal system.

It is also questionable whether shaming punishments are appropriate for crimes that are not so much "shameful" as "unseemly" and "embarrassing," like soliciting a prostitute, buying stolen furniture, cheating on taxes, or selling marijuana. These cases are probably better handled with fines, community service, home monitoring, or forcing the offender to attend educational seminars. Since the activities in question are not viewed as deeply shameful by many Americans, it seems excessive to make a public spectacle of the defendant's guilt.

Consider the decision to publish the names of men who are convicted of soliciting prostitutes. Many of these men probably feel that prostitution should be legal, as it is in Nevada and many European countries. The "john" will be ashamed when his name is plastered in the newspaper, and the release of this information may ruin his marriage (if it is not already ruined), but it is hard to see what society gains by making a public announcement of private affairs, especially when the criminal activity is simply driven further underground or rerouted to a new part of town. The only way to really cut down on this activity is through education, for example by teaching "johns" that prostitution is abusive, exploitative, and dangerous.

The same analysis applies in drug cases, which constitute a major percentage of recent convictions. When a drug dealer is arrested, several others step in to take his or her place because the trade is so lucrative. If these people are not deterred by 10- or 20-year sentences, they will probably not be deterred by being forced to walk around City Hall in a T-shirt proclaiming that they are drug dealers.

The point here is that shaming penalties would not seem appropriate for many cases that clog court dockets. Although shaming seems at first blush like a dramatic and powerful alternative to prison sentences, in reality there are very few opportunities where shaming would be appropriate, let alone effective.

The Rehabilitative Component

Although probation is supposedly aimed at rehabilitating the offender, it is hard to see how shaming penalties are rehabilitative. Forcing the criminal to publicly confess may give the impression of rehabilitation, but if the offender is simply going through the motions mechanically, there is no genuine rehabilitation. Subjecting the offender to public scorn reminds him of society's disapproval, but it has no component of teaching or instruction to help him become a better person. Not only does the shaming ritual fail to prepare offenders for re-entry into society, it actually marks them as persons of lesser worth in the eyes of their neighbors (it also stigmatizes their families). As a result, shaming sentences seem mean-spirited because they are motivated by the public's hunger to see offenders suffer, not by any attempt to rehabilitate. If there was a genuine concern to help criminals and to lessen criminality, then the shaming ritual would have to be complemented with a positive ritual that brings the offender back into the community.

Sociologist John Braithwaite has suggested one avenue in this direction by making an important distinction between "reintegrative shaming" and "stigmatizing shaming." Writing in *The British Journal of Criminology*, Braithwaite argues that the first type of shaming might work, whereas the second type will fail:

> For shaming to obtain its maximum effectiveness, it must be of a reintegrative sort, avoiding stigmatization. Stigmatization is shaming which creates outcasts where "criminal" becomes a master status trait that drives out all other identities, shaming where bonds of respect with the offender are not sustained. Reintegrative shaming in contrast is disapproval dispensed with an ongoing relationship with the offender based on respect[,] where degradation ceremonies are followed by ceremonies to decertify deviance, where forgiveness, apology and repentance are culturally important.[32]

Braithwaite's distinction between reintegrative shaming and stigmatizing shaming helps to explain why, if our goal is to lessen crime and to deter criminality, the shaming ritual must be followed by a reintegrating ritual, perhaps by having defendants meet with their victims and with people whom they respect, who can convey their disappointment at past conduct and their hope for future behavior. This element of reintegrative shaming is notably absent from the shaming sentences that have recently captured national attention, which tells us that public shaming is not really about stopping crime so much as venting public anger.

The resurgence of flamboyant shaming sentences has diverted attention from other nonincarcerative options that are perhaps less glamorous but more effective. The National Criminal Justice Commission has recommended several promising alternatives that appear more effective than prison, including intensive probation, drug treatment, halfway houses, day reporting centers, and work release programs.[33] These alternatives might combine the least intrusiveness and the lowest cost with the greatest potential for rehabilitation, yet we have heard very little about these options precisely because they lack the element of vengeance and retribution that accompanies public humiliation. To be sure, retribution and vengeance are important components of punishment, but it would be foolish to choose a method of punishment that satisfies only these goals at the expense of rehabilitation.

*****

There is a mean and gratuitous quality to the scarlet letter sentences that are gaining favor in courtrooms across the country. Although shaming is rationalized as a return to traditional values, its real motivation is simply to vent frustration. Shaming rituals are as close to a good old-fashioned whipping as contemporary society will allow.

It is true that a strong sense of shame prevents a person from committing a crime, but shame is a fall from grace, and a person who lacks self-esteem in the first place cannot fall very far. A better tactic in fighting crime is to elevate the criminal class to the point where they have something to lose by committing an illegal act. Focusing attention on the root causes of crime would be more fruitful than dusting off methods of punishment from the Dark Ages.

Notes

[1] Reske, *Scarlet Letter Sentences*, ABA Journal, January 1996, at 16. *See also* McMurry, *For Shame: Paying for Crime Without Serving Time, but with a Dose of Humility*, Trial, May 1997, at 12.

[2] Hoffman, *Crime and Punishment: Shame Gains Popularity*, New York Times, January 16, 1997, at A1.

[3] El Nasser, *Paying for Crime with Shame: Judges Say "Scarlet Letter" Angle Works*, USA Today, June 25, 1996, at 1A.

[4] Smith, *Judge Orders South Carolina Girl, 15, Shackled to Mother*, Chicago Sun-Times, December 15, 1995, at 30.

[5] Reske, *supra* n. 1, at 16.

[6] Spaid, *Humiliation Comes Back As Criminal Justice Tool*, The Christian Science Monitor, December 17, 1996, at Al.

[7] *Id.*

[8] *Id.* at 18.

[9] *See, e.g.*, West's Ann. Cal. Penal Code, secs. 1202.7, 1203.1(j).

[10] Will, *The Sting of Shame*, Washington Post, February 1, 1996, at A21.

[11] *Public Humiliations for Crimes: Ain't That a Shame*, ACLU News and Events, June 25, 1995, available on the World Wide Web.

[12] Goldschmitt v. State, 490 So.2d 123, 125 (Fla. Dist. Ct. App. 1986).

[13] Wooley v. Maynard, 430 U.S. 705, 97 S.Ct. 1428, 1435 (1977).

[14] *Supra* n.12 at 125-6; Lindsay v. State, 606 So.2d 652, 657 (Fla. Dist. Ct. App. 1992); U.S. v. Clark, 918 F.2d 843, 847 (9th Cir. 1990), *overruled on other grounds*, U.S. v. Keys, 95 F.3d 874, 878 (9th Cit. 1996).

[15] State v. Meyer, 680 N.E.2d 315 (Ill. 1997).

[16] State v. Burdin, 924 S.W.2d 82, 86 (Tenn. 1996).

[17] People v. Letterlough, 86 N.Y.2d 259, 655 N.E.2d 146, mot. den. 655 N.E.2d 698 (1995).

[18] State v. Bateman, 95 Or. App. 456, 771 P.2d 314, cert. den. 777 P.2d 410 (1989).

[19] Ballenger v. State, 210 Ga. App. 627, 436 S.E.2d 793 (1993).

[20] Andrews, *Punishments in Olden Times* (Littleton, Colorado: Fred B. Rothman & Co., 1993, orig. 1881).

[21] Rothman, "Perfecting the Prison," in Morris and Rothman, eds., *The Oxford History of the Prison* (New York: Oxford University Press, 1995).

[22] Beccaria, *On Crimes and Punishments* 46–47. Trans. David Young (Indianapolis: Hackett 1986).

[23] These statistics are reprinted in Dozinger, ed., *The Real War on Crime* 35 (New York: HarperCollins, 1996).

[24] *Inmate Count Doubles: Hit 1.6 Million in '95*, The Arizona Republic, August 19, 1996.

[25] *Supra* n.23, at 102.

[26] Kahan, *What Do Alternative Sanctions Mean?*, 63 U. Chi. L. Rev. 591, 631 (1996).

[27] *See* Massaro, *Shame, Culture, and American Criminal Law*, 89 Mich. L. Rev. 1880, 1944 (1991), arguing that shaming punishments are cruel and will not be effective.

[28] Cleaver, *Soul on Ice* 58 (New York: McGraw-Hill, 1968).

[29] Allen, *Starkweather: The Story of a Mass Murderer* (Boston: Houghton Mifflin, 1976).

[30] *See supra* n.2, at A11.

[31] *See* Reske, *supra* n.1, at 17.

[32] Braithwaite, *Shame and Modernity*, 33 Brit. J. Criminology I (1993).

[33] *Supra* n.23, at 200.

42

The Costliest Punishment
A Corrections Administrator
Contemplates the Death Penalty
Paul W. Keve

It's a provocative question—when most of the Western nations have abolished capital punishment why does the United States go resolutely against this humane current trend? Also a provocative question—why does this country sentence so many to death and then actually execute so few? The questions and their answers tell us much about the futility and counterproductive nature of this final penalty.

Ostensible support for capital punishment is seen in the fact that in 53 jurisdictions (the 50 states, the District of Columbia, the Federal justice system, and the U.S. Military), there are 37 that authorize the death penalty, and as of the end of 1991 the death rows of 36 of the states were loaded with a total of 2,547 men and women.[1]

The glut of condemned persons reflects an approving attitude which is encouraged by the frequent pronouncements of elected public officials. Every political campaign rings with cries for law and order, including reiterated declarations in favor of capital punishment by most candidates. Indeed, there have been particular campaigns in which the choice between two contestants has seemed to be determined largely by which one has called the loudest for more use of the death penalty.

But despite the proclamations in favor of it, and despite the steady accretions of death row populations, the country is persistently reluctant

Source: *Federal Probation*, Vol. 56, No. 1 (March 1992), 11–15.

actually to execute. During the last decade we have been adding an average of about 170 new cases each year to the death rows while the actual executions have been averaging only about 21 annually.[2]

And now in the year just past, 1991, the execution count dropped to only 14![3] Of course the quick response to this from the true believer in capital punishment is to argue that the pace must be stepped up; that the successive appeals must somehow be curtailed and executions expedited. But my argument is that the pace cannot be materially speeded, nor should it be. The only sensible way out of the cumbersome problems with this penalty is in its abolishment.

There are good and practical reasons why the appeals must not be curtailed, but additionally, can it be that even the politicians who demand the penalty actually do not want the executions to go forward any faster? A believable point. A full-scale rate of executions commensurate with the rate of sentencing to death would be the sort of bloodbath that might well cause a revulsion which could reverse or appreciably reduce the present support for the penalty. By loudly demanding the death penalty's availability and use legislators can maintain their image of being "tough on crime," while at the same time feeling assured that the mere token rate of actual executions will prevent what would become unacceptably barbaric results.

Any casual daily reading of the news makes it evident that the average citizen is unaware of the vast difference between the presumed high use of the death penalty and the paucity of executions actually accomplished. And the discrepancy is much greater than that suggested by comparing the execution count with the 170-plus annual additions to the death rows. For if all the original death sentences were sustained the growth rate would be nearly twice what it is, since actual sentences are 300 or more annually.[4] The shrinkage of nearly 50 percent tells much about why the appeals process is so valid and must be unabridged. It means that the appeals are indeed showing up defects in a high proportion of capital convictions.

It is a point on which the public seems to be deceived, and the news media seems quite willing to support the illusion that death sentences always are valid and will be carried out. The media, like the public generally, seems to prefer the illusion to the reality.

The public ought to be told—repeatedly—that the criminal justice system should not and cannot carry out the rate of executions that is now generally expected. For instance, suppose our rate of executing were to increase, let's say, to 25 per year. It would still take us fully a century to execute all the persons presently waiting on all the death rows! Furthermore, if the present rate of growth were to continue, there would be, during that century, another 17,000 or more new cases added to the backlog on the death rows! One writer calculates that for every person actually executed the U.S. courts are pronouncing 30 death sentences![5] Obviously the vast majority of ordered executions will never be carried out.

A Token Punishment

A sober look at the facts should persuade us that our constant effort to implement the capital punishment laws can never bring more than this kind of pretense. In effect, we are resorting to an occasional execution to keep ourselves persuaded that we are being tough on crime. It is a remarkably expensive pretense, and it adds to the anguish of all those involved in any murder and execution. Furthermore, if this corrections administrator's view is valid, the penalty serves no useful purpose and would be even less useful if executions were to keep pace with the sentencing.

The public's unawareness of how unlikely it is that a death sentence will result in actual execution is exceeded only by its unawareness of the exorbitant price we must pay to maintain our token death penalty. The public does know well enough that imprisonment is very expensive, and the mistaken inference, for most people, is that execution consequently must be much cheaper than life imprisonment. In a New York state poll, for instance, a 72 percent support for the death penalty dropped to 56 percent when the persons polled were informed that the death penalty is more costly than life imprisonment.[6]

As a useful example, in my state of Virginia the cost of keeping one person in prison is calculated at a current average of about $17,000 per year.[7] It is much too easy for the public to look at such a figure and think of what it would presumably cost if a young man of 20 or so would come into prison with a life sentence that might keep him inside for perhaps 40 years. The accumulated total would come to a staggering amount. Wouldn't it be much cheaper to sentence him to death and save all that imprisonment cost?

Not so. The dollar argument leads quite the other way.

In the first place, that figure for the annual cost of imprisonment is misleading. The costs in running a prison are mainly fixed costs; as long as the prison is there and operating it has a steady annual cost that is not affected by minor variations in its prisoner population. In other words, as long as we have the prison anyway we do not save money by taking one prisoner out either to turn him loose or to execute him. Nor does it increase the overall cost noticeably to add one more prisoner. So an execution cannot truly be shown to save any imprisonment cost at all, even when compared with a life sentence.

But the cost of executing—now that's another matter.

Capital Prosecutions: The Taxpayers' Burden

A principle that can be counted on absolutely is that the more severe the possible punishment, the more energetic will be the defense and the more costly the prosecution. The death penalty is the ultimate example of this. In 1976 the U.S. Supreme Court approved the principle which, in its opinion, would make the death penalty constitutional. In deciding three capital cases it specified that (1) the sentencing in such cases must be done in trials that are separate from the trials which determine guilt or innocence; (2) the sentencing hearing must examine both mitigating and aggravating factors, including pertinent features of the defendant's life and character as well as the conditions of the crime; and (3) each death sentence must be followed by an automatic right of appeal to the highest state court. Of course, each of these requirements imposes substantial additional costs.

In the first place, defendants in capital cases almost invariably are indigent and so must be served with defense counsel at the expense of the state. In a capital case the number of pretrial motions filed becomes excessive as compared with noncapital cases. "Jury selection is estimated to take, on the average, 5.3 times longer than jury selection for a noncapital case. . . . [and it takes] approximately 3.5 times longer to try capital cases than to try noncapital murder cases."[8] The trials are longer than in noncapital cases, requiring more time of judges, juries, and all court personnel. And even with all this, the trial is only the first stage of a torturous process.

In preparation for the penalty phase the defense must make extensive investigation of the defendant's life history, with all the costs of special investigators and usually considerable travel expense. The prosecution will also have to go over much of the same ground. And once the sentence is pronounced the required appeal process begins, with a certainty that reversals will occur in a high percentage of cases. According to one count, from 1976 to 1989 more than 1,400 death penalty cases in the United States were reversed by appellate courts. About half of death sentences are being overturned on appeals.[9] After a reversal the case must go back to square one and start over again.

Meanwhile the defendant is held in idleness on death row where the operating cost is far greater than in other prison units. Those who are finally executed wait there an average of 6 to 8 years, while those not executed often wait much longer before their sentences are reversed or commuted to life.

Such observations are barely able to suggest the overwhelming complexity that now characterizes legal procedure in capital cases. The extensive literature on the subject details a body of law so specialized and labyrinthine that few defense attorneys can be expected to master it, and few states can be expected to finance the defense of such cases adequately.

Several states have made serious efforts to assess the cost of implementing the death penalty, though the findings have been given remarkably little publicity considering their dramatic quality. In 1982 the New York State Defenders Association made a substantial study of what it would cost to restore the death penalty in that state; it was calculated that "the potential costs of litigating a model New York capital case across just the first three levels of review [would be] $1.9 million per case." [10]

In 1982 New Jersey adopted a death penalty despite an estimate that it would increase the state's criminal justice costs by $16 million annually. [11] In Kansas a move to reestablish the death penalty was defeated partially on the basis of a 1987 study by the Kansas Legislative Research Department that the presence of the death penalty would cost the state an extra $11,420,000 annually. [12] In 1989 a fiscal impact statement produced for the Indiana legislature found that the state would expect to save more than $5 million annually by abolishment of its death penalty. [13]

Florida, the state with the second most populous death row, seems to be paying at the highest level of any, with a calculated cost of each execution figured at $3,178,000. [14] Similar findings have been produced by fiscal studies in Ohio and Oregon. With prices like these it would seem much more practical to spend that money instead on more social services to prevent violent crimes, more police services, and more services to deal constructively with the needs of victims' families.

High Expenditures With No Gain

Of course, the issue of cost is the least worthy of any arguments regarding the merits of the death penalty, for we should not flinch at the cost necessary for reduction of such a heinous crime as murder. That raises the controversial question of the deterrent value of the penalty, an issue that cannot be finally resolved to everyone's satisfaction. My own viewpoint comes from experience of more than 50 years in the field of corrections, including responsibility for top administration of correctional systems in two states, one with the death penalty and one without. Over that half century I have had ample opportunity to know many men and women who had committed murder, some of whom were sentenced to death. Even though their crimes are brutal, it seems impossible to know these offenders well and to conclude that the threat of death would have stopped them. Often chronic misfits with years of failures behind them, they are driven by the towering impulse of the moment and incapable of making any fine distinction between consequences of imprisonment versus death. This observation agrees with the convictions generally of criminologists today who find no deterrent effect in the death penalty.

Some years ago a fellow corrections administrator, with years of experience in the California system, drew the same conclusion and noted the public's refusal to face the facts. "It is the unique deterrent value capital punishment is presumed to have that provides the mainstay of the arguments for retention of the death penalty. That this is true has been refuted year after year before the Legislature by a variety of witnesses—statistical experts, police officials from abolition states, psychiatrists, and criminologists among others."[15]

The Death Penalty as Provocative of Murder

There is another point about the nonutility of the death penalty—a point also unprovable but made convincing by years of experience. That is, I am convinced that I know of a number of murder victims who would still be alive if the death penalty had not been in effect. Sometimes a person has a wish to commit suicide at the same time that he has an incapacity to do it to himself. For some troubled people, at a subconscious level there is still a residue of the age-old suicide stigma that prevents the person from contriving his own death. But if the state will do it for him then his purpose is accomplished while he is relieved of the stigma. By committing a murder he callously exploits the state's willingness to abet a suicide. Sick and warped as it is, the pattern does exist and can be seen as the psychological condition in more than a few murders. One psychiatrist, observing the same phenomenon, commented that the death penalty "becomes a promise, a contract, a covenant between society and certain (by no means rare) warped mentalities who are moved to kill as part of a self-destructive urge."[16]

The pattern is reflected in the many cases of defendants who refuse to fight their death sentences, sometimes even bringing action to force the state to proceed with the execution. One writer points out that after the death penalty was reinstituted in 1976, five of the first eight men to be executed vigorously opposed any efforts by others to forestall their executions.[17] It becomes a bizarre perversion of the law's intent thus to reward the murderer by implementing the suicide which he wanted but which he could not do for himself.

In a similar category is the individual who suffers inwardly with intense frustration from never having accomplished anything of note in his unrewarding life. For this person the death penalty offers the chance, by committing a murder, to enjoy the spotlight with gripping notoriety for a brief season. Public excitement over his execution guarantees him the reward he seeks, the fame he has otherwise missed.

Restricting Appeals: A False Concept

With the prolonged and repetitive stages of appeals that keep capital cases languishing on death rows for years it is altogether natural that persons unfamiliar with the intricacies of the criminal justice system should see as a "solution" a drastic reduction of the prisoner's right to successive appeals. But here again there is vital reason for moving with great caution. The proven fact is that, contrary to popular assumptions about reliability of modern court processes, mistakes are still being made. Evidence for this has been gathered in very recent years by two researchers who have scouted all the U.S. cases since 1900 in which capital convictions were obtained but later set aside.

The project located a total of 350 men and women who were subjects of erroneous capital convictions! A detailed report of the findings was published in 1987, but the researchers still find evidence that such cases continue to occur.[18] And as another research team reports, "Wrongful sentencing of innocent people shows no sign of diminishing with the passage of time. Indeed the capital punishment system seems to be becoming even less reliable over time. In 1987, 1988 and the first seven months of 1989 alone, at least a dozen more men who had received death sentences have been released as innocent."[19]

The conclusion is inescapable that it is still all too easy for fatal mistakes to be made, and as long as this is so we cannot afford to curtail any defendant's right to contest his conviction. If the protracted and costly appeal process is considered too burdensome the only acceptable solution is just to eliminate the death penalty.

Meanwhile, however, if defendants are going to get the quality of defense that our society now considers minimal there must be a well funded and well trained defense counsel. But for many states the cost is beyond the resources the state is willing to commit. Adequate defense of a capital case calls for a great amount of time on the part of defense attorneys who have special knowledge and skill in this area of the criminal law that is so complex and so specialized that few are truly qualified. There is so much time involved for the attorney who would undertake it that most of them are reluctant to tolerate the resultant sacrifice of their law practice. An end result may often be to raise a constitutional question; a low limit set by a state on the amount allowed for a defense attorney's fee in a capital case has the likely effect of denying to the defendant the minimum legal defense that today's standards declare to be his right.[20]

Consider Feelings of the Victims

But there is still the question—what about the family of the victim? Don't we owe it to them to proceed swiftly to execute the murderer? Proponents of the death penalty seem to infer that if we do not we are grievously failing in the respect due to the victims. The response to that question can be brief. Murder victim families are entitled to all the help, comfort, and consideration that the state can reasonably give. But there is nothing whatever that we can do by executing the murderer which will restore his victim or bring serenity to the family. Experience shows that comfort and healing simply do not come to the victim families by means of the execution. They deserve from us a much more positive kind of help.

A thoughtful look at the alternatives makes clear that in a state with no death penalty the trial and sentencing are much sooner completed, and the ordeal for victims' families is more quickly over. By contrast, where the death penalty is used the families have a greatly prolonged period of anguish. Through successive appeals, successive execution dates, etc., they are repeatedly interviewed by the news media while their anger and distress are repeatedly revived, sometimes never to be resolved. The death penalty, instead of bringing comfort, actually denies the comfort and instead stretches out the agony endlessly.

In the final analysis, my own opposition to the death penalty is not based so much on its excessive cost, or even its failure to deter crime, but is simply found in these three successive points. (1) The act of murder reveals a lack of respect for human life. (2) In consequence then, we need to encourage a higher respect for life. But finally, (3) it defies all logic to suppose that we can encourage a greater respect for human life by the device of taking human life.

Notes

[1] *Death Row U.S.A.*, NAACP Legal Defense and Educational Fund, Inc., NY, Winter 1991.

[2] Information furnished to author by editorial offices of *Death Row U.S.A.*

[3] Ibid.

[4] Ibid.

[5] Dave Von Drehle, *Miami Herald*, July 11, 1988.

[6] James Alan Fox, Michael L. Radelet, and Julie L. Bonesteel, "Death Penalty Opinion in the Post-Furman Years," *New York University Review of Law and Social Change*, 18(2), 1990–1991, p. 515.

7 Information supplied to author by accounting services, Virginia Department of Corrections.

8 Margot Garey, "The Cost of Taking a Life: Dollars and Sense of the Death Penalty," *U.C. Davis Law Review*, 18(4), Summer 1985, pp. 1257–1258.

9 Robert E. Spangenberg, in speech (untitled) at Vanderbilt University, February 22, 1989. Also see, Barry Nakell, "The Cost of the Death Penalty," *Criminal Law Bulletin*, 14(1), January/February 1978, p. 69; and Margot Garey, op. cit., pp. 1221–1273.

10 Jonathan E. Gradess, *The Washington Post*, February 28, 1988.

11 Margot Garey, op. cit., p. 1261.

12 Dave Von Drehle, *Miami Herald*, July 13, 1988.

13 Indiana State Legislature, Fiscal Impact Statement for SB 0531 (replacing death penalty with life imprisonment), January 23, 1989.

14 Von Drehle, op. cit.

15 Richard A. McGee, "Capital Punishment as Seen by a Correctional Administrator," *Federal Probation*, 28(2), June 1964, p. 11.

16 Louis J. West, "Psychiatric Reflections on the Death Penalty," in *Capital Punishment in the United States*, by Hugo Adam Bedau and Chester M. Pierce, AMS Press, 1976.

17 Welsh S. White, *The Death Penalty in the Nineties*. Ann Arbor, University of Michigan Press, 1991, p. 164.

18 Hugo Adam Bedau and Michael L. Radelet, "Miscarriages of Justice in Potentially Capital Cases," *Stanford Law Review*, 40(1).

19 Ronald J. Tabak and J. Mark Lane, "The Execution of Injustice: A Cost and Lack-of-Benefit Analysis of the Death Penalty," *Loyola of L.A. Law Review*, 23(1), November 1989, p. 102.

20 Ronald J. Tabak, "The Death of Fairness: The Arbitrary and Capricious Imposition of the Death Penalty in the 1980s," *New York University Review of Law and Social Change*, 14(4), 1986, p. 76.